Els Menorets

The Franciscans in the Realms of Aragon From St. Francis to the Black Death

JILL R. WEBSTER

The visit of Saint Francis to Spain in the early thirteenth century set the stage for the remarkable expansion of his order in the realms of Aragon. The popularity of the Order of Friars Minor and its immediate acceptance by contemporary society, especially by the crown and the merchants, enabled the Franciscans to establish themselves in all the major urban centres.

This study is an attempt to reconstruct, primarily from unpublished archival sources, the early years of the Franciscans in the realms of Aragon, showing their rapid progress as trusted ambassadors, messengers, spiritual advisers and cultural leaders. As an integral part of the mosaic of late medieval urban social life, the *menorets* interacted with Christians, Jews and Muslims, inspiring artistic endeavour and the creation of charitable organizations, and thereby imparting much of the charisma of their founder to an increasingly complex world.

The primary evidence gathered in this volume should be of interest to many scholars. The appendices contain transcriptions of over fifty representative documents, alphabetical and chronological lists of all friars for whom there exists some documentary evidence, the names of those who held positions as provincial ministers, guardians, custodians and lectors, as well as other information.

Saint Francis handing the Rule to his followers: a panel from a retable by Lluís Borrassà (1415), painted for the convent of Santa Clara in Vic

STUDIES AND TEXTS 114

Els Menorets

The Franciscans in the Realms of Aragon From St. Francis to the Black Death

JILL R. WEBSTER

PONTIFICAL INSTITUTE OF MEDIAEVAL STUDIES

ACKNOWLEDGMENT

This book has been published with the help of a grant from the Canadian Federation for the Humanities, using funds provided by the Social Sciences and Humanities Research Council of Canada.

∞ Printed on acid-free paper.

CANADIAN CATALOGUING IN PUBLICATION DATA

Webster, Jill R. (Jill Rosemary), 1931–
  Els menorets : the Franciscans in the realms of Aragon from St. Francis to the Black Death

(Studies and texts, ISSN 0082-5328 ; 114)
Includes bibliographical references and index.
ISBN 0-88844-114-2

1. Aragon (Spain) – Church history. 2. Aragon (Spain) – Church history – Sources. 3. Aragon (Spain) – Social conditions. 4. Aragon (Spain) – Social conditions – Sources. I. Pontifical Institute of Mediaeval Studies. II. Title. III. Series: Studies and texts (Pontifical Institute of Mediaeval Studies) ; 114.

BX3644.A7W4 1993   255′.3′0094655   C93-093465-2

© 1993
Pontifical Institute of Mediaeval Studies
59 Queen's Park Crescent East
Toronto, Ontario, Canada M5S 2C4

PRINTED BY UNIVERSA, WETTEREN, BELGIUM

IN MEMORIAM

This book is dedicated to the memory of Daniel Rebull i Muntanyola (†1983), better known as Nolasc del Molar, OFM (Cap.), devout follower of Saint Francis, prolific scholar, loyal Catalan, faithful friend. His inspiration and encouragement over many years enabled me to complete this study, and so to realize something of the life-work of his confrere, Fr. Martí de Barcelona, who before his untimely death during the Spanish Civil War was working on a history of the Franciscans in the realms of Aragon.

ON THE PREVIOUS PAGE
Saint Francis receiving the Word:
a woodcut from the *Floreto de São Francisco* (Seville, 1492), sig. aiv

Contents

List of Plates ... ix
Abbreviations ... x
The Royal House of Aragon ... xi
Map of Realms of Aragon, Showing Franciscan Houses ... xii

PART ONE
The Development of the Order

Introduction ... 3
1 Legend and History ... 14
2 Security, Learning and Privilege ... 73
3 The Mosaic of Urban Life ... 103
4 The Cure of Souls ... 149
5 Life Within and Without the Cloister ... 175
6 The Second and Third Orders ... 220
7 The Cultural Impact of the Franciscans ... 260
Conclusion ... 290

PART TWO
Documents and Appendices

Documents ... 303
Appendix 1 Chronology of Franciscan Officers ... 355
Appendix 2 Franciscan Affairs and Organization ... 360
Appendix 3 Family Origins of Friars ... 368
Appendix 4 Chronology of Convent Residents ... 372
Appendix 5 Alphabetical List of Friars ... 383
Appendix 6 Chronological List of Friars ... 395

PART THREE
Glossary, Archival Sources, Bibliography and Index

Glossary	409
Archival Sources	411
Bibliography of Printed Sources	421
Index	437

Plates

Frontispiece Saint Francis handing the Rule to his followers: a panel from a retable by Lluis Borrassà (1415), painted for the convent of Santa Clara in Vic (courtesy of the Museum at Vic).

Facing page 408 An eighteenth-century map of Barcelona showing a Franciscan house near the waterfront.

Black-and-white plates follow page 456.

1 Morella, cloister and well (photo by Josep Martí Mayor, OFM, Archivist of the Arxiu històric dels Franciscans de Catalunya, Barcelona).
2 Morella, cloister (photo by J. Martí Mayor).
3 Cervera, interior of the Church of Sant Antoni de Padua (photo from Arxiu Josep Gavín, Valldoreix, near Barcelona, Ref. 1812-19).
4 Cervera, part of the nave of the Church of Sant Antoni de Padua (photo from Arxiu Gavín, Ref. 1812-21).
5 Cervera, cloister of the Church of Sant Antoni de Padua (photo from Arxiu Gavín, Ref. 2405-8).
6 Cervera, well and cloister of the Church of Sant Antoni de Padua (photo from Arxiu Gavín, Ref. R/41).
7 Vilafranca, cloister of the Church of Sant Francesc (photo from Arxiu Gavín, Ref. 2398-22).
8 Miramar, Majorca (from postcard).
9 Tortosa, the Church of Sant Francesc (photo from Arxiu Gavín, Ref. 801/15).
10 Santa Clara, Tortosa (photo from Arxiu Gavín, Ref. 801/8).
11 Montblanc, apse of the Church of Sant Francesc (photo by J. Martí Mayor).
12 Montblanc, entrance of the Church of Sant Francesc (photo by J. Martí Mayor).
13 Castelló d'Empúries, wall of the Convent of Sant Francesc (photo from Arxiu Gavín, Ref. 2125/15).
14 Castelló d'Empúries, part of the Convent of Sant Francesc (photo from Arxiu Gavín, Ref. 2125/16).

Abbreviations

For a complete list of archival sources see pp. 411–420

AC	Archivo/Arxiu (capitular) de la catedral/seo
ACA	Archivo de la corona de Aragón
ACF	Arxiu de la Curia Fumada
AD	Arxiu diocesà
ADM	Archivo del duque de Medinaceli
AE	Arxiu eclesiàstic
AFH	*Archivum Franciscanum historicum*
AH	Arxiu històric
AHC	Arxiu històric comarcal
AHFC	Arxiu històric dels Franciscans de Catalunya
AHM	Archivo histórico/Arxiu històric municipal
AHN	Archivo histórico nacional
AHRM	Arxiu històric del regne de Mallorca
AIA	*Archivo ibero-americano*
AIEG	*Annals de l'Institut d'estudis gironins*
AMP	Arxiu del monestir de Pedralbes
ECR	Escribanía de cartes reials
EF	*Estudios franciscanos/Estudis franciscans*
N	notarial manual
ORM	Ordenes religiosas y militares
RC	Registros de la Cancillería
REF	*Revista de estudios franciscanos*
RP	Real Patrimonio
T	manual of testaments (wills)

MEMBERS OF THE ROYAL HOUSE OF ARAGON

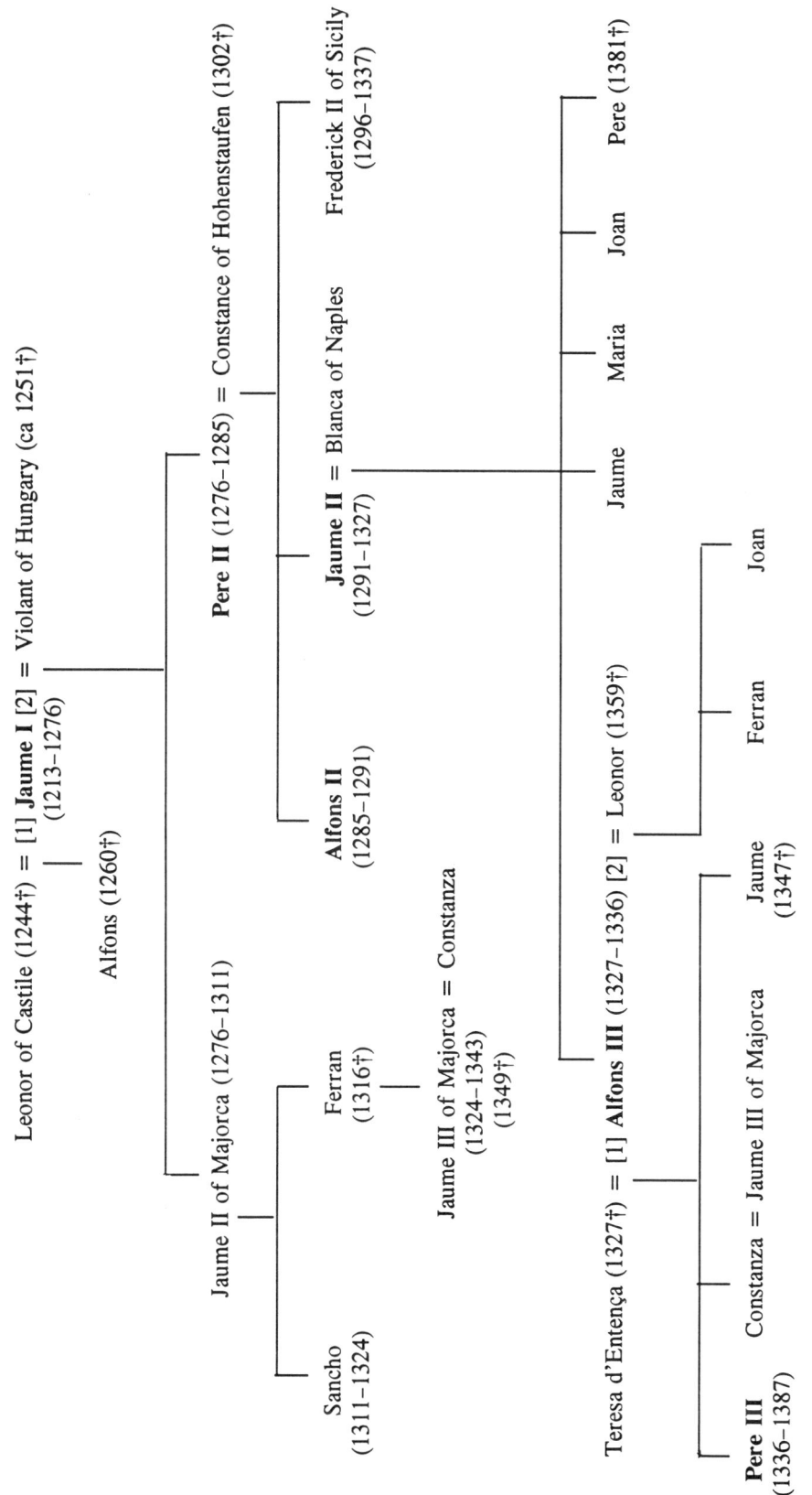

Note: Only members pertinent to this study are shown here. The names of the Aragonese rulers are in **bold** type. Dates in parentheses refer to the period of reign; an obelisk † marks the date of death.

PART ONE

The Development of the Order

ON THE PREVIOUS PAGE
The stoning of Ramon Llull at Bugia:
a woodcut from Llull's *Ars inventiva veritatis* (Valencia, 1515), sig. Cv

Introduction

The Iberian Peninsula in the late Middle Ages was a complex unit, comprising a number of different kingdoms, among them Aragon, Castile, Portugal, Navarre and the Moorish kingdom of Granada. The Crown of Aragon itself was a pluralistic entity, composed of widely different geographical regions whose historical and linguistic background was also equally diverse, a factor which was to become increasingly significant in subsequent years.

This diversity was complicated by religious diversity. James I succeeded to the throne at a very young age, at a time when his inheritance was in disarray, and in his early years he was placed in the custody of the Templars at Monzón in Aragon who were entrusted with his education.[1] The various territories were not at peace among themselves and the young king had a formidable task facing him, but it was one for which he proved more than fitted, for when he died he succeeded in handing on to his son and heir vast territories stretching from Montpellier to Valencia, across the Mediterranean Sea to the Balearic Islands and Sicily, westward to the borders of Navarre. His subjects followed different religious beliefs: Christians, Moors and Jews coexisted in a society increasingly intolerant of those who did not share the Christian faith. The reconquest of land from the Moors, the missionary attempts of the Franciscans and the violent eruptions in the Jewish quarters or *calls* from time to time emphasized this diversity and gave impetus to the royal crusade for Christian supremacy.

Religion, not surprisingly, was deeply embroiled in politics, and the period from the accession of James I to the incorporation of the Majorcan crown in 1344 was probably the most prosperous the Crown of Aragon was ever to enjoy. The largest mendicant orders, the Dominicans and Franciscans, quickly established their houses throughout the realms of Aragon during this period. Later the Carmelites and Augustinians

---

1 See Thomas N. Bisson, *The Medieval Crown of Aragon: A Short History* (Oxford, 1986), pp. 58–85, and Jocelyn N. Hillgarth, *The Spanish Kingdoms 1250–1516* (Oxford, 1976), 1: 3–15, to which I am indebted for much of what follows.

joined them, and together these friars were everywhere in the towns and journeying in pairs throughout the countryside, often preaching and conducting religious services from portable altars or primitive chapels adapted for the purpose.

Life in the realms of Aragon was a complicated series of conquests and social struggles, struggles in which the mendicant orders were to assume a prominent role. They acted not only as propagators of the faith but as instruments of royal policy, providing a bulwark against the encroachment of non-Christian ideas, and soon they became strong allies of the urban middle classes from which the majority of them came. Indeed, their activities were not confined to their spiritual mission; as a primarily educated class they undertook a variety of secular duties, acting as advisers and emissaries for church and state.

Here it may be useful to sketch briefly the cultural and political landscape. I shall attempt to describe as simply as possible the main characteristics of the area, which was at one time or another part of the Crown of Aragon under the rule of James I and his successors up to the time of the Black Death (1348), and to describe briefly their relevance for this study. The Crown of Aragon comprised the kingdoms of Valencia, Catalonia and Aragon and the Balearic Islands; but its territories also extended beyond the boundaries imposed by the Iberian Peninsula to take in the counties of Roussillon and Languedoc, which today are part of France. In the early part of the century the Albigensian Crusade made travel in this territory very dangerous; later, dissident views were to develop here that would threaten the very existence of the Order of Friars Minor. The region was the home of Peter John Olivi and several communities of béguins and béguines, many of whom infiltrated the Third Order, bringing to it similar unorthodox views to those held by the Fraticelli and Spiritual Franciscans.

Along the Mediterranean coast Barcelona and Valencia enjoyed great prestige both as trading cities and as centres of strong representational government. Valencia was one of the first cities to be reconquered from the Moors by James I, and it was there that the first Franciscan missionaries died on their way to convert the Moors in North Africa. Midway between these two cities the Balearic Islands constituted an important trading post in the Mediterranean; they were governed for part of this period by a branch of the Aragonese royal family, but were fully incorporated into the Crown of Aragon in 1344 by Peter III.

Inland were the important cities of Lerida and Saragossa, both places where merchants gathered to sell their wares and, in the case of the latter, where the powerful Aragonese nobles frequently opposed royal policy in an attempt to gain a greater measure of jurisdiction over their territories. Further to the west lay Navarre, an independent kingdom with the small towns of Borja and Ejea de los Caballeros on its borders, and in the interior to the north and south were the important Aragonese towns of Huesca, Daroca, Barbastro and Calatayud. Huesca, in particular, became a prominent bishopric and an important centre for the Friars Minor. All these towns had a multiracial population, segregating the Jews and Moors in special districts in accordance with juridical practice, laid down during the reign of Alfonso X of Castile in the *Siete partidas*, later to become the legal code for the entire Iberian Peninsula.

It is important to remember that the monarchs who ruled these kingdoms were closely allied matrimonially. Peter II's daughter, Isabel, known as Saint Isabel, was the wife of King Denis I of Portugal; the Castilian noble and writer Don Juan Manuel was the son-in-law of both James II of Majorca and James II of Aragon; Frederick, the latter's brother, was king of Sicily. This complicated network of relationships wove an intricate set of alliances and obligations that, in the thirteenth and fourteenth centuries, frequently determined the course of events. Messengers were constantly travelling between these states, bearing letters to family members, dealing with political matters and generally keeping alive the network of communications which existed among the Christian royal families. It is no coincidence that Franciscans were often employed to bear these tidings or to deal with secret affairs on the king's behalf, for in some ways they gave the seal of approval to royal policy, emphasizing the religious nature of the reconquest and the Aragonese policy of territorial expansion, while never themselves constituting a threat to the sovereignty of the monarch.

The composition of the Crown of Aragon gives rise to certain problems of semantics. No one term can be applied to the king of these widespread domains without causing confusion between Aragon and the larger Crown of Aragon (composed of Aragon, Catalonia, Majorca and Valencia, and, for a short period, Montpellier). As it is sometimes necessary to refer to Aragon as a separate entity I have had to resort to somewhat clumsy terms such as "the realms of Aragon," "the Aragonese crown" and "the Crown of Aragon" to denote the larger political entity and the activities of King James and his successors.

Some of the rulers of the Crown of Aragon can be a source of confusion in their turn, due to the fact that as kings of both Catalonia and Aragon they can be referred to by both Catalan and Castilian names and sometimes have different numbers (the numbers referring to the Catalan dynasty being one less than the corresponding numbers in the Aragonese). Peter "the Ceremonious," for example, who reigned from 1336 to 1387, is both Pere III of Catalonia and Pedro IV of Aragon. In the interest of simplicity I have decided to refer to kings by their English names, and to apply only the Catalan system of numbering. Thus the king mentioned above is always Peter III, and James is substituted for Jaume or Jaime. The simplified genealogical table on page xi should help clarify the positions of the members of the royal family whose names occur most often in this study.[2]

The names of friars present a unique and difficult problem, for it is often impossible to be sure of the regional origins of the friars themselves. In the majority of cases it is clear that they were Catalans or Aragonese, but in others I can only attempt to relate them to families of the same surname and thus deduce their geographical origin, aware that this may at times lead to erroneous deductions. For Valencia it is particularly difficult, as it is clear that both Aragonese and Catalan friars found their way to this area. In view of the fact that many more of the names encountered refer to friars from Catalan families, largely because extant archival sources in Catalonia are more abundant for this period, I have decided to use Catalan first names for all Catalans, Castilian for those from Aragon or beyond the confines of the Crown of Aragon (except of course those whom I know to have been French or Italian) and Catalan for all those whose origin is in dispute.

The names of cities present fewer problems. English names are used for the larger, well-known centres like Gerona and Saragossa. For smaller towns whose names have no English equivalent I have adhered to the forms used by the natives in each place.

The Crown of Aragon at this period followed the method of dating known as the Florentine incarnation year, in which 25 March was regarded as the first of the year. In this study, for dates between 1 January and 24 March I give first the incarnation year, followed in square brackets by the equivalent form in the Julian calendar. Dates falling between March 25 and 31 December are identical in both systems.

---

[2] The Catalan forms Alfons, Jaume and Pere (for Alfonso, James and Peter) are retained in the genealogical table only. Note that, as there is no English equivalent of Alfonso/Alfons, this name appears in its more usual Castilian form throughout the text and notes.

The currency in use in the realms of Aragon varied from one area to another. Although from James I's time onwards there was an increasing tendency to adopt the use of pounds, *sous, diners* (denarii) and *òbols,* these were not always worth the same amount throughout the territories; for instance the Jaca sous were worth more than those in Barcelona. Other coins are referred to infrequently: the *mazmutina,* of Moorish origin; the *florin,* used more extensively in the fourteenth century; the *morabatin* denoting a variable number of sous; the *ral* or *real,* names used for the *diner* in Valencia and Majorca more especially; the *tornés* of French origin; and the *croat* first used under Peter II. Many of these coins were made of an alloy of silver and copper while some were primarily made of silver or gold, but it is important to remember that their value was not fixed until well after 1348.

One final remark about nomenclature would seem to be in order: I use 'convent,' 'house,' 'friary' as synonyms, largely because the most frequent term used in contemporary studies was undoubtedly 'convent,' a word English writers tend to use only for houses of female religious. It will be noted that the Latin documents also use 'monastery' as a synonym for 'convent,' but I have avoided its use in this study for Franciscan houses, tending to use it for convents of female religious or when referring to monastic orders.

The large area comprising the Crown of Aragon has made my task of research especially difficult, and I have spent some fifteen years of painstaking work in archives and specialized library collections in southern France and Spain, gathering the documentation and examining all extant material relating to the thirteenth and fourteenth centuries which might conceivably bring some light to bear upon the Franciscans in the realms of Aragon.

Clearly, such a task was not undertaken lightly and in some cases was not made easier by the fact that the catalogues of some of the archives I visited were incomplete or non-existent, or that some archivists found it difficult to imagine why I would wish to go through so many parchments or notarial manuals to find material on Franciscans. The many hours of work were frequently inadequately rewarded; still, I collected thousands of references to Franciscans, many of which had little value in themselves but taken as a whole enabled me to piece together the conclusions I have set down here. Limitations of space and consideration for my readers have led me to omit much of this material here, although its existence has often enabled me to see patterns of behaviour which otherwise would remain obscure. Fortunately, some of the material lends itself to systematization in the form of lists, and I have attempted to include these either in the appendices or in notes, wherever appropriate. In the collection of documents I have given samples of letters and/or wills referred to in the text and illustrating some of the main concerns or interests of the Franciscans and their supporters. I hope that this will not only clarify the text itself but emphasize the universality of certain aspects of Franciscan life before 1348. For the names of friars I have had to resort to simplified chronological and alphabetical indices, partly because their presentation in any other format would have been complicated and cumbersome, and would not have added significantly to my study.

In view of the importance I place upon the material gathered and the difficulty of the archival work undertaken over the last fifteen years, I have elaborated more than is customary on the archival sources consulted (see pp. 411-420). I believe that I should emphasize here certain aspects of these sources and elucidate further the method of proceeding and the way in which I have chosen to present my conclusions.

As far as I am aware, no similar study of the Franciscans in Europe has yet been undertaken, largely because much of the material I was able to consult—royal registers, notarial manuals, wills and municipal documents—has long disappeared in most countries. The idea of such a study is not itself new, but previous attempts have fallen victim to civil disturbances in Spain over the years. During the period prior to 1936 several scholars were working on collecting material for the history of the Order of Friars Minor, a task truncated by the outbreak of the Civil War and the subsequent deaths of Fr. Andreu Ivars and Fr. Martí de Barcelona, the two most actively engaged in the preparation of this work. Unfortunately, some of the archival material contained in the archives of the Order itself, which were moved to "safety" from areas considered to be at risk, has disappeared and was probably destroyed during the war. The only complete collection of Franciscan documents now preserved is that for the Gerona house, although there are surviving documents from the Barcelona house in the Crown of Aragon archives, and isolated parchments have been preserved by the Order itself from other Catalan houses, most notably that at Berga. Neither Aragon nor Valencia have been so fortunate, and only a few documents for the Jaca house survive in the National Archives in Madrid. In these archives a few parchments relating to the Majorca house have also been preserved, but such fragmentary records are quite inadequate for any major study of the Order before 1348.

My research over the years has therefore been laborious, time-consuming and frequently regarded with some misgiving by archivists who failed to see the connection between my ostensible subject and the documents for which they were asked, and indeed, at times there was no immediate connection, only the possibility that a reference to the Franciscans would crop up in an unlikely place. In some cases I was able to enter the stacks and consult the material directly without filling up request forms, a much slower process, or without being limited to a specific quantity of volumes, a procedure which has recently been adopted in the archives of the Crown of Aragon. These archives contain some of the most valuable medieval documents in Europe, a fact of which many European historians are unaware: for the thirteenth and fourteenth centuries alone thousands of registers survive from the chancellery and treasury of the crown, as well as thousands of parchments covering not only civil but ecclesiastical matters.

A similar wealth of material exists in the major cathedrals, and it took several years to go through the parchments, notarial registers and other relevant documents in Barcelona, Gerona and Vic, perhaps the richest in Catalonia, where registers containing rough notes of wills to be drawn up, inventories, commercial transactions and the multifarious tasks entrusted to civil and ecclesiastical notaries, run into the thousands. In addition, these archives preserve hundreds of wills on parchment, account books, parish visitations, ordination registers and other matters relevant to cathedral or diocese. Much of this material contains nothing of relevance for the mendicant orders, but it was necessary to analyse all the available documents in order to determine their possible significance. At first it seemed an impossible undertaking, but after many years in the archives I have been able to complete it.

In an attempt to approach my study from a different angle, I extended my search beyond ecclesiastical and royal archives. I went through all the extant manuals in notarial archives, again an onerous task, especially as many of these manuals were in an advanced state of decay and tended to crumble at the touch. Despite these difficulties, the manuals contributed significantly to my overall view of the Franciscans, affording abundant evidence that the Franciscans owed much of their success to the traders in areas adjacent to their houses. The friars frequently came into contact with the municipal authorities, at times acting for them or allowing the use of their conventual buildings for meetings of the councillors. I checked through the minutes of meetings of these authorities, the privileges accorded them and the parchments relating to the areas of their jurisdiction, expecting to find valuable information, a task which took years but which was disappointing, as they proved to be much less productive than the other archives mentioned. In part, this was due to the loss of much material, but I was surprised that there were fewer references to the friars in these records than I would have anticipated.

Although requiring long hours of careful perusal, my time in the Catalan archives was well rewarded. I found some useful material in the archives of the Reino de Valencia, but mostly for the latter part of the fourteenth century. Access to the cathedral archives in Valencia is somewhat limited and I was unable to do as systematic a search through the parchments as I would have wished. All the same, I made several visits to these archives and found some interesting material. In Aragon, however, little remains from the thirteenth and early fourteenth centuries, and although I visited all the likely archives, spread over a vast area, I had to rely almost entirely on material in the archives of the Crown of Aragon. From Saragossa and Huesca I collected material for the latter part of the fourteenth century and a few documents for the earlier period, but little remains to attest to the important Franciscan presence in these vibrant medieval cities.

After collecting much seemingly insignificant material, I began to see a pattern developing, and this enabled me to decide on a chronological demarcation for my study and a format for its presentation. Despite the fact that my research covered material for the whole of the thirteenth and fourteenth centuries in all but the most extensive archives, I chose to limit my comments to the period prior to 1348, believing that after this date a very clear shift in emphasis in ecclesiastical life becomes evident. The aftermath of the Black Death, the papal schism and later the massacre of the Jews, were to raise many questions among the laity and were probably partially responsible for a change in the way the mendicant orders envisaged their mission. By this time they had consolidated their influence in the realms of Aragon and had acquired both property and a position of respect in the community, but among themselves there was an ever-increasing divergence of opinion as to the observance of their rule.

In presenting the material, I have tried to emphasize the period of development of the Order, stressing where appropriate the problems it faced and the support it received. The lack of any comprehensive study of Franciscan life during this period in the realms of Aragon suggested that too much detail would detract from its overall importance. At the same time, because much of the material I have collected has no parallel in other Franciscan studies, I regarded it essential to consign to notes or appendices particulars that might help elucidate the text or which I hope to elaborate upon in a subsequent study. The very nature of the sources has precluded consideration of certain aspects of the friars' lives; ordinary everyday affairs were unlikely to be recounted in legal manuals or to attract the attention of royal scribes. Sometimes these matters can be inferred from legacies in wills, from disputes with the clergy and from favours granted; but the sermons the friars preached, the sick they attended, the services they conducted can only be conjectured. Evidence of such matters is almost non-existent, but I have tried to reconstruct the average life of a Franciscan friar in Chapter 5, conscious that whole areas have had to be omitted for lack of evidence. In all, my aim has been to clarify the position of the Franciscans during this period and to indicate the significant role they played in the most prosperous years enjoyed by the realms of Aragon. It might have been interesting to compare the Franciscans with the Dominicans, and again with the Carmelites and Augustinians, but this must remain for a later study. Until the basic archival research is completed for all the orders a comparative study can at best only be indicative of trends, although even these cannot be determined with any accuracy.

I am indebted to a large number of organizations and individuals without whose help this study could never have been attempted, but as I have benefited from the advice of so many, it would be impossible to refer specifically to all those who contributed in one way or another to its completion. There are a few, however, who merit special mention: the Canada Council and its later and current incarnation in the Social Sciences and Humanities Research Council for the financial assistance that enabled me to spend extended periods in Spain and to travel to the different archives; and the archivists and librarians in the various cities I visited, many of whom have been very helpful, often going to extreme lengths to ensure that I was able to consult every possible and many probable sources for Franciscan activity in the thirteenth and fourteenth centuries.

Among the many individuals, I am especially indebted to Fr. Josep Martí Mayor, OFM, Librarian and Archivist at the Franciscan Provincial Archives in Barcelona, who not only made available the valuable collection of manuscripts and books contained there but personally advised, listened and encouraged me throughout the long process of gathering information; Rev. Robert I. Burns, SJ, of the University of California at Los Angeles, who was always available to give advice and assistance regarding all aspects of the Crown of Aragon, the use of the archives, difficult manuscript readings and other matters, besides offering help and encouragement on occasions when I encountered unforeseen difficulties; Rev. Josep Baucells i Reig, Archivist of the Cathedral Archives of Barcelona, who most generously provided references to the Franciscans in the archive's holdings, offered help and advice, especially in the early years, and who, throughout, has been a valuable source of information; Rev. Canon Miquel Gros i Pujol of Vic, Archivist of the Ecclesiastical Archives, who went out of his way on several occasions to make special arrangements so that I could use to the full the limited time available; Rev. Joaquim Colomer of Gerona Cathedral Archives; Rev. Josep Maria Marquès and especially his former assistant, known to all who used the archives as Mossèn Jordi, of the Gerona Diocesan Archives; Dr. Ramon Alberch of the Gerona Municipal Archives; Dr. Enric Mirambell of the Gerona Historical Archives, and his successors; Sebastià Bosom i Isern of the Puigcerdà Historical Archives, who enthusiastically produced hundreds of virtually inaccessible notarial manuals under less than ideal circumstances; Rev. Canon Josep Maria Gasol i Almendros of the Manresa Municipal Archives. If, inadvertently, I have omitted a name, I hope that this general appreciation will right the omission: all I can do here is to repeat my gratitude and hope that in some measure this book will show them that their labour was not in vain.

There is one person, however, whom I never knew personally but to whom I owe a special debt, the late Fr. Martí de Barcelona, OFM, who was assassinated in 1936 at the beginning of the Spanish Civil War. Fr. Martí had embarked on a history of the Friars Minor in Aragon, treading many of the same paths I was to take; sadly, his life was cut short when he had already completed a significant portion of his study. It was only some years after I had begun my own work that Dr. Michael McVaugh brought to my attention the existence of some recently discovered notes of Fr. Martí housed in the Capuchin Archives in Barcelona. I hastened to consult them and found that they were indeed the notes he had buried in the ground in 1936 when he realized the dangers he faced, and which he hoped someday he would be able to dig up again and continue his history. This was not to be, but the notes themselves had been unearthed by a friend of Fr. Martí's and kept for some years by that friend before they were turned over to the Capuchins in Barcelona. They bore the marks of their singular resting place, having suffered somewhat from humidity, but were still very legible. It took me many weeks to copy the notes and months to check the references they contained, but this study was greatly enriched by the additional material they afforded; in some ways too, they served as a checkpoint for some of my own research, as Fr. Martí de Barcelona had covered much similar ground. Without this windfall my work would have been the poorer, and I wish to record my thanks here to the Capuchin friars in Barcelona who allowed me to consult this invaluable material, at the same time paying tribute to the scholarly work of Fr. Martí de Barcelona from which I have frequently drawn when attempting to present an overall view of Franciscan endeavour in the realms of Aragon and to complement my own conclusions.[3]

As I was putting the finishing touches to this manuscript I learned with great sorrow of the death of one of the greatest Franciscan scholars of all time, Dr. John R.H. Moorman, a historian whose work is cited constantly in these pages and who was also a personal friend. I had hoped that he might have been able to read the study before it was published and give his valuable advice; instead I can only pay a written tribute to his scholarship and express my gratitude for his friendship and interest in my own work.

Finally, I would like to thank those who consented to read this manuscript: the late Rev. Michael Sheehan, CSB, of the Pontifical Institute of Mediaeval Studies, Toronto, who kindly read chapters as they were written and made many valuable suggestions; Anna Burko of the Centre for Medieval Studies in the University of Toronto for her tireless efforts in checking text, notes, archival and bibliographical references; Jean Hoff of the Pontifical Institute for her suggestions for improving the Latin; as well as Rev. Robert I. Burns, SJ, of the University of California at Los Angeles, Professor James Brodman of the University of Central Arkansas, Conway and Professor Jocelyn Hillgarth of the Pontifical Institute, all of whom read the finished work prior to publication and offered useful advice. Their suggestions ensured that many errors were eliminated, and that any that remain are entirely my own responsibility.

---

[3] Very recently the Capuchin friars have begun to publish manuscripts which Fr. Martí de Barcelona had completed at the outbreak of the Civil War. One of these posthumous works is included in the Bibliography.

1

Legend and History

The thirteenth century was an important landmark in the history of Christendom, for during these years changes were made that fashioned the shape of Europe and defined its spiritual direction. Two of the men who influenced these changes were central figures in the development of the Franciscan ideal within the realms of Aragon: Saint Francis of Assisi and King James I of Aragon.

Saint Francis, the founder of the Order of the Friars Minor, needs no more than a brief introduction. His concern for the poor and afflicted, his reputed love of animals and his life of prayer and meditation are known beyond the confines of the order he founded in 1209.[1] Born in Assisi about 1182, the son of the wealthy cloth merchant Peter Bernardone, Francis grew up with the aspirations of his social background, a desire to become a knight and do deeds of chivalry like other young men of his acquaintance. He was extravagant and abundantly endowed with the good things of life, but he soon became disenchanted with the life of ease, which he saw in vivid contrast to the poverty around him. He rejected the comfort and wealth to which he was accustomed, deliberately seeking poverty and suffering. Many thought him mad, and his father was furious when he sold cloth from the family business to help rebuild the church. Unable to persuade his son to return home and take his place in the business, he demanded the money back, and it was the dramatic gesture of Francis in giving to his father all the money he had and with it the clothes from his back that marked the beginning of a life of deprivation and evangelism.[2]

---

1 John R.H. Moorman, *A History of the Franciscan Order from its Origins to the Year 1517* (Oxford, 1968; repr. Chicago, 1988), p. 11.
2 Ibid., p. 7, and Rosalind B. Brooke, *The Coming of the Friars* (London, 1975), pp. 21–22, for Francis's dramatic renunciation of all his possessions and his family.

Much of his initial success was derived from the fact that he had not only given up a life of wealth and ease but also made peace a keynote of his mission at a time when strife was endemic in Italy and when the ordinary inhabitants of the city states were wearied with constant warfare. Assisi, which was to be the centre of the order founded by Francis, was also the place where he received the message "Go and repair my house which you see is in ruins."[3] Like many of the neighbouring cities it frequently became involved in the struggles between empire and papacy; Francis himself was captured and imprisoned for his participation in one of the frequent wars between Assisi and Perugia.[4] The poverty and peace which Francis preached were, therefore, foreign concepts to the Italian city states whose successful commercial undertakings often led to greed and strife.

Francis, however, was not the first to preach a life of poverty, nor was his the only mendicant order to be founded in the first decade of the thirteenth century.[5] A century earlier Peter Waldo or Valdes, a rich merchant from Lyons, repenting of the way in which he had made money through usury, also set forth to preach the message of poverty.[6] Like Saint Francis, Waldo was disenchanted with the life of the church around him and, by gathering a group of like-minded men who were prepared to live a life of austerity, hoped to become a better Christian.[7]

Certainly at the beginning they had no intention of separating from the church, and a description of his followers could well have been a

---

3 Brooke, *Coming of the Friars,* p. 21.
4 Ibid., p. 30.
5 The foundation and development of the Dominican order closely paralleled that of the Friars Minor, and the early life of Saint Dominic has much in common with that of Saint Francis. For the origins and growth of the order see William A. Hinnebusch, *The History of the Dominican Order* (Staten Island, NY, 1965). The Carmelites and Augustinians were both founded early in the thirteenth century, but their houses in Spain only date from the end of the century. A number of smaller mendicant orders were abolished at the Council of Lyons in 1274, in part because they were considered to be operating on the fringe of orthodoxy, but also because they were too small to maintain an independent existence.
6 G.G. Coulton, *Two Saints: St. Bernard and St. Francis* (Cambridge, 1932; repr. Folcroft, PA, 1974).
7 Martin Scott, *Medieval Europe* (London, 1964), p. 210; Coulton, *Two Saints,* pp. 76–81. See also Jeffrey B. Russell, ed., *Religious Dissent in the Middle Ages* (New York, 1971), p. 41, where the editor points out that there is no reliable evidence to support the name Peter.

description of the barefoot Franciscan friars who, dressed in their coarse sackcloth, went out to preach in the villages; yet there was one important difference: the Waldensians were condemned as heretics, while the followers of Francis remained within the church. The Humiliati, the Cathars and other religious sects of the twelfth century also abandoned orthodoxy and were condemned by the papal Inquisition. In them can be seen the beginnings of a popular movement for ecclesiastical reform, a movement which yearned for purity and which eventually culminated in the Reformation.[8] Furthermore, the contradictions and problems of the thirteenth-century church derived in part from the difficulties associated with the emergence of a powerful lay contingent in the towns and the spirit of nationalism which led to the development of independent states and vernacular languages.[9]

Ironically, it was to be the order founded by Saint Francis, which in some respects can be considered the successor of some of the unorthodox movements mentioned, that, together with the Dominicans, was to help in the extirpation of heresy. Some of the friars who followed Saint Francis themselves overstepped the bounds of orthodoxy, and in 1321 were condemned as heretics by Pope John XXII.[10] Together the followers of Saint Francis and Saint Dominic laboured towards a new world in which the ideals of peace and poverty were central. It was the example of the man from Assisi which most appealed to popular piety; at first the followers of Saint Dominic were characterized by their austerity and learning, although later in the thirteenth century there was little to distinguish them from the Franciscans.[11] What is more, they were joined by other orders such as the Augustinians and the Carmelites which, although they were never so numerous and could not hope to emulate the popular appeal of Saint Francis, nevertheless shared many of the same ideals. The commitment to poverty, simplicity and peace by the Franciscan order is as relevant today as it was in the thirteenth century. Thus, the cult which grew up around the name of Saint Francis with its emphasis on these ideals has not only survived to the present but

---

8 Scott, *Medieval Europe,* p. 100.
9 John H. Mundy, *Europe in the High Middle Ages 1150–1309* (London, 1973), pp. 515–520.
10 Ibid., p. 312. A discussion of the impact of the ideas of some of these friars in the Crown of Aragon is to be found in José María Pou y Martí, *Visionarios, béguinos y fraticelos catalanes (siglos XIII–XV),* rev. ed. (Madrid, 1991).
11 Coulton, *Two Saints,* p. 100.

has a strong appeal to contemporary man, accounting in part for the recent renewal of interest in Franciscanism.[12]

The second great figure in the thirteenth century who helped to promote the cause of the Franciscans and other religious orders in the Iberian Peninsula was King James I of Aragon. James lived from 1208 to 1276 and ruled a number of coastal realms "from the Rhone to Valencia."[13] At different times these realms comprised parts of the Mediterranean seaboard of southern France and northern Africa, Aragon, Catalonia, the Balearic Islands, Valencia and Murcia.[14] From 1225 onwards James led a series of successful invasions of Moorish Spain, conquering Majorca in 1232 and dying on the Valencian front over forty years later while he was attempting to contain the most serious revolt against his authority.[15]

Although James was primarily a warrior-king, his main contribution to subsequent peninsular history was the way in which he gradually reconquered the territory occupied by the Moors. In order to consolidate his newly-reconquered lands he encouraged their repopulation by Christians and promoted the establishment of religious orders. In strengthening the Christian presence in his territories, and by encouraging the proclamation of the Christian faith and the conversion of the non-Christian minorities, James hoped that the kingdoms would be protected from further incursions of his neighbours to the south.

The reconquest was a long and complicated process which falls beyond the scope of this study, but in essence it was the recovery of land from the Moors, followed by the fortification of the Mediterranean coasts by Christian repopulation and royal support for the church. Such a policy ensured the continual development of the mendicant orders, especially the Dominicans and Franciscans, throughout the thirteenth

---

12 The Faculty of Theology of Saint Pacià in Barcelona, with the collaboration of the three orders of Franciscans (the Friars Minor, the Capuchins and the Conventuals), inaugurated a course on Franciscanism in October 1983.
13 Robert I. Burns, "Castle of Intellect, Castle of Force: The Worlds of Alfonso the Learned and James the Conqueror," in *The Worlds of Alfonso the Learned and James the Conqueror: Intellect and Force in the Middle Ages,* ed. Robert I. Burns (Princeton, 1985), pp. 3–22, at 6; see also his *Society and Documentation in Crusader Valencia* (Princeton, 1985), p. 3.
14 For a full description of the territories over which James I ruled see Burns, "Castle of Intellect."
15 Ibid., p. 8.

century. The following chapter explains the extent to which the kings of Aragon protected the Franciscans and encouraged their work. In this chapter an attempt will be made to indicate the chronological foundation of the various houses throughout the realms of King James. From this it will be clear that the establishment of Franciscan friaries directly parallels the progress of James I's crusade against the Moors and is indeed an integral part of his political policy of Christianization.

THE FIRST FRIARS

Following the example of their founder, Saint Francis, the first friars divested themselves of their possessions and set out to begin a life of poverty and evangelism. At first their activities were limited to Assisi and the Marches of Ancona, but it was not long before they decided to take their message further afield. The people who lived in the war-torn cities of Italy, where corruption was rampant, greeted with enthusiasm this new message of hope brought to them by Saint Francis and his followers. Unlike the Waldensians a century before, Saint Francis and his friars were very careful to ensure that they followed the orthodox teachings of the church, giving the respect due to its hierarchy and clergy in the hope that they would be accepted without acrimony and obtain the necessary papal approval.[16] If the friars were to succeed in their mission, the Pope had to be convinced that Francis and his followers were serious in their desire to live lives of humility, poverty and devotion.

Moreover, it soon became evident that if they were to be effective in their missionary work some organization was needed, and Francis began to think about the future of the order he had founded. It is not known exactly what was in the original rule he drew up for his small band of followers because it has long since disappeared, but from the later version of 1221 (which might have suffered some modifications) it is clear that Francis and his disciples hoped to emulate the example of the first apostles and preach the Gospel to all people.[17] Subsequent chapters show that many friars found it impossible to achieve such a state of perfection, and for them the rule became little more than a

---

16 Brooke, *Coming of the Friars*, p. 31.
17 Ibid., p. 15.

guide, its provisions frequently being ignored or interpreted with a laxity which Francis would have found repugnant.

It is difficult to be precise about the first missionary journey undertaken by Francis outside Italy, because so much has been written about him that history and legend have, in some respects, become indistinguishable. This is also true of his missionary journey to the Iberian Peninsula, which led to the establishment of Franciscan friaries throughout the kingdoms of Aragon, Castile, Navarre and Portugal. Claims have been made by many of the towns he is said to have visited that he founded the Franciscan house there. In some cases the claim is obviously impossible; in others there is insufficient evidence to reach a definitive conclusion.

Surviving documentation, then, seems to suggest that the journey of Saint Francis provided the inspiration for the foundation of friaries, but that in most cases these were not established before his death in 1226. To dismiss legends as unhistorical would be to deny the way in which popular tradition is disseminated. If not accurate in their portrayal of events, legends by their very survival contribute to an understanding of the importance attached by medieval Christians to the Franciscan ideal. It was logical that one of the first places to be visited by Saint Francis and his friars should be the Iberian Peninsula, which, in the early part of the thirteenth century and prior to the accession of James I, was still partly under Moorish rule and therefore sorely in need of the Gospel message. The reconquest of the territory from the Moors was not to be completed until 1492, when Granada was incorporated into the then united kingdom of Spain under Ferdinand and Isabella, long after the death of James the Conqueror and well beyond the limits of this study.

Saint Francis Visits Spain

Accounts of the early years of the missionary work undertaken by Saint Francis and his friars vary significantly. The date of Saint Francis's departure for Spain is no exception and remains uncertain, although it probably took place in 1213 or 1214. One of his early biographers, Thomas of Celano, explains how Saint Francis, filled with an intense desire for martyrdom, set out for Morocco. It seems likely that he took the shortest route by sea to Barcelona and from there made his way across the northern part of the Peninsula to Burgos, to obtain from Alfonso, king of Castile, the necessary permission for his missionaries to enter Morocco.[18] He then intended to go to Santiago de Compostela to visit the shrine of Saint James, and probably achieved his aim before falling victim to what was to become a prolonged illness, and one which forced him to abandon his proposed journey to Morocco and return to Italy.[19] Tradition has it that while he was praying at the shrine of Saint James he became aware that he must set up houses for friars in Spain.

Little is known about those who accompanied Saint Francis on this journey, but it is probable that his only companion was Fr. Bernard. An alternative account of the journey suggests that other friars besides Fr. Bernard undertook the pilgrimage, but there is no evidence for this.[20] Atanasio López also suggests that along the route to Santiago many people were drawn to the order, but makes it clear that he can provide no names to corroborate or dispute his suggestion.[21] If the charisma of the saint from Assisi drew men to him, as would seem reasonable, it is likely that these early friars lived in small groups, perhaps never becoming officially integrated with the order. Some of them probably helped to spread the word about the order and later may have been of considerable help to those who wished to establish friaries. Extant documentation affords no indication of where the first friars came from nor what led them to found houses in the Iberian Peninsula.

---

18   Thomas of Celano, "The First Life of Saint Francis," trans. with intro. and notes by Placid Hermann, in *St. Francis of Assisi, Writings and Early Biographies: English Omnibus of the Sources for the Life of St. Francis*, ed. Marion A. Habig (London, 1972), pp. 225–355, at 274 (par. 55). In the first book of his *Crónica* (1738) Jaime Coll devotes considerable space to the journey of Saint Francis to Spain and suggests that he made the overland route through Southern France (Roussillon) to Barcelona, where he established a convent either in 1211 on the way to Santiago de Compostela or in 1214 on the way back to Italy. See Coll, *Crónica de la província franciscana de Cataluña: Parte primera*, secs. 12–17, facsimile ed., with intro. and indices by José Martí Mayor, Crónicas franciscanas de España 21 (Madrid, 1981), pp. 5–7.

19   Coll, *Crónica*, secs. 13–14, ed. Martí Mayor, pp. 5–6. I am particularly indebted to this work for its synopsis of Saint Francis's visit to Spain.

20   Pedro Sanahuja, *História de la seráfica provincia de Cataluña* (Barcelona, 1959), p. 20.

21   Atanasio López, *La província de España de los frailes menores* (Santiago, 1915), p. 13.

The Foundation of the First Convents

Although there is no factual information about the years which led up to the establishment of the Franciscans in the realms of Aragon, there are a number of legends which have grown up over the intervening centuries. Most of these refer to Catalonia, which was probably the first area reached by Saint Francis if and when he arrived by ship from Italy. Some writers have claimed an alternative point of entry to Spain, Navarre, but if their assertions are correct Saint Francis would have had to travel overland, a much longer and more hazardous journey and one which he might have preferred to avoid because of the dangers he almost certainly would have encountered en route and the extra time it would have taken him to reach his destination.[22]

It should be remarked here that Pope Innocent III's appeals to Count Raymond IV of Toulouse to ban heresy from his jurisdiction had fallen on deaf ears, largely because the count was unwilling to plunge his lands into the civil war he knew would ensue.[23] The excommunication of Raymond in 1207 and the Albigensian Crusade initiated a "Holy War" in Provence and Languedoc. Aragonese fiefdoms north of the Pyrenees were attacked, and King Peter I was killed at Muret in 1213.[24] For Saint Francis to have travelled through these war-torn lands would have been impractical. The tradition which claims that he arrived in Barcelona by boat, having taken the shortest route across the Mediterranean, and that he spent a few days there to rest before continuing his pilgrimage to Santiago, is not only the most logical but is supported by one of the earliest legends, which maintains that Saint Francis preached in the chapel of the hospital of Saint Nicholas, where he had a cell.[25]

Although he cannot be credited with having founded a house in Barcelona at this time, it is quite possible that he spent the few nights in the city at the hospital of Saint Nicholas, which was situated close to the port at which his ship would have docked. Some confusion must have arisen here over the date, which could not have been as early as 1211. This would suggest a merging of the visits of Fr. Gil and Saint Francis to the March of Ancona sometime after 1209, at which time only Fr. Gil proceeded to Spain. He was probably accompanied by Fr. Bernard, as

---

22 Sanahuja, *Història*, p. 21.
23 Scott, *Medieval Europe*, p. 213.
24 Ibid., p. 214.
25 Sanahuja, *Història*, p. 50.

was Saint Francis a few years later, and is also reputed to have made the pilgrimage to the shrine of Saint James in Santiago, although early writers do not agree on the dates for this journey, suggesting that it took place sometime between 1209 and 1215.[26] It is almost certain that Saint Francis did not accompany them on this occasion.

It was only in 1217, when the number of friars had grown considerably that Saint Francis, in the chapter held that year in the Porziuncola, decided to appoint provincial ministers who, accompanied by a few brothers, would go out to organize friaries and undertake missionary work in the various nations professing the Catholic faith.[27] As López explains, Spain was to receive a mission of several friars, whose names are not known today, although probably among them was Bernard of Quintaval as the first provincial minister.[28] The actual date of Fr. Bernard's arrival in Spain has been disputed and could even have been later than 1217.[29] He was probably accompanied by Fr. John Parente, who in 1219 was elected provincial minister of Spain and made the journey to his new destination with one hundred friars.

Saint Francis hoped that, through the sending of so many missionaries to Spain, a point of departure for the Moorish territories of Africa, the Christian faith could also be taken by them to those non-Christians. The coastal city of Valencia served as a midway point for those bound for the African missions, and two of the friars, purportedly on their way to Tunis, were martyred in Valencia by the Sayyid Abu Zayd, the Moorish leader who, with many of his relatives, later embraced the Christian faith.[30]

Many difficulties confront the historian of the early years of the Franciscans in Spain, not least of which is the intermingling of fact and fiction, making it impossible to establish a rigid chronological sequence for the foundation of friaries. For this reason, the early establishment of houses will be discussed by area, starting with Catalonia as the most likely to have been the first to have welcomed Saint Francis.

26 López, *La província de España*, pp. 4–12, where the pilgrimage of Fr. Gil is dealt with in some detail.
27 Ibid., p. 14.
28 Ibid., pp. 15–16.
29 Sanahuja, *História*, pp. 23–24, where Fr. Bernard's visit to Spain is discussed.
30 López, *La província de España*, p. 90.

However, before doing so, it may be relevant to examine the legends which grew up over the years around the visit of Saint Francis to Catalonia. Too much reliance cannot be placed on the dates they suggest, but the very fact that in some areas they are so numerous lends support for an early foundation in a given town.

A recent publication on this subject attempts to collect in one place these popular stories about the visit of Saint Francis to Catalonia.[31] The first excerpt included in this collection is taken from the *Libre del Crestià* of Fr. Francesc Eiximenis (or Examenis), a prominent fourteenth-century Catalan Franciscan who spent most of his productive life as a writer in Valencia. Fr. Francesc says:

> I would especially like to tell you a remarkable fact about the glorious virgin and martyr, Our Lady Saint Eulalia, who with our father, Saint Francis, came from the land of the Moors to Barcelona to preach in a small chapel dedicated to Saint Nicholas. It is still in our monastery today close to the chapel dedicated to Saint Louis ... . Then he [Saint Francis] said to them: "Be apprised that in this place there will be a famous monastery with friars belonging to my order. I commend them to you for the love of Jesus Christ."[32]

This story is the basis for the conclusion by all subsequent writers that the Barcelona house was founded by Saint Francis. Now, the long-standing popular tradition that claims him founder cannot be disregarded. Historians should not understand it strictly to mean that Francis personally supervised the building of the Barcelona house. The Saint's visit to Barcelona would have aroused the interest of the citizens, many of whom would have gathered round him, and some would probably have agreed to carry on the work he had started. If Saint Francis had arrived by sea, it is logical that the site chosen for the future convent should be adjacent to the shore. On these grounds, perhaps, his followers would have made a plea to their contemporaries for a piece of land which could be used for a convent, and in this inspirational sense Saint Francis could later be regarded as the "founder" of the Barcelona house.

---

31 *Sant Francesc d'Assís, "el Pobrissó" (1181[2]-1226): El seu pas per Catalunya* (Reus, 1968). Although this is a popular devotional pamphlet (paginated 481–507), it has drawn on all the available sources for the legends it includes and gives a very full bibliography and chronology to support the material.

32 López, *La província de España*, p. 491. The translation is taken from Jill R. Webster, *Excerpts from the Works of Francesc Examenis*, Folklore Seminar Papers 3 (Saint Andrews, [1982]), p. 6.

The same argument can be adduced regarding the foundation of houses at Lerida, Gerona and Saragossa. Other legends, surrounding private houses at Sant Joan Despí, the Llobregat valley, Santes Creus near Tarragona, Poblet, Reus, Gerona, Manresa, Prades, Vic and Sant Celoni, while not always providing the inspiration for the establishment of a convent, all have in common their personal contact with Saint Francis.

Recently Jordi Romero, a local historian from Sant Joan Despí, has published an article casting doubt upon the veracity of the legend associated with Can Codina, a house in that vicinity. It provides the best illustration of how legends are created, for tradition claims that Can Codina was built in 1090, while Romero can find no trace of a Codina family there until the sixteenth century. The first documented member of the Codina family is Guillem of Sant Boi, who in 1537 married a girl called Margarida from Sant Joan Despí. From this time on there was always a Codina family in Sant Joan, and so in 1738 the chronicler Jaime Coll referred to the very old tradition that Saint Francis received hospitality in a house called Can Codina in Sant Joan Despí.[33] Can Codina probably only took its name from its sixteenth-century inhabitants, but the tradition must have grown up around a previous house on the same site, later becoming associated with the Codina family. There are similar traditions connected with the other houses, and although many of these may owe much to popular devotion to Saint Francis it is also possible that on his visit to the area Saint Francis and some of his followers did in fact stay with local residents.

One of the more plausible of such legends is that connected with the Guerau family in Gerona. In 1334 Joan Guerau, son of Jofre, petitioned to reenter the Gerona Franciscan house, which he had left to "sow his wild oats." As it was not customary for such petitions to be granted, his father claimed that in this case an exception should be made in view of the devotion of the Guerau family to Saint Francis and the fact that the Saint had stayed at the family home when he had visited Spain.[34]

---

33 Jordi Romero, "Sant Francesc d'Assis i la tradició de que va posar a Can Codina de Sant Joan Despí," *La font del be* (Sant Joan Despí) 57 (julio–desembre 1984), 19–21, at p. 19.

34 Jill R. Webster, "Tradiciones y datos medievales para la història franciscana," *AIA* 44 (1984), 199–210, at p. 201. See also Josep Perarnau, "*Beatus Franciscus per Gerundam transiens*: Tradició del pas de Sant Francesc d'Assis per Girona," *EF* 85 (1984), 237–240, at pp. 237–238.

Whether or not these legends are true is in itself unimportant, but the fact that they are so numerous and have survived so long reinforces the impact the Saint's visit to the Peninsula must have had on his contemporaries, making the subsequent establishment of Franciscan friaries in Catalonia a logical outcome. This is further corroborated by extant documentation, especially the numerous wills which reflect the charitable preferences of contemporary citizens. The fact that some of the wills were never proved and the bequests nullified in no way diminishes their significance as an indicator of the popularity of these early friars. The following discussion of individual houses shows how these wills assist the historian in piecing together the sequence of events which contributed to the firm establishment of the order in the realms of Aragon.

Barcelona

Barcelona was probably the first Catalan town to be visited, if Saint Francis travelled by sea to the Iberian Peninsula and if the legend that he preached in the chapel of the Hospital of Saint Nicholas in 1211 is based on fact. The date given is almost certainly incorrect: no documentary source mentions the existence of a Franciscan house in Barcelona before 1229.[35] The friars needed the economic support of their contemporaries before they could build a permanent convent. They would first stay in private houses to make themselves known in an area; only a few years later would they be able to establish an official house.[36]

Unfortunately, extant documentation tells little of these early years. The earliest references to the house in Barcelona, described as "Saint Nicholas of the Minores," are found in the Barcelona cathedral archives in two documents of the same date, the first of which is no longer extant. Both refer to legacies in the amount of 12 diners to the work of the Minors of Saint Nicholas and are dated 23 May 1230.[37] The aver-

---

35 Jill R. Webster, "Dos siglos de Franciscanismo en Cataluña: El convento de San Francisco de Barcelona durante los siglos XIII y XIV," *AIA* 41 (1981), 223–255, at pp. 223–224.

36 Moorman, *History of the Franciscan Order*, p. 28; Jill R. Webster, "El desconocido convento de Puigcerdà," *AIA* 49 (1989), 167–194.

37 The non-extant document, listed in the *Index* of Caresmar, 1234–1771 (to be found in the Arxiu capitular de la catedral, Barcelona), refers to the will of Ermesenda, sister of Bernat de Palau; the extant document is the will of Ramon Bou (found in Barcelona, AC, Pia Almoina, perg. 4-17-71).

age lapse of time between the establishment of a house and the appearance of bequests in wills is usually about a year. If these premises are accepted, the date of foundation for the Barcelona house cannot be earlier than 1228, a date which would be in line with the establishment of other houses in Catalonia, such as those in Gerona and Vic, for which there is more documentary evidence.[38] Consequently the date of the chapter said to have been held in 1229, cannot have been correct and probably derives from a misreading of the Roman numerals of an earlier source.[39] It was not until 1233 that the reference to Saint Nicholas was dropped. Bernat de Polinyà's will of 27 January 1233 [1234] leaves 20 sous to the "mensa Fratrum Minorum" rather than to the table of the Minores of Saint Nicholas.[40] From this date on they are usually referred to as "Fratres Minores," and a noticeable increase in bequests is evident as the century progresses. The foundation date of the convent of Saint Nicholas, later known as Saint Francis, could not have been later than 1230 and possibly dates from much earlier.

Lerida

Barcelona was not the only house which claimed to have been founded by Saint Francis in 1211. The chronicler Coll states that he founded five convents, Barcelona, Cervera, Gerona, Lerida and Perpignan, and that two of the friars who accompanied him on that first mission, Fr. John Parente and Fr. Peter of Sassoferrato, lived in the Lerida convent.[41] Lerida was certainly one of the first friaries to be established, although the date of 1217 mentioned by some early Franciscan historians cannot be substantiated.[42] Lerida, according to tradition, owed its foundation to the miraculous conversion of a prominent citizen, Ramon de Barriac, with whom the first friars had stayed. Ramon de Barriac, who was very rich, was promised an increase in his wealth by God if he would build

---

38 For Vic see Sanahuja, *História*, p. 48; for Gerona, Jill R. Webster, "Col.lecció de documents del convent de Sant Francesc de Girona (1224–1399)," *AIEG* 28–30 (1985–1989), 28: 157–189, at p. 163.
39 The date of 1229 is given in *España sagrada: Teatro geográfico-histórico de la iglesia de España,* comp. Enrique Florez et al., 56 vols., 3rd ed. (Madrid, 1879–1957), 28: 335; repeated by Sanahuja, *História*, pp. 32, 51.
40 Barcelona, AC, Pia Almoina, perg. 4-3-250, 27 January 1233 [1234].
41 Sanahuja, *História*, pp. 43–44.
42 Ibid., p. 43.

a convent for the friars.[43] Sanahuja possessed a copy of the will of Ramon de Barriac, but since it was destroyed in the Spanish Civil War before he was able to write his monograph he could only remember that Ramon wished to be buried in the Franciscan cemetery and that his will was dated between 1221 and 1228. He cites another will dated 18 July 1227, which is among the first documentary evidence found for Franciscan houses in the realms of Aragon.[44] There is also evidence that on 12 January 1228 [1229] another legacy was willed to the friars of the Lerida house, making it likely that the house had been established the previous year, shortly before the will was drawn up.[45]

Vic

Curiously enough, Vic was not mentioned among the five houses Coll claimed were established by the first friars who arrived in the Peninsula, despite the fact that it possesses the first recorded document for any house in Catalonia. On 13 December 1225, Felip and Berenguera de Mayoles donated land to the Franciscans on which they could build their convent, provided always that they were subject to the jurisdiction of the bishop of Vic.[46] Such a condition was not in accordance with the way in which the order was to operate, and conflicts with the parish clergy became very frequent.[47] It is probable that work began on construction of the Vic convent in 1226 but was not completed until later. From 1230 onwards there are a number of documents attesting to the presence of the Franciscans in Vic, and unlike many of the other convents in Catalonia, its origins and development are consistently documented.

Gerona

Like Barcelona, Gerona claimed that Saint Francis had visited the city, and that he founded a convent there in 1211, a date disproved by extant

---

43 Sanahuja, *Història*, p. 44, where the miraculous story of Ramon de Barriac is told.
44 Ibid., p. 45.
45 Barcelona, ACA, ORM, Gran Priorato, arm. 28, perg. 117.
46 Sanahuja, *Història*, p. 48.
47 Jill R. Webster, "Documents relacionats amb els convents de Sant Francesc, Santa Clara i Santa Maria del Carme de Vic a l'edat mitjana," *Studium Vicensia* (Vic), in press. Includes documents outlining the way in which the Franciscans were to refrain from impinging on the duties and privileges of the clergy of the diocese of Vic.

documentation. Although it was one of the earliest houses to be established, there is evidence that in 1224 the land which was later to be incorporated into the building of the convent was still in private hands.[48]

The Gerona house is unique in that it possesses an almost complete archival collection of parchments and other records, dating from before the foundation of the house in 1231 [1232] and continuing well beyond the end of the Middle Ages up to the dissolution of the convent in 1836. There is also an archival catalogue listing the contents of the archives in the eighteenth century.[49] If, as tradition claims, Saint Francis stayed in Gerona, the question arises as to why the house was not built earlier, at least as early as Barcelona and Lerida; it is all the more puzzling because a later comment accords Gerona the second place among the houses.[50] Whether or not this refers to the date of foundation or to the importance of the house is impossible to determine from the cryptic remark in the notarial manual. It is clear from the extant documentation that the archival records date from the time that the Franciscans in Gerona planned to build a house. What is not so evident is if, prior to 1224, they lived in private houses, possibly having more difficulty in acquiring the economic support to establish a convent there than was the case in Barcelona, Lerida or Vic.

The preservation of most of the documentation for the Gerona house precludes further speculation about its origins, but it affords a way of determining what kind of documents were usually regarded as important enough to find their way into the Franciscan archives. The great majority of the earliest parchments refer to gifts and sales of land, making it possible to determine precisely where the house stood, which citizens supported it and what its dimensions were. None of the records refer to the daily activities of the friars, although some of these can be inferred from the type of document. Only one or two clauses in wills give any idea of the appointments of the convent or church. Later accounts suggest that the Gerona house was one of the most splendid within the

---

48 Webster, "Col.lecció de documents," pp. 182-189.
49 Ibid., p. 159, regarding the *Repertori de actes del convent de Girona*, preserved in the Arxiu històric dels Franciscans de Catalunya (AHFC), Barcelona, being an inventory of the parchments in the Gerona convent archives in the 18th century, some of which have since been lost.
50 Ibid., p. 166.

realms of Aragon, and an eighteenth-century sketch shows that it stood high up on the banks of the river Onyar, which now divides the old part of the town from the new.[51] Recent construction uncovered part of the old walls, an arch from the cloisters, a well and other fragments of the old convent, but sadly these archeological finds could not be preserved because development of the site had to proceed according to schedule.[52] Although the documentation preserved by the Gerona house dates from 1224, the foundation must be placed somewhat later, probably in 1231 [1232], the date of the first document referring to the existence of the house.

Cervera

One of the five mentioned by Coll as having been founded by Saint Francis, Cervera presents the historian with more difficulties, because little documentation survives from the early thirteenth century. The records kept in the old hospital, mentioned by Sanahuja, seem no longer to exist, and, as with Barcelona, erroneous dates have caused confusion over the date of foundation of the Cervera convent.[53] The earliest positive reference dates from 1235, when Joan de l'Hospital and Ermesenda founded two houses of charity to give shelter each night to two poor people in perpetuity. There is no indication that these houses had anything to do with the work of the friars, but among the legacies is one of twelve diners for the work of Saint Francis.[54] From then on there are many references to the Cervera house and, despite lack of documentary proof, Cervera was probably founded around the same time as the nearby house of Lerida—possibly in the early 1220s.

---

51 Webster, "Col.lecció de documents," p. 169, where the sketch is reproduced.
52 Numerous illustrations of fragments of the Gerona convent have appeared over the years in local periodicals such as the *Revista de Girona;* and some remains are still preserved in private houses, including a recently-opened art gallery, *El Claustre,* where, as its name suggests, arches from the cloisters and a well form part of the entrance. Other fragments are to be found both in Gerona and in the nearby coastal town of S'Agaró, but as all of these are relatively well known they have been omitted from the illustrations accompanying this study.
53 Sanahuja, *História,* p. 92. Attempts to locate the old Cervera hospital records have met with no success, although local residents believe they may still exist. Photographs have been obtained of the ruins of the convent from the Arxiu Gavin, and details will be found in the list of illustrations.
54 Pedro Sanahuja, "El monestir de framenors de Cervera," *EF* 45 (1933), 47–97.

Perpignan

Perpignan is the last of the five houses in the east said to be founded by Saint Francis, and although it is beyond the confines of Catalonia and now French territory, it is of direct relevance to the foundation of houses south of the Pyrenees, for if Saint Francis travelled through France on his way to Spain and not by sea to Barcelona, as is thought by many early historians, the traditions concerning his visit to the Iberian Peninsula would have to be reconsidered. There are as many stories about Saint Francis in southern France as in Catalonia, and it is likely that he did visit this area, though perhaps on a different occasion. Durieux accepts as most probable a date of 1213, midway between the two suggestions of dates for Saint Francis's visit to the Peninsula, 1211 and 1214.[55] Saint Francis is credited with having founded the Franciscan house in Perpignan and, according to two conflicting traditions, was given hospitality by the first Carmelites, possibly on his return from the Iberian Peninsula.[56] It is extremely doubtful that these hermits had established a convent by that time, but it is just possible that they extended hospitality to Saint Francis in the private houses where they lived in small groups before building their permanent convent.

Archival research has failed to corroborate or deny this tradition, and Durieux gives the date of foundation for the Franciscan house in Perpignan as 1243.[57] But this date is incorrect, as there is evidence that the friars were there nearly ten years before that: the first will referring to the Franciscans, in which Pere Albercha of Perpignan leaves 20 sous to help the friars with their work, is dated 1235.[58] By 1300 the convent at Perpignan was well established, having received a house which had

---

55 F.R. Durieux, "Approches de l'histoire franciscaine du Languedoc au XIIIe siècle," in *Les Mendiants en pays d'Oc au XIIIe siècle* (Toulouse, 1973), pp. 79-100. He says (p. 81) that an itinerary by sea to Spain excluding Languedoc is very unlikely in view of the numerous local traditions about Saint Francis. It is his view that if the saint went to Compostela via Languedoc he probably returned via Catalonia. Taking into consideration the legends concerning Saint Francis's visit to Santiago, it would seem more likely that in fact he returned via Languedoc, along what is known today as the Pilgrim's Route.

56 Jill R. Webster, "Els anys formatius dels franciscans i carmelites a Montpeller i Perpinyà," in *Montpellier, la Couronne d'Aragon et les pays de langue d'Oc (1204-1349)* (Montpellier, 1987), pp. 241-253.

57 Durieux, "Approches de l'histoire franciscaine," p. 84.

58 Webster, "Els anys formatius," pp. 247-248.

belonged to the Friars of the Sack and one which had been the property of the Templars. It also maintained a close relationship with the see of Elne, Bishop Bernat having left his "large" Bible and his psalter with glosses to the Franciscans, not without making a condition that they return to the church at Elne the *Sentences* and *Homilies* of Saint John Chrysostom which he had lent them.[59] In the fourteenth century Franciscans frequently occupied the see of Elne, including Fr. Francesc Eiximenis, the Catalan friar whose encyclopedic works provide a commentary on many aspects of life in the Crown of Aragon in the late Middle Ages. Clearly Perpignan early acquired a reputation, and the most probable date of its foundation was about 1220 or shortly thereafter, a date not supported by documentary evidence but postulated on the assumption that Perpignan was one of the earliest convents to have been founded.

Saragossa

Other convents were established in Catalonia as the thirteenth century progressed, but first consideration must be given to three other kingdoms within the realms of Aragon: Aragon itself, Valencia and Majorca, all of which were closely associated with the Friars Minor early in the thirteenth century.

According to Gerónimo Zurita, a sixteenth-century archival historian, the house at Saragossa, in Aragon, was founded by Saint Francis at the same time as the house at Barcelona.[60] The man who became general of the order after the death of Saint Francis, he says, was Fr. John Parente of Florence, who arrived in Saragossa for the feast of the Assumption of the Blessed Virgin Mary in 1219. The description which follows of the founding of the house can only belong to legend, as must the suggestion that the Friars Minor first said mass in Saragossa on Saint Augustine's day on the site of a subsequent Augustinian convent.[61] If the tradition associated with Barcelona is correct and Saint Francis arrived there in 1211, Zurita's date of 1219 is immediately suspect, the more so since that is the date of the appointment of the first provincial

---

59 Webster, "Els anys formatius," p. 248.
60 Gerónimo Zurita, *Anales de la Corona de Aragón, Libro II [1137–1228]*, ed. Antonio Ubieto Arteta, Maria Desamparados Pérez Soler, and Laureano Ballesteros Ballesteros, (Valencia, 1967), p. 218.
61 Ibid., pp. 219–220.

minister for Spain, an appointment which can only have been made once the Franciscan house had been established. Is it to this latter fact that Zurita is referring, and has he somehow confused the two missionary journeys of Saint Francis and Fr. John Parente? Certainly there is no evidence of a Franciscan house existing in Saragossa before 1256, and even this date is somewhat dubious.[62] Archives in Aragon contain very little early documentation of any kind, making virtually impossible the reconstruction of the early years of the Franciscans in Saragossa. The first extant document probably dates from 1256, but the Franciscan friars must have established a house there many years earlier, perhaps in the 1220s, at about the same time as the foundation of the Lerida house, although it is true that other Aragonese foundations were not established until the 1250s.

Tarazona

Situated on the borders of Aragon and Navarre, Tarazona was an important city in the thirteenth century; it was visited by James I just prior to the reconquest of Valencia.[63] According to one tradition, Saint Francis moved eastward to Saragossa, stopping at the small Moorish town of Tarazona, perhaps because he was too sick to continue the long journey overland.

The thirteenth-century documentation for this area was destroyed during the Hundred Years' War, and the only accounts of the visit of Saint Francis to Tarazona belong more to popular tradition than to proven historical fact. Like so many of the legends surrounding the visit of Saint Francis to Spain, there are many aspects that are difficult to reconcile. Tradition has it that, when Saint Francis reached Tarazona, the cathedral chapter gave him the hermitage of Saint Martin, in the vicinity of the cathedral.[64] Sanz refers to a document, *Lumen 20,* apparently originally to be found in the convent but now no longer

---

62 Saragossa, AC, Cartulario menor, f. 212, 11 August 12[5]6, preserves the will of Don Domingo Sanz, vicar of the church of Saint Bartholomew, Saragossa, in which he left 30 sous to the Franciscans and 20 to the Dominicans. Unfortunately the number referring to the decade is missing, and other documents give no help in determining whether or not the will belongs to 1256.

63 José Maria Sanz Artibucilla, *El convento e iglesia de San Francisco en Tarazona y el santisimo Cristo de la V.O.T.* (Tarazona, 1924), pp. 36–38, refers to other royal visitors to both city and convent.

64 Ibid., pp. 15–19.

extant, which stated that Saint Francis, once he had established the convent at Tarazona, took the road to Saragossa and on to Catalonia without founding any further houses on the way.[65] He also states that the house at Tarazona for some years bore the unusual name of San Martín de Frailes Menores, probably changed around 1230 to honour the canonization of the founder of the order. There are many irreconcilable elements and few facts, but Tarazona, like the other early houses for which there is no corroborating evidence to indicate that they were established in the lifetime of the Saint, probably received its inspiration from the visit of the first friars to the Iberian Peninsula.

The earliest document referring to the Tarazona house is a circular letter sent by the king in October 1279 to a number of Franciscan houses, regarding the sermons they preached in the Jewish synagogues.[66] Sanz also mentions a document of 1272, now no longer extant, supporting the hypothesis that there existed a convent at least before the 1270s.[67] In 1320 the Franciscans wanted to transfer the convent of Tarazona to the custody of Navarre, but the king, obviously having received protests from the convent in question, told the provincial minister of Aragon, Fr. Pere d'Atarravia, that the convent of Tarazona was quite satisfied to remain within the custody of Saragossa and should be allowed to do so.[68]

Valencia

Valencia, on the other hand, while still providing very little early extant documentation, has a long and interesting connection with the arrival of the friars in the Peninsula. The tradition claims that Fr. John of Perugia and Fr. Peter of Sassoferrato accompanied Fr. Bernard of Quintaval to Spain, possibly in 1217 or 1220.[69] In 1220, a year after his appointment as provincial minister for the province of Spain, Fr. John Parente is said to have presided over a chapter in Saragossa. A number of friars

---

65 Sanz Artibucilla, *Convento e iglesia de San Francisco,* p. 32.
66 Barcelona, ACA, RC 42, ff. 148v–149v, 8 October 1279. For more about the Franciscans and the Jews see below Chapter 3, pp. 103, 130–137.
67 Sanz Artibucilla, *Convento e iglesia de San Francisco,* p. 359.
68 Barcelona, ACA, RC 246, f. 80v, 21 July 1320. This document is printed in full as no. 355 in Johannes Vincke, ed., *Documenta selecta* (Barcelona, 1936), p. 255.
69 For the relationship between the first missions to the Iberian Peninsula and the visits of Saint Francis to Catalan cities, see López, *La província de España,* pp. 86–87.

asked his permission to go to Valencia to preach the Christian gospel to the Moors. They are said to have travelled first to Teruel, which López states was founded in 1220, then to Valencia where they stayed in the house of an Aragonese noble, Don Blasco de Alagón, who tried to dissuade them from preaching to the Moors, warning them that they would place their lives in jeopardy.[70]

Throughout the centuries much has been written about the martyrdom of these early missionaries to the Moors in Valencia, the earliest account by a Franciscan being that of Francesc Eiximenis.[71] At the time, the Moorish governor of Valencia was the Sayyid Abu Zayd, who later converted to Christianity and whose remains now lie in the Clarissan Convent of Purity in Valencia.[72] The Sayyid Abu Zayd's son, who had taken the name Fernando Pérez when he converted to Christianity, drew up his will in 1262 and appointed the guardian of the Friars Minor in Valencia to ensure that his wishes were carried out. He also appointed as his executor Fr. Gómez, a Franciscan from the same house, who was a relative, and his confessor.[73] The names Pérez and Gómez are two of the most common surnames, making it difficult to trace the family of the Sayyid Abu Zayd, and it may well be that these names were deliberately chosen to preserve a degree of anonymity and to prevent reprisals from Moorish relatives. Forty years after the traditional martyrdom of the missionaries, known as the martyrs of Teruel, the Moorish king had, in addition to his Christian son, other

---

70 A full account of the legends and stories connected with the visit of these friars is to be found in López, *La província de España*, pp. 86–107. Robert I. Burns, *El reino de Valencia en el siglo XIII (iglesia y sociedad)*, 2 vols. (Valencia, 1982), 2: 448, tentatively suggests that this date should be 1228.
71 López, *La província de España*, p. 93.
72 Webster, "Tradiciones y datos medievales," p. 206; see also the account of the discovery of the remains of the Moorish king in Benjamin Agulló Pascual, "Los restos del rey moro Zeit Abu Ceid, en el monasterio de la Puridad de Valencia," in *Crónica de la XI asamblea de cronistas oficiales del reino de Valencia 1976* (Valencia, 1978), pp. 1–6. On one of the rare occasions when these remains were brought out to show to a small group of people, I was privileged to be present, and was informed that medical evidence strongly suggests that these were in fact the bones of the Moorish king, the Sayyid Abu Zayd.
73 Webster, "Tradiciones y datos medievales," p. 206.

relatives who had taken the Franciscan habit, lending credence to the legends referring to the conversion of the Sayyid Abu Zayd's family.[74]

Apart from the contact with the Sayyid Abu Zayd, the earliest recorded reference to the Franciscans in Valencia dates from the time James I laid siege to the city.[75] In James I's army there were at least two Franciscans, Fr. Peter of the See and Fr. Il.luminat, whose name recurs with some frequency in the chancellery registers. Fr. Il.luminat "et Fratres Minores" are mentioned in connection with the siege of the city, and Ambrós de Saldes quotes the part of the *Repartiment* which implies that the Franciscans had a convent on the road to Ruzafa.[76] The mention of the Franciscans does not necessarily indicate that the Valencian convent had already been founded by 1238, as it was customary for individual friars to act as emissaries and/or religious advisers to the king, but it does suggest that Franciscan friars were living in houses on the road to Ruzafa; it would also seem that they had established a house there as early as 1230.[77] Was this the reason that some years later, in 1239, James I granted eighty-five fathoms of land on this same

---

74 Robert I. Burns, "Príncipe almohade y converso mudejar: Nueva documentación," *Sharq al-Andalus: Estudios árabes* 4 (1987), 109–122, where it is clear that a bull of Urban IV congratulates Abu Zayd on his conversion and "ffilii ac duorum nepotum tuorum."

75 López, *La província de España*, p. 99; Burns, *El reino de Valencia*, 2: 448.

76 Ambròs de Saldes, "La orden franciscana en el antiguo reino de Aragón: Colección diplomatica," *REF* 1 (1907), 414–417, at p. 416. A facsimile edition of the *Repartiment* has been published: *Libre del Repartiment del regne de Valencia*, ed. Maria Desamparados Cabanes Pecourt and Ramon Ferrer Navarro, 3 vols. to date (Saragossa, 1979–).

77 Gabriel Alomar Esteve, *Cátaros y occitanos en el reino de Mallorca* (Palma de Mallorca, 1978), p. 62, refers to a certain Fr. Bonanat, confrere of Pere Oller, a beghard (bégard) or béguin who preached on the island around 1220. Oller was burned by the Inquisition as a heretic, but Fr. Bonanat, whose name suggests that he was a Franciscan, managed to escape punishment. Was he one of those who lived in the primitive house on the Ruzafa road, or was it merely coincidence that his confrere Oller preached in Majorca? If Fr. Bonanat belonged to the "Ruzafa house," the Franciscans might have been in Majorca before the reconquest of the island by James I. This is not impossible, because Fr. John Parente had already been put in charge of the province of Spain, which then included Majorca. Alomar indicates that Majorca was the home of many béguins and Fraticelli, most of them Franciscans. It is not clear whether this was the case as early as the 1220s and 1230s.

road, close to the Boadella gate and near the cemetery, so that the Franciscans could extend their monastery?[78]

The will of Doña Toda Ladrón, dating from the previous year, raises the possibility that after a period of living in temporary quarters the friars had acquired a clientele prepared to support the building of a larger, more permanent convent.[79] Doña Toda, whose husband was a loyal subject of King James, was probably acquainted with Fr. Il.luminat and the other friars when they were living on the road to Ruzafa. Burns refers to Doña Toda as a rich widow, sister of one of the most powerful men in Aragon, who in her will left the sum of 100 sous for the house of the Friars Minor to be founded in the city.[80] James I, in his second will, drawn up in January 1241 [1242], only two or three years after the endowment of the convent, leaves 1000 morabatins to the Friars Minor in Valencia.[81] The following month Maria, wife of Macià Portaioyes, bequeaths 5 sous to the Franciscans in Valencia and to their table, suggesting that by this time the house had already been built.[82] A precise foundation date is again problematic, but the presence of the friars in a house on the Ruzafa road can safely be dated from 1230, the same year as the convent of Majorca is mentioned in the *Repartiment*.

Majorca

As with Valencia, it is thought that the Franciscans went to Majorca at the time of the reconquest of the island by James I at the end of

---

78 *Documentos de Jaime I de Aragon*, vol. 2, *1237–1250*, ed. Ambrosio Huici Miranda, Maria Desamparados and Cabanes Pecourt (Valencia 1976), p. 54, no. 289, gives the date as 11 January 1239, having allowed for the thirty-eight years of the Spanish era, but it is not clear whether this document is dated by the conception (normally referred to in Spanish documents as the "incarnation era") or by the birth of Christ. If it were the former the date would be 1240.

79 Saldes, "La orden franciscana," p. 415, publishes a document purporting to be the legacy of Doña Toda Ladrón to the fabric of the Franciscan house in Valencia; but the document refers only to the Dominicans.

80 Burns, *El reino de Valencia*, 2: 450. For the text of Doña Toda's will see *Documentos de Jaime I*, no. 272, ed. Huici Miranda et al., pp. 37–39.

81 Ibid., pp. 118–119.

82 Madrid, AHN, Clero, carp. 3271, perg. 13, 3 February 1241 [1242]. The document consulted is a copy dating from 1250.

1229.[83] The following year their convent is mentioned as being located in a place known as "Aboabdille Abnazach."[84] Garcías Palou suggests that they had been living in that area for about eight years when the king offered them another piece of land on which to build their convent.[85] López states that the primitive convent was built outside the walls and that only in 1238 that were they able to move to a different location within the city.[86] Berenguer d'Agut's will of that same year bequeaths sufficient money to the friars for the upkeep of a lamp which he had already given to the church of Saint Francis in Majorca, and it is reasonable to assume that this was the church attached to the Franciscan house.[87] The Majorcan convent was to become one of the most important in the Crown of Aragon, and it is not coincidental that Ramon Llull established the missionary college at nearby Miramar.[88]

The college was unique: no others were founded by the order and the Miramar experiment was not repeated. It was never properly integrated into the Franciscan organization and in its approach differed somewhat from the usual concept of mission espoused by the Franciscans, a divergence which it is generally believed was derived from its founder's interest in Dominican spirituality.[89]

Llull stipulated that there should be thirteen friars, a number which Francesc Eiximenis not only used for the books of his Christian encyclopedia but also recommended as ideal when the convent of the Holy Spirit was founded near present-day Sagunto. In the event that the symbolism should go unnoticed, he commented that the number represents Christ and the twelve apostles; in the case of Miramar this has an added meaning, as not only were the friars sent out to preach the gospel to

---

83 Sebastián Garcías Palou, *El Miramar de Ramon Llull* (Palma de Mallorca, 1977), p. 47.
84 Saldes, "La orden franciscana," p. 416, referring to the "Repartimientos de los reinos de Mallorca, Valencia y Cerdeña," includes the clause relevant to the Majorca convent. The complete document has been published in a facsimile edition: *Libre del Repartiment del regne de Valencia,* ed. Maria Desamparados Cabanes Pecourt and Ramon Ferrer Navarro, 2 vols. (Saragossa, 1979).
85 Garcías Palou, *El Miramar,* p. 48.
86 López, *La província de España,* p. 209.
87 Ibid.
88 See Garcías Palou, *El Miramar,* for a detailed study of this college.
89 E. Randolph Daniel, *The Franciscan Concept of Mission in the High Middle Ages* (Lexington, 1975), pp. 73-74.

non-Christians but the majority of them would suffer martyrdom. Garcías Palou comments that Franciscan missionaries were already established in Tunis in 1235 and it is possible that some of these set sail from Majorca, as by that time the Majorca convent would have been in existence for some six years, serving as a contact among the friars from the Italian communes, the Iberian Peninsula and North Africa.

The Creation of Provinces

Initially the followers of Saint Francis were itinerant preachers, but as they became more numerous and spread beyond the confines of Assisi some structure was needed. The first division of the order into administrative provinces was decided upon in the first general chapter, held in the Porziuncola on the feast of Pentecost in 1217. Eleven provinces were created, two of which were Spain and Santiago.[90] In 1219 Fr. John Parente was given charge of the new province of Spain, but it was not long before it had to be subdivided, as the territory covered was too large to make communication easy. Sanahuja concludes that this new division took place in the general chapter held in the Porziuncola in 1232.[91] At this time Fr. John Parente resigned as provincial minister and was succeeded by Fr. Elias de Cortona.[92] The province of Spain was divided into three: Castile, Aragon and Santiago, but further subdivisions almost certainly took place very soon after 1232.

The province of Aragon comprised Catalonia, Aragon, Navarre, Majorca, Valencia and an area called Serrania, which included the modern cities of Saragossa, Teruel, Calatayud, Daroca, Calamocha, Albarracín and Molina.[93] Later this province was subdivided into custodies, and alterations were made in the boundaries of the provinces. These divisions do not necessarily coincide with the territory understood to be under the dominion of the king of Aragon, and reference will only be made to convents outside his territories when their activities directly relate to the overall development of the Friars Minor in Aragon.

---

90 Sanahuja, *História*, p. 30.
91 Ibid., p. 34.
92 Ibid., p. 35.
93 Ibid., p. 40.

The Province of Aragon

From 1263 to 1270 the province of Aragon was said to contain five custodies and twenty-six convents. Golubovich lists the state of the provinces throughout the thirteenth and fourteenth centuries. It is known that the province of Aragon itself existed in 1234 but was subdivided into custodies at some later date. Eubel suggests that by 1334 there were six custodies.[94] Although this division takes place towards the end of the period under review, it probably reflects the situation during the latter part of the thirteenth and beginning of the fourteenth centuries. For the present purpose it proves to be a more useful division. The six custodies were to be known as Barcelona, Lerida, Valencia, Saragossa, Navarre and Serrania, although the convents of Calatayud, Daroca, Molina and Teruel, which properly belonged to the custody of Serrania, were in fact included in the custody of Valencia. Sanahuja concludes that in effect there were only five custodies within the province of Aragon, no doubt those mentioned in 1263.[95]

The Custody of Barcelona

Minorca (Ciutadella)

The first custody, that of Barcelona, comprised the convents of Barcelona, Majorca (Palma), Minorca (Ciutadella), Gerona, Castelló (de Empúries), Vic, Vilafranca del Penedès, Ibiza (Inca) and Tunis, in the land of the "Saracens," which became a vassal-state after the conquest of Valencia, paying a yearly tribute to the Crown of Aragon, a situation which continued throughout the reign of James II.

This group of convents covers a vast area and seems mainly to comprise those along or not far from the Mediterranean seaboard, either in the Peninsula itself, the Balearic Islands or North Africa. These coastal convents were probably among the first to be established, but the houses at Minorca, Castelló, Vilafranca, Ibiza and Tunis are included. Extant documentation for the islands of Minorca and Ibiza is very much less than that for Majorca. Minorca was reconquered in 1286, somewhat later than Majorca, but although both Sanahuja and Moorman give 1302

---

94 Hieronymus Golubovich, "Series provinciarum ordinis Fratrum Minorum, saec. XIII et XIV," *AFH* 1 (1908), 1–22; Conradus Eubel, *Provinciale ordinis Fratrum Minorium* (Quaracchi, 1892). See also Sanahuja, *História,* pp. 29–38 and 65–66.
95 Ibid., p. 64.

as the date of the foundation of the convent of Ciutadella, now the capital of the island,[96] this is incorrect, as an extant royal document places its foundation in 1287, the year of the reconquest of the island. On 1 March 1286 [1287] the king of Aragon conceded to Fr. Pere de Bellfort, guardian of the Barcelona house, and Fr. Pere de Quadres, guardian of the Majorca house, acting on behalf of the Franciscans, land in Ciutadella, free of all taxes, containing houses and a garden giving on to the public street, so that they could build a church and convent.[97] The friars established a house almost immediately; subsequent documentation confirms its foundation in 1287.

There is no evidence that a Franciscan convent ever existed in Ibiza, referred to incorrectly by Sanahuja when listing the convents within the custody of Barcelona.[98] The convent of Inca, which he mentions as being in Ibiza, was in fact on the island of Majorca, and according to both Moorman and Sanahuja was not founded until 1325, nearly a hundred years later than the house in the capital.[99]

Vilafranca del Penedès

The three convents to the south of Barcelona, Vilafranca, Montblanc and Tarragona are intimately connected with the visit of Saint Francis to the area, and although the convent of Tarragona belongs to the custody of Lerida, it is more appropriate to discuss it here.

Two of the legends referring to this visit concern the Cistercian monasteries of Santes Creus and Poblet. To the left of the door to the cloisters of the former, a small memorial stone of white marble dating from the thirteenth century referred to the altar of Saint Francis, built with the largesse of a certain Pons de Banyeres, who died in 1242.[100]

At the neighbouring monastery of Poblet, the tradition, which purports to derive from a document in the archives of Fontfreda, has Saint Francis preaching to the monks shortly after his arrival in Barcelona. Neither Vilafranca nor Tarragona are far from these two monasteries,

---

96 John R.H. Moorman, *Medieval Franciscan Houses* (St. Bonaventure, NY, 1983), p. 136; Sanahuja, *História*, p. 79.
97 Barcelona, ACA, RC 64, f. 163v, 1 March 1286 [1287].
98 Sanahuja, *História*, p. 65.
99 Moorman, *Medieval Franciscan Houses*, p. 229; see Sanahuja, *História*, p. 81.
100 *Sant Francesc d'Assís, "el Pobrissó,"* p. 492.

and it would have been possible for Saint Francis to travel from Barcelona first to Vilafranca, then to Montblanc and Tarragona.

The earliest references to the foundation of convents in this area date from the 1230s. López and Sanahuja, quoting from a document published in the *Revista de estudios franciscanos,* affirm that the Montblanc house existed in 1238.[101] The document in question, Berenguer d'Agut's will, is dated 26 June 1258, not 1238.[102] Both Montblanc and Vilafranca were important houses, and the king and his retinue often stayed in the former, at times being responsible for causing considerable damage to it.[103] In Vilafranca it was usual for the elections of the town rulers or councillors *(jurats)* to hold their elections in the convent, and Sanahuja describes it as having been built in the ogival style with some Romanesque features. Over the altar were canvasses depicting scenes associated with Franciscan spirituality.[104] The Vilafranca house became well known for a different reason: it was the home of many Spiritual Franciscans and béguins and seems to have been the centre of such activities in the late thirteenth and early fourteenth centuries.[105] The houses at Vilafranca and Montblanc would almost certainly have been in existence by the 1230s, but no extant documentation survives to confirm or refute these dates.

Tarragona

This old Roman town has a much older connection with the Friars Minor, for it was here that Fr. Daniel left some of his confreres when he himself, with three companions, went to preach in Morocco at the end of 1226.[106] Tarragona may well have been one of the first convents to be established, in view of the many legends linking the early Franciscans to the area. López mentions that the martyrs of Ceuta, Saint Daniel and his companions, spent some days in Tarragona before reaching Africa. If this is true, and a house existed at that time, Tarragona

---

101 López, *La província de España,* p. 206; Sanahuja, *História,* p. 96.
102 Barcelona, ACA, GPC, Gran Priorato, arm. 28, perg. 204.
103 See below Chapter 2, pp. 86–87.
104 Sanahuja, *História,* p. 77. See below Chapter 7, pp. 285–286.
105 See Josep Perarnau, L'*"Alia informatio beguinorum" d'Arnau de Vilanova* (Barcelona, 1978).
106 López, *La província de España,* p. 62.

would have had a Franciscan convent in 1227.[107] As this is approximately the same year that houses were established in other Catalan cities like Barcelona and Lerida, the possibility of a foundation date for Tarragona around 1225/1226, shortly before or after the establishment of the house at Vic, should not be discounted.

The first documentary evidence for a Franciscan convent there comes from the will of Bernat de Cobis dated 30 April 1248.[108] He left 5 sous to the Friars Minor of Tarragona. In 1254 the guardian of the Tarragona house was entrusted with an important task on behalf of the papal nuncio to Spain, Peter of Priverno. The archbishop of Tarragona, who had refused to pay to the papal see certain outstanding debts, was forbidden to enter his church, being suspended "a divinis." It was the guardian of the Franciscans in Tarragona who was permitted to relax the sentence imposed by the nuncio for a period of time up to the feast of Saint Michael and, finally, to pardon any irregularity committed by the archbishop.[109] In 1258 there was a further legacy to the Tarragona house, which, from the abundant references to its activities in the latter part of the thirteenth century, must have been one of the most important in the realms of Aragon.[110] A tentative date of 1227 or thereabouts for the foundation of the Tarragona house can only be postulated with great caution, and is largely based on its proximity in geographical location and the dates of foundation of the houses in Barcelona and Lerida.

Tunis

Before leaving the custody of Barcelona, reference must be made to one rather distant convent, that of Tunis, about which very little is known. Saint Francis, on his missionary journey to the Iberian Peninsula, intended to obtain permission from the king of Castile to venture into the land of the Saracens in North Africa, specifically Morocco. Missionaries sub-

---

107 López, *La província de España*, p. 206. He also refers to the fact that Gonzaga and Wadding both believed the Tarragona house was founded in 1248, in the vicinity of a chapel dedicated to the divine Saviour: see Francisco Gonzaga, *De origine seraphicae religionis*, 2nd ed. (Venice, 1603), Provincia Cathaloniae, conv. IV and Lucas Wadding, comp., *Annales Minorum*, 3rd ed., 28 vols. (Quaracchi, 1931-1947), 3: 234.
108 Sanahuja, *História*, p. 75.
109 López, *La província de España*, pp. 206-207, for a detailed exposition.
110 Sanahuja, *História*, p. 75: Pons de Ribas left 10 sous for the table of the Friars Minor of Vilafranca in his will of 13 April 1258.

sequently set out for North Africa, and the earliest reference to the presence of Franciscans in Tunis dates from 1234.

Both Dominican and Franciscan missionaries were working in the kingdom of Tunis at this time, and the latter had taken some difficulties they had to the pope, using as their intermediary the famous Dominican, Saint Raymond of Penyafort.[111] No documentary evidence attests to the presence of the friars in Tunis before this date, but a Franciscan house almost certainly existed there from the time of the early missionaries. Monarchs from the Iberian Peninsula also maintained political and commercial relations with the Saracens in North Africa, and these contacts might have helped to support the endeavours of the early Franciscans to establish a house in Moorish territory. In 1314, a letter from James II to his brother, King Frederick, mentions forty friars from the province of Tunis who are to go to Sicily to be disciplined by their order for some infraction of duty.[112] It is at about this time the famous Catalan writer, Ramon Llull, who tradition claims was a member of the Third Order and who founded the convent at Miramar in Majorca, was staying in the Tunis house.[113] Indeed, Tunis was to acquire notoriety over the conversion to Islam of Fr. Anselm Turmeda nearly a century later.[114]

As Tunis is really marginal to this study, its inclusion here is primarily intended to show the extent of the custody of Barcelona and to underline the missionary endeavour of the Franciscans. Little is known about their early attempts at converting the Moors and other non-Christians, but Tunis seems to have formed part of the custody of Barcelona from the time of the reconquest of Valencia.

The Custody of Lerida

Berga

The custody of Lerida cannot be entirely separated from that of Barcelona, in view of the traditions which concern the whole area covered by these custodies. It was one of the first for which there is extant docu-

---

111 Sanahuja, *História*, p. 80; López, *La província de España*, pp. 367-368.
112 Barcelona, ACA, RC 337, f. 337v, 25 September 1314.
113 Sanahuja, *História*, p. 81.
114 Martín de Riquer, *História de la literatura catalana: Part antiga*, 3 vols. (Barcelona, 1964), 2: 265-274.

mentation, but a number of unresolved questions arise in connection with the convents under its jurisdiction. According to the division of 1334 these were Lerida, Tarragona, Tortosa, Montblanc, Monzón, Cervera, Tàrrega and Morella.[115]

Two convents are omitted from this list, Berga and Balaguer, both of which have been omitted from the other custodies as well; yet by the date of the division into custodies both houses had been established, Berga on two different occasions. The first of these occasions dates back to 1244 or earlier. A document dated 24 February 1244 [1245] refers to the gift made by the abbess of the Cistercian convent of Valldaura, Aldiarts d'Anglesola, to Pere of Berga, of the *masia* of Escodo in the parish of Santa Cecilia de Fígols in exchange for certain houses within the town of Berga formerly occupied by the Franciscans.[116] The Franciscans had probably already abandoned these houses, and indeed in the 1330s there is evidence that the then abbess of Valldaura and the Franciscans came into conflict over the property, which, the latter claimed, was given to them, and on which by 1330 the Cistercian nuns had erected their convent. Sanahuja, basing his conclusion on the fact that the nuns had taken over the houses abandoned by the friars, believed that the Franciscans only returned to Berga in 1330 once royal approval had been obtained and it had been ascertained that the citizens of the town were in agreement that the convent should be rebuilt.

The matter is not quite so clear-cut, because there are other references to the Berga house between 1244 and 1330. In 1279, as mentioned later in the discussion on the Castelló house, Berga is listed among the convents which the king requests to use peaceful means to persuade the Jews voluntarily to accept Christianity. If it were not for the fact that in 1287 Ismael de Portella (a Jew of the royal household) gave Fr. Pere Emberart, a Franciscan at the Berga house, 50 sous for clothes, it might

---

115 Sanahuja, *História*, p. 65.
116 Ibid., pp. 82–83. There seems to be some confusion here: on 6 June 1334 Alfonso III, writing to Pere d'Alou and Ramon de Aciba (or Aciber? "Acipparia"), jurisperiti in Berga, refers to previous correspondence as follows: 14 June 1330, the Franciscans wish to rebuild their house; 21 October 1333, enfranchisment of land in Berga called *Los menorets* which must not exceed 80 *canes;* 6 June 1334 (the document at hand), King Alfonso orders the *batlle* of Berga to hand over the land mentioned previously to the Franciscans, so that they can build a spacious house. Unfortunately the document is in a very bad state and some words are illegible.

have been possible to suggest that the king had mistakenly included the Berga house in the list of convents.[117] There are references to the Berga house in 1309, 1311 and 1315, the first of these being a letter from the king to the guardian of the Franciscans in Barcelona, the prior of the Dominicans in the same city and the Hospitallers in Berga, all of whom were executors of the will of the late noble lady Beatrix de Malayn.[118] The subject of the letter is the legacy of this lady to the convent of Valldaura in the amount of 4000 sous, a sum which at the time of writing was still outstanding. The fact that the guardian in Barcelona was an executor of this will seems to suggest that in 1309 the Berga Franciscan house no longer existed. It also seems to suggest that it had ceased to exist very recently; otherwise why would Beatrix de Malayn have chosen the Barcelona guardian?

A similar situation might well have pertained for the Dominican prior, although no dispute is known to have existed between the Dominicans and the Cistercian nuns of Valldaura. In 1311 the king wrote an interesting letter to his officials in Berga regarding treatment of the Friars Minor in Berga.[119] He emphasized the devotion of the Franciscans to the divine cause and asked that they be treated well in Berga. This letter indicates that certain friars had brought a lawsuit against others within the same Order of Friars Minor and that as a result the people of Berga were not so enthusiastic about having Franciscans in their midst. The king enjoined his officials and the citizens of Berga to forget any ill-feeling they might have had for the friars because of this lawsuit, and to allow them to return, because they were friars, living in poverty and devoted to the propagation of the Christian faith. It would seem reasonable to conclude from this document that the friars at Berga had been evicted from their house, probably in 1309, because of internal squabbles, and possibly ones which involved some of the citizens of Berga.

The king's injunction fell on deaf ears, for in 1316 Berenguer Clarí, an inhabitant of Berga, was to be enfranchised as a reward for the hospitality he had given on several occasions to Franciscans and Dominicans who were passing through the town.[120] There is no doubt that the

---

117 Barcelona, ACA, RC 71, f. 156v, 17 October 1287.
118 ACA, RC 144, f. 92v, 4 June 1309.
119 ACA, RC 148, f. 196v, 16 October 1311.
120 ACA, RC 212, f. 81v, 11 January 1315 [1316].

convent of Berga had ceased to exist and that its restoration had not yet been authorized. Some citizens evidently still looked on the Franciscans with Christian charity, and perhaps it was these same people who were instrumental in helping them to reestablish their house in the 1330s.

Indeed, at the time the Franciscans proposed to return to Berga, the inhabitants of the town were first asked whether or not they believed themselves able to support a convent, suggesting, perhaps, that in addition to the legal problems incurred over the dispute (whatever it might have been), there were also economic difficulties which made it desirable for the Friars Minor to absent themselves for a while from Berga. In view of the numerous documents attesting to the reestablishment of the Franciscans in Berga in the 1330s, it would have been logical for the custody of Lerida to have included the house among those within its jurisdiction, although given the confusing circumstances surrounding the new foundation, it is not surprising that Golubovich overlooked it. The matter was still not settled in January 1334, and the house at Berga could not finally have been reestablished before that date.[121]

The king's orders were disregarded in January, for Prince Peter was forced to write again to the bailiff (*batlle*) of Berga on 10 August 1334, referring to the previous letter and emphasizing the harm that had been done to the Order of Friars Minor as a result of the delay.[122] This evidently had some effect, for the next extant evidence of the existence of the convent in Berga suggests that the friars had started to build their house but once again had come into conflict with the nuns of Valldaura. On 13 November 1334 Prince Peter again wrote to the *batlle* at Berga, informing him that he had heard from the guardian of the Franciscans there that the nuns of Valldaura were building their monastery on the land given to the Order of Friars Minor.[123] He ordered the *batlle* to see that the nuns were not allowed to undertake any building on that site.

The next letter dates from September 1337, when King Peter III wrote to the *batlle* of Berga on behalf of the guardian and friars of the house there regarding land for its enlargement.[124] Three years later Peter III wrote once more to the *batlle* of Berga, referring to his

---

121 Barcelona, ACA, RC 461, f. 180r–v, 16 January 1333 [1334].
122 ACA, RC 571, f. 45r–v, 10 August 1334.
123 ACA, RC 572, f. 131, 13 November 1334.
124 ACA, RC 589, f. 42v, 19 September 1337. The document is somewhat ambiguous as it refers to construction or enlargement.

previous letter dated 22 September 1337 and confirming that the procurator of the Franciscan house was exempt from taxation and military service in the normal way.[125] As he had been forced unjustly to pay taxes, all monies collected from him were to be returned. This letter removes all doubt that the Franciscans had established their second foundation in Berga sometime between August and December 1334, and that the letter dated 19 September 1337 indeed refers to extra land required for the enlargement of the convent.

Balaguer (Almatà)

Moorman found no trace of the convent of Balaguer before the beginning of the fifteenth century; in fact, in 1413 it was destroyed and not rebuilt until the middle of the fifteenth century.[126] There is documentation concerning Balaguer which dates from much earlier.[127] The old quarter of the city of Balaguer, situated to the north of the modern city, was called Almatà in the Middle Ages, and in the chancellery registers of James II there is a reference to the convent of Almazán or Almatà.[128] There was also a town in Soria by the name of Almazán, but it seems much more likely in this instance that the document relates to the old part of the city of Balaguer.

The Centelles family had always been faithful followers of James I, and extended their allegiance to the crown to his heir, James II, so that the fact that a member of the family, Bernat, was deposited after death in the Almatà convent of the Friars Minor should not come as a surprise. From the dates it must be concluded that this Bernat is Bernat (III) who died in 1277 and who placed the castle of Saint Stephen, over which he had full jurisdiction, in fief to Pere de Santa Eugènia in 1242.

Among James II's letters are some which refer to the transfer of Bernat Centelles's body from the convent of Almatà to the custody of his grandson, Gilabert. Bernat was indebted to many citizens in Balaguer, and his creditors probably took his body from the convent where it lay at rest and prevented Gilabert from moving it to some undisclosed final resting place, such as the family tomb, until they had received payment

---

125 Barcelona, ACA, RC 608, f. 35, 10 September 1340.
126 Moorman, *Medieval Franciscan Houses*, p. 48.
127 Webster, "Tradiciones y datos medievales," pp. 201-203.
128 The document in Barcelona, ACA, RC 131, f. 108v, dated 15 March 1303 [1304], refers to the convent of Almazán.

of Bernat's debts. It is the convent of Balaguer rather than the fate of Bernat's body which is relevant to this study, and if indeed this is the old quarter of Almatà rather than the convent at Almazán (Soria), which dates from a later period, and Bernat's body on his death in 1277 was placed in the convent, the foundation of the Balaguer convent should be placed within the reign of James I, or before 1276.

Other documents prove that it existed in 1303 and in 1321, and Sanahuja refers to a convent of Friars Minor in Balaguer in 1372.[129] He suggests that it was a small convent (*conventet*), intended to serve the Clarissan nuns who had a convent in Balaguer at that time. Why there is so little mention of the convent of Balaguer is difficult to determine, but if indeed its main purpose was to serve the nuns, like the *conventets* at Pedralbes and Manresa, it might well have contained a small number of friars until the fifteenth century when it joined the Observants.[130]

Castelló d'Empúries

An inventory of some of the documents in the Castelló archives, dated 20 April 1583, is still extant, although the documents it refers to have long since disappeared.[131] Most of the items listed bear no date, but among them is the will of Pons Hug, count of Empúries, who left 200 sous to be paid annually to the friars on the feast of Saint Michael to provide clothing for people from Castelló getting married. The date of this will is 19 December 1263, more than a decade prior to the first extant document referring to the house of Castelló, dated 22 January 1276 [1277].[132] It is the will of Hug, count of Empúries, who wished to be buried in the Franciscan cemetery in Castelló and left 500 sous of Melgeuil to the Franciscans for the purpose, together with a further 1000 for the work of their church and 500 for their food and clothing. Witness to the document was the guardian of Castelló, Fr. Pere de Romaní.

---

129 Barcelona, ACA, RC 131, ff. 108v and 116; RC 367, f. 100v. Sanahuja, *História*, p. 306 (1372).
130 Sanahuja, *História*, p. 307.
131 This inventory is preserved in the AHFC, Barcelona, and purports to be the documents kept in the cell of the guardian of the Observant monastery in Castelló d'Empúries. The entries are very faint and difficult to read.
132 Seville, ADM, Ampurias, legajo I, no. 6533, 22 January 1276 [1277]. These archives contain hundreds of documents referring to the counts of Ampurias which found their way into the Medinaceli family archives through marriage.

The following year Arnau de Vilaric left all his worldly possessions to the Franciscans of Castelló.[133] The next reference is a circular letter sent the following year to the Franciscan convents of Barcelona, Gerona, Vic, Vilafranca, Cervera, Montblanc, Lerida, Castelló, Tarragona, Monzón, Tortosa, Huesca, Saragossa, Tarazona, Ejea de los Caballeros, Berga, Calatayud, Daroca, Teruel, Valencia, Xàtiva, Jaca and Barbastro.[134] It is a follow-up of a letter sent by the king to some of these houses (Castelló not being one of those mentioned in the earlier letter), in connection with the preaching of the Dominicans and Franciscans, whose missionary sermons to the non-Christian communities had aroused excessive enthusiasm among the populace and provoked outbursts which threatened the lives of the Jews.[135] While the friars were to try and convert the Jews, the king enjoined them in his second letter to do so in such a way as they might accept the Christian faith voluntarily.[136] The fact that Castelló is not mentioned in the first letter, which in fact bears the same date, merely suggests that no scenes of crowd enthusiasm had endangered the non-Christians in that town.

The convent of Castelló was described as a splendid stone building, suggesting that it had been in existence for some time; and the reference in Wadding to a pact in the year 1276 between the friars and the count of Empúries, Pons Hug (or Huguet), reiterated by Sanahuja, should be regarded as accurate, as should be his postulated foundation date of 1246.[137] Castelló, like the not far distant Berga, was one of a series of foundations in the province of Gerona which date from the 1240s.

Tortosa

Half-way between Tarragona and Valencia, Tortosa also fell within the jurisdiction of Lerida and was one of the more active houses in the Middle Ages. Sanahuja, relying on the information given in Coll's chronicle, gives the incorrect date of 1267 for the foundation of the Tortosa convent.[138]

---

133 Seville, ADM, Ampurias, legajo I, no. 7381, 31 October 1278.
134 Barcelona, ACA, RC 42, f. 149v, 8 October 1279.
135 ACA, RC 42, ff. 148v–149, 8 October 1279.
136 Ibid., f. 149v, 8 October 1279.
137 Wadding, *Annales Minorum*, 5: 6; Sanahuja, *História*, p. 78.
138 Ibid., p. 99; Coll, *Crónica*, secs. 822 and 963–965, ed. Martí Mayor, pp. 240–241 and 286.

The first indication that the Franciscans founded a house in Tortosa dates from nearly twenty years earlier. In referring to this fact, Bayerri comments that the inhabitants of the town were well known for their extreme devotion to the Christian religion, and more especially for their generosity in giving to charity.[139] A document drawn up by a notary from Tortosa, Pedro de Tamarit, confirms the donation given by Ramon de Puig in 1248 to the Tortosa convent.[140] Although Bayerri does not mention the existence of the original parchment, it has in fact survived and is one of those which found its way into the state archives after the sequestration of the property of the religious orders in 1836.[141] As well, Ramona, Ramon de Puig's wife, confirms the gift made by her husband to Fr. Bernat Ferrer, guardian of the Tortosa house, to Fr. Alexander, provincial minister of Aragon, and to the Order of Friars Minor, of a piece of land and part of his vineyards, with the stipulation that it is for the use of the friars in the present and in the future.

The Tortosa house probably existed before 1248, as it was well established when Ramon de Puig made over his land to the friars. Tortosa was in a privileged position, having been reconquered from the Moors before the end of the twelfth century and settled by Christians at an early date.[142] At the beginning of the thirteenth century James I frequently visited the town, which by the time of the conquest of Valencia in 1238 already housed a number of religious orders: the Cistercians, the Trinitarians, the Mercedarians and the Dominicans in addition to the Franciscans.[143] It is indeed possible that the first Franciscan missionaries stayed in Tortosa on their way to Valencia. In any case, the Franciscan house must surely have been established there no later than 1238, when Valencia was reconquered from the Moors.

Morella

Three further convents in the custody of Lerida, those of Morella, Monzón and Tàrrega, remain for discussion. The first two of these are among the earliest of the foundations, but documentation is singularly

---

139 Enrique Bayerri y Bertomeu, *História de Tortosa y su comarca,* 8 vols. (Tortosa, 1933–1959), 7: 542.
140 Ibid., 7: 543.
141 Madrid, AHN, Clero, carp. 2900, perg. 11, 27 August 1248.
142 Burns, *El reino de Valencia,* 1: 114.
143 Bayerri y Bertomeu, *História de Tortosa y su comarca,* 7: 525–526.

lacking to corroborate this. An ancient walled town, Morella still preserves its medieval atmosphere, and in the square of Saint Francis stand the remains of the Franciscan convent and church (the latter now serving as a museum), both built in the Gothic style.

The history of Morella is more intricately bound up with the history of Valencia than with that of Lerida, as it was occupied by James I's men at the beginning of the campaigns in Valencia and finally became part of the Crown of Aragon in 1249.[144] Sanahuja states that, according to Antonio de Hebrera (one of the sources for Coll's *Crónica*), the Franciscan convent was built shortly after 1232, although Gonzaga and Wadding suggest 1272 as the more likely date.[145]

My research has failed to turn up any reference to the convent prior to the document granting enfranchisement to Guillem Moltó of Morella in [1301] 1302 as a reward for his services as procurator of the Franciscans.[146] He, like other procurators to the friars, was to be exempt from military service and from all royal taxes by reason of his office. He had almost certainly completed a period of time as procurator, for enfranchisement was only granted on completion of a term of office, or when the man in question had served for a period of years and was to have his appointment renewed. Despite this, the presence of James I's men in Morella in the 1230s and the significance of the town during the reconquest suggests that the Franciscans moved into Morella immediately after the conquest of the area by the king's armies, and that the house there was built sometime between 1232 and 1249.

Monzón

Monzón is even less fortunate in the preservation of its written records. Sanahuja states, on the authority of Coll and *España sagrada* (neither of whom can be relied upon for accuracy), that the Franciscan convent of Monzón was founded in 1235.[147] Situated outside the walls of the town, close to the river Sosa, on the road to Cinca, some archeological

---

144 Burns, *El reino de Valencia*, 1: 37-38.
145 See Sanahuja, *História*, p. 87, with Coll, *Crónica*, secs. 966-974, ed. Martí Mayor, pp. 287-289; Gonzaga, *De origine*, Provincia Valenciae, conv. II; and Wadding, *Annales Minorum*, 4: 410.
146 Barcelona, ACA, RC 200, f. 176v, 23 January 1301 [1302].
147 Sanahuja, *História*, pp. 88-89, with Coll, *Crónica*, secs. 966-974 and *España Sagrada*, 47: 239.

remains of the convent can still be seen.[148] In 1238 James I, on his way to lay siege to Valencia, stayed in Monzón to hold his *corts,* attended by the two friars minor in his retinue, Fr. Il.luminat and Fr. Peter of the See.[149]

The presence of these two friars does nothing to clarify the date of foundation of the Monzón house, as they were to continue to Valencia with the army of the king. Valencia was reconquered from the Moors that same year, after which the two Franciscans were given a plot of land on the Ruzafa road, close to where the king and his army had camped, on which to build a convent. Monzón can scarcely have possessed a Franciscan house before this time, despite the date of 1235 put forward by *España sagrada* as the date of foundation.

The first extant document dates from 1261, the year in which James I ordered that Pedro Sánchez, an official of the curia of Lerida, be paid the sum of 30 Jaca sous, which had been given to the Franciscans of Monzón at the time of their chapter.[150] The reference to the chapter indicates that the house had already been in existence for some time. Sanahuja states that the famous troubadour, Fr. Jofre de Foixà, credited with having given the name "catalanesc" to the language and honoured by the monarchs of Aragon, must have lived in the Monzón house at this time.[151] In 1269 Fr. Jofre was given permission by the guardian of the Monzón house, Fr. Guillem de Fraumir, to confirm a novena made by his brother Arnau, archdeacon of the Ampurdán.[152]

Another interesting document, the will of Master Arnau, rector of the church of San Martín, is dated 24 June 1273, and contains a list of charitable donations, including those bequeathed to a series of Franciscan convents, among them Monzón.[153] The list in itself is significant, as bequests are made to the Franciscans at Saragossa, Teruel, Daroca, Calatayud, Lerida, Monzón, Barbastro, Huesca, Ejea, Pamplona, Tudela

---

148 María Teresa Oliveros de Castro, *História de Monzón* (Saragossa, 1964), p. 469.
149 Sanahuja, *História,* p. 88, gives the name of the second friar as Fr. William of the See or Fr. Peter, but for lack of incontrovertible proof one way or the other the names have been adopted as they appear in Burns, *El reino de Valencia,* 1: 200.
150 López, *La província de España,* p. 191.
151 Sanahuja, *História,* p. 89; see also Joaquín Pla Cargol, *Gerona histórica,* 2nd ed. (Gerona, 1945), p. 64.
152 Sanahuja, *História,* p. 89.
153 Saragossa, AC, Cartulario menor, f. 158v.

and a place which seems to be Ruzafa, probably Valencia.[154] Morella is missing from this list, and the majority of the houses mentioned are in Aragon or Navarre, with the exception of Lerida and Valencia, which might have been included because they were important custodies at the time. For Monzón there is so little evidence of activity in the thirteenth century that to suggest a date of foundation for the Franciscan house is almost impossible. It must have taken place between the conquest of Valencia in 1238 and the chapter held in Monzón in 1261, and was probably part of the Christianization policy of the king in Aragon.

Tàrrega

Consideration of the custody of Lerida would not be complete without a brief reference to the date of foundation of the Tàrrega convent, traditionally believed to have been one of the last to be established in the realms of Aragon.

Extant documentation confirms the fact that John XXII's bull *Clara ordinis vestri* of 14 May 1318, allowing the Friars Minor to found a house in Tàrrega, became effective almost immediately.[155] Three documents in the chancellery registers are of interest here: on 25 June 1318 James II wrote to the *batlle* and *paers* of Tàrrega explaining that, because the Friars Minor were about to build a monastery in the town, the provincial minister of the Franciscans and some friars from the order were repairing to Tàrrega to choose a site. He ordered that four upright men from the town be chosen to evaluate the square or place chosen by the friars for their house, and that a sum of money equivalent to the price agreed upon as just be given to them by the officials of Tàrrega, so that they could begin construction.[156] The following month the king wrote again to the officials of Tàrrega, referring to his previous letter and making it clear that he had no intention of suggesting that the property belonging either to the Santes Creus monastery or to any other religious house in the town of Tàrrega should be expropriated for the building of a Franciscan monastery. He emphasized that he forbade the

---

154 The word Ruzafa appears as Roaff or Ruaff but is unclear in the document. As the only house with a connection anywhere near Ruzafa was Valencia, I assume that Master Arnau was familiar with the Valencian house by the name of its location.
155 Sanahuja, *Història*, p. 100.
156 Barcelona, ACA, RC 166, ff. 238v–239, 25 June 1318.

use of these properties for the said purpose.[157] The Privileges of Tàrrega confirm that in 1293 the Templars, Hospitallers and the monasteries of Poblet and Santes Creus belonging to the Cistercians, together with the monasteries of Sant Cugat, Vallsanta and Pedregal among others all held property within the municipality of Tàrrega.[158]

There were frequent conflicts there between the various religious orders, and it may be that the town had attempted to seize the property of one of the more troublesome of the orders in order to give it to the Franciscans. In August of 1318 the Dominicans also wished to build a house in Tàrrega, but this had led to a number of disputes in the town regarding the desirability of the plan. The king showed his displeasure at this attitude, and expressed the hope that peace could be restored so that the Dominicans might establish their house in Tàrrega.[159] These disputes were probably never settled amicably, as a Dominican convent was never established in Tàrrega.

The Franciscans obtained the support of the townsmen and in late August of 1318 acquired the property of the Confraternity of Saint Francis to help with the foundation of their new house.[160] A few years later the king gave them the house, vineyards, land and other property and income belonging to the lepers in Tàrrega, with the stipulation that they could sell it and use the proceeds from the sale towards the construction of the house, or for whatever other purpose they deemed necessary. The only condition attached to the king's generosity was that they should, both then and in the future, attend to the needs of all lepers born in the town.[161] A second document confirms that the property was indeed handed over to the Franciscans, as requested by the king.

In December of 1321 James II wrote to his officials in Lerida asking them to extend the credit given to the guardian of the Tàrrega house, Fr. Pere de Cervera, in the sum of 400 Jaca sous owed to them by Pere Delfrau for timber, for a period of two more years.[162] The heirs of Pere Delfrau were required to pay this debt, probably by selling a Bible

---

157 Barcelona, ACA, RC 166, ff. 258v–259, 7 July 1318.
158 Lluis Sarret i Pons, *Privilegis de Tàrrega,* facsimile ed. by Ignasi de L. Camps i Sarró (Tàrrega, 1982), p. 34, no. 3, 11 April 1293.
159 Barcelona, ACA, RC 165, f. 52v, 13 August 1318.
160 Ibid., f. 97, 28 August 1318.
161 Sarret i Pons, *Privilegis de Tàrrega,* p. 82, no. 43, 5 July 1322, and for the second document, p. 85, no. 46, 3 August 1325.
162 Barcelona, ACA, RC 172, f. 186v, 13 December 1321.

they had pawned, but to make sure that they met their obligation the Bible was to be placed in a safe place. In 1325 James II issued one of his many orders that the Friars Minor be protected from all harm within the town of Tàrrega.[163] The construction of the house began in 1318, and from that time on Franciscan friars resided in the town. At first they attended to the needs of the lepers; later they abandoned that aspect of their work and followed their more traditional role of ministering to Christians and of attempting to convert non-Christians to the Catholic faith.

The Custody of Valencia

The division of convents into custodies is somewhat arbitrary, as the custody of Valencia contains convents which would appear more properly to belong to that of Saragossa. The foundation of the principal house, Valencia, as dating from the reconquest of the city from the Moors has already been established. Only two of the convents within its jurisdiction belong to the Valencia region, Xàtiva and Murviedro (the modern Sagunto), although it will be remembered that Teruel was intimately connected with the early misfortunes of the missionaries to the Levante. The other convents in the Valencian custody but within the kingdom of Aragon were Calatayud, Daroca and Molina. These three houses with the addition of Teruel were later assigned to a new custody to be known as Serrania. Sanahuja believes this division took place in 1357, some years after the Black Death.[164] Before this time the convents of Calatayud, Daroca, Molina and Teruel fell within the jurisdiction of the Valencian custody.

Calatayud

Little has been done on the convents geographically situated in Aragon but regarded by the Friars Minor as forming part of the Valencian custody. This is understandable, as very few documents remain to help determine foundation dates. The first of these, Calatayud, is not mentioned by López in his chapter on the convents of Navarre and Aragon, possibly because he believed it dated from the fourteenth century; yet the plethora of documents referring to the activities of the Franciscans in

---

163 Sarret i Pons, *Privilegis de Tàrrega,* p. 85.
164 Sanahuja, *História,* pp. 65–66.

Aragon in the chancellery registers suggest that it was one of the most important houses from the end of the thirteenth century, if not before.[165]

The first indication that the Franciscans had established a convent in Calatayud dates from the time of Saint Francis.[166] If this is correct, the house was probably founded shortly after that of Saragossa in 1219, but the first extant documentation dates from much later.[167] The house at Calatayud was one of the beneficiaries of the 1273 will of Master Arnau, indicating that by that date the house had been in existence for some time, and from 1279 onwards Calatayud is mentioned continually in the royal registers. One of these, a letter addressed by the king to the corporation of the village of Calatayud, concedes a total amount of 4000 sous for a period of four years.[168] This amount was to be divided between the bishop of Tarazona and the Friars Minor at Calatayud, a singularly unwise provision given the constant conflicts between the clergy and the mendicant orders, and one which may well have provoked some of the trouble which will be discussed in a later chapter.[169]

Again in 1279, the king wrote to his faithful subjects in a number of Jewish quarters (*aljamas*) throughout his realms, including Calatayud, concerning the sermons which the Jews were obliged to attend. It had been customary for them to listen to these from outside the synagogues, but the religious fervour of the Christians would often become so great that they became incensed against the non-Christians in their midst, thus putting the Jews' lives in danger. In future, the king said, they were to listen to the sermons inside their synagogues, so as to prevent further occurrence of these violent incidents.[170]

Subsequent references to the Calatayud house emphasize the difficult and often contentious lives the Franciscans led in the town—indeed, this seems to have been true in most of the places where they had convents in the kingdom of Aragon. If the above references are any indication, a date before 1273, and perhaps considerably earlier, seems in order for

---

165 López, *La província de España*, pp. 174-193.
166 Moorman, *Medieval Franciscan Houses*, p. 100.
167 Zurita, *Anales de la Corona de Aragón*, pp. 219-220.
168 Barcelona, ACA, RC 46, f. 110, 30 September 1279.
169 See below Chapter 4, pp. 156-165.
170 Barcelona, ACA, RC 42, ff. 148v-149, 8 October 1279.

the foundation of the Calatayud house. Similar difficulties to those encountered for Calatayud make it impossible to give precise foundation dates for the other Aragonese convents within the jurisdiction of the Valencian custody.

Daroca

López states that the Friars Minor were already residing in Daroca in 1225, when James I conceded to them a sum of money accruing from salt.[171] Moorman seems to believe that the convent itself was built later, but there is evidence that it was completed in 1237, thanks to the generosity of King James.[172] Other concessions from the king's salt fields lead to the conclusion that construction of the convent along the banks of the river Giloche must have been under way by 1225, as, judging by surviving documentation, it was usual for the king to make these concessions only after the initial phase of construction had begun. The fact that Daroca was begun so early gives credence to the date of 1219 for the foundation of the convent of Saragossa, and possibly Calatayud too. Daroca is also mentioned in the list of beneficiaries of Master Arnau's will of 1273. In 1279 the Jews at Daroca, like those at Calatayud, were also enjoined to enter the synagogues to hear the sermons aimed at converting them.[173] The history of these two convents very closely parallels that of Saragossa, and all three houses probably date from the same time.

Molina

The convent of Molina presents insurmountable problems, as the only evidence that it ever existed comes from the will of the princess known as Doña Blanca de Molina, dated 1293.[174] She asked to be buried in the convent of San Francisco de Molina in Aragon and left 4000 morabatins (to be taken from the tax of 5000 paid by the Jews at Michael-

---

171 López, *La província de España,* p. 190.
172 It is curious that Toribio del Campillo, *Documentos históricos de Daroca y su comunidad* (Saragossa, 1915), did not include any documents referring to the establishment of the Franciscan convent in Daroca.
173 Barcelona, ACA, RC 42, ff. 148v-149, 8 October 1279.
174 Epifanio de Pinaga, "Testamento de la infanta doña Blanca de Molina, fundadora del convento de San Francisco de Molina de Aragón, año 1293," *AIA* 27 (1927), 394-400, includes the text of the will.

mas), which, she stipulated, would help to clothe and feed the friars. The wording of the will suggests that she was the founder of the house, which she referred to as "my monastery" and which she wished to be inhabited by Conventual friars ("frayles de claustra"). Fr. Pedro de Chilliella is mentioned as the guardian, and among the witnesses are two other friars, Fr. Domingo López and Fr. Nicolás de Moriella or Morella; yet the house is not contained in any of the lists of recipients of letters from the king, nor is it mentioned by López, although Sanahuja states that it was assigned to the custody of Valencia in the division of 1334.[175]

The house also appears in subsequent divisions, but the only information comes from Pinaga's article on the will of Doña Blanca, from which it appears that it was in existence by 1286, and a papal bull of 1441 which suggests that it was in need of reform.[176] The friars must have continued to live in Molina until that date, but the house must have been small and not involved in questions of a litigious nature requiring the services of a notary or necessitating arbitration by the king. The scanty evidence at least places it among the foundations of the 1230s or 1240s, and possibly shortly after that at Morella. It may even have come under the latter's jurisdiction during its early days, explaining, at least in part, why it did not appear among the houses listed in the king's letter of 1279 referred to above.

Teruel

Finally there is the house at Teruel, closely connected with the journeys of the early missionaries and with the Valencia house. The two martyrs, Fr. John of Perugia and Fr. Peter of Sassoferrato, probably lived in private houses in Teruel around 1220, although the Franciscan chroniclers prefer the date 1217.[177] It is highly improbable that the convent in Teruel could have been founded before 1225. One of the early guardians of the Teruel house, Marc Pérez, arouses interest, as it is possible that he was one of the descendants of the Sayyid Abu Zayd, who conver-

---

175 Sanahuja, *História*, p. 65.
176 See Pinaga, "Testamento," p. 395, and Moorman, *Medieval Franciscan Houses*, p. 308.
177 López, *La província de España*, p. 192; Moorman, *Medieval Franciscan Houses*, p. 474.

ted to Christianity after the conquest of Valencia.[178] Pérez, a very frequent surname in the Valencian region, was the name chosen by some of the Sayyid Abu Zayd's descendants, and it is difficult to be sure that Fr. Marc was in any way connected with the illustrious Moor. In the document quoted, a letter from King Peter written in Algeciras to two of his subjects in Albarracín, Fr. Marc is named as the king's emissary, bearing the king's command to them that none of their vassals or men were to enter or be received in his territories, according to the agreement between King James and the king of Castile.

A recently published article on the church of Saint Francis in Teruel, probably part of the old convent, refers to the concession of forty days of indulgences to those who visited the church, to diminish their period of suffering in the life to come. Issued by the archbishop of Saragossa in 1249, this document is included in the inventory of the convent's possessions, and Agulló Pascual concludes that the church referred to was in fact part of the old convent.[179]

There will be occasion to refer again to the church of Saint Francis in Teruel in the discussion of the influence of the mendicant orders on the architecture of the thirteenth and fourteenth centuries.[180] It was one of the most important of the convents in the Valencian region shortly after the reconquest of the area from the Moors, and was included in Master Arnau's will and in the list of convents urged to preach to the Jews inside their synagogues in 1279. From the 1270s on Teruel was frequently mentioned in the chancellery registers in a number of different contexts. From 1277 the Franciscans in Teruel were involved in a burial dispute with the clergy of the diocese, one of many bitter struggles between the mendicant friars and the diocesan authorities.[181]

King Peter's letter, the first of the two documents dealing with the subject, records the geographical situation of the convent of Teruel, which, it states, was situated outside the town, probably just outside the

---

178 Barcelona, ACA, RC 50, f. 230, 13 January 1281 [1282].
179 Benjamin Agulló Pascual, "Iglesia de San Francisco de Teruel," in *Celebración del 750 aniversario del martirio de los santos fray Juan de Perusa y fray Pedro de Saxoferrato, copatronos de Teruel, Valencia-Teruel, 1228-1978* (Valencia, 1979), pp. 43-96, at 51. See also León Amorós Payá, *Los inventarios del antiguo archivo del convento de San Francisco de Teruel* (Teruel, 1960), p. 13.
180 See below Chapter 7, pp. 280-281.
181 Ambròs de Saldes, "Documentació franciscana (1267-1285)," *EF* 45 (1933), 130-149; López, *La província de España*, p. 192.

walls, as was customary in other places. The cause of the dispute lay in the fact that the clergy claimed that burials within the town were under their jurisdiction, and although the king stated that the Franciscan convent could be considered inside the walls for all practical purposes, he referred the matter to the ecclesiastical authorities whose right it was to decide such questions.[182] Teruel, which was among the earliest houses in the Valencian region and was probably established in 1225, had an illustrious beginning, perhaps even claiming as its inspiration the two martyrs and counting among its residents at least one descendant of the Sayyid Abu Zayd.

Xàtiva

Two further convents were included in the 1334 custody of Valencia, Xàtiva in Aragon and Murviedro, not far from the city of Valencia. Xàtiva, to the south of Valencia, was one of the most strategic areas in the defence of Valencia; it was reconquered by James I as early as 1244.[183] Founded in 1248, the convent of Xàtiva was quite active during the latter part of the thirteenth and early fourteenth centuries, but was completely destroyed during the war between Castile and Aragon in 1372.[184] In 1296 the king, writing to the *jurats* of Xàtiva, referred to a communication from the guardian of the Franciscan house in which he stated that the late King James, when Xàtiva was reconquered [1244], had given a piece of land to the Franciscans on which to build their monastery and where they could live in perpetuity, at the same time conceding to them the right to draw water from a stream near the city walls for the purpose of irrigating their land.[185]

This suggests that there were Franciscan friars in Xàtiva from 1244, even though the official foundation of the convent may only date from 1248. The letter confirms that the friars did in fact build their house there, and were still in residence at the time of writing. In 1298 the Franciscans at Xàtiva were claiming the unpaid legacy bequeathed to them by Garcias Fernando de Varra for the construction of a

---

182 See below Chapter 4, pp. 149–165, where the whole question of relations between the friars and the diocesan clergy is discussed at length.
183 Burns, *El reino de Valencia*, 1: 30, 34.
184 Moorman, *Medieval Franciscan Houses*, p. 235.
185 Barcelona, ACA, RC 104, f. 58, 25 August 1296.

church.[186] It sounds as though they had been unable to build a permanent church, but maybe this legacy was really intended to be used for the enlargement of the existing church, as it is unthinkable that for a period of nearly fifty years the convent of Friars Minor, endowed with land in 1244 and established four years later, had remained without a church.

Murviedro

Earliest references to the convent of Murviedro date from the first decade of the fourteenth century, but the documents in question prove that the convent existed much earlier. Murviedro, an old Roman fortress, fell to the Christians at the time of the reconquest of Valencia and, following the pattern of the other foundations in the Valencia region, it seems likely that James I gave land to the Franciscans at least before 1250. The first documented evidence of the existence of this convent dates from 1301 [1302], when the king wrote to the justice of the town in connection with the legacy of the butcher Lope, a neighbour of Murviedro.[187] There is no doubt that by the date of the king's letter the house was well established, perhaps founded the same year as Xàtiva (1248); yet, if paucity of documentation even after 1300 is any indication, it was one of the least important Franciscan convents.

THE CUSTODY OF SARAGOSSA

Huesca

Eight convents make up the custody of Saragossa: Saragossa itself, Huesca, Tarazona, Barbastro, Ejea de los Caballeros, Jaca, Borja and Sariñena. The almost total lack of records for the early years of convents within the kingdom of Aragon makes it impossible to suggest even approximate dates for their foundation. This is particularly frustrating, as later documents show that they were among the most important mendicant foundations in the kingdom.

The foundation of the house at Saragossa, a strategic point in the line of fortification from Aragon to Valencia, has already been discussed, as has that of Tarazona, and it is therefore appropriate to turn to the nearby house of Huesca, which according to Wadding existed in 1235, the date

---

186 Barcelona, ACA, RC 110, f. 38, 27 April 1298.
187 ACA, RC 120, f. 215r–v, 15 January 1301 [1302].

Pedro de Les was given some houses situated in the quarter where the Friars Minor had their house.[188] Gonzaga suggests that 1280 was the date of foundation, but this is obviously incorrect, as extant documents date from 1251.[189] In the municipal archives at Huesca, in a document of 1260 which confirms the papal privilege to coin money in Jaca, the names of Fr. Il.luminat and Fr. William Bede appear, the latter presumably the same man mentioned earlier in this chapter as Fr. Peter of the See.[190]

There are also three signatures on behalf of the Dominicans, that of the famous preacher Fr. Ramon de Penyafort, Fr. Miquel and Fr. Guillem de Barberà. The duty of these friars was to watch over the way in which the king minted money, and the document is signed by James I. The presence of this document in Huesca does not necessarily confirm that there was a Franciscan convent there at that time, but it does show that the Franciscans and Dominicans were solicited by both crown and papacy as guarantors.

More pertinent to the history of the Huesca convent is the fact that Queen Violant, wife of James I of Aragon, left 50 maravedis to the friars in her will of 1251, and in 1275 Prince Peter, James I's lieutenant, granted them a safe-conduct which, if not obeyed, would result in a fine of 50 morabatins being levied on the person disobeying his orders.[191] In view of its proximity to Saragossa and its importance to the crown, there is little doubt that Huesca should take its place among the earliest foundations of the late 1220s or early 1230s, even though records from those dates have been lost. Remains of the old Gothic house can still be seen despite the fact that the provincial government now occupies a modern building erected on the site.

Barbastro

Of the other convents in the custody of Saragossa, Barbastro was one of the most significant. First mention of the Barbastro house is in 1235,

---

188 Wadding, *Annales Minorum,* 5: 104; see also López, *La província de España,* p. 193.
189 Gonzaga, *De origine,* Provincia Aragoniae, conv. X; see also López, *La província de España,* p. 193.
190 Huesca, AHM, Privilegios reales, s. XIII–XIV, L.1, R.1260 (98A), 12 August 1260. There is no way of ascertaining which of the two names is correct.
191 Barcelona, ACA, RC 37, f. 92, 9 July 1275.

when the church of Saint Francis attached to the Barbastro convent was the beneficiary of a will.[192] The source of this reference, *España sagrada,* is not always reliable, but in this case it is very likely that the date is correct, as it would mean that the house at Barbastro was founded at about the same time as the convents of Saragossa and Huesca. The first extant documentation refers to the year 1273, when Master Arnau included the Barbastro house in the list of beneficiaries of his will. Barbastro also appears in the subsequent list of the Franciscan houses enjoined by the king in 1279 to preach to the Jews inside the synagogue in order to prevent civil disturbance.[193] Despite the almost total lack of early references, the abundance of documents in the later chancellery registers referring to the Barbastro house, and the one reference to its existence in 1235, support its claim to a place among the early foundations.

Jaca

Jaca is one of the few convents for which part of the archives is extant, having been taken over by the state upon the sequestration of the property of the religious orders in the nineteenth century, but the early years seem to follow a similar trajectory to that of Barbastro.[194] Gonzaga notes that the convent existed in 1246, when Pope Innocent IV issued a bull granting an indulgence of forty days off purgatory to those who gave money towards the fabric of the Jaca house.[195] In 1257 the friars were granted permission to extract two hundred loads of wheat to use at their table. In 1278 [1279] the friars were having trouble with the chapter of canons in Jaca, and the king wrote both to the chapter and to his officials in the town, telling them that the friars had protection from the papacy and must not be interfered with in any way.[196] This injunction must have fallen on deaf ears, because conflicts between friars and clergy continued unabated into the fourteenth century. After this date documents referring to the Jaca house become very numerous, and it is a recipient of most of the circular letters sent to Franciscan convents

---

192 Moorman, *Medieval Franciscan Houses,* p. 50.
193 Barcelona, ACA, RC 42, ff. 148v–149, 8 October 1279.
194 These documents are now housed in the Archivo histórico nacional (AHN), Madrid, but unfortunately are incomplete and refer only to the fourteenth century.
195 Gonzaga, *De origine,* Provincia Aragoniae, conv. VIII; see also López, *La província de España,* pp. 191–192.
196 See Barcelona, ACA, RC 37, f. 92, 9 July 1275.

(such as the letter of 1279, cited earlier, concerning the preaching of the Christian message to the Jews). No definite date of foundation can be established for Jaca, but it can tentatively be placed sometime in the 1240s, shortly before Innocent IV's bull of 1246.

Ejea de los Caballeros

The convents of Ejea, Borja and Sariñena all date from the thirteenth century, but little is known about their activities prior to the 1270s. Ejea was founded in 1250, but the first surviving document is the will of Master Arnau, from which the house of Ejea was to receive 5 sous.[197] Ejea was also one of the convents which received the letters from the king in 1279, urging that sermons aimed at converting the Jews be preached from within the safety of the synagogue.[198] To judge from the extant documentation in the chancellery registers (the best source found for references to the Aragonese Franciscans in the thirteenth and fourteenth centuries), the Ejea house, although founded as early as 1250, must have been small and perhaps was eclipsed by the importance of the houses at Saragossa, Jaca, Barbastro and Huesca.

Sariñena

There is little surviving documentation for the house of Sariñena, which was founded in 1282, somewhat later than most of the other houses.[199] In that year the king wrote to the official acting on his behalf (the *superjuntario*), informing him that the Friars Minor proposed to build a monastery in honour of Saint Francis within the town of Sariñena. This is a standard letter of royal protection for the friars, repeated on many occasions, in which the king enjoined his officials to see that the friars were not impeded in their work and were allowed to build their monastery without interference. As their presence was often unwelcome to the diocesan clergy, letters of this sort must sometimes have been helpful in preventing trouble, although unfortunately conflicts between the friars and the clergy still arose on numerous occasions.

Founded in 1282, Sariñena, like Ejea, must have been a small house whose development was not dissimilar to that of the other friaries in

---

197 Moorman, *Medieval Franciscan Houses,* p. 170.
198 See Barcelona, ACA, RC 42, f. 149v, 8 October 1279.
199 Ambròs de Saldes, "Documentació franciscana (1282-1285)," *EF* 42 (1930), 86-96, at p. 90.

Aragon. Unlike these other friaries, it was later taken over by the Capuchin friars and still exists today, maintaining, at least in part, some of its medieval buildings.

Borja

Borja was probably a later foundation, possibly dating from the second decade of the fourteenth century, when the convents of Tàrrega and Puigcerdà were founded. The earliest references to its existence occur in two documents of 1325,[200] and indicate that the house had been in existence for some time and was very poor. The first document refers to 70 sous outstanding to the friars on account of a payment to be made by Martín Alfonso de Razazol in connection with his marriage; the second is a request from the king to the *jurats* and *prohoms* of Borja to pay 2000 Jaca sous to the Franciscans, who are in dire need of the money to pay for the fabric of their church.[201] As Borja was very close to the larger town of Tarazona, its development was probably much slower, and perhaps it was only in the 1330s, from which period more documentation survives, that it acquired the status of the other houses in Aragon.[202]

THE CUSTODY OF NARBONNE

Although outside the realms of Aragon for part of the period under review, three convents belonging to the custody of Narbonne had close connections with the Crown of Aragon and therefore come within the scope of this study. The convents of Perpignan, Villefranche de Conflent and especially Puigcerdà were situated within the territories of the Crown of Majorca, forming part of the amalgam of kingdoms which constituted the Crown of Aragon. Both Perpignan and Villefranche were founded in the thirteenth century and were well established by 1300, although most of their activities have more to do with France than with Aragon and are beyond the scope of this study. Perpignan has been

---

200   This is some forty years earlier than the date put forward by Wadding, *Annales Minorum,* 8: 217; see also Moorman, *Medieval Franciscan Houses,* p. 83.
201   Barcelona, ACA, RC 375, f. 20r–v, 4 July 1325.
202   The royal chancellery registers for the 1330s contain a number of references to the Borja house, which, it is interesting to note, does not appear in López, *La província de España,* nor among the lists referred to for the years 1273 and 1279.

mentioned earlier, as, like many of the convents in Catalonia and Aragon, it boasted of an association with Saint Francis. Montpellier, the city in which James I had been born, was also part of the Crown of Aragon. In 1243 James bequeathed it to his infant son James, who was later to become king of Majorca.[203] Consequently, until 1344, when it was sold to the king of France, the lordship of Montpellier was part of the kingdom of Majorca.[204] Despite this fact, and perhaps because of its geographical situation, the convent of Montpellier had little contact with the Franciscan province of Aragon, to which it never belonged.

We should now turn to the most significant of the convents belonging to the Narbonne province, that in Villefranche de Conflent, only a few kilometers from the French frontier with the Iberian Peninsula.

Villefranche de Conflent

This small town, situated in the Pyrenees close to the borders of the province of Gerona, had a fundamental role in the development of the house at Puigcerdà. In 1279 the house which had belonged to the Friars of the Sack was given by the papacy to the Franciscans at Villefranche.[205] Pladevall has accepted this date as the foundation of the convent, but it is quite probable that there were friars resident in Villefranche long before 1279.[206] Little is known about this house before the end of the thirteenth century, when it became one of the convents to espouse the apocalyptic ideas of Peter John Olivi, Joachim da Fiore and their followers.[207] Certainly from 1301 the notarial records in Puigcerdà suggest that the house at Villefranche was active and well known on both sides of the Pyrenees.[208] Its importance for this study lies not in its association with heretical ideas but rather in its relationship

---

203 Thomas N. Bisson, *The Medieval Crown of Aragon: A Short History* (Oxford, 1986), p. 69.
204 Ibid., p. 106.
205 Jerónimo Aguillo López de Turiso, *La provincia seráfica de Cataluña* (Barcelona, 1902), p. 36, *Nuper exponentibus*, dated 28 June 1279.
206 Antoni Pladevall and F. Català Roca, *Els monestirs catalans*, 4th ed. (Barcelona, 1978), p. 88.
207 Sanahuja, *História*, p. 73.
208 Puigcerdà, AHC, Ramon de Coguls and Pere d'Onzés, *Liber testamentorum* (4 July 1301–20 May 1302), f. 4. Subsequent manuals show a steady flow of donations to the Franciscans at Villefranche. Some photographs of the remaining part of the convent have been included among the illustrations in this book.

with Puigcerdà, the most important convent within the custody of Narbonne to remain within the Franciscan province of Provence after the conquest of the kingdom of Majorca by Peter III in 1344.

Puigcerdà

The town of Puigcerdà, situated only one kilometer from the French border, belongs administratively to the province of Gerona. In the thirteenth and early fourteenth centuries it was under the general jurisdiction of the king of Majorca and had close contacts with the Franciscan convents of Perpignan and Villefranche de Conflent, both more accessible than Gerona itself. Puigcerdà was one of the convents to be founded in the second decade of the fourteenth century, largely as a result of pressure from natives of the town who had entered the Order of Friars Minor and were resident in the convent of Villefranche, but wished to move nearer home.[209] The house at Puigcerdà was established in much the same way as that at Tàrrega, founded two years earlier; but in Puigcerdà the process emphasizes the close alliance between the Franciscans, the royal house of Majorca and the municipality, largely composed of prominent merchants. Some of the details of this process are relevant to the way in which the traders helped the friars to become established in the Crown of Aragon and will be mentioned again later.

The first evidence of the intention to found a house in Puigcerdà comes from a will of 1315, in which Fr. Pere Llaguna's sister, Berenguera, left her estate to the Franciscans at Puigcerdà if, by the time of her death, they had founded a house there. At this time Fr. Pere was resident at Villefranche, but after the foundation of the Puigcerdà house he transferred to his native town. Even before 1315 the friars probably had a hospice in Puigcerdà, or visited the town frequently, but it was not until 7 August 1320 that the house was founded officially.

The will of Berenguera also mentions that the Poor Clares had just established a convent in Perpignan, a fact confirmed by another legacy of approximately the same date, strongly suggesting that, as yet, neither they nor the friars had a house in Puigcerdà. It was customary, although not always the case, that the friars first established their own house and then helped the Poor Clares to found their convent in the same town.

---

209 Webster, "El desconocido convento de Puigcerdà," from which all of the details regarding the Puigcerdà house are taken.

The letter from King Sancho of Majorca acceding to the request of the municipality of Puigcerdà states that three upright citizens (*prohoms*) were to be appointed to evaluate the property of the late Bernat de Mornach, thus affording evidence of the friars' intention to make a permanent commitment to the town.

On 7 August 1320 the Franciscans paid a down payment of 50 Barcelona pounds towards the purchase price of 200 pounds, and promised to pay the remaining 150 pounds in two installments, 50 at Christmas of 1320 and the other 100 the following year on 24 June. This contract gave them the right to take possession of the property immediately, although they may not have moved into it until later, as they already had a hospice in Puigcerdà near the late Bernat de Mornach's house and probably wished to adapt the property they had purchased to make it suitable for a permanent convent. Between the date of purchase and 1333, the Franciscans were engaged in building a permanent convent, which was opened with due ceremony that year.

During the intervening years there are frequent references in the notarial manuals still extant in Puigcerdà, to the wills of merchants who included the Franciscans in their wills as beneficiaries, and to other documents pertaining to the affairs of the Puigcerdà house, many of which afford valuable information about the early inhabitants of the town and the families of the friars. From this source it is possible to reach the conclusion that by 1333 most of the friars who were natives of Puigcerdà had returned to their homeland. Puigcerdà, perhaps the most interesting of all the houses in the realms of Aragon because of its close contacts with southern France, belonged to the foundations of the second decade of the fourteenth century, and was in full operation by 1320.

THE ISLAND OF SARDINIA

One further area should be mentioned, Sardinia, which was fully incorporated into the territories under Aragonese rule with the siege of Cagliari in 1323, having previously been in the hands of the Pisans and Genoese.[210] In order to ensure that the mendicant houses did not

---

210 For a more detailed acount of the Aragonese resettlement of the convents on the island of Sardinia with Catalan friars, see Jill R. Webster, "The Early Catalan Mendicants in Sardinia," *Biblioteca francescana sarda* (Oristano, Sardinia) 2 (1988), 5-16.

maintain their contacts with their Italian confreres, King Alfonso III decided to resettle the houses with Franciscans from Catalonia. This was accomplished in Cagliari in 1325, and by 1329 there was a Catalan vicar on the island. In 1326, when Sassari and Vila Iglesias fell to the king, it was not long before Catalans replaced the Italians in those Franciscan houses too.

Again, the Aragonese monarchy's policy of Christian resettlement is evident, here carried one step further by the sending of Catalan friars to ensure that the island of Sardinia remained faithful to the crown. These houses, which had originally been founded in the first half of the thirteenth century and in the 1320s fell into Catalan hands, are only of very tangential interest to the main thrust of Franciscan development in the realms of Aragon. A few friars, especially from the province of Gerona, were transferred to the island but remained within the custody of Barcelona. Their activities in no way affect the present study, but the king probably used the mendicant orders to avoid possible treason by the hostile Pisans and Genoese, a decision which directly parallels James I's use of these friars to Christianize his territories in the kingdom of Valencia, and safeguard them from Moorish invasion.

Hospices

Research in the Crown of Aragon archives has turned up two interesting documents referring to a Franciscan hospice in Manresa, not far from Barcelona. The documents, which date from 1292 and 1297, are among the very few which suggest that the Franciscans had smaller enclaves outside the main nuclei, although this was certainly the case when there was a Clarissan monastery. For instance, the Friars Minor of the Barcelona house undertook the religious duties of saying mass and dispensing the sacraments to the nuns at the monastery of Pedralbes, founded in 1327.[211] It may well be, and this was certainly true later, that the friars who performed these duties lived in a house (or hospice?) close to the Pedralbes monastery; for the monastery would have been too far away for them to make frequent journeys from their house in Barcelona, in the area of the present Plaça de Medinaceli, close to the waterfront.

---

211 Barcelona, AMP, *Chronologia de la regla de Santa Clara,* discusses the early activities of the Friars Minor in relation to the convent at Pedralbes.

Manresa

A commercial town renowned in the Middle Ages for the fairs held on Ascension Day and the feast of Saint Andrew, Manresa became an important centre. The convent of Saint Clare was established in the fourteenth century, and the town also possessed a church dedicated to Saint Francis, although the modern church by that name dates from the Renaissance period. What is not generally known about the town is the fact that it also possessed a Franciscan hospice.

Normally a hospice of this kind would have been established for the priests who served the convent of Saint Clare, but since the sister house was not founded until 1322 the Franciscans probably first intended to found a house in Manresa. However, perhaps for lack of support or because both the Dominicans and Carmelites succeeded in establishing houses there around 1300, they decided to abandon the idea.[212]

The first of the two documents found, dated 21 April 1292, is a letter from King James II confirming the privileges accorded the hospice of the Friars Minor in Manresa.[213] These privileges exempted the hospice from the payment of all taxes and its procurator or almoner from military service. A note in the margin indicates that the letter was written "pro" Ferrer de Sala. The second document, dated 5 May 1297 and addressed to Berenguer de Mas of the king's household, at the instance of the Barcelona Franciscan house, refers again to Ferrer de Sala:[214] the king orders his official not to demand the half *bovatge* (a tax on livestock paid to the crown by all citizens) from Ferrer de Sala, who was exempt from all payment of taxes by reason of being the collector or distributor of alms for the hospice at Manresa.[215]

The Manresa hospice depended on the house at Barcelona, no doubt in much the same way as the group at Pedralbes later considered themselves part of the Barcelona convent, although the friars seem to have been drawn from the neighbouring convent at Vic. A similar document to that of 1292 refers to Fr. Pere de Roca, almoner of the Dominican

---

212 Jill R. Webster, "Els framenors de Manresa," *Miscel.lània d'estudis bagencs* (Manresa) 5 (1987), 127–137, where the situation in Manresa is discussed in more detail.
213 Ibid., pp. 128, 136.
214 Barcelona, ACA, RC 264, f. 6v, 5 May 1297.
215 Ferrer de Sala, according to the document of 1292, was the elemosinarius of the hospice at Manresa.

hospice of Manresa, which presumably fulfilled a function parallel to that of the Franciscan house, with the vital difference that the Dominicans were able to consolidate support for a permanent foundation there.

From an economic point of view, these hospices were run by the almoner, who probably acted on behalf of the hospice in much the same way as the procurator acted on behalf of the mother house. The almoner may even have had to account to the procurator at the end of each year. There is no evidence to confirm this conjecture, but if it is true, it would seem safe to assume that when a convent of nuns was established in a town which had no Franciscan or Dominican convent, a hospice was established, drawing on the nearest custodial house for its personnel.

There are no further references to a hospice in Manresa until the 1320s, when friars from the Gerona house lived in a small convent in the town to attend to the needs of the recently-founded convent of Saint Clare. The thirteenth-century hospice can only have been established with the aim of founding a convent, an attempt which was clearly unsuccessful; but there is nothing to explain why the later *conventet* was staffed from Gerona and not Vic.

Other Hospices

There are two further references to Franciscan houses or hospices which cannot be classified: a legacy from Guillem de Rocafull to the Franciscans in Alcira, near Valencia; and grants from the royal treasury to friars in Castellón del camp de Burriana, to the north of Valencia.[216] No reference has been turned up to confirm the existence of Franciscan friars in these places in the thirteenth and early fourteenth centuries, nor to suggest the existence of sister convents of Saint Clare which might have given a motive for their presence there. In the case of Alcira, Guillem de Rocafull's will describes the plot of land he was leaving to the Franciscans as being alongside the bridge and the road leading to Xàtiva; perhaps the legacy never became effective, or should be read as referring to the house at Xàtiva. In the case of Castellón, maybe some Franciscans worked there for reasons obscure to the modern scholar but possibly connected with their mission to the non-Christians.

---

216 See Madrid, AHN, Clero, Valldigna, carp. 3364, perg. 7 (I have to thank Father Robert I. Burns for this reference.)

The parallelism between James I and Saint Francis is best seen in the development of the first houses, intended, it would seem, both as a further bulwark against the Moors and as a way of integrating the new urban middle classes into the political scene. The success of this policy is evident in the reigns of subsequent kings, for, as indicated, a further cluster of Franciscan houses was established both in the 1270s and during the second decade of the fourteenth century, probably to ensure a continuing Christian presence in areas where the Jews had acquired significant commercial success, and to reaffirm the orthodoxy of the Franciscans when the Spiritual movement threatened to split the order apart.

It is a possible, if not an irrefutable conclusion, that these new houses were a means of convincing the crown that the Franciscans could still be of service in supporting its policies in an urban environment, where the rumours of heresy abounded and the excommunication of friars for infraction of their privileges was common in the early years of the fourteenth century. With the conquest of the island of Sardinia and the settlement of Catalan friars in the convents there, royal policy can again be seen as favouring political control through strategically placed mendicant houses. The threat of invasion of the island by Pisans and Genoese would have been much greater had Alfonso III allowed friars from these communes to remain in Cagliari, Sassari and Vila Iglesias. At best they would have been a constant irritant to Aragonese power and an invitation to their countrymen to attempt reconquest of the island. The friars were as important to the crown as the crown was to them, and it is significant that they continued to render numerous services to each other, frequently making demands or undertaking missions that in later centuries would have been unthinkable in a religious context.

By the end of the thirteenth century the disciples of Saint Francis had not only spread throughout Europe, but more especially had become established in the dominions of the king of Aragon; nearly forty houses and at least one hospice had been founded, and they had not yet achieved their peak of prosperity. Their progress closely parallels that of the monarchs who had done so much to help them to acquire the economic basis for their success. The following chapter will illustrate royal intervention in Franciscan affairs, discussing just how important royal protection was to these early friars, who in turn rendered many and varied services to the crown; how in some cases grants made to them were delayed for years and perhaps in others were never paid; and how their popularity in the realms of Aragon was to a very great degree dependent on the fortunes of the royal house.

2

Security, Learning and Privilege

The previous chapter discussed at some length the way in which Saint Francis influenced the development of Christian society by sending his friars to the Iberian Peninsula, where, with the aid of his near contemporary King James I, they were able to establish convents and acquire support from crown and people. When James I succeeded to the throne of Aragon, he became titular ruler over a series of loosely bound kingdoms covering a vast territory, the southern part of which was still under Moorish rule. James was born in Montpellier, orphaned at an early age and placed under the tutelage of his father's slayer, Simon de Montfort; but he was soon removed from the latter's influence by Pope Innocent III, who placed both king and kingdom under the protection of the Knights Templar.[1]

James's early upbringing laid the foundations for a reign which was to combine military prowess with religious piety. His character combined cruelty and devotion in equal measure and his behaviour was often loose and immoral. Yet in some ways his reign was a crusade, a landmark in the development of the Christian church in the Peninsula. It was not only essential but logical that, if he were to give strong leadership in the reconquest of his lands still under Moorish rule, he must avail himself of the binding forces of Christianity and ensure that he had the support of church and papacy. It was fortunate that his reign began at a time when the two major mendicant orders, the Dominicans and the Franciscans, were sending their first missionaries to the Peninsula, en route to Africa, for this gave him the opportunity to enlist them in his crusade.

---

1 Robert I. Burns, "Castle of Intellect, Castle of Force: The Worlds of Alfonso the Learned and James the Conqueror," in *The Worlds of Alfonso the Learned and James the Conqueror: Intellect and Force in the Middle Ages*, ed. Robert I. Burns (Princeton, 1985), pp. 3–22, at 7–8.

It was to the western Mediterranean that James first turned his attention. In the early 1230s he conquered the Balearic Islands, Majorca and Minorca, for if he was to move southward to Murcia and Valencia he had to be sure that he would not be attacked from these islands. Although the king granted land to the Majorcan house in 1233, it is in the campaign on the Valencian front that Franciscans attached to the royal army are first noted, by the presence of the Brother Il.luminat and Fr. Peter of the See mentioned in the previous chapter.[2] It is not clear what their function was, nor is it known what happened to them later, but they probably acted in an advisory capacity and attended to the spiritual needs of James's army. There is evidence that they were instrumental in helping found the first Franciscan houses in the realms of Aragon. Reconquest meant resettlement, and here the church could fulfil the important role of ministering to the Christians who moved into the newly-conquered areas. Not only did the friars and clergy attend to the needs of the Christians, but they also made every effort to persuade the non-Christian minorities to embrace Christianity through a system of voluntary or not so voluntary conversions.

Resettlement by Christians and the establishment of religious houses in the newly-conquered lands clearly benefited both the king and the friars, for just as James needed the approval and support of the church, so the church needed the assurance that the royal house would endow the new religious houses and protect them from harm. The *Chronicle* of James I frequently mentions the participation of the mendicants in royal affairs, and records that on one occasion a *menoret* from Navarre rose up in the *corts,* at that time being held in Saragossa, and claimed that he had had a vision of James I as the king appointed by God to restore Christianity to Spain by extirpating the Moors.[3] No doubt the chronicler included this story to give validity to the Conqueror's campaigns, and to emphasize the king's crusade on behalf of Christendom.

---

2   See above Chapter 1, pp. 35, 52; Sanahuja, *Història,* p. 54, for the land grant.
3   *Crònica del rei Jaume I, el Conqueridor,* cap. 389, in *Les quatre grans cròniques,* ed. Ferran Soldevila, 2nd ed. (Barcelona, 1983), pp. 1–402, at 144. The term used here is *Espanya,* not to be confused with the modern political denomination which came about from the union of the Crowns of Aragon and Castile at the end of the fifteenth century under Ferdinand and Isabella, known as the "Catholic kings." The friar's intervention is curious, in view of the fact that neither was he a subject of King James nor was the meeting of the *corts* being held in the convent of the Friars Minor at Saragossa. In fact the assembled company repaired to the Dominican church.

Initially, of course, it was through the king's bounty that the new mendicant orders were able to acquire property, and to develop contacts which gave them a significant following within a very short time of having established their first houses. The fact that they were to expand throughout Aragon was largely attributable to royal protection, generous grants in money and land and the exemption from taxation afforded them by the king.[4] The favourable treatment they received from the monarch was hardly destined to protect them from the jealousy and animosity of their contemporaries, and they frequently became embroiled in conflicts with the clergy or other orders, and also with prominent laymen. In the most troublesome disputes they appealed to the king to intervene on their behalf and help them obtain a favourable settlement.

It is not surprising that the mendicant newcomers should have met with opposition from established society. Still, their widespread popularity in a litigious age indicates that frequent references to disputes between the friars and their contemporaries should not be interpreted as having any overall significance on their development. The popularity of the mendicant orders is one of the phenomena of the later Middle Ages, and the timing of their arrival upon the spiritual scene was fortunate, coinciding with the rise of an active merchant class and the need for revival of effective pastoral work in the parishes, where the clergy seemed to have lost touch with their parishioners. Faced with a society in evolution, many of the parish priests were unprepared to meet the challenge of a new age. They often lacked the education and experience required for them to compete with the friars, whose preaching ability immediately gained them popular support.

In Chapter 1, it was suggested that the Franciscans could in some ways be compared to the Waldensians, Albigensians and other heretical groups who, at the turn of the century, threatened to undermine the established church. In particular, they seemed to have inherited some of the popular appeal of these groups, although at no time was their orthodoxy in question. The friars clearly learned much from these groups, benefiting from the novelty of their approach, especially in the eloquent sermons they preached. They might even have learned some of the techniques used by the heretics to draw the attention of the crowd, but, whatever the origin of their success, they made a direct appeal to their contemporaries which could not be matched by the parochial clergy.

---

4   Ch.-E. Dufourcq and J. Gautier Dalché, *História ecónomica y social de la España cristiana en la edad media* (Barcelona, 1983), pp. 198–199.

It was for their preaching ability that the followers of Saint Dominic and Saint Francis were primarily known in the early years; their sermons drew immense crowds, which was a major cause of tension between them and the parochial clergy, yet at the same time they won the support of many wealthy citizens. Although this is a crucial factor in any attempt to evaluate the causes of their meteoric success, the favour shown to the friars by the wealthy citizens alone could never have ensured their continuing prosperity, had it not been evident that the king gave his unqualified moral and economic support to the mendicant cause.[5]

While royal favour was essential to the progress of the order, at times it had a negative impact on the work of the friars. When political exigencies made it convenient for the monarchs to emphasize their need for church support, they showed great generosity to the endeavours of the friars; at other times, regular concessions granted to them often went unnoticed for years before they were paid. Even the legacies bequeathed by royalty did not always reach their beneficiaries, nor were the foundations for which they left their money always established. This prompts the suggestion that some of the great wealth which the numerous bequests seem to indicate never found its way into Franciscan coffers. If this were indeed true, and a definitive conclusion must await a later study of the final decades of the fourteenth century, certain concepts about the progress of the order might have to be reexamined.

Any analysis of the support given by the royal house to the Minors, and of its intervention in their affairs, must be seen in the context of the principal source from which it is drawn. Much of the extant documentation relating to Franciscan activities in Aragon comes from the royal archives, and there is a danger of over-emphasizing the role of the royal family in the promotion of the Christian church, especially since there are relatively few other records referring to the daily activities of the friars. If these had existed it might have been possible to assess more accurately the impact of royal support to the friars on the order itself, and on those who came into contact with it. Despite these drawbacks, the prevalence of documents in the royal archives referring to Franciscan life provides incontrovertible proof that the order played a significant role within the realms of Aragon.

A second major source can be used to supplement much of the information drawn from the royal documents, especially for the early

---

5 Robert I. Burns, *El reino de Valencia en el siglo XIII (iglesia y sociedad)*, 2 vols. (Valencia, 1982), 2: 446–452.

years: the extant wills, which by their very nature are limited in the comparative material they provide. The interdependence between the crown and the friars is so important, however, that it should never be overlooked when assessing the success of the mendicant orders, and the following comments will only serve to reinforce this conclusion.

Numerous privileges were accorded to the friars by the royal house of Aragon; these can be divided into two main categories: those which enabled the friars to establish a house and run it without difficulties, and those which pertained to the employment of individual friars for confidential royal business.

General Privileges

When the friars first arrived in the Peninsula, it was with the intention of proceeding to North Africa to convert the Moors, although they might also have had in mind the possibility of establishing houses along the route. It is not known just how much knowledge Saint Francis and his followers had of conditions outside the Italian communes, but the new order he founded shared the missionary fervour of thirteenth-century Europe, which derived much of its inspiration from the Crusades and the capture of Jerusalem by the Christians in 1099. It is no accident that the Franciscan order was given the papal privilege in later years to watch over the Holy Sepulchre in Jerusalem, a duty which to this day is a privilege the Catalan Franciscans share with representatives of other branches of the Catholic church. Upon the death of King Peter I of Aragon, his son, James I, had been placed in the custody of the Templars on the orders of Pope Innocent III, and pontifical regents were appointed to help him maintain an impartial administration. In 1220 they counselled the king to place his fiscal matters in Aragon and Catalonia under the supervision of this powerful military order, an order which in later years was to come under critical scrutiny, until it was finally dissolved.[6]

The challenge presented by a country partially controlled by Moorish rulers, and just across the Mediterranean, could not have failed to arouse the interest of the Friars Minor. Italian friars had first crossed to the Peninsula soon after the accession of James I, and in 1219 a provincial minister for Aragon had been named. It must also have been abundantly clear to the young king that, if he were to unify his domains, he could

---

6 Thomas N. Bisson, "Prelude to Power: Kingship and Constitution in the Realms of Aragon, 1175-1250," in *The Worlds of Alfonso the Learned and James the Conqueror*, pp. 23-40, at 32.

enlist the support of the church for his military campaigns against the Moors by presenting these wars as part of a crusade on behalf of Christendom. In this way he could take advantage of the need of the newly-founded mendicant orders to gain a firm foundation from which to operate. The surviving documentation shows how he exploited this opportunity to the full. It also indicates that many of the concessions were granted in perpetuity and renewed with each successive reign, making clear that his successors also understood the value of the "crusade." Can it be assumed, then, that the Franciscans, whose primary intent had been to convert the Moors in North Africa and perhaps help with their conversion in the reconquered lands, were persuaded by the king that they could best carry out their mission by allying themselves with his policy of reconquest and resettlement? Certainly there were many incentives for them to accept this role, which after all seemed to accord well with the spirit of the rule of 1221, which said that Friars Minor so inspired by God to work as missionaries among the "Saracens" might, upon receiving permission from their minister, go forth and preach the word to the unbelievers. An appeal to this spirit of mission and sacrifice by the king evidently met with a favourable reception.

The first documentary evidence for the king's interest in the mendicant orders is to be found in his will drawn up in Tarragona in 1232, in which he bequeathed 1000 morabatins to the Franciscans and Dominicans in his territories.[7] At this time, several houses had already been established, including those in Barcelona, Gerona, Lerida, Majorca, Saragossa, Valencia and Vic. The date of 1232 suggests that the friars were well known to the king and were beginning to acquire a position of some significance in the royal domains, a fact supported by the subsequent frequent concessions granted to them by the monarch.

Concessions of Land

The most basic concession made to the Franciscans by the king consisted of grants of money or land to enable them to build permanent houses. The discussion of the foundations of houses in the realms of Aragon in Chapter 1 has mentioned several occasions on which the king made a grant of land to the friars. Without such help these foundations might never have been established, while others would have had far greater financial problems in their early years. Many of these grants of money

---

7 Ambròs de Saldes, "La orden franciscana en el antiguo reino de Aragón: Colección diplomatica," *REF* 1 (1907), 90–92, 219–222, 279–282, at pp. 279–280.

or land date from the reign of James I and were confirmed by his successors. It was not unusual for subsequent grants to be made to the friars when convents were enlarged or changed their location. Such grants were probably made at one time or other to all the Franciscan and Dominican convents in the realm, and proportionately to the smaller mendicant orders.

The first extant evidence of this practice refers to the land given by James I to the Majorca house to enable the friars to move to a location within the city.[8] A year later, in 1239, the king also gave land on the Ruzafa road to the friars in Valencia.[9] It can surely be no mere coincidence that the two areas reconquered from the Moors were those to which James first lent his support, and it is tempting to conclude that the grants were intended as a reward for services rendered by the friars during the reconquest of Majorca and Valencia. Apart from any intention the king might have had to recognize the spiritual help given by the Franciscans during these campaigns, it would have been part of his policy of consolidation to ensure that the friars would support future royal endeavours. His generosity probably had more to do with political expediency than with a sincere desire to recompense the friars for their help at the time of the reconquest. Grants of land or money were insufficient to protect the Franciscans from those who envied them their success; indeed, they might have exacerbated the latent hostility of the secular clergy, who resented the intrusion of these newcomers into the domain which previously had been exclusively theirs.

This leads to the second basic form of support the Friars Minor received, in common with other religious orders in the realms of Aragon, the right to proceed unharmed on the king's highway.

Protection

In the thirteenth and fourteenth centuries it was quite common for travellers to be attacked by brigands on the highways, and it was unsafe to travel from place to place without some guarantee of protection from the king, a safeguard which was given on the understanding that any form of violence would be regarded as a crime punishable by the royal court of justice. This safe-conduct granted to the friars would identify them as royal messengers, irrespective of whether they were acting on behalf of the king, the pope, the municipal authorities, their religious su-

---

8   See above Chapter 1, p. 37.
9   See above Chapter 1, p. 52.

periors or other citizens who had entrusted them with missions of importance. There are many examples of Franciscans employed on delicate missions, and reference will only be made to the most representative here.

As in the case of the grants of land, the letters issued by the king followed a standard format, no doubt because the need to give the friars assurance of royal protection was both frequent and widespread. A slightly different form letter was needed to address complaints made by the friars that the diocesan clergy had interfered with their work, thus infringing the provisions made for the friars' welfare. These royal edicts should have protected the friars from harm, but in this regard too the king's commands were often disregarded; some of the diocesan clergy, resentful of the privileges which the friars enjoyed and economically disadvantaged by their popularity, saw the friars' journeys as an opportunity for aggressive assertion of their own position, and attacked the travellers when they were without the protection of their confreres. Although the Franciscans travelled in pairs, this precaution was inadequate to defend them from malicious attacks planned by those who had a grudge against them. The case of Fr. Aparicio and his confrere Fr. Pardo is the most outstanding example of the defenselessness of the friars on public highways.[10]

A similar privilege was subsequently extended to the friars when they had to rebuild or transfer an existing house to another location.[11] Yet another form letter was issued when interference came from the presence of women and others who disturbed the friars' acts of devotion, by carrying on trades such as prostitution outside the convent.[12] A frequent cause of conflict came from ambitious neighbours who wished to build onto property which was adjacent to the convent. The new

---

10 See below Chapter 4, pp. 162–165.
11 The royal chancellery registers in the archives of the Crown of Aragon preserve several letters of protection: general letters written in 1293 and 1328 (Barcelona, ACA, RC 96, f. 107v; RC 475, f. 124v); and letters for specific houses, as follows: Berga in 1333 (RC 487, f. 185); Calatayud, 1328 (RC 476, f. 186v); Saragossa, 1347 (RC 885, f. 38); Valencia, 1290 (RC 81, f. 4v); Vilafranca, 1292 and 1310 (RC 94, f. 44v; RC 207, f. 158v).
12 The frequency and ubiquity of this problem can be seen in the surviving documentary references: Daroca in 1316, 1317 [1318], 1326 and 1337 (Barcelona, ACA, RC 355, f. 79; RC 356, f. 152; RC 379, f. 212v–213; RC 481, f. 259); Huesca, 1322 (RC 370, ff. 227 and 245v); Saragossa, 1310 [1311] and 1331 [1332] (RC 146, ff. 29v–30; RC 565, f. 137); Valencia, 1301, 1323 [1324], 1330 [1331], 1335 and 1340 (RC 118, f. 68; RC 181, ff. 47 and 186v; RC 574, f. 189; RC 607, f. 83).

buildings were often planned with windows which overlooked the cloisters of the convent, thus depriving the friars of privacy, or they had walls which blocked the light from the windows of the convent. These are common aspects of urban life which will be discussed more fully in the next chapter, but all of them required the intervention of the king, emphasizing the way in which he often became personally involved in difficulties encountered by the friars.

These letters were not unique to the Franciscans. The problems incurred were general in affecting the well-being of all the mendicant orders in the thirteenth and fourteenth centuries, and were caused in part by the problems created by a developing urban society. Orders requiring the speedy removal of undesirables from the vicinity of religious houses were frequently issued in response to appeals made by the mendicant orders to the king. That they had to be repeated shows that they were often disregarded, and some of the most flagrant examples of disobedience of the king's laws will be discussed in subsequent chapters.

Individual Friars in the Royal Service

The earliest recorded evidence of the close association between the crown and individual friars is the document mentioned already and dating from the time of the reconquest of Valencia, when the king gave to Fr. Il.luminat and Fr. Peter land on the Ruzafa road on which the Franciscans could build a house; this was primarily a political move in an attempt to ensure that the Valencian frontier remained firmly in Christian hands. Such manifestations of generosity were not only to become common and diversified in the thirteenth and fourteenth centuries, but were to be repeated in many parts of King James's realms, not only during his own lifetime but throughout those of his successors. Some grants were made to the order as a whole; others to individual friars, who according to their rule were obligated to hand over any material property to the order, an ideal some found difficult to live up to.

What qualifications were necessary for a friar to be chosen to undertake difficult missions? Primarily, these messengers were chosen for two main reasons, the family they came from or the special qualities with which they were endowed. In 1281 Fr. Berenguer de Palmerola and Hug de Mataplana, bishop-elect of Saragossa, were required to deliver a letter from King Peter to Bernard, bishop of Oporto.[13] This letter

---

13 Ambròs de Saldes, "La orden franciscana," pp. 91-92. The heading to this document erroneously calls the bishop *cardinal* of Oporto.

requested the bishop to give advice and protection to Fr. Berenguer, who was to proceed to the papal court in Rome. A second letter of the same date, addressed to King Denis of Portugal, indicates that another friar minor, Domingo [of Jaca?], had been robbed near Teruel of the secret letters he was taking to King Peter from the queen of Portugal.[14] The thieves obviously thought he carried something more valuable than letters, for when they found out that there was no money they threw the letters from a nearby bridge into the river. Queen Isabel was King Peter's sister, known to later generations as Saint Isabel of Portugal, and although the content of the secret letters is not known, it must have been important enough to warrant the king's request that Fr. Domingo inform him of its import by word of mouth. Certainly he told Peter that his sister was well and being adequately provided for by King Denis. Special messengers had to be trustworthy, as, if this case can be regarded as typical, they were frequently apprised of the contents of the letters they carried or of the secret negotiations between the king and the recipients of his letters.

In some cases the friars were required to go overseas to negotiate with foreign powers, as evidenced by the negotiations which took place with King Robert of Sicily.[15] Fr. Pons Carbonell, one of the friars whom the king sent to Sicily in 1315, frequently undertook delicate missions for James II.[16] One of the favourite Franciscan ambassadors, who would seem to have been chosen for his special abilities, was Fr. Domingo de Jaca, elected provincial minister in the 1290s, the probable bearer of the letters to and from Queen Isabel.[17] He must have come from a prominent family, but there is insufficient information about his background to be able to establish this fact.

---

14 Saldes, "La orden franciscana," p. 91.
15 The negotiations regarding Sicily took place over a number of years. See Antonio Arribas Palau, *La conquista de Cerdeña por Jaime II de Aragón* (Barcelona, 1952); Vicente Salavert y Roca, *Cerdeña y la expansión mediterránea de la Corona de Aragón 1297-1314,* 2 vols. (Madrid, 1956); and Barcelona, ACA, RP 278, f. 56v (the accounts of the treasurer, Pere Marc, for the period from January 1314 until June 1315).
16 Pedro Sanahuja, *História de la seráfica provincia de Cataluña* (Barcelona, 1959), pp. 123-124. See also Barcelona, ACA, RC 299, ff. 143 and 202v (1314-1315); RC 337, ff. 210 and 353v (1315).
17 He seems to have gone to Sicily in 1295 (Barcelona, ACA, RC 252, ff. 20v and 146v-147); also to Castile in 1294 and 1295 (RC 262, f. 323v; RC 102, f. 139v), and to Rome in 1293 (RC 92, f. 97v).

Without doubt a prominent ancestry determined the selection of Fr. Sancho López de Ayerbe, great-grandson of James I and Teresa Gil de Vidaure, as special adviser to King Alfonso III, and subsequently his appointment as archbishop of Tarragona.[18]

One further example will suffice of the way in which the king employed the friars to undertake important tasks. Fr. Romeo Ortiz, also from a prominent Aragonese family, undertook many duties on behalf of the royal family of Aragon, and was appointed executor of the will of James II's brother Peter, an onerous task which was not fully accomplished by the time of his death from tertian fever in 1316.[19] His life will be discussed in more detail in a later chapter, as it is illustrative of many of the concerns which beset both the friars and the king in the late thirteenth and early fourteenth centuries.[20]

There is another group of friars who received protection from the king, but who were not directly in his employ: those who went overseas to study at the well-known universities in England, France, Germany or Italy. Saint Francis had no desire to see development of learning in his order, and he would have been surprised and dismayed to find that, as early as the middle of the thirteenth century, the Order of Friars Minor was regarded as one of the most learned institutions in the world.[21] As Saint Bonaventure was to stress, the chief task of the friars was to preach, and in order to do so satisfactorily they had to spend long years

---

18 Teresa of Vidaure was a noble lady who married James I in a clandestine ceremony; she was responsible for the foundation in 1265 of the abbey of La Zaidia in the kingdom of Valencia, where she herself was buried in the habit of a Cistercian nun in 1278. See Burns, *El reino de Valencia*, 2: 500-502. See also Sanahuja, *História*, pp. 146 and 195. Fr. Sancho López de Ayerbe was archbishop of Tarazona from 1343 until 1346, and of Tarragona from 1346 until his death in 1357. He was buried in the Franciscan cemetery in Tarragona, and a chapter of the seventeenth-century account of the archiepiscopate of Tarragona is devoted to him. See Josep Blanch, *Arxiepiscopologi de la santa esglèsia metropolitana i primada de Tarragona*, 2 vols. (Tarragona, 1985), 2: 43-48.

19 His interventions are so numerous that they cannot be cited here; suffice it to say that there are at least eighty-seven named instances of his work as executor of the will of Prince Peter, numerous unnamed references to the executors of the will, and an equal number of documents dealing with his position as executor of other wills. The references date from November 1296 until long after his death in 1316.

20 See below Chapter 5, pp. 204-207.

21 See John R.H. Moorman, *A History of the Franciscan Order from its Origins to the Year 1517* (Oxford, 1968; repr. Chicago, 1988), pp. 123-139, for a discussion of the friars and the universities.

in study, while the more able of them should be sent to the universities to obtain a thorough knowledge of theology.[22]

By 1229 the Franciscans had their own school on the outskirts of Paris, and it was not long before it had acquired a reputation for scholarly distinction. The same year a Franciscan school was founded at Oxford, with a layman, Robert Grosseteste, as its first master; and in 1230 the one at Cambridge is thought to have opened its doors.[23] From the middle of the thirteenth century, many friars from King James's territories made their way by land and sea to these centres of learning. The king not only issued safe-conducts to ensure that the friars were given protection on the journey, but also defrayed some of the expenses incurred, including those for tuition.

The frequency with which the friars attended universities in other countries seems to have increased from the middle of the fourteenth century, by which time centres of Franciscan studies not only existed in Oxford, Cambridge and Paris but in other parts of France, and in Italy and Germany. The Constitutions of Cahors in 1336 stipulated that all religious who wished to study in universities other than those at Paris, Oxford and Cambridge must first obtain the consent of the provincial chapter and minister general, and then receive papal dispensation to do so.[24] Theoretically the pope would then choose which university the friar would attend, but it was not unusual for these provisions to be disregarded. The recommendation of Pope Clement VI to the chancellor of the university of Paris that Fr. Roger de Pallars be admitted to the degree of Master of Theology is in line with the constitutions.

At times the Franciscans preferred to appeal to the royal family to support their intentions. Between 1329 and 1336 Queen Leonor of Sicily asked Alfonso III to recommend to the minister general that Fr. Gil de Navarra be sent to Paris.[25] The expenses incurred in this connection would have been considerable, and it is understandable that the friars would appeal to a member of the royal family with the expectation of receiving financial help towards their studies from the king. This help would not necessarily be a monetary grant but could consist of

---

22 Moorman, *History of the Franciscan Order*, p. 143.
23 R.W. Southern, *Robert Grosseteste: The Growth of an English Mind in Medieval Europe* (Oxford, 1986), p. 4, refers to the Oxford house of the Friars Minor as "recently established" outside the walls in 1230. The house at Cambridge was founded not long afterwards.
24 Sanahuja, *História*, pp. 176, 195-196.
25 Ibid., p. 177.

exemption from the payment of the usual tolls required of travellers, as was the case in 1335 when Fr. Pedro de Huesca required assistance for his journey to Paris to attend the Franciscan studium generale.[26] This exemption could be extended to the tax payable on the transportation of books from one place to another, and on at least one occasion the king exempted both the Dominicans and the Franciscans from paying the tax on the books they carried.[27] Indeed, the king sometimes had to intervene on behalf of individual friars so that they could obtain a degree or the position they sought.

By the end of the fourteenth century many Franciscans had received significant support and encouragement from the royal family to undertake university studies, and it became a commonplace of life from the end of the thirteenth century for outstanding friars to be called upon to fulfil roles which in later centuries would have been assigned to secular officials. The concessions made to the friars extended to almost every area of daily life, and the crown was even called upon to intervene in conflicts between individual friars when they had become so serious that they were threatening to interfere with the Franciscan mission.[28]

Concessions in Kind

Most of the other concessions granted by the royal house of Aragon concern the daily requirements of a religious house, for the Franciscans like the Dominicans had no large estates or livestock from which they could obtain a livelihood. The early mendicant friars lived in makeshift houses until they could establish permanent buildings suitable for a religious order, and that these were often large and luxurious reflects the attitudes of both the king and the subjects whose generous support provided economic stability. In the urban environment in which the friars lived and worked, many of the staples of life were scarce or expensive, and certainly beyond the reach of the mendicant orders had they not received support from the king and their neighbours. Royal concessions were made to them to provide supplies of water, grain, salt and other foodstuffs.[29]

---

26 Sanahuja, *Història,* p. 176.
27 Ibid., p. 124.
28 See below Chapter 5, pp. 211–212.
29 Among the references to water are those for Barcelona in 1293 (Barcelona, ACA, RC 260, f. 211v); Gerona, 1319 (RC 217, f. 101r–v); Saragossa, 1321 and 1347 (RC 220, f. 12r–v; RC 885, f. 37v); Sardinia, 1335 (RC 518, ff. 211v–212); Valencia, 1336 (RC 859, ff. 242v–243); Xàtiva, 1296 (RC 104, f. 58). Similarly,

These concessions were frequent and common to all areas of King James's territories, but they were accompanied by help of a less obvious kind, invitations to the friars to dine with the king. On these occasions the friars would have had meals which were far superior to those which they normally enjoyed. The first such documented invitation refers to the occasion in 1262 when the Franciscans from Montpellier were attending a chapter meeting in Calatayud and were invited to dine with the king, who at the time was waiting in the town before declaring war on Castile.[30] On some occasions it is known what kind of food they were served, as there is a record of disbursements made by the king's treasury during the early part of the reign of Peter III. The entries refer to several days during 1338 and 1339 when the Friars Minor had either dinner or supper at the palace, and disbursements were made for those meals for eggs, fresh fish, chicken and lamb.[31]

There is no explanation of why the friars were invited in this way, but since many of them acted as royal confessors and others undertook diplomatic missions for members of the royal family it is not difficult to see these invitations as partial recompense for services rendered. In general these meals were provided at times when the royal retinue was lodged in the Franciscan convent, or when a general or provincial chapter was being held and the number of mouths to be fed had increased beyond the capacity of the convent facilities.

Royal hospitality extended to the Franciscans was probably partial payment for the accommodation afforded. But the recompense given in the form of food and drink was frequently insufficient to compensate for the damage often done to the convent by the members of the king's retinue. The courtiers were wont to behave with total disregard for their hosts' property, which not infrequently suffered severe damage, inclu-

---

grain concessions were made to Murcia in 1296 (RC 340, f. 283); Oleron, 1322 (RC 370, f. 94); Tortosa, 1340 and 1341 (RC 868, f. 109v; RC 1114, f. 103r-v; RC 1115, ff. 130v-131). Salt concessions were made to Calatayud in 1308 and 1328 (RC 205, f. 136v; RC 476, f. 189r-v); Daroca, 1325 and 1329 (RC 227, f. 198; RC 478, f. 289v); Saragossa, 1347 (RC 885, f. 37v).

30 Barcelona, ACA, RC 12, f. 49. The phrase used is "die qua invitavimus fratres minores Montispessulani quando ibidem fecerunt capitulum" and does not refer to the kind of invitation issued.

31 Barcelona, ACA, RC 1524, ff. 15v, 16, 66v, 67, 110, 134v.

ding the destruction of walls and the burning of the buildings.[32] When damage of this kind occurred the Franciscans appealed to the king for reparation, but they often had to wait months and years before anything was done to compensate them for the careless behaviour of his men. Payments were eventually made to meet these extra expenses, and the king would regularly grant a sum of money, frequently 300 sous, to help defray the additional costs of a particular house at the time of a provincial or general chapter.[33] The records indicate that the number of friars present on any specific day in the year often varied considerably, making it very difficult for that house to provide sufficient food for the residents and visitors. Indeed, for Majorca between 1311 and 1330 the number of friars present on certain church festivals varies considerably, often increasing by as much as a third of the total number of residents.[34] No doubt a similar situation existed in other houses, and perhaps with an even greater variation in towns such as Barcelona, Valencia and Saragossa, where the number of visiting friars would probably have been far larger. To provide food and lodging for so many people must have placed a considerable burden on some of the larger convents.

A comparison can be made with the custom in England. Eleanor of Castile provided money for food and drink when provincial chapters of the Friars Preachers were held in Oxford in 1289 and 1290; in the latter year during Lent she also sent salmon to the Dominicans in Oxford, and the Franciscans received food and drink at her expense.[35] This lends

---

32 See Barcelona, ACA, RC 491, 2 December 1327, regarding the fire which occurred in the Montblanc house when the king and his men were staying there. The dates on which payments were made suggests that the invitations to the friars referred to major feast days such as Easter, St. John's day, the Assumption of the Blessed Virgin Mary and Christmas. Curiously enough the Friars Minor seem to have been privileged in this respect, as the Carmelites and Dominicans (both men and women) —the only other religious orders mentioned in this connection—received what appear to be monetary payments for food, although of course they might have been disbursements made when they dined at the palace.

33 See Appendix 2 for references to chapter meetings.

34 Jill R. Webster, "Política reial i suport ciutadà per a les cases religioses del regne de Mallorca," in *XIII Congrès d'història de la Corona d'Aragó (Palma de Mallorca, 27 setembre-1 octubre 1987): Comunicacions 1* (Palma de Mallorca, 1989), pp. 263-270.

35 John Carmi Parsons, *The Court and Household of Eleanor of Castile in 1290* (Toronto, 1977), p. 16. Parsons refers to the fact that Eleanor of Castile was called the "nursing mother" of the Dominican order in England, and the Friars Preachers

support to the evidence collected from other areas that the mendicant friars evoked practical expressions of piety wherever they settled, the royal gifts often enabling them to acquire a measure of security, which was necessary if they were to carry out their mission satisfactorily.

Royal grants in kind must have been essential to the friars' continued ability to maintain an active mission in the towns, whether the grants were received in the form of invitations to dine at the king's table or were concessions which enabled them to acquire staple products. Corn was perhaps the single most valuable commodity received by the friars in this way. The first recorded instance of a concession of grain is to be found in one of the earliest registers of James I. In 1257 the house at Jaca was granted permission to extract 200 loads of corn, a quantity measured according to the measurements of Jaca, an extremely valuable concession in a land which suffered from long periods of drought, where grain was both expensive and scarce and there was a prohibition on its being taken from one area to another.[36] Similarly, there is evidence in the fourteenth century that 5 *cafises* of salt, a quantity which was probably equivalent to 666 litres, was allowed to the Saragossa house from the salt fields of Castllà or Remolinos.[37] The document concerned is dated 1347, but it confirms an earlier concession made by James II in 1304. In the Middle Ages salt was used primarily for the purpose of preserving food, and the conquest of Sardinia in the first half of the fourteenth century by the Catalans helped to ensure that the supply of salt in the Crown of Aragon was adequate.

In addition to corn and salt, another daily need was the subject of numerous concessions to the friars, the right to draw water from the king's wells. The first recorded instance of this dates from Peter II's reign and is a confirmation of a privilege conceded by James I to the Friars Minor in Huesca.[38] The right to use wells on royal property

---

were the main recipients of her generosity. The book in which these items are to be found is the *Liber domini Johannis de Berewyk' de expensis in garderoba regine anno regni regis Edwardi .XVIII°. Berewyk'*. On p. 100 there is a reference to the Franciscans: "*Anniversarium Regis Castelle*. xj. die Aprilis apud Eynesham. solutam proputura fratrum predicatorum et minorum Oxon' pro anniversario Domini Alfonsi quondam Regis Castelle per manus Nicholi de Stalham. cum oblacione ad missas utrobique vij.li.xv.s.vij.d.ob." (This refers to the death of Alfonso X on 4 April 1284, the anniversary concerned having been celebrated in 1287.)

36 Saldes, "La orden franciscana," p. 222.
37 Barcelona, ACA, RC 885, f. 37v, 24 September 1347.
38 Ambròs de Saldes, "Documentació franciscana (1267–1285)," *EF* 45 (1933), 130–149, at p. 145, 17 August [1281].

must have made a significant difference to the friars, for the garden (*hort* or *huerta*) was an important part of any conventual establishment, furnishing the means whereby the friars could obtain fresh fruit and vegetables. Some of the documents confirming the right to draw water specifically mention that it was needed for the purpose of irrigation by the people of the town, and presumably also by the Franciscans whose land it traversed.[39] Mills and wells appear in royal documents with remarkable frequency, a fact easily understood in a land where climatic conditions made water and grain such valuable commodities. Other concessions covered the provision of olive oil and wine, both of these dietary staples in Mediterranean countries.[40]

On numerous occasions help was also given by the king for the purchase of cloth to make habits. One of the earliest such documents was issued by the king's bailiff, Aaron Abinaffia, to the convent at Teruel, giving them 300 sous for clothing.[41] That this practice extended beyond the confines of the realms of Aragon is confirmed by the knowledge that Eleanor of Castile gave money to at least two Franciscan friars to repair their habits.[42] Clothing was an expensive item, with which the royal family could give valuable assistance. Sometimes the right to a certain amount of cloth was granted by the king. In January 1344 Peter III confirmed the privilege of a weekly length of cloth amounting to 2 *canes* (equivalent to 16 palms or 3110 millimetres) from mills at Jaca, accorded to the French convent of Oleron on the borders of Aragon, a regular recipient of favours from the royal house of Aragon.[43] Since this amount would not have been enough to make a

---

39 Barcelona, ACA, RC 139, f. 367, 2 December 1307; RC 150, f. 218v, 6 November 1312. The Huesca house had complained here that the inhabitants of the town, when gathering water for their own use, climbed over the wall of the convent close to one of the windows of the house and disturbed the friars. Clearly it was a recurrent problem, as five years after the first document the matter was still one of concern.
40 References to these are found in Barcelona, 1288, 1289, 1290 and 1292 (Barcelona, ACA, RC 78, f. 17; RC 80, f. 137; RC 83, f. 99v; RC 95, f. 155); Soria, 1334 (RC 487, f. 232).
41 Saldes, "Documentació franciscana (1267–1285)," p. 142.
42 Parsons, *Court and Household of Eleanor,* p. 17. "Eodem die ibidem cuidam fratri Radulpho de ordine minorum ad habitum suum emendum de dono Regine" (p. 87). "Eodem die ibidem fratri Johanni de Lincoln' de ordine minorum ad unum habitum suum emendum de dono Regine" (p. 89).
43 Barcelona, ACA, RC 875, ff. 205v–206, 4 January 1343 [1344]. The earliest concession to this house was that of 7 August 1283, when King Peter granted the friars the right to extract from Aragon 50 *cafises* of grain, measured according to

habit, it can be concluded that the convent only received its allotment of cloth yearly, although the amount would have been computed on a weekly basis.

In Gerona the linen mill was situated close to the Franciscan house, and the friars complained more than once that when the wind blew in their direction the foul odours from the flax which had been laid out to dry wafted towards them.[44] The presence of these linen mills often caused problems for the convents situated outside the walls, where the mills had originally been located precisely to prevent the wafting of the smells in the direction of residential areas.

The king's concessions to the Franciscans embraced every aspect of life, from the basic grants which enabled them to establish houses and work in an area with some degree of safety to the provision of the daily requirements of food and drink. There is evidence that the king also attended to the spiritual needs of his subjects who attended Franciscan churches. In June 1335, for instance, Alfonso III gave to the friars at Teruel a triptych on which was painted the life of Saint Louis, a member of the Franciscan order, who had been canonized a few years earlier.[45] Few examples of such gifts are recorded, but they must have been quite frequent to enable the friars to decorate their churches in the splendid way commonly associated with the later Middle Ages.

BEQUESTS AND OTHER MONETARY PAYMENTS

The considerable benefits the friars received from concessions of land, water, corn, salt, cloth and other products were augmented by monetary grants, and by bequests in royal wills. When the Franciscans, through their procurator, received money from the crown which was not in direct payment for their services, it was not unusual for the grant to be accompanied by a condition as to how it was to be spent. The usual limitations placed on the money given by the crown required it to be used for a habit or for books, and reading between the lines it is possible to conclude that the king's help had been solicited by the friars. Other monetary payments were made to defray the costs of provincial or general chapters,

---

the requirements of Jaca, which they could take in four lots of 12 *cafíses* to Oleron (there is a miscalculation here, it would seem). See Saldes, "Documentació franciscana (1267-1285)," p. 143.

44 Jill R. Webster, "Col.lecció de documents del convent de Sant Francesc de Girona (1224-1399)," *AIEG* 28-30 (1985-1989), 28: 157-189, 29: 27-86, 30: 141-226.

45 Sanahuja, *Història,* p. 126.

which sometimes included an additional payment to meet the expenses incurred in providing hospitality for friars from other houses.[46] Financial recompense was made to the friars for services they had rendered, such as undertaking missions as ambassadors, acting as executors of royal or noble wills, providing the services for the royal chapel or acting as the king's or queen's personal confessor. Hundreds of such documents indicate by their very number the important functions the Franciscans carried out on behalf of the royal family. The more outstanding friars who undertook these tasks included such men as Fr. Romeo Ortiz and Fr. Arnau de Canelles, who are among the few whose activities are abundantly documented. The payments made to them went a long way towards the maintenance of the convents throughout Aragon. The monetary bequests made by members of the royal family to the order provided security and a solid economic base.

Finally, friars were often called upon to act either as executors or as advisers when members of the royal family drew up their last will and testament. Several members of the house of Aragon asked to be buried in the Franciscan habit and cemetery, and Moorman suggests that this practice provided a source of funds, as the dying person would leave a sum of money to pay for the costs of such a burial.[47]

Testamentary laws differed from place to place, but there is no doubt that they occupied a prominent place in medieval jurisprudence. The *Siete partidas,* a compilation of laws from a variety of sources and drawn up at the orders of King Alfonso X of Castile, was widely used by the other kingdoms in the Iberian Peninsula. The entire sixth *partida* deals with the laws relating to the last will and testament, and the need for legal expertise in this and other areas of life led to the creation of a class of royal notaries in the thirteenth century. Their proliferation and the effect they had on testamentary practice can be regarded as a parallel undertaking to the organization of the royal archives under James I.[48] Notaries and scribes, executors, advisers and witnesses were all needed

---

46 The many documents in the archives of the Crown of Aragon, in the collection of Royal Patrimony (Barcelona, ACA, RP), show that the Franciscans were frequently given grants between 1304 and 1348 to defray expenses on festivals such as Easter and Christmas, when a larger number of friars would be present in any given house.
47 Moorman, *History of the Franciscan Order,* p. 120. See also Sanahuja, *História,* p. 120.
48 Robert I. Burns, *Society and Documentation in Crusader Valencia* (Princeton, 1985), pp. 143-144. See also José Bono, *História del derecho notarial español,* 2 vols. (Madrid, 1979-1982).

to draw up these wills, which became increasingly complex in the later Middle Ages. Witnesses were not to know the contents of the wills, and apostates, or those who had reneged upon their commitment to a religious order, even if they later repented, could not act as signatories to wills.[49] James I himself made at least two wills; the first, drawn up in Tarragona in 1232, leaves the Franciscans in his realms 1000 morabatins but has a Dominican as signatory.[50] The second will, drawn up in Barcelona on 1 January 1242, confirms the legacy of 1000 morabatins but does not include any Franciscans acting in an advisory capacity.[51] This comes as no surprise, as the king relied mainly on friars from the Order of Preachers prior to 1250. After this date increasing importance was given to the Franciscans, and several members of the royal family requested burial in the Franciscan habit in the convent cemetery.

ROYAL BURIALS

The first recorded instance of an Aragonese monarch wishing to be buried in the Franciscan habit dates from 1281.[52] When Alfonso II made his first will, he not only requested burial in the Franciscan cemetery or, according to Muntaner, in the Franciscan church, close to the altar of Saint Nicholas, but he also bequeathed sufficient money to provide for one meal for the friars on each of three days of the week (Sunday, Tuesday and Thursday).[53] Six months later, in his second will, Alfonso asked that he not be buried in a royal tomb but in one customarily provided for the friars themselves, a symbol of even greater religious devotion and humility. He died in June 1291, but it was not until 1302 that James II and the provincial minister of Aragon, Fr. Arnau Oliba, with the guardian and procurator for the Barcelona convent, reached final agreement over the clauses of the will.[54] Royal

---

49 See Alfonso X, el Sabio, *Partidas* 6.1.2 and 6.1.9, *Las siete partidas del rey don Alfonso el Sabio*, 3 vols. (Madrid, 1972), 3: 361 and 364.
50 Saldes, "La orden franciscana," pp. 279-280.
51 *Documentos de Jaime I de Aragon*, vol. 2, *1237-1250*, ed. Ambrosio Huici Miranda, Maria Desamparados and Cabanes Pecourt (Valencia, 1976), pp. 116-120.
52 Sanahuja, *História*, pp. 108-109.
53 *Crònica de Ramon Muntaner*, cap. 143, in *Quatre grans cròniques*, pp. 667-1000, at 802-803; Sanahuja, *História*, pp. 108-109.
54 Barcelona, ACA, Pergamins, James II, no. 1826, 11 December 1302, refers to his final resting place. For the agreement between James I and the Friars Minor at Barcelona, see Sanahuja, *História*, p. 109. The entire text is in Ambròs de Saldes, "Franciscanismo: Documentos franciscanos," *EF* 17 (1916), 64-74, at pp. 69-74.

wills usually took some years to prove, but here the delay was likely caused by the fact that Alfonso was first buried in Santes Creus, regarded as a more appropriate burial place for a royal prince. At the intervention of his mother, and no doubt to comply with her late son's wishes, the body was moved to the Franciscan house in Barcelona in 1297.[55]

Although Alfonso's predecessor, Peter the Great, was not actually buried in a Franciscan cemetery but in Santes Creus, there were Dominicans and Franciscans at his funeral in 1285.[56] Ramon Muntaner states that there were as many as ten friars present from each of the houses in the realms of Aragon.[57] In 1300 Queen Constance died in Barcelona and was buried in the Franciscan convent, dressed in the Clarissan habit.[58] In 1327 Peter III's mother was buried in the Franciscan cemetery in Saragossa; her infant son Frederick was buried there also.[59] Alfonso III, who died of dropsy on 25 January 1335 [1336], wanted to be buried in the Franciscan convent at Lerida, but as he died in Barcelona his body was laid to rest in the house there and not moved to Lerida until 1369.[60]

---

55 The chronicler Ramon Muntaner refers to Alfonso's death and the fact that, as he had requested, his body was taken to the house at Barcelona for burial "ab gran professó" (*Crònica de Ramon Muntaner*, cap. 174, in *Quatre grans cròniques*, pp. 823–824), a reference taken up later by Bernat Boades, who states that his body was interred with great honour in the Franciscan house at Barcelona, "vestit ab l'àbit d'aquella religió del benayunturat pare monsènyer sant Francesch ...," *Libre de Feyts d'armes de Catalunya*, ed. Enric Bagué, 5 vols. (Barcelona, 1930–1948), 4: 139–140.

56 *Crònica de Ramon Muntaner*, cap. 143, in *Quatre grans cròniques*, pp. 802–803.

57 Ibid., cap. 121, pp. 778–779.

58 Ibid., cap. 143, pp. 802–803. Only one other recorded instance has been found of burial in the habit of Saint Clare: Guilleuma, widow of Bernat Gardiola, a tailor of Puigcerdà, drew up her last will and testament on 6 September 1363, and in asking to be buried "cum abit de sor menor" left 20 Barcelona sous for the purchase of the habit. It is relevant to note that the testator in this case belonged to the Confraternity of the Blessed Virgin Mary. Puigcerdà, AHC, Bernat Manresa, *Liber testamentorum* (12 September 1362–17 March 1365), ff. 58v–59.

59 *Crònica de Ramon Muntaner*, cap. 291, in *Quatre grans cròniques*, pp. 932–933. See also Peter III, *Chronique catalane de Pierre IV d'Aragon, III de Catalogne, dit le Cérémonieux ou del Punyalet*, 1.1.75–77, ed. Amédée Pagès (Toulouse-Paris, 1941), p. 14.

60 *Chronique catalane*, 2.1.14–16, ed. Pagès, p. 69. See also Andrés Ivars, "Sepulcro de Alfonso IV de Aragón en la iglesia de los frailes menores de Lérida," *AIA* 30 (1928), 107–113.

There were other infant princes who found their place of rest in Franciscan cemeteries, and the emphasis laid on the place of burial must have had some special significance which is largely lost on a modern reader of the documents. Close ties formed with a particular order, together with the political implications of that choice, evidently proved so strong that burial within that order became a natural result. Indeed Peter III, although he himself did not wish to be buried in a Franciscan cemetery but rather in Poblet, seemed to be obsessed with the arrangements for his funeral, and was constantly fearful that his wishes might be forgotten.[61] There is even a suggestion in his insistence that his wishes be carried out that he somehow feared that his legitimate right to the throne would be questioned, a fear which is difficult to understand today but which might have had its origin in slander or malicious gossip unknown to modern historians.

The choice of burial place must have been largely personal, but implicit in the choice might also have been political elements which can only be surmised, and which seem to derive from the popularity of a particular order at the time the testator drew up his last will and testament. Burial in a Franciscan cemetery can be regarded as only one further manifestation of royal devotion to and support for the Friars Minor, no doubt a consequence of the way in which individual friars looked after both the material and spiritual welfare of members of the royal house of Aragon.

Endowments

Members of the royal family, either through significant legacies or during their lifetime, endowed chapels and altars in the Franciscan churches, and, in one case at least, an important hospital was founded thanks to the generosity of the queen. Queen Constance, wife of King Peter, left a considerable sum of money in her will so that two hospitals could be established in Barcelona and Valencia. These were to be built

---

61 Barcelona, ACA, RC 1128, ff. 51v–52, 14 September 1347. Part of this document, which appears among those bearing the secret seal of the king, has been rendered illegible by injudicious repairs. Its contents suggest that on the day that the late King Alfonso was buried Fr. Arnau de Canelles preached a sermon, praising the monarch and referring to his revelation in the privacy of the confessional that "nunquam in sua vita rem carnalem habuerat cum aliqua muliere nisi cum propriis suis consortibus." It was in Peter's interests to find out exactly what had been said, in order to avoid claims to the throne by those purporting to be sons or daughters of Alfonso III.

close to the Franciscan houses and were to be under the direction of the guardian and friars.[62]

Extant documentation makes it very difficult to be precise about the way in which the queen's last will and testament was carried out. She died in Barcelona in 1300, but the will was not finally settled until more than a decade later. The queen left 18,000 sous to establish the Valencian hospital, and a further 1200 to provide beds, furniture and other necessities. For the hospital in Barcelona she only left 1410 sous, 2 diners and 1 òbol, together with 343 sous and 3 diners for the purchase of beds and other furniture. It is curious that Barcelona received less money, because the queen was buried in the house in Barcelona. Perhaps she thought that there were other possibilities there which would make it less expensive to establish a hospital, and these may not have materialized, making it impossible to found the Barcelona hospital as she had willed.

The correspondence concerning this matter refers to the purchase of a site in Valencia in 1310, when arrangements were made immediately to establish the institution known to this day as the Hospital de la Reina, for which a sum of 20,000 sous was made available, that is 2000 sous over and above the amount left by the queen. The king also gave money towards the purchase of beds and other necessities, and at the time of the foundation bought *censals* so that the hospital would receive a regular income. Three years later the money left for the hospital in Barcelona was transferred to Valencia, for by then it was quite clear that there was no question of opening a similar hospital in Barcelona, as the legacy was insufficient to defray the expenses.

By 1326, however, the Hospital de la Reina in Valencia was not without its problems and must have been in an impoverished state, as the king asked how many poor were attended to there, how much income was received and how it was administered, suggesting that there might have been some mismanagement. In 1333 a coadministrator was appointed and paid from the king's curia; but the hospital seems never to have been able to meet its obligations adequately, and by 1375, the year of a severe occurrence of plague, the friars could not even muster sufficient money to pay for shrouds in which to bury the dead.

---

62 Jill R. Webster, "La reina doña Constanza y los hospitales de Barcelona y Valencia," *AIA* 51 (1991), 375–390. This article discusses more fully the establishment of the Valencia hospital and indicates the reason why the Barcelona one was never established.

The city *jurats* agreed that it was necessary to give it substantial help, as it was in dire need of both buildings and financial aid. In 1379, after a number of negotiations, the Hospital de la Reina finally became the property of the city of Valencia, although the legality of this was disputed for some years and only finally resolved in 1383. Queen Constance would have been saddened by the fate of her legacy, but inflationary prices during the first half of the fourteenth century and the advent of the Black Death in 1348, together with other epidemics like that of 1375, had prevented compliance with her wishes. Her bequest had become a burden which the Franciscans were not equipped to bear, a fact which raises the question whether the Valencian house, after its initial prosperity during James I's reign, had fallen on hard times, or it was poor organization that was really responsible for the financial difficulties which beset the running of the hospital. Certainly, after it had given up responsibility for the hospital, the Valencian house was to gain distinction by the presence of Fr. Francesc Eiximenis and the theological *studium* in which he and other prominent friars taught their confreres.

OTHER BENEFITS FROM QUEEN CONSTANCE'S WILL

In 1300 the executors of the will of Queen Constance were ordered to pay the expenses of Fr. Pere d'Esplugues, his confrere and those who accompanied him to the royal curia.[63] The amount given to Fr. Pere is not mentioned, merely that he should receive from the queen's estate whatever was thought to be necessary to compensate him for the expenses of the journey. In accordance with the provisions of the Franciscan rule, the friars would not handle this money themselves, but it would be received on their behalf by the procurator. The appointment of these officials, whose duties will be discussed fully later, seems to have needed the royal stamp of approval before it became official; consequently it is not surprising that they were rewarded by the crown when their term of office had expired. The first evidence of this practice dates from 1257, when James I granted exemption from all taxes and military service to Bernat Ramon of Tamarit, thanks to the pleas made on his behalf by the Franciscan and Dominican custodians at Lerida.[64] In this case no reason is given for the king's favour, but subsequent practice suggests

---

63 Barcelona, ACA, RC 116, f. 123v, 11 September 1300.
64 For a detailed description of the royal archives see Burns, *Society and Documentation,* esp. 1: 15–32. For the exemption see Barcelona, ACA, RC 10, f. 8v, 12 August 1257.

that Bernat Ramon had probably been in charge of the financial affairs of the two orders in Lerida, and was thus reaping the reward for his services.[65] This shows that, right from the very early days the friars, whose rule prohibited them from handling money directly, had appointed a procurator.[66] But presumably because the houses of both Dominicans and Franciscans had little business to transact when they were first established, they shared the services of one man.

Concessions to Relatives and Associates of the Friars

Relatives of the friars were often able to obtain benefits by association. In 1345 the nephew of one of the king's confessors, Fr. Berenguer Amorós, was allowed to use as collateral the royal *foriscapium* (the tax due to an overlord) he held for an amount not to exceed 10,000 Barcelona sous;[67] this same Fr. Berenguer, in the *Crònica de Pere III* for 18 July 1344, is credited with having preached a sermon in Perpignan castle concerning the Aragonese union.[68] Members of the Third Order likewise benefited from the king's policy towards the Friars Minor, for they were treated in much the same way as the procurators and were rewarded by being granted exemption from taxation and military service. Among the early beneficiaries of this policy were Fr. Bernat Fuster and his brother Guerau, both tertiaries, who were given exemption from taxation and military service by Bernat de Sarrià, the king's official, in the county of Pallars, a privilege confirmed in 1299.[69] This family from Vilafranca was later to acquire notoriety for its associations with the béguin movement.[70]

---

65 In fact one of the first references to the appointment of one procurator and the exemption of another also comes from the convent of Lerida. In May 1288 Alfonso appointed Joan de Barriac, a citizen of Lerida, as procurator of the Franciscan house there and confirmed the fact that Ramon Soquet, who had been procurator, was now relieved of his duties. The latter was also rewarded for his services by receiving the royal privilege of exemption from taxes and military service. See Barcelona, ACA, RC 79, f. 51, 24 May 1288.
66 See the list of procurators in Appendix 2.
67 Barcelona, ACA, RC 879, f. 70, 4 December 1345.
68 Peter III, *Chronique catalane* 3.16.2-5, ed. Pagès, p. 212. See also English translation of Mary Hillgarth and J.N. Hillgarth, *Pere III of Catalonia (Pedro IV of Aragon): Chronicle*, 2 vols. (Toronto, 1980), 1: 356.
69 Barcelona, ACA, RC 114, f. 204, 3 December, 1299.
70 See below Chapter 6, pp. 250-251.

There were times when the advantages one member of the family received resulted in the arm of royal justice being brought down on another, who had in some way failed to fulfil his obligations. This can be seen very clearly in the intervention of James II on behalf of the two Ola brothers, one of whom belonged to the Order of Friars Minor.

The third brother, Juan de Ola, could have had little satisfaction from his brother's calling when, in 1300, at the request of Fr. Ramón [de Ola] de Huesca of the Order of Friars Minor, the king wrote to the *superjuntario* for Huesca and Jaca, demanding justice over the question of money accruing from a sale of the royal concession of 160 loads of oil. Juan had sold this to García Pedro de Blegua de Campdalchu, but had apparently retained the full proceeds; whereas, because the original royal concession had been made to their father in payment of an outstanding monetary debt, all three brothers should have received a share.[71] The fact that the matter was taken to the king suggests that Juan de Ola had hoped to avoid dividing the proceeds of the sale with his brothers, and that neither Fr. Ramón nor his brother Pedro Ximéno had been able to persuade him to give them their share.

One of the most interesting documents referring to the intervention of the king on behalf of relatives of the friars concerns a Gerona family which was popularly said to have given hospitality to Saint Francis when he passed through the city during his pilgrimage to Santiago.[72] In 1310 James II wrote to his officials in Gerona, Bernat de Llivià, the *batlle*, and Guerau de Abad, the judge ordinary for the area, informing them that it had come to his attention once again that Jofre Guerau, son of Pere Guerau, a Gerona citizen, had accidentally wounded Pere de Bell-lloc, another Gerona citizen.[73] The latter had gathered about him a crowd of people whom, the document states, he had wrongfully and unjustly incited against Pere Guerau with the intention of killing him.

The king commanded his officials to enquire into the matter and see that those responsible for the outrage were brought to justice. The Guerau family was well respected in Gerona from at least the beginning of the thirteenth century; its members were faithful servants of the crown and had a long tradition of devotion to the Order of Friars Minor. In the 1330s two members of the family, possibly sons of the Pere Guerau referred to earlier, entered the order.[74] One of the two sons found the

---

71 Barcelona, ACA, RC 115, f. 347v, 24–25 March 1299 [1300].
72 See above Chapter 1, p. 24.
73 Barcelona, ACA, RC 145, f. 69v, 1 August 1310.
74 Webster, "Col.lecció de documents," *AIEG* 30: 193.

discipline too severe for his liking and left after his probationary year, only being readmitted by special dispensation, granted to him as a result of his father's plea that the family had given hospitality to Saint Francis. Despite the emphasis placed on Jofre Guerau's having wounded Pere de Bell-lloc unintentionally, and on Fr. Joan Guerau's having sown his wild oats in the recklessness of youth, it is tempting to conclude that the Guerau family found it very useful to remind their contemporaries of their illustrious forebears precisely because their own reputations were far from unblemished. Certainly Pere Guerau might have found himself in an unenviable position, without the king's intervention.

Royal Recommendations

It was customary for the king to recommend the appointment of mendicant friars to vacant positions within the church. Some of these friars would have been proposed to the king by their contemporaries as suitable candidates for bishoprics, but others seem to have been recommended by the king himself, often in lands recently acquired by the Crown of Aragon. As indicated in the previous chapter, an excellent example of the king's desire to consolidate his territory by the appointment of Catalans to vacant ecclesiastical positions occurs after the occupation of Sardinia.[75] As the friars acquired a greater degree of learning and perhaps attracted more men from prominent ruling families, royal intervention in mendicant affairs was extended to other areas. At the end of the fourteenth century Fr. Francesc Eiximenis was told that he had to finish the book he was writing before he could leave Barcelona to take up residence in Valencia, where he was required to assist with the pacification of social unrest.[76]

There is a change in emphasis in relations between the king and the Franciscans here; royal patronage, for example, seems to have shifted from the earlier attitude of protection of the Franciscan order to a more authoritarian attitude involving control over the way in which individual friars occupied their time. This raises the interesting question as to how much the Franciscans' activities in the realms of Aragon were directly influenced by the need for royal approval. There is no clear answer to

---

75 Jill R. Webster, "The Early Catalan Mendicants in Sardinia," *Biblioteca francescana sarda* (Oristano, Sardinia) 2 (1988), 5–16. See also above Chapter 1, pp. 68–69.

76 Martín de Riquer, *Història de la literatura catalana: Part antiga,* 3 vols. (Barcelona, 1964), 2: 137.

this question, but the account which follows indicates that the crown played a fundamental role not only in the development of the Order of Friars Minor, but even perhaps in the way the order envisaged its mission in the western Mediterranean.

OBLIGATIONS NOT HONOURED OR DELAYED

Before leaving the question of the extent to which the Franciscans were beholden to the crown, it is necessary to look at the other side of the coin, for there were times when royal favour seems to have been turned in a different direction or when, through negligence or deliberate intent, privileges and concessions were not confirmed or payments were not made. Incidents are also recorded of the king supporting individual friars who had been defamed or suspected of heresy, such as Fr. Arnau Oliba or Fr. Sancho López de Ayerbe, or criticizing those who had behaved in a way inconsistent with their calling, especially the apostates whose arrest and return to the convent he ordered.[77] In these cases reprimands had been provoked, but the fact that the king directly intervened in conventual affairs seems to suggest that the mendicant friars in the thirteenth and fourteenth centuries enjoyed a very limited independence.

More serious than these isolated examples of frustration and chastisement are the numerous claims made by the Franciscans during the reign of Alfonso III and Peter III that monies due to them from James II's reign had not been paid.[78] The grants and donations seem to have been very generous, and the order prospered towards the end of the thirteenth and early fourteenth centuries; but after 1327 there appears

---

77 See Sanahuja, *Història*, p. 123. There are numerous references in 1311 to the scandal connected with the name of Fr. Arnau Oliba, whom James II described as "honest and upright" and whom he wanted treated with kindness in consideration of the good he had done (Barcelona, ACA, RC 239, f. 111, 19 July 1311). Clearly Fr. Arnau had the king to thank for his release from prison. Fr. Sancho López de Ayerbe had fallen into the hands of the Inquisition and the king showed his displeasure in a letter addressed to Fr. Bernat de Puig, provincial prior of the Dominicans and the inquisitor in this instance (RC 521, f. 7v, 25 March 1329). Fr. Sancho was a relative of the king and later was consecrated archbishop of Tarragona.

78 See Appendix 2 (Unpaid Accounts) for money due to the Franciscans.

to have been an increasing reluctance to honour commitments made before that time.[79]

Could it be that famine, economic instability and disease had dissipated some of the mendicants' popularity evidenced in their developing years? Certainly after 1327 conflicts between parish priest and friar became both more frequent and more hotly contested, possibly as a result of increased financial restraints which imposed hardship on friars and parish clergy alike. The friars themselves had departed somewhat from their founder's principles, and many had acquired positions of importance and university degrees, seeming in their lives to differ little from those who had not espoused vows of poverty. The urgent appeals to the crown for payments of concessions long overdue indicate that the Franciscans were finding it difficult to manage their affairs without these important sources of revenue. The Black Death of 1348, which did not distinguish between priest and layman, might well have helped the friars to regain their lost ascendancy, as their services would have been increasingly needed even though many of them fell victim to the disease.

There is no hint that at the end of the fourteenth century the Franciscans had fallen out of favour with their royal protectors; on the contrary, although rewards for services rendered were more frequent than concessions, the friars were still held in high regard by the crown. Royal support was a right they had come to expect, rather than a privilege for which they were grateful. An analysis of the way in which the crown and friars continued to work together after the Black Death must be left for another occasion, as no valid conclusions can be reached without careful perusal of documentation in the royal archives for the period between 1348 and 1400. The vast territories over which the king of Aragon held jurisdiction were by 1348 no longer in danger from Moorish invaders. During this period the Christian monarchs within the Peninsula were more concerned with the extension of their own political power than with the completion of the reconquest, an ambition which frequently brought them into conflict with each other rather than with their Moorish neighbours.

---

79 Out of 105 claims made by the Franciscans in the province of Aragon, just under half were made between 1328 and 1348. There are references in the chancellery records to the houses at Barbastro, Barcelona, Borja, Calatayud, Castelló d'Empúries, Cervera, Daroca, Ejea de los Caballeros, Gerona, Huesca, Lerida, Monzón, Murviedro, Puigcerdà, Saragossa, Sariñena, Tarazona, Tarragona, Tàrrega, Teruel, Tortosa, Valencia, Vilafranca and Xàtiva.

Their need for close cooperation with the mendicant orders seems to have remained unchanged and even strengthened in the latter part of the fourteenth century. The Franciscan mission could not have prospered with the support of the crown alone, as to a very large degree it had to rely on the goodwill and practical assistance of the urban dwellers to whom it was primarily directed. That it was the middle classes who gave their allegiance to the cause of the friars only offers further evidence of the political liaison in Aragon between the crown and the rising bourgeoisie, an alliance which proved an essential bulwark against the ambitions of a powerful Aragonese nobility.[80] Consideration must now be given to the main ways in which this trading class helped the Franciscans to become firmly entrenched throughout the realms of Aragon, and to how the role they played complemented that of crown and papacy.

---

80 Thomas N. Bisson, *The Medieval Crown of Aragon: A Short History* (Oxford, 1986), p. 88.

3

The Mosaic of Urban Life

The reconquest of the lands occupied by the Moors during the reign of James I set the scene for the development of Christian cities in his territories, and by the end of the thirteenth century a powerful class of burgesses had emerged. The complex organization of these lands is reflected in the diversity and multiracial nature of the urban scene.

Many urban dwellers made their living by means of some kind of industry or profession and included cloth merchants, money-changers, lawyers and doctors; some of these were converted Jews.[1] In most cities within the Crown of Aragon there were also important *calls,* or special areas set aside for the Jews, where those who still practised Judaism probably preferred to live. They were frequently employed as tax-collectors or financiers, and both James I and Peter II employed Jewish administrators.[2] Such positions made it easy for them to become money-lenders, and they were much in demand by the Christians, who were only too ready to lay the blame on the Jews when circumstances made it impossible for them to repay the loans. As they were not subject to Christian law, the Jews were allowed to charge high rates, a fact which helped to give them a bad name among their Christian contemporaries. There were also Jews who followed the same trades and professions as the Christians, and often entered into partnership or competition with them.

---

1   J.N. Hillgarth, *The Spanish Kingdoms: 1250–1516,* 2 vols. (Oxford, 1976), 1: 70–74.
2   Thomas N. Bisson, *The Medieval Crown of Aragon: A Short History* (Oxford, 1986), p. 82. Yitzhak Baer, *A History of the Jews in Christian Spain,* vol. 1, *From the Age of Reconquest to the Fourteenth Century,* trans. Louis Schoffman (Philadelphia: Jewish Publication Society of America, 1961), pp. 177–180, has argued that Jewish participation declined after 1250. But *batlles* (bailiffs) were frequently Jews in Barcelona, Lerida, Tortosa and Saragossa even after this time.

Less relevant to this study, but still an important component of the urban mosaic, were the Moors, many of whom had remained after the land had been reconquered by James I. In general, the Moors were agriculturalists, and in most of the territory of the Crown of Aragon had little to do with the Franciscans; only in Valencia is there any evidence that prominent Moors converted to Christianity, and that their descendants entered the Order of Friars Minor.

It was into this relatively tolerant society that the mendicant friars came with their city orientation, their concern for those who worked in an urban setting and their desire to carry the Gospel of Christ to non-Christian minorities. Saint Francis had come from a merchant background, and his followers regarded the towns as the area of primary focus of their mission. They complemented admirably the political aims of James I during the reconquest, and gave the seal of Christian respectability to the newly conquered lands, offering the prestige necessary to transform his imperialist aims into a crusade for the expansion of Christendom. The enthusiastic acceptance given to them by the king evoked a similarly generous response from their contemporaries, and even from some of the clergy, who were barred from entering many of the professions to which the Franciscans ministered; but others looked upon the arrival of the newcomers with some perturbation of spirit, regarding them as trespassers on their domain.

The Mediterranean towns were ideally situated to carry on trade with the Italian communes, France, North Africa and other countries which could be approached by sea. Barcelona was the first of these towns to embrace a highly-developed form of self-government, which by 1300 had been extended to the kingdom of Majorca.[3] In the interior, the cities of Saragossa and Lerida, both of which possessed royal palaces and a sophisticated municipal structure, were active trading centres in the thirteenth and fourteenth centuries and acted as focal points of government for their regions. Similarly, Gerona provided the link with the Catalan towns to the north of Barcelona and, as an important ecclesiastical centre, played a crucial part in the development of the Dominicans, Franciscans, Carmelites and Mercedarians.

The establishment of Franciscan houses directly parallels the formation and structure of these early cities. The location of convents

---

3 I am indebted to Hillgarth's *Spanish Kingdoms*, 1: 75-83, for the description of town life in the realms of Aragon.

and the custodies, grouped within the province of Aragon, in many ways follows quite closely regional divisions and political developments. The administrative organization of the Order of Friars Minor suffered modifications as and when political events interfered with former allegiances; this was exemplified most clearly when the kingdom of Majorca ceased to exist as an independent territory.

As in thirteenth-century Germany, the foundation of Franciscan convents was an important process in the urbanization of the country. The spiritual mission of the friars acted as a bulwark against unorthodoxy and helped to prevent heretical ideas from spreading among the burgesses. By ensuring that royal policies were carried out, and by caring for the spiritual needs of a class which was dependent for its livelihood on the success of a mercantile economy, the Franciscans filled a preeminently political role.[4] It could be argued that, to a very great degree, the Franciscans shared directly in the fortunes of the merchant class to which they ministered, and by the end of the thirteenth century, like it, acquired a position of stability and power.

In much the same way as the king called upon the friars to undertake diplomatic missions, rewarding them with recommendations to the papacy for ecclesiastical appointments when it seemed politically expedient, so these new burgesses, who came from the same milieu as the friars, made use of their services in a number of different ways, not least as a stamp of approval for their activities.

In this regard, the foundation of the Order of Friars Minor and the emergence of a class dedicated to commerce are two events which must be regarded as an integral part of the move towards an urban economy in the thirteenth century. The development of cities was extremely fortunate for the friars, because it meant that they immediately occupied a unique position in them. They were also able to enlist without much difficulty the support of the merchants, who until their arrival upon the scene had been regarded with less than enthusiasm by the church. The friars demonstrated that a Christian life was possible in an urban environment, that a profit economy or a trading orientation was not contrary to the teachings of the church and that their mission did not interfere with the rural life of the monastic orders, whose contemplative mission

---

4   See John B. Freed, *The Friars and German Society in the Thirteenth Century* (Cambridge, Mass., 1977), esp. pp. 51–53, for the rise of the friars in Germany.

away from the towns had become a tradition of the medieval countryside.

The enthusiastic response of the urban dwellers to the expedient arrival of the newcomers is abundantly documented in contemporary testaments, in the evidence they provide of acts of generosity which made it possible for the Franciscans to build splendid convents within a relatively short period of time. In some way these donations were probably made in the hope that they would mitigate the harmful effects the medieval church believed would accrue to those engaged in trade, a form of piety which was to bring great benefits to the mendicant orders, and of which they were not slow to take advantage.

Franciscan houses in the Crown of Aragon owed much to the significant donations of private citizens, which, along with the royal grants of land and money, gave the friars a solid base upon which to build. The initial generosity of these citizens pales before the ever-increasing support shown to the mendicant orders during the hundred years before the advent of the Black Death in 1348. The surviving documentation reveals a highly structured plan of giving, composed of a number of general categories that are most easily understood in the light of the development of three major houses. These will be described in some detail, and references to others under their jurisdiction will help complete the structure.

The most representative of the Franciscan houses have been chosen for this purpose, bearing in mind not only their importance for the order but the significance of their geographical position: Barcelona, possibly the most important of all the convents; Lerida, the foremost city in an agricultural area; and Gerona, which, besides being an administrative centre of some significance, has retained documents from 1224 until the dissolution of the religious houses in the nineteenth century.[5] In both Lerida and Gerona, two distinct periods of development emerge, one prior to 1300 and one during the first half of the fourteenth century.

While most Franciscan houses were founded in the thirteenth century, there are those like Tàrrega and Puigcerdà which were not established until the reign of James II, and others like Berga, where

---

5 One or two documents are missing from the collection, but apart from these the list contained and described in the *Repertori de actes del convent de Girona,* preserved in the Arxiu històric dels Franciscans de Catalunya (AHFC), Barcelona, provides details of all the records from the thirteenth to the eighteenth century.

there seem to have been two foundations. The possible reasons for this are inseparable from the development of the order and its function within the Crown of Aragon, and they have already been postulated at some length.

The economic and political circumstances pertaining to the different regions must also be seen as part of this development, as some aspects are of direct relevance to the role the friars played in the nascent urbanization of the lands of the Crown of Aragon. Briefer reference will be made, for reasons which will be evident in the discussion of these cities, to two more convents: Saragossa, the focal point of Franciscan activity in Aragon; and Valencia, the centre of the Levante and one of the houses founded as a direct result of the reconquest.

One other area should be included here, Majorca, not so much in the context of the parallel development of friars and city, although this was certainly the case, but more because of the very special circumstances pertaining to the island, which were unique in the Crown of Aragon and fundamental to the missionary work of the Franciscans. Three convents within the custody of Narbonne, Perpignan, Puigcerdà and Villefranche de Conflent, and the convent of Montpellier, were also under the jurisdiction of the kingdom of Majorca until 1344 and have a limited impact on the trajectory of the Franciscan province of Aragon. The houses at Pamplona, Estella and Tudela, which belonged to the kingdom of Navarre, are excluded from the discussion, as they never belonged to the Crown of Aragon and only tangentially affected its fortunes. As the Franciscans were a mobile group, often travelling extensively during their lifetime, among the friars in any given house were men from all the peninsular kingdoms, and from England, France, Germany and Italy. In the fourteenth century there were even friars from the North African provinces who had been converted by the Franciscan missionaries.

BARCELONA

By the end of the thirteenth century, Barcelona was one of the most vibrant commercial centres in the Mediterranean and a fundamental point of contact for traders from Africa and northern Europe. James I realized that his territorial ambitions could not be achieved without improvement of the resources of the port of Barcelona, and that Catalan and overseas traders had to be assured of a safe passage for their goods. In 1257, one of the most far-seeing attempts to control maritime trade was drawn up under the title of *Libre del consolat del mar,* the name having been taken from a guild court in Pisa and Genoa.⁶ A recent study emphasizes the intricacies of this trade and the advance in organizational techniques of the thirteenth century, among them the development of notarial expertise.⁷ Nowhere was this tendency more prevalent than in Barcelona, where economic advances on land and sea had laid the foundations for the creation of a wealthy urban patriciate; and nowhere is the presence of this wealth more evident than in the support the merchants gave to the mendicant friars.

Medieval traders in Barcelona not only profited from the burgeoning mercantile economy but were able to rely on an equally well-defined and well-organized administrative structure. From 1249 to 1274 Peter II experimented with a number of charters intended to balance royal and local autonomy, a process which in 1274 gave rise to the *Consell de Cent,* a general assembly of one hundred councillors responsible for the government of the city of Barcelona.⁸ The councillors were chosen from the prominent urban patricians, and many of them not only supported the Franciscans financially but contributed sons and daughters to the Order of Friars Minor and to the Poor Clares. It is mainly from the wills of these and other wealthy traders that some insight can be gained into the parallel rise of friar and patrician in late thirteenth- and fourteenth-century Barcelona.

The Crown of Aragon is unusual in its preservation of early wills, and Barcelona is fortunate in possessing the final copies in parchment form, together with hundreds of notarial manuals containing the rough notes made by the notaries before the finished copy was drawn up. These records provide the identities, the relative wealth and family backgrounds of those who supported the friars, at the same time revealing their interests and the charitable institutions they patronized. Using wills from cathedral archives in the two cities, comparative studies have been made of the bequests to charitable organizations by citizens of Barcelona and Vic. Although the data cannot be assessed on a numerical basis, because the wills do not always correspond chronologically and are somewhat

---

6   Hillgarth, *Spanish Kingdoms,* 1: 273.
7   For an excellent study of maritime practices see Arcadi García i Sanz and Maria-Teresa Ferrer i Mallol, *Assegurances i canvis marítims medievals a Barcelona,* 2 vols. (Barcelona, 1983), esp. 1: 47–48.
8   Bisson, *Medieval Crown of Aragon,* pp. 76–79. For the development of the crown archives under James I, see Robert I. Burns, *Society and Documentation in Crusader Valencia* (Princeton, 1985).

unequal in their distribution, they do provide sufficient facts to reach tentative conclusions regarding the relative popularity of the different mendicant orders in these two towns in the thirteenth century.

Extant documentation in other cities is less extensive, but the testaments consulted confirm that the Franciscans were supported primarily by traders, usually those owning some property, people who would now be classified as small proprietors. In most areas, there were significantly fewer bequests to the Franciscans from members of the upper classes, many of whom had a long and close relationship with the older monastic foundations. Among the Franciscan supporters were invariably those who had some connection with members of the royal family or who were responsible for the execution of royal or municipal policies, lending further credence to the traditional alliance in the Crown of Aragon between the non-noble classes and the crown. Many of these people in Barcelona occupied positions on the *Consell de Cent;* in other cities they similarly took an active part in municipal affairs. The very poor, of course, left little trace of the hardships they suffered: they had no need to make a will, and no doubt at times owed a debt of gratitude to the Friars Minor for their care in the hospitals which the Franciscans operated on their behalf.[9]

The documentation for the Gerona house shows that by the eighteenth century the friars no longer came from the wealthy urban traders but from those who had little or no property.[10] This was probably also true for Barcelona and other Catalan cities, and maybe for the Crown of Aragon at large. It would make an interesting study to compare this shift in the origin of Franciscan vocations with the economic conditions prevalent in Aragon in the eighteenth century, and to assess the likelihood that this change of focus was also reflected in the support given to the order; but such a study, of course, must be left for another occasion.

The first documentary evidence of the house in Barcelona known as Saint Nicholas is a bequest of 12 diners left in 1230 by Ermesenda, the sister of Bernat de Palau; this amount accurately represents the average

---

9 Jill R. Webster, "La reina doña Constanza y los hospitales de Barcelona y Valencia," *AIA* 51 (1991), 375-390. In Tàrrega, for a while at least, the Franciscans continued to run the leprosarium which they had been granted by the king on the condition that they looked after any lepers still living there.

10 See Jill R. Webster, "Els orígens socials dels franciscans," in *Actes del segon col.loqui d'estudis catalans a Nord-Amèrica, Yale, 1979,* ed. Manuel Duran, Albert Porqueras-Mayo, and Josep Roca-Pons (Montserrat, 1982), pp. 415-424.

bequest of most thirteenth-century testators.[11] A glance at the comparative table of Batlle and Casas reveals that out of a total of one hundred and twenty-eight legacies, the Friars Minor received 8104 sous, 4 pence and 4 besants, the rights to an *obrador* (workman?), books including a bible, clothing and a bed.[12] The amounts given ranged from 1 to 600 sous, and were paid from 1232 to 1299, the total received being somewhat less than the amount left to the Dominicans.[13]

It is not known how many of these legacies reached the Franciscans, as disputes with heirs became increasingly frequent and numerous appeals were made to the king to see that justice was done.[14] Unfortunately, the nature of the records for the thirteenth century is such that comparison of extant wills with letters in the chancellery registers to see whether any of them were disputed is quite impossible. An attempt has been made to do this for the fourteenth century, for which more information is available, although inevitably any conclusions drawn are far from reliable, as there is no guarantee that all documents survived. It is more likely that many did not, and the fact that a particular will is not disputed in the registers does not necessarily mean that the Franciscans actually received the amount stated.

The earliest records in the king's registers of non-payment of bequests date from the last decade of the thirteenth century, but only one of these concerns the Barcelona house and this one is not contained in the list of the wills analysed by Batlle and Casas.[15] The document in question is typical of all royal documents ordering payment of legacies to the Franciscans, although the greater complexities of certain wills required a more elaborate format. In the present instance, the king wrote to his vicar in Manresa and the area of the Bagès, ordering payment of Sibil.la de Castellet's legacy of 130 morabatins to the Franciscan house in Barcelona. Sibil.la's daughter of the same name, the widow of Umbert de Rocafort, seemed to be reluctant to honour her mother's bequest

---

11 See above Chapter 1, p. 25.
12 Carme Batlle i Gallart and Montserrat Casas i Nadal, "La caritat privada i les institucions benèfiques de Barcelona (segle XIII)," in *La pobreza y la asistencia a los pobres en la Cataluña medieval,* ed. Manuel Riu, 2 vols. (Barcelona, 1980–1982), 1: 117-190, at pp. 153-154 and 182-190.
13 Ibid., 1: 184 (unnumbered page).
14 References to unpaid accounts are listed in Appendix 2.
15 Barcelona, ACA, RC 92, f. 97, 21 May 1292.

to the friars of a mass on the anniversary date of her death, possibly because as a widow she herself was in need of money.

Using similar sources to those consulted by Batlle and Casas for Barcelona, an approximate estimate can be given of total legacies by Barcelona citizens to the Franciscans between 1300 and 1348, and this amounts to 32 pounds, 887 sous, 12 morabatins and 1000 besants, the latter a bequest of Marie of Lusignan, queen of Aragon.[16] References in the chancellery registers to conflicts over the payment of legacies during that period amount to twenty-seven, but only two refer to Barcelona. The late Pere Foix's legacy of an unspecified sum was still outstanding in 1316, as was the sum owed by a money changer, Bernat Sabater, on account of a deposit made by the Franciscans before Bernat's death; but neither of these bequests is included in the approximate amounts given above for 1300 to 1348.[17]

These figures are in no way representative of the support the mendicants received from their contemporaries, and any conclusion must be reached only after other factors are taken into consideration. Despite their obvious incompleteness, taken as a whole and in conjunction with other extant sources, the figures provide the historian with an approximate gauge to measure the popularity of the different mendicant orders and the average size of monetary bequests made to them. Grants of land, foundations of chapels, altars and other bequests in kind are not included in the figures given above, but were among the most significant donations the Franciscans received from their deceased supporters.

This raises the question of the origin of the furnishings of the Franciscan churches, and suggests that most of them were given to the order by wealthy benefactors rather than purchased with the money bequeathed to them by their contemporaries. As this aspect of the order has an intrinsic value for the study of Gothic art and architecture in the Crown of Aragon, it is sufficiently important to merit a chapter apart. It is enough here to remember that endowments of chapels and altars frequently expressed devotion to Saint Francis, the other saints and the

---

16 Pedro Sanahuja, *História de la seráfica provincia de Cataluña* (Barcelona, 1959), p. 99. Queen Marie made her will while she was in Tortosa in 1319, stipulating that she wished to be buried in the Tortosa Franciscan house, or, if she died elsewhere, in the Franciscan house in that city. In fact she died in Barcelona, in 1322, and was buried close to the chapel of Saint Stephen in the church of St. Francis belonging to the Friars Minor in Barcelona.
17 Barcelona, ACA, RC 159, f. 266 (1316 [1317]); RC 162, f. 40v (1316 [1317]).

Blessed Virgin Mary, and that tradesmen's guilds were established in honour of the founder of the order in many parts of the Crown of Aragon. In most cases, there is proof that bequests of this kind were honoured; but there is no doubt that some were not, primarily, perhaps, because when the will was proved there was insufficient money to carry out all the testator's wishes. It is both impossible and inappropriate to include here the names of all those who supported the Franciscans. Certain families not only gave generously to the order but had a close relationship with the friars because one member of the family had taken vows as a Friar Minor. The available information in this regard proves incontrovertibly the merchant origin of the majority of medieval friars in areas such as Barcelona and Gerona.[18] In these towns, unlike some of those in other areas, there is abundant evidence that the Minors actively participated in local events.

Gerona

Medieval Gerona was a vibrant commercial centre which, because of its inland position not far from the French frontier and on the direct route to Barcelona and the Levante, provided a focal point for foreign traders to all points within the Crown of Aragon. Most extant municipal records date from the fourteenth century, and it is difficult to assess accurately the pattern of urban development in Gerona from the time of the establishment of the Franciscans in the 1230s until after 1300.[19] One fact stands out: besides its importance as a commercial centre, Gerona was already a renowned ecclesiastical see, explaining, in part, why the Carmelites, Dominicans, Franciscans and Mercedarians all chose to found houses there prior to 1300.

The preservation of the Franciscan archives, unique in their import and range, make conclusions concerning the Gerona house far less tentative, and it can be said without hesitation that the Franciscans received support from the families who lived in the Mercadal area, which the friars had chosen as the location of their convent. They were indebted to their neighbours for much of the land on which their property was

---

18 See Appendix 3 for the family origins of known Friars Minor.
19 See Jill R. Webster, "Col.lecció de documents del convent de Sant Francesc de Girona (1224–1399)," *AIEG* 28–30 (1985–1989), 28: 157–189, 29: 27–86, 30: 141–226, for the documents from the Gerona Franciscan archives preserved in the AHFC, Barcelona.

situated, and for the continuing financial support which enabled the Gerona house to become one of the most splendid within the Crown of Aragon. After 1348 both the municipality and the diocesan authorities gave support in a variety of different ways, including allowances for food and other necessities which had been supplied to the friars by local traders.[20] Nowhere else are records of this kind extant, and it is curious that the diocese not only considered it necessary but was willing to subsidize the mendicant orders in this way. Could this be regarded as a special situation, in part arising from the difficulties the city of Gerona experienced in the fourteenth century from crop failures and the incursion of French raiders?[21] Certainly these were problems for both layman and ecclesiastic, and the friars were to suffer directly from the raids: on one occasion at least, the soldiers forced an entry to their convent and stole bedding.[22]

Like Barcelona, Gerona was a well-organized town where both ecclesiastical and lay records have survived the ravages of time. The extant documentation makes it clear that important schools of notaries developed in Gerona in the thirteenth century. Although for the capital no thirteenth-century notarial records survive, a few from the outlying towns of Perelada and Castelló d'Empúries, dating from the last years of the century, bear witness to the existence of a highly organized notarial system; and this is borne out by the large number of extant fourteenth-century notarial records for Gerona itself.

The documentation preserved for the Gerona house predates its foundation and makes it possible to trace the development of relations between friar and citizens from a very early period. The first document, of 1224, refers to the sale of a mill by Alamanda, the widow of Pere Metge, to Bernat Gros in the Mercadal, on a site which was later to be

---

20 Gerona, AD, *Libri notularum,* G.40 (39), 1360–1361. Although these payments were made later than the period under review, they support my belief that relations between the cathedral of Gerona and the friars were unusually cordial.

21 Joaquín Pla Cargol, *Gerona histórica,* 2nd ed. (Gerona and Madrid, 1945), p. 66, refers to 1333 as the year of the great famine, but this was a recurring problem in the fourteenth century.

22 The incursions of the French date from 1285, when they stole blankets and other bedding from the Gerona house (see Webster, "Col.lecció de documents," *AIEG* 28: 178).

the place the Franciscans built their convent.[23] Alamanda may also have been an ancestor of the famous Catalan writer, Bernat Metge, whose father was a doctor in Barcelona. In any case, it looks as though this sale was effected with the establishment of the friary in mind, but the particular piece of land sold to Bernat Gros is not mentioned again.

In February of 1231 additional land was given to the Franciscans by Bernat Esteve, a canon of Gerona cathedral, on behalf of the bishop and chapter; it was received for the friars by Fr. John Parente, minister for Spain, probably because, as this was the first step towards the establishment of a house at Gerona, there was no guardian or procurator who could take possession of the land. Three years later the bishop and chapter of Gerona cathedral gave a further plot of land in the Mercadal area, the site of the convent until its disappearance in the nineteenth century. Unlike other houses, the Gerona house was founded with the generosity of the bishop and chapter, and this might have prevented some of the animosity between friar and parish priest so typical elsewhere in Catalonia but recorded far less frequently for Gerona.

To what extent did the bishop and chapter of Gerona encourage the friars to establish a house there? The citizens were proud of the visit of Saint Francis to their city some years earlier, and the brothers who continued their ministry in Gerona after his departure might well have acquired a reputation which elicited unprecedented diocesan and citizen support. The first significant grant of land came from the diocese, a generosity which must have encouraged traders living in the Mercadal area to respond in like manner. It is not until 1249 that there is evidence of the existence of a building set aside for the friars' use under the administration of the guardian Fr. Ramon de Castelló, who, if his name is an indication, came from the nearby town of Castelló d'Empúries, which later had its own Franciscan house.

Gradually the citizens living in the Mercadal area either gave or sold to the Franciscans properties adjacent to or in the vicinity of those donated by the bishop and chapter. Among these was Pere Guerau, who in 1285 sold his property consisting of houses and gardens in the Mercadal to the Franciscans through their procurator, Martí Ermengol. Did Saint Francis stay in one of these houses when he was given hospitality by the Guerau family, or did the friars themselves live on the Guerau

---

23 Webster, "Col.lecció de documents," *AIEG* 28: 182, no. 1. Subsequent references to the Gerona house in this section are taken from this study.

property before building their own convent? Irrespective of the answers to these questions, from this point on the support of the citizens was guaranteed, and indeed, many families could boast of a son who had joined the order, giving them an even greater impetus to ensure that the convent had the wherewithal to fulfil its mission.

Thus, the thirteenth century saw the development of Gerona and Castelló d'Empúries; the fourteenth century added the convent of Puigcerdà, which, although in the province of Gerona, was situated in an area under the jurisdiction of the king of Majorca. For a time at least, it had less contact with houses in Gerona than with those in Majorca and southern France. The extant notarial records for Puigcerdà show that the merchant community was active in the first decades of the fourteenth century, and that certain families had a long history of trading in the city.

Devotion to the mendicant orders was also a longstanding tradition, as there were important houses of both the Dominicans and the Friars of the Sack in Puigcerdà itself, and those who wished to join the Order of Friars Minor had to cross into southern France, where they were welcomed in the convent of Villefranche de Conflent. The establishment of a Franciscan convent in Puigcerdà coincides with the founding of the house in Tàrrega. If the "double" foundation of Berga is excluded, the houses of Puigcerdà and Tàrrega were the last to be established in Aragon before the Black Death, and among the first to disappear, suggesting perhaps that the need for houses in these towns was far more temporary in nature than had seemed to be the case in 1318-1319.

Lerida

One of the first cities in twelfth-century Catalonia to be reconquered from the Moors by the early thirteenth century, Lerida was a mosaic of Christian, Jewish and Moorish inhabitants.[24] One of the first tasks of the Christians was to ensure that the church of Lerida responded to the needs of a city which had been recently reconquered. Ecclesiastical life in Lerida was organized in 1168, no doubt receiving further consolidation once the city had fallen to James I's Christian warriors, and the *Llibre vert,* or chronicle of cathedral life, makes available the names of many of the early settlers.[25] Little is known about their relation to the

---

24 José Lladonosa Pujol, *Lérida medieval,* 2 vols. (Lerida, 1974-1975), 1: 13-31.
25 See ibid., 1: 27.

foundation of the Franciscan house, except that it was one of the first to be established, thanks to the generosity of a merchant, Ramon de Barriac, a resident in the Calle Mayor.[26] By the 1220s Lerida must already have become a mercantile city of some reputation, and at least some of the traders resident there must have acquired considerable wealth. The city was held in high esteem by James I, who owed the men of Lerida a debt of gratitude for participating in the reconquest of Murcia in 1243.[27] When the Levante and Majorca were resettled after the reconquest of the Balearic Islands, many men had moved to these areas from Lerida, probably largely because the king had given them lands in recompense for their help in his defeat of the Moors.

The city of Lerida itself benefited directly from a number of royal privileges granted during the reign of James I and the compilation of the *Consuetudines Ilerdenses* in the early years of the century, amplified or modified later as events decreed, provided the city with a record of these privileges together with a reference guide to its traditional laws and customs. Municipal organization, without being a copy of that found in other Catalan towns, had much in common with the system pertaining in Barcelona. The mendicant friars, on their arrival in Lerida, found a city with an active and growing body of merchants. Fairs were held which were attended by traders from overseas, and Lerida was an agricultural centre for the towns of the Segre valley.

Sad to say, modern Lerida bears few traces of its illustrious history and has been singularly unfortunate in being the centre of numerous wars, which have not only destroyed buildings but made it impossible to preserve many of the records. Extant documentation has been sufficient to bear testimony to the importance of one memorable institution, the *estudio general,* an early institution which was attended by many Franciscans in the fourteenth century. Founded in 1300, it had a significant impact on the city, where the students lived as a distinct group, similar to the tradesmen and other inhabitants. Lladonosa Pujol describes in some detail the statutes of the university of Lerida, which he regards as unique, providing for a measure of democracy not found in the Crown of Aragon in other educational institutions of the early fourteenth century.[28] A large merchant class and a well-established

---

26 José Lladonosa Pujol, *Lérida medieval,* 1: 96.
27 Ibid., 1: 57.
28 Ibid., 2: 13–31.

ecclesiastical structure would have made it attractive to the first Franciscans, and Lerida's educational fame attracted scholars from far and wide.

It is extremely difficult to trace material elucidating the early activities of the Lerida friars, mainly because some of the material in the cathedral archives has either disappeared or remains to be catalogued and is not readily accessible to scholars.[29] If it were not for the pioneering work of Sanahuja, himself a native of Lerida, these lacunae would remain unfilled. Sanahuja states that Lerida had received Saint Francis and given him hospitality, welcoming his followers with the same degree of enthusiasm that they accorded to the founder of the order. The document which has traditionally been regarded as referring to the foundation of the house is Ramon de Barriac's will, which Sanahuja dates between 1221 and 1228.[30]

As the archives where it was housed were completely destroyed in the Civil War of 1936–1939, verification of the date is now impossible, but a reference to the Franciscans in another will at least confirms the presence of the friars in Lerida by the late 1220s: on 12 January 1229 Ferrer Pallarés and his wife, Berenguera, left a small donation of 2 sous to the Franciscans.[31] Similarly, in February 1231, Hug de Tolosa left 5 mazmutines to the Lerida house.[32] In 1236 Fr. Arnau, whose name also appears in connection with Majorca around the same time, and Fr. Il.luminat, Fr. William of the See and Fr. Guillem de Cervera respectively acted as witnesses to documents referring to the convent of Trinitarian nuns in Lerida.[33] In July of that same year the will of Guilleuma, daughter of Guillem Porquet, made provision for 10 mazmutines to go to the Franciscans for their table, and for other charitable

---

29   The parchments of Lerida's cathedral archives still remain largely uncatalogued and facilities for research are very limited, making it almost impossible to undertake an exhaustive study.
30   Sanahuja, *História,* p. 44.
31   Barcelona, ACA, ORM, Gran Priorato, arm. 28, perg. 117, 12 January 1228 [1229].
32   Ambròs de Saldes, "Documents inèdits per a la història de l'antiga província franciscana d'Aragó (segles XIII-XIV)," *EF* 46 (1934), 98–107, at p. 98.
33   Lerida, AHM, *Privilegis, statuts e ordinacions de la ciutat de Lleida 1299–1413,* p. 180 (old numbering: f. 168), dated 15 October 1236; Sanahuja, *História,* p. 45.

donations to institutions in Lerida; a few months later, in October, Pere Belló left 90 sous to his confessor, Fr. Guerau of the Lerida house.[34]

After this date there are many references to the house at Lerida, where in June 1246 the reconciliation took place between James I and Fr. Berenguer de Castellbisbal, the Dominican who was chosen as bishop of Gerona and whose tongue was cut out because he allowed it to wag too freely.[35] The majority of the extant documents refer to royal privileges granted to the house or to difficulties encountered in the late thirteenth and early fourteenth centuries; some of them were circular letters like the one sent by the king in 1279 to many Franciscan houses, enjoining them to use conciliatory methods to convert the Jews.[36] From the references which survive, and this would be logical given the geographical position of Lerida on the borders of Catalonia and Aragon, it is clear that the Lerida Franciscan house was supported by merchants and some noble families, a pattern more typical of the Aragonese towns than of their Catalan counterparts.

Saragossa

Like Lerida, Saragossa has suffered from numerous reverses of fortune through the ages, making it virtually impossible to draw even a sketchy picture of the medieval Franciscan house.

Very little has been published on mendicant activity in the city, largely because the documentation which would make this possible probably disappeared at a very early date. If this is true for Saragossa, the situation is much worse for the other houses in Aragon: Calatayud, Daroca, Huesca, Jaca, Tarazona, and the small houses of Ejea and Borja. Fortunately, the chancellery registers mention these convents with some frequency, but in many cases the picture they paint is far from flattering. Although there are the usual references to grants and favours, much of the emphasis in the fourteenth century seems to be placed on the difficulties the friars had with their clerical or lay neighbours. This aspect is exaggerated by the lack of preservation of any other documents to offset the negative impact the royal documents create on the reader. There must have been more positive aspects of the friars' ministry in

---

34 Sanahuja, *Història,* p. 45; Barcelona, ACA, ORM, Gran Priorato, arm. 28, perg. 164, 22 October 1236.
35 See below Chapter 4, pp. 152–153, and Sanahuja, *Història,* p. 46.
36 See above Chapter 1, pp. 33, 49, 64.

Aragon, given the fact that the houses there acquired notoriety and enjoyed some measure of economic stability; but sadly, records of them have not survived.

Saragossa was one of the most important cities within the realms of Aragon in the thirteenth and fourteenth centuries. Surrounded by walls, with the Franciscan convent situated outside the city itself, it was a frequent meeting place for the king's court. The king's retinue sometimes used the convent either as a meeting place or as a place of lodging, a custom shared with the Dominicans and one also observed in relation to the nearby house of Daroca.[37] Although permission was given to hold the coronation ceremony in Saragossa, it was not until 1276 that a king was actually crowned there.[38] Unlike the situation in Catalonia, Aragon's powerful aristocracy, especially the nobles who banded together in the union, was sufficiently bold to challenge the power of the king.[39] To a certain degree this highly aristocratic society prevented the development of a democratic governing structure, an aspect of Catalan life which had encouraged the emergence of the merchant class and ensured their continued prosperity.

In some ways Saragossa bears more resemblance to Valencia than to Catalonia. There existed a large Moorish population in addition to the extensive Jewish communities, although as in Lerida, the fairs held in the marketplace attracted merchants from far and wide, while the cathedral and its staff provided ecclesiastical direction for the numerous parish churches within the city and its environs. Much of the importance of Saragossa lies in the fact that it was the focal point for the agricultural communities of Aragon, which would take their produce and livestock to the city to trade it with the merchants who frequented the fairs. A highly-developed administrative structure to meet the needs of the citizens in the Aragonese capital would have been logical, and in some ways this was so, for it is clear that the *fueros* of Aragon provided the legal basis for officials, including those who were appointed to administer justice.

---

37 Barcelona, ACA, RC 535, f. 51v, 25 January 1333 [1334], refers to the construction of windows and doors in the house at Daroca for the king's visit; RC 862, f. 34v, 18 September 1337, suggests that the king frequently made use of the house in Daroca, which had been adapted for the purpose.
38 See Bisson, *Medieval Crown of Aragon,* p. 87.
39 Ibid., pp. 58–85. Peter II of Catalonia and III of Aragon was crowned in Saragossa in November 1276.

The chancellery registers also provide ample evidence that a clearly-defined system of justice was firmly entrenched in Aragonese society in the fourteenth century, but municipal government seems to reach its maturity much later than that of the Catalan towns, in part no doubt because the predominant aristocratic structure made it difficult for the nascent commercial traders to acquire a sure foothold. The first rudiments of such an organization only appear in the reign of James II, considerably later than was true of Lerida, for instance.[40] Among the officials referred to in the first municipal *ordenanzas* were those whose duty it was to oversee the affairs of the marketplace, suggesting that only in the late thirteenth century did Saragossa really attract traders in any numbers.

In view of the lack of early records, any degree of accurate assessment of the contribution of the merchants to the Franciscans in the thirteenth century is just not feasible; in the fourteenth the information is insufficient to permit more than very tentative conclusions. In both centuries there were talented Aragonese friars like Fr. Romeo Ortiz and Fr. Domingo de Jaca, whose aptitude for special missions was recognized by the crown. Some of these friars appear in the royal registers with the frequency expected when dealing with those who came from influential and highly-placed families. If they are to be regarded as typical of the friars who entered the Order of Friars Minor in Aragon, the conclusion must be that the friars from that region came from significantly more aristocratic backgrounds than those from Catalonia.

In outlining the difficulties inherent in any research on medieval Aragon, it is obvious that the lack of surviving documentation prevents an accurate assessment of the role the Aragonese merchants played in the development of the Franciscans. According to popular tradition, the convent of Saragossa was one of the first to be founded, and there is no doubt that it subsequently received continual support from the crown and from certain prominent families. In the fourteenth century it could be regarded as one of the most important in the Crown of Aragon. The renown in which the Saragossa convent was held is best seen in the illustrious example of 1251 when James I's queen, Violant, included among a number of legacies to Franciscan convents one to the house of

---

40 María Luisa Ledesma Rubió and María Isabel Falcón Pérez, *Zaragoza en la baja edad media* (Saragossa, 1977), pp. 86–88.

Saragossa, leaving it 100 morabatins.[41] This is the first extant document referring to the Saragossa house, but it was probably founded not too long after 1219, the date Fr. John Parente was said to have held a chapter in the city.[42] Subsequent chapters will constantly refer to certain Aragonese families whose devotion to the Franciscans is documented in the royal registers, but any conclusions drawn from these references are lamentably inadequate to explain the numerous occasions on which Aragonese friars participated in contemporary events.

VALENCIA

To the south of Saragossa and in the heart of a thriving Moorish agricultural centre, Valencia had the dubious distinction of witnessing the martyrdom of two early Franciscan missionaries, who had hoped to proceed to Africa to convert the Saracens.[43] It was also one of the areas reconquered by James I in the 1230s, and its resettlement in subsequent years gave strength to the diocesan system and the impetus to the mendicant orders to establish their houses: the Dominicans, Franciscans and later the Augustinians and Carmelites all made Valencia their home.[44] At least two Franciscan friars had accompanied James in his crusade against Valencia; thus, the order had been associated with James I's policies in the Levante from the very moment of the conquest of the city. Little documentation survives to explain the function of these friars in James I's army, nor are there any early references to the support given to them by the citizens.

Like the other towns reconquered from the Moors, Valencia was resettled by Christians, often by those who later received land in reward for their services. The Franciscans also benefited from the royal policy of Christianization, and the privileges and concessions they received from the king enabled them to establish their first convent in the city. Valencia, with its large population of Moors, many of whom remained in the city after the reconquest, presented a direct challenge to the missionary work of the Friars Minor.

---

41 Ambròs de Saldes, "La orden franciscana en el antiguo reino de Aragón: Colección diplomática," *REF* 1 (1907), 414–417, 478–482, at pp. 478–479.
42 See Sanahuja, *História,* p. 24.
43 Robert I. Burns, *El reino de Valencia en el siglo XIII (iglesia y sociedad),* 2 vols. (Valencia, 1982), 2: 447–448.
44 Ibid., 2: 445–480.

The conversion of the Sayyid Abu Zayd, the Moorish king who had ordered the martyrdom of the two Franciscans and was said to have repented of his sin, thereafter converting to Christianity and giving his palace to the Franciscans in atonement for his cruelty, could not have been the least of the order's achievements.[45] When he died he asked to be buried in a marble tomb in the Franciscan house, a request which can neither be proved nor rejected as untrue, although Chabás, by publishing the will of the Sayyid Abu Zayd's son Fernando Pérez, has laid to rest some of the legends regarding this Moorish king.[46]

The Sayyid Abu Zayd had two sons, one of whom, Fernando Pérez, was probably the offspring of his Christian wife. In 1296 Fernando Pérez became seriously ill and, expecting to die, drew up his last will and testament, in which he asked to be buried in Valencia cathedral.[47] He also requested that his confessor, Fr. Gómez, together with the guardian of the Valencian Franciscan house at the time of his death, distribute 200 royal sous among the poor. A subsequent clause in the same will mentions Fr. Gómez as a relative of the testator on his mother's side, and leaves him 800 royal sous. From his worldly goods and to atone for his sins, Fernando Pérez left 3000 royal Valencian sous to build a dormitory in the house of the Friars Minor of Valencia. His relative (possibly brother-in-law) and the guardian of the Franciscans were authorized to decide any questions arising from the will. The family of the Sayyid Abu Zayd had not only converted to Christianity, but one of its members had become a Franciscan friar, thus indicating that Moorish origins were not an obstacle to taking the habit of the Order of Friars Minor.

There are other early documents confirming the mosaical pattern of Valencian society. One of these is especially interesting as it concerns Fr. Ferrer, bishop of Valencia, who at the request of the Franciscans agrees to their receiving the mosque, cemetery and houses situated in the *carrer major* leading to the "turrem combustam," a property which had

---

45 Burns, *El reino de Valencia,* 2: 449. See also Roque Chabás y Lloréns, "Çeid Abu Çeid," *El archivo* (Denia) 4 (1890), 215-221, at pp. 215-216, where the story of the Sayyid Abu Zayd's conversion, burial in the Franciscan cemetery and the devotion of his family to the order is discussed in detail. Doubt is cast on the veracity of some of the ideas contained in P. Teixidor's *Antigüedades de Valencia,* 2 vols. (Valencia, 1895), which was responsible for circulating the legends.
46 See Chapter 1, p. 34 with n72 for the final resting place of the Sayyid Abu Zayd.
47 Roque Chabás y Lloréns, "Çeid Abu Çeid," *El archivo* (Valencia) 5 (1891), 283-304, at pp. 289-304.

belonged to Ramona Torpina, the wife of Pons de Soler.[48] The first reference to the Xàtiva convent dates from the end of 1283, but it is probable that it was established very much earlier; and if the mosque belonging to Pons de Soler was given to the Franciscans in Xàtiva in 1252, it is likely that either a house existed in the town at that date or the order had considered establishing one there. The Franciscans in Valencia had already obtained the Moorish palace on the Ruzafa road where the first martyrs had been killed, and had built their convent on the site; and it may be assumed from the fact that Pons de Soler's property in Valencia was given in perpetuity by Canon Bernat de Vilar of Valencia, in the name of Bishop Arnau and the chapter of the cathedral, to Arnau Guillem de Morlans, that it was either superfluous to the friars' needs or was situated in an area disadvantageous for their work.

The Franciscans tried to convert the Moors, having frequent contact with them, including the use of Moorish servants to undertake the manual work in the convent. In 1303 there is a reference to the will of Bartolomea de Moros, described as a servant of the Friars Minor, and by her name probably of Moorish origin.[49] How would a servant have enough goods to make a will, and why would she leave to her employers as much as 30 sous of Jaca money? A servant in a religious house, and one of non-Christian origin, would have been very unlikely to have received more than a living wage and might even have been a slave. It can only be assumed in this instance that she came from a wealthy Moorish family which had fallen on hard times as a result of the reconquest of the city, and that she was orphaned at an early age and forced to enter domestic service in order to survive. Even so, it is hard to imagine how she would have accumulated enough money to make a will.

Like Saragossa, Valencia seems to have enjoyed the support of wealthy citizens who, although not necessarily noble, were certainly not merchants. In 1255, for instance, the knight Ochoa Alemany requested burial in the Franciscan cemetery, leaving 300 royal Valencian sous to

---

48 Valencia, AC, perg. 1308, 21 October 1240, copy of 19 September 1270. Was the mosque referred to in 1252 as being located in Xàtiva the same one, as we are told it had also belonged to Pons de Soler? It is of course quite possible that Pons de Soler possessed two properties, one in the carrer major and another in Xàtiva.

49 Madrid, AHN, Clero, Valencia, carp. 3275, perg. 11, "dos dias per exir abril" [28 April 1303].

Fr. Ramon Cortell for a Bible.[50] Three years later Bernat de Bell-tall left 10 sous to the Franciscans in Valencia.[51] As Burns points out, it is rare to find a will after 1240 which does not leave some money to the Franciscans, and among the examples he cites there are those who might more properly fall within the classification of *mà major,* or upper classes, rather than the tradesmen who seem generally to have been the backbone of support of the mendicant orders.[52] Three canons of the cathedral, Bertrán de Teruel, Nicolás de Jungría (Hungría?) and Pedro Pérez, also asked to be buried in the good Franciscans' cemetery and not in the cathedral. This raises a question: why they were such strong supporters of the Franciscans when it was more usual for the diocesan clergy to maintain a certain distance in their relations with the mendicant orders.[53]

It is also curious to find a letter concerning the behaviour of the secular clergy addressed to the guardian of the Franciscan house. Was he expected to intercede with the unreasonable members of the diocesan hierarchy? Fr. Godofred from Rome wrote to the guardian of the Franciscans in Valencia in 1269, on behalf of the Holy See, while the papacy was vacant, to inform him that the dean and canons of the Valencian church had acted very harshly against those under their jurisdiction who had preached or written against the statutes of the Council of Lyons, placing them under the ban of excommunication. The offending clergy appear to have broken most of the ten commandments, but since they had erred more through ignorance than deliberate wrongdoing, they were to be reinstated in the good graces of the church, provided they refrained from such behaviour in the future.[54] An interference of this kind in diocesan matters on the part of the friars would have been unwelcome in most dioceses, and the clergy in Valencia would certainly not have tolerated it in the late fourteenth century.

An attempt has been made to emphasize the distinct aspects of early Franciscan life in Valencia, but of course the development of the order, its acquisition of property, bequests to it in wills and activities of the

---

50 Madrid, AHN, Clero, Valencia, carp. 3273, perg. 12, 6 February 1254 [1255]. Ochova is a variant of the Basque name Ochoa and the name "Ochova Alamay" in the manuscript has been interpreted as Ochoa Alemany.
51 Barcelona, ACA, ORM, Gran Priorato, arm. 28, perg. 340, 1 June 1258.
52 See Burns, *El reino de Valencia,* 2: 450–451.
53 Ibid., 2: 451.
54 Valencia, AC, perg. 5998, 20 October 1269.

friars followed much the same trajectory as elsewhere in the Crown of Aragon. Only in the fourteenth century did the convent of Valencia emerge as a distinct entity from the other Franciscan houses: the establishment of the hospital attached to the friary, and its administration for a period of some fifty years, placed a heavy burden on the resources of the friars, one which they could not sustain. All the same, towards the end of the fourteenth century the Valencian house reached the peak of its fame, developing an active school of theology. Among those who taught in this school was Francesc Eiximenis, who had gone there in 1383 as arbiter of a will and who had remained to give advice to the *jurats* and to help quell the violent popular riots disturbing the peace of the city.[55]

Majorca

Strategically situated in the western Mediterranean, the largest of the Balearic Islands, Majorca played a significant role in the development of commerce between the Iberian Peninsula, the Italian communes and, to the south, the continent of Africa.

Shortly after James I reconquered the island from the Moors, a Franciscan house was established, and in 1276 the famous Col.legi de Miramar, so intimately connected with the life of Ramon Llull, was founded. This house was unique and was largely the creation of Llull, who requested the king of Majorca to proceed with the foundation of a monastery where thirteen friars could learn Arabic as a preparation for their missionary work to the Moors.[56]

Initially endowed with royal grants, the Franciscans, like the other mendicant orders on the island of Majorca, owed their continued existence to the citizens who supported them. It is likely that the Majorcan house, as a focal point in the Mediterranean, served as a staging point for missionaries proceeding to Africa. The great variation in the total numbers of friars in the house at any given time seems to support this

---

55 See Martín de Riquer, *Història de la literatura catalana: Part antiga,* 3 vols. (Barcelona, 1964), 2: 137.
56 Sebastián Garcías Palou, *El Miramar de Ramon Llull* (Palma de Mallorca, 1977), p. 40.

theory.[57] There would certainly have been those who stayed in Majorca on their way to the Catalan and Valencian coastal towns, or maybe even on their way to other parts of Europe, making the house one of transit.

The friars were not the only people who regarded Majorca as an important base in the Mediterranean. From the time of the reconquest Catalan merchants had been interested in extending their activities to Majorca, an important midway point for traders to Mediterranean ports, and they realized that they could expect a very good return for any financial help they gave to James I in his reconquest of the island.[58] They were not disappointed, and many of them received generous grants of land from the king to settle on the island. The *Repartiment* gives the way in which this land was distributed, and among the beneficiaries were men from Tarragona and Lerida.[59]

Many of the original Moorish inhabitants seem to have remained on the island, working on the land or as artisans in the towns, and thereby providing a useful source of taxes for the crown.[60] The presence of these Moors also provided an opportunity for Franciscan missionary work, and helps to explain the fact that it was in Majorca that the Franciscans chose to establish their college to train missionaries.

A document of 1244 refers to one of the early settlers, a certain Pere Examenis, who seems to have been a native of Murcia and who might have been an ancestor of the famous Catalan friar, Fr. Francesc Eiximenis (or Examenis).[61] Witnesses to the document were two Franciscan friars, showing that this important merchant family, whose family connections with the Order of Friars Minor can be traced well into the

---

57 See Jill R. Webster, "Política reial i suport ciutadà per a les cases religioses del regne de Mallorca," in *XIII Congrés d'història de la Corona d'Aragó (Palma de Mallorca, 27 setembre–1 octubre 1987): Comunicacions 1* (Palma de Mallorca, 1989), pp. 263–270, at 267–268, for the royal grants to the friars in the early fourteenth century. These records show that the variation in the numbers of persons present in the convent at any given time was due, in part at least, to the fact that there were always visitors in addition to the residents of the house.

58 Josep M. Salrach and Eulàlia Duran, *Història dels paisos catalans dels orígens a 1714*, 2 vols. (Barcelona, 1982), 1: 580.

59 Hillgarth, *Spanish Kingdoms*, 1: 27.

60 Ibid., 1: 27–28.

61 See Jill R. Webster, "Una familia de mercaderes: Los Examenis," *AIA* 47 (1987), 63–78, at p. 64.

fifteenth century, probably first formed allegiance to the mendicant cause (they also supported the Dominicans) at the time of the reconquest.

Soon after the reconquest of the territory from the Moors a mercantile economy developed in Majorca, and maritime traffic plied between the eastern Mediterranean towns and the Peninsula with increasing regularity. For the greater part of the period under review the royal house of Majorca was independent of the Crown of Aragon, and merchants from the island were often in direct competition with those from the mainland.[62] Among the territories ruled over by the Majorcan royal house were those within the barony of Montpellier, and the lands to the south of the Pyrenees, which included the towns of Perpignan, Villefranche and Puigcerdà.[63]

When the Franciscan convent was established in Puigcerdà, King Sancho of Majorca was approached to give his permission for the evaluation and ultimate purchase of a property suitable for a convent. Ecclesiastically the island had close links with the diocese of Gerona, and it is not unusual to find friars from Majorca in Gerona and vice versa, suggesting that religious affiliations between the two areas extended beyond diocesan boundaries to include the mendicant orders.

For the friars, the presence of a large mercantile community in Majorca assured them of the support they needed to succeed in their missionary work. There is little documentation dating from the 1230s, but after 1240 there is continued evidence that the Franciscans were able to attract the support of the Majorcan merchants in much the same way as they did in Barcelona, Gerona and the other mainland areas. The main sources for this period are again the royal archives, the cathedral notarial manuals and a few parchments preserved from the Franciscan archives and now in the Archivo histórico nacional in Madrid. In addition to the house established in the 1230s, the college at Miramar, founded by Ramon Llull, had a short but illustrious history. Since it has been the subject of a separate monograph, there is no need to do more than refer to it briefly here.[64]

---

62 Salrach, *Història dels paisos,* 1: 580. See also Antoni Pons, *Història de Mallorca,* vol. 6, *História del reino de Mallorca* (Palma de Mallorca, 1970), for detailed comments on the Majorcan maritime trade.

63 J. Ernest Martínez Ferrando, *La tràgica història dels reis de Mallorca,* 2nd ed. (Barcelona, 1979), pp. 26–27.

64 See Garcías Palou, *El Miramar.* The first chapters deal with the college, but the few surviving records preclude a detailed study of the early years.

Documentation for the Majorca house, although not abundant for the years before 1240, at least confirms a continual progression in the fortunes of the Franciscans. Among the lands described in the *Repartiment* in 1230 is a garden by the name of Rial Aboabdille Abnazach, where the Friars Minor were said to be living.[65] Four years later the will of Guilleuma, wife of Guillem Hug, left 100 sous to the Franciscans in Castelló d'Empúries and 500 melgurien sous for a Holy Bible to Fr. Arnau of the Order of Friars Minor, should he still be alive and need the money; otherwise she wanted the residue of her estate to go the Franciscans in Majorca for books.[66] Fr. Arnau seems to have been alive at the end of 1237 when Guillem Hug himself entrusted to him the sale of his possessions and, provided he complied with this request, made him his universal heir.[67] Fr. Arnau was in Saragossa a year earlier, but he probably died sometime in 1238 or 1239, before Guillem Hug made his second will.[68] In this will, the custodians of the Dominicans and Franciscans between them were to act as executors and administer his estate, which seems to have been left entirely to the poor.

Two further documents preserved among the parchments in the Palma de Mallorca Franciscan file are of general interest: one of September 1231, to which Ramon Llull was a signatory, in which there is a reference to the gift of a house by Assalia de Gudal, acting on behalf of James I;[69] the other dated July 1247, in which García Examenis, *miles,* confirms to his wife Sibil.la, daughter of Bernat de Castellet, that her father and Saurina, her mother, paid to him on account of her dowry 200 morabatins of good, new Alfonsine gold.[70]

---

65 Sanahuja, *História,* p. 54. See also Saldes, "La orden franciscana," p. 416.
66 See Lorenzo Pérez Martínez, "Corpus documental Balear (V): Reinado de Jaime I," *Fontes rerum Balearium* (Palma de Mallorca) 3 (1979–1980), 1–48, at pp. 36–37 (no. 521). The fact that in many cases legacies were divided between the Dominicans and Franciscans meant that documents were frequently kept in both archives; thus where the Franciscan copy is no longer extant, and the Dominican preserved, the latter provides the missing data.
67 Madrid, AHN, Clero, Palma de Mallorca, carp. 78, perg. 3, 2 December 1237.
68 Madrid, AHN, perg. 17, 13 December 1239. The will is published in Pérez Martínez, "Corpus documental Balear (V)," pp. 36–37, no. 521.
69 Madrid, AHN, Clero, Palma de Mallorca, carp. 75, perg. 21, 6 September 1231. There is no indication, of course, whether this is the father of the writer Ramon Llull or another member of the family.
70 Madrid, AHN, Clero, Palma de Mallorca, carp. 81, perg. 8, 12 July 1247.

The fact that these two documents have been kept with those relating to the Franciscan house in Majorca surely cannot be a coincidence, especially since among the parchments is one referring to Fr. Francesc Eiximenis as lector of the Majorcan house.[71]

The support given to the Franciscans by the citizens of Majorca has been the subject of a recent article.[72] One interesting fact seems worth repeating in some detail here, because the inference it makes has wider repercussions for the order than the occasion noted. In April 1240 Berenguera, the wife of Martí Ferran, agreed to deposit her dowry with the Franciscans on condition that both she and her husband could have access to it when they wished.[73] They emphasized that the money they were depositing was not a donation to the friars but remained their property. At first glance, this might seem to display an unjustifiable lack of trust in the friars. Towards the end of the thirteenth century and early in the fourteenth century those who wished to reform the order, the Spirituals and later the Observants, criticized the way in which the friars had misappropriated money deposited in their convents.[74] Certainly 1240 is very early for such abuses to have become public knowledge, but almost immediately after the death of Saint Francis the desire for a more worldly style of life became apparent, and it would not have been impossible for an incident of misappropriation to have occurred in Majorca at this time.

The Majorcan house was one of the most prosperous in the thirteenth and early fourteenth centuries, and its development closely paralleled that of the Catalan houses of Barcelona and Gerona. Endowed with royal grants, concessions and frequent occasional benefits, the friars were able to secure a sure economic base with the financial and moral support of the merchants, who, like them, were comparative newcomers to the scene. The only unique factor about the Franciscan presence in Majorca was the existence of the Franciscan college founded at Miramar by Ramon Llull in 1276. In all other respects life for the Franciscans went on in much the same way as it did elsewhere in the Crown of Aragon.

---

71 Madrid, AHN, Clero, Palma de Mallorca, carp. 112, perg. 12, Wednesday, 15 December 136[7].
72 See Webster, "Política reial i suport ciutadà."
73 Palma de Mallorca, AHRM, ECR 342, 1239–1261, f. 9, 18 April 1240.
74 John R.H. Moorman, *A History of the Franciscan Order from its Origins to the Year 1517* (Oxford, 1968; repr. Chicago, 1988), p. 203.

Majorca is also intricately bound up with the fortunes of the Franciscan house at Puigcerdà, a town which fell within the dominions of its king. Founded in 1320, the house is probably the best example of the way in which the merchants helped the friars and were instrumental in obtaining royal approval for the establishment of a Franciscan convent, and it can be taken as representative of the way in which Franciscan houses were founded after 1300. Houses established after the end of James I's reign owed as much to the generosity of wealthy citizens as they did to the patronage of the crown. Puigcerdà seems to be a case in point and one which required the cooperation of King Sancho of Majorca, the consuls and the wealthy traders in the city before it could begin to build a permanent convent. It also lends support to the conclusion that the royal house of Majorca showed a similar concern for the establishment and well-being of the mendicant orders to that shown by James I and his successors. With the conquest of Majorca by Peter III in the 1340s, the commitments made by the Majorcan royal family to the friars were honoured by the house of Aragon.

Non-Christian Urban Dwellers

Although the Order of Friars Minor was mostly concerned with attending to the spiritual needs of the Christians, there was another aspect of their evangelizing work which has been the subject of much speculation and controversy, both among their contemporaries and by modern historians.[75] Cohen attributes the success of both the Dominicans and the Franciscans to the fact that in the thirteenth century both friars and traders were newcomers to the urban scene, and that they shared a common concern with the merchants.[76] He suggests that much of the animosity of the Christians towards the Jews stems from the fact that both were traders, and the Jews more especially were successful businessmen.

This may have been so, but there is no evidence in the thirteenth-century documents to suggest that the Jews were in any way disadvantaged in their commercial transactions because of their religion. It is true that James I and the archbishop of Tarragona, perhaps in an

---

75 See Robert Chazan, *Daggers of Faith: Thirteenth-Century Christian Missionizing and Jewish Response* (Berkeley, 1989).
76 See Jeremy Cohen, *The Friars and the Jews: The Evolution of Medieval Anti-Judaism* (Ithaca and London, 1982), p. 41.

attempt to curtail the activities of the Jews and reduce any influence they had on their Christian contemporaries, ordered the confiscation of all copies of the Talmud and had them examined by the Dominicans and Franciscans, and that James II asked Fr. Ramon de Mieres to examine a Hebrew Bible and other books for possible heresy.[77] It is perhaps significant that the Spiritual Franciscans regarded their mission to the Jews as extremely important, as they themselves were not free from the taint of unorthodoxy. As late as the end of the fourteenth century Jewish books were still being examined by the friars for heresy, an indication that the Jews in Aragon were still under close surveillance.[78]

In some areas of the Iberian Peninsula, including Barcelona, Valencia and Majorca, this was the time of the anti-Jewish massacres. There is no doubt that in these places by 1400 there was a more clearly distinguishable intolerance towards the Jews, exacerbated, it has been suggested, by economic problems and epidemics such as the Black Death of 1348, for which some Christians held the Jews responsible. Even in the last decades of the thirteenth century, when the friars extended their apostolate to trying to convert the Jews, they frequently aroused the populace to a frenzy of anti-Jewish feeling by the sermons they preached.[79]

Latent animosity against the Jews gradually became more overt, partly as a result of the preaching of the Dominicans and Franciscans, and no doubt fostered in the fourteenth century by those who exploited the popular belief that the Jews were the cause of natural disasters such as climatic changes, famines and epidemics. In the face of ignorance of the true nature of these events, such beliefs were stimulated by the need to find a scapegoat, and who better filled this need than the Jews, who had rejected Christ and thus indirectly were bringing punishment for their sins to bear upon the whole of Christendom?[80] In the end, the social need to convert may also have led some of the non-Christians to

---

77 Cohen, *Friars and Jews*, pp. 80-81. Cohen gives his name incorrectly as Miedas.
78 See Francesc Eiximenis, *Lo Crestià (selecció)*, ed. Albert Hauf (Barcelona, 1983), p. 10. The pogroms of 1392 led to the examination of these books, and Fr. Francesc clearly was disturbed by what he regarded as blasphemy against Christ and the Virgin Mary contained in the Hebrew books.
79 See above Chapter 1, p. 49.
80 Juan Manuel, *Libro de los estados*, ed. R.B. Tate and I.R. Macpherson (Oxford, 1974), explains that the Jews had been responsible for Christ's death and had thereby rejected the Christian faith.

be convinced by the friars' preaching and accept baptism, and in Gerona at least one family whose name suggests a Jewish origin lived in a house in the Mercadal, indicating perhaps that these were Jews who had converted to Christianity.[81]

The areas chosen as representative of Franciscan urban activity in the Crown of Aragon all had large Jewish communities, and the first of them, Barcelona, was perhaps the largest and most significant of all. The campaign against rabbinic literature, which aimed at bringing to light so-called blasphemous texts from the Talmud, has already been mentioned.[82] In the thirteenth century relations between the friars and the Jews were not always cordial, largely because these relationships were formed most frequently in the context of attempts by the friars to convert the Jews to Christianity.

Why was the problem of the Jews regarded so seriously in the thirteenth century? In part, this was the result of the study of contemporary Judaism and rabbinic literature, exacerbated by the public disputes between the mendicants (especially the Dominicans) and the rabbis on the relative merits of the Christian and Jewish faiths. Nowhere were these public debates so prevalent as in the territories of Aragon, where two disciples of the famous Dominican preacher Fr. Ramon de Penyafort waged an attack on contemporary Judaism.

Fr. Ramon Martí published his views in *Pugio fidei,* which Cohen regards as expounding the views of a particular school of thought initiated by Fr. Ramon de Penyafort and adopted by the Dominican order.[83] It was this polemical anti-Jewish ideology, he contends, that led to the famous Barcelona Disputation of 1263, which marked a change in the church's attitude to rabbinic Judaism. Even before this date Pope Gregory IX, in a letter to James I, had praised the king's declared intention of extirpating heresy from his lands.[84] In 1237 Franciscans acted as inquisitors in the process against the count of Foix, lord of Castellbó, among them a certain Fr. Esteve, possibly the same man who appeared in Lerida as provincial minister some years later.[85] It was

---

81 See Webster, "Col.lecció de documents," *AIEG* 28: 187-189, no. 4, where the house of Solomon, the son of Vidal de Dolça, is mentioned.
82 Cohen, *Friars and Jews,* pp. 78-81.
83 Ibid., p. 164.
84 Saldes, "La orden franciscana," p. 479.
85 An archival document (Barcelona, AC, Pia Almoina, perg. 1-6-796, 5 October 1272) indicates that a Fr. Pere Esteve was provincial minister of Aragon in 1272.

during this period that Catharism was at its height in the neighbouring lands of Languedoc, and some heretics were known to have found refuge in the adjacent territories of the count of Foix.[86] The process against the count lasted for some years, finally being resolved in the 1250s, and in character seems to be unique in Aragonese history.

The event is important not so much because of the heretical beliefs of the count, but rather because it marks the initiation of a royal campaign against heresy. James I had reconquered the island of Majorca from the Moors not long before; he was in the middle of a campaign to recover the land in the Levante, and it was vital that his territories to the north be free of any taint of unorthodoxy, from any source. In 1242 the king issued a decree, approved by Pope Innocent IV in 1246, in favour of Jews who converted to the Holy Catholic faith, at the same time ordering the archbishop of Tarragona, the bishops, Friars Preachers and Friars Minor to proclaim the word of God in towns where there were significant numbers of Jews and Moors.[87] The Jews, for their part, were expected to sit quietly and patiently while the friars preached the Christian gospel to them. To a modern historian the king's decree seems naive in the extreme, but James I seems to have believe that evangelization of his kingdom after the reconquest of the lands from the Moors could be achieved by peaceful means. This was not to be, and outbursts of popular fury against the Jews became increasingly frequent.

The Dominicans and Franciscans had been given both papal and royal authority to act as missionaries to the non-Christian minorities in Aragon, and there is evidence that they preached the word of God with extreme eloquence and enthusiasm throughout the crown territories. They embraced this aspect of James I's crusade for Christendom with such vigour that he was forced to intervene on behalf of the Jews. In 1268, the Jews of Barcelona were exempted from attending sermons preached by the Dominicans and Franciscans in the Jewish synagogues, because of the mockery and vituperations heaped upon them by the populace.[88] A curious corollary to this order appears: if the friars

---

86 See Jean Duvernoy, "Le Catharisme en Languedoc au début du XIVe siècle," in *Effacement du Catharisme? (XIIIe-XIVe s.)* (Toulouse, 1985), pp. 27–56, at 28–34.
87 Sanahuja, *História*, p. 104.
88 Barcelona, ACA, RC 15, f. 122v, published as document no. 73 in Francisco de A. de Bofarull y Sans, "Jaime I y los judíos," in *Congrés d'historia de la Corona d'Aragó dedicat al rey en Jaume I y a la seva época,* 2 vols. (Barcelona, 1909–1913), 2: 819–943, at pp. 892–893.

wished to preach in the synagogues they could continue to do so, but they were to take with them ten good Christian men and forbid entrance to the general public. Future events indicate that it was easier to write this order in a letter than to put it into practice.

The first recorded problems between Christians and Jews occurred in Barcelona, adding credence to Cohen's theory that the 1263 Disputation of Barcelona was responsible for arousing a frenzy of hostility and anti-Semitic feelings. The Jews had become heavily involved in credit for the campaigns of the reconquest, and this had much to do with the vehemence of the people's feelings.[89] It is probable that these emotions had been smouldering under the surface for some time, and the Disputation provided the excuse for them to be expressed publicly.

The Jews were a prosperous group, marginalized socially, and because of their financial ability frequently rose to positions of importance, although they could not accept appointments as vicars or judges.[90] As legal codes were drawn up for the towns under the jurisdiction of the Crown of Aragon, the life of the Jews became increasingly circumscribed by regulations which governed their behaviour. The very fact that the Jews were treated as a class apart marked them in the eyes of their contemporaries as outside Christian society, and it was only one step further in that thought process to regard them as unacceptable, and even dangerous outsiders. In 1279 Peter II was obliged to write to the *batlle* of Barcelona and to his officials elsewhere within his territories, enjoining them to forbid Christians from approaching the synagogues when the friars were preaching to the Jews.[91] The matter had become one of maintaining public order, and the friars were making the problem worse by attempting to coerce the Jews into converting, threatening them with violence and infamy if they refused.

An interesting series of documents from 1298 refers to the usurious practices of the Jews. Usury was against the precepts of the Christian church in the medieval period. The first of the documents refers to an Inquisition into these practices in Huesca, and an adjunct to the process is the guardian or lector of the Franciscans.[92] The document states that there had been reports of usury in the city and in the diocese of Huesca,

---

89 Bisson, *Medieval Crown of Aragon*, pp. 74–75.
90 Ibid., p. 75.
91 Sanahuja, *História*, p. 105.
92 Barcelona, ACA, RC 319, f. 24, 7 January 1297 [1298].

and that the Jewish quarter (*aljama*) was required to produce evidence of all the debts owed to the inhabitants in this connection. If it did not do so, the Jews would be punished by the royal arm of justice. The king, emphasizing that he was empowered to act in this way because of special favours to Aragon by the Holy See, demanded that any money collected by the Jews as usury be returned to those concerned. If there was a surplus, once all financial commitments had been met, it should be given to religious or pious uses, or to the poor.

The Franciscans stood to gain from these inquisitorial practices, and some of their enthusiasm in converting the Jews might well relate to the benefits they hoped to acquire thereby. It is perhaps relevant to the prevailing atmosphere of hostility provoked by the mendicants' sermons to note that the king referred to the Jews as "dogs," a term more frequently employed when talking of the Moors. Such terminology applied to the non-Christian minorities was not calculated to diminish the bitterness shown to them by the Christians, and scarcely seems to support the traditional view of tolerance towards them in the Middle Ages.[93]

A year later, in 1299, James II gave permission to Ramon Llull to preach the truth of the Catholic faith in all the synagogues of the Jews and Moors within his realm, perhaps to prevent mass disturbances occurring, but thereby seeming to confirm that the decrees of 1279 had had little or no effect on the continuance of this practice. The discovery of usurious practices within his realm had only exacerbated the king's desire to convert the Jews to Christianity.[94] The king was concerned that the intransigent attitude of the friars was leading to a dangerous situation of intolerance on the part of the populace towards the non-Christians. Had he been able to see what happened in 1391 in many parts of the Peninsula, he would have realized the wisdom of his decrees

---

93 See Américo Castro, *The Spaniards: An Introduction to Their History*, trans. Willard F. King and Selma Margaretten (Berkeley, Los Angeles and London, 1971), pp. 501–503. Castro claims that the intolerance *began* at the end of the fourteenth century and was largely caused by "the weakening of authority held by the seignoral class and ... the increase in the size of the Christian population." Castro's comments are primarily directed to Castile, but a parallel might be suggested between what happened here at the end of the fourteenth century after the sermons preached by Ferrant Martínez and others in Castile and what happened in the Crown of Aragon after the sermons preached there by the mendicant orders.

94 Antoni Rubió i Lluch, ed. *Documents per l'història de la cultura catalana mig.eval*, 2 vols. (Barcelona, 1908–1921), 1: 13–14.

recommending conversion by persuasion rather than by force, but much water was to pass beneath the bridges which led to the opening of the floodgates in the latter half of the fourteenth century.[95]

Little has been said of the conversion of the Moors, though the discussion of the reconquest and resettlement of their territory has amply illustrated the Aragonese king's crusade for Christendom in those areas. The conversion of the Sayyid Abu Zayd and the subsequent entry of some of his relatives into the Franciscan order provides evidence of the most significant of all attempts at conversion of the Moors. It is pertinent to remark that the attitude adopted by medieval rulers to the Moors was somewhat less intransigent than that shown to the Jews. The Jews were a prosperous group, marginalized socially and expected to wear distinguishing signs, but the disciples of Islam, although similar conditions pertained for them, were regarded as less inimical to Christianity than Judaism was, because they had not been responsible for Christ's death on the Cross.[96] The centralizing policy of the Aragonese monarchy could not tolerate the presence of any non-conforming groups: in this respect Jews, Moors and heretics all constituted a threat to the well-being of the corpus mysticum.

---

95 It is interesting to note here that the legal code of Alfonso X, in the section on the Jews, emphasizes the need to convert through peaceful persuasion rather than through force. See *Partidas* 7.24.6, where Jews who become Christians are protected from undue exertion of pressure because "nuestro señor Dios non quiere nin ama servicio quel sea fecho por fuerza" (our Lord God does not want nor does he like service which is given as a result of force). *Las siete partidas del rey don Alfonso el Sabio,* 3 vols. (Madrid, 1972), 3: 669–675, at pp. 672–673. The king's letter (Barcelona, ACA, RC 42, ff. 148v–149, 8 October 1279) has been mentioned in Chapter 1 above (pp. 44 and 49), since some of the Franciscan houses appear for the first time in the chancellery registers in this document. The list of Franciscan houses that received the king's letter is fairly comprehensive: Barcelona, Gerona, Vic, Vilafranca del Penedès, Cervera, Montblanc, Lerida, Castelló d'Empúries, Tarragona, Monzón, Tortosa, Huesca, Saragossa, Tarazona, Ejea, Borja, Calatayud, Daroca, Teruel, Valencia, Xàtiva and Barbastro, representing the convents in Catalonia, Valencia and Aragon. In all these towns there were nuclei of Jews, many of whom had risen to positions of trust in the royal administration, and it is clear that the conflagration which had started in Barcelona had rapidly spread to the rest of the Crown of Aragon.

96 Alfonso X, el Sabio, *Partidas* 7.24.11, *Las siete partidas,* 3: 675, refers to the sign to be worn by the Jews. In Partida 7 Alfonso devotes Title 24 (eleven laws) to the Jews, and Title 25 (ten laws) to the Moors.

Ramon Llull's permission to preach to both Jews and Saracens recalls his missionary zeal, a vocation which took him to Africa, where he is believed to have died in 1315 although his death probably occurred the following year in Majorca.[97] His establishment of the college of Miramar in Majorca was a significant step in providing training for Franciscan missionaries to Africa, and serves to emphasize the centrality of the Franciscan mission to convert the Moors. The custody of Barcelona was responsible for the missionaries who went to Tunis and to the land of the Tartars, referred to as Aquilonia tartaria. It is not surprising to find a similar order being issued to the Dominicans and Franciscans to preach the word of God to the Jews and the Saracens in all places within Aragon where they were found to reside.[98] Attempts at conversion continued and became a commonplace of the late thirteenth and fourteenth centuries.

Family Background of the Friars

It has been demonstrated that the majority of the friars were drawn from families of small traders in whose midst they lived, but others, especially in Aragon and Valencia, came from wealthier backgrounds; and a few examples of friars whose families supported the Franciscans will serve to illustrate the fact that it was mainly the merchants and lesser nobles who were responsible for the friars' acceptance in the towns and who, themselves, profited most from this association. To follow the fortunes of many of these medieval families requires long and tedious research, and it is only recently that attempts have been made to trace some of the prominent Barcelona families. The Examenis family perhaps provides the best example of several generations of devotion to the mendicant cause, but there are others, like the Guerau family in Gerona, who could boast of a similar tradition.[99] In most cases, it has been impossible to follow

---

[97] In October 1315 James II wrote to the provincial minister of the Franciscans, Fr. Romeo Ortiz, on behalf of Ramon Llull, asking him to release Fr. Simó de Puigcerdà so that he might go to Tunis and translate Llull's *Ars consilii;* but there is no evidence to suggest that he completed this task. See Garcías Palou, *El Miramar,* pp. 78 and 336.

[98] Sanahuja, *História,* p. 105.

[99] See above Chapter 1, p. 24 and Jill R. Webster, "Tradiciones y datos medievales para la história franciscana," *AIA* 44 (1984), 199–210, at p. 209. The names of the two Guerau family friars appear among those resident in Gerona in the 1330s.

the fortunes of more than one generation, largely because of the lack of documentation dating from the early thirteenth century.

One of the earliest references concerns Fr. Pascasi de Vall-llebrera, one of the most outstanding friars of his day. In 1311 the sale was recorded of a field by Franca, the widow of Andreu de Vall-llebrera of Castellfort in the village of Morella, to Bonafonat, another member of the Vall-llebrera family, who was a citizen of Lerida.[100] At this time Fr. Pascasi lived in the Saragossa house; he is registered as one of the executors of the will of the late noble Sancho de Antillón of Huesca, suggesting that his family was well known to the crown.[101] Similarly, in Puigcerdà one of those who wished to found a house in the *vila* was Fr. Pere Llaguna, whose sister's will predates by nearly five years the actual establishment of the Franciscan house and provides information relevant to the process of its foundation.[102] The Llaguna family appear to have been residents of Puigcerdà for some time, as there are references to several members of the family from 1315 until the late fifteenth century.[103] Like many other families, they continued to give their loyal support to the Franciscan cause in Puigcerdà, a situation which seems to have been characteristic of allegiances formed and main-

---

100 Barcelona, ACA, RC 146, f. 55r–v and 73, 13 February 1310 [1311].
101 Ibid., f. 218, 8 June 1311.
102 This has been discussed above in Chapter 1, p. 67; see also Jill R. Webster, "El desconocido convento de Puigcerdà," *AIA* 49 (1989), 167–194.
103 See also Puigcerdà, AHC, Mateu d'Oliana and Guillem Hualart, *Liber testamentorum* (29 June 1321–10 July 1322): f. 20v, 1 March 1321 [1322], where Ermesenda, wife of Guillem Llaguna of Puigcerdà, requests burial in the Franciscan house, for which she leaves 30 sous together with a further 20 sous for masses "ad notitiam" Fr. Pere Llaguna; and f. 24, 11 April 1322, where Matea, wife of Guillem Cerdà of Puigcerdà and daughter of Guillem Llaguna, requests burial in the Franciscan cemetery and leaves 40 sous for this purpose and 8 pounds to Fr. Pere Llaguna for prayers for her soul. In AHC, Arnald Embertad and Bernat Guillem de Lorà, *Liber testamentorum* (24 June 1324–27 April 1325), f. 3, 9 July 1324, Guilleuma, wife of Pere Llaguna of Puigcerdà, not only chooses burial in the Franciscan cemetery but appoints as her executor Fr. Pere Llaguna. She seems to have wanted an elaborate funeral mass in the parish church of St. Mary, at which thirty priests were to sing. Ten sous were to go to her executor, and Fr. Pere Llaguna and another resident of the Puigcerdà house and native of the town, Fr. Arnau Colomer, were to receive 40 sous and 5 sous respectively. The fifteenth-century document is preserved with the unclassified parchments for La Cerdanya in the archives of the abbey of Montserrat.

tained by citizens of many generations to religious orders in this mountain town.[104] Where documentation survives, analogous patterns could probably be drawn for many other towns within the Crown of Aragon, and some of these will be mentioned in the discussion of the participation of individual friars in conventual life.

For the present, a less agreeable aspect of medieval life must be mentioned. It might be concluded that, given the fact that the friars came from the merchant families in whose midst they lived and carried out their duties, relationships between the two would invariably have been amicable. This was not always so, and there were those who did not support the Franciscans, who envied them their success or whose own ambitions directly conflicted with the life of the friars. The secular clergy are one noteworthy example of this, but they were not alone in their opposition to the expansion of the Franciscan mission. Heirs to the wills which provide us with so much valuable information frequently disputed the legacies left to the friars, but not always because there was insufficient money to meet the bequests; in a number of cases their opposition stemmed from other causes. Some of these beneficiaries believed that the friars had used spiritual coercion to wrest legacies from the dying, thus unfairly claiming bequests which more properly belonged to the family of the deceased, a situation that was not uncommon in the thirteenth and fourteenth centuries. The friars often had a legitimate claim to a portion of the estate, which would include the fees due to them for performing the burial rites; but this would not make it any easier for them to convince the relatives of the deceased that they were also entitled to the bequests.

To understand some of the objections raised by heirs to the estates, it is necessary to bear in mind that many of the testators would not have had much interest in the well-being of the friars, but would have supported them for reasons of expediency, not least because they believed that in this way they would earn their passage to heaven. With

---

104 See Jill R. Webster, "El desconocido convento de Puigcerdà," *AIA* 49 (1989), 167-194, at pp. 167-194. Dated 1 November 1488, it refers to the foundation of an anniversary mass for the soul of Francesc Basseda, to be said in the chapel of All Angels in the Franciscan church at Puigcerdà. The executors of the will of Francesc Basseda de la Llaguna were Berenguer Llaguna of Ripoll, the guardian of the convent at Puigcerdà, and Fr. Francesc Esteve, master in theology. Some members of the family had obviously moved to neighbouring townships by the date of this will.

this in mind, most testators in the thirteenth and fourteenth centuries would expect to leave a nominal amount to pious causes and slightly more to the religious house or parish church they attended. Charitable bequests depended on the popularity of a particular cause at any given time; in cities such as Barcelona and Gerona, where the urban environment was well established by the early fourteenth century, nominal giving seems almost to have died out, and liaisons with one or more charitable or religious foundation to have been firmly established. In Majorca and Vic, the level of bequests does not seem to drop off after 1300, and it may be that there is a reason for this disparity which is not immediately apparent. For the moment the discrepancy can only be noted, as definitive conclusions require an extensive comparison of a number of factors, not all of which are available, given the state of extant documentation in some of the areas. The different pattern of giving is only relevant here in so much as the disputes between heirs to estates and the friars suggest that some of the donations were made, not from conviction, but because of interference from an external source.

If this is taken a step further, it is not difficult to give credence to the accusation that on some occasions the testator was pressured into giving to particular charities. Among the abuses prevalent at the end of the thirteenth century and brought to light by Franciscan reformers was the exertion of undue pressure by certain friars in order to ensure that a wealthy person left a large share of his worldly possessions to the order or, contrary to the rule of the order, even to individual friars for their own use.[105] In the Crown of Aragon, it was not uncommon for friars to receive special gifts of money to help them buy books or to meet other needs. Records do not say whether or not they handed this money over to the order, although one of the statutes of the general chapter held in 1279 decreed that under no circumstances should a friar be a beneficiary of a will, suggesting that some friars, not necessarily in Aragon, regarded the legacies as their own personal property.

The question of misappropriation or diminution of legacies prompts the raising of another question, to which no definite answer can be given but which is fundamental to any understanding of the thirteenth and fourteenth centuries. Is the apparent diminution of pro forma legacies to the Franciscans after 1300 an acknowledgment of the order's vows of poverty, or does it reveal a dissatisfaction with the way in which the

---

105 Moorman, *History of the Franciscan Order*, pp. 186-187.

friars had abandoned their early austerity of life, misappropriated legacies and acquired property and wealth? This will be brought up again in relation to the emergence of the Spiritual Franciscans, but the order had already strayed far from the vision of Saint Francis, for whom any sign of wealth or possessions was anathema and directly opposed to the ideal he had tried to convey in the rule of the order. The rule itself had only been drawn up under pressure from Pope Innocent III, who had been astute enough to see that there was a danger that the followers of Saint Francis would lapse into heresy if they were not given some form of coherent structure. Subsequent events proved the wisdom of Innocent's decision, but also the impossibility of preventing the spread of heretical ideas, even in a structured organization.

Before the Franciscans are condemned for having abandoned the way of poverty, or the citizens for their lack of generosity, it should be remembered that the end of the thirteenth century had witnessed the rise of two further mendicant orders, the Augustinians and the Carmelites, which made similar demands upon their contemporaries at a time when adverse climatic conditions and subsequent economic crises caused considerable hardship to many citizens. It is not surprising that wills were contested and disputes became more frequent as people tried to adjust to less prosperous times. Although these new orders had little impact on life in Aragon until the second half of the fourteenth century, the difficulties they had to establish themselves, and the poverty and poor conditions they had to endure, provided a clear contrast to the more comfortable life of the Dominicans and Franciscans, emphasizing in this way the wealth and property these orders had amassed by 1300.

For all that, disputed bequests were not confined to the Dominicans and Franciscans but extended to the new orders, which quickly faced the same resistance from relatives who saw their entitlement to the estates of deceased family members slipping from their grasp, in much the same way that the clergy saw their income disappearing into the coffers of the convents. Conflicts over wills frequently reached the point that the only way to resolve them was for both the friars and the beneficiaries to take the matter to court. It is from such records that the conclusion can be drawn that disputes of this kind must not only have been routine but at times extremely bitterly contested by the parties concerned. As might be expected, the conflicting interests of the friars and their neighbours were not confined to wills, but could be seen in the daily irritations typical of urban life. There were three main causes of such friction, the presence of those who plied undesirable trades in the vicinity of the convent, the ambitious building plans of people whose property adjoined the Franciscan house and interfered with their privacy, and the disruption of their devotions by those whose work produced noise and unpleasant odours. Like the disputes, these situations were not confined to any particular city but existed throughout the Crown of Aragon. Local courts had insufficient power to settle the matters at issue, and it was frequently necessary for the parties concerned to take the case to the royal court for arbitration. Even then there is evidence that the losers, almost invariably those who interfered with the friars' devotions, did not accept the decisions handed down to them and, whenever possible, tried on subsequent occasions either to ply their undesirable trades or to proceed with the aggrandizement of their property.

A few of the most persistent cases of citizens whose work or ambitions made it impossible for the Franciscans to enjoy their property exemplify an aspect of medieval urban life which has received little prominence in studies of the mendicant orders. These difficulties represent the adjustment of a predominantly rural society to a new way of life in an urban environment, where noise and pollution were inevitable, and they have an importance far beyond the problems they posed for the Franciscans. Environmentalists in the twentieth century frequently raise issues very similar to those which so concerned the Franciscans in the thirteenth and fourteenth centuries, showing that they are endemic to urban life. The first example of the prolonged conflicts between the friars and their neighbours is to be found in an official denunciation by Fr. Berenguer de Lledó, the guardian of the Vic house, of a citizen by the name of Pere de Camdeuna who was having a building constructed next to the garden and cloisters of the Franciscan convent, to the "prejudice and harm" of the friars.[106] Those present at the time of the denunciation all agreed that Pere de Camdeuna should remove the building. The response of the delegate of the procurators of the archdeacon of Vic, to whom the complaint had been sent, was immediate. If the friars wished to make an injunction against the citizen with the purpose of having the building demolished, they were to present it in writing before the following Friday (giving them about eight days to prepare their case). Pere de Camdeuna was also advised of the action to be taken by the Franciscans. The remaining pages of the notarial

---

106 Vic, AE, ACF, Manuals notarials, no. 19 (1281–1282), ff. 117, 119v and 122v (19 June, 17 June and 2 July 1282, respectively).

manual which might have provided the resolution of this quarrel between the friars and Pere de Camdeuna have been so badly damaged by water that they are no longer legible.

Similar complaints occurred in Barcelona and Gerona at the beginning of the fourteenth century. In Barcelona, there is the parchment preserved by the Franciscans themselves and letters from the king concerning the complaints of the friars against Felip de Otina. The matter seems to have been far more contentious than the complaint from Vic, perhaps because both parties concerned seem to have chosen to ignore James II's letter of 17 May 1292 to the *batlle* of Barcelona, ordering him to prohibit the construction of windows which overlooked the Franciscan convent or houses which were or would be situated on the public thoroughfare leading to Montjüic.[107] No building was to be permitted in the vicinity of the convent if it overlooked either the cemetery or garden of the Franciscans; nor was it permitted to have windows which looked over the square adjoining the cemetery, or to place sewers or rubbish dumps in any place that would result in the stench pervading the square. Felip de Otina, possibly perfectly cognizant of the king's decree, directly contravened its provisions and had a window built in his house which overlooked the square, one side of which was occupied by the Franciscan convent.[108]

The friars argued that the square belonged to them by reason of a gift made by the late Berenguer de Rubí and by Berenguera, the widow of Guillem de Vic, his nephew. The document describes the exact nature of the dispute: the friars for their part stated that the legal documents at the time the contract was drawn up declared the square between the convent and Felip de Otina's house to be their property; the councillors of the city of Barcelona, on the other hand, upheld the right of Felip de Otina to have a window which opened out on to the square, because, they said, it was public property.

As no agreement seemed to be possible between the two parties, an appeal was been made to James II to settle the dispute, and his letter subsequently made clear that certain types of businesses, workshops and

---

107 Barcelona, ACA, RC 260, f. 69, 17 May 1292.
108 Barcelona, ACA, ORM, carp. Franciscans, perg. L.6, 18 June 1315; and ACA, RC 212, ff. 18–20, of the same date. Both documents elaborate at length on the conflict between Felip de Otina and the Franciscans.

other buildings were not be erected in the vicinity of the convent.[109] As the square was adjacent to the seashore, the king stated, it was also prohibited to build ships there or to erect breakwaters without wooden supports ("molas sine ligamina") which in any way could interfere with the divine office. The by-laws, he contended, did not prevent Felip de Otina from having a window which overlooked the square, the rationale being that this in no way impeded the activities of the Franciscans. The window overlooking the square did not contradict his earlier provisions, although the Franciscans could claim that it was an intrusion on their privacy. A second letter from James II states that the owners of the houses in the street which led to the *dressanes,* or shipping arsenal, argued that, according to the customs of Barcelona, they had every right to have windows which gave on to the public thoroughfare. The friars had objected to these windows because they allowed their owners to look right into their dormitory and other rooms of the convent.

Some of these neighbours were also engaged in noisy trades, which disturbed the peace of the Franciscan house. This letter from the king reminded the parties concerned that both his mother, Queen Constance, and his brother Alfonso were buried in the Franciscan church, and out of reverence for the memory of these members of the royal family, if for no other reason, consideration should be given to the convent. Notwithstanding that it was not fitting that the inhabitants should be able to look into the dormitory or garden of the friars, there was no reason why doors and windows giving on to the public street should not be permitted, provided their owners did nothing which would interrupt the friars in their devotions. The king's decision, which was to be observed in perpetuity, was clearly an attempt at an amicable compromise, but nearly a century later there were still problems over Felip de Otina's property.[110]

The example from Gerona shows that again there was a bitter contest among the parties concerned. Two citizens were involved, Bernat Venrell, a cloth merchant who wished to rebuild a wall, and Ramon

---

109 The wording in the documents referred to in the previous notes is very specific: "tabulas nec envanam [protruding building] ... nec operatoria vel alia hedifici ... per que posset stringi dicta platea."

110 See Barcelona, ACA, ORM, carp. Franciscans, perg. 10 (B.15). King Martin on 26 June 1397 confirms the privilege granted by James II, protecting the Franciscans from intrusion on their privacy but repeating the details contained in the earlier document.

Calvet, junior, who claimed a piece of land between the Franciscan church and the river Onyar as his property, saying that he had permission to build on it.[111] A year earlier the Franciscans in Gerona had taken the first matter to the king, claiming that Bernat Venrell had begun to build a wall contrary to the established custom that no such construction was to take place close to the walls of the convent.[112]

In his reply Prince Alfonso, writing on behalf of the king, agreed that if the friars were able to prove in the presence of the bishop of Gerona or his representative that the wall concerned had belonged to the convent, then Venrell should not be allowed to build his new wall; if he did so, he would be subject to a penalty of 500 sous. Venrell's wall was situated to the west of the garden and east of the house owned by Calvet, who claimed that the construction of the wall also concerned him, and that he should be included in any agreement between the friars and Bernat Venrell. The custodian of the Gerona house, Fr. Arnau de Castllà, and the guardian, Fr. Joan de Roure, gave their consent to the construction of the wall.[113] Subsequent records show that Venrell continued to build on to his property, situating his linen mill immediately adjacent to the church and cemetery, and that the disagreements between the parties did not cease immediately.[114]

---

111 See Webster, "Col.lecció de documents," *AIEG* 29: 62–64, no. 31.
112 Barcelona, ACA, RC 372, f. 186, 1 May 1323.
113 See also Gerona, AH, G.1 (Arnau Despoll), no. 3, 17 February 1337 [1338], where Venrell is told that he cannot have an *envanam*, "protrusion," nor may his construction exceed certain specifications, among them the building of exits or entrances on to the square. The tenor of the document is very similar to the one concerning Felip de Otina in Barcelona.
114 Barcelona, ACA, RC 601, f. 126, 13 December 1339, is a letter from the king to Berenguer de Pujol, jurisperitus for Gerona, written on behalf of the Franciscans, who were still vexed over the question of taxes due to them "in emphiteosis" (a long-term lease in return for a small annual payment) from Ramon Calvet for the houses next to the church or cemetery of the friars and between the linen mill and the bridge leading to the church. This document refers to the fact that the friars had won their case against Ramon Calvet but, because of the guardian's unfamiliarity with the procedure, the taxes due to the royal chancellery had not been paid, as the reply was incorrectly drawn up. The king's letter reiterates the annoyance caused to the Franciscans by Ramon Calvet's linen mill, which disturbed them at mass. Berenguer de Pujol is asked to see that the matter is settled expeditiously so that the taxes due are received within a month from the date of his letter, and reminding him that the friars are mendicants and poor. On 7 November 1340 the

The question of the ownership of the land between the church and the river Onyar was important to Bernat Venrell and to the Franciscans, who, when they wished to enlarge their convent, could have expanded in that direction (a dubious privilege, given the river's propensity to flood and cause severe damage to property in Gerona built along its banks).[115] Ramon Calvet was able to prove that he had been given permission to build on that land, although it is clear that his property was still owned by the Franciscans and that he was required to pay taxes to them. It can only be conjectured that the friars were afraid that Venrell, had he been able to prove his claim to the land, would merely exacerbate the already untenable situation regarding the strong and unpleasant odours which wafted towards the Franciscan convent from the linen mill when the flax was laid out to dry. The activities of this linen mill seem to have been a perennial source of annoyance to the friars, largely because of the noise it made and the unpleasant smell of the flax.[116]

The very nature of life in a city is fraught with numerous difficulties, largely because people of all kinds gather in a relatively small geographical area and have different interests which they believe should be accommodated, even to the detriment of their neighbours. Traders arrive from overseas or from the surrounding countryside, travellers take their rest in the inns and friars visit their confreres; all this is to be expected, but without the cooperation of all citizens peaceful coexistence is unattainable. Even so, beneath the prosperity of every mercantile economy lies the "reverse side of the coin," the poverty and misery of the unemployed or unemployable, the diseased and the orphaned, and finally those who cater to the baser needs of mankind, the prostitutes and those who earn their living by exploiting their bodies. Homosexuality, regarded as a form of moral depravity in the Middle Ages, was rife in many medieval towns, and prostitutes must have found it worthwhile to congregate

---

king wrote to his jurisperitus in Gerona, repeating the contents of his earlier letter, and adding that he had been told by the Franciscans that other houses built in the same area were in fact owned by them, and the taxes on them should have been included in the original request. It is clear that Ramon Calvet held these properties "in emphiteosis" and refused to pay the taxes due on them.

115 Jaume Marquès i Casanovas, *Girona vella* (Gerona, 1979), pp. 52–56, where the incidence of floods caused by the river Onyar is described in detail.
116 See Webster, "Col.lecció de documents."

in areas close to the markets and the churches, where crowds constantly gathered, so that they could make their contacts with greater ease.[117]

Among the documents preserved in the royal registers are frequent complaints from all the mendicant friars that "viles mulieres" were plying their trades in the vicinity of their churches, thereby leading the faithful away from the care of their souls to the prostitution of their bodies. The friars repeatedly asked the king to order these women to move away from the vicinity of the convent, but it seems they often returned, no doubt because there they had a ready-made clientele and other areas of the city would have been less favourable for their rendezvous. In part they were responsible for another problem, the dumping of waste in the vicinity of the convent, which, the Franciscans complained with some justification, made the area unsavoury and impeded the movement of the faithful on Sundays and holy days. There is no evidence that the friars attempted to recall these women to the way of virtue, nor does there seem to be much concern on their part for the poor at this time. They worked in hospitals in at least two places, and perhaps elsewhere, and it may be that the lack of documentation is more to blame for this omission than the Franciscans themselves.

The inhabitants of a medieval town were not unlike the city dwellers of today, drawn from every class and condition of people. Lack of hygiene, poor nutrition and unmade roads led to terrible squalor and misery for the poor. Rising up from the poverty and darkness of medieval streets were the palatial dwellings of the merchants and the towers of the parish and conventual churches, providing a contrast which can still be appreciated in the surviving older areas of Barcelona, Gerona and other towns which preserve some of the Gothic streets. Although they would be unrecognizable to their medieval inhabitants, for modern city dwellers these streets are the only link with the intricate mosaic of medieval urban life in the Crown of Aragon.

The examples given to illustrate the strong connections between the friars and the urban traders help place these relationships within the

---

117 Among the many studies published recently on this topic, especially pertinent are those of John Boswell, *Christianity, Social Tolerance and Homosexuality* (Chicago, 1980), pp. 269–302; Vern L. Bullough, "Prostitution in the Later Middle Ages," in *Sexual Practices and the Medieval Church,* ed. Vern L. Bullough and James Brundage (Buffalo, 1982), pp. 176–186; and Bronisław Geremek, *The Margins of Society in Late Medieval Paris,* trans. Jean Birrell from the French ed. of 1976 (Cambridge and Paris, 1987).

context of a developing urban environment, with all its conflicting demands and interests. The conventual life of the friars and the individual tasks which distinguish them from their contemporaries, both illustrated in a later chapter, show how the bonds between the Franciscans and the traders were forged and strengthened through daily contact. Nowhere is this more apparent than in the wills of the thirteenth and fourteenth centuries, especially in Catalonia and Majorca, where the majority of testators were drawn from the urban environment in which the friars lived and worked.[118]

The close association between the friars and their neighbours was not only to their mutual advantage; at times it served as a useful bulwark against the non-Christian minorities in their midst, many of whom were engaged in direct commercial competition with the Christians. Cohen explains the support the friars received from the merchant classes in precisely these terms, regarding them as being more responsive to the needs of the traders and more in tune with the mores of the marketplace than perhaps traditional historians have implied.[119] This is an over-simplification of the situation in the thirteenth and fourteenth centuries, but there is no doubt that the majority of the friars at this time were the sons of prominent traders and not unnaturally shared the hopes and fears, the dreams and disappointments and the activities and achievements of the class to which they belonged.

---

118 See Batlle and Casas, "La caritat privada," where a comparative analysis is made of legacies to the mendicant orders and other charitable institutions in the wills of the Pia Almoina preserved in Barcelona cathedral. A similar unpublished analysis has been made for Vic: see Immaculada Ollich i Castanyer, "Aplicació sistemàtica d'ordinadors a la documentació medieval de la plana de Vic" (doctoral dissertation, University of Barcelona, 1981). These and the documents published by Webster, "Col.lecció de documents," give abundant evidence of the interaction and interdependence of the friars and the middle classes.

119 Cohen, *Friars and Jews*, p. 41.

4

The Cure of Souls

James I's crusade for the recovery of territory from the Moors and the parallel rise of burgesses and friars were not the only events of importance in the thirteenth century, for the church at large was to react to the impact of new situations arising from the presence of a larger urban population. At its helm, the pope was to encourage and support both James and the friars, and the parochial clergy must have felt threatened, not only by the newcomers, but by the fact that they often had to relinquish territory they considered indisputably theirs in favour of the Dominicans, Franciscans and other mendicant orders. To understand better the thirteenth-century revolution in ecclesiastical affairs in Aragon, we must take into account events taking place in the church in Europe and the relations between the spiritual and secular arms of Christendom. It is well to remember that the disputes which arose were occasioned largely by the emergence of national territorial rights, which did not always coincide with the politics of the papacy; and to bear in mind the significant increase in the numbers of those able to minister to their contemporaries, either through an unordained ministry, or more important for the parish clergy concerned, through the ordained priesthood.

Rivalry between the two spiritual groups, the friars and the clergy, was inevitable, for both were attending to the spiritual needs of their contemporaries and thereby both competing for the same material rewards. That the friars in the early part of the thirteenth century, initially the Dominicans and after 1250 the Franciscans, were better educated and more appealing to the new middle class, which regarded them as allies, must have dismayed the clergy, who foresaw the gradual erosion of their power. That the king and papacy supported the work of the friars, primarily because it suited their own political aspirations, must have caused bewilderment and disillusion among the parish priests, whose scanty preparation made them unready to meet the exigencies of a new age. It was perhaps unfair to expect them to respond to the new demands made upon them, and even less reasonable to expect that they would welcome enthusiastically those who seemed to have advantages which they could not hope to obtain.

The surviving documentation affords copious illustrations of the bitter animosity between the friars and the secular clergy, but first it is relevant to take a brief look at the motives behind papal protection of the friars and at the privileges the mendicant orders were given by the papacy which caused them to come into conflict with the parish priests.

The Order of Friars Minor had been approved verbally by Pope Innocent III, the first draft of a written rule dating from 1221 and the definitive version approved by Pope Honorius III in 1223.[1] At first, many of the Franciscans were not ordained, but they gradually assumed a greater similarity to the Dominicans in the way they fulfilled their mission, and by the middle of the thirteenth century many Franciscans also took holy orders.[2] This was like a declaration of war to the parish priests, who had seen the simple houses in which the Franciscans first lived transformed into splendid convents, thanks to the generosity of their parishioners. At first they were reluctant to accept these gifts, as their rule did not allow them to handle money, and to get over this difficulty Pope Gregory IX in his bull *Quo elongati* regarded the property used by the friars as still the property of the donors.[3]

Innocent IV in *Ordinem vestrum* transferred the ownership to the Holy See, no doubt foreseeing the inherent problems in allowing the original donors to retain even nominal ownership. In practice these provisions had little effect on the way the friars acquired both property and money, except that a third party, the procurator, was required to act as an intermediary in all transactions involving the handling of money. Such papal enactments as these would have conveyed to the parish priests the message that the support they could hope to receive from the papacy in their grievances against the friars was likely to be minimal.

---

1   David Knowles, *The Religious Orders in England,* 3 vols. (Cambridge, 1948–1959, repr. 1979), 1: 129–130. Much of the discussion in the following pages is taken from this work.
2   See John R.H. Moorman, *A History of the Franciscan Order from its Origins to the Year 1517* (Oxford, 1968; repr. Chicago, 1988), p. 54. Even before the rule had been drawn up priests were joining the group of friars, and it is clear from the activities of the Franciscans within the Crown of Aragon that many had accepted ordination.
3   Ibid., p. 120.

Much more serious were the subsequent papal bulls in favour of the friars, many of which directly affected the livelihood enjoyed by the parish priests. The friars, as they grew more numerous and spread throughout Europe, had gradually encroached on the economic and spiritual preserves of the secular clergy. The bishops had no objection to them coming into their dioceses, but they had to protect the interests of their own priests. Many of the friars had acquired a reputation as eloquent preachers and had lured away some of the faithful from the parish churches, hearing their confessions, conducting marriage ceremonies, burying their dead and undertaking exactly the same duties which had hitherto been the sole prerogative of the parish priests.[4] The clergy felt that they had been betrayed by the papacy, as they complained of the interference of the friars in the work of their parishes. Indeed, Saint Francis too might have felt betrayed had he seen how his simple band of men was gradually being transformed into a structured order which competed in many areas with the parochial clergy.

Throughout the thirteenth and fourteenth centuries appeals were made by the secular clergy to the pope, asking for clarification of the friars' rights and demanding that action be taken to prevent their usurping parochial territory. Innocent IV curtailed mendicant rights severely in his *Etsi animarum,* promulgated in 1254 but revoked by his successor Gregory X shortly after.[5] If the mendicants were to fulfil a useful role in the cities, it was clearly impractical for the papacy to accede to the demands of the parish clergy that the friars be prevented from preaching, hearing confessions, burying the dead or carrying out the functions of a parish priest, except on certain very clearly defined occasions.

With the growth of the Franciscan order the situation between priests and friars deteriorated. The mendicant orders were acquiring popularity and material prosperity, and in so doing were directly jeopardizing the continuity of the diocesan structure. In 1274 the question was once more raised at the Council of Lyons, but the friars were strongly represented there and Pope Gregory X merely confirmed the privileged position of the Franciscans and Dominicans, suppressing smaller mendicant orders like the Friars of the Sack.[6] Seven years later Pope Martin IV issued the bull *Ad fructus uberes,* which gave them full permission to preach

---

4   Moorman, *History of the Franciscan Order,* p. 143.
5   Ibid., p. 122.
6   Ibid., pp. 177–178.

and hear confessions; although there were other attempts on the part of the secular clergy to prevent the friars from encroaching on what they considered their territory, this bull of 1281 was really a victory for the mendicant orders.

This did not mean that relations between the clergy and the friars were peaceful in the urban centres where their interests were bound to conflict. In the realms of Aragon, and more especially in Aragon itself, disputes often became violent, at times threatening the lives of the friars or the sanctity of their burial grounds. Valencia provides the most extensive arbitration judgment on the rights of the two parties, but the fact that it dates from the end of the fourteenth century merely goes to show how bitter and long-lasting were these controversies.[7] By that time both the Augustinians and Carmelites had established houses throughout the Iberian Peninsula, and had carved up yet further the diminishing pie of the parish clergy. By the end of the fourteenth century economic and social conditions had worsened, and the Black Death, papal schism and increasing corruption in the church gave credence to fears of the millennium, problems which belong more properly to a subsequent study but which began to emerge even before the great epidemic of 1348.

There are many aspects of the relations between the papacy and the friars which bear closer examination, none so clearly documented as the support given to the Franciscans in the exercise of their spiritual mission in the cities and in the conversion of the Jews and Moors both at home and overseas. This can first be seen in the privileges granted to the order through its individual houses, and in the way in which they were entrusted with special duties, often carrying out delicate diplomatic negotiations, for which they had no specialized training. In King James's territory this was no different from elsewhere in Europe, a two-way arrangement by which either legates were sent from the papacy to Aragon or friars from the Peninsula were chosen as papal ambassadors when the occasion warranted.

The first Franciscan papal delegate to the realms of Aragon whose name is known was Fr. Desideri. His first task was a dubious one, that of bringing James to recognition of the terrible sin he had committed in having the bishop of Gerona's tongue cut out, and for which James had

---

7 See Jill R. Webster, *Per Déu o per diners* (Valencia, forthcoming).

been excommunicated.⁸ In August 1246 the king wrote to the pope, informing him that, thanks to the good counsel of Fr. Desideri, he had come to the realization of his crime and was prepared to do penance.⁹ No doubt there was an element of political sagacity in James's repentance: a king who touted his reconquest as a crusade for Christendom could scarcely remain at variance with the church on whose support he relied.

Be that as it may, Fr. Desideri had accomplished his mission successfully and was to be rewarded for his efforts with an even more difficult task, the coordination of the collection of the papal subsidy from the realms of Aragon.¹⁰ As the collection was to come from the entire Peninsula, Fr. Desideri could not undertake it unassisted, and for Aragon he appointed as his lieutenant Fr. Aimeric of the Gerona house.¹¹ In 1276 Pope Innocent IV wrote to the queen of Aragon, exhorting her to increase daily her devotion to the Holy Catholic Church and to receive graciously his delegate, Fr. Desideri.¹²

Saldes suggests that the business to be undertaken by Fr. Desideri probably related to the support the pope sought from the king of Aragon in the continuing struggle between the Holy See and the empire. Fr. Desideri must have been an old man by this time, and after 1276 his name disappears from the documents. The nationality of Fr. Desideri is unclear, but it is known that Fr. Aimeric was guardian of the Gerona house in 1246 and custodian in Valencia a year later, suggesting that he was probably a Catalan.¹³ As Linehan points out, it was customary for

---

8   Atanasio López, *La província de España de los frailes menores* (Santiago, 1915), pp. 380-388; and Peter Linehan, *The Spanish Church and the Papacy in the Thirteenth Century* (Cambridge, 1971), p. 195.
9   López, *Província de España*, p. 381.
10 Linehan, *Spanish Church and the Papacy*, pp. 195-196. See also Ambròs de Saldes, "La orden franciscana en el antiguo reino de Aragón: Colección diplomatica," *REF* 1 (1907), 90-92, at p. 90.
11 Linehan, *Spanish Church and the Papacy*, p. 196.
12 Saldes, "La orden franciscana," p. 91.
13 Linehan, *Spanish Church and the Papacy*, p. 196. It is curious that, among the documentation found for the Gerona house (the only complete Franciscan archives in the realms of Aragon), there is no mention of Fr. Aimeric. A Fr. Aimeric reappears in a series of documents between 1312 and 1315, mainly dealing with the dowry due to James II of Aragon as a result of his marriage to Marie of Lusignan, although he acted as ambassador for Henry II in the negotiations with James which took place in April of 1314.

friars to undertake the collection of papal subsidies in their native territory.

This is borne out by the appointment of another friar whose name appears frequently in the early documentation, Fr. Miguel de Tudela, to deal with the census. In November 1246 he had been sent to King James to inform him of the attempt made on Pope Innocent IV's life.[14] Perhaps because of the distance from his home territory, he delegated the duties connected with the census to Fr. Pere de Tarragona, who in 1247 was resident in the Franciscan house at Lerida.[15] In 1255, Fr. Pere de Tarragona with Fr. Bernat de Bach, custodian of the Lerida convent, was commissioned by the archbishop of Tarragona to undertake the triennial visit "ad limina" on his behalf, and later became a chaplain to Pope Alexander IV.[16] The Franciscan house at Tudela, situated close to the Aragonese border, although under the jurisdiction of Navarre and beyond the confines of this study, had close relations with Aragon during the thirteenth century, a situation which explains the seemingly curious appointment of a Navarrese friar to look after papal interests in Aragon.

The activities of these early friars have been discussed in some detail, because their role as papal delegates illustrates more clearly than anything else the way in which the papacy regarded the Franciscans as an extension of papal authority. The tasks which were entrusted to the friars, such as the collection of subsidies for the Holy See, were not likely to make them particularly popular among those who paid these tithes, in almost all cases the secular clergy. The friars chosen to illustrate this aspect were the first of many to undertake papal missions.

It is not long after these papal nuncios were sent to collect subsidies from the realms of Aragon that the first documentary evidence reveals the resentment of the secular clergy of the intrusion of the newcomers on their territory. It may even be, although this is impossible to prove, that the work of the papal nuncios was directly responsible for igniting the spark of a conflagration which was to burn brightly for years to come, and for which the scene had already been set when the mendicant orders chose an urban environment for their apostolate. When the friars first arrived in King James's territory their attention was mainly focused

---

14 Linehan, *Spanish Church and the Papacy*, pp. 197-198.
15 Ibid., p. 196.
16 See Pedro Sanahuja, *História de la seráfica provincia de Cataluña* (Barcelona, 1959), p. 47.

on the acquisition of land and buildings, and in any case few of them at that time were priests, so that the problems which were to plague relations with the diocesan clergy were not immediately evident.

By the middle of the thirteenth century the Minors had become a clerical body, able to hear confessions, preach and undertake all the duties of the parish priest.[17] These included the conduct of marriages, the burial of the dead and related ceremonies, and in every case, of course, the friars benefited from the fees due on those occasions. In the case of the death of a parishioner, the friars were often beneficiaries from his estate, a situation which led to a serious loss of income for the parish priest, who had previously been able to count on the entire fee accruing from whatever spiritual service he performed. Reaction to the pastoral activities of the Franciscans in Aragon seems to have come somewhat later than in Germany, where the resentment of the clergy can be seen well before 1250.[18] Although this could be attributed to lack of documentation for the early years, it is also true to say that in the Iberian Peninsula prior to 1250 the Dominicans were considerably more influential in the parishes than the Franciscans, who during those years probably caused relatively few problems for the diocesan clergy.[19]

The appointment of Benet de Rocabertí as archbishop of Tarragona in 1252 seems to signal the end of Dominican ascendancy and to symbolize the triumphal entry of the Franciscans on the diocesan scene, for Archbishop Benet replaced the Dominicans in his employ by Franciscans.[20] From this time on the position of the Franciscans seems to be assured, and although there is no documentary evidence that disputes in Aragon occurred before 1276, it is hard to believe that areas of conflict with the parish priests could possibly have been delayed for over twenty years after the Franciscans had acquired influence in the dioceses.

17 See above, p. 150 with n2.
18 See John B. Freed, *The Friars and German Society in the Thirteenth Century* (Cambridge, Mass., 1977), p. 35.
19 Linehan, *Spanish Church and the Papacy*, pp. 70–71, refers to the appointment of Fr. Pere de Centelles as bishop of Barcelona after the death of Bishop Berenguer Palou, who had died at the end of August 1241. He states that he was the first Dominican to be appointed to a bishopric south of the Pyrenees, but by 1248 there were five Dominican bishops in the province of Tarragona alone.
20 Ibid., pp. 86–87.

By examining the pattern of legacies to the Franciscans in the towns of King James's kingdom where records are extant for the years prior to 1250, and taking Vic as a model because the notarial records of wills date from the 1240s, it is evident that there is a significant increase in legacies to the Franciscans after 1250.[21] The parish clergy would certainly have been deprived of much income after this date, but had probably only been able to count on diminished resources from the very inception of the establishment of the Franciscan house. It could be that by the 1270s tolerance had reached its limit, but it is far more likely that either the early instances of conflict between the friars and the parish priests were not recorded or the documents outlining their vicissitudes have suffered the ravages of time.

The first recorded incident is typical of many subsequent conflicts. In 1276 an agreement was reached between Fr. Berenguer de Valls, custodian, and Fr. Berenguer de Guàrdia, guardian, and the friars of the Tortosa Franciscan house and the bishop of the diocese, in connection with the offerings due to the officiant of a funeral.[22] By the terms of the agreement, when a parishioner died a fourth part of all wax used for candles, together with the bed on which the deceased was borne to his last resting place, was to be divided equally between the friars and the diocese. It is not clear just how they intended to divide the bed, but perhaps this term was intended to comprise the bier and coverings at the time of burial. The desire for equality seems to have been paramount, since all bequests were to be shared between the two parties, and if the Franciscans were given money to defray burial expenses a portion of this was also to go to the diocesan clergy. In this case the matter seems to have been settled amicably between the two parties concerned, but on other occasions the Franciscans were obliged to appeal to the king to intervene on their behalf.

The first occasion on which the king was forced to act as arbiter occurred in Teruel in 1277, in connection with a difference of opinion

---

21 See Immaculada Ollich i Castanyer, "Aplicació sistemàtica d'ordinadors a la documentació medieval de la plana de Vic" (doctoral dissertation, University of Barcelona, 1981), and her analysis of the volume of wills in "Les entitats eclesiàstiques d'Ausona al segle XIII a través de les donacions testamentàries," Treball realitzat mitjançant la beca "Mossén Gudiol" per a estudis històrics, concedida pel Patronat d'estudis Ausonencs, Vic, Curs. 1974–1975 (mimeographed).

22 Tortosa, AC, Cartulari IV, carta 1, ff. 1-2, 13 November 1276.

as to whether or not the Franciscan house could be considered part of the town, situated where it was outside its walls.[23] The king replied that, although it was in the suburbs, the house could be regarded as an integral part of the town. He added that it was not for him to adjudicate the rights and wrongs of the conflict over burial rights, as this more properly belonged to the ecclesiastical courts.

Reading between the lines, we may say that the question of the situation of the convent arose because of the location of the cemetery, which, if within the parish boundaries of the Teruel church, would fall within diocesan jurisdiction, so that the Franciscans, if they buried a parishioner, would be required to pay a portion of the burial fees to the diocesan clergy. Records in Tortosa and elsewhere show that this was usually a quarter, hence the name canonical quarter, a significant portion which the Franciscans had probably refused to pay, claiming royal and papal privileges that exempted them from diocesan jurisdiction.

In 1282 the king wrote to the justice of Calatayud, concerning the dispute between the chapter of the parish church of Calatayud and the two mendicant orders (Dominicans and Franciscans) over the violence which had been perpetrated against the clergy by certain laymen at the time of a funeral.[24] Subsequent documents suggest that the cause of this dispute was the burial of a parishioner in the friars' cemetery, on which occasion the parish clergy almost certainly protested and were attacked by the relatives and friends of the deceased. Judging by the extant chancellery records, conflicts between friars and clergy in the kingdom of Aragon tended to be much more violent in nature than those which occurred in Catalonia, Valencia or elsewhere. The exact number of these disputes cannot be determined, as only those which proved difficult to settle were taken to the king; but other, more minor conflicts must have occurred on numerous occasions, especially when a wealthy citizen preferred to be buried in the cemetery of the friars rather than avail himself of the services of the parish priest.

The parochial clergy must have been sorely vexed when the friars arranged to bury a member of the royal family, as the fees in such instances would have been considerably larger than was customary. Queen Constance, the widow of King Peter, who left money to set up

---

23 Sanahuja, *História,* p. 118.
24 Saldes, Ambròs de. "Documentació franciscana (1267–1285)," *EF* 45 (1933), 130–149, at p.146, no. 41, 11 June 1282.

hospitals in Barcelona and Valencia, died in Barcelona and was buried in the Clarissan habit, in their cemetery.[25] In June of 1300, some three months after her death, which had occurred within the jurisdictional territory of the church of Saint Michael in Barcelona, the rector, Berenguer de Torre, was continuing to threaten the Franciscans because they had not paid him the canonical quarter which he regarded as his due. Queen Constance had taken vows in the Clarissan convent in Messina in Sicily, and when she returned to Barcelona in 1299, having no residence of her own, had stayed with the family of Pere Martí in the parish of Saint Michael, where she died some six months later. Berenguer de Torre not only claimed his share of the burial fee but maintained that the queen had not received the holy sacraments in any parish in Barcelona, implying that she had died without making her peace with the church.

When Berenguer continued to harass the friars, they were forced to take the matter to James II, in the hope of receiving confirmation that they were justified in keeping the whole burial fee, but the king was unable to resolve the matter satisfactorily. In October of 1300 Pope Boniface VIII wrote to the abbot of Sant Cugat, stating that he was doing so in response to a request from the Barcelona Franciscan house, and referring to the dispute between Berenguer de Torre and the friars.[26] In his letter he confirmed that Queen Constance, although buried in the Franciscan cemetery, had died in Barcelona within the jurisdictional territory of the church of Saint Michael and that the Rector had every right to claim the canonical quarter. He also added that the friars had explained that the Holy See had exempted them from this payment, but were unable to convince the rector that this was so. The parochial clergy must have been well aware that earlier that year Boniface VIII had issued the bull *Super cathedram* in an attempt to improve the tense situation which existed between the parochial clergy and the friars.[27] It was this bull that established the right of friars to bury in their churches and cemeteries, provided they gave one fourth of all fees and legacies to the parish priest. Boniface, instead of rebuking the Franciscans, as might have been expected when they refused to pay the canonical quarter, upheld their stance contrary to the provisions of *Super cathedram*.

---

25 Sanahuja, *História*, p. 108.
26 Barcelona, ACA, ORM, carp. Franciscans, perg. 17 (B.13), 24 October 1300.
27 Moorman, *History of the Franciscan Order*, p. 202.

Although the queen died in March 1300, a month after the papal edict, and her will was drawn up before *Super cathedram,* Boniface felt justified in defending the position of the Franciscans.

Subsequent events indicate that problems continued to arise, especially over royal funerals, and it is difficult not to feel some sympathy with the parochial clergy, who must have regarded the popularity of the friars with something akin to despair when they watched the large royal donations slip from their grasp. Their faith in the papacy must also have received a rude shock from the support given by Boniface to the Friars Minor, although the edict *Super cathedram* would still have been unknown to them, an edict which the friars regarded as a curtailment of their privileges, flooding the papal curia with their protests.

As a result Benedict XI, Boniface's successor, annulled the bull of 1300 with *Inter cunctas,* issued in February 1304.[28] In 1306, an agreement referring to the death of Alfonso II and his subsequent burial in the Barcelona Franciscan house raised once again the question of entitlement to the canonical quarter. In this case the parish church of Saint James was entitled to its share of the significant fees accruing from the ceremonies held in the royal palace in Barcelona at the time of the king's death, a fact which Pons Otger, a canon of Barcelona cathedral and rector of the church of Saint James, made sure was not forgotten. The agreement drawn up between the rector and Fr. Joan de Roure, guardian of the Franciscan house, confirmed that 580 Barcelona sous, representing the amount due from the royal funeral to the church of Saint James, in whose parish it was held, would be paid to Pons Otger by the friars.[29]

This was not to be the end of such conflicts, for in 1303, some three years after the publication of *Inter cunctas* and the death of the Franciscan bishop of Barcelona, Fr. Bernat Peregrí, the appointment of Pons de Gualba as his successor evoked a response from Fr. Francesc Vilagrassa, then in charge of the Barcelona Franciscan custody. He demanded confirmation in the presence of the new bishop of Barcelona that the

---

28 Moorman, *History of the Franciscan Order,* p. 202. The friars contended vigorously that *Inter cunctas* seriously threatened the efficacy of their pastoral work. It is not surprising to find confirmation of the important bulls of Clement IV (1265) and Benedict XI (1304) in a document preserved in the Franciscan archives for the Gerona house.

29 Barcelona, ACA, ORM, carp. Franciscans, perg. 6 (A.775), 14 March 1305 [1306].

friars were exempt from episcopal jurisdiction as a result of the papal privileges granted to them.[30]

Bishop Pons cannot have been unaware of the position of the mendicant friars, but despite this he seems to have attempted to claim jurisdiction over them, thus lighting a further spark to the smouldering grievances of the friars. There is evidence that he had great difficulty in collecting the taxes due to the church from prominent laymen, for after three requests for payment and numerous exhortations to the councillors of the city and the superiors of religious houses to help him obtain these tithes he was forced to ask all members of the ordained clergy to read out at their Sunday services a notice of excommunication against the recalcitrant laymen who had not paid their taxes.[31]

Threats were made against the ecclesiastics, and an order from the bishop gave the clergy permission to bear arms, no doubt to protect them from the wrath of the laity. Those who had been excommunicated appealed to the archbishop of Tarragona to absolve them from this penalty, but were denied absolution and again ordered to pay the taxes due. In a council convoked for the purpose, the metropolitan repeated the censure of the laymen concerned, but added the names of seventy-two religious who had supported them.[32] These mendicant friars had refused to read out the censure in their churches, because, if they had done so, they would have acknowledged implicitly the bishop's right to jurisdiction over them. Among those who were prohibited from celebrating the divine office or ministering in public, either in the city or in the suburbs, were twenty-five Franciscans from the Barcelona house, including the custodian, Fr. Francesc Vilagrassa.

---

30 See Sebastián Puig y Puig, *Episcopologio de la sede Barcinonense* (Barcelona, 1929), pp. 228–232. Bishop Bernat was buried in the chapel of St. Francis in Barcelona cathedral, a chapel it is said that he had built; but the 1355 document in the Barcelona diocesan archives (*Institucio tercii benefficii sanctorum ffrancisci et Ludovici constructi in dicto claustro sedis Barchinone*, Barcelona, AD, Registra dotaliarum, no. 1, ff. 326v–330) refers to the chapel built in the cloisters and endowed in his will by Francesc Examenis, son of the Francesc Examenis who was killed by brigands on the highway near Barcelona and probably a relative of Fr. Francesc Eiximenis (or Examenis).

31 Puig y Puig, *Episcopologio*, pp. 232–233.

32 Ibid., p. 233. See Barcelona, AD, Registra communium, no. 1, ff. 81v–82, 14 November 1307.

It is clear that his meeting with Bishop Pons had been to no avail and that the new provisions of *Inter cunctas* had failed to achieve the much-desired peace between the mendicants and the clergy. The Franciscans must have appealed to the minister general, Fr. Gondissalvo, to meet with Bishop Pons in an attempt to settle the difficulties which had arisen over the friars' position. The meeting between the two church dignitaries took place in the cloister of the Barcelona house, where the Constitutions of Tarragona, whose provisions had been contravened by the religious placed under interdict, were confirmed.[33] In this case the mendicants were at fault, although, in view of the unresolved question of the extent of episcopal jurisdiction, it would have been surprising had they acceded to the bishop's demands.

The whole matter of the mendicant position vis-à-vis the parochial clergy was finally taken before the Council of Vienne in the autumn of 1311, and Pope Clement V decided that the only practical solution was to return to the provisions of *Super cathedram*.[34] At first glance, this might have seemed to be a step in the wrong direction for the mendicants, but the complaints of the parochial clergy were so numerous and in some cases so extreme that the only compromise possible was to allow them part of the fees accruing to the friars when they conducted funerals of their parishioners or carried out other functions which fell within the purview of the secular clergy.[35] Certainly, if any measure of peace was to prevail in the urban environment in which both clergy and friars cared for the souls of their contemporaries, Clement V's decision was wise. Later events show that it was insufficient to prevent the ever-increasing conflicts between the mendicants and the parish clergy. The trajectory of these sordid episodes in the ecclesiastical history of Valencia can best be seen in *Per Déu o per diners* (For God or Mammon), which gives a transcription of the long and complicated arbitration judgment of the late fourteenth century compiled by the two arbiters, Cardinal James of Aragon, bishop of Valencia, and Fr. Vicent Ferrer, the famous Dominican preacher.[36]

The problem was one which had no easy solution, but the prevailing atmosphere of distrust was exacerbated by the tracts issued a year after

---

33 Barcelona, AD, Registra communium, no. 1, f. 85v, 15 February 1307 [1308].
34 Moorman, *History of the Franciscan Order*, p. 202.
35 Ibid., p. 203.
36 See Webster, *Per Déu o per diners* (Valencia, forthcoming).

the Council of Vienne by those who were not in agreement with the confirmation of the reinstatement of *Super cathedram*.[37] Among the tracts issued was one by a Dominican, Hervé Nédélec, provincial prior of France, putting forward the theory that all power belonged to the pope, who, if he wished, could diminish or withdraw authority from the bishops and parochial clergy and give it to the friars, an inflammatory suggestion which could only provoke anew the diocesan authorities. John of Pouilly took up the position of the secular clergy in the university of Paris in 1312, and the Franciscans brought a formal accusation against him in November 1317, declaring heretical some of his assertions.[38]

The incidence of disputes between the two branches of the ecclesiastical world in the realms of Aragon became not only more frequent as time went on but also more acrimonious, and perhaps, in part at least, this can be attributed to the deteriorating economic conditions of the fourteenth century.

There was little variation in the form of the disputes from one part of the kingdom to the other, but in Aragon there seems to have been a tendency for them to take on a more violent character.

One of the longest-lasting and seemingly most unwarranted attacks on the Friars Minor came from the diocese of Huesca, where the bishop's men waylaid two Franciscans on the public highway. The first indication of this conflict comes from a long letter from King Alfonso to the bishop of Huesca, Pedro, in August of 1331, referring to an incident the previous year which occurred on the public highway near a place called Casbas de Huesca, and describing some of the events.[39]

A further letter addressed to the *superjuntario* of Huesca the same month also explains in some detail the cause of the complaint from the Franciscans.[40] The details in the two accounts are not identical, and the following is an attempt to reconstruct the events as they appear from the extant documentation.

When Fr. Aparicio Serra and Fr. Pardo Serra of the Saragossa Franciscan house, who were travelling on royal business from Huesca to Barbastro, reached a place called Casbas de Huesca and were about to turn on to the public highway, they were suddenly accosted by a

---

37 See Moorman, *History of the Franciscan Order*, pp. 339-349.
38 Ibid., p. 141.
39 Barcelona, ACA, RC 565, f. xi-vii.v/xi.viii, 16 August 1331.
40 ACA, RC 447, f. 134, 19 August 1331.

number of hostile men on foot and on horseback. The men, supporters of the bishop of Huesca, immediately began to insult Fr. Pardo, who, when he had seen them approaching, had drawn aside. They asked him what had happened to Fr. Aparicio, who was carrying books, money and other things, and Fr. Pardo, fearing for his life, said that his confrere had gone on ahead, whereupon the bishop's men pursued him until they caught up with him in a valley through which he was riding. They not only insulted him verbally but even drew blood, as they stripped him of his habit and bore him and his people (presumably attendants on the journey) captive to Sesa, the place where the bishop of Huesca had his palace. There they showered him with further insults, treated him roughly, robbed and imprisoned him with murderers and other criminals.

The king, having received news of the assault and capture of Fr. Aparicio from both the Franciscans and from Garsias, a canon of Huesca cathedral, demanded that Fr. Aparicio and those captured with him be led to the *superjuntario,* and eventually to the royal curia. He also stated that proper legal action should be initiated according to the *fueros,* reminding the *superjuntario* that the Franciscans, who were travelling on the king's highway, were under royal protection and had taken a vow of poverty. The incident had not only physically harmed Fr. Aparicio and those with him, but had displayed contempt for the laws of the land and for the king himself. He enjoined his official to see that the criminals were apprehended and reparation made to the friars for their loss. He also wrote to the justice of Aragon at the same time, advising him of the occurrence and giving further details of what happened.[41] The two friars had reached the river Bero when the attack took place.

When Fr. Aparicio asked his attackers why they were accosting him in this manner, the men replied that they were acting on the orders of the bishop of Huesca, whereupon they took the friar to the "horrible castle" that served as his prison, where only the most despicable murderers and criminals were placed, bound him round the chest with a cord and kept him tied up for the whole time they held him prisoner. He remained in the prison for five days, and they would have kept him longer had he not been in danger of being killed by the other occupants. In January 1332 the king wrote again to Sancho Ximéno de Ayerbe, justice of Aragon, informing him that legal action taken against the

---

41 Barcelona, ACA, RC 447, f. 179, 31 August 1331.

bishop of Huesca's men should now be revoked.[42] It appears that the inquiry conducted by the justice had led to the payment of 3000 sous of Jaca by the vassals of the bishop, as a form of guarantee or "forfeit," which the king now ordered should be returned to them. The matter had come to an end, but the correspondence does not cease at this point.

Sympathy with Fr. Aparicio should not blind the reader to the very real aggravation caused to the parochial clergy in Huesca, especially in the light of a letter from the king to the bishop of Huesca dated August 1332, more than a year later, which suggests that the reason for the attack was the interference of the Franciscans in parochial matters. The way the letter is phrased unequivocally places the blame for the incident on the friars, a conclusion supported by the revocation of legal action by the king. The inquiries made by the justice must have uncovered certain long-standing problems between the friars and the clergy. The king, in his letter of 1332, referred to complaints by the bishop of the damage done to the diocesan clergy and to the faithful by the friars' sermons, hearing of confessions and receiving of alms and tithes. He again mentioned the vow of poverty the friars have taken, and suggested that the bishop might find some way in which both parties could continue to serve the spiritual needs of their flock without coming into conflict. For his part, he said, he would write to the pope to ask that measures be taken to prevent the Franciscans from impinging on the rights and duties of the diocesan clergy. A final settlement had not been reached.

In January of 1333 King Alfonso wrote to his brother, the patriarch of Alexandria, regarding the imprisonment of Fr. Aparicio in the castle of Sesa.[43] The letter emphasizes the injuries, insults and losses suffered by Fr. Aparicio, and the fact that he was led into the presence of the king by the other friars so that the bishop of Huesca could be confronted with his own wrongdoing and be forced to make amends. To pay for the medical expenses incurred by the aggrieved friar as a result of the incident, his confreres had been forced to pawn "aparamenta ac ornamenta," and the king asked his brother to advance them the money to enable these articles to be recovered, always bearing in mind that the Order of Friars Minor received protection from the Holy Roman Church. At the same time the king informed Sancho Ximéno de Ayerbe, the justice of Aragon, that the whole question had been taken to the

---

42 Barcelona, ACA, RC 526, f. 151, 29 January 1331 [1332].
43 ACA, RC 456, f. 90, 25 January 1332 [1333].

patriarch of Alexandria (also archbishop of Tarragona).[44] There is no further correspondence on this matter, and it is likely that a truce had been arrived at between the diocesan clergy of Huesca and the Franciscans. It rouses the historian's curiosity as to why so much attention should have been given to the Huesca incident.

A partial answer can be found in a letter King Alfonso addressed to all his officials in August 1328, two years before the attack on the Sesa highway.[45] The letter states that, as the result of a concession of the minister general of the Franciscans, the king was permitted to employ friars to undertake diplomatic missions on his behalf. With this in mind, he was sending Fr. Aparicio of Saragossa on a mission to an unspecified location, and he wished to remind his officials that Fr. Aparicio and his companion possessed a royal safe-conduct protecting them from harm or violent attacks. In the light of later events this seems ironical, but it might well indicate why the king was so upset. He would have regarded the matter, as indeed he inferred in his letter, as a direct insult to the royal house of Aragon. Not all conflicts were of such magnitude, but they were persistent and must have caused bitter feelings whenever they occurred. They were not confined to the Franciscan order: the other mendicants were troubled in much the same way, as the Valencian arbitration sentence of the late fourteenth century shows so clearly.[46]

THE FRIARS AND THE STRUGGLE BETWEEN POPE AND EMPEROR

A slight digression to comment briefly on relations between pope and emperor helps to elucidate the repercussions they inevitably had on the Order of Friars Minor and the Crown of Aragon and, more especially, contributes to an understanding of the Spiritual movement.

The problems which concern this study are best reflected in the struggle for supremacy between secular and national rulers, a situation which was further exacerbated in the fourteenth century by conflicting loyalties to the imperial ideal and divergent views on the apostolic mission of the Holy Roman Church. Pope John XXII had to resolve the most pressing aspect of this mission, the question of the Spiritual Franciscans, in an atmosphere fraught with intense political implications,

---

44 Barcelona, ACA, RC 456, f. 91v, 8 February 1332 [1333].
45 ACA, RC 520, f. 170v, 9 August 1328.
46 See Webster, *Per Déu o per diners* (Valencia, forthcoming).

because of the support lent to their cause by Frederick of Habsburg. These heretical doctrines infiltrated Catalonia, attaining a prevalence among the Franciscans which the condemnation of 1317 seems to have been powerless to prevent.

The first documentary intimation of this involvement comes from a letter of Pope Innocent IV to James I, informing him that Fr. Miguel de Tudela, a Franciscan from the kingdom of Navarre, had informed him of the wicked and horrible crime the emperor Frederick II had planned against him with men "who are called assassins."[47] The letter is dated 1246, four years before the death of Frederick, and relates to the period in which the pope was engaged in a battle with the emperor over the kingdom of Sicily. In the absence of a legitimate claimant to the papal fiefdom, Innocent hoped to find a ruler who would remove the island from the clutches of the Hohenstaufen family.

Meanwhile Frederick died, and in January 1252 his only surviving son, Conrad, returned to Italy to conquer his father's kingdom.[48] His premature death two years later did not end the struggle, and his illegitimate son Manfred asserted his rights to the island. Fr. Francesc Eiximenis, in his Christian encyclopedia, uses the story of Conrad and Manfred to exemplify what happened to those who tried to usurp territories rightly belonging to the Holy See.[49]

The details of the struggle between Manfred and the papacy, the annexation of the kingdom of Sicily by Peter II and his subsequent war with Charles of Anjou, whose grandiose plans were doomed to failure when his son was captured by Admiral Ruggiero di Loria, are too complicated to discuss here, as are the details regarding the defeat of Philip III by the Catalans and the peaceful settlement made by Peter the Great of Aragon.[50] When Peter died in 1285 the agreement collapsed, and after an unsuccessful attempt to assert his rights over Sicily, his younger son James, who had inherited the island, agreed to convey his

---

47 Saldes, "La orden franciscana," p. 91.
48 See Daniel Waley, *Later Medieval Europe from Saint Louis to Luther,* 2nd ed. (London and New York, 1985), pp. 29-34, for a succinct account of relations between pope and emperor.
49 See Francesc Eiximenis, *Dotzè llibre del Crestià: Segona part,* ed. Curt Wittlin, Arseni Pacheco, Jill Webster et al., 2 vols. (Gerona, 1986-1987), 1: 39 (cap. 484).
50 Thomas N. Bisson, *The Medieval Crown of Aragon: A Short History* (Oxford, 1986), pp. 87-90.

inheritance to the Holy See in return for certain sanctions.[51] Pope Boniface promised Sardinia and Corsica to James II in return for Sicily, but the islanders had their own candidate, and in 1296 elected Frederick of Sicily as king. In 1302 it was agreed that he should reign for life, and that after his death the kingdom should pass to Charles of Naples; but the provisions of the Treaty of Caltabellota for Sicily were in fact never carried out.[52]

The struggle for the empire continued during the late thirteenth century, and the subsequent death of the emperor, Henry of Luxembourg, who had received encouragement in his imperialistic ambitions from Pope Celestine V, led to a disputed election in 1313.[53] The two candidates were Frederick of Habsburg and Lewis of Bavaria, and the struggle which ensued led to the pope's excommunicating Lewis and claiming the imperial vicariate in Italy, a defeat from which the empire never really recovered. The papacy, on the other hand, had other difficulties to address, for it had already come under siege from nationalistic rulers in England and France, and was to go through a long period of unrest before finally emerging triumphant at the end of the Middle Ages.[54]

The problems in Sicily and the rivalry between pope and emperor had had direct repercussions on both the Crown of Aragon and the convents of the Order of Friars Minor in King James's territory. The Crown of Aragon had an important Mediterranean empire, and could not afford to let Sicily fall into the hands of an alien power; James II had already attempted to obtain the kingdom for his own son, Frederick, and by the Treaty of Anagni in 1297, in return for conveying Sicily to the Holy See, had received Sardinia and Corsica, becoming intimately involved in the fate of these Mediterranean outposts.[55]

---

51 Bisson, *Medieval Crown of Aragon*, p. 92.
52 Ibid., p. 93. See also J.N. Hillgarth, "The Problem of a Catalan Mediterranean Empire, 1229–1327," Supplement to *English Historical Review*, no. 8 (London, 1975), esp. pp. 28–31. Hillgarth emphasizes the change in Mediterranean policy of the rulers of Catalonia–Aragon after 1295, when they turned their attention to the conquest of Sardinia (p. 48).
53 Waley, *Later Medieval Europe*, pp. 65–66.
54 Ibid., pp. 46–59 and 96–115.
55 See Jill R. Webster, "The Early Catalan Mendicants in Sardinia," *Biblioteca francescana sarda* (Oristano, Sardinia) 2 (1988), 5–16.

In all these endeavours the Franciscans in Aragon found themselves used by both the papacy and the crown, dependent as they were on them for the continued success of their mission. At first this presented no problems, but as the political situation in the Mediterranean became less stable and the order itself became divided over the meaning of poverty, conflicts regarding the interpretation of their mission, such as the one leading to the deposition of the provincial minister of Aragon, Fr. Pere d'Artamara, inevitably occurred.

The Friars and the Papacy

The friars received protection from both crown and papacy; the letters which refer to the Franciscans as papal nuncios are complemented by a number of extant papal bulls which point to the way in which the friars either received direct commands from the pope or appealed to him when their circumstances so warranted. These date from before the death of Saint Francis and cover numerous aspects of the order's life, from the establishment of convents and the persecution of apostates to the confirmation of privileges and the appointment of inquisitors. They are to be found not only among the extant Franciscan documents and papal registers, but interspersed throughout the manuals and parchments preserved in state and cathedral archives. Referring to the continual dialogue between the Franciscans and the papacy, they are pertinent to every convent in the territories of the Crown of Aragon. Some are couched in complex legal terminology, others are brief and to the point; but reference to almost every aspect of mendicant life illustrates the international character of the friars and the significance of their mission. In the same way as the Franciscans depended on the support of the crown and on help from their contemporaries for their material needs, so did they also rely on papal direction for their spiritual mission.

The relevance of the papal letters can be grouped under three general headings: those which refer to the establishment, building and appointment of convents and the churches associated with them; those of a jurisdictional nature; and those which refer to individual friars, whether to honour or commission them in the service of the church, or to chastise and exhort them in the name of Christian obedience.

No Franciscan houses would have existed anywhere in King James's territories had it not been for approval from both crown and papacy of their apostolic mission.[56] It had been with great reluctance that Saint Francis had agreed to approach Pope Innocent III to obtain recognition for his band of followers, and later Honorius III for approval of the rule of the Friars Minor.[57] From the very first the Franciscans had acknowledged the need for papal support, and the records show very clearly that, at least initially, the friars had to obtain permission from the papacy before they could establish permanent houses. The placing of the order under the direct supervision of the papacy and exempting it from episcopal jurisdiction was the prime cause of the constant friction with the parochial clergy, but it also had both positive and negative effects on the lives of individual friars and on the efficacy of religious life.

When Saint Francis set out on his journey to Spain with his companions, he took no thought for his material needs. He had to rely on the hospitality of the Catalans and Aragonese.[58] The success of this journey helped his followers to obtain lodgings in private houses and gradually to win sufficient support to build permanent convents. Although during the early years most of the friars would have been lay brothers, the few priests among them would have required a place to say mass and their daily office.

This explains why in 1224 Honorius III gave permission for the Order of Friars Minor to erect portable altars for the celebration of the divine offices.[59] This provision can also be found among the extant documentation relating to the Dominicans and Carmelites, and as a provisional measure it must have been very successful, as it would have allowed the friars to say mass and the divine office in a number of different locations, eventually enabling them to choose suitable places for the building of their convents. In some areas, at least, the pope gave indulgences to Christians who gave alms for the construction of Franciscan houses.[60] The bequests to charities and religious orders in

---

56 See the foregoing discussion and above Chapter 2, pp. 73-92, passim.
57 Moorman, *History of the Franciscan Order*, pp. 18-19 and 53-59, for a description of the difficult decision which Francis had to make shortly before his death and which culminated in the 1223 rule, a shorter version than that of 1221, but the one still in force today.
58 See above Chapters 1 and 3, pp. 23-24, 30, 114.
59 Honorius III, no. 5194, 3 December 1224, *Regesta Honorii papae III*, ed. Petrus Pressutti, 2 vols. (Rome, 1888-1895), 2: 285.
60 Alexander IV, no. 304, 1 November 1257, *La documentación pontificia de Alejandro IV (1254-1261)*, ed. Ildefonso Rodríguez de Lama (Rome, 1976), p. 287.

the numerous wills which survive from the thirteenth century provide practical evidence of the benefits the testators hoped to obtain from supporting Christian endeavours. As late as 1330 indulgences were also given to those who enlisted in the armies fighting the Moors in Granada, an ongoing crusade, in view of the fact that several Franciscans had accompanied James II to Granada in his attack on Almería in 1309, some twenty years earlier.[61]

The friars' work could not proceed without manpower; it became necessary to prohibit the entry of young children into the mendicant orders, indicating, perhaps, that contemporaries regarded the religious life not only as a means of vicarious salvation but as providing a secure livelihood for their offspring.[62] Many of these novices would have been unsuitable for the life they entered, and the year's probation would have done little to prevent their taking vows which they were too young to understand. This helps to explain the high incidence of apostasy among religious orders in the late Middle Ages. As early as 1244 Innocent IV issued a bull giving licence to capture, bind and imprison apostates from the Franciscan order, wherever they might be found and in whatever habit or religious order they might have found refuge.[63] Frequent documents attest to the magnitude of this problem; fugitives

---

61 See below Chapter 5, p. 190 with n42, and Jill R. Webster, "Col.lecció de documents del convent de Sant Francesc de Girona (1224–1399)," *AIEG* 28–30 (1985–1989), 29: 27–86, at pp. 64–66, no. 32.

62 In Montpellier, Archives de la ville de Montpellier, arm. E, cassette 5, 1362, no. 4, Inventaire 2259, Urban V advises all religious superiors (including the mendicant orders) that in Montpellier young boys and girls who have not reached the age of puberty should not enter convents, for to do so might be damaging to their spiritual well-being. This was not new, as Alfonso X had said that those wishing to enter religious orders must be at least fourteen years old and women entering monasteries must be twelve years old (*Partidas* 1.7.4); those who had entered before puberty, even if they had taken their final vows, could leave the convent on the grounds that they had been too young to know what they were doing (*Partidas* 1.7.7). See *Las siete partidas del rey don Alfonso el Sabio*, 3 vols. (Madrid, 1972), 1: 298–299 and 300. Nicholas IV refers to the fact that he himself entered the order when he was very young. See no. 1, 23 February 1288, *Les Registres de Nicolas IV: Recueil des bulles de ce pape*, ed. Ernest Langlois, 2 vols. (Paris, 1886–1891), 1: 1–3, at 1.

63 Innocent IV, no. 67, 5 August 1244, in *Bullarium pontificium quod exstat in archivo sacri conventus S. Francisci Assisiensis (nunc apud bibliothecam Assisii)*, ed. Laetus Alessandri-Franciscus Pennacchi (Quaracchi, 1920), p. 14.

from most of the religious orders were actively pursued by the arm of justice.[64]

The Crown of Aragon was no exception, and there are several references to apostates from the Franciscan houses in Aragon, some referring to friars who had committed a criminal act and feared apprehension and punishment, others to those who had found the life distasteful to them and a third group who regarded transferring from one order to another as the answer to their problems.[65] The most privileged of such apostates was Fr. Joan Guerau, of the house at Gerona, who sowed his wild oats and, contrary to established custom, was readmitted to the order because his family had given hospitality to Saint Francis.[66] This raises the question of how many other friars were readmitted in this way after they had broken their vows and disgraced the order. The two friars from the house at Calatayud who in 1291 joined their brothers and raided the convent at Xàtiva, stealing valuable altar cloths and even wounding some of the residents, were surely treated with less tolerance, although extant documentation fails to elucidate this point.[67] Even so, their crime was mild in comparison with that of Fr. Gil Mercader, who had committed murder; yet he was to be given a light punishment because he had not intended to kill—an interesting commentary on early fourteenth-century justice.[68]

---

64 Nicholas IV in 1290 reiterates a prohibition against harbouring these apostates. See no. 3578, 1 November 1290, *Les Registres de Nicolas IV,* 1: 553.
65 Among the apostates and those who left the Order of Friars Minor either to enter monastic orders or to take up the life of a secular, were: Martín Pedro de Biel, 1283 (Ambròs de Saldes, "Documentació franciscana [1282-1285]," *EF* 42 [1930], 86-96, at p. 95); Ramonet Dublit, 1285 (Saldes, "Documentació franciscana [1267-1285]," *EF* 45 [1933], 130-149, at p. 149, no. 52); Ramon de Lluvià, 1289 (Barcelona, ACA, RC 81, f. 25); Pedro Martín and a man surnamed On[ten]iente, 1291 (RC 90, f. 106); Pere Laurador, 1294 (RC 100, f. 154); Jaume Robert and Pere Renovart, 1295 (RC 99, ff. 62v, 171r-v); Francesc de Morera, 1300 (RC 117, f. 220); Vicens, 1305 (RC 98, f. 262); Jaume Galindi, 1308 (RC 141, f. 199v); Guillem Treballós, 1310 (RC 145, f. 140; a man with the same name appears in the Tàrrega house in 1333, RC 123, f. 14); Martín Sanz, 1316 (RC 159, f. 171); Bernat Esquerrer, 1318 (RC 349, f. 57); Ermengol, 1319 (RC 168, f. 68v); Antoni de Pons, 1321 (RC 173, f. 30).
66 See above Chapter 2, pp. 98-99.
67 Pedro Martín and a man whose surname was On[teni]ente: see Barcelona, ACA, RC 90, f. 106, 17 November 1291.
68 Barcelona, ACA, RC 205, f. 121v, 2 January 1307 [1308].

In 1318 a letter from James II to Pope John XXII refers to Fr. Bernat Esquerrer, who fled from the Franciscan order, led a dissolute life for some years and then decided to enter the Benedictine convent at Montserrat.[69] Permission to do so was denied him, but despite this there is evidence that he rose to the position of prior at the nearby monastery of Ripoll. Extant records suggest that there was no change in his behaviour after his admission to the Ripoll monastery. He committed many crimes while he was there, including that of espousing heretical ideas; and when it was time for a new prior to be appointed, the king asked that his son James be considered for the position.

In lieu of evidence to the contrary, the historian must conclude that Fr. Bernat had come into contact with some of the heretical groups which had spread from southern France to Catalonia.[70] Only a few years earlier Pope John XXII had condemned the Spirituals, and these were quite prevalent in parts of Catalonia.[71]

In this connection the process against the Majorcan Spiritual, Fr. Pere Arnau, is of some relevance, for it had a curious twist, in that Fr. Pere d'Artamara, provincial minister of Aragon and one of those appointed by Pope John XXII to examine the case, appears to have disregarded the papal order.[72] Sanahuja concludes that he was deposed as a result of his disobedience, as there is no further mention of his role in the order.[73] Subsequent events suggest that Fr. Pere d'Artamara was a supporter of Fr. Michael of Cesena, minister general of the Franciscans in 1325, the date of the former's appointment to the commission in Majorca. After months of accusations and detention in Avignon, Fr.

---

69 Barcelona, ACA, RC 349, f. 57, 20 December 1318.
70 The Pamiers Inquisition documents refer to the presence of heretics in Puigcerdà, another frontier town, at this time. See Jean Duvernoy, *Le Registre d'Inquisition de Jacques Fournier, évêque de Pamiers (1318-1325)*, 3 vols. (Toulouse, 1965), 1: 410–421, for the confession of "Alazaicis uxoris Arnaldi Fabri quondam de Monte Alionis," held on 1 April 1321, "in foro Penitencie fratribus de Puigcerdà," probably the Franciscan convent, although there was also a Dominican house.
71 See Josep Perarnau, *L'"Alia informatio beguinorum" d'Arnau de Vilanova* (Barcelona, 1978).
72 Sanahuja, *História*, pp. 247 and 271.
73 Ibid., p. 247. See also José María Pou i Martí, *Visionarios, beguinos y fraticelos catalanes (siglos XIII-XV)*, rev. ed. (Madrid, 1991), p. 251, where the case is discussed at length, although the extant documentation fails to explain what errors or heretical views Fr. Pere Arnau was accused of supporting.

Michael was finally deprived of his position by the papacy.[74] John XXII believed that Michael was lending support to Lewis of Bavaria, a fact which received further corroboration when the emperor provided the minister general and his companions, after their escape from Avignon, with a boat from Aigües Mortes to Pisa. Moorman believes that Michael was probably innocent of the crime with which he was charged, and certainly the order supported him by reelecting him minister general against the pope's wishes.[75]

One further case of apostasy, which has nothing to do with the political situation, completes the commentary on Catalan apostates; it concerns Fr. Jofre de Foixà or Fuxà, a native of Gerona, a troubadour and the man credited with having given the name "catalanesc" to the Catalan language.[76] In 1295 Pope Boniface VIII dispensed him from the obligation to remain in the Franciscan order, which he had entered twenty years earlier.[77] He, like many other apostates, wished to follow the rule of Saint Benedict, this time at Sant Feliu de Guixols not far from Gerona, where he had made his profession as a Friar Minor. He was probably granted this dispensation because of the reputation he had acquired as a troubadour, but the rule of Saint Benedict was regarded as more severe than that of Saint Francis, making Fr. Jofre's request acceptable to the pope.[78] In other cases, the possession of an influential family or evidence of exceptional ability were distinct advantages, and those who were fortunate enough to enjoy them benefited in numerous ways.

The liaison between the pope and the friars and the relations of the latter with the secular clergy are fundamental to an understanding of the work of the Franciscans in the realms of Aragon: individual friars served both pope and king, and at times were employed by the bishops to

---

74 Moorman, *History of the Franciscan Order*, pp. 318-321.
75 Ibid., p. 520.
76 Joaquín Pla Cargol, *Gerona histórica*, 2nd ed. (Gerona and Madrid, 1945), p. 64.
77 Boniface VIII, no. 593, 11 July 1295, *Les Registres de Boniface VIII: Recueil des bulles de ce pape*, ed. Georges Digard, Maurice Faucon, Antoine Thomas, and Robert Fawtier, 4 vols. (Paris, 1884-1939), 1: 208.
78 Alfonso X, el Sabio, *Partidas* 1.7.29, *Las siete partidas* 1: 316, refers to the punishment of apostates who leave orders, suggesting that they lose eternal life; for, like fishes who cannot live out of water, so they cannot live outside the cloister. It also stresses that it is acceptable for a man to move from a less to a more severe religious order.

conduct services in the cathedral or elsewhere. Papal dispensations were required for any exception to canonical procedure, and the Franciscans frequently acted in the capacity of papal delegates on such occasions.

The spiritual concerns of medieval people were not limited to Sunday observance, nor could they be separated from municipal and national politics: they were a way of life, and as such directed the behaviour and aspirations of life on earth. Both crown and papacy needed the support of the mendicant friars, disguising their need as a crusade on behalf of Christendom, and the Crown of Aragon made use of the services of the friars as a means to consolidate relations with the rising merchant class from which many of them were drawn. In the pages which follow, an attempt will be made to reconstruct life within a typical medieval Franciscan house, explaining the structure of the order as it affected the realms of Aragon: the activities in which both average and outstanding friars were engaged, the relations they had with their contemporaries, lay or ordained, and the difficulties they encountered in following in the steps of Saint Francis.

5

Life Within and Without the Cloister

Saint Francis and his early companions had no splendid convent, no fixed abode, but went from place to place on foot, without thought for the morrow, begging food and living on the providence of God.[1] Reluctantly, Saint Francis was forced to realize that to be effective more organization was required and that a rule was necessary. There is no doubt that this was so, but the acceptance of an organizational structure led to a number of problems in the years after Saint Francis's death, not the least of which concerned one of the basic tenets of the order, poverty, and how this was to be interpreted within the urban environment in which the friars had chosen to work. This chapter will discuss the problem of the application of that rule, which was frequently at variance with daily life in the Crown of Aragon. Many friars were obliged to play a dual role, as they not only attempted to fulfil their apostolic mission but undertook secular duties which brought them into conflict with their founder's ideals.

Extant documentation, slanted as it inevitably is towards the secular life, shows that the Franciscans and other mendicant friars in King James's territories conceived of their mission in very broad terms: in fact, the lives of some of these men, who acted as king's advisers or undertook secret ambassadorial functions on the monarch's behalf, differed only slightly from those of their lay counterparts. From the provisions of the rule of 1221, it is clear that the founder's intention was that his followers should eschew all worldly activities and thus avoid the temptations that would inevitably lead them away from their spiritual mission. The point of this warning becomes increasingly evident as, during the thirteenth and fourteenth centuries, the members of the order

---

1   John R.H. Moorman, *A History of the Franciscan Order from its Origins to the Year 1517* (Oxford, 1968; repr. Chicago, 1988), pp. 10–17.

gradually incorporate into their way of life elements which their founder would have regarded as a denial of the basic principles of the rule. Saint Francis gave up a life of ease to dedicate himself to the poor; yet some of his followers south of the Pyrenees seem to have been given special privileges because of their royal, noble or wealthy family backgrounds.

The rule stipulated that the friars were to live in "obedience, without property, and in chastity," provisions that were immediately contravened by the erection of splendid churches and conventual buildings.[2] At first the title to these properties was held by a third party, and in the Crown of Aragon might have been held on their behalf by the crown, the municipal authorities or the friars' procurator; but in many of the instances to be discussed there is no evidence to suggest that they themselves were not the legal owners: on the contrary, in some cases it is clear that they waited until they had acquired sufficient funds before they bought property suitable for the house they intended to build or enlarge.[3]

The rule also required them to sell all their personal possessions, but they could not be received into the order until after a year's probation. Again, exceptions were made, and friars from wealthy families often continued to hold property and received special financial allowances, presumably to allow them to live in the style to which they had been accustomed; this suggests that within the Franciscan houses there was a differential scale, applied to the entering friars on the basis of social standing. Consider the following example.

Joan d'Aragó (cited in the document from which the example is taken as the brother of James II) was granted 1000 sous of Tours in February 1311 to pay for his studies.[4] It is assumed that this is the same man as Fr. Joan d'Aragó, the Franciscan who studied in Montpellier, acted as a messenger from the queen of Portugal to the king of Aragon in 1340, was responsible for enlarging the Franciscan house at Barcelona and was finally consecrated bishop of Cagliari in Sardinia, dying in 1368 or 1369, about the same time that another royal prince known as the Infant Pere took the Franciscan habit in the Barcelona

---

2 See "The Rule of 1221" and "The Rule of 1223," trans. Benen Fahy with intro. and notes by Placid Hermann, in *St. Francis of Assisi, Writings and Early Biographies: English Omnibus of the Sources for the Life of St. Francis*, ed. Marion A. Habig (London, 1972), pp. 27-53 and 54-64.

3 See Jill R. Webster, "El desconocido convento de Puigcerdà," *AIA* 49 (1989), 167-194, at pp. 167-172.

4 Barcelona, ACA, RC 147, f. 135v, 21 February 1310 [1311].

convent.[5] In May 1334 the executor of the will of Fr. Joan's father (also called Joan d'Aragó) discovered that the 500 sous due for Fr. Joan's studies had not been paid.[6] Fr. Joan's father had left a sum of 500 sous in his will to cover this payment. If this refers to studies undertaken during the second decade of the fourteenth century, payment has been delayed for approximately twenty years, a fact which seems to accord well with other delayed payments to the Franciscans. During the reign of Peter III Fr. Joan received an allowance of 400 sous of Jaca money ("in violarium") in September of each year for his "needs," with the stipulation that this was to be paid to him as long as he lived.[7] This is the first reference to this amount, and a further 1000 sous of Jaca money granted to him (surely not the 1000 sous granted for study in 1311?) dates from May 1337.[8] In 1338 200 sous of Jaca money were paid to him from the income received by the general bailiff for Aragon to cover the month of November; for that year, at least, he must have received the allowance granted to him.[9]

Some friars, particularly those of royal or noble extraction like Fr. Ferrer de Cruilles, drew up their last will and testament during the year of probation, an act which was essential for those who owned land and properties. Fr. Ferrer de Cruilles, the younger son of the late Ferrer and Dolça de Cruilles, was a novice in the Gerona Franciscan house in November 1267, when he made his will.[10] The Cruilles family was one of the most important in Gerona during the Middle Ages, and the

---

5   Pedro Sanahuja, *História de la seráfica provincia de Cataluña* (Barcelona, 1959), pp. 51, 196, 218–219, 235.
6   Barcelona, ACA, RC 569, f. 232, 9 May 1334.
7   The annual payment is recorded in Barcelona, ACA, RC 877, f. 129, 10 May 1345.
8   Barcelona, ACA, RC 1308, ff. 15v–16, 23 July 1345, contains the text of previous letters, written from Montblanc and Perpignan on 7 September 1337 and 4 May 1337, referring to the same subject.
9   Barcelona, ACA, RC 1298, f. 87, 13 September 1338. See Johannes Vincke, ed., *Documenta selecta* (Barcelona, 1936), p. 389, for doc. 524, which is a request for legitimization of Fr. Joan of Aragon of the Order of Friars Minor, as a blood relative of King Peter. It is curious that this request for the removal of the taint of illegitimacy comes as late as 1345, and it can only be concluded that previously this had not been a problem.
10 The will of Fr. Ferrer de Cruilles, Gerona, AH, Hospital de Girona, perg. 102, is printed below as Document 1.

carved effigy over the tomb of Jofre Gilabert de Cruilles dating from the fourteenth century is still preserved in the museum housed in the old church of Sant Pere de Galligans. Fr. Ferrer had as his executors the abbot of Sant Feliu, Gerona (probably the collegiate church of Sant Feliu and not Sant Feliu de Guixols), and his brother, the camerarius (treasurer) of Sant Miquel de Cruilles. The guardian of the friars acted as his adviser, and all his property was to go to the family, although there is a clause allowing for the poor of Jesus Christ to inherit, in which category he specifically included the Friars Minor.

The will is long and complex, but it shows that even in 1267 books were regarded as important, for Fr. Ferrer stipulated that, should the poor inherit, his property should be divided into two equal halves, one for the acquisition of books for the friars in Gerona and the other to allow payment of their debts. Other wills relating to novices or concerning members of the order are less complex, but include Franciscans among the witnesses; it is curious that in a will of such importance to the order the friars are conspicuous by their absence.[11]

---

11 Noteworthy also is the practice of giving the same names to two brothers. This often caused confusion, and in the will of Jaspert (Gisbert) Examenis we come across this same practice. For a very early will of some significance see Immaculada Ollich i Castanyer, "Aplicació sistemàtica d'ordinadors a la documentació medieval de la plana de Vic" (doctoral dissertation, University of Barcelona, 1981), no. 14, dated Vic, 22 June 1243. This is one of the earliest wills made by a Friar Minor. Bernat de Puigalt intended to enter the order and made his will before doing so. The will is quite long, and is especially interesting because it includes legacies to the would-be friar's sons, suggesting that he had been married and had decided to enter the Order of Friars Minor after the death of his wife. In June 1299 Fr. Guerau de Puigalt (possibly the same man but almost certainly from the same family), together with his socius Fr. Bernat Mora, received the king's permission to travel home to Catalonia from Naples (Barcelona, ACA, RC 113, f. 267). A number of friars with the family name of Mora are recorded in the fourteenth century as having resided in the houses at Barcelona, Gerona, Majorca and Vilafranca. One further series of documents is relevant here. In February 1263 [1264] Fr. Pere Vidal, who was serving his novitiate in the Franciscan convent at Vic, authorized his brother, Berenguer, to act as his procurator for the recovery of money owed to him from Tunis, Majorca and thereabouts, suggesting that he had gone to Tunis as a missionary, perhaps training in Majorca beforehand, although the famous college of Miramar had not yet been founded. Berenguer promised to undertake this for his brother and to hand over the money recovered to the guardian of the Vic house, Fr. Guillem de Blanes. Berenguer Vidal promised to give the Franciscans 100 Barcelona sous "de terno," which he had received from his

The primary obligations of the medieval Franciscan friar in the realms of Aragon were both spiritual and secular, and the interdependence of two directly opposing ways of life led to endless difficulties. The friars were to follow in the footsteps of Christ, applying his teachings to the best of their ability and saying the divine office or, if they were clerics, celebrating the liturgy. They were also required to pray for the living and the dead, say or sing Psalm 50 (the *Miserere*), one *Pater noster* for the faults and failings of the friars and one for their deceased confreres, together with Psalm 129 (the *De profundis*).[12] They were only to be allowed the books necessary for their religious exercises, and those lay brothers who could read were permitted a psalter.

At the time the rule was drawn up there was no thought of the friars attending universities or having their own theological schools, but it was not long before the Franciscans, like the Dominicans, became prominent in university circles.[13] Such a change of focus inevitably meant that some of the provisions of the rule concerning the possession of books could no longer be applied strictly.

Technically, of course, the books used by an individual friar belonged to the house in which he professed, and reverted to it at his death; but in practice there was little difference between that and outright possession. Although some of the houses possessed libraries by the fourteenth century, books were almost certainly also assigned to individual friars during most of the thirteenth century, and indeed, some friars are known to have acquired a number of books, especially those who went to study at the universities in England and France. Most of these men would have been priests or were studying for the ordained ministry. The apostate Juan Garçès clearly regarded the books he had in his possession

---

mother's will; the document also refers to the property at Boules. The friars were given 150 sous left by the late Ferrer de Boniles, and again the property at Boules is mentioned. Two years later, in March 1266, Fr. Pere Vidal was dead, leaving a will regarding the property in Boules and Malla which he had inherited through his mother; the 200 sous he received on that property was to pass to the Franciscans at Vic for the work of their church. Further documents refer to the same question, indicating that promises were made to see that the Franciscans received the 200 sous (Vic, AE, ACF, Manuals notarials, no. 9, unnumbered folios, dated 4 February 1263 [1264], 4 March 1265 [1266] (3 docs.), 13 April 1266 and 11 May 1266.

12 See "The Rule of 1221," in *St. Francis of Assisi: Omnibus of Sources,* p. 34.
13 See William J. Courtenay, *Schools and Scholars in Fourteenth-Century England* (Princeton, 1987), p. 185.

as his personal property and had no scruples about taking them with him when he left the order, refusing to return them to the Franciscans.[14] The custodian for the Saragossa custody took the matter to the king, who wrote a letter to the justice of Calatayud, ordering that Juan Garçès be compelled to return the stolen property. Books were valuable, and their loss would have been a matter of great concern to the friars.

Strictly speaking, in the early years, if the friars had been following the precepts of the rule, there would have been no problem regarding the ownership of books because they were not expected to study. The friars were "minors" and as such the most lowly of God's servants, dedicating their lives to prayer, praise and thanksgiving. Thus, few of the friars would have had any education at first, and during the period under review there would always have been a significant proportion of the number in any convent who were employed in purely manual work and for whom literacy was irrelevant. It is impossible to assess to what extent attitudes towards learning changed, for lay friars are seldom mentioned in the extant documentation. By the end of the Middle Ages the proportion of illiterate manual workers had almost certainly been reduced significantly. The rule stipulated that the friars were to regard all clerics and religious as their superiors, and to respect their office; but this provision was soon to change, as it was not long before the friars themselves joined the ranks of the ordained clergy, with whom they were frequently at loggerheads over ecclesiastical matters or the canonical quarter.[15]

Saint Francis considered it very important that the friars should understand the meaning of service to others, explaining that those who held office, especially the provincial and general ministers, were in fact the servants of the other friars, and on them rested the responsibility to assign those within their jurisdiction to the various houses in the provinces. Similarly, they were to look after the correction of those friars who fell into sin. Apostates such as Juan Garçès, when apprehended, were to be returned to the order for discipline. If unrepentant and not apprehended, they reverted to the lay state and came under civil jurisdiction, losing any privilege they had as members of a religious

---

14 Barcelona, ACA, RC 90, f. 50v, 23 September 1291.
15 See above Chapter 3, p. 139.

order.[16] Warrants were sent out for their arrest; but many probably escaped the clutches of the law, while others took refuge in monastic orders such as the Cistercian or Benedictine. Some, like Jofre de Foixà, mentioned in Chapter 4 (whose case might be considered exceptional), rose to the rank of abbot.

Work and service to others were the basis of the Franciscan ideal, and friars who had a trade could work at it, provided that they accepted no money and that it did not interfere with their spiritual life. Friars were not to handle money in any circumstances, and for this reason the procurator was appointed to look after their economic needs.

In King James's territories this procurator was given certain privileges, including exemption from taxation and military service.[17] An unusual document dating from 1302 declares that any such exemption or privilege was not valid on that occasion, that is, during the final stages of the war against Sicily.[18]

The privilege was greatly appreciated, as all male citizens, unless granted exemption, were expected to render military service when the need arose. The completion of the reconquest in the Crown of Aragon by the end of the thirteenth century decreased the significance of municipal militias, and exemptions from this service became increasingly frequent.[19] The same procurator often served for many years, and in some families holding the office became a tradition; one such was the Fuster family of Vilafranca, who supported the Third Order and the Spirituals from the turn of the thirteenth to the fourteenth century and from whom came Fr. Bernat Fuster, who was imprisoned in Majorca for

---

16 See Alfonso X, el Sabio, *Partidas* 1.7.29 and 1.7.31, *Las siete partidas del rey don Alfonso el Sabio,* 3 vols. (Madrid, 1972), 1: 316–317.

17 See below Appendix 2 for a list of procurators, and Documents 9, 16, 52 for transcriptions of the form letters granting them such exemptions.

18 The war came to an end in 1302; see Thomas N. Bisson, *The Medieval Crown of Aragon: A Short History* (Oxford, 1986), p. 93. Barcelona, ACA, RC 307, f. 40, Lerida, 8 April [1302], reads: "*Capitols que En Johan den Uchs aporta de part del senyor infant et de son Consell.* Item: los frares menors i els preycadors han privilegi que lurs procuradors no són tenguts d'anar en host e lurs procuradors són dels bons i dels cummals de la vila. És resposta del senyor rey que negun privilegi ne neguna gràcia no.ls escusa en aquest cas."

19 See James F. Powers, *A Society Organized for War: The Iberian Municipal Militias in the Central Middle Ages, 1000–1284* (Berkeley, 1988), pp. 81–84.

many years for his unorthodox views.[20] The epithet "Friar" was frequently prefixed to the names of procurators who belonged to the Third Order, making it extremely difficult to distinguish between them and members of the Friars Minor. Some members of the Third Order also took holy orders, but it is not known whether they became parish priests or undertook some other kind of work.

For the Friars Minor money was a symbol of worldliness and greed, and the rule condemns the friar who collects or keeps money as "a fraud and a thief and a robber and a traitor."[21] By the middle of the fourteenth century some friars were clearly infringing the provisions of the rule, for the Castilian poem, the *Libro de buen amor,* written about this time, paints a very uncomplimentary picture of those who, in addition to being followers of Don Amor, are scarcely able to wait for the dying man to draw his last breath before they swoop down like crows on their prey and take possession of anything they can lay their hands on.[22] In a similar vein and slightly later, the *Friar's Tale* of Chaucer suggests that the medieval friar lived and fed well, a description with which English readers are very familiar. In this context, perhaps, it is easier to understand the differential treatment afforded to those friars who came from prominent families.

---

20 See below Chapter 6, pp. 241-253 for descriptions of the Third Order and similar organizations.
21 See "The Rule of 1221," in *St. Francis of Assisi: Omnibus of Sources,* p. 39.
22 Juan Ruiz (Arcipreste de Hita), *Libro de buen amor,* ed. G.B. Gybbon-Monypenny (Madrid, 1988), pp. 212-213 (quatrains 505-507):

> "Commo quier que los frailes non toman los dineros,
> bien les dan de la çeja do son sus parçioneros;
> luego los toman prestos sus omnes despenseros.
> Pues que se dizen pobres, ¿qué quieren thessoreros?
>
> "Monges, frailes, clerigos, que aman a Dios servir,
> si varruntan que el rrico está ya para morir,
> quando oyen sus dineros que comiençan a rretenir,
> quál dellos lo *levará,* comiençan luego a rreñir.
>
> "Allí están esperando quál avrá más rico tuero;
> non es muerto, ya dizen: 'Pater Noster' a mal agüero;
> commo los cuervos al asno, quando le desuellan el cuero:
> Cras, cras nós lo avremos, que nuestro es ya por fuero."

It was customary for each friar to have a companion (*socius*), and for the two friars to travel together on the highways begging alms, a very dangerous undertaking in the Middle Ages, when robbers and vagabonds frequently attacked the unsuspecting traveller.[23] In this they were following the precepts of their rule, and the picture of the friars on their travels has become a commonplace of literature, contributing to the fiction associated with the image of the medieval mendicant friar.

The Italian friar Salimbene refers to his experiences in Pisa, where he was assigned "a certain fickle and lightheaded lay brother" as his socius to accompany him, a remark that suggests that the companion was assigned rather than selected by the individual friar, and that at times the person chosen was not to his liking.[24] Aragonese friars were wont to experience hardship on their way through the countryside, not necessarily from brigands but more usually from incensed clerics who set out to attack them in retaliation for the loss of income that derived from "infringement of their territory."[25] In these instances the brothers followed the provisions of the rule enjoining them to look after each other under all circumstances, and not to abandon those who were sick or in trouble.

At times, looking after a socius meant incurring danger, as in the extreme case of Fr. Aparicio mentioned in Chapter 4. In such instances, it would have been virtually impossible to have lived up to the gospel exhortation to turn the other cheek, or if deprived of their cloak, to be prepared to give up their coat. The normal mode of travel for the friars was on foot, but in certain circumstances they were later allowed to ride on horseback or on a mule, no doubt because the secular duties they were required to undertake demanded a certain amount of despatch. Men like Fr. Sancho López de Ayerbe were given horses and mules by the king, partly in reward for the services they had rendered, but probably also because the king intended to call upon them again in the immediate

---

23 Some names of socii are known, but the majority were probably not ordained members of the order.
24 Salimbene da Parma, *The Chronicle of Salimbene de Adam*, trans. Joseph L. Baird, Giuseppe Baglivi, and John Robert Kane (Binghampton, NY, 1986), p. 18.
25 The case of Fr. Aparicio is described in the previous chapter (pp. 160–163), but there were many other similar instances of aggression against friars.

future.[26] The king's requirements could not have been met on foot, and when the friars accompanied the army, as in Valencia or Granada, they would have been expected to ride on horseback. In all things, the friars were enjoined to love one another and not speak ill of their confreres, but the documents show that this requirement was easier to make than to keep. Some friars got into violent fights, others suffered from the slander spoken against them by enemies from within the order and apostates even returned to their erstwhile convent to take revenge for past slights, wounding and even killing their former confreres. Some apostates were responsible for break-ins, and the most extreme case resulted in the death of Fr. Martín Fernando at Calatayud and the wounding of several other friars.[27] The instinct for revenge was very

26 In Barcelona, ACA, RC 1299: f. 54v, 29 February 1338 [1339], Ramon de Boyl, the king's treasurer, is instructed to pay Fr. Sancho López de Ayerbe 1000 Barcelona sous for the purchase of a mule; ff. 54v-55, 6 March the same year, payment to Fr. Sancho is again requested for a mule (perhaps the same one as in the document of 29 February) to be used in the king's service; f. 61v, 8 March (two days later), the account is still outstanding and payment is ordered again. RC 1300, f. 130r-v, 7 September 1339, again addresses Ramon de Boyl, ordering him to pay Fr. Sancho 800 Barcelona sous for a black mule used in the king's service. RC 1304, ff. 66v-67, 4 August 1341, is addressed to Bernat de Oltzinelles, doctor of law and royal treasurer, ordering him to send immediately to Fr. Sancho, the king's confessor, 300 sous for a dark chestnut mule which he had bought to use on the king's service; as the document points out that the original order for payment was 1 March 1337 [1338], Fr. Sancho had to wait several years to receive the money. In RC 1117, f. 7, 4 April 1343, the king writes again to his treasurer, ordering payment of 1200 sous to Fr. Sancho, to buy a mule. See also Ambròs de Saldes, "Franciscanismo: Documentos franciscanos," *EF* 17 (1916), 64-74. On 17 January 1290 [1291] Arnau Bastida was ordered to see that Fr. Alberic was provided with mounts to enable him to undertake a mission for the king. These horses were to be bought from the provincial minister of the Friars Minor.

27 Barcelona, ACA, RC 106, f. 28v, 7 October 1297, addressed to the judge of the royal curia, Sancho Muñoz, refers to the death of the friar and the harm caused to his confreres; the perpetrators of this break-in had evaded capture. A similar case, referring to another Aragonese convent, was reported to the king by Fr. Romeo Ortiz, provincial minister of Aragon (ACA, RC 351, f. 181, 29 April 1313): Andrés de Pozo with a band of armed men had committed sacrilege, entering the Monzón convent and seizing Fr. Martín Dendestre, but on this occasion the friar escaped death. The intruders had treated Fr. Martín roughly and had stolen items, including books, from the convent. In his reply Prince James assured Fr. Romeo that such behaviour could not be tolerated, and ordered his officials to capture Andrés and the accomplices named by Fr. Andreu de Copons and impose a sentence on them.

strong in the Middle Ages, condoned by the code of chivalry explained in detail by Ramon Llull and Juan Manuel and set out legally in the *Siete partidas* of Alfonso X.

Two outstanding friars, Fr. Arnau de Castllà, royal chaplain for many years, and Fr. Francesc Gener of the Gerona convent, also suffered from the malicious gossip of their enemies.[28] In the cloisters of the Gerona convent in 1370 Fr. Francesc Gener had a violent encounter with the guardian, Fr. Pere de Pont, and some years afterwards, when he was in Perpignan, slanderous lies were spread regarding his behaviour, although on this occasion witnesses were able to prove that they were the work of his enemies.[29] The king took a strong view of such cases, especially when they concerned his chaplain or confessor.[30]

28 The name Castllà has a number of variant spellings and the most usual one has been adopted here. See *Pere III of Catalonia (Pedro IV of Aragon): Chronicle,* trans. Mary Hillgarth and J.N. Hillgarth, 2 vols. (Toronto, 1980), 1: 356, n. 212, where Arnau dezcastlar (or Dezcallar) is referred to as a member of an important Roussillon family; he should not be confused with the Gerona family of Castellar.

29 See Jill R. Webster, "Unlocking Lost Archives: Medieval Catalan Franciscan Communities," *Catholic Historical Review* 66 (1980), 537–550, at p. 548. This is the clearest case of ill-will against an individual, for it seems that the animosity shown by the guardian of the Gerona house, Fr. Pere de Pont, to Fr. Francesc Gener in 1370 continued in 1372 when, as provincial minister, he was staying in Perpignan and fell victim to malicious gossip. On the latter occasion the innkeeper and his wife, Pere and Jacma Cauders, in whose inn Fr. Francesc and his socius, Fr. Pere, seem to have stayed, swore before a notary that the two men, wearing their habits, had done no harm but had lodged in his inn without causing trouble (Perpignan, Archives départementales des Pyrénées-Orientales, sér. B, no. 125, f. 32, 6 April 1372). As Perpignan was part of the custody of Narbonne at this time, Fr. Francesc was probably provincial minister of the province of Provence and not of the province of Aragon, where Fr. Nicolau Sa Guàrdia is recorded as occupying that position in 1371 (see Sanahuja, *História,* p. 253).

30 Barcelona, ACA, RC 1115, ff. 130v–131, 22 September 1341. A letter from Peter III to the minister general, Fr. Gerard, expresses surprise at the gossip concerning Fr. Arnau de Castllà, a man of exemplary life and virtue, assiduous in the king's service and with an excellent reputation. A second letter of the same date was sent by the king to Fr. Ramon de Bas, the provincial minister, emphasizing the king's displeasure at learning of the seditious libel and false gossip against the good reputation of Fr. Arnau. A legal process had been initiated against the good friar and Peter III ordered that it be stopped at once. A further letter was sent to the cardinal holding the title of St. Cyriacus in Thermis, repeating the king's belief that Fr. Arnau was a deeply religious and honest man, endowed with an abundance of irreproachable qualities. There is no hint as to what the gossip entailed, but he was

The Franciscan rule states that it should be a delight for the friars "to live among social outcasts, among the poor and helpless, the sick and the lepers, and those who beg by the wayside," and if they are in want they should beg alms. This "delight" was to be dimmed, no doubt, by the violence they often encountered on the highways, and there is little evidence that the followers of Saint Francis shared his delight in living as social outcasts, or indeed that they devoted much of their time to disadvantaged members of society. The friars did, for a short period, attend the sick in Valencia in the hospital founded by Queen Constance, but their lack of financial means doomed the undertaking to failure.[31] In some cases old leprosaria were given to the friars for their convents, as in Tàrrega and Cervera; in the case of the former the friars did care for the lepers for some years, at least, but in Cervera there is little evidence that they used the buildings for anything other than conventual purposes.[32]

On many occasions they even made representation to the king against the presence of social outcasts, prostitutes and those plying low trades in the vicinity of their churches, asking that they be required to go to another area of the town: requests which do not suggest a love for these people (a distinction should be made, however, between those who were merely poor and those who plied immoral wares).[33] Fr. Francesc Eiximenis, writing for the *jurats* in Valencia in the 1380s, refers to those on the fringes of society, but shows no special concern for their welfare; his

---

almost certainly reproached for adherence to Spiritual ideas, like Fr. Arnau Oliba in the first decade of the fourteenth century, who was imprisoned for a brief period and later reestablished. Whatever the cause of the problem, Fr. Arnau continued to act as royal confessor and executor of the will of Alfonso III without any apparent difficulty.

31 See above Chapter 2, pp. 95–96.
32 Josep Maria Segarra i Malla, *Història de Tàrrega amb els seus costums i tradicions, I (segles XI–XVI)* (Tàrrega, 1984), p. 91, referring to the fact that the Franciscans treated the lepers so well that James II decided to place them under his protection. The lepers had to be moved outside the city, as their presence constituted a threat to the inhabitants. Food was left for them halfway up the hill of Saint Eloy, to which they had been forced to retire. It is relevant that Saint Francis kissed the hand of a leper he met by chance and later attended to the needs of those who dwelt in the leper-house. See Moorman, *History of the Franciscan Order*, p. 8.
33 See above Chapter 3, pp. 146–147.

concern is to ensure that their habits will not impinge on the lives of hardworking citizens.[34]

Neither the Franciscans nor the other mendicant orders appear to have had any desire to care for or reform those whom they regarded as nuisances, disturbing the peace and preventing the faithful from attending divine service. Immorality was regarded as a sin against God, and of greater magnitude than murder or theft. No attempt seems to have been made by the friars to help those entrapped in a life of prostitution, a curious lack of concern in the light of Christ's treatment of Mary Magdalene. It is also in direct contrast to the care shown by these orders for those convicted of crimes, and it is not uncommon to learn that the Franciscans harboured criminals in their houses until they were brought to justice; at times they helped them to escape punishment for their crimes.[35] By taking refuge in the convent they placed themselves

---

34 See Francesc Eiximenis, *Regiment de la cosa pública,* cap. 24, ed. Daniel de Molins de Rei (Barcelona, 1927), pp. 169-170.
35 A few cases will suffice to exemplify this concern. In 1337 Peter III requested the *batlle* at Vilafranca del Penedès to see that the murderers of Berenguer Llaurador of Vilafranca were removed from the Franciscan convent, where they had been held pending the imposition of the sentence (Barcelona, ACA, RC 594, f. 191v, 19 April 1338). In 1340 he wrote to the guardian and friars of the Tàrrega house, indicating his suprise that the Franciscans were harbouring criminals to the detriment of the well-being of the city, and ordering them to see that the wrongdoers left convent and city without delay; if they did not do so immediately, they would be liable to a fine of 100 morabatins (RC 1056, unnumbered folios [62v-63], 7 March 1339 [1340]). In 1329 Alfonso III wrote to the guardian and house of Barbastro, stating that Ramón de Mur, a squire and the killer of a man called Gómez de Suelbes, had taken refuge in the Franciscan convent in an attempt to avoid the penalty for his action; he should be taken prisoner, as he had committed a horrible crime (RC 577, ff. 33v-34, 8 April 1329). On 11 March that same year Domingo de Fuentes of Saragossa, fearing for his own life after the murder of his brother, asked the Franciscans to take him in (RC 563, f. 21). In yet another case, Peter III wrote to the justice for the criminal court of Valencia, on information received from Fr. Ramon de Bas, the provincial minister, ordering that Fernando Posanes, convicted of murder (for which the penalty was mutilation of limbs), be pardoned because the justice, in attempting to arrest him in the Franciscan convent whither he had fled, had infringed ecclesiastical law (RC 874, ff. 15v-16, 5 November 1342). This document shows clearly that criminals sought asylum in religious houses to escape the penalty their actions warranted. RC 584, f. 25v, 22 September 1328, refers to two men who had been found guilty of crimes and who to escape the punishment took refuge in the Franciscan house at Cervera.

beyond the arm of civil justice, and strictly speaking should then have come under the ecclesiastical courts, which were reserved for clerics; in this way they fell between two stools and eluded the arm of the law.

The charity shown by the friars to criminals extended to the relatives of those who had been hanged and whose bodies remained on the gallows for a year and a day for all to see and take heed of their folly. It was often the friars who asked that the body be removed after the legal period had elapsed, contending that to leave it there any longer was undesirable. In the case of the corpse of Guillermo Andrés of Saragossa, which had been hanging in Tamarit for the required period, the intercession of the Franciscans resulted in King Alfonso III's giving permission for his remains to be buried according to the rites of the church, a favour which was not usually granted to those condemned to death.[36] The crime he had committed is not known, but the friars' intercession on his behalf suggests that he had not committed murder, a mortal sin which would have deprived him of the right to receive an ecclesiastical burial. According to Sanahuja, Benedict XIII ("Papa Luna"), the antipope who refused to accept his deposition (scarcely a criminal in the true sense of the word, but certainly a refugee from ecclesiastical "persecution"), found asylum in the Franciscan house at Morella and endowed the church with many valuable relics, including two thorns from the crown of thorns worn by Christ at the Crucifixion.[37]

It was fitting that some friars, following the tradition of Saint Luke, should study medicine, the cure of the body so closely connected with the care of the soul, and at least two Franciscans in the realms of Aragon became physicians to the queens of Aragon and Castile.[38] Fr. Arnulf was physician to James II's consort, Queen Marie, and was

---

36 Barcelona, ACA, RC 575, f. 122, 28 December 1331.
37 Sanahuja, História, p. 88. M. Aragonès i Virgili, *Benet XIII: Una obstinació proverbial* (Reus: Patronat del Castell, 1987), p. 228, refers to the five-day meeting in Morella between the antipope and Ferran I on 18 July 1414, but does not mention the venue. Benedict's having taken refuge in the Franciscan house at Morella does not appear in other documents; Sanahuja may in fact be referring to this meeting.
38 Barcelona, ACA, RC 140, f. 107, 16 March 1307 [1308], James II's letter to Fr. Gondisalvo, minister general of the Franciscans, confirming that Fr. Fernando García, custodian of Valencia, would go to see him (implying that he had replaced the king's physician, Fr. Albert, who was needed by both king and queen for health reasons [ACA, RP 620, f. 142v, 1294]). Both Fr. Albert (RP 269, f. 24, 1295) and Fr. Arnulf (RP 279, f. 2v, 1315) received payments for their services.

frequently required to attend both the ailing queen and Don Juan Manuel, a high Castilian noble known for his support of the order.[39]

The last chapters of the rule reaffirm the Franciscan spiritual mission among both believers and unbelievers, their preaching of the word of God, the holding of chapters at Michaelmas whenever appropriate, and the requirement to attend the general chapter at St. Mary's of the Porziuncola at Pentecost once every three years. The friars who accompanied James I in the reconquest of Valencia, and those who went to Almería with James II early in the fourteenth century, probably rejoiced in the privilege of being able to preach to the "Saracens."[40] Relations worsened between James II and the ruler of Granada in 1308, largely because of the presence of some Aragonese ships off the Mediterranean coast which Mohammed III regarded as threatening hostilities against his kingdom.[41] He ordered a number of raids near

---

39 Barcelona, ACA, RC 245, f. 30r–v, 17 September 1318. See J. Ernest Martínez Ferrando, *Jaume II o el Seny Català, Alfons el Benigne*, 2nd ed. (Barcelona, 1963), pp. 243–244. In 1318 James II reorganized the household of Queen Marie, making drastic reductions in personnel, and asked Fr. Arnulf, her confessor, to inform her in detail of the measures taken. The king's actions must have distressed the queen, who saw all her favourite ladies-in-waiting disappear, and the next we know of the queen is her illness, which was described as "alarming." The king took the news seriously and made arrangements for her funeral in case she died, but in the meantime, thanks to the medical attention of Fr. Arnulf, the queen's health improved to such an extent that the friar expressed the hope that she would soon be perfectly cured. The queen fell ill again in 1322, and no doubt Fr. Arnulf was once more called upon to attend her. See Juan Manuel, *Libro de los estados*, ed. R.B. Tate and I.R. Macpherson (Oxford, 1974), p. 281, where the author states that there are two orders which are beneficial for salvation and which exalt the Catholic faith. They are the Friars Preachers (Dominicans) and the Friars Minor (Franciscans).
40 Barcelona, ACA, RP 272, ff. 62 and 102, 1 June (?) and 1 July (?; dates unreadable) 1309. Ten Franciscan friars accompanied the king on his crusade to Granada, receiving 600 Barcelona sous for their expenses: see Jill R. Webster, "La contribución de los registros del patrimonio real a la história de los frailes menores durante la primera mitad del siglo XIV," *AIA*, in press. One of them, Fr. Fernando García, was given a dispensation ("non obstante illegitimitatis macula") in 1304 so that he could become a bishop (see Benedict XI, no. 364, 26 February 1304, *Le Registre de Benoit XI: Recueil des bulles de ce pape*, ed. Ch. Grandjean [Paris, 1905], p. 256), but clearly by 1309 he had not been consecrated in any bishopric.
41 Martínez Ferrando, *Jaume II*, and his *Jaime II de Aragón: Su vida familiar*, 2 vols. (Barcelona, 1948), 1: 195. See also Angel Masià i de Ros, *Jaume II: Aragó, Granada i Marroc* (Barcelona, 1989), pp. 337–393.

Alicante, Denia and Javea, with the result that both Castile and Aragon made preparations to protect the coast by conquering Almería and Algeciras. The mendicants were well represented in the party led by James II against Granada, and not only Franciscans but Augustinians, Carmelites and Dominicans all participated.[42] In a crusade against the Moors it was expedient to have the representatives of Christendom, for both chaplains and confessors would be required to attend to the sick and hear the confessions of the dying.

The Order of Friars Minor had come into being at a time when the Albigensian Crusade was still raging in southern France, and when the extirpation of heretical views like those of the Waldensians and others was still a source of concern in ecclesiastical circles. This helps to explain why the rule emphasizes that all friars were to be Catholics. The friars resembled the Waldensians in many ways, and Saint Francis had to reassure the pope that his followers were entirely orthodox in their acceptance of the Holy Roman Church.

Organization of the Order

It was after the first rule had been drawn up that the organization gradually took the form it was to maintain in future years. In 1217 eleven provinces were designated, including one for Spain; a provincial minister was given the administration of each and was directly responsible to the minister general.[43] After the death of Francis the choice of a successor to direct the affairs of the order frequently became a matter of contention, and the ministers elected were expected to interpret the practical meaning of the Franciscan rule.

Under the provincial and general ministers were those responsible for each house or group of houses, the guardian, first appearing at the time of Saint Francis's Testament, and the custodian (*custos*), a later necessity when provinces were subdivided into smaller entities. There was also a vicar, whose task it must have been to replace the guardian when the

---

42 Their names appear in Barcelona, ACA, RP 272, f. 102r-v, 1 July (?—date unreadable) 1309, but some are not legible. In addition to the four Franciscans mentioned earlier, Fr. Dalmau [Mansolí], Fr. Berenguer Fiveller, Fr. [Pere] Oliba and Fr. Pere Jofre, with two further confreres (one the unnamed socius of Fr. Pere Jofre and one whose name is no longer legible), also accompanied the king to Granada in 1309 and received 100 sous each for their expenses.

43 Moorman, *History of the Franciscan Order*, p. 62.

latter was called away on other business, as must have happened on numerous occasions in houses such as Barcelona, Saragossa and Valencia, although the most frequent use of this term in the documents consulted is for the Puigcerdà house, where the vicar seems to have been the alter ego of the guardian and replaced him constantly. Most of the foundations for this structure were in place prior to the establishment in the 1220s of the first houses within the realm of Aragon, a fact which is clear from the description in Chapter 1 of the organization of the province of Aragon.

Within the province and custodies, the most important centre of activity was the convent, where the friars lived and worked, and the church, to which they attracted large crowds of faithful supporters. One of the most difficult tasks the historian faces in assessing the role of the medieval mendicant orders is that of determining the precise nature of the life awaiting the average friar within the cloister. The surviving documentation is concerned with exceptional events or behaviour, and makes but little reference to the spiritual and material aspects of the daily routine which must have continued within the convent walls. Some of these have been postulated earlier in this chapter from the accounts of Salimbene and others, but the very real possibility that local customs, not always identical to those described, prevailed should not be disregarded.

As the order developed, it became impossible to follow to the letter the rule of 1221, and certain modifications were inevitable. The friars were not an isolated group, for they lived in a society which was undergoing profound social and economic changes, changes to which they contributed significantly but which in turn forced them to reconsider certain aspects of their mission. Their lives were to a great degree dependent upon the support of the papacy, the crown and the urban patricians, and were frequently at variance with the lives of the parish clergy or the ambitions of neighbouring merchants.

Despite the advantage they had in being the custodians of the spiritual destiny of their contemporaries, a fact which cannot be ignored in the Middle Ages, some compromise was required on the part of the friars in return for the support they received. By the fourteenth century the educated among them were much in demand to undertake the multifarious duties associated with an expanding economy and the ever-increasing complications of the diverse components of the Crown of Aragon, including the development of highly skilled notarial practices to which this study is so greatly indebted. Inevitably this led them away from a simple, unstructured life of poverty to a situation in which they were the close allies of crown and merchant, versed in theology, philosophy and the learning which came from their university studies. This progress was not unattended by the taint of heresy, the prevalence of unorthodoxy and the polemics over the meaning of the central purpose of the rule of Saint Francis, which at the end of the fourteenth century was to lead to a split between the two groups who were later known as the Observants and the Conventuals.[44]

The first and primary material consideration of the friars was undoubtedly the need to eat, and for this purpose certain members of the convent were appointed to look after the procuring of food and its preparation for the table. In this category could be counted those who worked in the house and in the garden, and, of equal importance, those who begged from door to door.

The second activity basic to the welfare of the convent related to all matters connected with the church: the hearing of confessions, the administration of the sacraments and the attendance upon the sick and dying. The missionary endeavours of the friars, the preaching to the non-Christians and the contact with the convents in North Africa all fall under this heading. Indeed everything pertaining to the care of souls, and the rewards the friars received for this aspect of their work can be placed within this category.

The third group of miscellaneous secular tasks is perhaps the largest and most diverse, proceeding directly from the second but not forming an integral part of it. It is here perhaps that the mission of the friars in the Middle Ages differs more significantly from their role in modern times, for the plethora of political tasks entrusted to them has no parallel in the life of the order in the twentieth century. These tasks are more abundantly documented than any, and are also of more interest to the social historian, as they show just how much the monarch relied on the religious orders for the fulfilment of functions only indirectly connected with the spiritual purpose of the order.

The political and organizational structure of the Crown of Aragon cannot be discussed in any detail, but the possession of overseas territories, the reconquest of lands from the Moors and the relations with Sicily, Sardinia and Majorca made it essential for the king to have at his command skilful and trustworthy ambassadors who would convey his

---

44 Moorman, *History of the Franciscan Order*, pp. 441–456.

despatches expeditiously and secretly. The key to the success of the friars in any such endeavour can be attributed to the fact that they had no material benefit to gain from these secret missions, beyond the stipend they were granted for their services. Unlike the nobles, they had no territorial aspirations; trading was forbidden to them and they could not personally accept money, goods or titles, although some were recommended for bishoprics when they fell vacant. The king had at his behest a group of people who constituted no threat to his sovereignty and who could be relied upon to undertake the tasks entrusted to them without thought of the reward they would receive. The advantages of such a system need not be spelled out, as they are immediately apparent.

Not all the friars were involved in these royal missions, and even those who were must at some time or other have participated in conventual life, although how many of them were given special privileges is an unresolved question. For the average friar life within the cloister would have been his primary concern, and extant records suggest that community living was even more difficult in the Middle Ages than it is today.

Unfortunately, only these instances of conflict survive, and any attempt to give a fuller portrait of life within the cloister in the thirteenth and fourteenth centuries can only be conjectural. One fact emerges incontrovertibly: the numbers in the medieval Franciscan houses varied considerably from one place to another, and at different periods. It might be true to say that the average friary consisted of fifteen to twenty friars, and that the more important friaries had reached a total complement of between sixty and seventy by the end of the fourteenth century. In some houses there were also slaves, whose function must have been purely menial, perhaps looking after much of the cleaning and preparation of food, although there is no evidence to support this.[45]

A medieval friary differed from a modern one in that it was normal for a number of laymen to live in it, perhaps because they had nowhere else to go, or because they were staying in the town temporarily. Some of these visitors would have been from noble families, and indeed the

---

45 Palma de Mallorca, AC, Protocols, no. 14574, unnumbered folio, 1 April 1359. Fr. Jordi Prat, bishop of Belgrade in the province of Rumania, concluded a deal with Pere Amat of Ibiza in which he exchanged his light-skinned slave, Margarida, for a light-skinned "Saracen" slave called Mohamet. Fr. Jordi also paid Pere Amat 23 reials of fine Majorcan gold to cover the value of the slave he received and Pere Amat paid him 24 reials of fine Majorcan gold for Margarida, indicating that the woman slave, who is not designated as a "Saracen," was worth more.

king himself frequently lodged in the larger houses in the realms of Aragon, not always to the advantage of the friars. Others would have been workers employed by the Franciscans, or those who had retired from active work and who, because of an agreement they had made with a particular house, were able to live out the remaining years of their lives without care for the morrow.[46]

Although at the beginning of the thirteenth century most of the friars would have been lay brothers and would therefore have had little part in the saying of mass, hearing of confessions and other similar duties, after 1250 the proportion of ordained Franciscans equalled or even exceeded in ever-increasing numbers that of their non-ordained brethren. If this is correct, there would have been fewer friars available to undertake the menial tasks, thus explaining the presence of slaves, servants and workers. The majority of the friars came from reasonably affluent families and would not have been used to performing many of these tasks, and it would have been unthinkable for them to have carried out the roughest and most menial work. It would have been enough that they had given up material aspirations to beg for their food, without having to stoop to do the work of servants. It would have been nothing unusual to see two friars, accompanied by a servant and probably, in some cases, a mule, being sent to procure the food for the house.[47] It is likely that these duties would have been rotated among the members of the convent and that one of these friars, the socius, would have been a lay brother.

Life in the friary could not have varied much from one place to another, and it is from Salimbene's *Chronicle* that the best picture can be obtained of what a young man entering the Order of Friars Minor might have expected to find within the cloister. Certainly, he would not have expected to break off the ordinary relations of life, nor avoid his fellow men, and the very need to beg for food would have ensured con-

---

46 The only document found of this type of agreement is in Puigcerdà, AHC, Arnald Embertad with Ramon Guillem de Lorà and Jaume Mercer, *Liber firmitatis*, 25 March 1338–14 January 1339, f. 17v, 17 April 1338. It refers to Bartomeu Borrell, a tailor of Puigcerdà, who made over all his property (20 pounds) to the friars on the condition that they should then allow him to live in the Puigcerdà house for the rest of his life, in sickness or in health, provide him with meals and clothing and attend to any other needs he might have. The document consists of the sworn statement of the donor followed by that of the guardian, lector and all the friars resident in the Puigcerdà house.

47 See Andrew G. Little, *The Grey Friars in Oxford* (Oxford, 1892), p. 91.

tinual contact with the world.⁴⁸ To test his fitness for the life he had chosen, a year's probationary period was required, but it is clear from the number of apostates and the means which were taken to make them return to the convent that the year served little purpose.

It has been mentioned elsewhere that some novices entered the order when they were too young to understand the significance of the step they were taking, a practice which was condemned by Pope Urban V, who took measures to ensure that it was discontinued.⁴⁹ That many friars entered the convent before the age of puberty goes some way towards explaining why there were so many apostates. An extreme case was that of Arnau Guillem, who entered the Order of Saint Augustine at the age of seven but left when he was fourteen.⁵⁰ Strictly speaking, a friar who left without completing his probationary year, and then at a later date wished to reenter the convent, was prohibited from so doing by ecclesiastical law. Only in exceptional cases was a renegade friar readmitted to the life he had abandoned so willingly.⁵¹ In theory, those who did not conform to the discipline of the cloister were reprimanded or punished severely, depending on the gravity of the matter in which they had erred. All the same, according to Salimbene, the average friar did not conform to all the rules because, in his opinion, they were only "pious aspirations."⁵² The scanty evidence for the Crown of Aragon corroborates this account, as there is no doubt that many of the friars caused trouble to their superiors, not only when they first entered the order but throughout their lives.

The examples of such behaviour are those which required the intervention of a higher authority, but there must have been many more which were settled within the Franciscan house itself and of which no

---

48 See G.G. Coulton, *From St. Francis to Dante: Translations from the Chronicle of the Franciscan Salimbene (1221-1288)*, paperback ed. (Philadelphia, 1972), p. 63. For a full translation see Salimbene da Parma, *Chronicle,* trans. Baird et al.
49 See above Chapter 4, p. 170n62.
50 Barcelona, ACA, RC 598, f. 64v, 8 October 1338. The fact that he left with the knowledge and consent of his confreres and that he had entered at such an early age exempted him from punishment. Arnau, who went to live with his brother, was captured four years later at the prior's instigation, and took his case to the king. The present document confirms that, because of his age, the order had no claim on him and could not force him to reenter.
51 See above Chapter 1, p. 24.
52 Coulton's translation, *From St. Francis to Dante,* p. 65.

record has been found. Concerns of this type would first be reported to the guardian of the convent, and if unresolved would be taken to a conventual chapter or perhaps, if more serious, to a provincial one, all the friars in the house having been gathered in the refectory or other large room at the ringing of the church bell. These conventual chapter meetings were convened regularly to conduct the affairs of the house, but if any major decision had to be made, such as the purchase of a piece of land or the transfer of the friary to a new location, an extra meeting would be held.[53]

The medieval friar differed little from his contemporaries: he shared their values and code of behaviour, and often became embroiled in their concerns and quarrels. Usually he lived in a convent which still formed part of the neighbourhood in which he had grown up, and which owed much to the wealthy citizens around it, perhaps even to his immediate family.[54] For this reason it was inevitable that friars maintained an interest in family affairs and interceded on behalf of relatives when a problem arose, usually in connection with a legacy, to ensure that the king looked favourably upon them. There are many instances of such favours granted to individuals or to families solely because of their connection with a Franciscan who had undertaken services for the king.

Crises must have occurred quite frequently for one reason or another, not the least when food was scarce, or the house had been broken into by those with criminal intent or serious damage had been done to its furnishings by the king's retinue. In some of the larger houses, where there were frequent visitors, there would have been constant movement, with some friars coming and going on business and others transferring from one house to another.[55] In common with society at large, hygiene would not have been of prime importance, and accounts of Saint Francis present him as having a dirty tunic and an unprepossessing person, suggesting that he took little thought for his

---

53 A list of chapter meetings will be found in Appendix 2.
54 The most obvious instance of this is in Puigcerdà, where the family connections of most of the friars can be traced. The Llaguna family, which supported the Franciscans from before the foundation of the house to the sixteenth century, and the families of Colomer, Espanyoll and Puig were among the founding families.
55 See Jill R. Webster, "Política reial i suport ciutadà per a les cases religioses del regne de Mallorca," in *XIII Congrés d'història de la Corona d'Aragó (Palma de Mallorca, 27 setembre–1 octubre 1987): Comunicacions 1* (Palma de Mallorca, 1989), pp. 263–270.

clothing.[56] On different occasions the king gave money for the purchase of a habit, at times even commenting that the friar in question was much in need of new clothing.[57]

Fr. Francesc Examenis in his *Crestià* describes this habit as being the colour of a sack (*burel*), adding that in winter it was customary to wear skins, while in summer only the threadbare habits were worn because then it was more difficult for the bugs to lodge in them.[58] Like Salimbene, he comments on the presence of fleas, noting that they were able to snuggle into the fur and cause their wearer extreme discomfort.[59] It is known that some habits were made of a light-coloured rough woollen cloth known as *cadin,* commonly used in the Middle Ages.[60] The fact that the friars also made use of the services of a barber suggests that their hair and beards were trimmed, and early pictures of the friars portray them with a a tonsure and a short haircut.[61] There is no evidence to suggest how frequently the barber attended; however, it is known that in 1330 in Saragossa he was a "Saracen."[62]

---

56 Moorman, *History of the Franciscan Order,* p. 24.
57 Tàrrega, AHM, Llibres del Consell, no. 2 (1342-1360), f. 28v, 29 October 1342. Fr. Ramon Gornall, as guardian of the Tàrrega house, was to be given 30 sous for a habit, in recognition of the many things he had done for the town.
58 See Jill R. Webster, "Eiximenis and the Society of His Day" (M.A. dissertation, University of Nottingham, 1964), p. 222.
59 Ibid., and Coulton, *From St. Francis to Dante,* pp. 62-75.
60 See J. Angel Sesma Muñoz and Angeles Líbano Zumalacárregui, *Léxico del comercio medieval en Aragón (siglo XV)* (Saragossa, 1982), p. 127. In Perpignan in 1295 the cloth used by the Franciscans was known as "drap de frares menors," but it is not known whether or not this Catalan material was the same as the coarse cloth described here and used by the Aragonese. See Miguel Gual Camarena, *Vocabulario del comercio medieval* (Barcelona, 1976), p. 322. It should also be noted that the material used by the Dominicans was known as "drap de prehicadors," suggesting perhaps that the quality of the cloth was similar for all religious orders (Gual Camarena, *Vocabulario,* p. 398).
61 Gabriel Llompart, *La pintura medieval mallorquina,* 4 vols. (Palma de Mallorca, 1977-1980), 2: facing p. 161, depicts Saint Jerome with a tonsure; see also Josep Gudiol and Santiago Alcolea i Blanch, *Pintura gótica catalana* (Barcelona, 1986), illustration 339.
62 Barcelona, ACA, RC 482, f. 14v, 8 October 1330. Alfonso III granted the request of the guardian of the Saragossa convent to enfranchise the friars' barber and exempt him from payment of the tax levied on Saracens. His name is not given, but we are told he was the son of Audalle Pex, a barber of Saragossa.

Many of the documents suggest that it was not too difficult to gain entrance to medieval Franciscan convents for those who were determined to do so, although in general they were considered safe enough to be used for the guarding of money and jewels. The royal family and those who had valuables or documents which they wished to lock away entrusted them to the guardian of the nearby Franciscan convent.[63] In the case of documents, it was usual for three keys to be supplied, one to be retained by the owner, one handed over to the guardian of the convent and one to a third person, either the executor of a will or a friend of the owner. A problem sometimes arose when one of the persons died, especially if that person was the guardian of the convent or an executor of the will; in most cases all three persons were required to agree to a document's being removed from safekeeping, and to be present when this happened.[64]

Life in the cloister was not very different from life outside, except, perhaps, insofar as an attempt at poverty led at times to hardship and deprivation. The royal documents constantly refer to the Franciscans as poor and in need of economic help, and as the year of the Black Death approached some convents, at least, seem to have had difficulty in eking

---

63 The following references give some indication of the importance of the convents as a place of safekeeping. For money: in Barbastro, Majorca and Saragossa in the year 1295 (Barcelona, ACA, RC 101, f. 218); Barcelona, 1275, 1296, 1317, 1324 and 1326 (RC 37, f. 97v; RC 252, f. 158v; RC 162, f. 40v; RC 285, f. 4, 229v; RC 286, f. 2); Gerona, 1299 and 1336 (RC 265, f. 267; Vic, AE, ACF, Testaments 1306-1336, Testament 5.12.1336); Majorca, 1240 (Palma de Mallorca, AHRM, ECR 342, f. 9); Saragossa, 1330 (Barcelona, ACA, RC 524, f. 157v). For documents: in Barcelona in 1314 (RC 241, f. 162); Calatayud, 1283 (Ambròs de Saldes, "Documentació franciscana [1282-1285]," *EF* 42 [1930], 86-96, at p. 95); Ejea, 1306, 1309 and 1312 (Barcelona, ACA, RC 138, f. 258v; RC 289, f. 95; RC 150, f. 233r-v); Huesca, 1302 (RC 125, f. 109v); in Tortosa in 1329 (RC 435, f. 171); Saragossa, 1330 (RC 524, f. 157v). For miscellaneous other items, including: in Barcelona, a crown and jewels in 1311 (RC 272, f. 37v), keys in 1339 (RC 1055, f. 175v), and a chest in 1309 (RC 212, ff. 65v-66); a chest in Ejea in 1312 (RC 150, f. 233r-v); a shield in Gerona, 1290 (Sanahuja, *História*, p. 122); and a corpse in Morella, 1308 (Barcelona, ACA, RC 205, f. 195v).

64 The king wrote to the councillors of the city of Barcelona, asking them for one of the two keys (not three in this case) to the deposit box containing the documents regarding the inquiry into the death of Francesc Examenis. The keys were held by his father, Jaspert, and the guardian of the Franciscan house in which the documents had been placed for safekeeping. See Jill R. Webster, "Una familia de mercaderes: los Examenis," *AIA* 47 (1987), 63-78.

out a bare subsistence. A distinction should be made between the splendid houses of the major cities and the lesser friaries, where life might have been very much more difficult. Convents like Borja and Monzón seem to have had a relatively quiet existence and to have disappeared at a very early date, leading to the conclusion that their main functions were to ensure the Christianization of Aragon in the years following the reconquest of those territories.

Almsgiving was one of the major sources of income, a fact confirmed by the numerous bequests which mention that they should be used for the Franciscans' table, their clothing, the work of their church, books or other needs. The king and royal family constituted the most important almsgivers, and there were frequent occasions on which the Franciscans shared their table.[65] This happened in England too, but in Aragon account books survive that give the provisions of lamb, eggs and fish paid for out of the royal exchequer on some of the occasions the friars joined the royal family for meals.[66] The friars were invited to

---

65 One example of this was during 1314, when the incidence of the plague led to a sojourn in the Montblanc house of two sons of James II (see Sanahuja, História, p. 96), who probably took their meals with the friars. In Tortosa in 1334 the king of Majorca stayed in the Franciscan house while the king of Aragon was in the castle with the rest of the party (see Barcelona, ACA, RC 536, ff. 31v–32, 19 July 1334); certainly the king of Majorca took some of his meals with the friars.

66 Barcelona, ACA, RC 1524, ff. 15v–212 passim, records the expenses of Peter III for 1338–1339. They include the following items when the Franciscans were at the palace: on Thursday, 25 June [1338] (f. 15v), an item of 6 sous for eight pounds of lamb; on Wednesday, 26 June [1338] (f. 16), 2 sous for eggs and 14 diners for fresh fish, on the occasion that the Franciscans dined with the king; on Monday, 7 June (probably should read July) [1338] (f. 66v), 6 diners for fish for the Franciscans and Dominican nuns; on Tuesday, 8 October [1338] (f. 67), 3 diners for fish; on Tuesday after Easter [1339] (f. 110), 3 sous less 2 diners for two chickens, for the evening meal; on Sunday, 16 May and for the feast of Quinquagesima (presumably the one just past) [1339] (f. 134v), 2 sous 8 diners for two chickens to the Franciscans and "la senyora" (no indication of who she is), for dinner; on Wednesday, 8 September [1339] (f. 180), 3 sous for four pounds of lamb; on Wednesday, 29 October [1339] (f. 194), 2 sous 8 diners for eggs; on Saturday, 30 October [1339] (f. 194 [item 2]), 2 sous 8 diners for eggs; on Wednesday, 29 December [1339] (f. 205), 6 diners for bread for En Galcerán, Samuel and the Franciscans; on Wednesday, 21 February [1339, i.e. 1340] (f. 212), 2 sous 6 diners for eggs. It is not clear whether the amounts refer to expenditure for the meals the friars shared with the royal household, or whether they were given the money afterwards to buy the commodities mentioned. A comparison of these

dine not only by the royal family, but by the municipal authorities in some towns, and probably by rich families.[67] Apart from the friars whose task was to go begging in the streets, there would doubtless have been others who were in charge of collecting alms at all the masses and other services held in the Franciscan church. Since no Franciscan account books have survived from this time, it is impossible even to guess at the amounts they might have received in this manner. There seems little doubt that, regardless of the amount collected during or after services, the regularity of these alms would have helped to pay for the upkeep of the friary and the replenishment of the convent pantry.

The primary purpose of the convent, the successful completion of the Christian mission the friars had vowed to uphold, was an aim relegated to second place, not because of its lack of importance but rather because the energies of the first friars must have been divided between their material needs and their spiritual commitment. There is abundant evidence that the Franciscans undertook most of the duties associated with the parochial clergy, and like them probably visited the homes of their neighbours, becoming familiar figures as they wandered through the streets in their sacklike habits.

When they had to travel from one town to another and particularly from one country to another, the friars were granted safe-conducts by the king, and they were also allowed to erect portable altars for saying mass when there was no church or convent in the vicinity.[68] This may have contributed to their popularity, and it surely helped them to make the acquaintance of their contemporaries who lived in less accessible areas on the periphery of the towns.

Associated with the spiritual functions of saying mass and administering the sacraments were others which were purely secular. Up to the

---

amounts with those listed as given to the bishops of Barcelona and Valencia at the time of Peter's journey to Toledo in 1269 (see Ferran Soldevila, *Pere el Gran*, 2 vols. in 4 [Barcelona, 1950-1952], 1/2: 247), lends support to acceptance of the latter possibility.

67 In Tàrrega the *Consell* wished to invite the minister of the Framenors and put aside 30 sous for the purpose. Tàrrega, AHM, Llibres del Consell, no. 2 (1342-1360), f. 13, 14 April 1342.

68 Honorius III, no. 5194, *Regesta Honorii papae III*, ed. Petrus Pressuti, 3 vols. (Rome, 1888), 2: 285. The full text of the bull is printed in Lucas Wadding, *Annales Minorum*, 28 vols., 3rd ed. (Quaracchi, 1931-1947), 2: 671-672 (or, in numbering of 2nd ed., 599-600).

time of the Black Death, although in the second quarter of the fourteenth century in some towns the practice was less evident, Franciscans acted as witnesses to legal documents and advisers to testators. This gave them the opportunity to exert pressure on the sick and thus obtain a share of the estate; some were unscrupulous enough to do this, hanging "round the corpses of wealthy men like dogs round carrion."[69] The guardian or another friar often gave advice to testators, and in many instances apparently received no monetary or material benefit for his efforts. Many took on the role of executor, either acting jointly with a member of the deceased's family or other prominent person, or in some cases in conjunction with friars from other orders or, less frequently, with the parish priest. It was not unusual for the confessor, adviser or executor to be mentioned in the will as the recipient of a sum of money, books or bedding, a valuable commodity in the thirteenth and fourteenth centuries.

It is from this source that the names of the friars listed in Appendix 5 have been drawn, and in some cases their names reappear in the royal documents, enabling brief biographies to be compiled. The most interesting of these form the basis of the discussion of the tasks undertaken by the medieval friar, for many a Franciscan was constantly on the move, having little or no time for conventual life. It is also evident that certain friars were chosen for specific duties because of their family connections, and that the superior of the convent had little or no choice in the matter, having been requested by king, pope or provincial minister to allow a particular friar to undertake a special mission.

On occasions when a friar was considered of devout and upright life and showed qualities of leadership, municipal authorities exerted pressure on the order to have him appointed guardian in the convent in their city. Such was the case of Fr. Guillem de Campllong of Gerona, who had been transferred to Majorca, much to the disgust of his native town, but whose return the *jurats* of Gerona requested, on the grounds that he had previously done so much to make the Gerona convent one of the best in Catalonia.[70] In Tàrrega too there is evidence that pressure

---

69 Moorman, *History of the Franciscan Order,* p. 201. The English chronicler's opinion of the friars is not unlike that of Juan Ruiz (see above p. 182n22).
70 Gerona, AHM, Acords, no. 6, f. 24, 26 March 1366. Fr. Guillem de Campllong, at the time of the document guardian of the Franciscan house in Majorca, was urgently required by the *jurats* of the city to return to Gerona, leaving his position as guardian of the Majorca house to someone else. Unfortunately, part of this document has been so seriously damaged by water that it is not legible.

was exerted on the order to appoint a particular guardian, and it is clear that decisions of this nature were not left entirely in the hands of the Franciscans.[71] This can be understood if the purely secular functions that the medieval convent fulfilled are borne in mind, as it was in their interests that the guardian be a trustworthy and upright man. In addition to receiving important guests like the king, the convent was used on a regular basis for public meetings, including those of the municipal authorities.[72]

The friars also had an important function to fulfil in connection with the convents of the Poor Clares; they acted as visitors, chaplains, confessors and advisers.[73] In Barcelona, the Clarissan monastery at Pedralbes was important enough to need the services of more than one friar and a *conventet* especially for those friars who undertook duties for the nuns was built in the vicinity. In smaller towns this would not have been necessary, but cities, as they became more important commercially, frequently demanded that the friars build a convent there; this happened in the case of Tàrrega and Puigcerdà, two of the group of convents founded during the second decade of the fourteenth century.[74] There is little doubt that, prior to the foundation of these convents, the friars were well known in the area, travelling from neighbouring towns or staying in hospices, as in Manresa, to get to know the townspeople. Whatever their duties, one fact is evident: the friars travelled extensively, both within the Crown of Aragon and beyond its borders to Castile, Portugal, Navarre and the university cities of Europe.[75]

It would be tedious and repetitive to describe the individual lives of the majority of friars, not only because for many of them the extant

---

71 Tàrrega, AHM, Llibres del Consell, no. 4 (1376–1378), f. 21, 24 October 1376: "Item comana lo dit honrat Conseyll als dits honrats pahers sobre un provesió real que ha aguda lo guardià dels frameno[r]s que lo portal del carrer de Belloch stigue ubert que la puxen fer revocar i scriure al ministre dels frameno[r]s que deye mudar altre guardià e açò per algunes rahons [not given]."
72 Gerona, AHM, Correspondència, I (1329–1333), f. 10, 12 April 1330; f. 88, 17 August 1334; and ff. 100 and following, passim, 7 September 1334. Surviving parchments from the 1330s and 1340s refer to the gathering of the "universitas" of Gerona in the Franciscan house as a habitual event. For example, AHM, perg. 253, 1 January 1336; perg. 295, 1 January 1341; and perg. 305, 1 January 1342, record instances when the election of the *jurats* was held in the convent.
73 See below Chapter 6, pp. 234–235.
74 See above Chapter 1, pp. 53–55, 67–68.
75 See below Chapter 7, pp. 263–265.

references to their activities are insufficient to allow a picture of them to be formed, but also because the activities in which they engaged were very similar. There are a few men whose lives, taken together, cover the main functions the order undertook in the late thirteenth and fourteenth centuries; the six chosen include three Aragonese and three Catalans, Fr. Domingo [Ola] de Jaca, Fr. Romeo Ortiz and Fr. Sancho López de Ayerbe from Aragon; Fr. Pons Carbonell, Fr. Arnau Oliba and Fr. Arnau de Canelles from Catalonia. There are others from these regions who could have been included, but limitations of space have made it necessary to omit them.

Fr. Domingo [Ola] de Jaca

Documents relating to the activities of this friar cover a period of some fifty years. The earliest references occur in wills, and there is no proof that the Fr. Domingo mentioned in them is in fact Fr. Domingo de Jaca, but after 1289 his place of origin is mentioned and from 1292 he was provincial minister of Aragon.[76] In 1295 he seems to have been given the bishopric of Silves; but again the evidence is not conclusive.[77] Throughout his life he was often called upon by the king to act as his ambassador. A few examples will suffice to indicate his importance. In 1295 the king appointed Simó de Llor, a knight, and Fr. Domingo to advise him on the succession to the throne of Sicily.[78] The following year Fr. Rodrigo Pons, master of the Order of Calatrava, joined these two men as royal nuncios to Queen Mary and Prince Ferdinand.[79]

---

76 See Sanahuja, *Història,* p. 244.
77 Barcelona, ACA, RC 100, f. 391r–v (2 docs.), 17 March 1294 [1295], and RC 101, f. 6, 27 March 1295. The first two documents refer to a Fr. Domingo as bishop of Silves but do not mention that he was from Jaca. They say that he was required to go to Portugal to talk to Queen Isabel on the king's behalf and must, therefore, travel through Castile. This must have been the same man referred to in Pius Bonifacius Gams, *Series episcoporum ecclesiae Catholicae* (Ratisbon, 1873), p. 106, as Fr. Domingo, of the Order of Preachers, bishop of Silves from 27 May 1292 until 1 March 1297. The third document refers to a safe-conduct granted to Fr. Domingo de Jaca together with four horses; in view of the date, I believe it endorses the conclusion that the three documents concern Fr. Domingo de Jaca.
78 Barcelona, ACA, RC 252, f. 19v, 10 August 1295.
79 Ibid., f. 20v, 5 August 1295; ff. 146v–148v and 151–152v, 16 April–18 September 1296, all of which refer to royal missions to be carried out by Fr. Domingo, mediator and ambassador.

Fr. Domingo was also appointed by the king to go to Pope Boniface VIII in connection with this matter, to discuss the relative merits of Prince Frederick's suitability for the throne of Sicily. He was to be paid 2000 silver sous of Tours for his expenses, and Bernat de Sarrià, the king's official, was told to go immediately to Barcelona to hand over the money to Fr. Domingo, as the mission on which he was to go was very urgent.[80] The king did not have the money and had to borrow from the Chiarenti Company of Pistoia. In 1297 Fr. Domingo de Jaca was to be paid by Alfonso de la Cerda, a claimant to the Crown of Castile, a sum of 1000 Barcelona sous of silver money as an instalment of the 10,000 Barcelona sous changed into Castilian money by the king of Aragon.[81]

Fr. Domingo's talents as an ambassador must have been considerable, as the Sicilian question needed careful handling if it were to be settled in favour of the Crown of Aragon, and James II would not have entrusted him with the recovery of such a large sum of money from Castile if he had not considered him reliable and trustworthy. Jaca was an important episcopal town in the Middle Ages, and in 1288 Alfonso II and Edward I of England met there to try and resolve the conflicts which had arisen over the occupation of Sicily.[82] Was it at this time that Fr. Domingo first came to the attention of the king? Once in royal favour, how did Fr. Domingo manage to fulfil his obligations to the crown, to his order as provincial minister and to his episcopal duties? These questions must remain unanswered, as must the question of his family origin, which undoubtedly played an important role in his subsequent success.

Fr. Romeo Ortiz

Fr. Romeo Ortiz was also Aragonese, and probably professed in the convent of Ejea de los Caballeros, where he served as lector and custodian for the custody of Saragossa, having as his socius Fr. Martín

---

80 Barcelona, ACA, RC 263, f. 40, 16 May 1296.
81 ACA, RC 264, f. 28, 30 May 1297.
82 Some of the problems arose because of the powerful Aragonese union, an alliance of nobles who posed a threat to royal sovereignty, demanding control over foreign policy, the royal household, lands and revenues. See J.N. Hillgarth, *The Spanish Kingdoms: 1250-1516*, 2 vols. (Oxford, 1976), 1: 260-261; and also Peter III, *Crònica general de Pere III el Ceremoniós, dita comunament Crónica de Sant Joan de la Penya*, ed. Amadeu-J. Soberanas Lleó (Barcelona, 1961), p. 154.

de Ejea.[83] On 10 May 1286 he was referred to as confessor of Peter, the son of Peter the Great, king of Aragon, and the following year he attended the general chapter of his order held at Assisi.[84] When Peter died, it was to Fr. Romeo Ortiz that the long and complicated process of executor to his will was entrusted, a task which was not completed at the time of his death and which Fr. Pascasi de Vall-llebrera had to undertake in his place.

Among the many activities Fr. Romeo undertook was a journey to Avignon in 1309, to defend his friars against the charge of being sympathetic to the doctrines of the Spirituals.[85] In 1311 Fr. Romeo was present at the Council of Vienne to confirm the election of Sr. Clara de Gener as abbess of the convent of Sant Antoni in Barcelona, a position which she certainly held in 1290 and again in 1316, although it is not clear whether her tenure there was uninterrupted.[86] There are many Franciscans with the surname Gener, and some of them, at least, seem to have come from the same family.

Fr. Romeo seems to have been a favourite of James II, who on more than one occasion sent him on diplomatic missions to Naples and Sicily. In 1316, shortly before his death, James II entrusted him with three letters to take to Naples, whither he was going to attend the general chapter, in the hope that an end could be negotiated to the war between the Angevins of Naples and the kingdom of Sicily.[87] Fr. Romeo must have been a learned man to fulfil the position of lector in Saragossa, so it is not surprising that the king commissioned him to copy a Bible for him and to arrange for it to be illuminated.[88] It was to Fr. Romeo that the king wrote to say that Fr. Simó de Puigcerdà's presence was required in Tunis to translate from Catalan to Latin a book of Ramon Llull's.[89] The Franciscan house at Tunis formed part of the custody of Barcelona, and Fr. Simó was obviously an expert translator, for he is

---

83 In some documents he is incorrectly cited as Fr. Ramon, but the overwhelming majority of the references to him name him as Fr. Romeo. See Barcelona, ACA, RC 89, f. 104, 5 June 1294.
84 See Sanahuja, *História,* p. 194.
85 Ibid., p. 246.
86 Ibid., p. 247.
87 Ibid., p. 214.
88 See Antoni Rubió i Lluch, ed., *Documents per l'història de la cultura catalana mig.eval,* 2 vols. (Barcelona, 1908–1921), 1: 59, no. 49, 21 August 1313.
89 Sanahuja, *História,* p. 205.

credited with having translated several of the works of Ramon Llull, including the *Ars consilii*. The last mission the king requested of Fr. Romeo Ortiz was destined to be undertaken by others, as the illustrious friar was stricken with tertian fever and probably died shortly afterwards, that is, in May 1316.[90] Certainly he was dead before November of that year, and as there is no further reference to him alive after May he probably died then.

What kind of a man was Fr. Romeo? He probably came from a prominent Aragonese family, possibly from the Ortiz of Setia, Ejea de los Caballeros, who are mentioned in February 1333 in connection with a legal matter which one of them, a certain Lope, was appealing.[91] He is said to have led a good life and to have been ready to do the king's bidding, not fearing nevertheless to place the affairs of the Friars Minor ahead of the royal command, as happened in [1314] with the provincial chapter which was to be held in Lerida that year and which he had to attend.[92]

A letter of James II, written in 1308 to the bailiff of Barcelona, explains that Fr. Romeo Ortiz, then provincial minister of Aragon, and Fr. Berenguer Folcrà, guardian of Barcelona, expressly renounced the grant made to them by the late King Alfonso, of 250 quartans of oil taken from the royal vineyards and mills in Caldes de Montbui and Barcelona.[93] There is no indication as to why they renounced this concession, but it would seem that the king had need of this oil for provisions for the men who were to accompany him on the joint Castilian/Aragonese venture against Mohammed III of Granada.[94] The Franciscans might have believed that it was their duty to forego the benefits of the concession in the interests of defeating the unbeliever. Among the extant letters from the reign of James II are one or two written or dictated by Fr. Romeo, but unfortunately, like many of the others

---

90 Barcelona, ACA, RC 337, f. 305v, 15 April 1316.
91 ACA, RC 568, f. 172v, 26 February 1332 [1333].
92 Barcelona, ACA, Cartas reales, James II, caja 36, no. 4507, 9 May 1312; caja 96, no. 11658, s.a. [1314].
93 The *quartà* is a measurement of oil equivalent to approximately 4 litres. The measurement standards followed were those for Barcelona. See Barcelona, ACA, RC 296, f. 216v, 7 September 1308.
94 See Bisson, *Medieval Crown of Aragon*, p. 95.

consulted, some bear no indication of the year they were written.[95] In all, the references to Fr. Romeo are perhaps more numerous than those to any other fourteenth-century Franciscan friar, largely because the beneficiaries of Peter's will made endless demands upon the executors and Fr. Romeo's name constantly appears in this connection.

Fr. Sancho López de Ayerbe

The last of the Aragonese friars is Fr. Sancho López de Ayerbe, who rose to a position of importance during the reign of Peter III. Fr. Sancho was the great-grandson of James I, already a distinct advantage for future promotion, and it was not long in coming.[96] He is first referred to at the beginning of 1329, appearing both as guardian of the Saragossa house and as lector in Huesca.[97] That same year he was accused of speaking to the dishonour of Pope John XXII, and was due to be investigated by the Inquisition; but the pope, out of respect for the king of Aragon, agreed not to punish him if he would retract what he had said.[98] Fr. Sancho denied ever having spoken against the pope on the subject of absolute poverty and the position of the Spirituals, and went so far as to say that he would preach in public against the very errors which he was reputed to have supported; whereupon Alfonso III ordered the Inquisition enquiry to be suspended at once.

In 1337 Fr. Sancho was sent to the minister general, Fr. Gerard, in connection with the election of Sr. Beatriz of Saragossa as abbess of the house of Poor Clares at Xàtiva, where there had been some difficulties in placing suitably good-living nuns as residents of the new convent.[99] It is ironical that Fr. Sancho, whose sermon had given rise to Inquisition proceedings only a few years earlier, was now requested to intervene with the minister general over the Xàtiva question, in which another friar, Fr. Pedro de Huesca, much to the king's amazement and annoyance, was accused of having made clear his opposition to the king's

---

95   Some of those bearing a date are Barcelona, ACA, Cartas reales, James II, caja 27, no. 3438, 6 March 1308 [1309]; caja 29, no. 3668, 7 May 1309 (no. 3669, also 7 May 1309, refers to Fr. Romeo although it is not written by him); and caja 36, no. 4507, 9 May 1312.
96   Sanahuja, *História*, p. 146.
97   Barcelona, ACA, RC 475, f. 60, 6 January 1328 [1329].
98   Sanahuja, *História*, p. 146.
99   Barcelona, ACA, RC 1054, f. 111, 19 July 1337.

choice of abbess for the Xàtiva convent, and with Fr. Berenguer d'Ivorra had persuaded the provincial minister to agree to the election of Sr. Agnès.[100]

After 1340, references to Fr. Sancho are very frequent: in 1341 his socius was Fr. Pardo, raising the question whether this is the same man who acted as socius to Fr. Aparicio at the time of the attack on the highway outside Huesca in 1330.[101] Fr. Sancho spent some years in the royal court, where he acted as spiritual adviser to the king and his family; from 1335 he was confessor to Alfonso's successor, Peter III, who referred to him as his "beloved confessor" and who, on several occasions, gave him money to buy a mule.[102] In 1339 Fr. Sancho also received a grant of 12 golden florins to buy a book, and at that time his socius was Fr. Pere d'Artasona.[103] In 1340 Peter III asked the bishop of Barcelona, Fr. Ferrer, to pay, out of the money left by James II for the health of his soul, 400 Barcelona pounds to help with the work of the church of the Franciscans in Saragossa, this amount to be sent to Fr. Sancho López de Ayerbe so that he could pass it over to the procurator of the convent.[104]

Some of these documents bear the name of Fr. Sancho at the end, and were probably dictated by him. The constant grants to the Saragossa house owed much to the presence of Fr. Sancho at court. He was commissioned to purchase a Bible on behalf of the royal scribe, Bertran de Valls, for which he was to be paid 1200 Barcelona sous. The same Bertran is recorded as having given the sum of 200 sous of Jaca money to Fr. Pardo in 1341, to buy a Bible for his confrere Fr. Sancho, although, as frequently happened, the money was not paid immediately and had to be claimed by the friar.[105]

In 1342 Fr. Sancho was a witness to the signing of the process against the king of Majorca, part of the proceedings in connection with

---

100 For the Xàtiva house of the Poor Clares see below Chapter 6, pp. 238-240.
101 Rubió i Lluch, *Documents per l'història,* 1: 120-121, no. 107.
102 Barcelona, ACA, RC 1008, f. 84v, 2 March 1334 [1335], records his appointment as special procurator to the king. See also above, p. 184n26.
103 ACA, RC 1299, ff. 54v-55 and 61r-v, 6 and 10 March 1338 [1339].
104 ACA, RC 1302, f. 168, 7 October 1340. Like most of the royal grants this was not paid immediately, and the following month the *mestre racional* of the king's curia was told to send 2000 sous of Jaca money to Fr. Sancho for the work of the Saragossa Franciscan church (RC 1303, ff. 39v-40, 25 November 1340).
105 Rubió i Lluch, *Documents per l'història,* 1: 120 and 122-123, nos. 106 and 109.

the conquest of Majorca by Peter III, completed in 1344.[106] In 1344 he became bishop of Tarazona, a position he held until 1346, when he was translated to the archbishopric of Tarragona.[107] The king asked Fr. Sancho to go to the court in October 1356, and on the tenth of the month wrote to the friar saying he was sorry to hear that he was ill and excusing him from attendance.[108] The illness must have been serious, for he now disappears from the records and died less than a year later, on 22 August 1357, being buried in the Franciscan convent of Sant Francesc de Tarragona.[109] Despite the many documents referring to Fr. Sancho, his personality remains more obscure than that of Fr. Romeo, possibly because few references refer explicitly to his character or to his expertise.

The Catalan friars came from less prominent families than men like Fr. Sancho, but they reflected the thriving merchant economy in Catalonia.

Fr. Arnau Oliba

Fr. Arnau Oliba first appears as lector in Majorca in 1284, at which time he received a legacy of 100 sous for books.[110] By 1300 he had taken over the position of provincial minister from Fr. Romeo Ortiz, who for a brief period had succeeded Fr. Domingo de Jaca and Fr. Pere Esteve, and was involved in the arrangements for the funeral of Queen Constance; he was also one of the executors of her will.[111] The king had discussed with Fr. Arnau the situation of the legacy of 4000 sous given by the late King Alfonso to the Franciscan house in Barcelona, where both Alfonso and his mother were buried; but it was Fr. Romeo Ortiz who actually went to speak to the guardian of the Barcelona house, perhaps because he was from a more distinguished family and likely to

---

106 Barcelona, ACA, RC 618, f. 79, 16 September 1342.
107 See Sanahuja, *Història,* p. 146; and Barcelona, ACA, RP 322, f. 45, 1 January 1343 [1344].
108 Barcelona, ACA, RC 1136, f. 92, 10 October 1356.
109 Sanahuja, *Història,* p. 195.
110 The will is no. 118, dated 18 January 1284, ed. Pau Mora and Lorenzo Andrinal, *Diplomatari del monestir de Santa Maria de la Real de Mallorca* (Tarragona, 1982), 1: 365.
111 Barcelona, ACA, RC 266, f. 171v, 20 April 1300; and RC 268, f. 251, 17 December 1300.

have more expertise concerning the way in which royal wills were executed.[112]

Like Fr. Romeo, Fr. Arnau, as executor of the will of Queen Constance, was to have a considerable amount of work to do, work which extended over a period of years. The numerous legacies and the complicated disposition of royal estates frequently caused the executors unforeseen difficulties, as in fact happened when Queen Constance's assets were insufficient to allow for the building of the hospital next to the Franciscan house in Barcelona.[113] In the early years of the fourteenth century he seems to have been highly esteemed and very active both in the service of the king and in that of the order.[114] With Fr. Vidal de Four, a lector in Toulouse and later a cardinal, he was entrusted with the delicate task of visiting the Franciscan houses in Provence, where the Spirituals were very numerous.[115] He wrote a *Memorial* of this visit to the minister general, Fr. John of Murovalle, combating some of the doctrines of Peter Olivi.[116]

In 1302 his name appears in connection with an agreement drawn up between him, in his capacity as provincial minister, and James II over testamentary clauses in the will of Alfonso II, a document bearing the signatures of thirty-two friars from the Barcelona house who acted as witnesses.[117] That same year, again acting in an official capacity, he interceded with the king on behalf of Jaume de Calou of Berga, whose goods had been forfeited unjustly since he was not to blame for his unpaid debts.[118] At the beginning of 1303 James II wrote to Fr. Arnau and Fr. Domènec de Fontana in connection with the will of the nobleman Artaldo de Alagón. In 1304 the friar apparently attended the general chapter of the Franciscans held in Assisi, and was granted 200 Barcelona sous for his expenses.[119]

---

112 Barcelona, ACA, RC 268, f. 274, 28 January 1301 [1302].
113 See above Chapter 2, pp. 94–95.
114 Among the documents transcribed concerning Fr. Arnau Oliba see Vincke, *Documenta selecta*, pp. 55–56 and 150–151, nos. 100 and 224.
115 Sanahuja, *Història*, pp. 244–245.
116 See José María Pou i Martí, *Visionarios, beguinos y fraticelos catalanes (siglos XIII-XV)*, rev. ed. (Madrid, 1991), p. 30.
117 See Sanahuja, *Història*, p. 109.
118 Barcelona, ACA, RC 200, f. 144, 11 December 1302.
119 ACA, RC 126, f. 215, 8 January 1302 [1303]; RC 294, f. 171, 5 March 1303 [1304].

The outstanding qualities of Fr. Arnau can best be appreciated when it is recalled that his name was put forward to the Holy See as a possible candidate for cardinal; the kings of Aragon were anxious to have a Catalan cardinal, but had no success until 1357, when Fr. Nicolau Rossell was elevated to the position.[120] In July 1306 Bernat de Fonollars, acting as general procurator for Catalonia, was reminded by James II that a special favour of 400 Barcelona sous had been granted to Bernat Oliba, to be paid out of the 600 sous which Bernat de Vic of Berga, also known as Bernat de Rena, owed to him.[121] This man must have been a relative of Fr. Arnau's, and as such expected to receive special favours from the king.

In 1307 Fr. Arnau informed the king that the clergy and laity in Vilafranca had interfered with a funeral in the Franciscan church, and the officials of the town of Vilafranca were required to look into this and to allow the friars to bear the body of the deceased to the parish church without molestation by the clergy.[122] The following year Fr. Arnau, Fr. Dalmau Mansolí and the bishop of Barcelona, Pons de Gualba (not a Franciscan), accompanied by the prior of the Dominicans, attended the council held in Tarragona, where the bishop of Barcelona preached a sermon which caused the sacristan to rise and declare the friars to be heretics.[123] They were accused of having divided the body of Jesus Christ into two parts, referring of course to Paul's rebuke to the faction-ridden Corinthians, "Has Christ then been divided into two parts," and implying that the arrival of the mendicant friars had divided Christ's church and caused conflict between them and the parish priests.[124] As a result, the following month a large number of friars, not only Franciscans and including Fr. Arnau and Fr. Pons Carbonell, were placed under interdict.[125]

The accusation, and perhaps Fr. Arnau's earlier connection with the Spirituals, even though at that time he did not support their cause, led to his being suspected of sympathizing with heretical views, with the result that he was imprisoned in the house at Barcelona in 1311. The

---

120 Rubió i Lluch, *Documents per l'història,* 1: 180-181, no. 177.
121 Barcelona, ACA, RC 203, f. 179, 11 July 1306.
122 ACA, RC 139, f. 120v, 5 January 1306 [1307].
123 Barcelona, ACA, Cartas reales, James II, caja 86, no. 10510, 4 January s.a. [1308].
124 See Corinthians 1.12.
125 See Sanahuja, *Història,* pp. 69-70.

king said that the reason for his imprisonment was the malice and envy of his confreres and intervened on his behalf, urging that Fr. Arnau be released; and by the end of the year he was again in liberty.[126]

Fr. Arnau de Castllà had also suffered from the malicious gossip of his confreres, and in his case the king showed his displeasure that a man of exemplary life and virtue, who had diligently undertaken royal missions and had an excellent reputation, should be so defamed, ordering that the enquiry into these false rumours should be discontinued immediately.[127] Friars who served the king could expect his support in difficult circumstances, but after Fr. Arnau Oliba was imprisoned in the Barcelona convent he was no longer referred to as provincial minister, and it would seem that Fr. Romeo Ortiz took charge of the province of Aragon once more. All the same, Fr. Arnau Oliba was obviously reinstated in the king's good graces, and in July 1314 both he and Fr. Pons Carbonell were requested to go to Lerida to see him; the bailiff in Barcelona was to provide them with the money they needed for the journey and two horsemen to accompany them.[128] The last reference to Fr. Arnau Oliba is in a letter from Bishop Peter of Barcelona, dated March 1316, regarding the innocence of Jaspert Examenis, a parishioner of the church of Sant Just, Barcelona and probably an ancestor of Fr. Francesc Eiximenis, who had been accused of wrongdoing during his term as sub-vicar of Barcelona; it is likely that he died shortly afterwards.[129]

Fr. Pons Carbonell

He accompanied Fr. Arnau to Lerida in 1316 and had a long and distinguished career, but historians have confused him with another man of similar name. In their zeal to point out his good qualities, they have imputed to him positions which he almost certainly never held. The eighteenth-century chronicler Coll, whose reliability has been called into question on a number of occasions, talks of him as a man of saintly life, and describes at length the many worthy deeds he believed could be attributed to him; it is at this time, perhaps, that the mythical Fr.

---

126 See Sanahuja, *Història*, pp. 245 and 135-136.
127 Barcelona, ACA, RC 1115, ff. 116v-117, 19 September 1341. This document is no. 515 in Vincke, *Documenta selecta*, p. 381.
128 Barcelona, ACA, RC 275, f. 35v, 24 July 1314.
129 Barcelona, AD, Registra communium, no. 3, f. 25, 31 March 1315 [1316].

Carbonell first came into existence.[130] Much of Coll's account is inaccurate, explaining some of the misconceptions about Fr. Pons, who, to judge by documents, was neither more nor less distinguished than other friars of the early fourteenth century.

Fr. Pons probably professed at the Barcelona house sometime during the last quarter of the thirteenth century, and there are references to him early in the fourteenth century. It is possible that he instructed Saint Louis of Toulouse when he was held captive in the Barcelona house, but no documentary references exist in support of this assumption.[131] Certainly a chapel to Saint Louis was built in the convent at the Barcelona house sometime during the early part of the fourteenth century, and in 1320 Fr. Carbonell was paid 1000 sous from the royal treasury for having said mass in that chapel.[132] As guardian of the Barcelona house in 1308, Pons Carbonell received 30,000 sous, being half the amount promised to Fr. Arnau Oliba, when he was provincial minister, from the will of Queen Constance. In 1311 he was paid 190 sous 1 diner from the royal treasury to cover expenses in connection with two covers bought by him for the tombs of Alfonso II and Constance, both of whom were buried in the Barcelona Franciscan house.[133]

The first document of any real significance, however, predates these payments from the royal treasury. In 1307 Fr. Pons Carbonell appears as custodian of the Barcelona house at a time when the interdict was placed on a number of mendicant friars, forbidding them to preach or

---

130 See Jaime Coll, *Crónica de la província de Cataluña: Parte primera* (1738), facsimile ed. with intro. and indices by José Martí Mayor, Crónicas franciscanas de España 21 (Madrid, 1981).
131 See Sanahuja, *História,* pp. 222-223. On p. 127 he states that Fr. Pons Carbonell did not teach Saint Louis but that the saint was placed under the tutelage of two of his confreres, Fr. Francesc Bruny and Fr. Pere Escarrer. Sections 579-600 of Coll's *Crónica* (ed. Martí Mayor, pp. 168-175), are entirely dedicated to the life of Fr. Pons Carbonell.
132 Barcelona, ACA, RP 557, f. 108, 1 April 1320.
133 Barcelona, ACA, RC 296, f. 180v, 4 June 1308. Of the 60,000 Barcelona sous owed to the Franciscans from Queen Constance's will, 9687 sous 6 diners had already been paid, together with 7500 silver sous of Tours. See also RC 147, f. 238, 5 September 1311, on which occasion the Dominicans also received money. Fr. Pere d'Esplugues, together with his socius, was granted payment of the expenses he incurred when he helped with the winding up of the queen's estate in 1300 (RC 116, ff. 123v-124, 11 September 1300).

hold divine services within the churches of the diocese of Barcelona.[134] He was custodian of the house again in later years, and also held the position of guardian intermittently from 1308, rising to provincial minister for a short period of time at the end of his life in 1336. Tradition has it that he was buried under the bell tower of the Barcelona Franciscan house, but since the original convent was destroyed in 1500 there is now no way of ascertaining the truth of this statement.[135]

Two copies of the *Apostilla,* or commentary on the Bible, which he wrote around 1328-1329, were placed in the library of his native convent, but in 1374 Pope Gregory XI asked for and received one copy, and the second was taken to the convent of San Juan de los Reyes at Toledo during the reign of Ferdinand the Catholic.[136] The removal of this work to Toledo may have been the cause of the misconception that Fr. Pons was archbishop of Toledo, just as the fact that he visited the patriarch of Alexandria's house was probably misconstrued into his becoming patriarch.[137]

In fact Joan, the patriarch of Alexandria, James II's second son, was Alfonso's brother and the brother-in-law of Don Juan Manuel, the Castilian writer who dedicated his *Libro de los estados* to the patriarch, including in his discussion of contemporary society a section on this dignitary's position.[138] Unfortunately there is no year to the document referring to Fr. Pons's visit to the patriarch's house, nor to that advising that the letter he had carried to the king of Jerusalem had reached its destination.[139] In view of the mention of the consecration of Fr. Ferrer as bishop of Neopatria three days earlier, the visit probably took

---

134 Ambròs de Saldes, "Documents inèdits per a la història de l'antiga província franciscana d'Aragó (segles XIII-XIV)," *EF* 46 (1934), 67-107, at pp. 102-104.
135 Sanahuja, *Història,* p. 249; see also Bernardo Comes, *Libro vero è original,* 2 vols. (Barcelona, 1725), 1: 37.
136 Ibid., pp. 206 and 249.
137 Barcelona, ACA, Cartas reales, Alfonso III, caja 34, no. 12, s.a. (see below Document 49). Joan d'Aragó became patriarch on 16 August 1328; this letter was thus likely dated sometime in 1329 or 1330. See also Manuel, *Libro de los estados,* p. xl.
138 Manuel, *Libro de los estados,* p. xl; and Josep Blanch, *Arxiepiscopologi de la santa esglèsia metropolitana i primada de Tarragona,* 2 vols. (Tarragona, 1985), 2: 25-38.
139 Barcelona, ACA, Cartas reales, Alfonso III, caja 34, no. 12 (see below Document 49); caja 99, no. 12326, dated 15 August [1322].

place in 1334, shortly before the patriarch's death on 19 August that year.[140] The patriarch, who was also archbishop of Tarragona from 1327 until his death, lived in the cathedral city, and it is not surprising that Fr. Pons visited him there.[141] Indeed, while Joan d'Aragó was archbishop he ordered both the Dominicans and the Franciscans to preach in Tarragona cathedral, and accorded them the right to eat in the cathedral refectory on those days.[142]

Fr. Pons and a number of other theologians acted as advisers to Pope Benedict XII, who by his bull *Redemptor noster* of 28 November 1336 promulgated the statutes known as "Benedictines."[143] Clearly Fr. Pons distinguished himself not so much in the service of the order as in that of two kings, James II and Alfonso III, to whom he was confessor from at least 1317 until his death in 1336, and in that of the church at large, which he served faithfully throughout his life. During the secret and often difficult negotiations with Frederick of Sicily concerning the presence of Spiritual Franciscans on the island, Fr. Pons acted as royal legate, and he also intervened on James II's behalf in the struggles between King Robert of Naples and King Frederick of Sicily, attempting to bring them to a peaceful agreement.[144] For the work the friar did in Sicily in 1314, Fr. Pons was paid 600 Barcelona sous.[145]

It is relevant in this connection that his socius was Fr. Bernat de Vilanova, probably a relative of Arnau de Vilanova, one of the greatest supporters of the Spiritual cause and a man favoured by James II.[146] This suggests that Fr. Pons was himself sympathetic to the Spirituals, and perhaps for that reason was chosen to head the delegation. On the

---

140 The two letters are dated 12 and 15 August s.a., but in view of the probable difference in years they may have had nothing to do with each other.
141 Barcelona, ACA, RC 466, f. 44, 28 July 1334.
142 See Blanch, *Arxiepiscopologi*, 2: 29.
143 Sanahuja, *História*, p. 248.
144 Sanahuja, *História*, pp. 110, 213-214.
145 The accounts of Pere Marc, royal treasurer (1314-1315), Barcelona, ACA, RP 278, f. 56v, refer to this journey to Sicily and the payment of 600 sous. See Webster, "Contribución de los registros," *AIA*, in press.
146 Barcelona, AD, Registra communium, I, ff. 81v-82, 14 November 1307. The names of mendicant friars (Franciscans, Dominicans and Carmelites) who contravened the Constitutions of Tarragona and who were excommunicated as a result include twenty-six Franciscans from the Barcelona house, among them Fr. Bernat de Vilanova, Fr. Arnau Oliba and Fr. Pons Carbonell.

advice of learned theologians, the king convened a special court in 1318 to look into the matter of repayment of royal debts incurred by his predecessors, and to draw up *ordenaciones* so that they could be paid. Eight people formed the court and included Fr. Bernat de Puigcercós and Fr. Joan Llotger from the Dominicans, Fr. Arnau Oliba and Fr. Pons Carbonell from the Friars Minor, two clerics and two lawyers.[147]

This is important in the light of the many outstanding royal concessions to the Franciscans, some of which were paid after this date while others awaited a later, more opportune moment before they were liquidated. Fr. Pons was both active and able, but the confusion concerning the nature of his connection with the patriarchate of Alexandria has obviously helped to create an unduly favourable reputation for him; in truth, his life differs little from that of many of his equally distinguished confreres.

Fr. Arnau de Canelles

A near contemporary of Fr. Pons Carbonell, Fr. Arnau de Canelles or Canyelles, also from Barcelona, had a career which bears a marked resemblance to that of Fr. Pons. There are references to Fr. Arnau from 1302 to 1347, and it is likely that he died shortly afterwards of the plague. He was a lector and provincial minister, but again distinguished himself more in the service of the king than in that of the order. Like Fr. Pons he was intimately connected with the Spiritual Franciscans, and in fact was required to act as one of the judges of the works of Arnau de Vilanova, which were condemned as heretical in 1316.[148] Later, as one of thirty religious asked to look into the accusations against Fr. Pere Arnau, lector of the Majorca convent who had supported the deposed Franciscan general, Fr. Michael of Cesena, he came under censure himself for declaring unjust the condemnation of the Majorcan friar.[149]

Pope John XXII showed his disappointment at the way in which Fr. Arnau had handled the case, and clearly objected to his serving as provincial minister, from which position he was deposed but, it seems,

---

147 Sanahuja, *Història,* pp. 124 and 245.
148 Ibid., p. 135. The others involved in this case were Fr. Bernat de Pim, lector in Lerida, and Fr. Guillem Sa Roca, lector in Tarragona, as judges; Fr. Pere Cervera and Fr. Pere Ferrer were present at the trial.
149 Ibid., pp. 143–145 and 271.

reinstated later.[150] Alfonso III supported his confessor vigorously in a letter to the minister general, Fr. Gerard, protesting that his chaplain was a man of religious and honest life whose discretion and good advice had been put to test on various occasions.[151] The king requested that all action against him be dropped at once, as it was displeasing to him, for he held Fr. Arnau in high regard.

Alfonso's reliance on the good services of this friar are abundantly clear, for he entrusted him with the safekeeping of the papal dispensation from his vow to be buried in the monastery of Santes Creus, so that his eternal resting place could be in the cemetery of the Friars Minor of Barcelona.[152] Chapter 2 referred to the letter of September 1347 regarding the confession Alfonso III made to Fr. Arnau, stating that he had not lain with any woman other than his wife, and therefore had had no illegitimate offspring. This is the last reference to Fr. Arnau, whose name now disappears from the chancellery registers.

Despite the difficulties Fr. Arnau encountered during his lifetime, there is little doubt that he was a man of upright life and concerned about the welfare of his order. In September 1321 he wrote to James II about the religious who were living immoral lives and perverting the good state of the "res publica," at the same time defending one of the accused, Fr. Galcerán d'Aguilar, whom he believed to be innocent of any wrongdoing.[153] Fr. Arnau obviously asked the king to arrest the friars who had left the order and return them to the Barcelona convent for disciplining, as in December 1321 James II, writing to his bailiff in

---

150 See Sanahuja, *Història,* p. 147. The provincial who supported Pope John XXII against Fr. Arnau de Canelles may have been Fr. Pere de Lavinyac, who is recorded as having been provincial in 1331 (see Barcelona, ACA, RC 562, f. 237v, 3 June 1331), or Fr. Guillem Rubió, who took over from Fr. Arnau Canelles in 1333. There is a discrepancy here between the dates given by Sanahuja and the fact that Fr. Arnau de Canelles, after a brief period, perhaps when he was deposed, again took the position of provincial in 1333. Certainly, until the death of Alfonso III in 1335, he acted as royal chaplain and confessor, and the king held him in high regard (in RC 581, f. 127, 14 March 1335 [1336], he is still mentioned as adviser for the will of Alfonso III).

151 Barcelona, ACA, RC 562, f. 246, 13 June 1331, preserves the king's letter recommending the exemplary conduct of his chaplain, Fr. Arnau, to the minister general, Fr. Gerard, and asking him to intercede on the friar's behalf with the pope.

152 Sanahuja, *Història,* p. 86.

153 Barcelona, ACA, Cartas reales, James II, caja 55, no. 6823, 20 August 1321.

Barcelona and the Vallès and all other officers of the law, ordered them to apprehend these apostates.[154]

The following year Fr. Arnau attended the general chapter under the minister, Fr. Michael of Cesena, for which the king granted a sum of 1000 silver sous of Tours.[155] In subsequent years he was sent on a number of missions for the king, including one to Queen Elisenda, Alfonso's stepmother, in the early part of 1332 [1333].[156] In 1327 [1328] he again attended the general chapter at Assisi under Fr. Michael of Cesena, who was deposed in 1328 shortly after many friars had supported him at the chapter; these friars probably including Fr. Arnau, whose troubles must largely have arisen from this support and from his obvious sympathy for the Spirituals, a sympathy shared by James II and probably by Alfonso III, but almost certainly repudiated by Peter III.[157] Alfonso confided many missions to his chaplain, and there are references to regular payments to him for the services he had undertaken; the most numerous references are to the purchase of books on the king's behalf, for which each time a payment of 5 sous was made.[158] As in the case of other payments made by the king, the friar often had to wait some months or even years before he received the money.

The lives of these friars illustrate certain aspects of medieval mendicant activity: on the one hand, their significant contributions to diplomatic relations with the Italian communes and the kingdom of Sicily, their intervention in ecclesiastical and political matters concerning the pope or other church dignitaries; and on the other, their reliance on royal favour to protect them from their confreres or superiors. They represent those friars whose qualities and educational background fitted

---

154 Barcelona, ACA, RC 368, f. 16, 2 December 1321.
155 ACA, RC 301, f. 201, 15 March 1321 [1322].
156 ACA, RC 534, ff. 86v and 89v, 4 February and 2 January 1332 [1333].
157 Fr. Arnau was given money for the general chapter to be held in Assisi, which he was to attend: see Barcelona, ACA, RC 519, f. 1, 18 March 1327 [1328]. For Fr. Michael's deposition see Moorman, *History of the Franciscan Order,* pp. 320-321.
158 Barcelona, ACA, RP 302, f. 111, 1 December 1332; RP 303, f. 115, 1 December 1333; RP 307, f. 82v, 1 December 1335. RC 500: f. 153, 22 December 1332; f. 170v, 13 January 1332 [1333]; f. 192v, 8 February 1332 [1333]; f. 218, 15 March 1332 [1333]; f. 230v, 27 March 1333. RC 501: f. 11, 1 June 1333; f. 42v, 13 July 1333; f. 111v, 30 October 1333. RC 502: f. 136v, 8 December 1333; f. 161, 23 January 1333 [1334]; f. 180v, 1 March 1333 [1334]; f. 189v, 15 March 1333 [1334]. RC 503: f. 24v, 22 August 1334; f. 165, 1 September 1335.

them for royal service, but there were many others whose lives were spent preaching, hearing the confessions of their contemporaries, saying mass and undertaking the tasks normally associated with religious life. Early in the thirteenth century these would also have included notarial functions such as drawing up documents, acting as scribes and advising on legal matters, but by the middle of the fourteenth century such tasks had long been left in the hands of a professional class of notaries.

Over a period of less than one hundred and fifty years the friars had grown from a small band of poverty-stricken men to a powerful group of advisers to the pope, the king of Aragon and other secular rulers, in constant demand as confessors, chaplains, intermediaries and arbitrators and called upon for numerous other tasks, many of which led them to interpret very liberally their rule and to be almost indistinguishable from their lay contemporaries. Only the fact that the influence they exerted and the economic benefit they received were not for personal gain but for the well-being of their order and, by extension, for that of the kingdom of God on earth, saved them from being condemned as more interested in worldly affairs than in immortal human souls.

6

The Second and Third Orders

The personal example of Saint Francis and the sacrifice and devotion of the group of men who gathered round him to found the Order of Friars Minor was to have repercussions which were to extend the ideals of poverty and self-abnegation to both men and women who had not entered the religious life but who were occupied in a trade or profession. There were also those who, in their zeal to follow the example of Saint Francis, interpreted poverty in a way which led them to embrace ideas condemned by the church; among them were the Spirituals, as they were called, who, by adopting the apocalyptic views of Joachim da Fiore and Peter John Olivi, threatened the very unity of the Franciscan movement. Within the territories of the Crown of Aragon prominent members of the Order of Friars Minor and many tertiaries were associated with the Spirituals.

THE SECOND ORDER

The implications of Saint Francis's friendship with the young girl Clare must first be considered, for it led to the foundation of the second order in the Franciscan family, the Order of the Poor Clares. The progress of this order in the realms of Aragon is a subject which merits a study apart, as there is abundant extant documentation (as yet unpublished) in all the archives consulted for this study. Remarks in this chapter can only be regarded as a tentative sketch of the development of certain aspects of the Order of Poor Clares in Aragon, and their main purpose is to illustrate the involvement of the Friars Minor with the sister order. In some cases indications will be given to show that the Poor Clares established specific houses earlier than was hitherto believed, and that in general the foundation of their convents followed that of a house of the Friars Minor by approximately ten to fifteen years.

The story of the friendship of Saint Francis and Saint Clare is well known, as are the words he is said to have cried out to the peasants who were restoring the church of Saint Damian, later to be the home of the Poor Clares: "Come and help me with this monastery of San Damiano, for here there will be an order of ladies whose fame and holy life will glorify the heavenly Father in his whole Church."[1] Clare, like Francis, came from a wealthy background, and her mission, like his, was to be to the poor and deprived. The spiritual relationship which developed between the two led to the acceptance by Francis of Clare's profession to serve God with the Order of Friars Minor, yet because she could not join the brothers some permanent solution had to be found to the problem of the way in which her vows of poverty could be used to the best advantage. She had to face opposition from her family, which fought her decision and that of her sister, Agnes, who within a very short period of time joined her. The example of the two girls soon drew the attention of other women, who were inspired to follow Clare and Agnes, and it was clear that a sister order would have to be founded and that Saint Francis' prophecy at the church of Saint Damian was being fulfilled, perhaps more quickly than anyone could have foreseen.

For the first three years Clare and her followers lived as a community without any particular rules, but it was evident that if the group increased in numbers it would require a rule, in much the same way as had been the case with the Friars Minor. Thus, in 1215 a rule for their common life was drawn up, and although it has disappeared it is thought to have contained rules about fasting, poverty and the relations between the "Poor Ladies" of Saint Damian and the friars. This primitive rule met the needs of the first small community, but as the "Poor Ladies" increased in number it became apparent that a revision was necessary.

From the very beginning the life of Clare and her followers was very austere, although there is no evidence that she envisaged the cloistered life which the Poor Clares were to adopt in subsequent years; on the contrary, this was a negation of the mission embraced by both Saint Francis and Clare herself. By 1219 the number of houses had risen to at least four, and a more comprehensive rule was obviously required. In the drawing up of the first rule of the Order of Saint Clare, Cardinal

---

1   John R.H. Moorman, *A History of the Franciscan Order from its Origins to the Year 1517* (Oxford, 1968; repr. Chicago, 1988), p. 32, has provided the basis for this section on the Poor Clares.

Ugolino, whom Pope Honorius had commissioned to attend to the matter, seems not to have consulted Francis and to have given the Poor Clares a rule not dissimilar to that followed by the Benedictine nuns; it provided for the closest claustration, a provision which distressed Clare and, as indicated, was contrary to the first intentions of the order. In fact, the rule had little that was specifically Franciscan about it, but it was to be observed strictly by both Clare and her followers.[2]

To serve the Poor Clares was not only a duty but a privilege, and at first the friars were responsible for collecting alms and attending to the needs of their sisters in Christ, a task which became increasingly more difficult and finally impossible, as both friars and Poor Clares grew in numbers and moved out into different communities beyond the confines of their native Assisi. Although it provided the basis for the Second Order, the Benedictine rule had never really been wholeheartedly accepted by Clare, her sister Agnes or their followers, despite their strict compliance with its provisions. Many exceptions were made to it over the years, leading finally to the new rule of 1245, by which the Poor Clares became dependent on the Friars Minor.[3]

Unlike the original informal dependence, the sisters were placed under the direct supervision of the minister general and provincial ministers of the Friars Minor, who were to appoint visitors for the convents, approve the election of superiors, hear confessions and appoint chaplains. Clare was not satisfied, and regarded the new rule as a betrayal of the first ideals of the sisters; she drew up her own rule, which was approved two days before she died in 1253. The main difference between the rule of Saint Clare and the previous rules was the emphasis on the ideals of Saint Francis, poverty and renunciation, and the closer links forged with the Order of Friars Minor. Not all houses were bound to accept the revised rule, and the last years of the thirteenth century witnessed further variants, most of them laying even more stress on the close relationships between the friars and the sisters. In some cases men and women lived in the same building, a situation which the friars contended prevented their completing their work satisfactorily.[4]

---

2 For a discussion of the rule and its various modifications see Ignacio Omaechevarría, "La 'Regla' y las reglas de la orden de Santa Clara," *Collectanea Franciscana* 46 (1976), 93–119.
3 Moorman, *History of the Franciscan Order,* pp. 212–213.
4 Ibid., p. 214.

A compromise was reached in the Urbanist rule of 1263, so called because it was drawn up during the pontificate of Urban IV, by John Gaetano Orsini, who had been the protector of the Clarissas under an arrangement reached between the friars and Urban IV two years previously. It is thought that he probably drew up the new rule with the help of Saint Bonaventure. Its most important effect was to remove total responsibility for the Poor Clares from the Order of Friars Minor. By this new arrangement the friars continued to act as spiritual directors for the sisters, but were not expected to provide for their material needs. Saint Francis would not have approved of this change, for he envisaged the Second Order as an integral part of his own group of brethren, whom he regarded as responsible for the sisters' well-being.

The first monastery of the Poor Clares to be founded in Spain was Santa Engracia in Pamplona, which was probably established in 1228.[5] Although Pamplona formed part of the administrative and political kingdom of Navarre, it belonged at first, before the subdivision into custodies effected in the fourteenth century, to the Franciscan province of Aragon.[6] The first houses of the Friars Minor were founded at much the same time, and it is clear that the development of the Second Order proceeded on similar and often parallel lines to that of the first. The monastery of Santa Elisabet in Saragossa dates from 1234, that of Sant Antoni de Padua in Barcelona, which later passed to the Benedictines, and the monastery in Lerida from the late 1230s or early 1240s, while the year 1240 saw the foundation of monasteries in Calatayud and Tarazona. From this time on monasteries of the Poor Clares could be found not only in most of the towns where the friars had a house, but also in others like Manresa, where it is possible the friars intended to build a house for themselves but finally abandoned the idea in favour of a *conventet* with the primary function of serving their sister order.[7]

---

5   Pedro Sanahuja, *Història de la seráfica provincia de Cataluña* (Barcelona, 1959), pp. 761–766, has supplied the information for much of this section on the Poor Clares in Spain; and the more recent work of John R.H. Moorman, *Medieval Franciscan Houses* (St. Bonaventure, NY, 1983), pp. 537–688, has been used to corroborate dates and to provide added material. My own research in some ways extends or modifies conclusions contained in these earlier studies, but is necessarily incomplete and superficial.
6   See above Chapter 1, "The Province of Aragon," pp. 38–39.
7   See Jill R. Webster, "Els framenors de Manresa," *Miscel.lània d'estudis bagencs* (Manresa) 5 (1987), 127–137.

Friars in the territories of the Crown of Aragon took their duties seriously: small houses of friars, or *conventets,* were established in places where there was no Franciscan house, as in the case of Manresa. Their sole purpose seems to have been to provide spiritual direction for the sisters, although in some cases they might have undertaken other duties. Manresa is the earliest documented example of this, but later evidence suggests that these *conventets* were found elsewhere, and were probably far more numerous than extant records suggest. The most famous of these small groups of friars, the *conventet* attached to the Clarissan monastery of Pedralbes, on the outskirts of Barcelona, was founded in 1327 under the patronage of Queen Elisenda. A community of sisters endures to this day; the old buildings still stand, although the Poor Clares themselves have recently been granted a new convent so that the medieval complex could be opened to the public as a museum.

Houses of the Poor Clares

Like that at Pedralbes, houses of the Poor Clares were often to be found in the vicinity of a Franciscan friary, and the pattern of their development closely resembled that of the first Order. The earliest monasteries in the territory of James I were located in the areas associated with both the journey of Saint Francis through northern Spain and the reconquest of territory from the Moors: from Barcelona south to Tarragona, from Lerida west to Navarre and in Valencia and the Balearic Islands of Majorca and Minorca. As far as possible, the progress of the sisters of Saint Clare will be followed both chronologically and geographically.

Catalonia

Pope Gregory IX in his bull of 18 February 1236 recommended that a monastery of *menoretes* or Poor Clares be established in Barcelona, and the house of Sant Antoni was founded shortly afterwards; from 1237 Barcelona citizens included the Poor Clares among the beneficiaries of their last wills and testaments. Innocent IV exempted Sant Antoni from episcopal jurisdiction in 1243, praising Bishop Peter of Barcelona for what he had done for the sisters.[8] Despite the fact that the bishop was

---

[8] See Innocent IV, no. 4, 4 August 1243, and no. 59, 1 June 1244, *La documentación pontifícia de Inocencio IV (1243–1254),* ed. Augusto Quintana Prieto, 2 vols. (Rome, 1987), 1: 25 and 80. The latter bull is reissued on a number of occasions.

no longer responsible for the nuns, he continued to give them his protection.[9] Likewise the pope accorded them special privileges, such as attending mass behind closed doors in time of interdict, and mitigation of their strict rule regarding food and clothing, while granting indulgences to those who visited the convent on saints' days and recommending both abbess and sisters to the people of Barcelona.[10]

Similarly, Pope Gregory's bull of 17 December 1240 set the stage for the establishment of a house of Poor Clares in Lerida. and it is likely that the actual monastery was founded sometime during 1241.[11] Unlike Barcelona, the Clarissan house there does not seem to have awakened the same papal concern, and it can only be surmised that the people of Lerida did not in any way interfere with the life of the nuns. Only Sant Antoni in Barcelona continued to receive special concessions from the papacy, and the constant intervention of the pope can only be attributed to local conditions. There seems to have been a Clarissan monastery in Tarragona in the late 1240s, although the nearby town of Montblanc did not have a community of Clarissas until 1296.[12] There is evidence that the Carmelites wanted to establish a house in Montblanc, because of the miraculous appearance of the Virgin on the site which was later given to the Poor Clares;[13] but in the end the long Franciscan tradition in the area prevailed over the desires of the later arrivals, and probably the presence of a Franciscan house in Montblanc itself led to the choice of the Poor Clares rather than the Carmelites.

The house at Vilafranca, founded as the result of a legacy from Queen Blanca of Naples, wife of James II, in 1308, had the honour of including among its first inhabitants Sr. Agnès, whose brother Fr. Pere

---

9 Innocent IV, no. 87, 8 January 1245; ed. 1: 98.
10 Ibid., nos. 62, 81, 136, 222, 223; ed. 1: 82, 95, 157, 257, 258.
11 See José Lladonosa Pujol, *Lérida medieval,* 2 vols. (Lerida, 1974–1975), 1: 95. Moorman, *Medieval Franciscan Houses,* p. 606, cites a number of different suggestions for the foundation date, opting for the monastery's existence in 1236; but the existence of a papal bull similar to the one which recommended the establishment of a monastery in Barcelona would seem to suggest that the date of 1241 is far more likely.
12 Sanahuja, *História,* p. 806.
13 Barcelona, ACA, RC 101, f. 196, 19 July 1295.

Guerau was one of the first tertiaries in Catalonia.[14] To the south of Tarragona, in Tortosa, the Poor Clares established a community which still exists today, although the archives, which were transferred to Barcelona on a provisional basis, were totally destroyed as a result of anti-clerical demonstrations during the Tragic Week of 1909.[15] Enrique Bayerri accepts Wadding's date of 1267 for the foundation of this house, but given the fact that the Friars Minor established their house much earlier, it would seem more likely that the monastery of the Poor Clares existed prior to 1267 and possibly from the 1240s, like the neighbouring houses of Lerida and Tarragona.[16] A pattern seems to emerge: a group of foundations established prior to 1250, a few further monasteries at the turn of the century and another significant group around 1340, a pattern which seems to follow very closely the clusters of foundations in the realms of Aragon for the First Order.

Most Franciscan houses were in place before 1300, while others (in northern Catalonia) were not founded until the early years of the fourteenth century. The majority of Clarissan houses followed a similar chronological pattern, but there were some, like Gerona, which seemed to diverge somewhat from this general practice. The house of the Friars Minor at Gerona was one of the first to be established, yet the sister order had some difficulty in founding a house there and was not successful until 1309 (not 1319, as has traditionally been accepted as the date of foundation); whereas Castelló d'Empúries, with a similar Franciscan tradition, had a monastery of the Second Order as early as 1260.[17]

Extant records suggest that the Franciscan house at Cervera was in existence long before the Poor Clares managed to establish their monastery in 1344, but in this case it is probable that the lack of records referring to an earlier establishment could account for the apparent

---

14 See Sanahuja, *Història,* pp. 810-811; and Barcelona, ACA, RC 232, f. 128, 5 September 1311: Sr. Agnès was granted 150 Barcelona sous each year for the rest of her life, payment of which was to be made from money existing in the secretariat of the vicar and bailiff of Vilafranca, where her brother worked as a scribe, at the rate of 12.5 sous per month.
15 See Ramon Miravall, *Necròpolis, sepultures i inhumacions a Tortosa* (Tortosa, 1986), p. 111.
16 Lucas Wadding, comp., *Annales Minorum,* 3rd ed., 28 vols. (Quaracchi, 1931-1947), 4: 315; Enrique Bayerri y Bertomeu, *História de Tortosa y su comarca,* 8 vols. (Tortosa, 1933-1959), 7: 540.
17 See Sanahuja, *Història,* p. 798.

anomaly. The Franciscan convent at Cervera seems to have been very active in the thirteenth century and, unlike the case of Gerona, where extant documentation is relatively abundant, few documents have survived to prove or disprove the 1344 date.[18]

This hypothesis seems to be supported by what is known about the nearby town of Tàrrega, which follows the pattern, as the friars founded their house in 1318 and the convent of the Poor Clares was established prior to February 1347, when Peter III wrote to the officials of the city of Tàrrega concerning the newly-established convent of Saint Clare.[19] It is possible, of course, that there had been no attempt to establish a Clarissan convent in Cervera before the foundation of the Tàrrega house, and that rivalry between the two towns had led to the demand from the citizens of Cervera that the Poor Clares open a convent there too, especially since the Franciscans had already acquired popularity and support. If in fact permission had been given to found the Tàrrega house in 1344, as seems likely, it would not be unreasonable to postulate a similar date for the Cervera house.

In Puigcerdà, in the greater province of Gerona, the friars acquired a property in 1320, although they seem to have lived in a hospice in the town for some years previously; the Poor Clares did not arrive in Puigcerdà until 1351, a date for which there is documentary evidence.[20] The *Dietari,* a later work recording some of the events of the fourteenth

---

18 In some cases deficient archival material may account for what appears to be a later date, and these dates are offered very tentatively; subsequent research on the Poor Clares may well overturn the conclusions drawn here.

19 Barcelona, ACA, RC 642, f. 218v, [?] February 1346 [1347]. Unfortunately the document is in such a bad state of preservation that it is only possible to see that the house had been founded under the Regular Observance of the Order of Saint Clare and was in the process of being built. By 1 June 1350 the house was already in full operation, as the king issued the usual letter of enfranchisement to the procurator of the convent of Saint Clare at Tàrrega (Lluis Sarret i Pons, *Privilegis de Tàrrega* [Tàrrega, facsimile ed., 1982], p. 178). It is curious that Josep Maria Segarra i Malla, *Història de Tàrrega amb els seus costums i tradicions, I (segles XI-XVI)* (Tàrrega, 1984), makes no mention of the Clarissas.

20 See Maties Delcor, "Le Diétari de Puigcerdà: Texte et notes, deuxième partie," *Etudes Roussillonnaises: Revue d'histoire et d'archéologie méditerranéennes* (Perpignan) 4 (1954–1955), 135–150, at p. 149; and Jill R. Webster, "El convent de Santa Clara, Puigcerdà: Algunes consideracions preliminars," *Ceretania: Quaderns d'estudis cerdans* (Puigcerdà and Bourg-Madame) 1 (1991), 107–116, at p. 108.

century, seems not to have had knowledge of this document and does not attempt to date the convent of the Poor Clares. It attributes its foundation to Manethedei, a rich Florentine merchant, whose tomb was said to have been close to the entrance to the choir of the church.[21] The account states quite explicitly that the monastery of Saint Clare was not as old as the house of the Franciscan friars, a statement which has been proved correct and attests to the fact that Franciscanism in Puigcerdà followed the pattern established elsewhere in the Crown of Aragon.

It is extremely unlikely that the monastery of Saint Clare was in fact founded by the merchant Manethedei, whose name is not mentioned in the document of 1351 which states explicitly that the house was founded on the property formerly belonging to Andreu Mornach and Jaume Capdevila, the father or uncle of a Friar Minor by the same name.[22] Andreu Mornach on 31 March 1348 made over properties which he owned along the Querol road to the Franciscans on the condition that the friars should hold an anniversary of his death on the day of the Blessed Virgin in March and pray for the eternal rest of his soul.[23] If his will of 28 June 1348 is any indication, and certainly his name ceases to appear in the notarial manuals after this date, he probably died of the plague at the end of June or early in July 1348.[24] The Mornach family had supported the Franciscans from the very beginning, and their first property had belonged to a member of this family. The first document listing names of the inhabitants of the newly-founded Saint Clare house makes no mention of the Agnès Coch who, with some other suitable ladies, had been instrumental in the establishment of the house in 1351, nor does her name appear in the record of those present at the chapter meeting of 1361.[25] Perhaps, by the time the house was operative, she had either taken her vows elsewhere, lost interest in the religious life or died.

---

21 Salvador Galcerán Vigué, *Dietari de la fidelíssima vila de Puigcerdà: Transcripció literal del text i comentari original* (Barcelona, 1977), p. 30.
22 See Delcor, "Diétari de Puigcerdà," p. 149.
23 Puigcerdà, AHC, Bernat Manresa with Guillem Castells and Joan Montaner, *Liber firmitatis* (26 March 1348–24 March 1349), f. 10, 31 March 1348.
24 Puigcerdà, AHC, Bernat Manresa with Francesc Esteva, Guillem Castells and Joan Montaner, *Liber testamentorum* (2 April 1348–31 August 1349), ff. 73v–74, 28 June 1348.
25 Puigcerdà, AHC, Bernat Manresa and Guillem de Quer, *Liber firmitatis* (22 January 1361–23 December 1361), f. 98, 19 July 1361; f. 187v, 13 December 1361.

Vic, with its numerous religious houses, many of them dating from the thirteenth century, seems like Cervera to diverge somewhat from the pattern for Catalonia as a whole, perhaps because of the importance of the bishopric and diocesan structure and the relative proximity of Barcelona, Manresa and Gerona. The convent of the Poor Clares in Vic was not established until 1383, although the friars founded a convent in Vic as early as 1225. There is evidence that attempts were made to found a house in 1287 and again in 1343, and on the latter occasion a possible abbess, Clara Sa Sala, was highly recommended by the king.[26] Initially territory in the area of Sentfores and Cestanyol was set aside for the house of Poor Clares, but because this had been common land, the bishop and chapter opposed the construction of the convent there. An enquiry was held and although the document giving the result has not been discovered, it can be assumed that it was unfavourable to the Franciscans, who had to establish the convent of their sister order in the area of Puig de Reig, now known as Santa Clara la vella. The enquiry lasted a very long time, as forty years elapsed between the initial attempt at foundation and the successful opening of the convent of Saint Clare in 1383.[27] Once again, as was true of Gerona, the Poor Clares did not manage to found their house without considerable difficulty, largely due to the worsening economic and social conditions from the late 1340s until some years after the 1348 plague, making the populace more sensitive to the acquisition of common land for building purposes.

Two houses of the Poor Clares seem to defy any attempt at establishing a pattern for foundation: one in Conques de Tremp (1342), where no Franciscan house existed either at that time or in subsequent years, and the other in Balaguer (1351) where, like in Manresa (1322), there was only a *conventet* for the friars to say mass for the sisters and attend to their spiritual needs until the Observants established the convent of Santa María de Jésus almost a century later.[28]

---

26 See Jill R. Webster, "Documents relacionats amb els convents de Sant Francesc, Santa Clara i Santa Maria del Carme de Vic a l'edat mitjana," *Studium Vicensia* (Vic), in press.

27 Vic, AE, ACF, Monestirs i convents, undated document. Sanahuja, *História,* p. 846, using a copy originally housed in the Arxiu de Santa Clara, Vic, gives the date as 18 December 1383.

28 See Sanahuja, *História,* p. 306. The *conventet* is known to have existed in October 1372; in view of the earlier foundation of the Poor Clares, it probably existed at least twenty years earlier than this.

The Balearic Islands

In the Balearic Islands and Aragon the situation was not too dissimilar. Palma de Mallorca, reconquered from the Moors in 1230, had one of the earliest and most important Franciscan houses, and in 1257 a monastery of the sister order was established.[29] Minorca was reconquered in 1286, and the Franciscans established a house in Ciutadella that very same year.[30] The following year Alfonso II gave the Poor Clares land to found their monastery in Ciutadella, probably in a renewed attempt to ensure that the island was resettled quickly with Christians, so that there would be no opportunity for the Moors to regain sovereignty of the Balearic Islands.[31]

Valencia

Like Majorca, Valencia was a city with a large Moorish population, resettled after its conquest in 1238 by the followers of James I, who, to ensure its rapid absorption into his Christian kingdom, encouraged the establishment there of many religious orders, among them the Franciscans, a fact explained at some length in Chapter 1. It is logical that the Poor Clares were given land to found a house there in 1251, and that subsequently houses were founded in the nearby towns of Murviedro, the present-day Sagunto, and Xàtiva. There seems to have been some trouble with the establishment of the latter house, which belonged to the third cluster of foundations, a problem raised and considered in some detail later in this chapter.

Aragon

The Clarissan convents in Aragon seem to follow a similar chronological pattern: Saragossa, one of the first cities to have a Franciscan house, also seems to have had one of the earliest of the foundations of the Poor Clares, their monastery having been established in 1234, about the same

---

29 See Sanahuja, *História*, p. 797. Although Alexander IV's bull addressed to the bishop of Majorca, advising him that the Poor Clares were to establish a house there, is dated 18 March 1256, it would seem that the land was only granted by James I the following year. It will be recalled that this was the land first occupied by the Friars Minor (see above Chapter 1, pp. 36-38).
30 See above Chapter 1, pp. 39-40.
31 Sanahuja, *História*, p. 804.

time as the convent of Sant Antoni in Barcelona.[32] Similarly, in 1240 (or 1235, as suggested by Moorman) a house was established in Calatayud, and also in 1240 one in Tarazona.[33] Other houses established in Aragon include Teruel (1366–1367), Huesca (1264) and Morella, which was probably in existence by 1330 but which seems to defy all attempts at even suggesting an approximate date for its foundation.[34]

A few houses of the Poor Clares, beyond the geographical boundaries of this study, frequently received concessions from the Crown of Aragon, or their activities were closely connected with those of the neighbouring jurisdiction, among them the house at Soria, founded as early as 1244, and that at Almazán, also in the province of Soria and established in 1253.[35] The house at Perpignan, established in 1270, in later years was closely associated with the house at Puigcerdà, as it too belonged to the province of Narbonne.[36] Citizens south of the Pyrenees frequently left legacies to the house at Perpignan, and it was probably with the help of the Poor Clares in that city that the Clarissan monastery was finally established in Puigcerdà in 1351.

One further convent seems to warrant mention, although it is really beyond the scope of this study: it is the house at Messina in Sicily,

---

32 Sanahuja, *Història*, p. 782.
33 Ibid., p. 763.
34 See Moorman, *Medieval Franciscan houses*, pp. 670, 598. Neither he nor Sanahuja mention the existence of a house at Morella, nor indeed has any other reference been found except one in a register of King Peter III (Barcelona, ACA, RC 1008, f. 153, 20 August 1338), referring to the legacy left to the Poor Clares by King Alfonso II. Perhaps the Poor Clares intended to establish a house in Morella before the death of Alfonso, but never succeeded in doing so. If this were the case, the reference to the house by Peter III is not easily explained, as it was not customary for the chancellery records to be incorrect.
35 Barcelona, ACA, RP 321, f. 159v, 1 December 1343: Peter III grants the town of Almazán in the kingdom of Castile 50 Barcelona sous. Peter I of Castile stayed in the Almazán house and it may be that it received these grants because of connections with the royal family of Aragón. Similarly, in RP 314, f. 39v, 1 January 1339 [1340], the house at Soria receives a grant from the king, but unfortunately a hole appears in the manuscript where the amount should be.
36 Moorman, *Medieval Franciscan Houses*, p. 644, gives the foundation date sometime between 1263 and 1270; Sanahuja, *Història*, p. 764, gives 1270. But Berenguera, wife of Cerdany Unnes of Puigcerdà, in her will dated 28 May 1315, refers to the convent of Saint Clare at Perpignan as though it were still under construction: see Puigcerdà, AHC, Guillem Cog and Guillem Hualart, *Liber testamentorum* (25 June 1314–25 April [June] 1315), f. 43.

founded by Queen Constance of Aragon in 1294.[37] The queen was herself a member of the order, and when she died in Barcelona in 1300 she was buried in the Clarissan habit, in the cemetery of the house of the Friars Minor in Barcelona.[38] In her will she left considerable sums of money to both the friars and the Poor Clares throughout her husband's domains.

The dates of foundation of the main convents of the Poor Clares within the realms of Aragon have been discussed in some detail because they help complete a picture of a very strong Franciscan presence and elucidate many of the points taken up elsewhere in this study. Research into the history of the sisters has only been fragmentary at best, and in some cases little is known about their activities south of the French border. The Poor Clares were indirectly under the jurisdiction of the officers of the Friars Minor, and this relationship can best be understood by examining the documents in the archives of the Pedralbes house, and supplementing them with comments on the material relating to the particular circumstances of houses elsewhere in the realms of Aragon, especially that at Xàtiva in the Valencia region.

The Pedralbes house, on the outskirts of Barcelona, may have certain characteristics which were not shared by most of the houses, as it was clearly not one of the earliest and was probably the most richly endowed of all; largely due to its royal patronage, it was also spared the difficulties encountered in Gerona and Xàtiva. It is one of the few houses which, because it preserves intact its medieval archives, and allows access to them, enables events to be assessed in a chronological sequence.[39] Sanahuja describes the monastery of Santa Maria de Pedralbes as the most remarkable convent to be built under the rule of Saint Clare in Catalonia.[40] Pope John XXII authorized Queen Elisenda to have a monastery of Saint Clare sisters built within the province of Tarragona, stipulating that it should not be closer to an urban centre than one league but should be located in an area where the provincial minister of the Friars Minor of Aragon could be responsible for its well-being,

---

37 See Sanahuja, *História*, pp. 106–108.
38 See above Chapter 2, p. 93.
39 The house of the Poor Clares in Majorca also preserves its archives, which until some years ago were open to researchers; this is no longer so and it was impossible to consult this important material said to date from the thirteenth century.
40 Sanahuja, *História*, pp. 817–819, is the source for much of the description of this house.

suggesting that this official resided in the Barcelona house, a practice which is still observed today. The archives preserve the document of foundation, written in Catalan and bearing the date 1327; this gives the number of sisters who should form the community, and other provisions which should be followed.[41] The minister of the Friars Minor for the province of Aragon, Fr. Ramon Bancal, with many other friars from the order, and other religious and clerics from Barcelona, were present at the inaugural ceremony, which was held with great solemnity. The names of the first fourteen sisters are given, and they include that of the first abbess, Sobirana de Saus or Olzet.[42] All were clearly from well-connected families, a pattern which was common to the early houses of the Poor Clares.

The *Chronologia* of the convent makes possible some general conclusions, not only in connection with the Pedralbes convent but relevant to the other communities of the Poor Clares in the Franciscan province of Aragon as well. The first pages of the *Chronologia*, not numbered, describe the steps taken to establish the provisions of the rule of 1263, which the Pedralbes convent still preserves in a fifteenth-century edition.[43] This was adopted by the sisters in the province of Aragon, and subsequently, and more particularly here, by the convent of Santa Maria de Pedralbes. The steps followed to ensure its observance were as follows: the protector of the order, John, cardinal deacon of Saint Nicholas, wrote to the provincial minister of the Order of Friars

---

41 See Sanahuja, *Història,* p. 817.
42 The name should probably be Saus, not Olzet as appears in Sanahuja, *Història,* p. 818. The names of the sisters are not very legible in the original document, but some differ from those given by Sanahuja. He states that the other sisters were Francesca Sa Portella (the queen's niece), Alamanda de Mas-Lino, Constanza Seguera, Constanza de Vilardell, Dolça Lulla and her sister or niece Maria Lulla, Sauria de Junqueres, Margarita de Bomilla, Constanza Fiveller and her sister or niece Serena, Sancia Nagera, Clara de Castellet and Romeva de Sanguinyols. There were fourteen, and apart from the two Lull sisters the names should probably read Alamanda de Mansolí, Saurina de Jonques, Constanza de Vilardell, Sibil.la, Constanza Finesterra, Constanza de Molins, Margarida de Bonvila, Serena Fivaller, Sobirana de Saus (abbess), Francesca Sa Portella (niece of the queen) and Constanza Seguera.
43 It was Urban IV's rule of 1263 which stipulated that the order be called the Order of Saint Clare. The pages containing the rule of 1263 belong to an early printed edition, but are kept with the *Chronologia* of the convent at Pedralbes, compiled in the monastery on 10 July 1798, and housed in the AMP, Barcelona.

Minor in Aragon on 8 December 1263, recommending that the visitor selected from among the Friars Minor be of upright and suitable life.[44] At the same time the minister general of the Order of Friars Minor wrote to the provincial minister, charging him with the appointment of the visitor.[45]

The new rule contained twenty-six chapters, including among the provisions the requirement that the friar appointed as visitor should make his visits at two-weekly intervals to ensure that the nuns under his care were not in any way guilty of dereliction of duty. The *Chronologia* refers to Boniface VIII's bull of 1296, confirming the rule of 1243, but it is clear from the existence of the printed version of the 1263 text that the sisters of Santa Maria de Pedralbes adopted the Urbanist rule.[46]

After the foundation of the monastery in 1327, permission was obtained for a friar to act as confessor to the sisters and to be allowed to enter the cloister. Similarly, the sisters were granted the right to have their own burial ground, which, of course, would be served by the friars. In October 1328 the guardian of the Friars Minor in Barcelona was authorized by Pope John XXII to appoint four friars to be always available to conduct religious services, hear confessions and attend to the other spiritual needs of the sisters, especially to celebrate the festivals of important saints such as the Virgin Mary and the founders of the first and Second Orders. The cardinal protector, Arnold, granted permission for five or six friars, or secular priests, to enter the cloister on other important feastdays such as Palm Sunday, provided these men left immediately the religious service was over.

As the convent grew in size, so the number of friars allowed to conduct religious services there or to hear the confessions of the sisters became more numerous, and their visits were made more frequently. This made it imperative that a *conventet* be established close to the

---

44 The text is found in Barcelona, AMP, *Chronologia de la regla de Santa Clara*, 1263 (unnumbered page 1): "ab particular recomendació de que fes elecció de visitador en Religiós discret; y probat com ho exigia la comissió que deixaba a son zel ... ."

45 The contents of the letter are given in the *Chronologia* for 18 October 1264. The minister general is referred to as Fr. B. (Saint Boniface).

46 See also in this regard Margarida González i Betlinski and Anna Rubió i Rodón, "La regla de l'orde de Santa Clara de 1263: Un cas concret de la seva aplicació, el monestir de Pedralbes de Barcelona," *Acta historica et archaeologica mediaevalia* 3 (1982), 9–46. The study includes the Catalan transcription of the rule.

monastery, and the sisters were obliged to provide each friar with bread and wine on a daily basis and 50 sous each September. Nothing else was to be given to the friars unless the abbess of her own free will decided to offer them more.

One friar was to act as confessor to the sisters, and the remaining priests were to say a daily mass for the souls of the late king and queen, at the time and in the place laid down by the abbess. They were also to say or sing masses at other times as required by the community, and to attend the saying of the hours. If they failed to fulfil these obligations, they were to be deprived of their daily ration of bread and wine. These friars would have very little time to attend to other duties or to beg for alms, which explains why the Poor Clares were responsible for their material well-being.

The monastery at Pedralbes was entirely surrounded by high walls, and entrance was obtained through a heavy door which clanged shut behind the visitor. Two other doors existed in the Middle Ages, one to the south and one to the west, and it was next to this latter entrance that the *conventet* was built, with room for the six priests and the confessor. The monastery itself had space for sixty sisters and was virtually self-sufficient, with its own hospital, cemetery and grounds. It was so well endowed by the queen that it is easy to see why it had few of the problems encountered in some of the poorer monasteries in Aragon. With some variations, no doubt, and in different degrees of material well-being, similar conditions prevailed throughout the realms of Aragon, although unfortunately the fact that most of the monastic archives have disappeared makes it difficult to do more than make conjectures about the life in many of the other monasteries of the Poor Clares.

The material preserved in the royal, municipal and cathedral archives allows an overall impression to be obtained of life in the Order of Saint Clare, but this should be taken for what it is, an impression based on references to matters which required the intervention of a third party, usually the king or a notary. Their main value here lies in the way they show that the duties of the friars often went beyond the spiritual direction of the sisters, extending to assistance with land disputes, the recovery of legacies which the executors or heirs showed reluctance to pay and other similar matters. In some cases, the friars were required to improve the discipline of the convents they visited, or even to move sisters from one house to another, either because a new foundation needed help or because some problem had arisen which needed to be addressed.

The development of the convents of Poor Clares in the realms of Aragon progressed at much the same rate as those of the Friars Minor, most houses containing from twenty to sixty sisters; in some cases the number of Poor Clares in a particular convent on a given day is known, because, like the First Order, the sisters received alms from the king on special feastdays.[47] The names which have survived suggest that those who professed were almost always from the upper classes, some of them even coming from the royal family.[48] In many ways this directly parallels the situation in the friaries, where a large number of friars came from the merchant or noble classes. In Aragon, more especially, the friars were frequently from landowning families, unlike the Catalan friars, who were predominantly the sons of merchant traders. Valencia seemed to combine the two, but in the case of the sisters there seems to have been a tendency to follow the Aragonese pattern. These ladies would have had "serving sisters," as provided for in the rule of Saint Clare, and in Valencia the nuns were known to have had Moorish servants.[49] It was also customary for other people to live in the monasteries: some might be there to fulfil some function on behalf of the sisters, others because they had been assigned to the monastery for "safekeeping." Such was the case of Violant de Vilaragut, the wife of James III of Majorca, after the cession of the Majorcan branch of the crown to Peter III in 1344.[50]

---

47 See Jill R. Webster, "La contribución de los registros del patrimonio real a la história de los frailes menores durante la primera mitad del siglo XIV," *AIA*, in press.

48 Barcelona, ACA, RP 309, f. 105v, 1 November 1336. The king made a special payment to the Valencian convent of the Poor Clares for bread, wine and other provisions to be used on the day that the princesses Maria and Blanca took the habit of Saint Clare. The total payment amounted to 345 Barcelona sous. These two princesses were probably the daughters of Alfonso III, a fervent supporter of the Franciscans.

49 Moorman, *History of the Franciscan Order*, p. 408.

50 Violant seems to have been dissatisfied with her life in the monastery of the Poor Clares in Saragossa, to which she had been assigned for her own and the kingdom's protection, and asked for a transfer to the Dominican nuns in Valencia (Barcelona, ACA, RC 1154, f. 39r-v, 5 April 1350). A letter written two months later gave Pons de Santa Pau permission to carry to her a message from the king, possibly the transfer she had requested, although this is not stated (RC 1154, f. 79, 9 June 1350).

There is a curious dichotomy in the way the Poor Clares followed the precepts of their founder. Like the Friars Minor, the Poor Clares were enjoined to live a life of poverty and beg for their food. Since they were bound by a rule that forbade their leaving the cloister, at first the friars were obliged to undertake this duty on their behalf; but as the two orders expanded, it became more difficult to get enough food for both the Poor Clares and themselves. By the beginning of the fourteenth century other factors had to be taken into account. The Carmelites and Augustinians had established communities south of the Pyrenees, and they too were mendicants; there were crop failures and subsequent famines, epidemics and economic deprivation, which adversely affected the revenue the friars obtained from their benefactors. The hardship experienced by many of the Clarissan convents seems to be reflected in the letter from the *jurats,* consuls and city of Gerona which states that the sisters were living in extreme poverty and had had to leave the cloister to seek the basic necessities, a situation the authorities felt should not be allowed to continue and which was dangerous for the sisters.[51] Among the fourteenth-century documents there are many referring to concessions of money granted by the crown, which had not been paid; some of them had even been outstanding for as long as ten years.

Legacies to the mendicant orders were frequently disputed, and these disputes dragged on for years before they were finally settled; in the meantime, both friars and sisters had to live and were forced to seek other means of revenue. It is for this reason that monasteries founded in the fourteenth century were usually endowed by royalty or by wealthy citizens, to ensure that the sisters were self-sufficient. The houses at both Pedralbes and Xàtiva, in the Valencian region, are examples of this new policy.[52] Individual sisters were given clothing, money and jewels, and there is evidence of this practice in more than one convent. The princesses Maria and Blanca were provided with 30 ells and 2 palens of camelot (camel hair cloth) from Brussels, which was purchased from a Valencian draper, Guillem Rabassà, and was to be used when they took the habit in Valencia.[53] For their cloaks they were given two fur ruffs,

---

51 Gerona, AHM, Correspondència, I (1336–1337), f. 73, 23 May 1337.
52 See Moorman, *History of the Franciscan Order,* p. 409, for a discussion of this situation.
53 Barcelona, ACA, RP 309, f. 136v (doc. 1), 1 December 1336. The term *palens* is not found; *pelam*, used for an animal skin or length of fur, may be intended here.

for 140 sous from Pere Cescala, a furrier in Valencia.[54] Another noble lady, Sibil.la de Antillón, a Clarissan nun in the Saragossa convent, also received 50 sous for fur for her coat, and another 50 sous for alms the day she professed.[55] The original tenet proscribing possessions had become unworkable; indeed the *conventet* at Pedralbes provided for the food and lodging of the friars appointed to attend the spiritual needs of the sisters, a direct reversal of the situation pertaining in the early days, when the friars often begged on the sisters' behalf.

The friars continued to look after the sisters' welfare, and to determine the daily running of their monasteries, making sure that the number of inhabitants never exceeded the resources available.[56] They were called upon at times to correct the sisters and see that they followed faithfully the rule of their order, a duty sometimes made difficult by third parties and causing them to have recourse to the king, so that he could order his officials to allow them to proceed without hindrance.[57]

The behaviour of the friars themselves was not beyond reproach, as the correspondence concerning the foundation of a Clarissan house at Xàtiva shows. The first indication of trouble dates to 1336, when Peter III, wrote to Fr. Ramon de Bas giving the provincial minister permission to transfer nuns from Valencia to the newly-built convent of Xàtiva.[58] The following year the king sought permission post facto for Maria and Blanca, members of the royal family, to enter the Order of Saint John of Jerusalem.[59] As they had been residents of the Poor Clares up to that time, they probably had no wish to leave Valencia, and for that reason requested their transfer to the Order of Saint John of Jerusalem. Subsequent events were to prove that they were not alone in wishing to

---

54 Barcelona, ACA, RP 309, f. 136v (doc. 2), 1 December 1336.
55 Ibid., f. 144, 1 December 1336.
56 See Moorman, *History of the Franciscan Order,* pp. 411–412.
57 Barcelona, ACA, RC 144, f. 146v, 7 March 1309 [1310]. Apparently some unspecified persons had interfered with the provincial minister when he was attempting to restore discipline to the Huesca house. RC 271, f. 102r-v, elucidates the reason for Fr. Romeo Ortiz's need to correct the sisters: they were living a "scandalous" life and bringing their Order into disrepute.
58 Barcelona, ACA, RC 1053, f. 207, 18 October 1336. See also María Pilar Andrés Antón, *El monasterio de la puridad: Primera fundación de Clarisas en Valencia y su reino. Siglos XIII–XV* (Valencia, 1991), pp. 328–337.
59 Barcelona, ACA, RC 1054, f. 51 (2 docs.), 9 April 1337; see also Andrés, ibid., pp. 487–490.

remain in the capital. Later that same year Peter informed his officials in Valencia that, on the orders of both the papacy and the minister general of the Friars Minor, twelve nuns must leave the Clarissan monastery of Santa Elisabet in Valencia and go to the new house at Xàtiva, built as a result of a legacy from the late noble lady Saurina de Entenza.[60] The officials were to see that they were accompanied to Xàtiva, and that the guardian of the Franciscans there knew that they were to be transferred. It is not difficult to understand why such protection was necessary, in the light of the letter the king sent to the minister general, Fr. Gerard, complaining of the behaviour of some Franciscans, who, it seems, had opposed the transfer of the nuns to Xàtiva.[61]

The problem is set out at length in the king's letter: Fr. Berenguer d'Ivorra and Fr. Pedro de Huesca, among others, had supported the election of Sr. Agnès as abbess of the new monastery at Xàtiva, against the wish of the king, who had proposed Sr. Beatriz from the Saragossa convent. Fr. Pedro had made his views known in public sermons, and another friar, of whose name the king was unaware, had maligned the reputation of the sisters. Fr. Gerard was urged to see that Sr. Beatriz was elected, and the king's relative, Fr. Sancho López de Ayerbe, was to take the present letter to Rome. The king strategically issued letters to all persons concerned: the officials in Xàtiva, the executor of the will of Saurina de Entenza, and the guardian and friars in Xàtiva, informing them that part of the legacy was to be withheld until the matter was settled satisfactorily.[62] The matter was further complicated by the opposition of the Saint Clare house at Tortosa to the transfer of the twelve nuns to Xàtiva from Valencia and not from houses elsewhere, suggesting that there were those in Tortosa who would have liked to move to the new house. It can only be assumed that the Xàtiva convent had some facilities not available in the older establishments, and that these sisters wished to avail themselves of the better conditions.

Fr. Berenguer d'Ivorra and Fr. Pedro de Huesca, however, did not let the matter rest there, and clearly encouraged Sr. Agnès to appeal to the Holy See against the appointment of Sr. Beatriz as abbess.[63] The

---

60 Barcelona, ACA, RC 1054, f. 81v (2 docs.), 10 June 1337; see also Andrés, *Monasterio de la puridad,* pp. 488–489.
61 Barcelona, ACA, RC 1054, f. 111, 19 July 1337.
62 Ibid., ff. 112r-v, 113r-v, all documents dated 22 August 1337.
63 Ibid., f. 160v, 6 October 1337; cf. Andrés, *Monasterio de la puridad,* pp.330–331.

king, in the letter to Fr. Gerard, the minister general, used strong language to express his views on the difficulties surrounding the election of the abbess, and confirmed the appointment of Sr. Beatriz to the Xàtiva house. The Franciscans still seem to have been unwilling to comply with the king's wishes, and Peter was obliged to write to Fr. Gerard again at the end of December 1337, making clear his displeasure at their obstinate stand and disobedience of royal commands.[64] After this, the dispute continued on a low key and was only settled finally in 1345, when Pope Clement was urged to accept an episcopal recommendation that the building of the Xàtiva house be initiated.[65]

Turning away from the difficulties of populating new convents to another, less contentious, aspect of Clarissan life, the need for workmen to enter the monastery to undertake heavy duties, there is less documentary evidence to determine what in fact happened in the realms of Aragon. Moorman suggests that lay brothers would do the heavy work in the monasteries, but none of the documents consulted make any mention of this practice in Aragon (although the fact that no documentary evidence exists, does not automatically exclude the possibility). It is extremely likely that skilled craftsmen were employed on numerous occasions, and that gardeners, builders and other workmen were frequently required, especially in the nuns' convents. It is to be assumed that Ferrer and Arnau Bassa spent long periods in the Pedralbes monastery when they painted the murals of the chapel of Saint Michael, and that they could not have been unique in this respect.[66]

The general pattern of almsgiving and concessions is similar to that associated with the friars; many of the same problems, such as the presence of garbage or undesirable trades close to the monastery, or the reluctance of executors and heirs to pay legacies to the sisters, were experienced by the Poor Clares. The crown made concessions of water, corn and oil to the Poor Clares, gave special donations for feastdays, helped individual ladies with their clothing and generally supported the order. Like the Friars Minor, the Poor Clares could not handle money, and a procurator was appointed to take care of this important aspect of their life. He received the same exemption from military service and taxation as the procurator for the other mendicant orders.

---

64 Barcelona, ACA, RC 1054, f. 187v, 31 December 1337.
65 ACA, RC 1059, f. 165v, 15 January 1344 [1345].
66 See Manuel Trens, *Ferrer Bassa i les pintures de Pedralbes* (Barcelona, 1936).

The Third Order

The Franciscan ideal was not confined to those who entered the religious life; a Third Order of laymen, whose members became increasingly numerous in the fourteenth century, also made a very valuable contribution. Many of these people had close ties with the Order of Friars Minor, some of them acting as economic procurators for the friars. Some were to stray from the paths of orthodoxy and become involved with the Spirituals, although it is difficult to assess with any degree of accuracy the impact of the Fraticelli on Franciscan life as a whole south of the Pyrenees: certainly some of the laxities they criticized and divergences from the rule they condemned were clearly evident, and by the end of the fourteenth century were to lead to a rift in the Order of Friars Minor.

In Catalonia there were many Friars Minor and members of the Third Order who were affected to some extent by the ideas of Peter John Olivi and Joachim da Fiore, and by the influence of the royal physician Arnau de Vilanova, an enthusiastic supporter of the Spirituals and probably a tertiary himself. The ideal of absolute poverty preached by Saint Francis had been questioned by the friars, many of whom had acquired property such as books, vestments, ornaments and other goods.[67] Splendid friaries had been built, and in many cases the friars were living in greater luxury and wearing habits of better cloth and more elaborate design than the coarse habits mentioned in the previous chapter. In some cases individual members of the order controlled their own finances, in direct contradiction to the rule of Saint Francis.

This movement away from the ideals of the founder caused concern and consternation to many of the more ascetic friars, who saw in it a shift towards a more worldly life and the dawning of the millennium; they themselves embraced apocalyptic ideas, in the hope of persuading their contemporaries of the dangers of materialism. The question was one which had exercised the minds of many Franciscans from shortly after the death of their founder, but the more it became associated with unorthodox doctrines the more necessary it was to clarify what the doctrine of absolute poverty really meant.

Towards the end of the thirteenth century a rumour spread that at the general council in Lyons in 1274 the pope was going to bring forward

---

[67] See Moorman, *History of the Franciscan Order*, pp. 177–187, esp. 184–187, for a discussion of privilege and property.

the question of the right of the mendicant orders to possess property, with the express aim of allowing them similar privileges to those held by the monastic orders (which, of course, would have been a complete negation of all that Francis and his followers had stood for and which, in effect, would nullify the mission of the friars).[68] Some, like Angelo of Clareno, protested and were reprimanded at a provincial chapter, deprived of their habits and shut up in distant hermitages; but this was only the beginning of a movement for greater austerity, which was to plague the order for some time to come and which brought in its wake a deviation by some from orthodox beliefs.[69]

At the same time, and thus giving impetus to a force for reform, a similar protest movement had arisen in Provence, where the influence of Hugh of Digne's *Expositio regulae* and other writings had urged extreme poverty and the renunciation of all excesses. He has been called the "father of the Spirituals," although it was not he but his successor, Peter John Olivi, who was to inspire others to follow his lead and embrace the Joachimist heresy. It is interesting to note that Joachim, like many of his contemporaries, had entered the Friars Minor at the age of twelve, a practice condemned by successive popes: Boniface VIII, Clement VI and Urban V, who strongly endorsed the condemnation and reissued it under his own name.[70]

A third group of Spirituals, or *zelanti,* originated in Tuscany under the leadership of Ubertino de Casale, who, when he returned from his studies in Paris, fell under the influence of three remarkable people, among them Angela of Foligno, whose works were popular among Catalan friars. The protest movement had widespread support, and there were indeed practices within the Order of Friars Minor which were contrary to the ideals of their founder. Raymond Geoffroi, who was made minister general in 1289, sympathized with the Spirituals but could

---

68 Moorman, *History of the Franciscan Order,* pp. 188-189.
69 Ibid., p. 189.
70 Ibid., p. 189; and Montpellier, Archives de la ville de Montpellier, arm. E, cassette 5, no. 4, Inventaire 2259, being a copy of the bull of Urban V in the first year of his pontificate (2 January 1362 [1363]), confirming an earlier bull of Clement VI sent during the third year of his pontificate (27 April 1345), and addressed to the consuls and people of Montpellier and all superiors of convents and monasteries, both male and female, enjoining them not to admit young boys and girls who had not reached the age of puberty. Some years earlier Peter John Olivi actually became lector to the friars at Montpellier, where this papal bull is preserved.

not control those who believed that unity must be preserved at all costs.[71]

The extent to which the order had moved away from its origins led Olivi to predict the imminence of the milennium, preceded by a thousand years of tribulation, and to classify the ages of man, asserting at the same time that the church's claim that the righteous are separated from the unrighteous in this present life was clearly an error.[72] Pope John XXII's bull *Quorumdam exigit* of 1317, followed by *Super omnia* and *Gloriosam ecclesiam,* expressed the unacceptability of these doctrines, which he condemned as heretical.

The struggle which ensued between the papacy and those who supported Olivi and the Spirituals is beyond the scope of this chapter, but the bull *Ad conditorem canonum* of 1322, on the legal problems of use and ownership, two concepts which the pope regarded as inseparable, called into question the basic tenet of the Franciscan rule that the friars could use but not own property.[73] A year later Pope John published his bull *Cum inter nonnullos,* in which he dogmatically affirmed that to deny Christ and his apostles the lawful right of possession was not only contrary to biblical evidence but heretical.[74]

The minister general of the Friars Minor, Fr. Michael of Cesena, issued a letter saying that, before publishing anything, friars were to make sure that it had been approved by the general chapter or by deputies of the minister. He seems to have tried to prevent the trouble which ensued; but the march on Rome by the emperor, Lewis of Bavaria, accompanied by a few friars and thus exploiting the Franciscan controversy for his own political battle with the pope, led to the deposition of Fr. Michael, on the grounds that the general had encouraged the march. His deposition, flight and the controversies which followed led to a plethora of treatises, on the one hand defending the doctrine of absolute poverty on which the order had been based, and on the other supporting the papal position and condemning absolute poverty as heretical.

---

71 Moorman, *History of the Franciscan Order,* p. 191.
72 See Charles T. Davis, "Le Pape Jean XXII et les spirituels: Ubertin de Casale," in *Franciscains d'Oc: Les Spirituels ca. 1280-1324* (Toulouse, 1975), pp. 263-283, at 265.
73 Moorman, *History of the Franciscan Order,* pp. 316-317.
74 Ibid., p. 317.

In the late fourteenth century the latter group became known as the Conventuals; they conceived of an Order of Friars Minor subservient to the church, and thus were more concerned with obedience and submission than with rigorous application of evangelical poverty. South of the Pyrenees and elsewhere the rift between the Conventuals and Observants led to the formation of separate houses, and effectively splitting the order. The division was only healed at the Reformation with the establishment of two new orders—the Conventuals and the Capuchins.

In this context, after the middle of the fourteenth century, Jean de Roquetaillade, a friar minor who had studied at Toulouse and who had suffered several terms of imprisonment for his own brand of apocalypticism, ensured that Joachimist ideas were not forgotten.[75] He believed that Lewis of Bavaria was the awaited Antichrist and that the end of the world was at hand, and emphasized the even more urgent need to convert the Jews and infidels before it was too late. He died in Avignon around 1365.

The influence of the Spirituals and the details of the rift between them and the Conventuals is a complex subject which has more relevance for the study of the order in the late fourteenth and early fifteenth centuries than for the period prior to 1348. For this reason it is necessary to limit comments here to aspects of its origins which lie within the framework of the present study, and to include only certain basic facts regarding Peter John Olivi's life and ideas which bear directly upon developments in Catalonia from the first decades of the fourteenth century.

In 1289 Peter John Olivi began his teaching in Montpellier, at that time still under the Crown of Aragon, and drew many to him by his deep spirituality and pure life.[76] A group was formed, calling themselves béguins, and it is to this group that reference will be made when discussing the development of the Third Order south of the French border. Suffice it to say that it was not a group to be dismissed lightly: as already suggested, Arnau de Vilanova, the king of Aragon's physician, was probably a member of the Third Order and certainly a

---

75 See E. Randolph Daniel, *The Franciscan Concept of Mission in the High Middle Ages* (Lexington, KY, 1975), pp. 95-96.
76 Moorman, *History of the Franciscan Order,* p. 197.

supporter of the ideas of Peter John Olivi.[77] He had studied in a Dominican studium, had learnt Hebrew under the Dominican Fr. Ramon Martí and in his thought combined elements he had derived from the latter with an intense interest in the evangelical life and apocalyptic conversion central to Joachimism.[78]

Many prominent friars were to be associated with the ideas of the Spirituals; although he is beyond the chronological framework of this study, the Infant Pere, Alfonso III's younger brother, became a friar minor in Barcelona in 1358 and was responsible for a book of "revelations," clearly inspired by Joachimist principles, which was condemned by Pope Urban V in 1365.[79] The movement for purity and austerity which started in Provence and northern Italy found a considerable degree of acceptance south of the Pyrenees. It is also evident that a similar strain of protest ran through the members of the Third Order.

The origins and development of this group of laymen whose fortunes were so intricately bound with those of the First Order bear closer examination. Initially the Third Order consisted of a small group of unordained men and women who would have liked to enter the Order of Friars Minor or the Poor Clares but who could not do so for some reason such as being married and having a family. At first there was no

---

77 Francesco Santi, *Arnau de Vilanova: L'obra espiritual* (Valencia, 1987), pp. 83-93. Arnau knew Arabic, a fact which leads to speculation about the identity of Fr. Arnau de Vilanova, who heard the confession of Jaume de Rassals when the latter lay dying at the siege of Almería in 1309 (Barcelona, ACA, RC 147, f. 9, 8 August 1310, one of the few documents written in Catalan). Arnau de Vilanova did not die until a year after the date of this letter, which in any case refers to 1309. It would seem likely that Fr. Arnau de Vilanova came from the same family as the king's physician.

78 Daniel, *Franciscan Concept of Mission*, pp. 92-94, discusses Arnau de Vilanova's contribution to the mission of the Franciscans and shows the influence he had over Frederick II of Sicily, his popularity at the court of James II and his deep commitment to the conversion of the Jews.

79 José María Pou y Martí, *Visionarios, béguinos y fraticelos catalanes (siglos XIII-XV)* (Vic, 1930), pp. 349-350. The date Pere defended his *Revelations* coincided with the probable death of Jean de Roquetaillade, and there is no doubt that he was influenced by Jean. Since this study was completed the new edition of Pou i Martí's work has appeared (Madrid, 1991); the introduction and bibliographies have been brought up to date, and reference is made to Joachimist manuscripts which have recently come to light in Spain.

need for a rule, but as the group became larger it was necessary to lay down some basic precepts for tertiaries.

Moorman suggests that two points were clear immediately: the male members of the order should not bear arms, nor should they be required to take oaths other than those demanded by the Holy See.[80] In King James's territories the procurator of the Franciscans shared in this exemption from military service and also benefited by not having to pay taxes; his function was to receive the alms given to the friars and to look after all economic transactions. In the fourteenth century, among those who fulfilled these functions were some described as "friar," suggesting that they belonged to the Third Order. Like that of the Poor Clares, their early history was beleaguered by attempts to define their position within the Franciscan movement, and it was not until Nicholas IV's bull of 1289, *Supra montem,* that they acquired what was to be their one and only rule. It was after this date that the question of evangelical poverty and possession of property became a question of supreme importance among certain religious and laymen.

The rule of 1289 stressed the connection between the members of the Third Order and the Friars Minor: the visitor and ministers of any fraternity of tertiaries were to be nominated by the friars, whose duty it was to advise and direct them. The members of the fraternity were to attend the Franciscan church on the first Sunday in each month. Many altars in cathedrals and parish churches were dedicated to Saint Francis, and it was in these chapels that the fraternities would say mass and conduct other religious services. In many Aragonese, Catalan and Valencian cities after 1289 there seems to have been an increase in the establishment of such fraternities; some followed the pattern described above, others maintained devotion to Saint Francis and gathered in a chapel dedicated to him, but otherwise had little connection with the Friars Minor.[81]

Part of the mission of the mendicants was to minister to the poor, but this is much harder to document than the activities which brought

---

80 Moorman, *History of the Franciscan Order,* pp. 216–225. Moorman's account of the early tertiaries has provided the basis for comments here.
81 See Webster, "Els framenors de Manresa," p. 130, regarding the confraternity of Saint Francis in the cathedral of St. Mary, a group which apparently had little connection with the Franciscans. In Saragossa, on the other hand, the fraternity of notaries was constituted in the Franciscan house there, with the guardian present, and maintained a close connection with it through prayer and spiritual exercises.

them to public notice. The tradesmen who made up the majority of the fraternities were directly affiliated with a religious order, in this case the Order of Friars Minor, and frequently acted as dispensers of charity to the poor and needy, or at times to the sick.[82] It is not difficult to see how these groups gradually acquired a particular identity, and in some cases became religious communities themselves.

The organization of these confraternities belongs to a later section of this chapter; for the moment it is only necessary to indicate that male members of the Third Order were drawn primarily from the merchant class, and many belonged to trade associations. Groups of women, usually unmarried or widows, frequently became tertiaries and opened houses for the poor or sick. Bernat dez Clapers, known to the Castilian writer Don Juan Manuel, and a friend of Arnau de Vilanova, who was closely connected with the community of béguines in Valencia, established a hospital "pro anima sua."[83]

Shortly afterwards a man called Arnau or Ramon Guillem Català founded the hospital *dels béguins* in Valencia, about which very little is known except that béguins could live there in perpetuity, suggesting that it was more like an almshouse than a hospital for the sick.[84] Sr. Soriana, a member of the Third Order, known for the way in which she had helped many women to convert to a life of penitence, can probably be regarded as the foundress of a house for female penitents in Valencia.[85] The king urged the bishop and clerics of Valencia to buy a house either in the city or outside, where the women of the Third Order of Saint Francis could live together, suggesting that they could pay up to 4000 royal Valencian sous for it, despite the prohibition contained in the *fueros,* and commanding that his officials there observe the provisions of this concession. Other references to Sr. Soriana appear in the chancellery registers for the same year, including a concession of 15 Barcelona sous to the "Penitent" for expenses connected with her marriage, confirming

---

82 Michel Mollat, *The Poor in the Middle Ages: An Essay in Social History,* trans. Arthur Goldhammer (New Haven, 1986), p. 126.
83 See Agustín Rubió Vela, *Pobreza, enfermedad y asistencia hospitalaria en la Valencia del siglo XIV* (Valencia, 1984), p. 28.
84 Ibid., pp. 28 and 34.
85 The first reference to Sr. Soriana dates from 14 May 1345, when the *jurats* of the city of Valencia granted her 500 sous and their patronage, provided that the house was satisfactorily run (Valencia, AHM, Manuals del Consell, A.4, 1340–1345, f. 493v). See also Barcelona, ACA, RC 880, f. 185, 29 May 1346.

that the béguines were not always single women.[86] A payment to friars, sisters and "Ladies of Penitence" (a name frequently given to the béguines), and to hospitals in 1372 leads to the conclusion that both men and women were allowed to live either in the hospital *dels béguins* or another similar institution in Valencia, possibly the one the king had ordered established in 1346.[87] Alas, very little evidence survives for the activities of either béguines or female tertiaries, indicating perhaps that they were not so numerous as their male counterparts; this would no doubt be attributable in part to the flourishing female religious orders, which provided services elsewhere carried out by lay women.

Although strongest among the merchant class, the Third Order attracted a wide diversity of people, including mystics and hermits.[88] This very versatility seems to have led to trouble: in the early fourteenth century many tertiaries believed that they could better fulfil the aims of their calling by living a common life. In this shift of emphasis, they were really diverging from the original intentions of the Third Order and moving towards the formation of a new religious order. In some ways these men and women were filling the void left by the dissolution of the Order of Penitents of Jesus Christ, or Sack Friars, in 1274, an order which owed its origins to the Franciscan movement and whose founder, Raimondo or Raymond Athenulf, had in fact been a Friar Minor.[89]

The béghards or béguins and béguines were drawn from this group, and much has been written about their activities. They were very active within Catalan territory, especially in Majorca, Vilafranca and perhaps immediately south of the Pyrenees in Puigcerdà.[90] The béguinages of

---

86 Barcelona, ACA, RC 1309, f. 131v, 12 June 1346. This same register contains other references to Sor Soriana and the establishment of a house for the béguines of Valencia, referred to as Penitents of the Third Order of Saint Francis.

87 Isabel of Portugal, the sister of James II, entered the Clarissan convent in Coimbra as a tertiary when her husband died in 1325, and there are several documents in the chancellery registers referring to messages sent to her by her brother. Although it is clear that she wished to live a life of piety, the atmosphere of corruption and immorality at the Portuguese court made her life very difficult.

88 See also Santi, *Arnau de Vilanova: L'obra espiritual*, p. 151, for those who lived according to the Third Order in Barcelona but apparently ran no charitable institutions such as the hospital *dels béguins* in Valencia.

89 Robert I. Burns is preparing a full study of the Sack Friars.

90 See the case of Fr. Arnau Muntaner, resident in the Puigcerdà house after the Black Death (Sanahuja, *Història*, p. 150).

northern Europe, some of which were suspected of harbouring heretics, often ran hospitals or almshouses for the poor and elderly, and this pattern is also found south of the Pyrenees.[91] Elsewhere too they had already formed houses, but they continued to go out into the community and work as seculars.[92] In some places later in the fourteenth century they began to form enclosed communities. Many also began to diverge somewhat from orthodox teaching, and in an attempt to clarify their position Pope John XXII in 1319 declared that the Third Order lived "under the care and teaching of the Order of Friars Minor."[93] There is evidence that the béguins frequently espoused heretical doctrines, and some were called to account by the papal Inquisition on this account.[94] Arnau de Vilanova, whose own apocalyptic views brought him into disrepute, states that many béguins and béguines were cruelly persecuted by preachers and rulers alike, with defamations, calumnies and accusations of heresy; but not all members of the Third Order embraced these doctrines.[95]

Until recently very little has been known about the early years of the Third Order in the Crown of Aragon: its origins, its first members and even its whereabouts are obscure until the last decade of the thirteenth century. Josep Perarnau has done much to elucidate the activities of the béguins in Catalonia, and it is largely because of the existence of his studies that it is possible to add important supplementary data; but in his attempt to document this aspect of Franciscan history, he has tended to overemphasize their importance.[96]

---

91 See Mollat, *The Poor in the Middle Ages*, pp. 181–182.
92 See Moorman, *History of the Franciscan Order*, p. 419.
93 Ibid., p. 421.
94 Pou i Martí, *Visionarios, béguinos y fraticelos catalanes*, rev. ed. (Madrid, 1991), pp. 20–22; Sanahuja, *Història*, pp. 890–892; and Jean Duvernoy, *Le Registre d'Inquisition de Jacques Fournier, évêque de Pamiers (1318–1325)*, 3 vols. (Toulouse, 1965), which contains the proceedings of the inquisitors when dealing with different types of heresy brought to their attention. Navarra Bruni, the mother of a Franciscan, Fr. Pons Bruni, was brought to trial on 10 March 1319, after her son's death (Duvernoy, 1: 551). Franciscans and Carmelites sometimes acted as witnesses, as did Fr. Guillem Flequer (a Franciscan), on 6 April 1321 (ibid, 1: 451). In Pamiers the accused frequently had some connection with the Franciscans.
95 See Arnau de Vilanova, "Raonament d'Avinyó," in *Obres catalanes*, vol. 1: *Escrits religiosos*, ed. Miquel Batllori (Barcelona, 1947), pp. 167–221, at 206.
96 See Josep Perarnau, "Una altra carta de Guiu Terrena sobre el procés inquisitorial contra el franciscà fra Bernat Fuster," *EF* 82 (1981), 383–392.

The first documented reference found to the Third Order in the realms of Aragon dates from May 1298 and concerns a citizen of Vilafranca del Penedès, a town to the south of Barcelona which had strong contacts not only with the tertiaries but with the Spiritual Franciscans.[97] In a letter to his bailiff in Vilafranca, James II, writing on behalf of Fr. Bernat Fuster of the Third Order of Saint Francis, who claimed that a tax of 15 sous had been levied on him because he had not enlisted in the army of the count of Pallars, states that the man should not be required to pay this because he is a "religious person."[98] Exemption from military service could sometimes be obtained through payment of a tax, as in this case; but as a "religious person" Fr. Bernat was not required to do military service, nor to pay a tax in lieu, and the bailiff was to see that the 15 sous extorted from him by the worthy men of Vilafranca were returned to him. It is probable that this man comes from the same family as Bernat Fuster of Sant Boi, who in his will of March 1296 left 200 sous to the Franciscans of Barcelona, as subsequent documents suggest that the Fuster family were strong supporters of the Spiritual cause.[99] The document of May 1298 is the earliest yet found referring to the presence in Catalonia of members of the Third Order of Saint Francis. The following year (1299), a further letter from King James to his bailiff at Vilafranca, shows that the matter was still not settled, as both Fr. Bernat Fuster and Fr. Pere Guerau, also a member of the Third Order, had been required to pay the tax determined by the king's councillor, Bernat de Sarrià, for those who wished to buy their exemption from military service.[100]

There are several references to Fr. Pere Guerau of Vilafranca after 1299. Procurator for the Franciscan house in 1309 and 1315, he was

---

97 Barcelona, ACA, RC 111, ff. 225v–226, 20 May 1298. See below Document 14.
98 Ibid. Fr. Bernat came from a family well known for its association with Joachimist ideas. Josep Perarnau has written extensively on this subject: see his article "Noves dades sobre béguins de Girona," *AIEG* 25 (1979–1980), 237–246; 26 (1981), 383–392.
99 Barcelona, AC, Pia Almoina, perg. 4-3-110, 15 March 1295 [1296].
100 Barcelona, ACA, RC 114, f. 204, 3 December 1299. There is a reference to béguins in Gerona in 1304, when Berenguera, the wife of Joan Gili, procurator of the Castelló house, left 5 sous of Melguiers to Fr. Jaume, a béguin (Gerona, AH, C.73bis (T.1303–1310), Pere Perrini, f. 18, 1 October 1304). This suggests that the procurator at Castelló was a member of the Third Order and might well have been a béguin himself.

active with Fr. Bernat Fuster (they both bear the epithet "friar,") in the Third Order from the latter years of the thirteenth century.[101] Indeed, Fr. Bernat Fuster's son became a friar minor, and distinguished himself in 1321 by being brought before the Inquisition at the instigation of the Carmelite bishop of Majorca, Fr. Guy Terreni, for espousing heretical ideas; he was condemned and imprisoned for over ten years in the papal palace at Avignon.[102] He and his father had been influenced by the views of Arnau de Vilanova, and no doubt the latter's comments on the life of the béguins in Catalonia can be taken to describe the group in which the family of Bernat Fuster was prominent.

Arnau de Vilanova, who had studied medicine in Montpellier and perhaps had been influenced there by the men and women who called themselves béguins, described their life as that of a group living on the fringes of society.[103] Briefly, Arnau refers to the life of mendicity and poverty adopted by Saint Francis and his friends, a life without property or possessions, dedicated to the greater glory of God and his Gospel. The treatise exalts the advantages of having a spirit that is not fettered by earthly cares, that eschews all learning, a frequent cause of "perdition," and it emphasizes the desire of the béguins to avoid deviation from the ideal of evangelical poverty.

Arnau himself believed that he was writing in the sixth age of the church, an age which had probably begun at the turn of the fourteenth century and which could not last beyond 1340, an opinion which made clear his acceptance of the milennium predicted by Joachim da Fiore and his followers.[104] Others believed that the year 1400 would mark the beginning of a thousand years of tribulation before the final day of judgment brought the second coming and glorious kingdom of Christ, and saw the Black Death, the papal Schism and the corruption of the church as signs that the end was near.

---

101 Barcelona, AD, Registra communium, I, ff. 104v–105, 2 August 1309; and Barcelona, AC, Pia Almoina, Llibres notarials, Bernat Vilarrubia, 28 July–28 October 1315: f. 14v, 1 August 1315. I am indebted to Rev. Josep Baucells i Reig for these references.

102 See Josep Perarnau, "Una altra carta," pp. 383–392, which gives the chronology of the proceedings against the friar minor.

103 Josep Perarnau, L'"Alia informatio beguinorum" d'Arnau de Vilanova (Barcelona, 1978). Perarnau transcribes the text of this treatise by the famous physician to James II, and my comments in this section are taken from this edition.

104 Ibid., p. 166.

Arnau, and those who espoused the ideas of the Spirituals, also defended the equality of all Christians before Christ, basing their views on the primitive church. If this were so, it followed that laymen could be effective bearers of the Gospel, a view hotly disputed by those who believed that ordination conveyed a special sense of charisma and a certain undisputed privilege to preach the word of God.[105] By implication, Arnau was not only criticizing the ordained clergy and suggesting that there were others more worthy to fulfil their functions, but also casting doubt on the validity of the sacrament of ordination. It is not too difficult to see in the Spiritual movement an embryo of some of the more extreme forms of Protestantism introduced from the time of the Reformation. Doctrinal implications are not so relevant here, however, as the way in which the divergence of beliefs affected the Third Order.

Documents referring to the Fuster and Pere (or Guerau) families show the Third Order active in Vilafranca, if not elsewhere, as early as the last decade of the thirteenth century. It seems to have been customary there, at least, for tertiaries to fulfil the functions of procurator and thus to manage the friars' economic affairs. The king's physician, Arnau de Vilanova, shared the views of the béguins and was probably in close contact with them. The royal family tolerated "spiritual" beliefs. The king's brother, Frederick of Sicily, was especially sympathetic and gave asylum to Arnau in September 1309 when he was censured by James II for associating him with the Spirituals.[106] A group of forty Franciscan Spirituals also fled to Sicily and sought the protection of Frederick in order to escape papal persecution.[107] Elsewhere in the present study it has been shown that this same group of forty Franciscans was given a safe-conduct by the king, who probably felt relieved that they were leaving the Iberian Peninsula.

---

105 Perarnau, L'"*Alia informatio beguinorum,*" p. 173.
106 See Arnau de Vilanova, *Aphorismi di gradibus,* ed. Michael R. McVaugh, vol. 2 of *Opera medica omnia,* ed. L. Garcia-Ballester, J.A. Paniagua, and M.R. McVaugh (Granada and Barcelona, 1975), pp. 75–77.
107 Clifford R. Backman, "Frederick III of Sicily and the Franciscan Spirituals" (an unpublished paper read at the 103rd annual meeting of the American Historical Association, Cincinnati, 1988, under the auspices of the American Academy of Research Historians of Medieval Spain), discusses the prevalence of "these degenerate sons and followers of Satan who feign sanctity while moved by diabolical motives," delivering an exceedingly strong condemnation of a group of men who were aghast at the worldliness of the Church and of their confreres.

Up to now discussion has centred on the male members of the Third Order, who, because of their similarity to friars of the Spiritual movement, have more bearing on a study of the order in the realms of Aragon. There were many female béguines engaged in charitable works: the running of hospitals like that in Valencia, or homes for the poor, orphaned or widowed, although the extent of their activities in the Crown of Aragon is difficult to chronicle for lack of evidence.[108]

In Gerona, for example, there were both male and female members of the Third Order of Penitence (of Saint Francis) who ran a hospital, and who had been sentenced by Fr. Arnau Burguet, a papal inquisitor, and excommunicated.[109] One of them, Ferrer Morell of Llambilles, had confessed that he was a member of the Third Order, and the bishop of Gerona and the papal inquisitor Fr. Felip Alfons seem to have accepted his confession and given him absolution, probably on the recommendation of the guardian of the Friars Minor. Another document contains the permission for Fr. Francesc Joan of the Third Order of Saint Francis, a priest, to be given extreme unction.[110] This suggests that not all tertiaries could be given the last rites, and implies that those who had embraced heretical views were excommunicated and thus excluded from the sacraments. There were also houses of béguins in Majorca in 1339, but it is not clear if both men and women resided in them or what function they fulfilled, as there is less extant documentation on them.[111]

---

108 See Agustín Rubió Vela and Mateu Rodrigo Lizondo, "Els béguins de València en el segle XIV: La seva casa, hospital i els seus llibres," in *Estudis en memòria del professor Manuel Sanchis Guarner: Estudis de llengua i literatura catalanes*, 2 vols. (Valencia, 1984), 1: 327–341, which refers to professions of men and women tertiaries in the years 1316–1317, the period when their activities in the Crown of Aragon seem to have been most abundant.

109 Gerona, AD, Registra litterarum, no. 6, 1334–1343, f. 15v, 13 October 1335. A note is appended in Catalan: "se mana tornar vestir lo hàbit d'un terciari de Sant Francesch."

110 Gerona, AD, Registra litterarum, no. 7, 1339–1344, f. 69r-v, 26 June 1346. Documents preserved in Gerona for the towns of Castelló and Gerona show that these areas were fertile ground for the Penitents, a conclusion confirmed by the studies of Josep Perarnau i Espelt, referred to in notes 102 and 103 above.

111 Palma de Mallorca, AC, Protocols, no. 14552, unnumbered folio, dated 19 August 1339, refers to the will of the late Francesc Sa Costa, who wished to be buried in the Franciscan house in Majorca and left 500 pounds for the purpose, including among his legacies 5 pounds for provisions for the house, 20 for masses, 3 for both ordained and lay friars and 30 sous for "dominabus beguinis."

THE CONFRATERNITIES

The position of the confraternities or *cofradías* within the Franciscan movement is even more difficult to assess, because undoubtedly trade confraternities existed which had nothing to do with tertiaries. Extant evidence is sketchy and may give a totally erroneous picture of the geographical prominence of such organizations, but, despite this, the relatively incomplete documentation encountered makes an important contribution to the understanding of the confraternities in the late Middle Ages. One of the major problems in determining the affiliation of these confraternities and the extent to which their members belonged to the Third Order lies in the fact that trade confraternities existed long before the foundation of the mendicant orders, many of them having as their patron a saint or the Virgin Mary. Clearly these organizations had nothing to do with the movement of lay men and women associated with the friars, but the fact that they often bore similar names makes it virtually impossible to disentangle them from those confraternities run by tertiaries.

One of the earliest references to a guild or confraternity associated with the Franciscans is from Valencia is dated to September 1290, about the time when the Third Order made its appearance in the realms of Aragon. On this occasion the king granted the carpenters of Valencia permission to found a confraternity in the church of the Friars Minor, dedicated to the Blessed Virgin Mary, Saint Francis and All Saints.[112] There is nothing to suggest that the carpenters belonged to the Third Order, and it is probable that, like many such organizations elsewhere, they merely wanted to dedicate their guild to the Virgin and Saint Francis at a time when their popularity was at its height; consequently they might well have adopted the rule of the Third Order to give their organization validity.

The earliest reference found to the association in Saragossa dates from 1294, when the members asked the king for permission to participate in a fair to be held in the city.[113] A later document mentions the privileges given to the guild by King James, probably James II, and

---

112 Ambròs de Saldes, "Franciscanismo: Documentos franciscanos," *EF* 17 (1916), 64–74, at p. 67.
113 Barcelona, ACA, RC 97, f. 253, 24 January 1293 [1294].

possibly referring to the 1294 document.[114] While it is clear that Saint Francis's influence led to the formation of guilds like this one, extant documents do not elaborate on the constitutions of this guild or its relation to the Franciscan house in Saragossa. It is known, for instance, that a consortium dedicated to the Blessed Virgin Mary and Saint Francis existed in Parma in 1292, and it may be that the confraternity of Saint Francis in Saragossa belonged to this group.[115] Only from documents of 1328, when two more guilds—for scribes and notaries—were founded in Saragossa and Huesca, is it clear how these organizations were established in Aragon and that they bear similarities to the Parma consortium. They are the best extant examples of Aragonese confraternities closely associated with the friars showing the direct involvement of the guardian and officers of the Friars Minor in the guild's formation.

The Saragossa confraternity was established on 6 January 1328 and its statutes ratified on 1 May (the same year), while the Huesca confraternity was constituted on 4 September 1328 and its statutes ratified one month later.[116] The Huesca statutes were drawn up at a chapter meeting of the organization convened for the purpose, and begin (like the Saragossa statutes): "In the name of the Holy Trinity and indivisible unity of Father, Son and Holy Spirit. Amen." They state that they refer to the chapter of the confraternity of notaries, scribes and *jurados,* constituted to the honour of the Blessed Virgin Mary and Blessed Louis, comprised of all who are of one spirit and one mind in the Lord and who unanimously wish to live together in harmony, as expressed by the

---

114 Barcelona, ACA, RC 640, f. 29v, 28 March 1346. Santiago Sobrequés, "La época del patriciado urbano," in *História de España y América social y económica,* vol. 2, *Baja edad media,* ed. J. Vicens Vives, 2nd ed. (Barcelona, 1971), pp. 7–406, at 198, refers to the guild of notaries in Saragossa as dating from 1320, Huesca from 1328 and Daroca from 1337, all of them dedicated to Saint Louis. Other guilds were established during the second half of the fourteenth century.

115 See Bonaventura Giordani, "Statuta consortii B. Mariae Virginis et S. Francisci Parmae saec. XIV," *Archivum Franciscanum historicum* 16 (1923), 356–368, drawn to my attention by Rev. Josep Martí Mayor.

116 The Huesca statutes, the best preserved, are included below in Document 35. The Saragossa document of 1 May 1328 refers to a meeting of the chapter of the confraternity held at Epiphany (6 January) 1328, in the convent of Friars Minor, in the presence of Fr. Sancho López de Ayerbe (at the time guardian of the house) and all the friars, for the purpose of drawing up the statutes (Barcelona, ACA, RC 475, ff. 60–61, dated 1 May 1328). Comparison of this document with the Huesca statutes suggests that a similar formula was followed.

psalmist, "Ecce quam bonum et quam jocundum habitare fratres in unum." In the presence of the entire house of Friars Minor the members agreed to lead a common spiritual life, and expressed their desire that the organization be dedicated in perpetuity to the honour of Blessed Louis of the Order of Friars Minor. Saint Louis of Toulouse, the Saint Louis referred to here, was long thought to have been a tertiary, but this misconception arose from the fact that the other Saint Louis, King Louis IX of France, probably belonged to the Third Order, while Saint Louis of Toulouse had been held captive in Aragon and placed under the tutelage of the Friars Minor, himself subsequently taking the habit.[117]

The statutes state that members were to look upon the friars as their brothers and to submit to being directed and corrected by them, a provision included in the rule of the Third Order of 1289. The entire chapter of the friars readily consented to receive the confraternity members as confreres. The statutes also confirmed that henceforth the confraternities and their members would be bound by charity to the friars, emphasizing that this allowed the brothers to participate in all spiritual activities in both life and death (masses, prayers, fasting, abstinence, vigils, good works, preaching, confessions, etc.). The guardian or his substitute was to be informed when a guild officer died, so that a subsequent appointment could be made with the full consent of the house of Friars Minor.

Although there is no direct reference to the Third Order, it is very likely that the confraternities of Saint Francis in both Huesca and Saragossa were in fact composed of tertiaries, as the wording of the statutes follows exactly the format of a similar gathering held in Bologna in 1289.[118] There were other confraternities, very similar to this one, which only had a working relationship with the Franciscans and could not be considered part of the Third Order, even though they followed the same rule and were indistinguishable from the order.[119]

---

117 See Sanahuja, *Història*, pp. 53 and 127. He was the uncle of the Infant Pere, who became Fr. Pere d'Aragó. See also Moorman, *History of the Franciscan Order*, p. 221, and Pou i Martí, *Visionarios, béguinos y fraticelos catalanes*, which deals at length with the Infant Pere's life and associations with Joachimist views.
118 Moorman, *History of the Franciscan Order*, p. 219.
119 See Antoni Maria de Barcelona, "La regla del terç orde franciscà," *EF* 27 (1921), 246-261, at p. 257 (the issue is dedicated to the 700th anniversary of the foundation of the Third Order). To a transcription of the 1515 Catalan edition of the rule of the Third Order, is added the statutes of a similar organization, not affiliated to the Third Order, registered in the parish of Falset in 1320 and 1400.

In Tàrrega, where the establishment of the Friars Minor was somewhat later, James II granted permission for a guild to be founded in the name of Saint Francis.[120] In Tàrrega, unlike Saragossa, the guild encountered opposition, and the royal concession was revoked; it was only renewed in 1344, as a result of pleas from the guardian and friars of the Tàrrega house. They were enjoined to reestablish the guild in exactly the way it had been established originally, with the confreres and sisters whom the guardian wished to admit, and anyone opposing the king's command would incur his wrath. No mention is made of a particular trade or profession, and it may well be that this confraternity was more general in its scope since it admitted both men and women. If this were the case, and not merely that the extant document omits the affiliation because it is referring to a previous longer document, now no longer extant, it might not be inappropriate to hazard a guess that the reason for revocation of the privilege was in some way connected with the confraternity's membership: perhaps it was a community of béguins and béguines, who were not acceptable to the people of Tàrrega after the condemnation of the Spirituals by Pope John XXII.

The confraternities in the Crown of Aragon followed almost exactly the phrasing of the rule of the Third Order; the first rule of the Third Order drawn up in 1221 includes provision for abstinence, fasting, prayer, the sacraments, a special mass and meeting each month (one of the prime functions of the confraternities), a chapter concerning the correction and election of officers, and enjoins the members to visit the sick and bury the dead.[121] This rule existed in a number of different local versions, and to ensure uniformity Nicholas IV in 1289 issued the bull *Supra montem*, which remained in force until the late nineteenth century.[122] There were no substantial changes to the 1221 rule in 1289: its main purpose was to clarify unclear provisions, ensure that affiliation of the Third Order with the Friars Minor was spelt out officially and that the rule was in every way consistent with the aims and

---

120 Barcelona, ACA, RC 876, f. 38, 12 March 1343 [1344], published in Sarret i Pons, *Privilegis de Tàrrega*, pp. 161-162.
121 See "The Rule of the Third Order (1221)," trans. James Meyer, ed. with intro. and notes by Placid Hermann, in *St. Francis of Assisi, Writings and Early Biographies: English Omnibus of the Sources for the Life of St. Francis,* ed. Marion A. Habig (London, 1972), pp. 165-175, at 168-175.
122 "Rule of the Third Order," in *St. Francis of Assisi,* ed. Habig, p. 168.

aspirations of the tertiaries.[123] The confraternities in the Crown of Aragon must have had this before them, using it as a model for their own organizations. A Catalan version dating from 1515 survives in an incunabula printed by the well-known printer Joan Rosenbach.[124] The confraternities are mentioned very frequently in wills and in the royal chancellery registers in connection with the mendicant orders from the earliest documentation preserved for the Crown of Aragon, lending credence to the significant role the trades and professions played in the development of these orders. The confreres of the confraternities, probably in the main members of the Third Order, shared in the aspirations of the mendicant friars, helping them to extend their mission in the towns to the realms of everyday life. In some cases the confraternities acquired privileges and property, and their members lived together in a quasi religious community, carrying on their trade or profession but living under the provisions of the rule of 1289.[125] Since confraternities were exempt from taxes and military service, it has been suggested that the male members, by claiming the status of a religious order, sought to evade their civil duties and thus abused the system; but it is difficult to accept this argument, as there is no doubt that the king granted them privileges in exactly the same way as he did to the Friars Minor and other mendicants. He would hardly have been ignorant of their existence, and clearly regarded them as an extension of the Friars Minor and Poor Clares. The friars themselves seem to have accepted the tertiaries and béguins very readily, and it is often difficult to differentiate between members of the First and Third Orders.

---

123 Moorman, *History of the Franciscan Order*, pp. 217–218.
124 See Barcelona, "La regla del terç orde francisca." See also Fregando de Amberes, "La orden tercera de San Francisco de Asís: Su difusión e influencia política en el siglo XIII," *EF* 29 (1923), 42–53, which refers to the way in which Pier delle Vigne, Frederick II of Sicily's chancellor, accused the Franciscans and Dominicans of making public recriminations against him: "Y para acabar de debilitar nuestro poder y enajenarnos cada vez más de la adhesión popular han fundado dos nuevas fraternidades, que reciben hombres y mujeres indistintamente. Todos acuden a incribirse y raro es el que aún no les ha dado su nombre." Although there is some dispute over whether or not Pier delle Vigne actually used these words, it is clear that fraternities of men and women were common in Sicily at the end of the thirteenth century, and that these were in some way associated with the Franciscans and Dominicans.
125 Moorman, *History of the Franciscan Order*, p. 220.

By 1348 the followers of Saint Francis were not only found in the Order of Friars Minor, the Poor Clares and even the Third Order, but had also spread to trade or charitable guilds. By so doing they helped to bind the friars even closer to the merchant classes, and through them to the economy of the country. The crown, in turn, took advantage of the popularity of the mendicant friars and the philosophy they preached to consolidate its alliance with the middle classes, thus forming the most effective check against the ambitions of the powerful nobles referred to in Chapter 3. The ever-increasing number of educated men amongst the mendicants meant that their influence over their contemporaries in an age of development could not be rejected lightly, and the cultural significance of the friars will be discussed at some length in the following chapter.

7

The Cultural Impact of the Franciscans

No study of the Franciscans would be complete without some reference to the way in which they influenced the cultural scene of their day. It is perhaps here more than anywhere else that the extraordinarily rapid move made by the friars away from the simple life advocated by Saint Francis is evident. In the acquisition of learning and more material well-being, the friars with their fine buildings, increasingly elaborate in ornamentation, gradually came to play a part in the social life of the later Middle Ages that had little to do with their founder's view of the apostolic life.

This chapter discusses some of the ways in which the Franciscans took the lead in cultural affairs, emphasizing their contribution to the scholastic movement of the fourteenth century, their support of the doctrine of the Immaculate Conception and the significant impact they had on artistic and architectural endeavour in the cities of the Crown of Aragon. In view of Saint Francis's attitude to learning, and the emphasis in the rule that only those books necessary for religious observance should be in the friars' possession, it is ironical that his followers, like the Dominicans, should have been prominent in the scholastic movement of the thirteenth and fourteenth centuries. By the end of the fourteenth century friars like Francesc Eiximenis had made a name for themselves as encyclopedic writers and had acquired considerable libraries.

The early Friars Minor had lived in simple dwellings, probably in private houses, but not long after the founder's death their order thought nothing of acquiring splendid convents and properties, accentuating the order's move away from the simple ideal of Saint Francis. The rule as it had been drawn up was inadequate to meet the demands of a changing society, and it was inevitable that there should be some deviation from its provisions.

The previous chapters have shown how the Franciscans, like the other mendicant orders, acquired support and property in the Crown of

Aragon, undertaking difficult missions for the king, preaching to the Jews and Saracens and participating actively in fraternal organizations set up by the trade guilds. The friars were bound by family ties to many prominent merchants and statesmen, and it was from them that they both expected and received the financial benefits that led to the construction of magnificent churches and convent buildings. Hundreds of skilled tradesmen were required to plan and erect these buildings, and the influence of mendicant art and architecture on the late Middle Ages cannot be overemphasized. The carvings, paintings and other adornments which followed, and the heavy demand for their services inspired many artists to give of their best, especially since their products could be regarded as pious works and earn them a reward in the afterlife.[1]

Pope Innocent IV and his successors encouraged the faithful to give money to the Friars Minor and the Poor Clares so that they could either build their houses or add chapels and other improvements, as was the case for the Franciscan house at Cervera and the Clarissan convent of Sant Antoni in Barcelona; in return they would receive indulgences to help mitigate their suffering in purgatory.[2] To judge by the number of bequests to the Franciscans during the last three decades of the thirteenth century, the admonition was not taken lightly, and the promise of a reward in the afterlife provided sufficient incentive to part with worldly goods. Edicts like that of the archbishop of Tarragona in 1246 in favour of Cervera were probably issued in other dioceses, and may help to explain the pattern of giving to the mendicant orders.[3]

No religious orders offered such scope for artistic endeavour as the Dominicans and Franciscans; Saint Dominic, Saint Francis, Saint Antony and later Saint Louis of Toulouse all provided abundant material for creativity. Chapels, altars and retables, dedicated to these saints or containing scenes depicting their lives, could be found throughout western Europe, and the realms of Aragon were no exception.

---

1 Rotha Mary Clay, *The Mediaeval Hospitals of England* (London, 1966), p. 85, believes that the pious motives for medieval giving have been overemphasized and that care for the sick and poor also lay behind some of the legacies and donations attributed to a concern for the soul.
2 See Innocent IV, *La documentación pontifícia de Inocencio IV (1243-1254)*, ed. Augusto Quintana Prieto, 2 vols. (Rome, 1987). There are numerous references throughout this work to the practice of giving indulgences. See also Pedro Sanahuja, *História de la seráfica provincia de Cataluña* (Barcelona, 1959), p. 92.
3 See Sanahuja, *História,* p. 92.

Similarly, the works of theology and the studies more suitable for less specialized readers which the Franciscans produced, and their prominence and influence in university circles in the thirteenth century, is truly remarkable. It has much to do with the education which they themselves received, and which inspired the creation of other centres of higher learning in the fourteenth century. The present study can only include a brief discussion of the educational framework which produced this literary revolution, and make reference to the names of some of the writers in the Crown of Aragon and to the principal ways in which they influenced Franciscan thought. To attempt to do more would not only extend this study beyond acceptable limits but lead to a distortion of the Franciscan mission in the early years, when it was primarily concerned with the cure of souls and the firm establishment of a network of houses.

There were no international centres of study like those at Oxford or Paris in the Crown of Aragon, except Montpellier for a time, when the attempt to found one in Valencia was aborted by the studium generale founded in Lerida in 1300. Apart from Montpellier, this was probably the earliest institution of higher learning, and by that time the order was not only established but had a clearly-defined image which subsequent events could only modify. This image was largely derived from the way in which the friars had interpreted their rule and from the education they had received, often in the best universities of Europe, but it was one Saint Francis would have regarded with surprise, perhaps even distaste.

The international character of the Order of Friars Minor, especially during the first two centuries of development, meant that conditions prevailing in one area seldom differed significantly from those pertaining in another. Thus, it is fitting to turn to Moorman's *History of the Franciscan Order* for a description of the way in which a regular system of study had been devised by 1254. Each convent was to have its lector, who would be responsible for teaching theology to all the friars while preparing the most able for higher education elsewhere. Sanahuja suggests that from the early thirteenth century it was customary for the friars to study theology or the holy scriptures by comparing the texts with those of the church fathers and with the *Sentences* of Peter Lombard, a standard textbook for all clerics in the late Middle Ages.[4]

---

[4] Sanahuja, *História*, p. 173. The friars also possessed works by Duns Scotus, John of Wales, Ovid, the *Flos sanctorum* and the *Decretales*, all of them, with the exception of those by Ovid, standard volumes in the medieval Franciscan friaries.

Before entering the novitiate a potential friar would be expected to have completed the basics of Latin grammar and preferably also of logic. Once he had finished his novitiate he would receive an introduction to the arts and philosophy, and then continue with theological studies. Most friars would not proceed further, but those who showed some aptitude for university work would be sent to Paris, Oxford or Cambridge, where they would study under masters such as Duns Scotus or William of Ockham.[5] On their return to the Iberian Peninsula they would take up positions as lectors in local convents, teaching the latest views on theological questions which they had studied in England or Paris.[6]

The earliest references to the lector in the Crown of Aragon date from the late thirteenth century, and after that an increasing number of students were given permission to travel abroad and/or to carry books from one place to another without having to pay the tax levied on the transportation of scholastic materials.[7] This was a special privilege accorded to the mendicants, who clearly had no reason to pay a toll which was primarily an attempt to prevent expensive books from leaving the country. As study became more prominent in convents such as that at Barcelona in the late fourteenth century, foreign scholars of some note were frequently appointed as lectors for a term of one or more years.[8] This enabled them to keep the friars abreast of recent theological developments, and indeed to spread some of the more unorthodox ideas of the Spirituals with greater facility.[9]

---

5   Alfonso III ordered executors of the will of Gil Pérez de Tauste to return concordances to the Bible and writings on the *Summa* of Scotus to Fr. Miguel de Almenara, lector of Saragossa, who had been given these books by the deceased before his death. See Antoni Rubió i Lluch, ed., *Documents per l'història de la cultura catalana mig.eval*, 2 vols. (Barcelona, 1908-1921), 1: 101, no. 84, 23 August 1330.

6   Two of the earliest lectors were Fr. Romeo Ortiz, then at the convent at Ejea but later a famous provincial minister and royal adviser, and Fr. Pere de Torrents of Barcelona, whose brother (?) was guardian of the Barcelona house at the same time.

7   Barcelona, ACA, RC 159, f. 190, 27 December 1316; and RC 357, f. 149v, 11 July 1318.

8   See the case of Fr. Alfredo Gonter, whose life has been the subject of a study by León Amorós Payá, "Anfredo Gontero, OFM, discípulo de Escoto y lector en el estudio general de Barcelona," *Revista española de teología* 1 (1941), 545-572.

9   Fr. Alfredo had studied at Paris with Duns Scotus, and among other things wrote the tract *De paupertate Christi* while in Barcelona (Amorós Payá, "Anfredo Gontero," pp. 547-550).

In the latter part of the fourteenth century in Barcelona and Valencia both the Franciscans and the Dominicans had important schools of theology, where prominent Catalan theologians and writers such as Fr. Francesc Eiximenis and Fr. Vicent Ferrer carried on a not always friendly rivalry.[10] Studies had become as important for the Franciscans as for the Dominicans, and the lector was therefore a prominent member of the community to whom a certain respect was due, one of the few privileged enough to have a private room.[11]

Some of the friars left their home convent to study elsewhere; in the thirteenth century in Aragon this usually meant that they travelled abroad, although in 1294 the provincial minister of Aragon, Fr. Domingo de Jaca, was granted royal permission to allow Fr. Aloysius of Sicily, who fell within his jurisdiction, to study in Castile, probably because Fr. Aloysius came from a Castilian background.[12] The king stated that he was in favour of Fr. Aloysius being given this opportunity, because he held him in high regard; but all the same he was careful to emphasize that the expenses incurred were to be met by the provincial minister. This was the usual practice, unless an individual convent wished to defray the cost of study abroad for one of its members not sponsored by the Franciscan province. Friars selected for study by either the provincial chapter or the individual house were first expected to study for three or four years at their own house, then to proceed abroad to follow the course leading to the Master of Theology degree, so that on their return they too could occupy the role of lector.

Among those who attended the medical school at Montpellier was the king's physician, Arnau de Vilanova, and no doubt the two Franciscan royal physicians referred to in Chapter 5, Fr. Albert and Fr. Arnulf. The proportion of friars who attended these universities was probably initially fairly small, but as the order became more established and economically more able to finance the studies of these students, the numbers increased, and extant records suggest that by the end of the fourteenth century the proportion of educated friars had risen considerably.[13] This is scarcely

---

10 See Martín de Riquer, *Història de la literatura catalana: Part antiga*, 3 vols. (Barcelona, 1964), 2: 140.
11 John R.H. Moorman, *A History of the Franciscan Order from its Origins to the Year 1517* (Oxford, 1968; repr. Chicago, 1988), p. 123.
12 Barcelona, ACA, RC 100, f. 175v, 23 October 1294.
13 Rubió i Lluch, *Documents per l'història,* and Sanahuja, *Història,* both refer to many friars who went abroad to study in the latter half of the fourteenth century.

surprising in view of the predominance of Franciscan thought in fourteenth-century Paris and Oxford, thanks largely to the influence of John Duns Scotus and William of Ockham.[14] The impact of the Franciscans on the curriculum and their relations with the townsmen, not always harmonious, have been discussed at length elsewhere; but it is clear that the majority of students from south of the Pyrenees made their way to these two centres of learning, where they were able to meet with, and be influenced by, the greatest theologians of the time. Such a system enabled Franciscans from many nations to study together, and was probably responsible to some degree for the extraordinary influence the friars exercised in fourteenth-century Europe.

Theology was the prime object of study, and most of the Franciscan literature of the later Middle Ages was strongly theological or mystical in tone. The theological allegories of Alain de Lille, the poems of Jacopone da Todi and others and the popularity of Marian songs all contributed to a body of Franciscan literature which became popular throughout Europe. Among the many works of theologians and philosophers, none were more significant to the Order of Friars Minor than those of Saint Bonaventure, Duns Scotus and William of Ockham. Ascetic strength was found in these works of spirituality, through meditation on poverty, penance and contemporary evils such as greed and usury, but this phenomenon was not confined to any particular geographical area.[15] The Franciscans in the Crown of Aragon, through their study abroad and their interaction with friars from other countries, shared these same cultural influences, and there were few native writers of any stature to emerge before 1348. The popularity of certain Franciscan authors, such as Saint Bonaventure and Angela of Foligno, led to the production of Catalan versions, although it is impossible to say exactly when the first translations were made.[16]

Two outstanding writers of the late thirteenth and early fourteenth centuries drew their inspiration from Franciscan and medical themes and

---

14 William J. Courtenay, *Schools and Scholars in Fourteenth-Century England* (Princeton, 1987), pp. 185-190.

15 For a more detailed account of Franciscan spirituality and the influence of mendicant literature see John V. Fleming, *An Introduction to the Franciscan Literature of the Middle Ages* (Chicago, 1977); see also Moorman, *History of the Franciscan Order*, pp. 278-294 and 390-405.

16 A translation of Bonaventure's *Lignum vitae* was published by Nolasc del Molar, "Una traducció antiga del *Lignum vitae* de Sant Bonaventura," *EF* 79 (1978) 63-81.

wrote in both Catalan and Latin: Ramon Llull and Arnau de Vilanova. They represent the two currents of Franciscan thought: the ideas of those who observed orthodoxy, and of those who embraced the apocalyptic vision of Peter John Olivi and Joachim da Fiore. The support of James II for these ideas helped to ensure that the Order of Friars Minor became firmly established south of the Pyrenees. Father Basili de Rubí credits Llull with having been one of those instrumental in explaining the doctrine of the Immaculate Conception to the Franciscans of Barcelona.[17] Certainly he was not alone in this, as evidence exists that a number of friars in Aragon came under the direct influence of Scotus, and passed on his teachings to their confreres when they returned to their native convents.

The significance of the writings of Fr. Pons Carbonell has already been mentioned: he was probably one of the earliest Barcelona friars to acquire prominence as a theologian who followed the teachings of Duns Scotus. All the same, the extent of the latter's influence can best be seen in the theological writings of Fr. Alfredo Gonter of Brittany, who held the position of lector in the house at Barcelona in 1322.[18] Fr. Alfredo had studied under Duns Scotus in Paris during the first decade of the fourteenth century, and had defended the most commonly-held view of the Franciscans of his time, that Christ and his disciples had lived in absolute poverty. Among the many treatises he wrote, most of them composed while he was teaching in Barcelona, is the *Quaestio de paupertate Christi,* which defends his views on this subject. The studium generale in Barcelona was later to produce many outstanding scholars, and even before 1348 could boast of Pere Oriol, another supporter of the Immaculate Conception; Guillem Rubió, a pupil of Duns Scotus; Guillem Monrodó, later inquisitor in Narbonne for Benedict XIII's curia; and Joan Bassols, who received his doctorate in Paris and was regarded as having been the first pupil of Duns Scotus in Paris.[19]

Less is known of those who studied elsewhere in the studia generalia of the friars, but certainly later in the century the studium at Valencia

---

17 Basili de Rubí, "La escuela franciscana de Barcelona y su intervención en los decretos inmaculistas (siglos XIII–XIV)," *EF* 57 (1956), 363–406.
18 Amorós Payá, "Anfredo Gontero."
19 Rubí, "La escuela franciscana," pp. 375–376, gives a list of those who distinguished themselves during the fourteenth century and who were in some way connected with the Barcelona house.

was to rival that of Barcelona. It may be reasonable to suppose that the principal house in each custody had a studium, to which selected friars would be expected to go before proceeding to universities in France and England. In most smaller houses, only basic theological studies were probably available, but all friars were expected to familiarize themselves with the holy scriptures and probably with preaching aids such as bestiaries, manuals of exempla and other similar collections. However, many lay brothers would have lacked the education or incentive to progress beyond the minimal studies needed for their own religious observance.

The books studied can also be seen, for example, in the king's request to the friars in Tàrrega for Books 1-4 of Saint Isidore's *Sentences,* a book of Alain of Lille, the Gospel of Saint John, a *Flos sanctorum,* some Old Testament books, a book on the passions of the saints and a book of epistles, possibly the Epistles of the New Testament and the *Letters* of Saint Gregory.[20] In 1295 Jaume de Riusec, living in Valencia, son of the late Jaume de Riusec, left books to the Franciscans including a copy of the Bible and a book of the *Sentences,* presumably the standard textbook of Peter Lombard.[21] Such books would have been in most Franciscan libraries at the time, as they formed part of the educational programme of the friars. As early as 1286 friars also had libraries of their own: in his will, Ramon Aperrer (?) of Castelló left 100 sous of Melguiers to his son, Fr. Ramon of the convent of Castelló d'Empúries, for books.[22] That these books were to revert to the convent after his death stressed his temporary ownership of them and his compliance with the rule, but curiously enough, the clause which stipulates that if he was in need of money he could sell them makes no provision for that money to go to the convent.

The king made other demands on the friars relating to books, and it may be that friars like Fr. Romeo Ortiz copied books with some regularity, for in 1321 the king requested Fr. Juan de Ejea, custodian of the Saragossa custody, to send him a book which he referred to as Bernard's *Ad Eugenium,* which Fr. Romeo, before his death some four years earlier, had arranged for the king to have.[23] No archival references have

---

20 Barcelona, ACA, RC 289, f. 44, 13 December 1318.
21 ACA, RC 101, f. 273 12 August 1295.
22 Gerona, AH, C.15 (1286-1291), Bernat Fontcuberta, 11 July 1286.
23 Barcelona, ACA, RC 246, f. 172, 15 February 1320 [1321]. This was probably Bernard of Clairvaux's *De consideratione.*

been found to the presence of a scriptorium in the Franciscan convents, but it was customary for friars to copy books when requested to do so. Such work would have been highly remunerated and would have repaid the long hours spent laboriously copying manuscripts by candlelight. On one occasion James II helped the Franciscans to recover books stolen from them by a Jew from Vilafranca, Guillem de Tarasco, a native of Vilacubells, by ordering his arrest; among the books were a copy of the Bible, the *Decretales* and a *Flos sanctorum*.[24]

Books were so valuable that in times of hardship the friars were able to pawn them. In 1310 the cleric Bernat Tomàs of Perelada acknowledged receipt of books from Fr. Bernat de Puig of Canet which he had pawned: the Acts of the Apostles, Cato of Theodosius, Tobias, Ovid's *De remedio amoris* (a somewhat strange choice for a Franciscan), Aesop's *Fables,* Ovid's *De luppo facetus de Maria Egipthiaca* (possibly a conflation of two titles, one of which would be the Life of Saint Mary of Egypt), also incomplete lessons of grammar, logic and natural philosophy, all on papyrus, together with three-quarters of the questions on logic on parchment. In exchange Fr. Bernat received 40 sous of Melguiers for the books, and Bernat Tomás promised him that if he paid him 40 sous plus something for his trouble the books would be returned to him.[25] Despite the numerous books in Franciscan libraries, and the theological writings emanating from the studium generale of Barcelona, the main literary prominence of the Franciscans in the realms of Aragon belongs to the latter half of the fourteenth century.

That is not true for the significant impact their development had on architecture and art, and probably on all forms of visual representation of the Gospel and the lives of the Saints, especially that of Saint Francis. Construction of churches and convents in the thirteenth and fourteenth centuries must have given employment to thousands of artisans, both skilled and unskilled. By the end of the fourteenth century many of these buildings were richly decorated with carvings, retables, paintings and images, some of which are still extant today. At the present time art

---

24 Barcelona, ACA, RC 160, f. 188v, 27 May 1316.
25 Gerona, AH, P.11 (1307, 1309–1310), Jaume Barraca, 27 September [1310]: "et bona fide convenio dicto fratri Bernardo quod quecumque de ipse persolvat michi dictos XL solidos quod ego reddam tunc et deliberem dicto fratri Bernardo vel alicui a[lteri] persone potenci nomine et ratione ipsius libros sepedictos." The list of books is incomplete, as part of the document is no longer legible and keywords are missing.

historians are attempting to reconstruct the contribution of the Franciscans to Gothic architecture in the Iberian Peninsula, and the comments here should only be regarded as indicative of an area which has received little attention until now but which emphasizes most clearly the extraordinary influence of the friars on their contemporaries.

Before referring to individual examples of Gothic art and architecture, there is one aspect of the Middle Ages which is frequently ignored, largely because the buildings now associated with Gothic architecture lack the wall-paintings, chapels and images which must surely have been in place in their prime: the bright colours which must have met worshippers as they entered the church would have been a prominent factor in the popularity acquired by the mendicant churches.

It is evident today that cinematographic techniques have changed the face of modern life, bringing to the homes of the majority of citizens in the western world through television a whole range of images which not only broaden their horizon but radically alter their outlook. There is no need to emphasize here the way in which the mass media, largely through its visual impact, affects the attitudes of all twentieth-century citizens. If this effect is transposed to the medieval period and the reaction of the churchgoer faced with the splendour of construction is imagined, the side chapels with their paintings, the high altar with its retable and the general atmosphere of colour, it is only logical to conclude that a similar revolution was taking place and one which was largely attributable to the presence of the mendicant orders. Church festivals, held far more frequently than today, were social occasions which brought all the people together. They were eagerly awaited as providing respite from the drudgery of the daily routine, and they too relied heavily on processions, during which brightly coloured floats would parade the streets and the guilds would come out in full regalia. It is from them, perhaps, that it can best be understood how significant was the visual contribution of the friars to contemporary thought and behaviour.

These colourful, noisy festivals drew much from the liturgical calendar and the way it was observed by the friars, and although no documentary evidence has been found of Franciscan involvement in liturgical drama, it can scarcely have been absent. At least there must have been mimed representations of biblical scenes, dramatized sermons (which in any case regularly included exempla drawn from numerous manuals, especially those which portrayed animals with human characteristics).²⁶ To these should be added the homiletic use of pictures and other "props," including the stained glass windows and decorations in the churches, which would illustrate themes of the preacher's sermon.²⁷

The visual effect of the new buildings, the skilled carvings, the religious paintings which adorned every church and the colourful festivals should not be overlooked in any assessment of the way in which the followers of Saint Francis helped to effect a radical change of attitude on the part of their contemporaries. Songs and imitations of birds and animals almost certainly accompanied the visual aids, and it was only a step from these dramatizations to the performance of sacred plays. Little is known about these areas, and they are more difficult to assess today than buildings or paintings, especially since sophisticated methods of visual presentation blind the twentieth-century critic to the effects of more primitive ways of illustrating a theme; also, much of the impact of these buildings is lost, now that their original splendour has faded.

Heavy reliance on symbol and allegory in the late medieval period should also be kept in mind: Saint Bonaventure's works, such as the *Lignum vitae,* were extremely popular, influenced writers like Llull and Eiximenis and frequently gave inspiration to painters. It would be true to say that allegorical representations of biblical stories can be seen in all forms of literary output, from theology to works for a more general public, in paintings, carvings and other forms of artistic expression, and especially in architecture, where elaborate figures or scenes were carved in stone on the façades and portals of churches and cathedrals. Some of these, like the grinning gargoyles which look out from cathedral buttresses, seem crude today, but medieval people were accustomed to view them as representations of the evil which might befall them, were they to sin. The devil was as familiar a concept as Christ or the saints, and was portrayed in all his ugliness as a constant reminder of God's punishment for wrongdoing. The Gothic buildings remaining today and

---

26 Francesc Eiximenis, the famous Catalan writer of the late fourteenth century, best exemplifies this trend. See his *Contes i faules,* ed. Marçal Olivar (Barcelona, 1925), and other works. See also Sandro Sticca, *The "Planctus Mariae" in the Dramatic Tradition of the Middle Ages,* trans. Joseph R. Berrigan (Athens, GA and London, 1988), pp. 14–18. He attributes much of the importance of medieval drama in England to Franciscan spirituality and especially to the semi-dramatic structure of the friars' sermons.

27 See Fleming, *Introduction to Franciscan Literature,* pp. 126–128.

the sculptured figures adorning them help to reveal the psychology of an age which in many ways seems very remote, but which in others bears a remarkable resemblance to the twentieth century.

Gothic architecture has been compared to the scholastic movement which sought to clarify the Christian faith through the *Summa* or theological compendium, appealing to man as a rational being, but at the same time seeking to prove by means of scholastic reasoning the incontrovertible truth of the Gospel.[28] To aid understanding an appeal was made to the imagination, for it was thought that understanding could best be attained through the senses; in this way the imagination could be brought to bear upon the resolution of difficult theological concepts. Exempla, whether in the form of illustrative stories in sermons or by means of allegorical paintings, could be regarded as the visual expression of this scholastic movement.

Many medieval manuscripts were richly illustrated with exquisite miniatures, while even the choral books were so beautifully produced that they themselves could be regarded as works of art. Man, uplifted through the senses, could savour the full beauty and meaning of the liturgy of the church, and the skilful preacher realized to the full the desirability of making use of both sight and hearing to reach those who came to hear the word of God. If this is taken into account it may be less difficult to understand why structural uniformity played such an important role in ecclesiastical buildings. The very fact that these buildings were structurally homologous emphasized the importance of the one true religion, seen as a logical and uniform organization. According to Panofsky, this seemed to offer a direct parallel to the *Similitudines* of Thomas Aquinas, where the human species was described in similar terms, in essence constituting a kind of Everyman.[29]

---

28 The discussion on the relation between scholasticism and Gothic architecture is largely taken from Erwin Panofsky, *Gothic Architecture and Scholasticism* (Latrobe, PA, 1951).

29 Ibid., p. 49. No clearer indication of the way in which art was used as an appeal to the senses and as an aid to teaching spiritual truths can be found than Giotto's paintings in the Bardi chapel at Assisi (see Rona Goffen, *Spirituality in Conflict: Saint Francis and Giotto's Bardi Chapel* [University Park, PA and London, 1988], where the allegorical meaning of these paintings is discussed). Although no similar murals survive in place for the Crown of Aragon, many of the paintings of Saint Francis and other saints housed in a variety of Catalan museums show that a similar style did in fact exist in the Middle Ages in Catalonia.

Two men seem to symbolize the more popular concerns of the Franciscans: Jofre de Foixà, the late thirteenth-century friar minor who later left the order to become a Cistercian monk, and called his own poetry "catalanesc"; and a century later Francesc Eiximenis, who believed it important to write in Catalan so that a wider public could appreciate the truths he was explaining. Not only do these men reflect the concern the Franciscans had to make their works accessible to those who had no knowledge of Latin, but this concern seems to embody the ideals of the mendicant friars and add a further dimension to the popular appeal of Saint Francis and the national crusade of James I.

Catalan Gothic architecture reflects this same logical yet popular approach, explained by some as attributable to the primarily materialistic Catalan merchant society of the late thirteenth and fourteenth centuries, which regarded undue ornamentation as unnecessary and even extravagant.[30] Of course, the main purpose of the mendicant orders in building their churches was to gather in them as many people as they could. As they were designed for public worship, they had to be built with a minimum of obstructions, so that all could see the high altar and hear the words of wisdom emanating from the preacher.

Extant documents suggest that the Franciscans first built modest churches of this kind, more akin in structural form to the older Romanesque style, but they proved to be inadequate for the numbers they attracted and most of the houses were forced to extend the buildings at a later date to accommodate the enormous crowds attracted to them by the preaching of the friars. Few records refer to the buildings of the first Franciscan convents built in King James's territory, but those that do exist allow a composite picture to be formed, outlining their general characteristics.

The original Franciscan church in Barcelona was destroyed by a storm and rebuilt in 1500, but descriptions of it state that it was fairly elaborate, having twenty-three chapels and a huge vaulted roof, and that it was finished in 1247.[31] The Franciscan chronicler Coll states that the church was consecrated in the presence of Saint Louis, the son of

---

30 See Bernard Bevan, *History of Spanish Architecture* (New York, 1939), p. 87. See also Pierre Lavedan, *L'Architecture gothique religieuse en Catalogne, Valence et Baléares* (Paris, 1935), where reference is made to the Franciscan churches at Gerona, Majorca and Vilafranca del Penedés.

31 See Bernardo Comes, *Libro vero è original*, 2 vols. (Barcelona, 1725), 1: 37.

Charles II, king of Naples, bishop of Toulouse and a friar minor himself, and that the foundation stone was to be found in the cloisters.[32] Although the primitive church might have been completed in 1247, the consecration in the presence of Saint Louis probably refers to a much enlarged church with several chapels, including one to Saint Louis himself. A recent attempt to reconstruct the plan of the Barcelona convent in its various phases of construction emphasizes the basic simplicity of the buildings, although, for lack of extant documentation, it can be regarded at best as an approximation of the early Franciscan church and conventual complex.[33]

Sanahuja makes reference to two of the other early Franciscan churches, those in Montblanc and Castelló d'Empúries. The Montblanc church, somewhat similar to the church of Sant Just in Barcelona, was sixty feet long by seventeen feet wide, basically Gothic in conception, but showing some of the features associated with the Romanesque style.[34] The convent itself was built on two levels, planned in such a way that only one of the upper storeys looked out on to the ogival cloister, which belonged to the earliest parts of the complex. Parts of the walls, the façade with its doorway and the rose window are still standing, until recently in a lamentable state of neglect but now restored to some of their former glory.[35] The convent at Castelló d'Empúries was probably very similar in style, but the only evidence of its existence today are a few ruins and the retables which found their way to the Poor Clares' house and the parish church when the Friars Minor's convent was totally destroyed.[36] The primitive Franciscan church in Majorca, completed in 1244, was square or rectangular in shape, with arches and a roof with wooden beams.[37] Its large cloister still stands, and several tombstones dating from the thirteenth and fourteenth centuries remain in place.

---

32 See Jaime Coll, *Crónica de la província franciscana de Cataluña: Parte primera* (1738), facsimile ed. with intro. and indices by José Martí Mayor, Crónicas franciscanas de España 21 (Madrid, 1981), pp. 45-46 (secs. 132-133).

33 See Anna M. Giné i Torres, "El convent de Sant Francesc de Barcelona: Reconstrucció hipotètica," *Acta historica et archaeologica medievalia* 9 (1988), 221-243.

34 Sanahuja, *História*, p. 96.

35 See below Plates 11 (apse) and 12 (entrance).

36 Sanahuja, *História*, p. 79. See also Plates 13 and 14 below.

37 See M. Durliat, *L'Art dans le royaume de Majorque* (Toulouse, 1962).

Convents in important cities like Barcelona and Majorca were built on a more lavish plan, while those in the smaller towns were much simpler and their churches were reminiscent of some of the earlier Romanesque parish churches. It is probable that in many, if not all, cases the convent complex consisted of more than one building: the living quarters built on one or two storeys; the church, usually adjacent to the house and perhaps connected to it; and outhouses for keeping animals, grinding corn, and accomplishing the other tasks necessary for the community's well-being. These buildings would have been set in an uncultivated area of land, part of which would have served as a kitchen garden or orchard and part for recreation, although the cloisters, which always adjoined the convent, would have been used for exercise and for the location of lavatories.

Although at first the friars would have used a private house or houses lent by the citizens and eventually bought from them, as in Puigcerdà, they would also have had a chapel either in one of the rooms of the house or built somewhere in close proximity to it. In Vic evidence of the primitive chapel still remains, and was used for many centuries as a wayside shrine. Gradually, as the friars became more established, and as their economic situation improved, they added first the church, then the cloisters and convent buildings; often these had to be extended later, as their needs increased. One of the few extant references to the building of cloisters is in connection with the convent at Morella, whose church still stands.[38] To help defray the costs of building the cloisters, Peter III in 1341 granted the Friars Minor in Morella 1000 Barcelona sous, to be taken from the money that the royal judge Pedro de Ciutadella had received by way of fines collected from the inhabitants of Morella.[39] It is unlikely that there were no cloisters before this date, as Morella was one of the early houses, founded at the time of the reconquest of Valencia in the 1230s; thus the document of 1341 may refer to the building of larger cloisters or to their ornamentation. There are no further references to this matter, suggesting that on this occasion, at least, the friars received the money they had requested.

There are many references to later additions or enlargements made to the Franciscan convents, especially to those within the kingdom of Aragon, perhaps because at this time they frequently gave hospitality

---

38 See below Plates 1 and 2.
39 Barcelona, ACA, RC 1115, f. 131, 23 September 1341.

to the king and his men, and maybe also because some of the friars came from prominent Aragonese families. Chapter 5 has shown that families of friars who required special favours exerted pressure on the king, and although there is no mention of this in connection with the improvements to the Franciscan houses, there is no doubt that the friars who acted as royal advisers, confessors, chaplains and ambassadors made sure that they received some return for their services both in financial compensation and in assistance towards the needs of the order.

In 1306, 8000 sous of Jaca money promised to the Saragossa house for the building of their church was claimed by the friars from the king, who then ordered the money to be paid by the royal curia.[40] Two weeks later the king wrote to the bishop of Valencia, Abbot Jofre de Foixà and those responsible for collecting the *decimas,* saying that he could not pay the entire amount at the time because he had many other payments.[41] In 1314 the full amount had not yet been paid, and James II suggested to his *comendador major* in Montblanc, Artau d'Orta, that 3000 be paid from the royal curia to Fr. Ramón de Huesca, the guardian of the Saragossa house, towards the work of the church and convent.[42] Nine years later, in 1323, James II wrote to his *merino* in Saragossa, Guillermo Palazini, telling him that the amount to be paid by the royal curia to the Franciscans in Saragossa for their dormitory should be taken from money the Jew Mahil de Roda had in his possession.[43] In 1331 the Franciscans in Saragossa were still waiting for the payment, and the king gave a further order, this time to the general bailiff for Aragon, Pedro de Martorell, for the disbursement to be made, so that the friars could put it towards the work done on their dormitory.[44] One of the more important convents, Saragossa frequently seems to have needed enlargement. In 1343 the king's counsellor and *salmedina* (judicial officer) in Saragossa, Blasco de Ayusa, was told that, in view of the need the friars had to extend their convent, houses next to it should be expropriated and their owners forced to sell them to the Franciscans at a just price.[45] Surely it is no coincidence that at this time Fr. Sancho

---

40 Barcelona, ACA, RC 270, f. 164, 27 June 1306.
41 Ibid., f. 168v, 13 July 1306.
42 ACA, RC 276, f. 229v, 24 July 1314.
43 ACA, RC 284, f. 71, 21 July 1323.
44 ACA, RC 498, f. 203, 11 October 1331.
45 ACA, RC 1117, f. 5, 7 April 1343.

López de Ayerbe, later archbishop of Tarragona, was the king's confessor, and that he was a native of Ejea in the province of Saragossa.

There are also frequent references to improvements made to the Daroca house, especially to money left for the construction of the friars' dormitory, indicating that this might have been situated in a separate building.[46] In 1318 James II, writing to his *porter major* and the mayor of Albarracín, referred to a quantity of timber which the Franciscans in Daroca had paid for but never received.[47] Was this intended for the construction of the dormitory referred to above? The king had also promised money to the friars for the building of their convent, but this had to be claimed, and only five years later, when the matter was regarded as extremely urgent, did the king order that the unspecified amount be paid to them without delay. Despite the urgency, the money may well not have been paid immediately, if other instances are any indication of the way in which the king's treasury worked.

All the same, the convent building at Daroca must have gone ahead with the timber, because in 1333 both the house and the church had been damaged by fire and 50 sous had to be paid to the friars immediately so that they could repair the church; the administrators of the town of Daroca were to take this money from the amount set aside for repair to the walls of the town, because to allow the church to remain in a ruined state, the king said, would only be to the dishonour of Saint Francis.[48] A year later the Franciscans were to be granted 1000 sous, half from the account of the count of Urgell (also viscount of Ager) and half from the royal curia to pay for the repairs, which must have been more extensive than at first thought.[49] Timber was a valuable commodity which was sometimes granted to the Franciscans by way of alms, as in 1318, when the king suggested that, because the friars were so poor, they should be given one of the royal galleys from the arsenal in Barcelona which was beyond repair for navigational use.[50] The high number of fires which occurred during the Middle Ages can probably be attributed to the extensive use of wood in buildings where cooking and heating would have been by means of an open fire.

---

46   Barcelona, ACA, RC 284, f. 71, 21 July 1323.
47   ACA, RC 356, f. 151v, 16 January 1317 [1318].
48   ACA, RC 501, f. 118v, 17 October 1333; f. 134v, 28 December 1333.
49   ACA, RC 576, f. 50v, 24 August 1334.
50   ACA, RC 279, f. 125, 28/29 February 1317 [1318].

On 15 February 1336 Prince Peter wrote to Domingo de Añone, vicar of the parish church of Borja, in connection with the dispute between the executors of the will of the late soldier Juan Pedro de Gambe and the friars over a provision to build a chapel in the Franciscan church.[51] It appears that the friars had not complied with the funeral rites, and Domingo de Añone was ordered to see that a remedy was found which was in line with the *fueros*.

One of the more interesting documents referring to the rebuilding of a Franciscan church dates from the beginning of January 1337, when Prince Peter, writing to his *justícia* (or chief justice) in Borja, a small Aragonese town not far from the borders of Navarre, stated that the people of the town had given a sum of money to a Saracen, Jucef Duzenem from Pedral, to rebuild the church of Saint Francis in Borja.[52] Only part of the church had been rebuilt and not all the money given by the town had been spent, and the people now wished the unspent quantity to be returned to the town. Jucef, the Saracen, had given a guarantee that the work for the friars would be done, but because of illness he had been unable to follow through on his promise and the church was only partly built. It is relevant to note the involvement of the Saracen in the rebuilding of a Christian church, a not unusual occurrence at this time; but in this instance there is doubt that the church was ever completed.[53] These are the last references found to the Borja house.[54]

Sometimes the work done was not for the direct benefit of the friars but because the king and his retinue were coming to stay. In 1315 the Daroca house was obliged to have built a number of rooms and "palaces," the term used for large reception rooms, and other buildings, so that the king could stay there because "we have no house in that town in which we can stay better, or which is more suitable than the house of

---

51 Barcelona, ACA, RC 573, f. 174, 15 February 1335 [1336].

52 ACA, RC 574, f. 194, 13 January 1336 [1337].

53 For a discussion of the contribution of the *mudejars* (Moors living in Christian territory) as artisans within the realms of Aragon, see J.N. Hillgarth, *The Spanish Kingdoms: 1250-1516*, 2 vols. (Oxford, 1976), 2: 128-129.

54 John R.H. Moorman, *Medieval Franciscan Houses* (St. Bonaventure, NY, 1983), refers to dates before 1343, suggesting that it became an Observant house in 1425. If this were so, did it disappear after the damage to the church and was a new convent later established under the Observants? This would seem the most likely explanation for the complete silence after 1335.

the Friars Minor."[55] On such occasions it was usual for the king to pay for the alterations, but not always in advance, and the friars had to remind him that he owed them the money for the construction which had been undertaken on his behalf.

In the case of Daroca it was not the king's treasury which was responsible for the payment but the procurators, scribes, *sesmerinos* (judicial officers) and people of the town of Daroca. They were requested to pay a subsidy to the friars for the work to be done, but were also to discuss the matter with the guardian before any amount was agreed upon. What kind of construction was undertaken at such short notice? It must have been of a purely utilitarian nature, possibly merely adapting the existing buildings to their new use. In August 1328 the king asked his treasurer, García Lloriz, to pay the Daroca house 150 sous of Jaca money to cover certain buildings which he would require when he went to stay there.[56] In January 1334 Alfonso III wrote under his secret seal to his counsellor and *mestre racional*, advising him that Juan Guillermo de Cantaventayuelo, bailiff of Daroca, must have windows and doors made in the reception rooms that the king intended to use when he went to stay in the Franciscan convent at Daroca, and that he must be given money to meet the expenses incurred.[57] The house at Daroca seems to have been a royal favourite, but mendicant convents were often the largest and most convenient buildings for the king and his retinue to use as they travelled throughout the many areas which comprised the Crown of Aragon. In September 1334 Alfonso made plans for the king of Majorca to stay in the Franciscan house at Tortosa, while he and his men remained in the castle.[58]

Medieval towns were proud of their mendicant convents and frequently helped towards the building of additional accommodation, as in Tàrrega, where Master Joan de Montrós, clearly a skilled worker employed in the Franciscan house with the support of the *Consell,* was told to finish the work of the refectory satisfactorily because a chapter in honour of Saint Francis was to be held there, and it would redound

---

55 Barcelona, ACA, RC 276, f. 175v, 10 September 1315: "et in dicta villa non habemus hospicium in quo hospitari possimus melius et habilius quam in domibus fratrum predictorum"; and RC 278, f. 14v, 13 November 1315.
56 Barcelona, ACA, RC 559, f. 179v, 16 August 1328.
57 ACA, RC 535, f. 51v, 25 January 1333 [1334].
58 ACA, RC 536, ff. 31v–32, 18 September 1334.

to the shame of the town if the refectory were not completed in time.⁵⁹ On this occasion it was in the interests of both town and friars to improve the sleeping accommodation, so that visitors to the chapter would have somewhere to stay.

In 1327 the roof of the doorway to the Franciscan house in Montblanc was accidentally set on fire while the king and his men were staying there, and Alfonso ordered his bailiff in Montblanc to use the money from the bailiff's account to pay for the work of rebuilding or repairing. The doorway was to be restored to its original height, and the work was to be done without delay, because the Franciscans needed the door repaired. The king also took the opportunity to remind his bailiff in Montblanc that King James II's ordinance must be observed; here it must be assumed that he was referring to the protection order issued routinely by each monarch, threatening with the king's displeasure those who interfered with the friars' well-being. In the nearby town of Tarragona, damage was done by the king's men when the royal party stayed in the Franciscan house, and in May 1330 Alfonso III ordered the general bailiff for Catalonia, Ferrer de Lillet, to pay 500 Barcelona sous from his funds to the friars, for the repair or rebuilding of the wall surrounding their garden which had been knocked down by the royal retinue.⁶⁰

Repairs were not only needed to deal with the damage done by fire or by the king's retainers to the Franciscan houses; the elements also played their part, for example the terrible storm on Friday, 5 July 1326, which seriously damaged the Xàtiva house. In a letter addressed to the king from Fr. Benvingut de Granollers, guardian of the Xàtiva house, and Fr. Berenguer d'Ivorra, custodian for the custody of Valencia, it is stated that the wall around the friars' garden had fallen down.⁶¹ The following day huge hailstones fell and destroyed their vines, corn and other crops—such a storm, they said, had never been known in living memory. It does not take much imagination to realize that they were

---

59 Tàrrega, AHM, Llibres del Consell, no. 3 (1361–1367), ff. 89v–90, 4 August 1365: "veent la gran vergonya de la vila si lo dit refretor no est acabat ans que lo dit capitoll." A year earlier En Joan de Montrós had been appointed worker of the monastery with En Simó Caynt, who was already working there (see f. 65, 20 May 1364).
60 Barcelona, ACA, RC 491, f. 22v, 2 December 1327; and RC 495, f. 98, 30 May 1330.
61 Barcelona, ACA, Cartas reales, James II, caja 72, no. 8867, 7 July 1326.

appealing to the king for money to repair the wall and make reparation for the damage done, nor would it be too unreasonable to suggest that they had to wait a long time before the money for the repairs was forthcoming. Repeated requests and reminders were necessary, but in most cases subsequent documents suggest that eventually the money was paid.

One final example has its own value: so little is known about those who worked on the buildings that the reference to Fr. Eximeno Coscollola, operarius of the Barbastro church, is of special interest.[62] The document in question concerns the legacy of 100 sous of Jaca money which the late Estefania de San Vicente had left to the Franciscans in Barbastro and which was to be paid to them from the will of her late husband, Pedro Ahones de San Vicente, possibly a relative of the friar Bertran Ahones.[63] The document is complicated, and contains mention of a further 80 sous of Jaca money owed to Fr. Eximeno Coscollola by Tolomeo d'En Peirón, notary of Barbastro, presumably in payment of some work he had done in connection with the Franciscans' church. The fact that he is referred to as Fr. Eximeno suggests that he was probably a lay brother; if so, it could reasonably be conjectured that much of the skilled and unskilled manual work in the Franciscan houses was done by lay brothers, whose names would have no occasion to appear in the primarily legal documents that are the main source for Franciscan life in the Middle Ages.

By the end of the fourteenth century many of the major convents had expanded significantly. Some had been rebuilt after fire or other damage; all were far more elaborate than they had been a century earlier. The majority of these churches possessed one wide central nave, with narrow collaterals to give an impression of spacious simplicity. No doubt internal buttresses supported the vaulting and protruded into the church so that side chapels could be located between them, and from the many legacies specifying their use as chapels it is evident that these churches possessed many side chapels. The extant church of Teruel, built at the end of the fourteenth century, and the description of the church at Barcelona, rebuilt in 1500, both suggest that it was customary to have numerous altars and chapels. Windows, however, were frequently small, possibly for reasons of economy, but they had the effect of making the churches very dark.

---

62 Barcelona, ACA, RC 604, f. 153, 2 January 1339 [1340].
63 Ibid.

At first ornamentation was often kept to a minimum, but by the end of the fourteenth century much of the early simplicity was lost.[64] The church at Teruel shows the way Franciscan architecture had evolved, and it is difficult to understand why Bevan states that, although Aragon gave its name to the glorious empire of James I, it "remained both culturally and geographically the hinterland, and watched apathetically from behind [the] mountains."[65] Aragon was not as commercially active as Catalonia or Valencia, largely because of its geographical position and different social distribution, but it had a significant cultural role. Aragonese friars, like Fr. Sancho López de Ayerbe, Fr. Domingo de Jaca and Fr. Romeo Ortiz, all acted as royal ambassadors and/or provincial ministers of the Order of Friars Minor, and similar distinction was evident in artistic endeavour. Unfortunately, except for the church at Teruel, little of this remains; Aragon suffered more from the ravages of war than Catalonia, and many artistic treasures have since disappeared. Catalonia has no such outstanding examples of Franciscan Gothic architecture as the church at Teruel, although part of the house at Vilafranca del Penedès is still used by a convent of nuns, and ruins of the houses at Cervera, Gerona and elsewhere have been discovered in recent years.[66]

Some of the arches discovered recently for the Gerona convent support the view that decoration became an integral feature of most medieval Franciscan convents.[67] Although Catalan is the name given to this variation of Gothic architecture, largely because it flourished first in Catalonia, a similar style, with local variations, could be seen in the other kingdoms under the rule of the Aragonese monarchy; indeed, apart from the church at Teruel, it is in Valencia that the best examples of Franciscan churches dating from this period can be seen today.[68]

---

64 See Benjamin Agulló Pascual, "Iglesia de San Francisco de Teruel," in *Celebración del 750 aniversario del martirio de los santos fray Juan de Perusa y fray Pedro de Saxoferrato, copatronos de Teruel, Valencia-Teruel, 1228-1978* (Valencia, 1979), pp. 43-96, at 55-63.

65 Bevan, *History of Spanish Architecture*, p. 87.

66 See below Plates 3-6 (Cervera).

67 Examples can be seen in the Galería de arte *El Claustre* in Gerona, situated on the site of the old convent. The stores and hotel in the same block also have parts of the old convent walls. However, the Galería has recently closed; there is no public access at present to the Franciscan ruins.

68 Enric A. Llobregat and J.F. Yvars, *Història de l'art al país valencià*, 2 vols. (Valencia, 1986-1988), 1: 95-115.

Morella, founded in 1272 and initially part of the Valencian custody, has a single wide nave, which can be regarded as typical of the Catalan Gothic style, with its chapels tucked away under the buttresses and the vaulted roof with wooden beams.[69] Alongside is the cloister, very similar in design to that of the church of St. Francis in Palma de Mallorca referred to earlier. In Xàtiva, the church built between 1366 and 1373 still maintains these main features, although a greater element of ornamentation seems to have crept in.[70] It is sad that the Franciscan house in Valencia itself has long since disappeared.

In the high vaulted roofs, the spacious naves and the chapels dedicated to popular saints, a symbol of the greatness of God's kingdom is observed, emphasizing the glory and majesty of God the Father and the accessibility of God the Son, concepts so familiar to the medieval worshipper but often interpreted differently in the modern world. The numerous workers engaged in the design and building of these churches were united by a strong sense of brotherhood, usually bound together in close association through their guild, and very naturally they possessed a marked degree of professional pride, which no doubt was much enhanced by the structured apprenticeship which led to the position of the master and an esteemed reputation within that guild.[71]

When the magnitude of the task confronting these tradesmen is considered, the technical complications, the acquisition and transportation of building materials and the organization of hundreds of workers, some of whom had to be housed and clothed, their accomplishments can only amaze the modern scholar. Little enough is known about these workers in the realms of Aragon, although there are a few references to those who either defaulted in their obligations or died before they could complete their task.

One of the earliest and most explicit references to construction work in a Franciscan house has to do with Vic, one of the first convents to be founded. In 1262 two artisans, Guillem de Verdaguer of Vic and Master Simó Peris, promised the then guardian, Fr. Guillem de Blanes, that they would build seven arches for the church, smoothing the stone and

---

69 Llobregat and Yvars, *Història de l'art*, 1: 118.
70 Ibid., 1: 150.
71 For a brief discussion of the way in which the building was organized in the late Middle Ages, see Hans Jantzen, *High Gothic* (London, 1962), esp. pp. 80-98.

working it until all the arches were in place.[72] Payment had already been made by the friars at the rate of 5 sous per slab, and the two artisans had accepted the price and had agreed to do the necessary work to move the lamps, so that the arches could be put in place without requiring any further payment. The document suggests that the friars had first intended to have ten arches, but perhaps for lack of money had reduced that number to the seven agreed with the two tradesmen mentioned above. In this context it is pertinent to note that already in 1232 the convent at Vic had a bell-tower with figures of friars and the name of the first guardian, Fr. Segimon des Lledó, carved on it.[73]

Turning to another early convent, in 1301 Master Joan Jaume, painter, of Barcelona had been hired to paint the chapel of Saint Mary in the Franciscan church at Barcelona, for which he was to receive £18.[74] The price raises the question whether, in fact, this referred to paintings such as those commissioned by the king from Ferrer and Arnau Bassa later in the fourteenth century, or it was a payment for painting the walls of the chapel. For the years 1363-1365 the cathedral receipts refer to the work of a stonemason by the name of Rafart, who seems to have been doing some work for the Barcelona friars but receiving payment for it from the cathedral.[75] It was not unusual for a cathedral to give alms to the Franciscans, and the payment perhaps should be regarded in this light.

One final reference of some interest is to the Barbastro convent, which had hired a man called Domingo Spinelli to do some stonework in the church, but he had died before completing it. The first document referring to this matter is a letter of 1330 from Alfonso III to Juan Negro, jurisperitus of Barbastro, on behalf of the guardian and friars of the Barbastro house.[76] Domingo Spinelli of Barbastro had been con-

---

72 See Jill R. Webster, "L'art gòtic i els framenors segons alguns documents de Barcelona i de Vic," *Ausa* (Vic) 12 (1987), 203-208.
73 See Sanahuja, *História,* p. 48.
74 Barcelona, AC, Pia Almoina, Llibres notarials, Bernat Vilarrubia, 15 June–October 1301, f. 13v, 20 June 1301. My attention to this document was drawn by Rev. Josep Baucells.
75 Barcelona, AC, Obra de la catedral, Llibres d'Obra 1361-1363, ff. 6-7v, 18v, 26v, 28. Thus, "Item: Rehebi d'En Rafart, manobre per l'acapte dels frares manors e de Santa Maria de la Mercè, pagant a ell per sos treballs XXV sols, resten quantitatis 130 sols. 1 diner" (f. 6v); other entries are similar.
76 Barcelona, ACA, Cartas reales, Alfonso III, caja 9, no. 1270, 26 August 1330.

tracted, some time prior to the king's letter, to build a stone chapel inside the monastery and also to provide the chalice and other ornaments necessary for the chapel, without which, the king stated, the perfection of the chapel was flawed. Many people argued that Domingo's heirs were bound to meet these obligations, while others maintained that this was not so. The king stressed the poverty of the friars, but suggested that the jurisperitus of Barbastro call the complainants together to see whether an agreement could be reached without recourse to law. In July 1336 Prince Peter, writing to Juan Negro on behalf of the guardian and friars of the Barbastro house, stated that the friars had still not received the money owed to them from the estate of Domingo Spinelli.[77]

A third request two years later, addressed by the king to Guillermo Pedro d'En Peirón, jurisperitus of Barbastro, on behalf of the guardian of the Friars Minor, repeated the Franciscans' claim that Domingo had been paid for work he had not done and that the money advanced to him should be returned to the convent.[78] Domingo had been paid for a stone chapel inside the church, and was to have undertaken further work in connection with the tombstones in the cloister, but for this it appears that he had not been paid at the time of his death. In fact the non-completion of these tombstones, as indicated in the earlier letter, had aroused the ire of relatives of the deceased and prevented their paying the bequests to the friars.[79] The Franciscans, as usual, continued to plead poverty and requested that Domingo's heirs be forced to return the money he had been paid before his death. The fact that the matter had already been taken to the king eight years before suggests that the meeting in 1330 had come to nought, and in 1338 the friars were once again appealing to their benefactor to intervene on their behalf.

77 Barcelona, ACA, RC 588, f. 3, 22 July 1336.
78 ACA, RC 595, f. 179, 20 July 1338, transcribed in full in Document 54. A heading appears above this document giving the name of the worker as Domingo Borberali, whereas the document itself refers to him as Domingo Spinelli. His name suggests that he was not a native of Barbastro but an Italian; many workers left their home countries in search of employment, and it is quite possible that Domingo was among their number.
79 Barcelona, ACA, RC 588, f. 3, 22 July 1336; RC 595, ff. 164v and 179, 6 July and 20 July 1338. Although the first document does not refer to the cause of the case before the jurisperitus of Barbastro, the second is quite specific and goes into lengthy detail about the money owed by the relatives of the late Domingo Spinelli.

Examples of disputes over payments to workers are infrequent, and may be due to the general lack of documents referring to workmen employed by the Franciscans rather than to the honourable intentions of the workers and their relatives. The friars were free to engage in any activity, always on condition that they followed the provisions of the rule and did not personally receive any money for their labours. Indeed, the rule emphasized the importance of useful work.

Painters must have been in great demand to decorate the walls of the chapels and paint scenes from the Bible and lives of the saints for retables, so that these would appeal visually to the worshippers. Many of the paintings could be interpreted allegorically, others would symbolize the importance of the Virgin Mary and saints such as Francis, Antony and Louis; they would often be executed by the most expert painters, who would be paid by the king. The most well-known Catalan painter seems to have been Ferrer Bassa, who was responsible for the magnificent chapel of Saint Michael at the Pedralbes Clarissan convent.[80] He had been asked to paint a retable for the convent at Valencia, the subject of which was to have been the life of Saint Francis; but death prevented completion of the work and the Franciscans subsequently claimed the return of the money which had been advanced to the painter.[81] Ferrer Bassa was also asked by the king to paint a retable for the Franciscan church in Teruel, for which he would be paid a total of 2000 sous.[82] This time the subject was to be the life of Saint Louis, but this painting seems to have disappeared, possibly when the house at Teruel was destroyed during the second half of the fourteenth century, not long after the death of Ferrer Bassa himself.[83] Paintings were also commissioned for the Franciscan house at Vilafranca del Penedès, and for the Poor Clares at Vic: clearly Ferrer Bassa had an interest in painting scenes referring to Franciscan life.[84] Another well-known painter, Lluis Borrassà, who lived at the end of the fourteenth century, carried on the tradition; he painted a retable of Saint Francis for the

---

80 See Manuel Trens, *Ferrer Bassa i les pintures de Pedralbes* (Barcelona, 1936).
81 Josep Gudiol and Santiago Alcolea i Blanch, *Pintura gótica catalana* (Barcelona, 1986), p. 44.
82 See Webster, "L'art gòtic i els framenors," p. 205.
83 See Agulló Pascual, "Iglesia de San Francisco de Teruel," p. 55. See also León Amorós Payá, *Los inventarios del antiguo archivo del convento de San Francisco de Teruel* (Teruel, 1960).
84 See Gudiol and Alcolea i Blanch, *Pintura gótica catalana,* p. 44.

church at Vilafranca, and a retable for the Poor Clares at Vic depicting the three Franciscan orders with Saint Francis.[85]

Llompart, in a recent comprehensive work on medieval painting in Majorca, refers to several paintings from the convents of Saint Francis and Saint Clare, Majorca.[86] These include retables of the saints, such as Francis, Antony, Clare and others associated either with the Friars Minor or with the Poor Clares. Most significant, perhaps, is a document dated 23 March 1349, in which Francesc Comes, a master stained glass painter, agrees to undertake the glass for the rose window in the church of Saint Francis of Palma.[87] Stained glass must have been much in demand, and painters skilled in this art would have been sure to find employment, although extant records turn up few names of skilled stained glass tradesmen before the latter half of the fourteenth century. Similarly, references to painters before 1348 are few in number, but there is no doubt that many were hired by the mendicant churches between 1250 and 1350. The king frequently paid for the work, but wills show that citizens were also disposed to leave money to the friars for a retable.[88] Some of these legacies were probably delayed until arguments between the various heirs and the friars had been resolved, and it is possible that not all painters were paid in advance and that some had to wait for their money.

Friars were sometimes commissioned to copy bibles or other theological books for the king, and painters were hired to illustrate them. In 1301 Fr. Pere Alegre and Fr. Bernat, royal chaplains, bought for the chapel and had illuminated a psalter and the collects, also an antiphonary.[89] Just as Fr. Romeo Ortiz, for many years provincial minister of the Franciscan province of Aragon, copied a bible for the king, so Master Bernardo Gunter or Gonter was paid to illustrate it.[90] Whether he accomplished his task is a moot point, as three years later the king, after attempts to urge Master Bernardo to get on with his work, in

---

85 Gudiol and Alcolea i Blanch, *Pintura gótica catalana*, pp. 73-74 and illustrations on pp. 233, 331, 338, 348, 349, 384 and 386. Part of Borrassà's painting is reproduced in the frontispiece to this study.
86 Gabriel Llompart, *La pintura medieval mallorquina*, 4 vols. (Palma de Mallorca, 1977-1980).
87 Ibid., 4: 117.
88 See Webster, "L'art gòtic i els framenors," p. 206.
89 Rubió i Lluch, *Documents per l'història*, 1: 27, no. 22, 20 September 1301.
90 Barcelona, ACA, RC 241, f. 6, 21 July 1313.

exasperation asked him to return the bible to him.[91] It is only known that Master Bernardo lived in the vicinity of Daroca, where some of the money he was to be paid was deposited with the Franciscans; no other references to his work have been found, but he must have been a distinguished miniature painter to have been employed by the king. He obviously wanted part of the payment for his work on the bible in advance, and his reluctance to complete the work might well have derived from the fact that he was waiting to reassure himself that the money for the rest was on deposit at the Daroca Franciscan house.

There are also frequent references in notarial manuals to the endowment of chapels and altars, but there is no way of knowing how many of these actually came into existence, as the churches in question have long since disappeared and only isolated fragments of some buildings survive.[92] Artistic works such as carvings in silver and other metals, sculptures and overlaid woodwork must have been common, but it is more difficult to find records which refer to these, even though there are examples of sculpted images of the Virgin Mary and some of the saints still preserved in museums in Catalonia, Aragon and Valencia.

Finally, although strictly speaking it has little to do with culture, a passing reference must be made to the frequency with which the names of Saint Francis, Saint Bonaventure, Saint Louis and Saint Antony were used, not only for ecclesiastical buildings but also for ships, perhaps with the idea that the saint would protect the sailors from all harm.[93] The ships probably bore paintings depicting the saint on their hull or masthead, but in any case the fact that these saints were so popular only serves to stress the widespread influence of the Friars Minor.

Franciscan popularity extended beyond the strict limits of religious observance, and it has been shown that it was especially evident in education and artistic achievement. The simple life of poverty and humility appealed to a predominantly uneducated populace, and ensured the centrality of the Franciscan mission with its emphasis on the suffer-

---

91 See Webster, "L'art gòtic i els framenors," p. 206.
92 The cathedral archives at Vic, among the richest in the old Crown of Aragon, have notarial manuals dating from the 1240s, and references to chapels in the Franciscan church are numerous; however the fact that these references are mostly from the 1340s supports the suggestion that the friars spent more on decoration from this time on.
93 Barcelona, ACA, RC 252, for the years 1292-1300, makes mention of ships called Sant Francesc (f. 101) and Sant Bonaventura (f. 110v).

ings of Christ. The spirit of sacrifice of many friars, the call for penitence and conversion through example, were ideas which all could understand and share. The figure of Saint Francis himself, the unique position of the Virgin Mary, the example of saints like Bonaventure and Antony continued to exert a powerful influence over the faithful who attended the Franciscan churches.

The friars made a valuable contribution to the cultural life of the later Middle Ages, changing it in many ways, not least in the popular element they brought to festivals, paintings, images and illuminated manuscripts. Many men and women in the thirteenth and fourteenth centuries were proud to carry the names of the Franciscan saints, and many trade guilds gathered at the church of Saint Francis in the local convent or, if there was no convent, at the altars of these saints in other churches or cathedrals, as in Manresa where the altar of Saint Francis, erected at the end of the thirteenth century, bore witness for centuries to come of the devotion to the "Poverello" in Catalonia.

The instability of the fourteenth century, the division within the church and the natural disasters which seemed to have no end helped to create a propitious atmosphere for prophecies, miracles and an interest in anything which might possibly cast light on the troubled days in which the people lived. Joachim da Fiore, and later Jean de Roquetaillade, with their predictions of the approaching millennium followed by the final conversion of all humanity, attracted friars and lay people alike, who saw in them the answer to many of their problems. Although some of the ideas they propagated were regarded with suspicion by the orthodox church, they had a great influence on the Order of Friars Minor and contributed towards the subsequent split into Conventuals and Observants.

During the period under review, the greatest tribute to the extent of the influence of the Friars Minor in the Crown of Aragon lies in the way their image permeated every walk of life; it led to the creation of theological studia where doctrines such as the Immaculate Conception were discussed at length, to the writing of original commentaries on medieval theological thought, to the inspiration of architects and artists, builders and craftsmen, to the enjoyment of pageantry and colour, and more importantly to the development of a vibrant, prosperous and forward-looking Christian community, ready to serve church and king in a world of increasing uncertainty.

By 1348 both crown and friars had reached a peak of achievement, largely thanks to their alliance with the increasingly prosperous merchant class. After the Black Death the creativity of these early years was to continue for some time and to receive a new impetus with the creation of universities and the building of yet more splendid churches—a far cry indeed from the simple beginnings of the Minors.

Lurking in the shadows of this success were the dark spectres of the papal schism, anti-Semitic outbursts, dynastic troubles and the rift in the Order of Friars Minor itself, which threatened to tear it apart and which culminated in the separation of the Conventuals and Observants. A new era was dawning and new conflictive elements disturbed western Europe, and the Crown of Aragon itself suffered from dynastic troubles which were to terminate in its absorption by the new predominantly Castilian monarchy. The church too faced the same imminent threats to its existence, problems which were to lead to the Reformation and which for the Friars Minor meant the emergence of two new Franciscan orders, the Capuchins and the Conventuals; these are questions which, although they lie beyond the scope of the present study, have their roots in the philosophical discussions which took place before the advent of the Black Death and were especially prevalent in the latter part of the fourteenth century. Neither Saint Francis nor James I could have foreseen the course their mutual alliance was to take, nor could they have realized the impact which the mendicant orders were to have on the universities and the cultural life of their contemporaries.

Conclusion

The story of the first century and a half of Franciscan endeavour in Aragon is one of extraordinary success in both material and spiritual affairs, and one which had a significant impact on the way the Crown of Aragon perceived its mission. The foregoing chapters have emphasized some of the ways in which the early friars had gained the support of the crusading king and his successors, serving as the spiritual arm of the crown during the period of reconquest of land from the Moors and the years of expansion in the Mediterranean. By virtue of their mission they had helped the monarchy to consolidate its Christian territories, preaching to Jews, Moors and Christians alike and contributing towards the respectability of the monarchy and the renewal of the church within the Crown of Aragon. The endowments of property they received, the monetary grants and the concessions in kind they enjoyed, ensured their continual development and prosperity, a progress which closely paralleled the rise of the Crown of Aragon as a powerful force in the Mediterranean.

Despite the success the order had in establishing convents beyond the confines of Assisi, shortly after the death of Saint Francis it became evident that the rule of 1221 and the revision of 1223 would make it difficult to maintain internal unity, as differing interpretations of the meaning of poverty, the cause their founder had so faithfully espoused, were bound to cause dissension. Some friars regarded any attempt to broaden the scope of the rule or any compromise concerning its ideals as a denial of their founder's mission. No doubt these dissensions had been present from the foundation of the first convents in Aragon, but the first major threat to internal unity in the realms of Aragon dates from the end of the thirteenth century, when the apocalyptic views of Peter John Olivi and Joachim da Fiore infiltrated convents south of the Pyrenees. As might be expected from its geographical location, they were particularly prevalent in Catalonia, and fired the enthusiasm of those who believed that the order's original ideas of asceticism and poverty had given way to the very worldliness Saint Francis had warned his followers to avoid. In essence, they resulted from the disillusion some Franciscans felt with the way in which the rule was being interpreted, but they probably also owed much to a feeling of bewilderment at the changing pattern of life.

Towards the end of the fourteenth century this dissatisfaction was to lead to a division of ways, as both Conventuals and Observants maintained their separate convents, a situation which would have been difficult to prevent in view of the way in which the order had developed in the preceding decades. Similar problems were noticeable among the members of the Third Order of Saint Francis, many of whom supported Joachimist ideas and embraced the ideology of the beguin movement, an extreme form of asceticism which warned against the evils of the coming millennium, a period of tribulation preceding the end of the world and one which, in the opinion of some, seemed to be drawing very close.

Until the early fourteenth century the energies of the friars had largely been directed towards the establishment of their houses within the realms of Aragon, the acquisition of sufficient economic support to carry on their mission and the consequent building program which culminated in the splendid Gothic churches associated with the mendicant orders. In Catalonia this coincided with the rise of the merchant class, from which many of the friars came, giving them an unprecedented opportunity to draw on the resources of an increasingly wealthy sector of the population; this group itself depended greatly on the support it received from the crown, as it attempted to create a powerful bulwark against the power of the nobility. Elsewhere in the Crown of Aragon a similar development was occurring, although in Aragon itself many of the friars had noble or royal origins, a fact reflected in the number of these men chosen by the king to undertake ambassadorial tasks, such as the carrying of secret messages to other monarchs or to the pope, especially to Italy, Sicily and the neighbouring peninsular kingdoms. Indeed, some of these friars were given special privileges within the order, a direct negation of all that Saint Francis stood for and in direct contravention of the rule.

It would be true to say that the Franciscans within the realms of Aragon received an enthusiastic welcome from all but the parish clergy, who resented their immediate popularity, realizing that the friars' appeal to the people would seriously impinge on their own terrain and deprive them of the economic benefits they had come to expect. This situation was exacerbated by the fact that the friars were not under episcopal jurisdiction, and so freed from some of the constraints placed on the clergy. It did not help, either, that they were frequently better educated and more able to attract people to their services, especially to their illustrative and often dramatic sermons. It is true that their rule stipulated that they were to treat the clergy with respect, but it made but scant mention of what they were to do once they themselves took holy orders, as Saint Francis had never expected so many of his followers to become part of the ecclesiastical establishment in this way. He would have been surprised to see that Franciscans were given bishoprics, most of them, no doubt, either because they were related to the royal family, like Fr. Sancho López de Ayerbe, or as a reward for their services in helping to further Christendom (and the power of the Crown of Aragon), as was the case with Fr. Francesc Gosalt in Sardinia. Clearly these actions were politically motivated, for it was in the interests of the Aragonese king to appoint bishops loyal to the crown, especially in newly-conquered territories like Sardinia; but the ultimate prize escaped both James II and Alfonso III, who tried unsuccessfully to persuade the pope to appoint a Franciscan cardinal from their realms.

The very fact that some friars were given preferential treatment seems to deny the basic tenets of the order; yet in the Middle Ages the validity of such actions would probably not have been questioned, as the range of activities undertaken by the mendicant orders at that time was considerably broader than it is today.

The second order, or the Poor Clares, is in some ways a direct contrast to the Friars Minor, for many houses like that at Pedralbes were not only privileged to have a royal founder but drew on wealthy noble or merchant families for their postulants. The crown did not confine its patronage to the foundation and support of such convents, but frequently intervened in ecclesiastical appointments, in an attempt to see that a particular abbess was chosen. As has been shown, this happened in connection with the newly-founded Xàtiva house, when the king recommended an abbess from Saragossa, and in Vic, where he unsuccessfully tried to influence the councillors to allow a house of Poor Clares to be established in 1343 with a royal appointee as abbess.

The Franciscan order in the Middle Ages was more than a religious organization; it wielded considerable political power through its connections with royalty, from whom it received significant economic support. Although the friars themselves were unable to enjoy personally either the political power or the financial benefits they received, many of their relatives had no such scruples and were granted special favours, ranging from pardons for crimes and the successful resolution of disputes to grants of land and exemption from taxation and military service. These latter favours were also enjoyed by the procurators who looked after the economic affairs of the friars, and by those who undertook work on their behalf, such as craftsmen, gardeners, barbers and others occupied in similar tasks. Some of these procurators were already closely allied to the nearby Franciscan house through their membership in the Third Order; others probably had relatives who worked in the convent or who themselves took the habit.

The picture painted by this study of the Franciscans within the realms of Aragon is one of both spiritual and worldly success, but it is evident that there were also difficulties which cannot be assessed accurately by the historian: among them the non-payment of legacies and grants, and the long delays in meeting financial obligations, especially noted in the transactions connected with the royal treasury or the proving of wills. The lay brothers and all those who held no position of importance are shadows whose names, at best, may flit through the ordination registers only to disappear into the oblivion of time; yet these were probably the people who kept the houses running smoothly, while the friars who acted as ambassadors or travelled to other places spent months on the road, paying more heed to their secular duties than to the daily routine within a convent.

The Franciscan house in any large town was constantly used for secular purposes: it gave lodging to the king's retinue and frequently housed those who had nowhere else to go or who were employed within its precincts, while the convents of the Poor Clares sheltered noble ladies who required protection and the confraternities associated with the Third Order grouped men and women of particular trades who believed in the Franciscan ideal, some of them even living together as a community. Valuables, both money and jewels, were placed for safekeeping in the guardian's care; royal treasures and even the crown of Queen Constance were kept in the Barcelona convent. Legal documents, like the record of the investigation into the death of Francesc Examenis on the public highway, and title deeds to property were also confided to the friars, whose participation in all walks of life gave them a position of prominence which had little to do with their religious profession.

It should come as no surprise that some of those who entered the order were not able to meet the obligations placed on them, while others seem to have participated little in conventual life. After all, many of the young men who entered the Franciscan order probably had little or no vocation, and some were quite unfitted for life within the convent. The more daring left, some returning to take revenge on their enemies or to rob the convent of valuables on deposit; but the majority probably endured the hardship and, at times, the malicious slander, envy and violence which troubled their lives, depriving them of the peace or sense of fulfilment which comes to those with a true vocation. Those friars who were captured in their attempts to flee the religious life were subject to the discipline of the convent, if they were caught, and evidence shows that some were; the type of punishment meted out at the hands of the guardian is not known, but in the fifteenth century the errant friar would be confined to the convent until he submitted to discipline. The average friar, however, probably stayed in one or two houses throughout his life, fulfilling the duties required of him, preaching, hearing confessions and burying the dead; but his activities can only be conjectured, for they are not recorded.

Close to the Franciscan houses were often to be found prostitutes, tramps and those marginalized by their contemporaries, largely because, as urban centres grew in size and importance, the poor and less welcome elements on the fringe of society were forced to withdraw to areas outside the walls, where the gallows would also have been located. This may help to explain why the friars were frequently harbouring criminals, either to protect them from officers of justice or at times to give them shelter until their case was heard. It was not uncommon for the Franciscans to intercede on behalf of a hanged man's relatives, so that, after the regulatory year and a day required by law, the corpse could be taken down from the gallows and given a Christian burial.

To place the comments on the Franciscans into the wider context of medieval mendicant history, it would seem appropriate to make some reference to the geographical distribution of the Franciscans vis-à-vis the other mendicant orders, and especially in relation to the Dominicans and Carmelites, whose work most closely paralleled that of the Friars Minor. Consultation of the archives for the period under review reveals an interesting pattern. Up to 1250 the Dominicans were preferred by the royal family as emissaries, chaplains, confessors and ambassadors, and were recommended for vacant bishoprics. After this date, once the Franciscans had acquired an adequate economic base to found convents throughout the realms of Aragon, they too were chosen to fulfil such roles, while during the latter part of the thirteenth century the two orders vied for positions in the royal household, and indeed for the goodwill and financial support of their contemporaries. The popularity of the Franciscans seems to have increased while that of the Dominicans remained constant, as the development of the two smaller orders, the

Augustinians and the Carmelites, made further demands on the generosity of crown and people.

A look at the distribution of convents shows that in the large cities such as Barcelona, Saragossa and Valencia the names of both Dominicans and Franciscans appear as beneficiaries of wills with much the same regularity. In smaller towns there seems to have been some difficulty in sustaining two large mendicant houses, and in Puigcerdà, where the Dominicans were established before 1300 and the Franciscans a quarter of a century later, the latter eventually were forced to withdraw for lack of financial support. In Vic, the early Franciscan house was the only mendicant order there for more than a century, and the order was unable to establish support for the Poor Clares until the late fourteenth century.

In the nearby town of Manresa, on the other hand, it was the Dominicans who founded a convent, being joined there in the early fourteenth century by the Carmelites; the Friars Minor never succeeded in attracting sufficient support to establish a house in Manresa, although they did manage to found a convent of the Poor Clares in the 1320s. A similar pattern seems to pertain for most of the areas mentioned, but it is of interest to note that the Carmelites frequently acquired land and buildings formerly occupied by the Friars Minor, as in Perpignan and Saragossa. At times they established houses, such as that at Perelada, where economic support was not shared with the Dominicans and Franciscans and where they became very influential indeed. The Augustinians rarely seem to have threatened the economic support given to the other orders; it was only after the Black Death that they became more numerous and, especially in the kingdom of Valencia, extremely popular.

Unfortunately, detailed research on the early years of the Dominicans and Augustinians has been confined to individual houses, and as a result any conclusions offered in this study have to be tentative. There is no doubt that in many respects the Friars Preachers were the main rivals of the Friars Minor, but in the early years the greater emphasis they placed on the importance of learning detracted somewhat from their popular appeal and this may explain, in part at least, the Franciscan success in the second half of the thirteenth century. Saint Dominic was not nearly as popular as the charismatic figure of Saint Francis and the cult of poverty surrounding him.

The eremetical origin of the Carmelites and the difficulty they had in resolving the nature of the order made it difficult for them to compete with the two larger orders, but in their approach to poverty they most closely resembled the Franciscans. They were seldom found in small towns where there were both Dominican and Franciscan houses, although of course in the larger centres there was sufficient popular support to sustain three and even four mendicant orders.

Up to the time of the Black Death, the Franciscans were probably the most popular of the mendicant friars, and perhaps for that very reason the most susceptible too to heretical and unorthodox ideas. My research suggests that numerically, both in terms of the number of houses and the friars who professed, there was little difference between the two larger orders.

The Spiritual Franciscans, beguins and beguines might have made it seem that the Order of Friars Minor attracted greater numbers, but the influence of the Friars Preacher in Barcelona, Saragossa and Valencia and in some smaller towns should not be overlooked. The largest and most important convents of both Dominicans and Franciscans would have had fifty or sixty friars, while the lesser houses would seldom have reached a total of more than twenty. The larger Carmelite and Augustinian houses would have attracted fifteen to twenty, while in the smaller towns ten would have been regarded as an unusually high number. In addition to the religious in these houses there would have been a number of laymen, and their numbers might be expected to follow similar proportions. The Carmelites and Augustinians never managed to gain the same popular appeal as the followers of Saint Dominic and Saint Francis, and outside the large centres tended to settle in places ignored by the two larger orders.

In the absence of a detailed study of all the orders, it would seem reasonable to posit a tentative conclusion that, except in the large cities, the population was frequently too small to sustain more than one or two male convents and perhaps one order of nuns, and that the selection of a site for the foundation of religious houses in these small towns was directly related to the assurance of economic support. In places like Borja, Molina, Berga and Puigcerdà this seems to have reflected the short-lived political and commercial significance of those towns. When circumstances changed after the Black Death, convents which had been prosperous fell victim to the economic crises of the late fourteenth century.

The foregoing chapters elucidate an area of medieval life in the realms of Aragon which not only has importance for ecclesiastical history but also affords abundant material for prosopographical studies and social history. The names of hundreds of individuals who took the habit, and their connections with royalty, municipal authorities and the merchants of the towns, provide a better understanding of urban life in the thirteenth and fourteenth centuries. The problems they encountered and surmounted, the support they received and the way in which the order itself had to modify its approach cannot but prove fascinating.

Yet it is more than that, for James I and his successors realized the potential for a centralized economy based on the support of the middle class as a counterweight to the ambitions of the Aragonese nobles, and capitalized on it by enlisting the aid of the Franciscans, an international group disinterested in worldly gains and highly respected by the papacy. The friars, forbidden by their rule to accumulate wealth of their own, or even handle money, constituted no threat to the crown; rather they provided an excellent group of intermediaries, unconnected with diocesan structures, linked through Rome to convents throughout Europe, in touch with life beyond the borders of the realms of Aragon; and because many of them were highly literate, they were able to help the king in a number of ways, especially in the acquisition and maintenance of power and prestige.

The followers of Saint Francis in the space of less than one hundred and fifty years had become the spiritual arm of the Aragonese king, the friends of the merchant class and the new scholastics, popular wherever they went, more numerous as the years went by and ever more beset by the contradictions which their activities implied. On the eve of the Black Death the king was aware that he had no more powerful allies within the Crown of Aragon than the *menorets,* their convents had double the number of residents they had had fifty years earlier and many friars were prominent writers and theologians.

But the humility urged by Saint Francis was in danger of being forgotten in the desire for worldly success. The end of this study coincides with the Black Death, not so much because the epidemic itself had any immediate significance for Franciscan life, except perhaps the direct effects of the high mortality rate in some areas, but rather because after 1348 there was a perceptible shift in emphasis within the order itself and in its relations with church and state. The Black Death of 1348 spread more rapidly through urban areas, where people lived close together, frequently with inadequate provisions for hygiene and sometimes in dwellings which by any standards would have been considered little more than hovels. The poor were more susceptible to disease, mainly because of poor nutrition and crowded living conditions, and the friars who ministered to them frequently fell victims to the epidemic.[1]

This study cannot hope to determine the demographic and economic effects of the plague, but there is no doubt that the moral confusion which ensued after 1348 can in part be attributed to an epidemic imperfectly understood by those who survived to describe it. Indeed, in a search for the causes, a number of scapegoats were found: the Jews, the poor and even the Friars Minor, who heard the confessions of the dying and thus were blamed for having helped to spread the disease.[2]

A shift in attitudes towards the church after 1348 was to be expected, as was a disregard for many of its moral teachings. The church itself had difficulty in coming to terms with contemporary events, and more so perhaps, with people beginning to question the validity of some of its teachings. Doubts of this kind were responsible to a greater or lesser degree for dissension within its own ranks, the papal schism, the conflict among the friars themselves over the interpretation of the rule in the light of changing social circumstances and, in a more general sense, the gradual weakening of the Mediterranean as an economic base.[3]

---

1   See Michel Mollat, *The Poor in the Middle Ages: An Essay in Social History*, trans. Arthur Goldhammer (New Haven, 1986), pp. 193-210, for a detailed account of the effects of the plague in medieval Europe. There is no direct evidence of Franciscan deaths from attending the sick, but more immediate contact with the disease meant that the death rate among the friars in some areas was greater than in others.

2   For documents illustrating many of the problems encountered as a result of the Black Death, see Amada López de Meneses, "Documentos acerca de la peste negra en los dominios de la Corona de Aragón," *Estudios de edad media de la Corona de Aragón* 6 (1956), 291-447; and Mollat, *The Poor in the Middle Ages*, p. 197. Mollat cites the report of the provost of Narbonne, dated 17 April 1348, who took note of the confessions of "paupers and mendicants of all nations," accused of throwing potions into the waters, houses, churches and food supplies with the express purpose of killing the populace. Such exaggerated conclusions were drawn by many in an attempt to find a reason for the devastation inflicted by the epidemic, the worst of many in the fourteenth century.

3   Antonio Ubieto Arteta, *Ciclos económicos en la edad media española* (Valencia, 1969), p. 101 says that the prosperity of the first half of the fourteenth century was abruptly terminated by the Black Death of 1348: both agriculture and commerce stagnated, leading to two centuries of Catalan economic depression. This is an over-simplification of a depression difficult to assess, as J.N. Hillgarth points out in *The Spanish Kingdoms: 1250-1516*, 2 vols. (Oxford, 1976), 2: 9-10.

All these problems heralded the approaching end of the Middle Ages and the dawn of a new era, a factor easily determined today but which in the fourteenth century constituted a threat to the very fabric of existence, with its focus on salvation and preparation for the after life.

The Franciscans were no longer the group of destitute men who had followed Saint Francis, for they had achieved prominence in political and educational circles and had gained recognition as preachers, theologians and men of letters, their numbers having increased to a degree their founder could never have envisaged. Many of the founder's ideas of extreme poverty and asceticism had been modified to suit perceived contemporary needs, and in some ways the order had paid a high price for its active participation in political life.

The late fourteenth century marked the end of an era and the beginning of a troubled time for both crown and friars; dynastic problems and the discoveries in the Atlantic led to a shift in power away from the Mediterranean, and to the final absorption of Aragon into a united Spain dominated by Castile; the papal schism, dissent within the church and divisions within the Franciscan order led to problems which were only partially solved with the Reformation. The implications of these changes, exacerbated by dynastic problems and a changing socio-economic focus, really belong to a subsequent study; but it is clear that the alliance of crown, friars and middle classes was largely responsible for the prosperity which the Aragonese monarchy was to enjoy in the fourteenth century. The unstable conditions after 1348 were to extinguish many of the political achievements of the crown, but the Friars Minor, in their devotion to king and people, had gained the acceptance of their contemporaries as able administrators in both spiritual and temporal affairs and thus had carved out a permanent position for themselves in the Iberian Peninsula.

PART TWO

Documents and Appendices

The documents transcribed here aim to provide a selective but representative record of Franciscan life in the realms of Aragon before 1348.

The appendices that follow are based on references in the documents consulted and on some secondary sources such as Sanahuja's *Història* and the articles by Saldes (see Archival Sources and also Bibliography of Printed Sources below, pp. 411–436).

Appendix 1 lists the names of the provincial ministers, guardians, custodians and lectors recorded for the Franciscan province of Aragon. Appendix 2 illustrates organizational aspects of the Order of Friars Minor in the years prior to the Black Death: the provincial and general chapter meetings held to discuss financial and other matters, such as the appointment of officers; a list of the names of some laymen who undertook the task of procurator; and references to unpaid accounts, which became a constant problem not only for these procurators but also for the order itself.

Appendices 3–6 are included for prosopographical purposes. Although care has been taken to render the Latinized friars' names in their most appropriate form, orthographical variants and the use, in some cases, of one Latin form for several different names make it impossible to be certain that the correct name has been chosen in every instance.

The references to family origins of the friars collected in Appendix 3 provide an example of the way in which the documents may be analysed from the point of view of social history. Most friars took their vows and remained in the same convent or custody for the greater part of their lives. Other friars, however, were more mobile; this is evident from the chronology of convent residents in Appendix 4, which places the friars in a geographical context.

Alphabetical and chronological lists of all friars can be found in Appendix 5 and Appendix 6 respectively. The time various friars spent in different convents is usually impossible to determine, and throughout these appendices the dates given refer to the entire period of activity documented (an obelisk † marks the date, where known, of the death of a friar).

ON THE PREVIOUS PAGE
Bernat Fenollar (1438?–1516), canon of Valencia cathedral,
with Moreno, Gassull and Portell i Vinyoles at a literary gathering:
an illustration from *Lo procés de les olives* (Valencia, 1497), sig. Av

Documents

METHOD OF TRANSCRIPTION

The original Latin orthography of the documents has been maintained, with these exceptions: *i, y* and *j* have been transcribed as *i,* and double letters at the beginning of a word have been reduced to a single letter. Classical Latin *ti* is usually written *ci* in these documents; for the sake of clarity the latter form is adopted throughout. The orthography has also been maintained in the Catalan documents; however, accents have been added in accordance with the rules established by the Institut d'estudis catalans for modern Catalan. Parentheses have been used to enclose superfluous words or letters or an editorial comment. Essential additions to the text have been inserted in angle brackets.

LIST OF DOCUMENTS

1. Will of Fr. Ferrer de Cruilles: 1267
2. Royal order to capture an apostate: 1283
3. Permission to purchase a property in Majorca: 1286
4. Concession of Miramar to Franciscans: 1286
5. Concession of water to Majorca house: 1286
6. Concession of land in Ciutadella: 1287
7. Letter enjoining Franciscans at provincial chapter in Lerida from observing interdict: 1286
8. Plan to establish a convent in Sariñena: 1292
9. Enfranchisement of Ramon de Valls of Vilafranca: 1293
10. Concession of water to Barcelona house: 1293
11. General conditions for appointing procurators: 1293
12. Concession of water to Xàtiva house: 1296
13. Prince Peter's legacy to the Franciscans: 1296
14. Exemption from military service for Bernat Fuster of Vilfranca: 1298
15. Exemption from taxes granted to a Jewish physician: 1302
16. Enfranchisement of procurator of Vilafranca house: 1302
17. Letter concerning deposit by relative of Fr. Sancho López de Ayerbe in Ejea house: 1309

18	Contravention of building laws along Barcelona shore: 1309
19	Royal request for services of two Franciscans for war against Granada: 1309
20	Letter to *mestre racional* regarding payments to Fr. Pere de Puig of Lerida house: 1310
21	Letter to guardian of Ejea house regarding documents on deposit requested by abbess from Estella (Navarre): 1312
22	Letter to guardian of Saragossa house regarding documents deposited in Ejea house: 1312
23	Letter to Eximeno Pedro de Salanova, justice of Aragon, regarding documents on deposit in Ejea house: 1312
24	Two-year extension on payment for Fr. Pere de Cervera of Tàrrega house: 1321
25	Order to remove women of ill repute from vicinity of Huesca convent: 1322
26	Request by Bernat Venrell to build close to Gerona house: 1323
27	Letter naming Fr. Arnulf executor of queen's will: 1324
28	Safe-conduct for two friars going to England: 1325
29	Order to officials to respect safe-conduct issued to two friars: 1325
30	Edict to remove prostitutes from vicinity of Daroca house: 1326
31	Refusal of heirs to pay legacies to Vic house: 1326
32	Order to repair roof of Montblanc house: 1327
33	Order to officials in Cervera and Tàrrega to ensure that estate of Berenguer de Almenara is settled and legacy to Franciscans paid: 1327
34	Appeal by Fr. Sancho de Marra to King Alfonso to help him recover money owed by two Jews: 1328
35	Statutes of confraternity at Huesca: 1328
36	Apprehension of Mateu Miguel in Xàtiva house: 1328
37	Concession of grain to Tarragona house: 1328
38	Request to Bishop Gaston of Gerona to ensure that Bertran de Sa Mas of Castellfollet is not compelled to enter the Order of Friars Minor: 1329
39	Request for reestablishment of Berga house: 1329
40	Request for documents relating to murder of Francesc Examenis deposited in Barcelona house: 1330
41	Grant for repair of Franciscan house at Tarragona: 1330
42	Order to Bishop of Sardinia not to persecute members of Third Order: 1330

43	Permission to remove body of criminal from gallows and bury it in Franciscan cemetery: 1331
44	Order that chalices pawned by Master Domingo of Perpignan be redeemed: 1332
45	Order for recovery of legacy of Ferrer de Bruguera for Vic house: 1333
46	Order to officials in Cervera to ensure that Franciscans receive legacies made to them: 1333
47	Letter concerning dispute between Franciscans of Berga and monastery of Valldaura: 1333
48	Letter concerning Sardinians wrongly captured in Llençà: 1333
49	Letter to Fr. Pons Carbonell while at house of patriarch of Alexandria: <1334>
50	Letter to *batlle* of Berga regarding reestablishment of Franciscan house: 1334
51	Letter advising guardian of Teruel house of the gift of a retable: 1335
52	Appointment and enfranchisement of procurator of Lerida house: 1336
53	Order to Justice of Aragon to ensure that legacies are paid to Barbastro house: 1336
54	Order to jurisperitus of Barbastro to recover money owed to Franciscans by relatives of the late Domingo Spinelli: 1338
55	Letter referring to cleaning up of property in Moorish quarter of Saragossa: 1340
56	Concession to Franciscans at Tortosa to take grain out of city: 1340
57	Grant to repair chapel of Saint Louis in Teruel: 1345
58	Grant to lector of Teruel house to study theology at Paris: 1346
59	Permission to remove body of criminal from gallows and give it Christian burial: 1346

1

THE WILL OF FR. FERRER DE CRUILLES, A NOVICE IN THE FRANCISCAN HOUSE AT GERONA

14 November 1267   *Gerona, AH, Hospital de Girona, perg. 102*

In Christi nomine, ego frater Ferrarius de Crudiliis, filius maior Ferrarii de Crudiliis olim defuncti, existens novicius in ordine Fratrum Minorum, meum facio testamentum ac de bonis et rebus meis meam ultimam ordino voluntatem. In quo meos eliguo manumissores venerabiles abbatem Sancti Felicis, Gerunde, prepositum helemosine quam A<rnaldus> de Scala quondam in sede statuit Gerundense qui pro tempore fuerint, Ferrarium de Crudiliis, camerarium Sancti Michaelis de Crudile, fratrem meum, ac Raimundum de Caciano civem Gerunde; quibus, rogando eos, dono plenariam potestatem quod ipsi absque eorum dampno distribuant omnia bona mea prout hic invenerint ordinatum.

In primis, dimito monasterio Sancti Michaelis de Crudiliis homines et feminas quas et quos habeo et modo habitant in parrochia de Vilasacher, ad eorum voluntatem perpetuo faciendam in restitucione et emenda iniuriarum et dampnorum siqua intuli monasterio supradicto.

Item: in restitucione illius temporis quo ego non feci ardere lampadem quam pater et avus meus dimiserunt ardendam ante altarem Sancte Marie in eodem monasterio, dimito et instituo unam lampadem que ardeat coram dicto altari de nocte; tantum ad cuius institucionem dimito pro alodio francho in perpetuum illos tres solidos et quatuor denarios censuales et unum par gallinarum et tascham que omnia accipio, et accipere debeo, in vinea et terra in qua sedet quam tenet nunc En Cabrera, rusticus de Celrano, in loco videlicet qui dicitur de Aspirano, et omnia iura et dominia que accipio et accipere habeo et habere debeo in eadem. Quos inquam dictos tres solidos et quatuor denarios censuales et gallinas trias ego emi ab isto Bernardo de Scala, iuvene filio Bernardi de Scala olim defuncti.

Item: dimito pro alodio francho in perpetuum helemosine quam A<rnaldus> de Scala in sede statuit Gerundense ob remedium anime mee post obitum domine Dulcie, matris mee, totam meam partem quam habeo et accipio, et accipere iure domini consuevi, in mansis quorum unum habitat R<aimundus> de Riardo et alium R<aimundus> de Lantu in parrochia Sancti Felicis de Celrano, cum hominibus et feminis censibus agrariis terrarum ac cum omnium rerum dominiis et accionibus meis michi in dictis mansis pertinentibus vel pertinere debentibus quoquo modo, ad omnem voluntatem officii dicte helemosine perpetuo faciendam.

Item: dimito Ferrarie, sorori mee, 10 aureos post obitum domine matris mee quos Ferrarius, frater meus laicus, heres meus universalis, eidem solvat. Sed eos non teneatur solvere quousque 100 aurei quos ego solvere teneor qui inferius continentur quos mater mea sibi retinuit quando michi dedit honorem de Celrano fuerint persoluti, prout est inferius declaratum. Item: dimito iure institucionis domine Dulcie, matri mee, omnia feuda que ego et antecessores mei tenere consuevimus per dominum Castri de Barba vetula. Et omnes illas domos quas teneo per preposituram sedis Gerunde in villa de Celrano quas emi ab A<rnaldo> dez Parains de Celrano. Et totum bladum, vinum, bestiarium grossum que ipsa habebit tempore mortis sue et unum lectum pannorum completum scilicet de culcita capciali, linteaminibus, coopertorio et vanoa, ad omnem suam voluntatem perpetuo faciendam.

Item: dimito eidem domine matri mee, de vita sua, (tantum) totum honorem meum et omnia alia que ego habeo, teneo et possideo pro alodio francho in parrochia Sancti Felicis de Celrano; post mortem antedicte domine matris mee dimito Ferrario de Crudile laico, fratri meo, totum meum honorem quem habeo et possideo pro alodio francho in parrochia de Cilrano, excep(ta)tis hiis que superius dimito monasterio Sancti Michaelis de Crudile, et helemosine Arnalli de Scala, et excepto campo de Petron<e>; et quod dictus Ferrarius, frater meus laicus, donet et teneatur dare dicte domine matri mee tempore mortis sue, vel cum ipsa mandaverit solvi verbo vel testamento, 100 aureos quos ipsa sibi retinuit tempore videlicet quo michi dedit honorem de Cilrano; vel si dictus frater meus non solveret dictos 100 aureos manumissoribus matris mee, aut cui ipsa eos solvi mandaret, manumissores ipsius domine matris mee, vel ille quem ipsa mandaret, teneant et explicent dictum honorem tanto tempore et tamdiu donec dicti manumissores fuerint ex dictis 100 aureis satisfacti; et quod dictus Ferrarius, frater meus, non possit tenere dictum honorem quousque ipse solveret 100 aureos supradictos vel quousque manumissores matris mee vel ille quem ipsa mandaret essent ex ipsis 100 aureis satisfacti; postquam autem manumissores matris mee vel ille quem ipsa mandaret qui tenerent dictum honorem essent soluti ex 100 aureis supradictis, dictus Ferrarius habeat et teneat illum honorem.

Volo preterea, atque mando, quod dictus frater meus laicus restituat omnes iniurias meas et debita patris mei et omnium illorum quorum ego teneor restituere et solvere. Et si dictus Ferrarius, frater meus, decederet sine prole legitima, vel et cum prole que non perveniret ad 12 vel 14 annum, volo et mando atque ordino quod manumissores mei qui tunc temporis supraessent vel viverent emparent et accipiant omnia que ei dimito et ea vendant et precium ipsorum dent pro anima mea ad cognicionem guardiani Fratrum Minorum, Gerunde, qui tunc temporis esset, salvo sibi semper toto eo quod dictus Ferrarius solvisset de suo in dictis aureis matri mee vel illi cui ipsa mandaret solvendos, aut in debitis et in iniuriis meis vel patris mei aut <omnium> illorum quorum ego teneor, quod heredes dicti Ferrarii semper deducere in <iure> possent. Post mortem ante<dicte> domine matris mee prefati manumissores mei, illi scilicet qui superviverent, emparent campum de Petrone qui est meum alodium et illum vendant et de precio quod in <iure> habebunt, volo quod preconizetur in omnibus foris que sunt in villis, scilicet Gerunde, Balneolis, Bisulduni, Baschere, Petralate, Castilioni, Turrucelle, Petreincise, Monellis et Calidis, ut siquis est vel siqua cui pater meus Ferrarius de Crudile vel ego, frater Ferrarius, fuerimus iniuriati in aliquo veniant ad manumissores meos et eis illud restituatur infra mensem postquam fuerit eis significatum vel denunciatum, et hoc de consilio et voluntate guardiani Fratrum Minorum, Gerunde, scilicet de precio dicti campi.

Item: residuum precii dicti campi volo quod detur, medium per medium, in libros ad opus Fratrum Minorum, Gerunde, et ad debita domus eiusdem loci persolvenda, et hoc ob remedium anime patris mei et mei ipsius et illorum quibus pater meus vel ego teneremur; exceptis in <iure> 200 solidis qui dentur amore Dei ad cognicionem meam. Extunc non post illum mensem elapsum omnes iniurias meas et patris mei teneatur restituere heres meus, Ferrarius de Crudile laicus, quem heredem meum generalem et specialem in omnibus bonis meis ubicumque fuerint instituo, exceptis hiis que superius legavi et assignavi personis aliis sive locis, et ipse teneatur firmare vendicionem illius campi quantumque per manumissores meos in <iure> fuerit requisitus. Et si forte dictus Ferrarius nollet vendicionem predictam firmare et voluntantem meam adimplere in legatis meis et in iniuriis et debitis persolvendis, vel aliquam calumpniam seu impedimentum in aliquo huic meo testamento intulerit, volo quod privetur penitus omni iure institucionis in meo testamento contento et nominato, ac omni actu legitimo qui racione mei in aliquo ad ipsum pertineret; et instituo heredes meos speciales et generales pauperes Ihesu Christi inter quos intelligo Fratres Minores. Et si contingeret iste casus, dimito ipsi Ferrarii laico, fratri meo, 20 aureos quos sibi dimito super omnibus locis meis. Insuper hec omnia dono plenariam potestatem meis iamdictis manumissoribus et cuilibet eorum insolidum omnia bona mea et iura petendi, exigendi, recuperandi, atque recipiendi, et omnes personas quas michi in aliquo teneantur si necesarium fuerit in causam trahendi, et omnia alia faciendi que in persona mea propria facere ego possem, et quicquid per ipsos vel eorum alterum in hiis factum fuerit ratum in perpetuum habere permito.

Hec est autem ultima mea voluntas quam volo iure testamenti valere et si non valet iure testamenti, volo quod valeat iure codicillorum vel iure mee cuiuslibet ultime alterius voluntatis. Quod est actum XVIII Kalendas Decembris, anno Domini millesimo ducentesimo sexsagesimo septimo.

Signum: fratris Ferrarii de Crudiliis predicti, existentis novicii in ordine Fratrum Minorum qui hoc testamentum facio, firmo firmarique rogo. Signum: Domine Dulcie de Crudiliis, matris dicti fratris Ferrariis de Crudiliis que hoc testamentum et omnia que in ipso continentur firmo, laudo et concedo et promito non contravenire, cuius firmamentum est hic appositum per manum mei Michaelis de Ulmo, XI Kalendas December anno prefixo; presentibus A<rnaldo> de Montefolrano, traginerio, et G<uillermo> Barralli de Cilrano, testibus.

Testes rogati et ad hoc specialiter vocati sunt: Michael de Trulars, faber de Gerunda, Berengarius Bonelli de Sancto Andrea de Alodio, Guerallus Sabaterius de Campolonguo, Raimundus, faber de Gerunda, Berengarius de Podio, faber de Gerunda, Matheus Poncii de Lambillis qui habitat in Gerunda et Berengarius dez Cariet de Sancto Stephano de Lemena.

Signum: Michaelis de Ulmo qui hec scripsit mandato Bernardi de Vicco, publici, Gerunde. Signum: Bernardi de Vicco publici, Gerunde, qui hoc subscripsit.

2

A ROYAL ORDER TO CAPTURE AN APOSTATE

5 July 1283   *Barcelona, ACA, RC 61, f. 166*

Universis officialibus ex parte custodis et Fratrum Minorum propositum extitit coram nobis quod Frater Martinus Petri de Biel de ordine eorum post professum exivit de ipso ordine et vadit in scandal(i)um ipsius ordinis. Quare mandamus vobis quatenus super capiendo ipso Martino Petri dictis fratribus predictis consilium et iuva<men>tum <detis> quandocumque per ipsos fueritis requisiti. Datum Exee, III nonas Iulii, <1283>.

3

THE FRIARS MINOR ARE GIVEN PERMISSION BY ALFONSO II TO PURCHASE A PROPERTY IN MAJORCA

13 January 1285 [1286] *Barcelona, ACA, RC 63, f. 21*

Nos, Alfonsus, Dei gracia rex Aragonum, Maioricarum et Valencie, ac comes Barchinone, concedimus vobis, guardiano et conventui Fratrum Minorum, civitatis Maioricarum, quod ad opus dicti ordinis seu domus vestre possitis emere domos de Na Figera et corrale d'En Companyó que sunt contigua vestro monasterio predicto. Datum Maiorico, Idus Ianuarii, 1285.

4

CONCESSION TO THE FRIARS MINOR OF THE PLACE CALLED MIRAMAR

13 January 1285 [1286] *Barcelona, ACA, RC 63, f. 21v*

Fidelibus baiulo Maioricarum vel eius locum tenenti, salutem et graciam. Cum pro anime nostre remedio ac progenitorum nostrorum <comendav>erimus et dederimus ordini Fratrum Minorum locum qui dicitur Miramar, prout in donacione nostra inde constans plenius continetur, mandamus vobis firmiter et districte quatenus sine dilacione et mora de reddibus nostris plenarie satisfacere curetis guardiano et fratribus dicti loci in centum XXX tribus libris et tresdecim solidis et quatuor denariis regalium qui eis remanent ad solvendum de quantitate eis assignata pro suis necessariis anni presentis, ut nobis const<a>t per compotum Bernardi Bertrandi olim thesaurarii incliti dompini Iac<obi>, avunculi nostri, alias veras soluciones et pagas faciatis guardiano et fratribus dicti loci predictis singulis annis de cetero sicut in donacione nostra predicta ordinatas inveneritis ac eisdem fratribus in posterum faciendas. Datum ut supra. <Datum Maiorico, Idus Ianuarii, 1285>.

5

Confirmation of concession of the right to draw water from the royal wells in Majorca

13 January 1285 [1286] *Barcelona, ACA, RC 63, f. 21v*

Fidelibus suis baiulo et vicario Maioricarum, salutem et gratiam. Cum dompinus Ia < cobus > , avunculus noster, concesserit conventui Fratrum Minorum Maioricarum quod de aqua ceqie que intrat dictam civitatem possint recipere in loco ubi eos magis expedie(n)t aliquam quantitatem quam possint ducere ad eorum monasterium per canones; et mandaverit baiulo et vicario Maioricarum quod cum consilio proborum hominum dicte civitatis assignarent dictis Fratribus Minoribus certam formam quam recipere debeant de dicta aqua quam dictis Fratribus Minoribus et eorum monasterio cognoverint sufficere et esse competentem.

    Volumus ac vobis dicimus et mandamus quatenus iuxta concessionem predictam assignetis dictis Fratribus Minoribus et eorum monasterio formam quam recipere debeant de aqua predicta quam cognoveritis eis suficere et esse competentem. Datum ut supra. < Maiorico, Idus Ianuarii, 1285. >

6

Concession of land to the Friars Minor to build a convent in Ciutadella (Minorca)

1 March 1286 [1287] *Barcelona, ACA, RC 64, f. 163v*

Noverint universi quod nos, Alfonsus etc. ad honorem Dei et Beate Marie et ob remedium animarum parentum nostrorum damus, offerimus et concedimus per nos et nostros, domino Deo et beato Francisco et ordini Fratrum Minorum et vobis fratri Petro de Belloforti, guardiano Fratrum Minorum, Barchinone, et fratri Petro de Quadris, guardiano Fratrum Minorum, Maiorice, ortum in Ciutadella qui ortus vocabatur Ortus de l'Arrays et domus ex utraque parte contiguas ipsi orto ad opus, videlicet, ecclesie et monasterii vestri ordinis construendi ibidem. Qui quidem ortus et domus affrontant in carraria publica et in via inferiori usque ad viam superiorem, et in prato sive patuo ante turrem, et ex partibus inferioribus in terris seu ortalibus nostris que nondum sunt aliis assignata. Ita quod dictus ortus et domus sicut terminate et terminatus seu affrontatus sunt, habeat ordo Sancti Francisci per hed<if>i-cat<ionem> ipsam, franchum et liberum, tam in spiritualibus quam temporalibus sine contradiccione aliqua ad habendum, tenendum etc., sicut melius etc., sub condicione tamen quod dictas domos semper populatas teneatis et aliqui fratres ipsius ordinis ibi faciant residenciam personalem; mandantes etc. Datum Ciutadelle, Kalendas Marcii, 1286.

7

ALFONSO II WRITES TO THE FRIARS MINOR WHO ARE HOLDING A PROVINCIAL CHAPTER IN THE LERIDA HOUSE ENJOINING THEM NOT TO OBSERVE THE INTERDICT IMPOSED

3 May 1286 *Barcelona, ACA, RC 66, f. 65*

Alfonsus etc., religiosis viris Fratrum Minorum provincie Aragonum ceterisque fratribus apud Ilerdam in provinciali capitulo congregatis, salutem et dileccionem.

Licet super facto interdicti positi, ut dicitur, contra dominum patrem nostrum inclite recordacionis et terram nostram indebite in predictis pater noster et nos parati fuerimus et sumus quibuscumque de nobis querelantibus facere iusticie complementum, vobis nostras litteras miserimus per co<n>ventus quatenus ad vestrum ordinem affectamur amore intimo et dileccione eciam speciali. Timentes ne inter nos et vos racione interdicti predicti perpetuum †iniciamur seu supplicante aliquorum simplicium† scandalum oriatur, vobis scribendum duximus, cum sciamus discord(i)es ex nobis et maiores de provincia in presenti provinciali capitulo congrega<n>tis, ne si aliud, quod absit, inter nos et vos oriat ignorancia vos excuset.

Quare volentes predictis scandalis obviare, mandamus vobis tam prelatis quam subditis ac eciam ceteris fratribus universis nunc in dominacione nostra morantibus ac deinceps moraturis quatenus interdictum predictum nullatenus observetis nec sustineatis quod alius quicumque, sive sit de nostro dominio sive non, seu eciam venerit aliunde, interdictum predictum teneat vel inter vos ponat, seu in terminum nostrum intromitat; scientes quod si contrarium <inven>iemus introducentes, sustinentes ac consencientes et eciam observantes capitali sentencia puni(r)emus. Nos eciam facimus predictam nostram dominacionem decretum seu mandatum quod volumus universaliter sub pena gravissima ab omnibus observari, quod si aliquem vel aliquos cuiuscumque status, condicionis seu dignitatis invenerimus qui predictum interdictum observaverint seu aliquos alios induxerint ad servandum inducentes et inductos conservantes videlicet officiales nostri capiant et captos ac ligatos ad nostram presenciam deferant et adducant. Nos enim huiusmodi proponimus taliter corrigere quod sint omnibus audientibus in exemplum. Quia vero vos diligimus et ad vos afficimur supra omnes religiosos tanquam nostris specialibus, vobis scribimus familiarius ut ab huiusmodi cautatis ne habeamus in vos et vestros tirannidem exercere. Datum Osce, 5 Nonas Maii, 1286.

8
The Friars Minor at Huesca plan to establish a convent in Sariñena

4 December 1292 [1293] *Barcelona, ACA, RC 94, f. 9*

Exemino Petri, divina permissione abbati Montisaragone etc. Cum Fratres Minores Osce proponant hedifficare monasterium in Sara-\<n\>yena et suplicaverint nobis quod vobis deprecatorie scribere deberemus quod ecclesiam Sancti Michelis que est in Sara\<n\>yena eisdem fratribus pro monasterio hedificando ibidem ob honorem nostri concedere deberetis, ipsorum suplicacione admissa, rogamus vos quatenus predictis fratribus ecclesiam Sancti Michelis sitam in Sara-\<n\>yena honore et precibus nostris concedatis ad monasterium construendum. Hoc enim gratum habebimus et acceptum et regraciabimur vobis multum. Datum ut supra. \<Bolee, 2 Nonas Decembris, 1292\>.

9
Enfranchisement of Ramon de Valls, a worker at the Vilafranca house

19 March 1292 [1293] *Barcelona, ACA, RC 260, f. 189v*

Noverint universi quod nos, Iacobus, Dei gracia etc., ob graciam et preces venerabilis guardiani Fratrum Minorum Villefranche enfranchimus et franchum fecimus vos, Raimundum de Valle, operarium domus dictorum Fratrum Minorum, ab omni exercitu et cavalcata et redempcionibus eorundem. Ita quod, dum geratis officium antedictum quod dictis Fratribus Minoribus, non teneamini ire in exercitum vel cavalcatam, nec mittere aliquem loco vestri, nec solvere aliquid pro redempcionibus eorundem. Mandantes vicariis et baiulis Villefranche et universis aliis officialibus et subditis nostris quod presentem graciam nostram firmam habeant et observent, et faciant observari, ut superius est expressum. Datum Barchinone, 14 Kalendas Aprilis, 1292.

10

CONCESSION OF WATER TO THE FRANCISCAN HOUSE IN BARCELONA

25 May 1293 *Barcelona, ACA, RC 260, ff. 211v–212*

Noverint universi quod nos, Iacobus, Dei gracia etc., ob remedium anime nostre damus et concedimus vobis, venerabilibus et dilectis guardiano et conventui Fratrum Minorum Barchinone, presentibus et futuris in perpetuum, quartam partem aque unius occuli mole molendini accipiendam de regno nostro comitali Barchinone. Ita quod ipsam aquam faciatis adduci ad dictum monasterium vestrum sine preiudicio iuris alterius ac de ipsa aqua possitis rigare ortum vestrum et facere alia necessaria domus vestre, et servicium ipsius aque h<ab>eatis vos et vestri perpetuo franchum et liberum sine omni censu et servicio annuo et perpetuo. Mandantes vicario et baiulo Barchinone et universis aliis et singulis officialibus et subditis nostris presentibus et futuris quod in predictis vel aliquo predictorum nullum impedimentum vel contrarium faciant, vel fieri permitant, immo concessionem nostram predictam observent et observari faciant inviolabiliter ut que <nullate>nus contraveni<a>nt et non contraveniant nec aliquem contravenire permitant aliqua etc. Datum Gandie, 8 Kalendas Iunii, 1293.

11

ROYAL PROVISION FOR THE APPOINTMENT OF PROCURATORS
WHO ARE TO BE EXEMPT FROM TAXATION

7 September 1293 *Barcelona, ACA, RC 260, f. 246*

Universis iusticie, iuratis et omnibus comunariis locorum Aragonie in quibus Fratres Minores habent monasteria sive domos, salutem et graciam. Noveritis quod nos concessimus Fratribus Minoribus Aragonum quod in quolibet loco Aragonie in quo habeant monasteria possint habere unum hominem qui in ipso loco negocia monasterii ipsorum Fratrum Minorum faciat et procuret, et quod ille excusetur a prestacione exaccionum regalium dum tamen ille non sit de dictoribus ipsius loci. Quare placet nobis quod ad cognicionem nostri possint eligere dicti fratres in loco ubi monasteria habent unum hominem sufficientem et ad predicta negocia prestandum, qui non sit de dictoribus ipsius loci, et ipsum de prestacione dictarum exaccionum excusetis et excusatum habeatis qui in ipsa negocia pro dictis Fratribus Minoribus procurabit. Datum Cesarauguste, 7 Idus Septembris, 1293.

12

JAMES II CONCEDES TO THE XÀTIVA HOUSE THE RIGHT TO
DRAW WATER FROM THE ROYAL WELLS FOR IRRIGATION PURPOSES

25 August 1296 *Barcelona, ACA, RC 104, f. 58*

Ia<cobus> etc. fidelibus suis, iusticie et iuratis ville Xative, salutem et graciam. Intelleximus ex relacione guardiani necnon conventus Fratrum Minorum, Xative, quod inclite recordacionis dominus Iacobus quondam rex Aragonum, avus noster, tempore capcionis ville Xative concessit et dedit Fratribus Minoribus quendam locum ad construendum monasterium eorum et inibi perpetuo habitandum: in quo quidem solo dicti fratres monasterium construxerunt et morantur ibidem. Concessit eciam eis aquam de cequia comuni que labitur iuxta murum ville predicte pro usibus eorum et <ad> ortum quod ibi habent irrigandum, de qua aqua prout eis concessa fuit disser<u>erunt se usos fuisse pro usibus eorum et rigando orto predicto. Et quia timent super possessione dicte aque per aliquos indebite agravari, nobis humiliter suplicarunt ut super possessione et usu dicte aque ipsos manuteneri et defendi mandaremus; quorum suplicacione benigne admissa, vobis dicimus et mandamus quatenus fratres predictos conventus Xative prefati super possessione et usu in qua sunt dicte aque manuteneatis et deffendatis in iure nec permittatis eisdem per aliquos violenciam seu gravamina fieri seu inferri. Datum Valencie, 8 Kalendas Septembris, anno predicto <1296>.

13

A LEGACY TO THE FRIARS MINOR IN THE WILL OF PRINCE PETER

8 November 1296　　　　　　　　　　Barcelona, ACA, RC 105, f. 224

<Iacobus etc. > fideli suo G<uillelmo> Treni etc. Cum inclitus dominus infans Petrus bone memorie, carissimus frater noster, instituerit nos manumissorem suum in suo ultimo testamento et in eodem legaverit capellam suam Fratribus Minoribus, Cesarauguste: idcirco auctoritate manumissorie predicte qua fungimur in hac parte, vobis dicimus et mandamus quatenus capellam predictam quam vos, ut dicitur, deposuistis in domo Fratrum Predicatorum Cesarauguste, tradatis incontinenti dictis Fratribus Minoribus vel cui voluerint loco sui. Nos enim facimus alios manumissores dicti fratris nostri haberi procuratores pro tradicione capelle predicte et vos eciam indempnes penitus conservare. Datum Barchinone, 6 Idus Novembris, anno predicto <1296>.

14

THE BAILIFF OF VILAFRANCA IS REMINDED THAT BERNAT FUSTER
AS A MEMBER OF THE THIRD ORDER IS NOT REQUIRED
TO DO MILITARY SERVICE OR PAY TAXES

20 May 1298　　　　　　　　　　Barcelona, ACA, RC 111, ff. 225v–226

Ia<cobus> etc. fideli suo baiulo Villefranche vel eius locum tenenti, salutem et graciam. Ex parte fratris Bernardi Fusterii, habitatoris Villefranche, qui est de tercio ordine beati Francisci, fuit nobis expositum conquerendo quod, quamquam ipse pretextu sui ordinis in exercitu ire minime teneatur, iurati et probi homines Villefranche, pro eo quia ipse frater Bernardus non ivit in exercitum de Pailars, ipsum in quindecim solidos taxavere eundemque ad solucionem dictorum XV solidorum pignorant et compellunt; quapropter, ad instanciam et suplicacionem nobis pro parte dicti fratris Bernardi factam, vobis dicimus et mandamus quatenus cum ipse frater Bernardus sit persona religiosa et ire in exercitum minime teneatur, eundem vel bona sua ad solvendum predictos quindecim solidos in quibus taxatus est racione supradicta compelli nullatenus permitatis. Immo pignora ea facta vel quicquid ab eo per iuratos et probos homines predictos est habitum et extortum racione predicti exercitus ea sibi restitui faciatis predictos iuratos et probos homines et bona eorum ad hec cohercione debita compellendo. Datum Barchinone, 13 Kalendas Iunii, anno predicto <1298>.

Note: This is the first known reference to the Third Order in Catalonia.

15

JAMES II GRANTS EXEMPTION FROM TAXES TO A JEWISH
PHYSICIAN OF VALENCIA WHO HAS LABOURED LONG
IN THE SERVICE OF THE FRANCISCANS

24 March 1301 [1302] *Barcelona, ACA, RC 196, f. 296*

Nos, Ia<cobus> etc. attendentes te Homer<um>, fisicum iudeum, Valencie, de arte tua in serviciis religiosorum Fratrum Minorum civitatis Valencie fideliter laborasse et quia eis servire cotidie tenearis, ideo in dictorum serviciorum remuneracionem ad instanciam et preces religiosi fratris Ferdinandi, doctoris conventus predicti, concedimus tibi de gracia speciali quod te prius solvente et contribuente pro bonis tuis in tributis, peitis, questiis ac aliis exaccionibus regalibus et serviciis quibuscumque partes tibi (MS te) contingentes prout est consuetum fieri inter alios iudeos aliame Valencie non capiaris in persona tua nec claudantur tibi hostia domorum tuarum nec bona tua pignorentur postquam solveris partem tibi contingentem in omnibus et singulis questiis, tributis et aliis exaccionibus et serviciis supradictis nec compellaris eciam per aliamas regni Valencie seu quoscumque officiales aut portarios nostros ad obligandum te et tua bona, et ad faciendum fidancias in manuleutis nec in debitis aut in aliquibus contractibus quos predicta aliama iudeorum Valencie ex nunc factura est, te tamen prius solvente partem tibi contingentem in obligacionibus, manuleutis, debitis, aut contractibus supradictis. Mandantes per presentem cartam nostram procuratori regni Valencie necnon baiulo generali ac aliis officialibus et subditis nostris regni eiusdem, presentibus et futuris, quod predictam graciam et concessionem nostram firmam habeant et observent et faciant ab omnibus, ut continetur, perpetuo inviolabiliter observari et non contraveniant nec aliquem contravenire permitant aliqua racione. Datum Valencie, 9 Kalendas Aprilis, 1301.

16

ENFRANCHISEMENT OF THE FRANCISCAN PROCURATOR IN VILAFRANCA DEL PENEDÈS

16 September 1302   *Barcelona, ACA, RC 125, f. 70*

Fidelibus suis vicariis, baiulis, porteriis, collectoribus et universis aliis officialibus suis ad quos presentes pervenerint etc. Cum nos ob gratiam ac preces guardiani et conventus Fratrum Minorum Villefranche enfranchiverimus et franchum fecerimus Petrum de Romanino, habitatorem Villefranche, procuratorem ipsorum fratrum dum procurator fuerit eorundem, ab omni questia, servicio, subsidio, exercitu, seu cavalcata, et a qualibet alia exaccione regali ac redempcionibus eorundem cum carta nostra ut in ea continetur. Idcirco mandamus et dicimus vobis quatenus franchitatem predictam observetis eidem Petro, ponendo in compoto nostro partem ipsi (MS ipsam) contingentem in predictis prout in carta dicte franchitatis videbitis contineri et ipsum Petrum contra formam franchitatis predicte in aliquo non gravetis. Datum ut supra. <Barchinone, 16 Kalendas Octobris, 1302>.

17

DEPOSIT IN EJEA DE LOS CABALLEROS BY A POSSIBLE RELATIVE OF FR. SANCHO LÓPEZ DE AYERBE

22 February 1308 [1309]   *Barcelona, ACA, RC 289, f. 98*

Blancha etc. Religioso viro guardiano domus Fratrum Minorum de Exea, salutem et dileccionem. Intelleximus per nobilem dominam Iolant, uxorem nobilis Petri domini de Ayerbe filiamque inclite infantisse de Grecia quondam consanguinee nostre, quod vos tenetis in deposito seu comanda quedam instrumenta quibus ipsa indiget super proprietate locorum de Lienas et de Apies que vendita fuerunt per abbatissam et conventum monasterii Sancte Marie de Sales de <E>stella dicte infantisse de Grecia. Quapropter vos requirimus et rogamus quatenus ipsa instrumenta tradatis dicte domine Iolant vel cui voluerit loco sui prout dictus dominus rex iam super hoc vobis scripsit. Datum Barchinone, 8 Kalendas Marcii, anno quo supra <1308>.

18

CONTRARY TO ROYAL DECREE
BUILDINGS HAVE BEEN CONSTRUCTED IN BARCELONA
ALONG THE SHORE FROM THE FRANCISCAN HOUSE
TO THE HOUSE OF GUERAU DE TRILLA

13 April 1309   *Barcelona, ACA, RC 206, f. 29*

Iacobus, Dei gratia rex Aragonum etc. fideli suo baiulo Barchinone presenti et qui pro tempore fuerit etc. Significamus vobis quod nos personaliter accedentes ad edefficia et domos que edificate sunt in ripparia civitatis Barchinone, a domo videlicet Fratrum Minorum usque ad domos Gueraldi de Trilea inclusive—que edificia dicebantur esse situata in littore maris ipsius civitatis et sic edificata esse in preiudicium iuris nostri—edifficia ipsa vidimus occulis nostris quod subieccimus sic quod taliter providimus fieri super eis: quod ille antipar<at>e sive constructure que constructe sunt in prospectu maris—post parietes domorum quas Gueraldus de Trilea predictus et Felicius de Vallibus fusterius et Castilionus ancorerius ibi habent et quedam eciam domuncula fustea que constructa est in prospectu ipsius maris post parietes domorum heredum A<rnaldi> Gavarre quondam—amoveantur omnino eo quia nimis maris fluctibus appropinquant. Quibus amo(n)tis si autem ipsos parietes domorum illi quorum dicte domus sunt ob tuicionem fluctuum ipsius maris voluerint facere aliquantum antiparatum consimilem illi quam Fratres Minores fecerunt fieri parietibus qui sunt ante ecclesiam ipsorum Fratrum Minorum, eis facere seu facere fieri permittatis. Alia vero edifficia que alii cives Barchinone habent a dictis domibus Geraldi de Trilia et Felicii de Vallibus fusterii usque ad dictam domum Fratrum Minorum quia ea vidimus situata seu edifficata circa domos dictorum Geraldi, Felicii et Castilionis nec tantum maris fluctibus apropin<qu>ant, ea intacta volumus remanere. Sic quod a procedendo per vos super eis seu contra eis ex premissa causa desisti volumus et mandamus. Per hec autem non intendimus quod illi, qui ipsa hedificia habent, possint de cetero edifficando vel alius edifficia ipsa adcrescere seu protrahere versus mare, immo volumus quod acrescendo et protrahendo ea ulterius quam nunc sunt cessetur penitus eciam et desistatur. Quare per presentem cartam nostram mandamus vobis quatenus huiusmodi provisionem nostram observetis et observari faciatis sub forma premissa, ut superius continetur. Datum Barchinone, Idus Aprilis, 1309.

19

The king requests the services of Fr. Pere Jofre and his socius for the war against Granada

12 June 1309   *Barcelona, ACA, RC 308, f. 66*

Religioso fratri Petro Iaufridi de Ordine Minorum etc. Cum nos, pretextu licencie per nos obtente a venerabili et religioso viro fratre Romeo Orticii ordinis predicti ministro de ducendis nobiscum fratribus in presenti viagio quod Deo duce fecerimus contra regem Granate et gentes suas, fidei ca<to>lice inimicos, vos inter ceteros fratres ituros nobiscum in dicto viagio duxerimus eligendum: idcirco rogamus et dicimus vobis quatenus ad nos veniatis cum socio quem vos duxeritis eligendum vobiscum, <ut> in dicto viagio progrediamur. Datum Barchinone, 2 Idus Iunii, anno predicto <1309>.

20

To Pere Marc, treasurer, from Pere Boyl, mestre racional, regarding payments to Fr. Pere de Puig of the Lerida house

8 August 1310   *Barcelona, ACA, RC 308, f. 66*

Fideli thesaurario suo, Petro Marci, salutem etc. Viso quodam albarano dilecti magistri racionalis nostre curie, Petri Boil, tenoris sequentis: Jo, En Pere boyl, maestre racional del senyor rey, atorch a vos, frare Pere des Puig, guardià de la casa dels Frares Menors de Leyda, que avets mostrada a mi una carta pública feta per En Francesch Sa Vila, notari de Barcelona, i de tota la senyoria del senyor rey. E fo feta en lo setge d'Almaria, V Idus Ianuare, anno Domini MCCCIX, en la qual era contengut qu'En Jaume de Raffels, <qui tingué> grant malalt<i>a en lo dit setge d'Almeria, ordonà que frare Arnau de Vilanova de l'orde dels Frares Menors del convent de Tortosa, i En Berenguer de Morel<l>a ab ell ensemps, i en defaliment lur, vos, dit guardià, i En Iohan de Morella, rector de la església de Peralta, poguessets pagar i restituir algunes iniúries i torts que. l dit En Jaume de Raf(f)als avia dit (MS diets) en sa confesió al dit frare Arnau de Vilanova, i a pagar aquelles iniúries i tortes assignà algunes robes i coses que l'avia, estant en lo dit setge d'Almeria, les quals se contenen en la dita carta. E axí mateix hi assignà un deute que. l senyor rey li devia de mille solidos Barchinones.

E encara ço que li era degut per lo dit senyor rey per rahó del dit viatge d'Almeria segons que assó en la dita carta era largament contengut. E per declarar ésser compte d'assó que era degut per la cort al dit Jaume de Raffals mostràs a mi, i albarà fet per N'Arnau Ça Bastida sa enrere maestre racional de la Cort del dit senyor tramès als clavaris de la cullera de la cisa de Cathalunya, i fo fet en Barchinona kalendis marci anno Domini 1300 ab lo qual eren deguts al dit En Jaume de Raffels sa enrere per quitació sua del viatge de Sicília en lo qual fo en servey del senyor rey. E per esment(i) de cavayls que perd en lo dit viatge 2,182 solidos Barchinones, el dors del qual albarà era scrit que. n foren pagats per los dits clavaris en 7 paguès 956 solidos 6 diners Barchinones. Item: que'n foren pagats per En Pere dez Soler, scrivà del senyor rey 245 solidos 6 diners Barchinones, les quals pagues que són en summa 1,201 solidos Barchinones ab aiudes de la dita quantitat romanen a pagar del dit albarà, lo qual jo hé cobrat 982 solidos Barchinones. E no trop que altres pagues no sien estades fetes. si emperò a avant apropien no tinch al senyor rey que diguessen ésser ab aiudes de la quantitat damunt dita. En testimoni de la qual cosa fag aquest albarà(na) segellat ab lo segell del dit meu offici qui fo fet en Leyda primer dia d'Agost, anno Domini 1310.

Idcirco recuperato i per cautelam cure lacerato in cancellaria nostra albarano predicto, vobis dicimus et mandamus quatenus que peccunia cure nostre que est vel erit penes vos tribuatis et solvatis predictis personis in dicto albarano contentis quantitatem predictam prout iuxta tenorem dicti publici instrumenti de quo in dicto albarano fit mencio inveneritis faciendum. Et facta solucione(m) presentem recipiatis litteram cum apocha de soluto et † nichilominus † transumptum factum in forma publica predicti publici instrumenti. Datum Ilerde, 6 Idus Augusti, anno Domini millesimo CCCX. Guillem de Ruvira ex albarano magistri racionalis.

21

LETTER TO THE GUARDIAN OF THE EJEA HOUSE REGARDING DOCUMENTS ON DEPOSIT REQUESTED BY THE ABBESS OF THE MONASTERY OF OUR LADY OF SALAS, ESTELLA (NAVARRE)

9 December 1312 *Barcelona, ACA, RC 150, f. 2r–v*

Iacobus etc. Religiosis viris guardiano et conventui domus Fratrum Minorum Exee, salutem etc. Noveritis quod pro eo quare venerabilis abbatissa monasterii Sancte Marie de Salis de Stella nunc in nostra presencia constituta supplicando asseruit quedam privilegia et instrumenta et alias scripturas que sunt intus quandam caxiam dudum in domo vestra predicta sub depositi nomine positam faciencia, ut dicitur, pro dicto monasterio sibi debere tradi, providimus et ordinamus ut de privilegiis a <c> instrumentis ac scripturis predictis fiat quod faciendum fuerit, quod omnia ipsa privilegia, instrumenta ac quecumque scripture existencia intus caxiam predictam mittantur per vos guardiano et conventui domus Fratrum Minorum Cesarauguste, tenenda et custodienda per eos in domo predicta et hostendenda iusticie Aragonum quocienscumque ea infra ipsam domum videre voluerit, ac ordinando per ipsum iusticiam iuxta comissionem inde sibi cum alia littera per nos factam prout ipse cognoverit et duxerit requirendum.

Quocirca vobis dicimus et mandamus quatenus visis presentibus privilegia et instrumenta ac scripturas predictas mitatis intus dictam caxiam clausam et sigillo vestri dicti guardiani sigillata <m> sub fida custodia cum sumptibus (tamen) dicte abbatisse, guardiano et conventui supradictis, quibus nos per aliam litteram nostram scribimus super istis. Datum Ricle, quintus idus December anno Domini MCCCXII.

22

Letter to the guardian of the Saragossa house regarding documents deposited in the Ejea house

9 December 1312   *Barcelona, ACA, RC 150, f. 233v*

Iacobus etc. Religiosis viris guardiano et conventui domus Fratrum Minorum Cesarauguste, salutem etc. Noveritis quod ipso quare venerabilis abbatissa monasterii Sancte Marie de Salis de Estella nunc in nostra presencia constituta supplicando asseruit quedam privilegia et instrumenta ac alias scripturas que sunt intus quandam caxiam dudum in domo Fratrum Minorum Exee sub depositi nomine positam faciencia, ut dicitur, pro dicto monasterio sibi debere tradi, providimus et ordinamus ut de privilegiis et instrumentis ac scripturis predictis fiat quod faciendum fuerit, quod omnia ipsa privilegia, instrumenta ac quecumque scripture existencia intus caxiam predictam mittantur vobis per guardianum et conventum domus predicte de Exea, tenenda et custodienda per vos in domo vestra et hostendenda iusticie Aragonum quocienscumque ea infra domum vestram videre voluerit, ac ordinando per ipsum iusticiam iuxta concessionem inde sibi cum alia littera per nos factam prout ipse cognoverit et duxerit requirendum.

Quocirca vobis dicimus et mandamus quatenus et recipiendo predictam, cum vobis ea miserint guardianus et conventus predicti quibus per aliam litteram nostram super hac mandatum misimus, teneatis et custodiatis ipsam fideliter intus domum vestram predictam, hostendendo tamen ea prelibato iusticie quociens infra domum ipsam ea videre voluerit ac faciendo insuper ex eis quod idem iusticia cognoverit et duxerit ordinandum. Datum Ricle, 5 idus December anno Domini MCCCXII.

23

LETTER TO EXIMENO PEDRO DE SALANOVA, JUSTICE OF ARAGON, REGARDING THE DOCUMENTS ON DEPOSIT IN THE EJEA HOUSE

9 December 1312　　　　　*Barcelona, ACA, RC 150, ff. 233v–234*

Iacobus etc. Dilecto suo Eximenio Petri de Salanova, iusticie Aragonum, salutem etc. Noveritis quod pro eo quare venerabilis abbatissa monasterii Sancte Marie de Salis de Stella nunc in nostra presencia constituta supplicando asseruit quedam privilegia et instrumenta <et> alias scripturas que sunt intus quedam caxiam dudum in domo Fratrum Minorum Exee sub depositi nomine positam faciencia, ut dicitur, quod <a> venerabili Constancia de Beireno (MS Beoreno) quondam abbatissa dicti monasterii et nomine <eius> pro dicto monasterio sibi debere tradi, providimus et ordinamus ut de privilegiis a<c> instrumentis ac scripturis predictis fiat quod faciendum fuerit, quod omnia ipsa privilegia, instrumenta ac quecumque scripture existencia intus caxiam predictam mittantur per dictum guardianum et conventum dicte domus de Exea, guardiano et conventui domus Fratrum Minorum Cesarauguste, tenenda et custodienda per eos et in domo predicta et hostendenda vobis quocienscumque ea infra ipsam domum videre volueritis, ac ordinando per vos iuxta formam inferius expressatam.

Quocirca vobis dicimus et mandamus quatenus vocatis qui fuerint evocandi visis et recognitis diligenter privilegiis et instrumentis ac aliis scripturis predictis decernatis et faciatis super eis fieri quod fuerit faciendum. Nos enim super hiis vobis auctoritate presencium comitimus vices nostras. Datum Ricle, 5 idus December anno Domini MCCC duodecimo.

24

JAMES II INFORMS HIS VICAR AND THE CURIA AT LERIDA AND THE PALLARS THAT AS A SPECIAL FAVOUR FR. PERE DE CERVERA, GUARDIAN OF THE HOUSE AT TÀRREGA, WILL BE ALLOWED A TWO-YEAR EXTENSION ON THE PAYMENT OF THE 400 SOUS HE OWES

13 December 1321　　　　　　　　*Barcelona, ACA, RC 172, f. 186v*

Ia<cobus> etc. fidelibus nostris vicario et curie Ilerde et Pallariense ceterisque off<icialibus> nostris vel eorum locum tenentibus ad quos presentes pervenerint etc. Noveritis nos, de speciali gracia, elongasse fratrem Petrum de Cervaria, guardianum Fratrum Minorum, Tarrage, et debitores et fideiussores, si qui pro eo obligati fuerunt, et bona eorum a solucione cuiusdam debiti quadringentorum solidorum iaccensium in quo tenebatur Petro Delfrau quondam civi Ilerde quod fusta quam ab eo emi<t> pro ecclesia sui monasterii dicte ville Tarrage hinc ad duos annos a dato (MS datum) presencium continue subsequentes, dum tamen aliter pro dicto debito a vobis non fuerit elongatus. Ita videlicet quod in fine dictorum duorum annorum solvat heredibus dicti Petri debitum supradictum, aliter quod lapso dicto termino possint iidem heredes vendere quandam bibliam quam pro dicto debito tenent pignori obligante.

　　Quare vobis dicimus et mandamus quatenus elongamentum nostrum predictum observetis et observari faciatis per dictum tempus, ut superius contine<tur>; non obstante quod dictum pignus traditum fuerit pro serenitate seu solucione debiti supradicti, iniungendo eisdem heredibus ne interim dictum librum distrahant, immo ipsum in loco tuto conservent. Datum Dertuse, Idus Decembris, 1321.

25

PRINCE ALFONSO ORDERS HIS OFFICIALS IN HUESCA TO SEE THAT WOMEN OF ILL REPUTE ARE REMOVED FROM THE VICINITY OF THE FRANCISCAN HOUSE

10 July 1322　　　　　　　　*Barcelona, ACA, RC 370, f. 245v*

Infans etc. fidelibus suis iusticie, iuratis et probis hominibus civitatis Osce etc. Ex parte Fratrum Minorum et aliquorum civiu<m> Osce prope eorundem fratrum monasterium habitancium, nobis extitit humiliter suplicatum quod cum quedam mulieres meretrices et vilis condicionis circa eorum monasterium comorentur et ibi faciant residenciam, faciendo a<c> comitendo turpia a<c> plurima inhonesta que non solum (MS solo) ipsis fratribus qui Deo morem habent (MS habere) et divina oficia administrare immo eorum vicinis ac eciam aliis per eundem locum existentibus tedium, gravamen et dampnum non modicum genera<n>tur, dignaremur sibi super hiis de opportuno remedio providere. Quare, supplicacione benigne admissa, vobis dicimus et mandamus quatenus mulieres illas que male fame aut vilis condicionis existant quas morari preveneritis, et dicto monasterio Fratrum Minorum usum ad populacionem regiam incontinenti reserveritis, a<c> ab eodem loco per vicum expellatis.

26

Bernat Venrell wishes to build close to the Franciscan house in Gerona

1 May 1323   *Barcelona, ACA, RC 372, f. 186r–v*

Infans etc. fideli suo baiulo Gerunde vel eius locum tenenti etc. Intelleximus ex parte guardiani et conventus domus Fratrum Minorum, Gerunde, quod Bernardus Venrelli, habitator civitatis eiusdem, contra voluntatem et in prejudicium conventus ipsius incepit edificare ac incitare, et intendit domos construhere super quodam pariete domus ipsius contra iuris equitatem ac predictorum fratrum ordinis honestatem. Cum autem ut percipimus dicti fratres coram episcopo Gerundense vel eius officiali per testes idoneos et alia documenta legittima proba-v<er>in<t> dictum pariete<m> existere dicte domus, nosque pati vidimus sicuti nec decet ordinem ipsum quem in iure fovere tenemur per quemquam curam iusticie in ali<qu>o molestari; propterea vobis dicimus et mandamus expresse quatenus si dicti fratres vobis ostend<er>int legittime se probasse coram dicto episcopo vel officiali e<iusde>m dictum parietem domus predicte nullatenus permittatis dictum Bernardum super dicto pariete aliquid construhere neque per eum in edificiis ibi construhendis vel aliter minus iuste dictis fratribus vel conventui eorundem inferri molestiam vel gravamen, immo fratres ipsos defendendo quantum iusticie paciatur inhibeatis ex parte nostra dicto Bernardo sub pena 500 solidorum pro iis exigenda, si locus afuerit quod ad construendum opus aliquid super dicto pariete <i>mmo procedat. Datum Barchinone, kalendas Madii, anno Domini MCCCXXIII.

27

Fr. Arnulf named executor of the Queen's will

25 July 1324 *Barcelona, ACA, RC 225, f. 286*

Iacobus etc. Venerabilibus et dilectis prelatis religiosis ordinis minorum ceterisque presentes litteras inspecturis etc. Tenore (MS teneor) presencium volumus fieri vobis notum quod religiosus vir frater Arnulfus dicti ordinis olim confessor clare memorie domine Marie regine Aragonum carisime consortis nostre capellanus et familiaris noster dilectus affectans saluti anime dicte regine providere et circa exequcionem testamenti seu ultime voluntatis eiusdem regine tam in comissis sibi quam aliis effectivam operam adhibere a tempore mortis dicte regine etc. de beneplacito nostro in hiis partibus morare traxit et in (MS in et) premissis assiduam et efficacem diligenciam perhibuit (MS probuit) et ea ad statum perfeccionis deduxit.

Mandamus cum dictus frater Arnulfus a nostra recedens presencia ad partes alias personaliter accedat quem ob sui probitate<m> et merita speciali prosequimur prerogativa favoris: idcirco vos et quo<s>libet vestrum rogamus incontinenti quatenus memoratum fratrem Arnulfum velitis honore nostri benigne recipere ac ipsum tanquam domesticum et capellanum nostrum cum socio et familia sua favorabiliter pertractare. In hoc autem nobis plurimum complacebitis et regra<cia>bimur vobis multum. Datum Barchinone, 8 Kalendas Augusti, 1324.

28

James II grants a safe-conduct allowing Fr. Berenguer Folcrà and his socius Fr. Pere d'Oliver to go to England

20 November 1325 *Barcelona, ACA, RC 339, f. 359v*

Iacobus etc. Religioso viro fratri Berengario Folcrandi de ordine Fratrum Minorum etc. Cum dudum a tunc generali ministro dicte ordinis nobis assumendi atque mittendi ad quascumque partes pro nostris negociis de fratribus ipsius ordinis fuerit concessa facultas vosque propterea tanquam idoneum pro quibusdam negociis incliti infantis Petri, carissimi filii nostri, Rippacurene comitis, ad partes Anglie providimus destinandum: idcirco de discrecione vestra probitate et fidelitate plene confisi volumus et auctoritate dicte licencie vobis iniungimus quatenus assumpto vobis in socio religioso fratre Petro de Olivariis dicti ordinis ad dictas partes Anglie visis presentibus vos personaliter conferatis pro dictis negociis inibi peragendis et feliciter actore domino procurandis. Datum Barchinone, 12 Kalendas Decembris, 1325.

29
James II orders his officials to respect the safe-conduct issued to Fr. Berenguer Folcrà and his socius

20 November 1325   *Barcelona, ACA, RC 339, f. 359v*

Iacobus etc. Universis et singulis officialibus et subditis atque devotis et amicis nostris presentes litteras inspecturis etc. Cum nos mittamus ad aliquas partes pro quibusdam negociis incliti infantis Petri, carissimi filii nostri, Rippacurene comitis, religiosum virum fratrem Berengarium Folcrandi de ordine Fratrum Minorum presentis exhibitorem: idcirco vobis officialibus et subditis nostris dicimus et mandamus vosque amicos et devotos vestros intente rogamus quatenus iamdictum fratrem Berengarium cum eius socio ire et transire libere permittentes, eosque amicabiliter pertractantes, nullum eis aut familie vel rebus ipsorum in eundo, stando vel redeundo disturbium, impedimentum vel contrarium faciatis aut fieri permittatis quinimmo provideatis eis si necesse fuerit de securo transitu et conductu. Datum Barchinone, 12 Kalendas Decembris, 1325.

30
The Justice of Daroca is ordered to see that prostitutes are removed from the vicinity of the Daroca house

10 March 1326 [1327]   *Barcelona, ACA, RC 379, ff. 212v–213v*

Infans etc. fideli suo iusticie Daroche vel eius locum tenenti etc. Aborrenda nimium et eciam stupenda ad nos quedam incongruitas quinimo si verum est enormitas delata; intelleximus siquidem pro parte religiosorum Fratrum Minorum, domus Daroce, quod nonnulle mulieres meretrices publice volumptantes carnis illicitas nequiter exquirentes, <a> maligno (MS maligne) ducte spiritu, et accedentes circa monasterium dictorum fratrum ubi divina officia ac alia pia opera ad cultum nominis Domini nostri, Ihesu Christi, et totius Catholice fidei, per eos ad illa exsequenda obsequia deputatos iugiter ac sollempniter celebrantur, abiecto timore Domenico inpudenter plura detestanda scelera et crimina aborrenda comitere publice non verentur que non solum divini nominis immo eciam dominacionis regie et honestatis fratrum ipsorum contemptum pariunt et derisum verum cum laudabili eorum fame et honestati morum posset multum propterea detrahi et eciam non modicum derogari.

Igitur nos, <vo>lentes eorum tam iustis necessitatibus providere et obviare negociis, ut convenit, perversorum, cum dicti fratres ad nostrum presidium duxerint humiliter succur<e>ndum, ea propter vobis dicimus et mandamus quatenus deceero studeatis totis viribus ac eciam quantumcumque poteritis pro<h>ibere nec in locis circun-stantibus monasterio prelibato per aliquem vel aliquas prefata crimina vel alia sordida aliquatenus comitantur, apponendo primitus penam quam quibuslibet transgressoribus quociens in eam inciderint penitus infligatis, videlicet quod in vestro carcere ad panem et aquam capte per decem dies continuos teneantur, ut ex impunita licencia aliis non crescat audacia delinquendi. Sic in premissis omnibus vos habere totaliter studeatis quod a dictis locis circumvicinis monasterio antedicto cunctam negociam expellatis, ut loca ipsa ab omnibus viciorum sordibus expientur dictique fratres devocius valeant Altissimo famulari.

Et ut mandatum nostrum plenius exequatur et ne dicta scelera seu alia inhonesta per dictas meretrices sive personas alias fieri valeant seu comiti circa loca predicta convicina monasterio supradicto, volumus quod inhibeatis sub pena superius posita ac preconitzari publice faciatis, ut a loco vocato La puent d'Archa usque ad posticum ville quod est propinquum domui dictorum Fratrum Minorum alique de predictis mulieribus non presumant ingredi vel morari ullo modo racionibus supradictis.

Nos enim per presentes damus potestatem et licenciam plenariam Quilicio Bosso iuniori, Iohanni de Faricia, Iordano de Rubiolis et Bartholomeo de Rubietis, vicinis ville predicte, quod possint dictas mulieres infra loca superius assignata quociens eas illic invenerint capere, vel capi facere, easque captas vobis statim ducere ac eciam tradere ut infligatis eisdem penam quam propterea incurrerint iuxta presentis littere nostre seriem et tenorem, taliter super hiis vos habendo, quod inobedienciam aliquam circa predicta vel aliquid predictorum vos incurrisse minime audiamus, quod si feceritis vos graviter punire nullatenus (c)omitemus. Datum Daroce, 6 Idus Marcii, 1326.

> **Note:** The notation "sine precio qua mendicantes" appears against the document, indicating that the mendicants were not required to pay transaction fees.

31

REFUSAL OF HEIRS TO PAY LEGACIES TO THE FRIARS MINOR AT VIC

9 December 1326　　　　　　　*Barcelona, ACA, RC 188, f. 152r–v*

Iacobus etc. Dilectis (MS dilecto) et fidelibus suis, vicario Ausone, Vici, Rivipulli et Rivipullene et Campi Rotundi et de Regali et baiulo civitatis Vici predicte vel eorum loca tenentibus, salutem etc. Intelleximus pro parte religiosi guardiani domus Fratrum Minorum dicte civitatis quod nonnulli civitatis ipsius qui deffuncti sunt fecerunt legata ad pias causas domui et fratribus supradictis quodque (MS quosque) heredes sive successores aut bonorum dictorum defunctorum detentores non curant satisfacere de bonis defunctorum predictorum legata, ut predicitur, ad dictas pias causas ordinata. Cumque fratres predictos ob proprietatem sui ordinis predictos heredes, successores ac detentores dictorum bonorum in dictis legatis coram vobis non deceat convenire: idcirco volumus vobisque dicimus et mandamus quatenus compellatis districte omnes illos et singulos heredes, successores aut bonorum detentores dictorum defunctorum ad persolvendum et dandum dicto guardiano seu procuratori domus predicte legata predicta ut proinde voluntates defunctorum predictorum ex legatis ipsis valeant adimpleri, reiectis maliciis, difugiis ac dilacionibus quibuscumque. Datum Barchinone, 14 Kalendas Ianuarii, 1326.

32

ALFONSO III ORDER HIS BAILIFF AT MONTBLANC
TO SEE THAT THE ROOF OF THE PORCH OF
THE FRANCISCAN HOUSE IS REPAIRED

10 October 1327　　　　　　　*Barcelona, ACA, RC 491, f. 22v*

Alfonsus, etc. fideli nostro baiulo Montisalbi vel eius locum tenenti etc. Cum tectum sive cohopertura cuiusdam porticus domus Fratrum Minorum dicte ville fuerint casualiter combusta dum nos hac vice in dicta domo hospitati fuimus et volumus quod ipsa porticus reficiatur seu reparetur, ita quod dictum tectum seu eius cohopertura extollantur seu eleventur altius quam erant tempore incendii supradicti. Propterea vobis dicimus et mandamus expresse quatenus, de quibuscumque denariis officii dicte baiulie vobis commisse, faciatis dictam porticum seu opus eius reparacionis fieri et compleri sub forma predicta, taliter faciendo quod ipsum opus omnino fiat et dilacione postposita compleatur, cum sit necessarium fratribus dicte domus nosque velimus ne in hiis dilacio vel deffectus aliquatenus apponatur. In hiis tamen ordinacionem per serenissimum dominum Iacobum, felicis memorie regem Aragonum, patrem nostrum, factam super suis debitis et iniuriis exsolvendis volumus observari. Mandamus itaque per presentes magistro racionali nostre curie aut alii cuicumque a vobis compotum recepturo (MS recoperto) quod id quod vos in opere dicte reparacionis posueritis seu convertendum duxeritis vobis in compoto recipiat et admittat. Datum Monte Albano, 4 Nonas Decembris, 1327.

33

ALFONSO III ORDERS HIS OFFICIALS IN CERVERA, TÀRREGA AND URGELL TO ENSURE THAT THE ESTATE OF BERENGUER DE ALMENARA IS SETTLED AND THE LEGACY TO THE FRANCISCANS PAID

29 December 1327 *Barcelona, ACA, RC 428, f. 37v (1)*

Alfonsus etc. Dilectis suis vicariis Cervare et Tarrege necnon et Urgelli vel eorum loca tenentibus etc. Ex parte Bonanati Carbonelli, civis Gerunde, procuratoris iconomi vel actoris ecclesie et conventus domus Fratrum Minorum, Gerunde, fuit propositum coram nobis quod cum Berengarius de Almenara quondam Guillelmo de Cerviano quondam in septem mille solidis Barchinone ex causa mutui teneretur dicti Guillelmi, erga dictum ordinem zelo devocionis accensus, donavit atque concessit etiam ac in suo ultimo testamento legavit ecclesie, domui ac conventui supradictis pietatis intuitu predictam peccunie quantitatem. Cumque dictus procurator, iure sibi cesso a manumissoribus et exequtoribus testamenti Guillelmi predicti in quantitate predicta, intendat eandem de bonis dicti Berengarii de Almenara recipere et habere suplicatum nobis sibi super hiis de oportuno remedio subvenire, nos (vobis) qui pia loca et religiosa<s> possessione<s> in iure specialius ceteris tenemur fovere, et vobis mandamus quatenus vobis constit<ut>o de premissis compellatis heredes, manumissores vel exequtores aut detentores bonorum predicti Berengarii de Almenara et bona ipsorum ad solvendum et tribuendum predicto Bonanato, nomine quo supra, predictam peccunie quantitatem procedendo in predictis breviter, summarie et de plano et absque strepitu et figura iudicii, prout in causis defunctorum et pauperum mendicantium est breviter procedendum, taliter quod ob defectum iusticie vel negligenciam non habeant ad nos recurrere iterate.

34

Fr. Sancho de Marra appeals to the king to help him recover the 150 Jaca sous owed him by the Jews, Vidal de Alcolea and his son Jahuda

20 March 1327 [1328]   *Barcelona, ACA, RC 430, f. 291r–v*

Alfonsus etc. fideli nostro baiulo Osce vel eius locum tenenti, salutem etc. Nostram adiens presenciam frater Sancius de Marra, ordinis Fratrum Minorum, exposuit humiliter coram nobis quod cum Guillelmus de Marra, vicinus Osce, pater ipsius fratris Sancii, feceri(n)t cessionem et donacionem eidem de centum quinquaginta solidis iaccensibus qui sibi debentur per Vitalem de Alcolea et Iahudanum eius filium, iudeos civitatis predicte, cum instrumento publico prout in eo lacius, dicitur, continetur. Et dictus licet frater Sancius de licencia sui (MS seu) maioris requisiverit iudeos ipsos ut dictam sibi quantitatem exsolverunt iuxta donacionem et cessionem, ut predicitur, sibi factam, iidem tamen iudei postponunt exsolvere quantitatem ipsam dicto fratri Sancio pretextu cuiusdam elongamenti quod ipsi iudei a vobis asserunt se habere. Verum cum dictus frater Sancius intendat ire ad studium (MS sedictum) et pro libris emendis habea(n)t dictam quantitatem valde necessariam, supplicaverit quod vobis ut ipsam sibi non o<b>stante elongamento predicto exsolvi facere mandaremus. Ideo supplicacione ipsa benigne suscepta, vobis dicimus et mandamus quatenus constit<uto> vobis de predictis compellatis cohercione debita predictos iudeos et eorum bona ad dandum et solvendum incontinenti dicto fratri Sancio vel cui voluerit quantitatem predictam non obstante dicto elongamento aut quovis alio facto vel faciendo iudeis predictis singulariter vel cum aliqua aliama. Cum dictus frater Sancius licenciam obtinuerit sui maioris petendi et recuperandi a iudeis predictis quantitatem ipsam ut constat per alberanum guardiani <et> conventus Cesarauguste, nos enim quodcumque elongamentum factum dictis iudeis quo<d> ad quantitatem ipsam presentibus revocamus et ipsos ad solvendum eandem statim per vos, ut predicitur, compelli volumus et iubemus etc.

35

ALFONSO III APPROVES THE STATUTES OF THE CONFRATERNITY
OF THE BLESSED VIRGIN MARY AND SAINT LOUIS AT HUESCA

4 October 1328　　　　　　　　*Barcelona, ACA, RC 476, ff. 230v–232*

Nos, Alfonsus etc. Visis quibusdam capitulis super confratria ad servicium et honorem domini nostri Ihesu Christi et beatissime gloriose virginis Marie, matris eius, ac beati Lodovici, episcopi et confessoris ordinis Fratrum Minorum, facta sive statuta per notarios civitatis Osce, quorum tenores tales esse noscuntur:

In nomine Sancte Trinitatis et individue unitatis, patris et filii et Spiritus Sancti Amen. Hec est carta confratrie scriptorum sive notariorum iuratorum civitatis Osce, facta ad honorem Sancti Spiritus qui in nomine Domini congregatos facit unum cor et animam unam in Domino et unanimos in gaudio et concorditer habitare iuxta salmistam qui dicit "Ecce quam bonum et quam iucundum habitare fratres in unum." Idcirco predicti scriptores sive notarii, Sancti Spiritus consilio inspirati cor unum et animam unam habere in Domino cupientes ad domum Fratrum Minorum domus Osce convenerunt super die Dominica, 2 nonas Septembris, anno Domini 1328, et eorundem fratrum capitulum intervenerunt qui congregato Fratrum Minorum conventu, et venerabilibus fratre Sancio Luppi de Ajerbio, custode Cesarauguste, et fratre Nicholas de la Naia tunc g<u>ardiano Osce, et toto conventu instanter et humiliter postularunt ut ipsos bonorum suorum spirit<u>alium participes facerent et consortes. Insuper ibidem suum laudabile propositum expresserunt, videlicet quod confratriam suam volebant ad honorem et invocacionem beati Lodovici (MS Ledovici) ordinis Fratrum Minorum perpetuo et inviolabiliter instituere, tam pro se quam pro omnibus successoribus in officio scribanie, ut non solum haberent fratres supradicti conventus tanquam confratres et socios set quasi patres et correctores ad dirigendum et corrigendum si quid in ipsa confratria et eciam in confratribus et in ipso officio notarii indecens videretur.

Predicti vero custos et g<u>ardianus totusque conventus voluntarie et liberaliter concesserunt quod venerabiles scriptores petebant humiliter et instanter, recipientes eos (MS res) in confratres suos et beati Lodevici tam ipsos presentes quam eciam suos in posterum successores, vincientes (MS venientes) eos suo monasterio perpetuo vinculo caritatis, eisdem insuper scriptoribus et omnibus aliis confratribus presentibus et futuris huius confratrie scriptorum, que est ad honorem et invocacionem beati Lodevici ex promissione inmutabili unanimiter instituta, concedentes tam in vita quam in morte participacionem in omnibus bonis videlicet missis, oracionibus, ieiuniis, abstinenciis, vigiliis, laboribus, predicacionibus, confessionibus, ceterisque huiusmodi que per confratres conventus Osce fieri dederit actor bonorum omnium Dei filius dominus Ihesus Christus, ordinantes nichilominus quod cum aliquis confrater huius confratrie beati Lodovici migraverit ab hac luce maiorales confratrie confratres sui obitum denuncient guardiano Fratrum Minorum domus Osce vel sui tenenti locum ibidem et tunc ipse g<u>ardianus vel tenens locum animam defuncti confratris devote in capitulo suo fratrum oracionibus recomendet et faciat pro eo oraciones fieri speciales.

Instituta est igitur hec confratria scriptorum iuratorum civitatis Osce predicte in conventum Fratrum Minorum, Osce, a scriptoribus qui tunc temporis erant in officio notarie, quam confratriam constituerunt tam pro se quam eciam pro suis successoribus in ipso officio, perpetuo et inmutabiliter ad honorem Domini nostri Ihesu Christi et gloriose beate Marie virginis, matris eius, et specialiter ad honorem et invocacionem beati Lodovici necnon aliorum sanctorum anno, die et loco prefixo, in salutem animarum suarum et parentuum suorum et omnium fidel(li)ium tam vivorum quam eciam defunctorum, salva tamen semper et ubique fidelitate, reverencia et iurediccione illustrissimi domini regis et tocius populi civitatis Osce, confratriam hanc constituerunt et statuta bona acque (MS adque) utilia unanimiter dederunt per que sciant tam concorditer inter se debeant vivere in officio suo quam fideliter se habere.

In primis, statuimus quod in omnibus capitulis nostris generalibus, scilicet quandocumque comede<n>tur in confratria, statim in sequenti die ad domum Fratrum Minorum omnes confratres conveniant simul, et ibi missa pro defunctis confratribus celebretur. Post missam vero intrent capitulum, et antequam aliud ibi tractent si aliquis confrater vel aliquis frater de conventu Osce decesserit illo anno, eorum obitus coram confratribus nuncietur, ut fiat pro defuncto fratre conventus Fratrum Minorum quicquid pro confratribus nostris defunctis constituimus faciendum; postquam il<l>o obitus confratrum et fratrum coram omnibus et capitulo fuerit recitatus et oracio que eis facta fuerit statim inmediate legatur hec et ordinatio confratrie tota usque ad finem ne de hac tam sancta et utili ordinacione per oblivionem aliquid negligatur; que cum tota usque ad finem perlecta fuerit, tunc tractent inter se si quid ad utilitatem et promocionem confratrie et eciam ad concordacionem confratrum fuerit pertractandum.

Item: statuimus quod si aliquis confrater huius tam venerabilis confratrie in peccato mortali fuerit manifeste corrigatur secreto a maioralibus confratrie, que si se pro eis non emendaverit, tunc publice coram omnibus in nostro capitulo corrigatur. Si autem nec sic vitam suam voluerit emendare, tunc tanquam maledictus et reprobus et indignus de hac tam sancta et reverenda confratria ac societate nostra, quousque se correxerit, expellatur; si vero postea vitam suam emendaverit et in capitulo misericordiam petierit, ad nostram confratriam et societatem misericorditer admitatur.

Item: statuimus siquidem ut, per singulos menses prima Dominica mensis, omnes confratres ubi maiorales concordaverint ad capitulu < m > conveniant ad confratrie negocia pertractanda et excessus confratruum debite corrigendos; et si quis confratruum ad capitulum convenire neglexerit, si sanus in civitate fuerit et nuncium maioralis audierit per se vel per alium cui nuncius ipse dixerit, persolvat maioralibus ad opus confratrie mediam libram cere nisi iustam excusacionem (MS excusacionis) tamen habuerit, ut est dictum.

Item: statuimus quod si aliquis confrater in dicta civitate infirmus fuerit, alii confratres ipsum visitent et de salute anime sue illi consulant, et si non habet unde vivat confratres provideant ei in necessariis suis. Si aliquis autem confrater hobierit et tam pauper fuerit quod de suo non posset sepelliri, de confratria sepelliatur; et audito precone, omnes confratres ad vigiliam veniant, sequenti autem die omnes confratres cum illo eant ad ecclesiam et ipsi confratres eum deferant et omnes in manibus cereos teneant, donec corpus fuerit confectum sepulture. Interim dum missa celebrabitur singuli singulos donent denarios qui in pane pauperibus dividantur.

Item: generaliter statuimus quod unusquisque confrater in suo obitu dimitat V solidos iaccenses confratrie; quilibet confrater a maioralibus pro culpa sui pignoratus aut pignorari iussus pignus pignoratori paciente dimitat; si vero rebellis extiterit et dictum pignus noluerit pignoranti dabit V solidos confratrie.

Item: statuimus siquidem quod omni tempore comedant omnes insimul semel in anno in festivitate beati Lodovici.

Item: statuimus quod si aliquis intrare voluerit in hac sancta confratria et societate, veniat in capitulo; et si omnibus confratribus vel maiori et seniori parti placuerit, recipiant eum in confratr<i>am, et donet viginti solidos iaccenses confratrie. Tamen confratres possint introitum ipsius confratrie augmentare, si eis expediens videatur.

Item: statuimus similiter quod quilibet confrater teneatur consulere confratri suo in oficio scribanie, si ab aliquo confratre fuerit requisitus.

Item: statuimus quod una die in qualibet septimana omnes confratres bene (MS bone) mane teneantur ire ad ecclesiam beati Francischi, et ibi in altari beati Lodovici faciant missam celebrari ad honorem beate Marie virginis que est principium totius boni et efectum. Faciant confratres et teneantur dare singulos denarios pro cereis manutenendis.

Item: cum omnes confratres dividentes esse non possint, statuimus quod confratria de conventu emat unum pannum procureum quod ponatur supra corpus confratris defuncti, et faciant duos cereos sive brandones qui deferantur ante crucem, cum corpus confratris defuncti portetur ad sepelliendum.

Ideo ad dictorum notariorum humilis suplicacionis instanciam laudamus, aprobamus, confirmamus acque (MS adque) ratificamus confratriam et capitula supradicta necnon contenta in eis, salvis tamen semper nobis et nostris fidelitate reverencia et iurisdiccione ac dominio nostri et successorum nostrorum in omnibus sicut decet.

In cuius rei testimonium presentem cartam nostram inde fieri iussimus, et nostro sigillo appendicio roborari.

Datum Barchinone, 4 nonas Octobre, anno Domini MCCCXXVIII.

Guillelmus de Villa, mandato regio, causa domini Infantis Petri.

Signum: Alfonsi, Dei gratia regis Aragonum, Valencie, Sardinie et Corsice ac comitis Barchinone.

Testes sunt: Infans Petrus, Rippacorcie et Impuriarum comes, frater dicti domini regis.

Infans Raimundus Berengarii, comes montanarum de Pradis, frater dicti domini regis.

Reverendus Petrus Cesarauguste, archiepiscopus domini regis cancellarius.

Otho de Montechateno, Guillelmus de Cervilione; fuit clausum per Guillelmum de Villa, scriptorem dicti domini regis.

Datum Barchinone, 4 Nonas Octobris, 1328.

36

MATEU MIGUEL IS APPREHENDED BY THE JUSTICE OF XÀTIVA IN THE DORMITORY OF THE FRANCISCAN HOUSE

21 October 1328   *Barcelona, ACA, RC 430, f. 53r-v*

Alfonsus etc. fideli suo iusticie Xative vel eius locum tenenti, salutem etc. Cum vos extraxeritis ut fertur de dormitorio Fratrum Minorum dicte ville Matheum Michelis predicte ville occasione invasionis per eum facte Antonio Sesmoles in domo sua propia et abscisionis pugni desteri et dubitetis sentencialiter procedere contra eum pro eo quia allegatur per ipsam vitam et membram per vos se salvari debere. Idcirco vobis dicimus et mandamus quatenus in predicto negocio usque ad sentenciam procedatis et processum inde factum ad cancellariam nostram sub sigillo nostro mitatis ut possimus super eo mandare fieri quod fuerit racione.

37

ALFONSO III MAKES A CONCESSION OF GRAIN TO THE FRANCISCANS AT TARRAGONA, ALLOWING THEM TO TAKE IT FROM TORTOSA

1 December 1328   *Barcelona, ACA, RC 477, f. 67r-v*

Nos Alfonsus etc. Compacientes inopie religiosorum Fratrum Minorum, domus Terrachone necnon propter affeccionem quam beato Francisco et eius ordini gerimus et habemus, ut prefati guardianus et conventus onera expensarum quibus nunc sufficere nequeunt valeant facilius supportare, cum presenti carta nostra concedimus dictis guardiano et conventui quod, non obstante inhibicione quacumque facta vel eciam facienda, possint extrahere seu extrahi facere de civitate Dertuse anno quolibet ducenta kafficia tritici, defferenda vel transmittenda ad civitatem Terrachone, racione provisionis fratrum ipsorum. Mandantes per presentem baiulo Dertuse necnon quibuscumque aliis officialibus nostris, presentibus et futuris, quatenus observan<te>s concessionem nostram huiusmodi, super extrahendis dictis ducentis kafficiis tritici de dicta civitate anno quolibet et deferendis ac mittendis ad civitatem Terrachone predictam, iamdictis guardiano et conventui vel alicui alii eorum nomine dictum triticum extrahenti nullum impedimentum seu obstaculum apponeant seu per aliquos apponi permittant, quin immo ipsum triticum extrahi absque aliqua contradiccione permittant. Intendimus tamen servare volentes capitulum super hoc factum in generali curia Gerundense quod dicti guardianus et conventus extrahi faciant dictum triticum et quod graciam huius concessionis nostre non possint dare, vendere aut in alium transferre, quod si fecerint non valeat gracia supradicta. In cuius rei testimonium presentem cartam nostram inde fieri iussimus nostro sigillo munitam. Datum Ilerde, Kalendas Decembris, 1328.

38

Alfonso III requests Bishop Gaston of Gerona to ensure that Bertran, son of Bertran de Sa Mas of Castellfollet, is not compelled to enter the Order of Friars Minor

17 February 1328 [1329] *Barcelona, ACA, RC 438, ff. 43v–44*

Alfonsus etc. Venerabili in Christo patri Gastono, divina providencia Gerundensi episcopo, ceteris episcopis infra dominacionem nostram constitutis eorumque vicariis seu officialibus ad quos presentes pervenerint, salutem etc. Intelleximus per fidelem nostrum Bertrandum de Ça Maso de Castrofolleto quod Fratres Minores civitatis Gerunde mulcendo Bertrandum filium suum ipsum contra voluntatem et consensum ipsius Bertrandi in eorum ordine receperint inducendo ei habitum ordinis supradicte. Cum auctorari nullatenus blandiciis set proprio motu et ex disposicione divina ingredi debeat ipsum ordinem, vos requirimus et rogamus quatenus ipsum Bertrandum poni faciatis in loco idoneo, et si habitum elegerit, et remaneat in dicto ordine; si vero voluerit laicaliter conversari, ipsum dicto patri suo, expulso habitu, faciatis deliberari et tradi, cavendo ne per aliquos valeat contra eius propositum informari.

39

Alfonso III informs his bailiff in Berga that the Franciscans want their house there to be reestablished

27 March 1329 *Barcelona, ACA, RC 438, ff. 43v–44*

Alfonsus etc. fideli suo baiulo Berge vel eius locum tenenti, salutem et graciam. Pro parte guardiani et conventus Fratrum Minorum, civitatis Vici, fuit nobis humiliter demonstratum quod tunc olim in villa Berge esset monasterium Fratrum Minorum, quod monasterium propter defectum victus et aliorum necessariorum fratres eiusdem habuerunt dimittere. Quia nunc dicta villa et populus (MS popules) eiusdem incrementum suscepit et conventus ipsorum fratrum potuerit inibi plene vivere et habere necessaria ad sustentacionem vite, universitas ville predicte requisivit, ut fertur, quod fratres predicti ordinis reedificerent monasterium supradictum.

Ex quo dicti fratres volunt et intendunt ipsum monasterium construere in loco quo esse consueverat ab antiquo. Cum autem abbatissa monasterii Sancte Marie Vallislaure, ordinis Cisterciensis, cum aliquibus monialibus suis velit de novo iuxta locum predictum ubi fratres predictum monasterium habuerunt suum monasterium construere in dampnum et preiudicium, ut asseritur, ordinis supradicti ac contra privilegium seu rescriptum a sede apostolica indultum fratribus supradictis: idcirco ad ipsorum fratrum supplicacionem humilem nobis prelibatam, vobis dicimus et mandamus quatenus non permittatis construi monasterium dominarum ipsarum iuxta monasterium dictorum fratrum contra formam rescripti seu privilegii supradicti, nisi aliqua iusta racio (MS racione) seu raciones in contrarium pro ipsis dominarum opposite fuerint que obsistant. Quas curie nostre statim sub sigillo nostro mittatis, ut possimus super eisdem mandare fieri quod fuerit racionis, interim vobis volumus (MS velimus) ac vobis mandamus non faciatis supersedere in opere supradicto. Datum Barchinone, 6 Kalendas Aprilis, 1329.

40

CONCERNING THE DOCUMENTS ON DEPOSIT IN THE BARCELONA
HOUSE RELATING TO THE MURDER OF FRANCESC EXAMENIS

13 February 1329 [1330]   *Barcelona, ACA, RC 532, f. 57v*

Alfonsus etc. Dilectis et fidelibus (MS dilecto et fideli) suis vicario et subvicario Barchinone presentibus et qui pro tempore fuerint vel eorum loca tenentibus, salutem et dileccionem. Cum nos negocium inquisicionis facte super morte perpetrata in persona Francisci Exeminis, civis Barchinone, cuius processus est depositus in domibus Fratrum Minorum, civitatis Barchinone, in quadam caxia, ad instanciam Gisperti Examinis patris dicti Francischi quondam nobis vel dum nos a Cathalonia abfuerimus procuratori generali nostro vel eius vices gerenti in Cathalonia duxerimus reservandum: idcirco vobis dicimus et mandamus quatenus diffinicionem aliquam seu remissionem de iamdicta morte alicui minime faciatis. Que si per vos facte fuerint ipsas diffinicionem et remissionem tenore presencium decernimus non valere. Mandantes insuper vobis dicto vicario quatenus in dicta caxia que est in dictis domibus Fratrum Minorum, faciatis fieri duas diversas clausuras de quibus unam clavem teneant consiliarii civitatis Barchinone et aliam pater seu amici dicti Francischi ne iamdictus processus perdi possit seu per aliquos modo quolibet occultari. Per hec tamen non intendimus prohibere vobis quando possitis procedere ad persequcionem ac capcionem illorum qui comiserunt mortem predictam, immo mandamus quod ad eorum capcionem procedatis, et cum eos vel eorum aliquem ceperitis aut capi fec\<er\>itis, id nobis vel dicto procuratori nostro seu eius vices gerenti in Cathalone protinus intimetis. Datum Terrachone sub nostro sigilo secreto, Idus Februarii, 1329.

41

ALFONSO III ASKS FERRER DE LILLET, GENERAL BAILIFF FOR CATALONIA, TO SEE THAT 500 SOUS SENT WITH THE PRESENT LETTER ARE USED TO REPAIR THE FRANCISCAN HOUSE AT TARRAGONA

30 May 1330   *Barcelona, ACA, RC 495, f. 98r-v*

Alfonsus, etc. Dilecto consiliario suo Ferrario de Lilleto, baiulo Cathalonie generali, salutem etc. Cum nos venerabili et religioso guardiano et conventui Fratrum Minorum, domus Terrachone, pro refeccione seu construccione cuiusdam clausure orti que diruta extitit, nobis in dicta domo presentibus, quingentos solidos Barchinone, amore Dei, duxerimus concedendos, quos quidem quingentos solidos, de iuribus et proventibus baiulie vobis commisse, eisdem fratribus et conventui tribui volumus et exsolvi: idcirco vobis dicimus et expresse mandamus quatenus, de iuribus et proventibus dicte baiulie, tribuatis et solvatis dictis guardiano ac conventui vel cui loco sui voluerit quingentos solidos Barchinone supradictos, non obstantibus aliquibus assignacionibus piis factis, cum nos amore Dei et pietatis intuitu concessionem predictam duxerimus faciendam. Datum Ilerde, 3 Kalendas Iunii, 1330.

42

ALFONSO III ORDERS BISHOP GUIU OF SARDINIA NOT TO
PERSECUTE MEMBERS OF THE THIRD ORDER OF SAINT FRANCIS

2 June 1330   *Barcelona, ACA, RC 510, f. 209r–v*

Alfonsus etc. Reverendo in Christo patri fratri Guidoni, divina providencia Tirene et Arborene archiepiscopo, consiliario nostro dilecto, salutem etc. Iam nos scripsisse vobis recolimus ut, intuitu Dei et consideracione nostri qui beatum Franciscum et eius ordinem devocione affectuosa et sincera dileccione complectimur, fratres eiusdem ordinis occulo pio respicientes commendatos habeatis et tanquam pastor bonus et pater pius eos defendetis ab iniustis persecutoribus et oppressoribus eorundem: verum ut fidedigna relacione comperimus vos, et onere litteris nostris contemptis ac rogaminibus spretis, eosdem fratres verbis ac minis et factis multipliciter agravatis ac agravari a vestris clericis indebite et contra iusticiam sustinetis.

Cum enim declaratum sit per constitucionem domini Pape Iohannis vicesimi secundi peccata semel fratribus predicatoribus et minoribus confessa non teneri confitentes sacerdotibus parrochialibus iterum confiteri, vestre diocesis ecclesiam nisi eadem peccata numero eis confiteantur nolunt sacramenta ecclesiastica ministrare in mortis articulo constitu<i>tis, quod quidem impium sit et errorem constituit eadem et veridica<m> racione manifestat. Ceterum cum Ordo Fratrum et Sororum de Penitencia qui comuniter de Tercia Regula nuncupatur sit a beato Francisco institutus, et ab ecclesia approbatus, et a multis summis pontificibus confirmatus ac novissime diebus istis et <a> domino Papa Iohanne approbatus et confirmatus, sicut habere eiusdem auctoritatem que in terris istis et aliis habent(ur) clarissime comprobant et ostendunt; vos eundem ordinem asseritis publice fore tassatum et anullatum; personam quod eiusdem ordinis compellitis habitum deponere, et nisi h<ec> faciant in termino iam a vobis, ut dicitur, statuto cominatus estis, quod contra eos tamquam contra hereticos procedetis. Super qua re plene non sufficimus admirari quod cum hic tercius ordo vigeat Avinione ubi nunc est Romana Curia et in provincia aliisque regionibus tam citra quam ultra montanis quorum vos hoc toti mundo tam certum in partibus illis in dubium revocatis. Rogamus igitur iterum et requirimus ut ab hiis protinus abstineatis, et Fratres Minores ac illos de tercia regula beati Francisci nec in hiis nec in aliis molestetis; alias cum reges et principes teneantur omni(a) lege pauperes ac personas miserabiles defensare, et eciam nobis in speciali per summum pontificem fratrum beati Francisci in regnis et terris nostris commorantium cura et tuicio sit comissa huiusmodi, alias ut contra ipsos iniurias non possemus continentibus occulis pertransire vel quomodolibet tolerare et pro certo taliter facerem<us> quod esset aliis in exemplum. Datum Ilerde, 4 Nonas Iunii, 1330.

43

ALFONSO III TELLS HIS VICAR AT GERONA THAT THE FRANCISCANS MAY REMOVE THE BODY OF DALMAU DE VILAR FROM THE GALLOWS AND BURY IT IN THEIR CEMETERY

13 June 1331 *Barcelona, ACA, RC 483, f. 207v*

Alfonsus etc. Dilecto suo vicario Gerunde et Bisulduni vel eius locum tenenti, salutem etc. Cum nos, ad supplicacionem et preces religiosi fratris Dalmacii de Mansulino, de ordine Fratrum Minorum, concesserimus et velimus quod Dalmacius de Vilario, qui nuper suis exigentibus demeritis ad ultimum supplicium condempnatus extitit, amoveatur a furcis tradaturque ecclesiastice sepulture, ea propter vobis dicimus et expresse mandamus quatenus visis presentibus corpus prefati Dalmacii de Vilario a furcis removeri faciatis ac tradi religiosis Fratribus Minoribus conventus Gerunde, ut ipsum in eorum cimiterio sine omni contradiccione tradi valeant ecclesiastice sepulture. Et hoc aliquatenus non mutetis. Datum Barchinone, Idus Iunii, 1331.

44

ON BEHALF OF THE FRANCISCANS AT TERUEL ALFONSO ORDERS THAT THE TWO CHALICES AND PATENS PAWNED BY MASTER DOMINGO OF PERPIGNAN, A SURGEON AT TERUEL, BE REDEEMED

11 January 1332 [1333] *Barcelona, ACA, RC 456, f. 36r-v*

Alfonsus etc. fideli nostro iudici Turolii vel eius locum tenenti, salutem etc. Ex parte guardiani fratrum <et> conventus Fratrum Minorum Turolii fuit nobis expositum quod ipsi compacientes paupertati magistri Dominici de Perpiniano, cirurgici de Turolio, quia valde oppressus per aliquos eius creditores erat, ne propter debita in quibus tenebatur caperetur vel aliter contra eundem procederetur, mutuarunt eidem duos calices cum eorum patenis ob hoc ut super eis reciperetur aliqua manuleuta. Qui magister Dominicus manulevavit trecentos solidos iaccenses super ipsis. Postea ille qui dictos calices pignori tenebat, videns quod dictus magister non <vol>ebat redimere dictos calices, et eosdem posuit ad l<eu>dendum, quos trescentos solidos dicti fratres ne dicti in alios transferentur exsolvere habuerint. Verum cum dictus magister Dominicus, pluries per dictos fratres requisitus, contradicat, ut dicitur, eisdem fratribus exsolvere dictam peccunie quantitatem, et propterea pluries feceri(n)nt missiones (MS massiones): idcirco ad supplicacionem dictorum guardiani et fratrum vobis dicimus et mandamus quatenus de predictis nobis constituto eundem magistrum Dominicum debite compellatis ad solvendum dictis g<u>ardiano et Fratribus Minoribus dictam pecunie quantitatem cum dampnis et missionibus per eos sustentis magistri Dominici, procedendo in predictis breviter, simpliciter, et de plano prout de foro et racione fuerit faciendum. Datum Valencie, 3 Idus Ianuarii, 1332.

45

ALFONSO III ORDERS HIS BAILIFF IN VIC TO RECOVER THE
LEGACY OF FERRER DE BRUGUERA FOR THE FRANCISCANS AT VIC

24 April 1333 *Barcelona, ACA, 462, ff. 18v-19*

Alfonsus etc. Dilecto nostro vicario et baiulo civitatis Vici vel eius locum tenenti, salutem etc. Procurator conventus Fratrum Minorum civitatis eiusdem nostri baiuli peticionem monstravit quod Ferrarius de Brugeria, quondam civis dicte civitatis, in vita sua suum ultimum condidit testamentum in quo inter cetera legavit, ut dicitur, fratribus dicti ordinis omnia bona sua. Et cum subsequenter post dictum testamentum conditum infirmitatem demencie incurrisset, fuit sibi per vos, dictum vicarium et baiulum, ut dicitur, dictus curator, videlicet Berengarius Negrelli, civis civitatis predicte. Qui Berengarius, mortuo dicto Ferrario, contra ius et iusticiam retinuit et retinet dicta bona ut asseritur penes eum, pretendens quod ad uxorem ipsius Berengarii pertinent ipsa bona, sic quod dicti fratres legatum ipsum habere non possunt, cum executores dicti testamenti bona dicti Ferrarii non habeant seu possideant. Sane, cum dictus Berengarius qui ut curator dicta bona recepit non possit causam possessionis mutare quinimo, quia finitum est officium dicte cure, debeat compotum reddere <de> administratis per eum in dicta bona ac reliqua restituere vobis dicto baiulo qui ea sibi tradidistis. Ea propter pro parte procuratoris conventus predicti fuit nobis humiliter supplicatum ut super hiis dignaremur eidem de iusticie remedio providere. Qua supplicacione benigne suscepta, vobis dicimus et mandamus quatenus, vocatis qui fuerint evocandi, compellatis curacionem predictam iuris remediis quibus poteritis ad reddendum vobis et dictis manumissoribus compotum de receptis gestis et adminis<tracion>ibus per eum nominibus executoriis supradictis, et ad restituendum reliqua manumissoribus supradictis ut voluntatem eiusdem deffuncti valeant adimplere seu ducere ad effectum, et procedendo s<iqu>idem in predictis prout de iur<e> et racione fuerit faciendum. Enim nos vobis super premissa plenarie comittimus vices nostras etc. Datum Montealbano, 8 Kalendas Madii, 1333.

46

ALFONSO III ORDERS VICARS, BAILIFFS AND OFFICIALS TO ENSURE THAT LEGACIES MADE TO THE FRANCISCANS OF CERVERA ARE PAID

25 April 1333   *Barcelona, ACA, RC 462, ff. 25v-26*

Alfonsus etc. Dilectis et fidelibus suis vicariis, baiulis aliisque officialibus nostris, presentibus et futuris, vel eorum loca tenentibus ad quos presentes pervenerint, salutem etc. Licet exigente iusticia quibuslibet subditis nostris quod summa est reddi cupiamus, attamen religiosis presertim mendicantibus, tanto in eorum iure favorabilius adesse nos convenit quanto eorum condicio qui observanciam regularem ad Dei servicium elegerunt exposcat ut eis circa premissa debiti favoris suffragium impendatur. Cum igitur pro parte guardiani et conventus Fratrum Minorum Cervarie fuerit expositum coram nobis quod aliqui degentes in villa et vicaria Cervarie ac aliis locis Cathalonie tam ex legatis testamentariis quam aliter tenentur eisdem guardiano et conventui in aliquibus peccunie quantitatibus quas eisdem indebite, ut asseritur, solvere contradicunt: idcirco cum ex summa paupertate ipsorum cui se voluntarie submiserunt pie consideracionis inducamur affectu ut erga eos favorabilis pietatis suffragio succurramus, vobis et vestrum cuilibet et expresse percipiendo mandamus quatenus quilibet vestrum infra iurisdiccionem sibi comissam omnes illos quos invenire poteritis in aliquo teneri eisdem guardiano et conventui ad dandum et solvendum eisdem id in quo sibi tene<n>tur cohercione debita compellatis, sic in hiis sollicite et favorabiliter vos habendo, quod satisfaciendo celeriter eisdem fratribus in iusticia possitis de diligencia merito comendari. Datum in Montealbano, 7 Kalendas Madii, 1333.

47

ALFONSO III WRITES TO HIS COUNSELLOR FERRER DE LILLET, GENERAL BAILIFF FOR CATALONIA, ABOUT THE DISPUTE BETWEEN THE MONASTERY OF VALLDAURA AND THE FRANCISCANS IN BERGA

25 April 1333 *Barcelona, ACA, RC 461, f. 180*

Alfonsus etc. Dilecto consiliario nostro Ferrario de Lilleto, baiulo Cathalonie generali, salutem etc. Cum inter sindicos universitatis proborum hominum ville Berge ex una parte, et religiosos Fratres Minores ex altera, questionis materia sit exorta, super eo videlicet quod ipsi Minores pretextu licencie sine consensu et voluntate, ut asseritur, dicte universitatis obtente de construhendo monasterio infra vel iuxta ipsam villam, intendunt construhere ipsum monasterium in quodam loco nuncupato els Palomers iuxta locum quem universitas supradicta destinaverat ac deputaverat abbat<iss>e monasterii de Valldaura pro translatando inibi monasterium ipsum. Et asseritur (MS asseratur) per sindicos universitatis predicte quod si constructio monasterii dictorum Minorum fieret in loco predicto, esset, ex causis coram vobis propositis, valde dampnosum dicte ville et habitatoribus eiusdem possetque proinde magnum scandalum suboriri: idcirco cum regiam deceat dignitatem subdictorum scandalis et periculis precavere (MS precautem), vobis dicimus et mandamus quatenus, cum in mora versetur periculum, incontinenti aliis pretermissis ad dictam villam Berge personaliter accedendo, predictis partibus evocatis auditisque (et) collectis plenius racionibus eorundem, inducatis illis viis et modis competentibus quibus vobis videbitur partes predictas ad avinenciam seu composicionem premissorum faciendam, taliter quod dicti fratres, quos ex helemosinis populi monasterium supradictum hedificare et <in> vita eorum ministrare opportet, cum beneplacito dicte universitatis locum habeant competentem, ipsaque universitas excitetur ad beneffaciendum et erogandum in predictis que pia opera contrahere preterdubio dinoscuntur. Et si dictas partes ad concordiam reducere minime volueritis, faciatis in premissis et dirimatis parcium auditis racionibus quod de iure et racione inveneritis faciendum. Nos enim super hiis et dependentibus, emergentibus seu ea tangentibus, vobis per presentes comitimus plenarie vices nostras. Datum Montealbano, 7 Kalendas Madii, 1333.

48

ALFONSO III WRITES TO PRINCE PETER, COUNT OF RIBAGORZA AND AMPURIAS, REGARDING FIVE SARDINIANS WRONGLY CAPTURED IN THE PORT OF LLENÇÀ IN CATALONIA

30 March 1333　　　　　　　　　　*Barcelona, ACA, RC 457, f. 246v*

Alfonsus etc. Inclito infanti Petro, carissimo fratri nostro Rippacurrie et Impure comiti salutem etc. Scire vos volumus pro parte guardiani domus Fratrum Minorum de Sassero nobis fuisse expositum reverenter quod nuper in quodam lembo, qui propter maris et venti impetum apellere habuit in loco de Lançano, era<n>t quedam mulier et duo homines sardi de Sassero et alii duo de Alguerio qui una cum lembo iamdicto et rebus in eo sistentibus fuerunt in dicto loco retenti et adhuc capti detinentur, credendo ipsos esse ianuenses. Cum autem non sit decens quod subditi nostri per aliquem in terris nostris potissime capti detineantur absque aliqua iusta causa, propterea vos requirimus et rogamus quatenus vobis constituto predictos captos de locis ipsis esse et non ianuenses a capcione qua detinentur nisi aliud iustum oppositum fuerit quod obsistat deliberari faciatis ac eis restitui bona sua que in lembo ipso <cum> eis capta fuerunt. Datum Barchinone, 3 Kalendas Aprilis, 1333.

49

LETTER ADDRESSED TO FR. PONS CARBONELL WHEN HE WAS STAYING IN THE HOUSE OF THE PATRIARCH OF ALEXANDRIA

<1334>　　　　　　　　　*Barcelona, ACA, Cartas reales, Alfonso III,*
　　　　　　　　　　　　　　　　　caja 34, no. 12, s.a.

Al molt honrat i religiós (MS relagios) frare, Pons Carbonel<l>, de mi En Simó(n) Ricart, saluts ab tota reverència i honor. Bé sabetz, Senyor, que lonch temps ha que jo vaig dar<r>era Monsenyor lo Patriarque per què pog\<u\>és anar al Sant Sapulcre de Iherusalem i el\<l\>, per bontat sua, avie'n mes tostemps en gran esperanse per què é entés que l'honrat En Go\<n\>salbo García hi deu enguany anar per què'n clam mercè que'm comanetz en gràcia (MS gran) del molt alt Monsenyor lo Patriarque i que'l pregetz qui m'endr\<eç\>és que jo pusqué anar enguany ab lo dit Go\<n\>salbo.

> Note: Other documents found in this envelope date from the year 1334. A note on the reverse of the letter states: "A l'honrat relagiós frare Pons Carbonel\<l\> en caçe del molt alt senyor patriarque d'Alexandria."

50

ALFONSO III WRITES TO THE BAILIFF OF BERGA
CONCERNING THE REESTABLISHMENT OF THE BERGA HOUSE

24 June 1334   *Barcelona, ACA, RC 465, f. 233v*

Alfonsus etc. fideli suo Raimundo de Obena, baiulo Berge, salutem etc. Vos ignorare non credimus qualiter nos, ob devocionem integram quam ad beatissimum confessorem Sanctum Franciscum a tenere etatis nostre tempore citer gessimus atque gerimus puro corde, hedificari providimus in villa Berge monasterium sub invocacione et titulo eiusdem beatissimi confessoris. Sane quia, ut intelleximus, vos et quidam alii votis nostris huiusmodi vos adversarios ostenditis nostrum pium propositum, ut credimus, ignorando: idcirco volumus vobisque dicimus et expresse mandamus firmiter iniungentes quatenus si beneplacita nostra suscipere intenditis ac prosequi vero corde super construccione et operacione ipsius monasterii, vos adiutorem et favorabilem exhibicionem operis amodo ostendatis taliter quod mediante vestri favoris auxilio dictum monasterium, ut optamus, penitus sortiatur effectum. Aliter scire vos volumus quod si in hoc negligens vel remissus sitis (MS ssetis), magnum inde nobis deservicium f\<e\>ceritis, et providimus confestim, ut nostra interest aliter super eo. Datum in Sarrione aldea Turolii, 8 Idus Iunii, 1334.

51

Alfonso III advises the guardian of the Teruel house that he is sending by Arnaldo Sanz a retable in three pieces depicting the life of Saint Louis

26 July 1335 *Barcelona, ACA, RC 536, f. 71*

Alfonsus etc. Dilecto guardiano domus Fratrum Minorum Turolii (MS Terolii), salutem et dilect<ion>em. Significamus vobis quod per Arnaldum Sancii, museu<m> de domo nostra, mittimus vobis unum reetaule et sunt tres pecie in quibus depicta est vita beati Lodovici (MS Ledovici). Quare volumus ut recepto penes vos dicto reetaule ipsum ponatis in capella per nos constructa in dicto monasterio sub invocacione dicti beati Lodovici (MS Ledovici). Nolumus tamen quod dicto Arnaldo nec alicui alii tradatis aliquid pro missionibus cum iam sibi satisfactum est plenarie de eisdem. Datum Barchinone sub nostro etc. 7 Kalendas Augusti, 1335.

52

Appointment and enfranchisement of the procurator for the Lerida house

11 July 1336 *Barcelona, ACA, RC 859, f. 185r-v*

Nos Petrus etc. Attendentes quod ubi aliquid generaliter prohibetur quod expresse non conceditur, intelligitur denegatum et fratribus ordinis minorum generaliter prohibetur, considerata sui status inmunitate ne pro ulla re temporali possint nec debeant in iudicio experiri sed in laboribus spiritualibus, oratoriis et studiis sedule occupari: idcirco nos, cupientes ipsis circa bona temporalia providere cum presenti carta nostra ex plenitudine nostre potestatis, facimus et constituimus vos, Petrum Timor, civem Ilerde, procuratorem certum et specialem ad petendum, exigendum et recipiendum omnia et singula debita et legata ipsis Fratribus Minoribus debencia seu pertinencia, qualicumque tenore seu causa; dantes, concedentes vobis plenam et liberam potestatem quod vice et nomine nostri possitis dicta debita et legata ipsis Fratribus Minoribus quoquomodo pertinencia petere, exigere et recipere, et de ipsis apochas et diffiniciones (MS diffinidores) facere easque convertere in utilitatem et comodum dicti monasterii necnon quascumque personas que ipsis

Fratribus Minoribus modo aliquo tene<ntur> et bona eorum convenire et agere, rependere, defendere, excipere et replicare a<d> ius; seu quibuscumque bonis fir<m>are sacramentum calumpnie et veritatem discordie, et cuiuslibet alterius generis iuramentum prestare, testes instrumenti et alia probicionum genera providere, et sentenciam vel sentencias tam interlocutorias quam diffinitas audire, et ab ipsa vel ipsis, si vobis visum fuerit, appellare et apell<aci>o<nes>s petere et recipere, et appellacionem vel appellaciones prosequi, partes <d>are et requirere, et procuratorem vel procuratores super predictos substituere ante litem contestatam et post. Et alium seu alios (MS illos) revocare, et alium seu alios subrogare, et negocia sive lites reservare quando et quociens vobis videbitur faciendum. Et omnia alia facere in predictis et circa predicta quecumque ipsi fratres, si facultatem habuissent, facere possent scilicet personaliter interessent.

Quoniam vobis in predictis et circa predicta generalem et liberam a divinis <procu>racionem comitimus per presentes, et volentes vos relevare ab omni onere satisdandi ac fideiubentes in hiis pro vobis, promittimus vobis quod id eo per vos actum et gestum fuerit in premissis et circa premissa id teneri et observari ab omnibus faciemus. Volentes et statuentes quod in compensacionem laborum racione dicte procuracionis sustentorum sitis franchus, liber et inmunis ab omni questia, subsidio, exaccione et alia servitute regali necnon ab omni exercitu, hoste et cavalcata et redempcione eiusdem dum procurator fueritis monasterii antedicti, mandantes cum presenti curie et vicario Ilerde et Pallariene necnon baiulo et aliis officialibus nostris present<ibus> et futuris quod concessionem franchitatis predicte vobis dum procurator dicti monasterii fueritis observent et faciant observari et non contraveniant aliqua racione. In cuius rei testimonium presentem cartam nostram inde fieri iussimus nostro pendenti sigillo munitam. Datum Ilerde, 5 Idus Iulii, 1336.

53

PETER III ORDERS THE JUSTICE OF ARAGON TO ENSURE THAT LEGACIES OWED TO THE FRANCISCANS IN BARBASTRO ARE PAID

22 July 1336   *Barcelona, ACA, RC 588, ff. 3v–4*

Petrus etc. Dilecto consiliario suo Peregrino de Aç<t>orario, iusticie Aragonie, necnon superiuntariis, meriniis, iusticiis, çalmedini(i)s ceterisque iudicibus et offic<ia>libus nostris in regno Aragonie constitutis vel eorum locum tenentibus ad quos presentes pervenerint, salutem etc. Pro parte guardiani et conventus domus Fratrum Minorum Barbastri fuit expositum coram nobis quod aliqui degentes in dicto regno nobiles, milites, infanciones, cives et persone alie dicti regni, tam ex legatis testamentariis quam aliter, tenentur eisdem guardiano et conventui in aliquibus peccunie quantitatibus ad aliquas operas (MS operis) in monasterio conventus faciendas quas eisdem indebite, ut asseritur, solvere, in opera facere seu complere contradicunt(ur). Quare cum ex summa paupertate ipsorum fratrum cui se voluntarie submiserunt pie consideracionis inducamur affectu ut eisdem favor<a>bilis pietatis suffragio sucurramus, vobis et vestrum cuilibet expresse dicimus et mandamus quatenus quilibet vestrum infra <i>urediccionem seu distr<ict>um sibi comissa omnes et singulos quos invenire poteritis in aliquo te<neri> eisdem guardiano et conventui ad dandum et solvendum eisdem vel ad operas quascumque in dicto monasterio faciendas, seu fideli nostro Iacobo Balestarii, iurisperito civitatis Barbastri, eorum procuratori seu substituto vel substituendo ab eo, totum id in quo, vel ad quod, sibi tenentur cohercione debita compellatis, non obstantibus aliquibus frivolis ac dilatoriis seu maliciosis dilacionibus in contrarium oppos<itis> vel eciam opponendis. Nos enim, dicto Iacobo et in eius absencia vel deffectu (MS deffectum) procuratori per eum substituto vel substituendo, exigendi, petendi ac recipiendi dicta legata, elemosinas et alia dictis fratribus et conventui suprap<r>efati monasterii pertinencia, tenore presencium de voluntate dictorum fratrum concedimus potestatem; in hiis sic sollicite et favorabiliter vos habendo quod possitis inde a nobis de diligencia comendari. Datum Morelle, 11 Kalendas Augusti, 1336.

54

PETER III ASKS HIS JURISPERITUS IN BARBASTRO TO RECOVER MONEY OWED TO THE FRANCISCANS BY RELATIVES OF THE LATE DOMINGO SPINELLI

20 July 1338 *Barcelona, ACA, RC 595, f. 179*

Petrus etc. fideli suo, Guillelmo Petri den Peiron, iurisperito civitatis Barbastri salutem etc. Pro parte guardiani et conventus monasterii Fratrum Minorum dicte civitatis fuit expositum coram nobis quod

Domenicus Spinelli, quondam vicinus civitatis eiusdem, tenebatur et erat obligatus eis a magno tempore circa cum publico instrumento ad construendam quandam capellam lapideam intus ecclesiam monasterii antedicti, et eciam calicem et alia ornamenta necessaria ad dictam capellam pertinencia exhibere, sine cuius perfeccione capelle non potest, ut dicitur, procedi comode ad opus dicti ecclesie consumandum. Sunt eciam multi ut dicitur qui tenentur et remanent obligati pro illis in quorum bonis successerunt sepultis ea condicione seu pacto in dicti claustro monasterii ad faciendas operas in ipso claustro, qui licet moniti et rogati per ipsos fratres ipsi facere noluerunt. Precipimus insuper quod nonnulli, tam in dicta civitate quam extra ipsam degentes, tenentur dicto conventui ad elemosinas largiendas et ad aliquas operas exercendas de quibus parentes et predecessores eorum quibus faciendum bonis ordinarunt seu disposuerunt, quas nolunt, ut fertur, effectui anticipare (MS naticipare). Enim que ex nostro debito voluntarie in summa paupertate Domino famulari misericorditer iter miserii quod circa <omni> officii teneantur talibus personis que ad id effectu nostri animi inclinantes, vobis dicimus, committimus et mandamus quatenus, vocatis qui fuerint evocandi de predictis omnibus et aliis que occurrerint, cognoscatis breviter, summarie et de plano absque litigiorum administratoribus eis sine debito terminetis, maliciis et diffugiis omnibus pretermissis, <illorum> nichilominus quos (MS quas) taliter, ut supradictum est, obligatas esse inveneritis cohercione debita si opus fuerit compellendo. Nos enim, ex certa sciencia revocantes comissionem per nos de predictis factam Iohanni Nigri, iurisperito Barbastri, vobis super hiis tenore presencium comittimus plenarie vices nostras. Datum Cesarauguste, 13 Kalendas Augusti, 1338.

> Note: The note "sine precio qua mendicantes" again appears in the margin, indicating that the mendicants were not required to pay transaction fees.

55

PETER III REFERS TO A PREVIOUS LETTER ABOUT THE CLEANING UP
OF PROPERTY IN THE MOORISH QUARTER OF SARAGOSSA
USEFUL TO THE TOWN AND FRIARS

8 April 1340 *Barcelona, ACA, RC 868, f. 76r–v*

Nos Petrus etc. Attendentes cum generalis procuracionis officio fungebamur fecisse vobis, fideli de scribania nostra, Garsie Merivello, donacionem et concessionem infrascripti patui terre cum carta nostra continentie subsequentis.

Nos, Infans Petrus, illustrissimi domini regis Aragonum primogenitus ac eius generalis procurator, ad supplicacionem humilem per vos, fidelem de scribania nostra, Garsia de Merivello, habitatorem civitatis Cesarauguste, nobis exhibitam reverenter, prospicientes fore decencius et utilius dicte civitati et monasterio Fratrum Minorum ipsius civitatis erga quod patuum subscriptum extitit (MS BIS quod ... extitit) quod patuum ipsum popule(n)tur et ab infeccionibus et secretoribus inibi existentibus mundificetur, tenore presentis carte nostre firmiter valiture damus et concedimus vobis, dicto Garsie et vestris, in perpetuum graciose quoddam patuum terre quod est in moraria civitatis Cesarauguste et confrontatur ex una parte cum currali et orto Fratrum Minorum dicte civitatis, et cum orto domorum molendini vocati de Bardaxino, et ex alia cum orto et domibus Eximeni Petri de Salanova iusticie Aragonum quondam et cum domibus Ali fierro sarraceni et cum via publica, prout dicte confrontaciones ipsum patuum concludunt, ab aliis possessionibus condividunt et distingunt.

Ita quod deinceps vos et vestri et quos vos volueritis habeatis, teneatis, possideatis et exple<c>tetis patuum predictum ad usus vestros (perp) et ipsorum pacifice, quiete atque perpetuo absque omni honere servitutis, sine tamen iure preiudicio alieni, ad dandum, vendendum, imp<ignoran>dum, aut ad quomodolicet alienandum patuum antedictum, et ad faciendum eciam de ipso et in ipso omnes vestras et vestr<um> omnimodas voluntates, dum tamen preiudicium inde alicui nullum fiat.

Hanc itaque donacionem et concessionem vobis, dicto Garsie et vestris, facimus in perpetuum, sicut melius et utilius ad vestri et vestrorum comodum et utilitatem, ac bonum, sanum et sincerum intellectum potest intelligi acque dici, mandantes per presentem cartam nostram merino Cesarauguste, çalmedine, iuratis et aliis officialibus dicte civitatis ceterisque officialibus dicti domini regis et nostris et eorum loca tenentibus presentibus et futuris, quod donacionem et concessionem nostram huiusmodi firmam habeant et observent et faciant vobis et vestris in perpetuum inviolabiliter observari. In cuius rei testimonium presentem cartam nostram vobis fieri et sigillo nostro appendicio iussimus comuniri.

Datum Cesarauguste, 3 Kalendas December anno Domini 1335.

Et nunc vos, dictus Garsias, nobis duxeritis humiliter suplicandum ut donacionem et concessionem ipsam laudare et probare et confirmare de benignitate regia dignaremur: idcirco nos supplicacioni huic favorabiliter inclinati donacionem et concessionem ipsam et omnia et singula in preinserta carta contenta prout in ea melius et plenius continentur laudamus, aprobamus, ratifficamus et vobis, dicto Garsie, huius serie confirmamus, mandantes procuratori nostro generali eiusque vices gerenti necnon merino, calmedine et iuratis Cesarauguste ceterisque officialibus nostris vel eorum loca tenentibus quatenus donacionem et confirmacionem nostram huiusmodi firmas habeant et observent et faciant ab aliis inviolabiliter observari, et non contraveniant nec aliquem contravenire permittant aliqua racione. In cuius rei testimonium presentem cartam nostram vobis inde fieri iussimus nostro sigillo pendenti roboratam. Datum Cesarauguste, 6 Idus Aprilis, 1340.

56

CONFIRMATION OF CONCESSION TO THE FRANCISCANS AT TORTOSA TO TAKE GRAIN OUT OF THE CITY

8 June 1340 *Barcelona, ACA, RC 868, f. 109v*

Attendentes serenissimum dominum Alfonsum recolende memorie regem Aragonum, patrem nostrum, pietatis intuitu ac elemosinarie concessisse guardiano et conventui monasterii Fratrum Minorum Dertuse pro opere monasterii antedicti, quod Guillelmus Cirer mercator et civis eiusdem civitatis posset extrahere seu extrahi facere nomine ipsorum guardiani et conventus ab ipsa civitate duo milia cafficii tritici ad mensuram dicte civitatis, vel loco unius kaficii tritici, duo kaficia ordi, seu alicuiuscumque bladi defferenda ad quascumque partes regnorum Valencie et Maiorice, vel ad partes Cathalonie sue iurediccioni subiectas, non obstante prohibicione quacumque generali vel speciali facta vel eciam facienda; et vigore concessionis eiusdem dictus Guillelmus Cirer seu aliquis alius nomine dictorum guardiani et conventus nullam de dicta civitate frumenti vel alterius bladi extraxerint quantitatem prout inde nobis extitit facta fide. Nosque ad suplicacionem humilem memoratorum guardiani et conventus volentes eis ipsam concessionem et graciam licet tempus in ea prefixum lapsum sit observari, concedimus cum presenti elemosinarie et intuitu pietatis facultatem plenariam imperpetuum guardiano et conventui supradictis seu dicto Guillelmo Cirer eorum nomine dictam frumenti seu bladi quantitatem extrahendi a civitate predicta et ad partes nominatas superius licite deferendi (MS defenderi). Mandantes huius serie universis et singulis officialibus nostris quod presentem concessionem et gratiam intuitu liberaliter observando, nullum apponant impedimentum seu obstaculum in eadem. Recipiant tamen idoneam caucionem ab extrahentibus dictum triticum seu ordeum quod infra certum temporis per eos prefigendum quod eisdem vel eorum alteri dicti extrahentes testimonialem exhibuerint albaranum per quem appareat in locis predictis seu aliquo ipsorum dictum frumentum seu ordeum discarricatum fuisse ac sollicite caveant ne huius nostre concessionis pretextu maior frumenti seu ordei quantit(at)is possit extrahi per quoscumque. Presentem vero, quam post duos annos a dato presenti continue numerandos minime valere volumus, in abstraccione dicti frumenti seu ordei per dictos officiales retineri volumus et iubemus. Datum Valencie, 8 Kalendas Iunii, 1340.

57

PETER III MAKES A GRANT TO THE FRANCISCANS AT TERUEL SO THAT THEY CAN REPAIR THE CHAPEL OF SAINT LOUIS

24 August 1345   Barcelona, ACA, RC 1308, f. 24v

Petrus etc. fidelibus suis, procuratori et scriptori aldearum Daroce, salutem etc. Cum nos, ob devocionem quam erga beatum Lodovicum et ordinem Fratrum Minorum pie gerimus et habemus nec minus pietatis intuitu et misericordie inducti, guardiano et conventui fratrum monasterii ville Turoli ordinis supradicti, pro reparacione et construccione capelle beati Lodovici predicti que ex inundacione aquarum pluvialium per fluvia discurrencium persepe per quendam torrentem propinquum vel quasi contiguum monasterio predicto cominatur ruinam, mille solidos iaccenses tenore presentis graciose duxerimus concedendos. Idcirco vobis dicimus et mandamus quatenus, de primis denariis cuiuscumque demande per nos quam primum (MS primo) f<ac>iende hominibus aldearum predictarum, tribuatis et solvatis iamdictis guardiano et conventui, vel cui loco sui voluerint, mille solidos supradictos, recuperando ab eisdem presentem loco apocham <sol>vendam. Mandantes per presentem magistro racionali curie nostre, vel cuicumque a vobis compotum audituro de administracione dictorum predictorum, quod, vobis exhibendo eodem tempore vestri raciocinii presentem, a vobis in compoto recipiat quantitatem peccunie supradictam. Datum Perpiniani, 9 Kalendas Septembris, 1345.

58

PETER III GRANTS 100 BARCELONA SOUS TO FR. EXIMENO DE SAYAS, LECTOR OF THE FRANCISCAN HOUSE AT TERUEL, FOR HIS STUDIES IN THEOLOGY AT THE UNIVERSITY OF PARIS

27 June <1346> *Barcelona, ACA, RC 1309, f. 122*

Petrus etc. Dilecto consiliario et thesaurario nostro, Iacobo Rubei, salutem. Cum nos, fratri Eximino de Saias, lectori Fratrum Minorum, Turolii, qui in presenciarum ad studium Parisiense pro Sacre Theologie sciencia adipiscenda iter suum dirigit, centum solidos Barchinone graciose duxerimus concedendos: idcirco vobis dicimus et mandamus quatenus, de peccunia curie nostre que est vel erit penes vos, tribuatis et solvatis predicto Fratri Eximino, vel cui voluerit loco sui, centum solidos Barchinone supradictos. Et facta(m) solucione(m), presentem ab eo recuperetis litteram cum apocha de soluto. Datum Valencie, 5 Kalendas Iunii, anno predicto <1346>.

59

PETER III GIVES PERMISSION FOR FR. GABRIEL ORTOLÀ OF THE MAJORCAN HOUSE TO REMOVE THE BODY OF PERE DE FRAGA FROM THE GALLOWS AND GIVE IT CHRISTIAN BURIAL

25 September 1346 *Barcelona, ACA, RC 1411, f. 145*

Petrus etc. Dilecto consiliario nostro, Philipo de Boil, gubernatori Maioricarum, vel eius locum tenenti, salutem et dilect<ion>em. Contemplacione fratris Gabrielis Ortolani, ordinis Fratrum Minorum, conventus Maioricarum, nobis pro hiis humiliter supplicantis, vobis dicimus et mandamus quatenus incontinenti visis (de) presentibus deponi faciatis de furchis patibularibus civitatis Maioricarum, Petrum de Fraga ipsius civitatis, quem vos suspendi fecistis suis demeritis, annus est vel quasi elapsus, cuius corpus tradi faciatis aut permittatis ecclesiastice sepulture, eciam si corpus ipsum aut eius pars de furchis ceciderit antedictis. Et hec nullatenus inmutetis. Datum Ilerde, 7 Kalendas Octobris, <1346>.

Appendix 1

Chronology of Franciscan Officers

PROVINCIAL MINISTERS

1220: John Parente
1232: Elias de Cortona
1236: Alfonso Martín
1238: Serafí San Tiberi
1246: Vivià
1248: Alexander
1270–1282: Pere Esteve
1292: Domingo de Jaca
1294: Domingo de Jaca
1295–1297: Arnau Oliba
1297: Pere Esteve
1298–1304: Arnau Oliba
1304–1309: Romeo Ortiz

1309–1310: Ramon de Giniac
1310–1316: Romeo Ortiz
1320: Pere d'Atarravia
1321: Arnau de Canelles
1323: Arnau de Canelles
1325: Pere d'Artamara
1326–1327: Ramon Bancal
1329: Ramon de Bas
1331: Pere de Savinyac
1333: Guillem de Rubió
1335–1336: Ramon de Bas
1336: Pons Carbonell
1338–1349: Ramon de Bas

CUSTODIANS

BARCELONA
1276: Berenguer de Valls; 1307: Pons Carbonell; 1307 [1308]: Francesc Vilagrassa; 1314, 1315, 1320, 1325: Pons Carbonell; 1328: Arnau de Castllà

LERIDA
1255: Bernat de Bach; 1329: Ramon de Bas

SARAGOSSA
1300, 1304: Romeo Ortiz; 1307, 1309: Pascasi de Vall-llebrera; 1320: Juan de Ximénez; 1320 [1321]: Juan de Ejea; 1321: Ramón de Huesca; 1324: Aparicio Serra

VALENCIA
1247: Aimeric; 1307, 1308: Fernando García; 1308: Pascasi de Vall-llebrera; 1312, 1314: Fernando García; 1326: Berenguer d'Ivorra; 1333: Gil de Medina

GUARDIANS

BARBASTRO
1300: Guillermo de Alcalá

BARCELONA
1261: Pere de Gener (Janua); 1262: Bernat de Gualba; 1270: Pere Boada; 1277: Bernat de Gualba; 1278: Arnau Bonastre; 1279: Berenguer de Palmerola; 1280: Joan de Ciurana; 1285: Bernat de Bianya; 1286, 1287: Pere de Bellfort; 1288: Bernat de Bianya, Pere de Puigfort; 1289: Berenguer de Palmerola; 1297: Pere de Bellfort; 1299: Arnau d'Esplugues; 1300: Bernat Torrents; 1302: Bartomeu de Bosc; 1305 [1306]: Joan de Roure; 1307 [1308]: Pere de Torrents; 1307, 1308: Berenguer Folcrà; 1308, 1311: Pons Carbonell; 1312: Joan de Ciurana; 1314, 1315: Pons Carbonell; 1315: Berenguer Folcrà, Joan de Roure; 1316–1320: Pons Carbonell; 1323: Jaume de Vernet; 1324: Jaume Bonhom (Bononia?); 1325, 1326: Pons Brusca?; 1338: Francesc Màrgens; 1345: Tomàs Pere

BERGA
1333, 1334: Tomàs Pere; 1334: Ramon de Déu; 1336: Pere Fuixà

CAGLIARI
1335: Guillem Cendròs

CASTELLÓ D'EMPÚRIES
1276: Pere de Romaní; 1295: Arnau de Vilatenim; 1301, 1303: Pere de Forn; 1305: Guillem Ramon, Guillem Guitard; 1306: Jaume de Terrer (Terreni); 1309: Pons Rossinyol; 1339: Pere Isern

CERVERA
1305: Bernat Ade, Arnau d'Esplugues; 1322: Guillem de Valls; 1331: Berenguer Queralt; 1332: Jaume de Lillet; 1332: Bernat Requesens; 1332: Jaume Ros; 1338, 1343: Berenguer Queralt; 1348: Ramon Granell

DAROCA
1275: Fernando de Cetina

GERONA
1246: Aimeric; 1249: Ramon de Castelló; 1295: Pere Negre; 1305: Guillem de Sant Feliu, Arnau de Vilatenim; 1327: Guillem Gilabert; 1328: Joan de Roure; 1331: Berenguer Cerdà, Ferrer Gener; 1335: Pere Florit; 1337, 1338: Francesc Gener

HUESCA
1273: Gil; 1283: Rodrigo de Gúdar; 1305: Martín de Alcolea, Nicolás de la Naya; 1328: Sancho López de Ayerbe

LERIDA
1283: Joan de Barriac; 1291, 1293: Miquel Jordà; 1304: Guillem Castelló; 1305: Miquel Jordà; 1330: Joan Maler

MAJORCA
1281: Pere de Vilagrassa; 1282: Guillem Bonet; 1283: Berenguer Garí, Pere de Quadres; 1344: Bernat Sans

MINORCA
1283: Berenguer Garí; 1304: Guillem de Lles; 1344: Francesc Esteve

MOLINA
1293: Pedro de Chilliella

MONTBLANC
1305: Guillem de Valls, Guerau de Valls; 1330: Jaume Ros

MONTPELLIER
1282: Esteve Dardas; 1294: Arnau de Rocafull (at Lunel)

MONZÓN
1269: Guillem de Fraumir; 1272: Pere de Copons; 1275, 1282: Francisco

MORELLA
1272: Antonio Bonarres

MURVIEDRO
1304: Fernando de la Reina

PERPIGNAN
1295: Guillem Ferranco, Guillem Ferrer; 1295: Ramon; 1347: Bernat Geli

PUIGCERDÀ
1320: Ramon Talló; 1335, 1338, 1339: Bernat Geli; 1340, 1341: Guillem Canals; 1342: Ramon Ansurrà, Joan Bar, Berenguer Juli; 1344: Ramon Avezurrán?, Pere Llaguna; 1346: Joan dez Torrents; 1347: Pons de Capbreu, Ramon Colomer, Joan dez Trenils

SARAGOSSA
1288: Rodrigo de Gúdar; 1314: Ramón de Huesca; 1329: Sancho López de Ayerbe

SARIÑENA
1327, 1328: Nicolás de la Naya

TARAZONA
1337–1338: Pere de Maler

TARRAGONA
1254, 1255: Guillem d'Ager

TÀRREGA
1321: Pere de Cervera, Pere de Ses Gunyoles; 1342: Ramon Gornall

TERUEL
1281: Marc Pérez

TORTOSA
1248: Bernat Ferrer; 1276: Berenguer de Guàrdia; 1330: Bernat de Vilagrassa

TUNIS
1304: Guillem Guitard, Joan de Roure

VALENCIA
1268: Sauner; 1283: Pere de Tous; 1288: Martín de Vilella; 1329: Bernat Constans

VIC
1232: Segimon des Lledó; 1262–1264: Guillem de Blanes; 1263: Arnau de Forn; 1265: Guillem Ferrer; 1272: Guillem de Montmajor; 1275: Guerau Miró; 1281, 1282: Berenguer de Lledó; 1283: Arnau de Forn; 1295: Guerau d'Osor; 1330: Tomàs Pere; 1333: Bernat de Vilafant; 1342: Antoni de Vilanova; 1344: Pere Fuixà, Arnau Serra; 1347: Pere de Gualba

VILAFRANCA DEL PENEDÈS
1304: Guillem de Sant Feliu; 1320, 1321: Ferrer d'Alemany; 1335: Bernat Pellicer; 1347: Tomàs Pere

XÀTIVA
1283: Pere Roc; 1295: Miquel Jordà; 1326: Benvingut de Granollers

LECTORS

BARCELONA
Dates unknown: Pere de Torrents, Pere Vigué; 1281: Jaume Riuprimer; 1322: Alfredo Gonter

CASTELLÓ D'EMPÚRIES
1307: Berenguer Folcrà

CALATAYUD
1307: García Martínez

GERONA
1320: Arnau de Castllà; 1339: Pere de Sa Carrera

HUESCA
1329: Sancho López de Ayerbe; 1325: Martín Romeo

JACA
1321: Ramon de Borau

LERIDA
Date unknown: Lluis d'Escala; 1316: Bernat de Pim

MAJORCA
1284: Arnau Oliba; 1325: Pere Arnau

NARBONNE
1321: Berenguer Talló

PERPIGNAN
1321: Berenguer Talló

SARAGOSSA
1298, 1305: Romeo Ortiz; 1330: Miguel de Almenara

TARAZONA
1320: Juan de Bonell; 1329: Martín Romeo

TARRAGONA
1316: Guillem Sa Roca

TERUEL
1325: García Martínez, Joan de Montfort, Garino Valentín; 1346: Eximeno de Sayas

VIC
1314: Guillem de Sa Carrera

Note: Jeroni de Catalunya was lector at the papal court of Avignon (1321); see Sanahuja, *Història,* pp. 135, 139–140, 104–195, 218.

Appendix 2

Franciscan Affairs and Organization

CHAPTER MEETINGS

Chapter meetings were usually held in the Paschal season or at Pentecost, and it was customary for the king to pay 300 sous to the convent acting as host. The dates below are as given in the archival and secondary sources named and do not necessarily report actual dates of chapter meetings; it is unlikely, for example, that meetings were held in Montblanc in both August and September 1322, or that the Tarragona house hosted meetings in both April and May 1290. These dates may reflect only the vagaries of the sources; in any case the actual dates are difficult to ascertain. Asterisks * indicate convents located in the Franciscan province of Navarre.

BARBASTRO
15 May 1290: provincial (Saldes, *EF* 17 [1916], 67; Sanahuja, *História,* p. 122)

BARCELONA
28 August 1229: provincial (Sanahuja, *História,* pp. 32 and 51 [reference incorrect: see above Chapter 1, p. 26]); 23 September 1285: general (Barcelona, ACA, RC 58, f. 52); 16 April 1292: general (Finke, *Acta Aragonensia,* 3: 16–19); 27 November 1292: provincial (RC 95, f. 172); 23 June 1294: general (RC 88, f. 229); 11 June 1299: general (Barcelona, AC, Pia Almoina, perg. 1-6-1339); 17 September 1310: provincial (AC, Pia Almoina, perg. 4-3-188); 4 June 1313: general (RC 298, f. 229v); 13 June 1316: general (RC 300, f. 126v); 17 May 1323: provincial (RC 302, f. 51v); 17 April 1324: provincial (RC 397, f. 51v); 7 July 1343: provincial (RC 1117, f. 45v)

CALATAYUD
18 January 1304 [1305]: provincial (Barcelona, ACA, RC 134, f. 209)

CERVERA
18 April 1312: provincial (Barcelona, ACA, RC 298, f. 79)

DAROCA
25 August 1316: provincial? (Barcelona, ACA, RC 277, f. 253v); 17 September 1340: provincial (RC 1302, f. 138v)

EJEA DE LOS CABALLEROS
13 March 1308 [1309]: provincial? (Barcelona, ACA, RC 297, f. 82)

ESTELLA
11 May 1336: provincial (Barcelona, ACA, RC 1052, f. 96r–v)

GERONA
1 December 1328: general (Barcelona, ACA, RC 477, f. 67r–v)

HUESCA
3 May 1286: provincial? (Sanahuja, *História,* p. 122); 28 May 1287: provincial? (Barcelona, ACA, RC 71, f. 54); 25 July 1302: provincial (RC 294, f. 64); 13 February 1325 [1326]: provincial (RC 285, f. 147)

JACA
[7] April 1320: provincial (Barcelona, ACA, RC 282, f. 6); 26 April 1320: provincial? (RC 423, f. 18v); 15 May 1320: provincial? (RC 245, f. 1v)

LERIDA
7 May 1286: provincial (Barcelona, ACA, RC 66, f. 65); 26 August 1289: provincial? (Saldes, *EF* 45 [1933], 141–142; Sanahuja, *História,* p. 119); 11 December 1289: provincial? (Sanahuja, *História,* p. 47); 6 March 1307 [1308]: provincial (RC 290, f. 31)

MONTBLANC
13 August 1322: provincial (Barcelona, ACA, RC 386, f. 81v); [13] September 1322: provincial (RC 301, f. 296v)

MONZÓN
7 July 1261: provincial? (Saldes, *REF* 1 [1907], 220)

PAMPLONA
11 August 1301: provincial (Barcelona, ACA, RC 268, f. 167v)

PERPIGNAN
27 October 1330: general (Barcelona, ACA, RC 560, f. 267); 23 May 1331: general (RC 533, f. 91v); s.d. 1331: general (Sanahuja, *História,* p. 173)

SARAGOSSA
23 August 1276: provincial? (Sanahuja, *História,* p. 117); 12 March 1314 [1315]: provincial (Barcelona, ACA, RC 299, f. 204v); [31] August 1331: provincial (RC 443, ff. 106v–107)

TARAZONA
6 April 1337: provincial? (Barcelona, ACA, RC 1296, f. 52v)

TARRAGONA
19 April 1290: provincial? (Saldes, *EF* 17 (1916), 64); 19 May 1290: provincial? (Sanahuja, *Història,* p. 122); 24 April 1302: provincial (Barcelona, ACA, RC 294, f. 119); 9 March 1331 [1332]: provincial (RC 444, f. 172r–v)

TERUEL
24 April 1324: provincial (Barcelona, ACA, RC 302, f. 135)

TORTOSA
19 April 1316: provincial? (Barcelona, ACA, RC 277, f. 123v); 22 June 1327: provincial (RC 303, f. 186)

TUDELA
10 May 1330: provincial (Barcelona, ACA, RC 533, f. 22v)

VALENCIA
3 September 1295: provincial (Barcelona, ACA, RC 101, f. 312); 26 April 1321: provincial (RC 282, f. 227); 8 May 1335: general (RC 468, f. 184)

VILAFRANCA DEL PENEDÈS
12 September 1328: provincial (Barcelona, ACA, RC 531, f. 38v); 1 March 1347 [1348]: provincial (RC 1312, f. 147); 7 April 1348: provincial? (Sanahuja, *Història,* p. 76)

XÀTIVA
18 April 1311: provincial (Barcelona, ACA, RC 147, f. 167v)

PROCURATORS

BARBASTRO
Ramon de la Cardosa: 20 July 1338 (Barcelona, ACA, RC 595, f. 164v)

BARCELONA
Pere Ferrer de Vic: 1275–1314 (Sanahuja, *Història,* pp. 53, 109, 118, 119); Arnau de Busquets, Sr.: 7 July 1314 (Barcelona, AC, Pia Almoina, Llib. not. Bernat Vilarrúbia, 1314, ff. 89v–90); Fr. Ramon Jovell or Tovell: 2 April 1334 (Llib. not. Jordi Vilarrúbia, 1334, f. 65v); Fr. Guillem Llobet: 8 March 1345 [1346] (Jordi Vilarrúbia, 1345–1346, f. 38v)

CALATAYUD
Eximeno de Teruel: 26 June 1323 (Barcelona, ACA, RC 224, f. 15v)

CASTELLÓ D'EMPÚRIES
Joan Barrot (Barroca?): 7 August 1304 (Gerona, AH, C.76 [1301–1305], Bernat Junquera, f. 58v), 8 April 1305 (AH, C.78 [1304–1305], Bernat Junquera, f. s.n.); Joan Gili: 1 October 1304 (AH, C.73bis [T.1303–1310], Pere Perrini, f. 18); Pere Moner, sacristan: 2 March 1339 [1340] (Gerona, AD, Lib. not. G.14 [13], 1338–1339 [1340], f. 107)

CERVERA
Borras Llorac: 31 December 1283 (Sanahuja, *Història*, p. 92); Guillem Calb: 4 April 1305 (Sanahuja, *Història*, p. 92); Ferrer de Na Burguesa: 1316–1351 (Barcelona, ACA, RC 212, f. 125; Turrull, *Règim municipal*, p. 150); Pere de Nogueres: 1331–1340 (Turrull, *Règim municipal*, pp. 113–114; Cervera, AHC, Clavari 4 [1340], f. 2v), 10 April 1348 (Barcelona, ACA, RC 586, f. 224v); Ramon Serra: 6 June 1348 (Cervera, AHC, N.I.4 [1346–1348], Pere Dan, f. 61v)

DAROCA
Fernando, rector of Coll: 19 February 1333 [1334] (Barcelona, ACA, RC 464, f. 2v); Bertran Arnaldo: 22 October 1337 (RC 862, ff. 62v–63)

GERONA
Martí Ermengol: 3 January 1285 [1286] (Webster, *AIEG* 29 [1987], 42–43, doc. 15); Bonanat Carbonell: 29 December 1327 (Barcelona, ACA, RC 428, f. 37v); Arnau Raffart: 11 March 1343 [1334] (RC 876, f. 35)

LERIDA
Bernat Ramon: 12 August 1257 (Barcelona, ACA, RC 10, f. 8v); Joan de Barriac: 24 May 1288 (RC 79, f. 51); Ramon Soquet: 9 August 1312 (RC 150, f. 44v); Arnau de Morell: 23 October 1320 (RC 218, f. 136); Pere Timor: 11 July 1336 (RC 859, f. 185r–v)

MAJORCA
Guillem Arnau d'Illa: 8 March 1344 [1345] (Palma de Mallorca, AHRM, Lletres comunes 5, ff. 291v–292)

MANRESA (hospice)
Ferrer de Sala: 5 May 1297 (Barcelona, ACA, RC 264, f. 6v)

MONTBLANC
Arnau Sastre: 1313–1315 (Barcelona, ACA, RC 211, ff. 209, 328); Arnau Alanya: 1326–1328 (RC 229, f. 156v; RC 474, ff. 158, 287v); Arnau Alamany: 7 March 1343 [1334] (RC 876, f. 40r–v)

MORELLA
Guillem Moltó: 23 January 1301 [1302] (Barcelona, ACA, RC 200, f. 176v); Nicolau de Pi: 21 March 1327 [1328] (RC 474, f. 195)

MURVIEDRO
Pere Ferradoll: 7 May 1306 (Barcelona, ACA, RC 203, f. 162v); Berenguer Armengol: 1 September 1336 (RC 859, f. 230v)

SARAGOSSA
Juan Martín Serrano: 26 April 1320 (Barcelona, ACA, RC 169, f. 177); Domingo de Tarba: 1330–1340 (RC 482, f. 14; RC 868, f. 29); Pedro Martín de Martorell: 8 March 1332 [1333] (RC 486, f. 47v)

TÀRREGA
Jaume de Bas: 14 January 1318 [1319] (Barcelona, ACA, RC 216, f. 109r–v)

TERUEL
Pere Sanz: 18 January 1304 [1305] (Barcelona, ACA, RC 134, f. 209); Simó de Altariba: 1335 (RC 574, f. 124r–v, 165v)

VALENCIA
Bernat de Vilallonga: 6 November 1300 (Barcelona, ACA, RC 198, f. 214v); Jaume de Valls: 27 January 1303 [1304] (RC 201, f. 102)

VIC
Pere Miró: 12 July 1280 (Vic, AE, ACF, N.17 [1279–1282], f. 27); Berenguer Pinosa: 1288–1320 (ACF, N.25 [1287–1288], f. 83; N.27 [1290–1291], f. 121; N.28 [1290–1293], f. 208; N.29 [1294–1296], f. 156; N.40 [1304], f. s.n.; N.41 [1304 (–1305)], f. s.n.; N.50 [1308–1309], f. s.n.; N.67 [1317 (–1318)], f. 120v; N.78 [1320–1323], f. 28); Bononat de Ulmeto: 15 November 1303 (ACF, N.39 [1303], f. s.n.), 17–20? [21?] September 1308 (N.49 [1308], f. s.n. and f. 26 [both loose sheets]); Pere Calet: 26 January 1312 (AE, AC, Perg. 693); Bernat de Cases: 23 July 1318 (ACF, N.67 [1317 (–1318)], f. 120v); Francesc Fuster: 5 May 1322 (AE, Veg. 1321–1322, f. s.n.); Guillem de Marbuschi: s.d. 1324? (Veg. 1323–1328, f. s.n. [loose sheet likely part of documents of 1324])

VILAFRANCA DEL PENEDÈS
Bernat Fuster: 20 May 1298 (Barcelona, ACA, RC 111, ff. 215v–216); Pere de Romaní: 16 September 1302 (RC 125, f. 70); Guerau Pere: 2 August 1309 (Barcelona, AD, Reg. comm. I, ff. 104v–105), 1 August 1315 (Barcelona, AC, Pia Almoina, Llib. not. Bernat Vilarrúbia, 1315, f. 14v)

XÀTIVA
Jaume de Guàrdia: 14 June 1309 (Barcelona, ACA, RC 144, f. 106v), 15 November 1342 (RC 874, f. 7v)

UNPAID ACCOUNTS

GENERAL
26 February 1289 [1290] (Barcelona, ACA, RC 81, f. 45v); 7 December 1306 (RC 139, f. 96v); 17 January 1306 [1307] (RC 139, f. 128v); 17 November 1335 (RC 470, f. 260v)

BARBASTRO
1 March 1292 [1293] (Barcelona, ACA, RC 255, f. 31); 25 November 1293 (RC 93, f. 346v); 1 July 1307 (RC 139, f. 333); 22 January 1312 [1313] (RC 151, f. 70); 23 January 1313 [1314] (RC 152, f. 231); 13 December 1314 (RC 352, f. 117); 2 July 1336 (RC 588, f. 3v); 2 January 1339 [1340] (RC 604, f. 153)

BARCELONA
19 January 1271 [1272] (Saldes, *EF* 45 [1933)], 135-136); 17 May 1300 (Barcelona, ACA, RC 117, f. 83r-v); 25 June 1306 (RC 270, f. 159v); 22 May 1316 (RC 160, f. 190v); 28 February 1316 [1317] (RC 159, f. 266); 15 November 1340 (RC 608, f. 162)

BORJA
21 April 1335 (Barcelona, ACA, RC 574, f. 9); 28 October 1335 (RC 574, f. 122)

CALATAYUD
18 January 1304 [1305] (Barcelona, ACA, RC 134, f. 209r-v); 26 June 1306 (RC 138, f. 265); 17 December 1320 (RC 246, f. 144v); 19 August 1337 (RC 590, f. 276v)

CASTELLÓ D'EMPÚRIES
18 May 1298 (Barcelona, ACA, RC 111, f. 203)

CERVERA
21 June 1330 (Barcelona, ACA, RC 437, f. 96v); 9 June 1332 (RC 454, f. 109); 21 October 1339 (RC 601, f. 62v)

DAROCA
5 December 1307 (Barcelona, ACA, RC 106, f. 35); 7 March 1315 [1316] (RC 354, f. 77v); 23 March 1315 [1316] (RC 354 f. 100v); 25 March 1322 (RC 385, f. 154); 22 October 1337 (RC 862, ff. 62v-63); 12 October 1347 (RC 649, f. 47)

EJEA DE LOS CABALLEROS
25 February 1314 [1315] (Barcelona, ACA, RC 352, f. 161v)

GERONA
9 December 1327 (Barcelona, ACA, RC 428, f. 37v)

HUESCA
22 May 1301 (Barcelona, ACA, RC 124, f. 169); 22 January 1305 [1306] (RC 137, f. 102r-v); 6 August 1316 (RC 355, f. 9); 7 September 1316 (RC 355, f. 43); 21 October 1325 (RC 185, f. 119v); 1 July 1338 (RC 596, f. 186); 30 December 1338 (RC 596, f. 131v); 29 November 1345 (RC 638, f. 1v)

LERIDA
30 June 1301 (Barcelona, ACA, RC 121, f. 89); 11 July 1336 (RC 859, f. 185r-v)

MONZÓN
13 September 1329 (Barcelona, ACA, RC 479, f. 197v)

MURVIEDRO
1 September 1336 (Barcelona, ACA, RC 859, f. 230r-v); 9 May 1347 (RC 644, f. 131v); 5 February 1347 [1348] (RC 886, f. 164)

PUIGCERDÀ
7 January 1344 [1345] (Barcelona, ACA, RC 629, f. 103)

SARAGOSSA
4 March 1295 [1296] (Barcelona, ACA, RC 103, f. 275); 10 November 1301 (RC 120, f. 138); 13 July 1306 (RC 270, f. 168v); 27 June 1306 (RC 270, f. 164); 10 November 1307 (RC 141, f. 89); 5 January 1311 [1312] (RC 149, f. 36); 21 July 1323 (RC 284, f. 71); 23 March 1329 [1330] (RC 495, f. 23v); 27 March 1331 (RC 495, f. 26v); 11 October 1331 (RC 498, f. 203); 7 March 1339 [1340] (RC 868, f. 29); 25 October 1340 (RC 1303, ff. 39v-40); 25 September 1347 (RC 649, f. 90); doubtful references: 16 August 1292 (RC 86, f. 183v) and 5 November 1301 (RC 119, f. 119v)

SARIÑENA
30 October 1324 (Barcelona, ACA, RC 374, f. 137); 6 May 1342 (RC 619, f. 62)

TARAZONA
6 April 1337 (Barcelona, ACA, RC 1296, f. 84); 7 June 1307 (RC 139, f. 299); 16 August 1316 (RC 355, f. 18v); 31 July 1320 (RC 375, f. 59v); 14 October 1332 (RC 575, f. 165v); 13 December 1337 (RC 591, f. 215); 26 June 1338 (RC 596, f. 187)

TARRAGONA?
18 September 1346 (Barcelona, ACA, RC 642, f. 31v)

TÀRREGA
30 June 1301 (Barcelona, ACA, RC 121, f. 89); 16 March 1310 [1311] (RC 144, f. 159v); 19 March 1334 [1335] (RC 503, f. 50v)

TERUEL
24 March 1295 [1296] (Barcelona, ACA, RC 103, f. 319); 21 August 1315 (RC 353, f. 141v); 29 August 1334 (RC 466, f. 112v); 6 May 1337 (RC 861, f. 234); 29 May 1325 (RC 373, f. 203); 30 September 1337 (RC 589, f. 72); 28 November 1337 (RC 591, f. 195v); 13 February 1338 [1339] (RC 599, f. 22r–v); 3 August 1340 (RC 607, f. 145v); 23 July 1345 (RC 1308, ff. 15v–16);

TORTOSA
28 February 1343 [1344] (Barcelona, ACA, RC 624, f. 198v)

VALENCIA
23 May 1298 (Barcelona, ACA, RC 111, f. 241); 15 January 1306 [1307] (RC 139, f. 128v); 5 September 1308 (RC 142, f. 186v); 18 April 1312 (RC 149, f. 138v); 5 October 1329 (RC 435, f. 259); 15 May 1329 (RC 434, ff. 104v–105)

VILAFRANCA DEL PENEDÈS
31 March 1302 (Barcelona, ACA, RC 118, f. 77v)

XÀTIVA
23 May 1298 (Barcelona, ACA, RC 111, f. 241r); 15 February 1303 [1304] (RC 258, f. 84); 20 April 1306 (RC 138, f. 186v); 5 September 1308 (RC 142, f. 186v); 16 March 1310 [1311] (RC 144, f. 159v); 6 December 1311 (RC 148, f. 246); 19 March 1334 [1345] (RC 503, f. 50v)

Appendix 3

Family Origins of Friars

An important aid to the proper identification of friars named in the archival documents is the occurrence of references to members of their families. The following is a representative list of such references for a selected number of friars. Familial references are abundant in the documentation from Puigcerdà, as most of the friars there came from local families; only the most frequent of these are listed here, dating from the time just before and shortly after the foundation of the Puigcerdà house. The terms *family* and *relative* are used in cases where the documentary references are too vague to allow relationships to be specified, or the relationships themselves are too complicated to explain briefly.

BERNARDO DE AHONES
family (Barcelona, ACA, RC 115, f. 347v, 24 March 1299 [1300]; RC 137, f. 102v, 22 January 1305 [1306]; RC 119, f. 119v, 5 November 1301)

BERENGUER D'AMORÓS
nephew (Barcelona, ACA, RC 879, f. 70, 4 December 1345)

RAMON APERRER?
father (Gerona, AH, C.15 [1286–1291], Fontcuberta, f. 3v, 3 July 1286)

JOAN D'ARAGÓ
royal family (Barcelona, ACA, RC 877, f. 129, 10 May 1345)

BERNAT ARCEGELL
father (Puigcerdà, AHC, d'Oliana/Hualart, *Lib. test.* [1321–1322], f. 3, 25 September 1321)

FRANCESC D'ARENA
family (Vic, AE, ACF, N.39 [1303], f.s.n., 31 August 1303)

BERENGUER BORRELL
relative (Vic, AE, AC, T.1346–1348, f. 88, 21 July 1346)

GUILLEM DE CAMPLLONG
father (Gerona, AH, G.35 [1339–1348], Transfort, f. 4, 2 July 1348)

BERNAT COLOMER
father (Puigcerdà, AHC, Embertad/Lorà, *Lib. test.* [1324-1325], f. 1v, 24 June 1324)

BERNAT COMAS
relative (Vic, AE, AC, T.1331-1334, f. 64, 16 October 1333)

BERNAT ESPANYOLL
parents (Puigcerdà, AHC, Hualart/Garriga, *Lib. test.* [1320-1321], f. 10v, 10 February 1320 [1321])

PERE GUERAU
family (Barcelona, ACA, RC 145, f. 69v, 1 August 1310)

RAMÓN DE HUESCA (DE OLA)
brother (Barcelona, ACA, RC 115, f. 347v, 24 March 1299 [1300])

GUILLEM JORNET
brother (Barcelona, ACA, RC 391, fi. 105v-106, 29 September 1325; RC 392, f. 158v, 6 February 1325 [1326])

PERE LLAGUNA
father (Puigcerdà, AHC, Cog/Hualart, *Lib. test.* [1314-1315], f. 41, 22 May 1315); sister (ibid., f. 43, 28 May 1315); family (Puigcerdà, AHC, d'Oliana/Hualart, *Lib. test.* [1321-1322], f. 20v, 1 March 1321 [1322], and f. 24, 11 April 1322; d'Oliana/Hualart, *Lib. test.* [1322-1323], f. 24, 16 May 1323; Embertad/Lorà, *Lib. test.* [1324-1325], f. 3, 9 July 1324)

GUILLEM DE LLES
mother (Gerona, AH, C.13 [1295-1296 (1297)], Pere Serra, f.s.n., 1 June 1297)

MIQUEL DE MONTAGUT
family (Sanahuja, *Història,* p. 117, 7 November 1277)

GUILLEM DE MUSEROS
brother (Barcelona, ACA, RC 205, f. 139, 17 February 1307 [1308])

RODRIGO NAVARRET
mother (Barcelona, ACA, RC 440, f. 226, 17 November 1330)

ARNAU OLIBA
family (Barcelona, ACA, RC 203, f. 179, 11 July 1306)

ROMEO ORTIZ
family (Barcelona, ACA, RC 137, f. 102v, 21 January 1305 [1306])

TOMÀS PERE
sister (Puigcerdà, AHC, Alb/Roquer, *Lib. test.* [1328-1329], f. 11v, 5 February 1329 [1330])

BERNAT DE PILES
father (Vic, AE, AC, T.1348, f. 54v, 20 June 1348)

BERNAT PINTOR
mother (Barcelona, ACA, RC 416, f. 109, 23 December 1314)

MATEU PINTOR
mother (Barcelona, ACA, RC 1295, f. 92, 10 July 1336)

BERNAT PUIG
brother (Puigcerdà, AHC, Alb, *Lib. test.* [1321-1322], f. 15, 13 October 1321)

FR. RAMON
sister (Puigcerdà, AHC, Alb/Roquer, *Lib. test.* [1328-1329], f. 11v, 5 February 1329 [1330])

RAMON DE REI
brother (Barcelona, ACA, RC 166, f. 10, 14 March 1317 [1318])

JAUME DE RIUPRIMER
family (Sanahuja, *Història,* p. 117, 26 February 1273 [1274])

ARNAU DE ROCAFULL
brother (Madrid, AHN, Clero, Valldigna, carp. 3364, perg. 7, 19 January 1273 [1274])

MARTÍN DE ROSAL
sister (Saldes, *EF* 45 [1933], 134-135, 25 June 1279)

ARNAU DE ROVIRA
brother (Barcelona, AC, Pia Almoina, perg. 4-15-145, 12 February 1271 [1272])

PERE SES GUNYOLES
brother (Barcelona, ACA, RC 377, fi. 133v-134, 4 September 1326)

RAMON DE SOTSROCA
parents (Vic, AE, ACF, T.18, f. 116v, 14 September 1288?)

GUILLEM TREBALLÓS
parents (Barcelona, ACA, RC 121, f. 89, 30 June 1301; ibid., f. 102, 12 July 1301; RC 148, f. 79, 23 August 1311; RC 123, f. 14, 21 February 1332 [1333])

PASCASI DE VALL-LLEBRERA
brother-in-law (RC 64, f. 30v, 17 April 1280); family from Morella (Barcelona, ACA, RC 146, f. 55r-v, 73, 13 February 1310 [1311])

PERE VIDAL
mother (Vic, AE, AC, T.1265-1266, f.s.n., 4 March 1265 [1266])

BERNAT DE VILAERT
uncle (Gerona, AD, Perg. Mitra, C.24, no. 50, 7 May 1291)

BERNAT DE VILAFANT
relative (Vic, AE, AC, T.1331-1334, f. 64, 16 October 1333)

BERENGUER DE VILAGRANADA
mother (Vic, AE, ACF, T.1279-1286, f. 19, 18 July 1280); father (Barcelona, AC, Pia Almoina, perg. 4-8-14, 13 August 1280)

Appendix 4

Chronology of Convent Residents

ALCIRA, Kingdom of Valencia (no known convent, but it might have had a hospice in the thirteenth century)

BALAGUER (old part of the town was known as Almatà; founded before 1276, but no names found)

BARBASTRO (founded ca. 1235)
1300: Guillermo de Alcalá; 1313: Martín Dendestre; 1340: Eximeno Coscollola

BARCELONA (founded in the 1220s)
Dates unknown: Ferrer Sala, Pere Vigué; 1240: Guillem Escatar; 1248–1267: Bernat Ferrer; 1259: Guillem de Pujol; 1260–1280: Bernat Ferrer; 1261–1293: Pere de Gener (Janua); 1262: Bernat de Gualba; 1262–1284: Guillem de Blanes; 1262–1322: Ferrer d'Alemany; 1265–1338: Guillem Ferrer; **1270**: Pere Boada; 1271: Arnau de Rovira; 1273–1281: Jaume de Riuprimer; 1273–1295: Berenguer Garí; 1273–1324: Guillem de Lles; 1277: Bernat Oliver; 1278–1325: Arnau Bonastre; 1279: Berenguer Ozarí?; 1279–1289: Berenguer de Palmerola; **1280**: Jaume Polinyà, Berenguer de Vilagranada; 1280–1297: [Pere?] Tomàs; 1280–1298: Pere de Bellfort; 1280–1316: Joan de Ciurana; 1281: Pere Falcó; 1281–1316: Bernat Gil; 1281–1327: Pere de Quadres; 1282–1300: Bernat Peregrí; 1282–1316: Arnau Oliba; 1284: Jaume de Rovira, Ferrer de Sant Miquel, Bernat de Terrassa; 1285–1288: Bernat de Bianya; 1285–1291: Bernat Draper; 1286: Frimago?; 1287–1307: Pons Ullà; 1288: Bernat Arbitre, Pere de Puigfort; 1288–1308: Ramon de Sotsroca; **1290**: Joan de Morés; 1290?: Francesc Bruny; 1290–1309: Alberic; 1291–1306: Guerau d'Osor; 1292–1295: Ramon; 1292–1317: Arnau d'Esplugues; 1293–1307: Pere d'Esplugues; 1293–1324: Pere de Forn; 1295: Berenguer de Romaní, Bernat d'Alp; 1295–1296: Jaume de Forn; 1295–1331 Arnau de Vilatenim; 1296: Guillem de Canals, Ramon de Guàrdia; 1296–1299: Pere Negre; 1296–1307: Joan d'Alp; 1297–1309: Simó de Montsec; 1297–1329: Guerau de Prat; 1298–1307: Marc Godencs; 1298–1316†: Pere Guerau (Third Order); 1299–1307: Pere de Torrents; 1299–1333: Jaume Nadal; **1300**–1307: Berenguer Aguilar, Guerau Bonastre, Bartomeu de Bosc, Guillem Clarà, Pere de Cornudella, Berenguer de Fort, Romeu de Fuixà, Francesc de Preixana, Salvador de Roure, Pere de Sabenyà; 1300–1308?: Bernat Torrents; 1300–1309: Berenguer Fiveller, Pere Jofre, Arnau de Riera; 1300–1310: Francesc de Vilagrassa; 1300–1336: Pons Carbonell; 1300–1340: Dalmau Mansolí; 1301: Marc de Sarrià; 1301–1302:

Guillem de Roca, Gil de Sars, Sancho de Taxonera, Jaume de Venècia; 1301-1337: Ramon Puig; 1302: Pere d'Arenys, Jaume Boià, Berenguer de Cardona, Bernat Cardona, Bartomeu Cases, Nicolás de Ejea, Bernat Galcerán, Rafael Gener (Janua), Jaume Martí, Gil R[amon] Otger, Peravalls?, Rafael de Porta, Galter (Galcerán) Queralt; 1302-1308: Bernat de Cases; 1302-1321: Ramon de Borau; 1302-1324: Jaume de Bosom, Jaume de Vernet; 1302-1325: A[rnau] d'Armenter; 1302-1336: Joan de Castelló; 1302-1350: Pere de Sa Roca; 1303-1317: Guillem Guitard; 1306-1307: Joan de Lluçà; 1306-1328: Joan de Roure; **1307**: Berenguer d'Abat, Jaume d'Abat, Berenguer Abeyà, Berenguer d'Aguda, Nicolau Bosom, Bernat Burdils, Berenguer de Caral, Juan de Castella, Mateo de Castella, Bernat Company, Pere Demestre, Ramon Ferrer, Mateu de Fuixà, Juan de Galícia, Pere Ivern, Pere Llop, Guillem de Maserac, Domènec Mieres, Andreu Moré, Guillem Ollers, Pere Olloghet?, Andreu d'Orts, Pons de Pau, Arnau de Perellada, Pelegrí de Perugia, Martim de Portugal, Pere de Prat, Ferrer de Preixana, Guillem Ros, Pere de Sabé, Pons de Sant Jordi, Pere de Santa Eugènia, Bernat Senechs, Pere de Tornavell; 1307-1314: Guillem de Sa Carrera; 1307-1315: Bernat de Vilanova; 1307-1316: Ramon de Costa; 1307-1318: Bernat de Déu; 1307-1321: Pere Carbonell; 1307-1327: Guillem Gilabert; 1307-1328: Berenguer Folcrà; 1307-1335: García Martínez; 1307-1339: Guillem de Puig; 1307-1344: Arnau de Castllà; 1307-1348: Pons Carles; **1310**: Alberot (Alberic?), Francesc de Cardona; 1310-1354: Bernat Puig; 1311-1345: Pere Ferrer; 1311-1348: Pere Muntaner; 1312-1315: Simó de Puigcerdà; 1314-1330: Castelló Botinyà; 1314-1347: Tomàs Pere; 1315: Miquel Abeyà; 1316-1347: Arnau de Canelles; 1316-1364: Guillem Sala; 1317: Joan de Molina, Pere Guerau de Sant-Hipòlit; 1317-1324: Pere Besalú; 1317-1345: Romeu de Falques; 1319-1325: Jaume de Bonhom (Bononia?); **1322**: Ferran Bertís, Angelo de Genoa; 1322-1325: Alfredo Gonter; 1324: Bernat d'Alfam[er]a, Llorens d'Antoni, Guillem Bogar, Simó de Bullada, Pere de Burdils, Guillem Busquet, Francesc, Guillem de Gravera, Jaume Llers, Pere Mateu, Guillem Menor, Arnau d'Ort, Alexandre de Perugia, Bonadono de Perugia, Pere de Rostey, G[uillem] de Rubera, Juan de Sevilla, Angel de Terra Llaurador, Jaume de Trilla; 1324-1325: Joan de Montlleó, Pere d'Oliver, Joan Peiró; 1324-1344: Guillem Oliver; 1324-1357: Pere Fuixà; 1325-1334: Pons Brusca?; 1325-1342: Jaume Moler; 1325-1347: Francesc Esteve; 1326: G[uillem] Ballester, Andreu Batlle, Guillem Calvet, Francesc Carbonell, Bernat Casells, Arnau de Cases, P[ere] Dalmau, Paquet, Bernat Quintana, Bartomeu Rovira; 1326-1328: Francesc Segarra; 1326-1333: Pere Sa Capella; 1326-1338: Francesc Clarà; 1326-1345: Ferrer Senechs; 1327: R[amon] Teixidor; **1331-1332**: Berenguer Basella; 1332: Pedro de Castella, Prisc de Notó; 1333: Berenguer Tolrà; 1333-1356: Francesc Rovira; 1334: Pere Comabella, Barceló Marcador, Francesc Mellot; 1334-1338: Guillem Vidal; 1335-1342: Guillem Cendròs; 1335-1351: Francesc Batlle; 1335-1368: Bernat Pellicer; 1336-1374: Joan Carmenço; 1336-1382: Pere de Sicília; 1337-1338: Bernat Andreu; 1337-1374: Francesc Ros; 1338-1373: Nicolau Tanyà; 1339: Guillem Gavarra; 1339-1378: Guillem Pere de Rexach; **1340**: Guerau Rafart; 1340-1370: Pere de Pont; 1342-1345: Nicolau Agut; 1343-1350: Berenguer Rovira; 1343-1385: Jaume de Mora;

1344–1352: Guillem Llobet; 1344–1374: Arnau Renart; 1344–1375: Guillem Jordà, Ramon Moliner, Guillem Rafart; 1345: Jaume Julià, Francesc Màrgens, Ramon Sicart; 1345–1350: Ramon de Torrents; 1345–1393: Bartomeu Sant Martí; 1346–1382: Pere de Puig; 1347: Berenguer Cordelles; 1347–1386: Bernat Bru

BERGA (founded [1] ca. 1244; [2] ca. 1334)
1287: Pere Emberart; 1314–1347: Tomàs Pere; 1317–1336: Ramon d'Estany; 1321–1336: Pere Burgué; 1324–1357: Pere Fuixà; 1330–1336: Francesc Cabà, Francesc Llaurador, Jaume de Montsec; 1333: Berenguer Tolrà; 1333–1334: Ramon de Déu; 1336: Bernat Feliu, Berenguer de Mas, Pere de Matamala; 1336–1337: Francesc d'Arenys; 1336–1342: Francesc d'Hostòles; 1346–1365: Pere Domènec

BORJA (founded ca. 1320; no names found)

CAGLIARI (founded ca. 1325)
1335–1342: Guillem Cendròs; 1326–1339: Pere Isern

CALATAYUD (founded before 1273)
1281–1296: Marc Pérez; 1286: Pons de Cros; 1286–1292: Romeo de Teruel; 1292: Vicente Gallego; 1297†: Martín Fernando; 1297–1316: Romeu de Bosom; **1300**: Juan de Calatayud; 1302: [H]ispano; 1304: Simón de Calatayud; 1307–1335: García Martínez; 1312: Pedro Muñoz; 1313–1326: Ramon de Mieres; 1316: Miguel de la Cida?; 1317–1319: Beneyto Bueno; 1320–1321: Martín de Samara; 1321–1322: Geraldo; 1325: Garino Valentín; 1326–1327: Guillermo Sayas; 1337: Juan de Figuerola?; 1344: Juan Pérez

CASTELLÓ D'EMPÚRIES (founded ca. 1246)
1249–1276: Ramon de Castelló; 1265–1338: Guillem Ferrer; 1273–1324: Guillem de Lles; 1276: Pere de Romaní; 1280–1302: Berenguer de Sa Nespleda; 1286: Ramon Aperrer?; 1293–1309: Pons Rossinyol; 1293–1324: Pere de Forn; 1295: Pere Gomar; 1295–1302: Pere de Vilanova; 1295–1331: Arnau de Vilatenim; 1297–1309: Simó de Montsec; 1297–1317: Guillem Canavells; **1301**: Ramon de Roca; 1301–1303: Ramon Pere; 1302: Guillem Paradís, Bernat de Rubió; 1302–1350: Pere de Sa Roca; 1303: Bernat Terrós; 1303–1306: Jaume Terrer (Terreni); 1303–1317: Guillem Guitard; 1304: Pere de Navarra; 1305: Ramon Pocoví?; 1306: Guillem Torelló; 1307–1328: Berenguer Folcrà; 1308: Ebrí?; 1311: Bernat Carcassó, Joan Sifré; 1317: Pere Proeta, Jaume Segur; 1317–1322: Bernat Fuster; 1317–1324: Pere Besalú; 1317–1331: Pere Junyer; 1318–1331: Berenguer Cerdà; 1328: Bartomeu Fuster; 1332–1335: Francesc Gosalt; 1326–1339: Pere Isern

CASTELLÓN DEL CAMP DE BURRIANA (no known house, but there was probably a hospice there in the 1330s)

CERVERA (founded in the early 1220s)
Date unknown: Nicolau de Porra; 1292-1317: Arnau d'Esplugues; 1299-1333: Jaume Nadal; 1305-1306: Bernat Ade; 1305-1322: Guillem de Valls; 1312-1315: Simó de Puigcerdà; 1314-1336: Bernat Pintor; 1316-1321: Pere de Cervera; 1326: Ramon Mon[t]reclús; 1330-1343: Jaume Ros; 1331-1343: Berenguer Queralt; 1332: Jaume de Lillet, Bernat Requesens; 1334-1336: Mateu Pintor; 1339: Berenguer de Fustenyà; 1345-1346: Pere Desquo?; 1348: Guillem Fuster, Ramon Granell, Guillem Olomar, Guillem Porta, Guillem Revell, Arnau Sant Domí

DAROCA (founded in the 1220s)
1277: Fernando de Cetina; 1296: Domingo Merced; 1316: Eneco Martín Vigana; 1329-1345: Gil de Medina; 1334: Pedro Ramón, Jaime de Sayas; 1337: Sancho de la Nuca

EJEA DE LOS CABALLEROS (founded 1250)
1286-1316: Romeo Ortiz; 1316: Juan de Gargeto

GERONA (founded ca. 1231)
Date unknown: Ferrer Sala; 1249-1276: Ramon de Castelló; 1254-1255: Bernat de Bach; 1265-1338: Guillem Ferrer; 1267: Ferrer de Cruilles; 1273: Ferrer Serra; 1291: Bernat de Vilaert; 1291-1318: Bernat d'Ullà; 1295: Guerau Massó; 1295-1331: Arnau de Vilatenim; 1295-1337: Pere de Palau; 1296-1299: Pere Negre; 1297-1303: Guillem Banc; 1297-1317: Guillem Canavells; 1297-1329: Guerau de Prat; **1300**: Guillem de Cuiga; 1300-1310: Francesc de Vilagrassa; 1301-1337: Ramon Puig; 1302-1308: Bernat de Cases; 1302-1324: Jaume de Vernet; 1303: Berenguer Fabra, Jaume de Palau, Bartomeu Peregrí; 1303-1317: Guillem Guitard; 1304-1329: Guillem de Sant Feliu; 1305: Pere de Vilatenim; 1305-1353: Jaume Ferrer; 1306-1307: Joan de Lluçà; 1306-1347: Sancho de Navarra; 1307: Guillem de Bonastre; 1307-1311: Bernat d'Alemany; 1307-1328: Berenguer Folcrà; 1307-1327: Guillem Gilabert; 1307-1339: Guillem de Puig; 1307-1344: Arnau de Castllà; **1310**-1354: Bernat Puig; 1313: Joan; 1314: Ramon Alemany, Francesc Comte; 1315-1328: Joan de Roure; 1318-1329: Pere de Cab[an]elles; 1318-1331: Berenguer Cerdà; 1319: Guillem de Roca; **1320**-1334: Guillem de Rubió; 1324: Llorens d'Antoni; 1324-1326: Berenguer Ferrer; 1324-1333: Pere de Terradelles; **1325**: Ferrer Bolla, Joan Jordà, Jaume Negrell, Pere Ses Oliveres, Jaume Teuler; 1325-1342: Jaume Moler; 1325-1347: Francesc Esteve; 1326: Pere Calahug, Ramon David, Guillem Pomar, Guillem de Prat, Francesc Saquer; 1326-1328: Francesc Terrassa, Francesc Solà, Francesc Segarra; 1326-1333: Pere Sa Capella; 1327-1335: Bernat Ferrer; 1328: Bertran Sa Mas; 1329: Pere Artau, Firm[íc] Closa, Joan Marçal, Firm[íc] Provençal, Pere Quintana; 1329-1334: Berenguer Argilés, Ferrer Llobet, Pere Martí; 1329-1345: Bernat Sans; **1330**-1342: Francesc Miquel; 1331: Ferrer Gener; 1332-1335: Francesc Gosalt; 1333: Esteve Lluch, Pere Meder, Guillem Miquel, Nicolau de Puig, Bernat Trassera; 1333-1336: Ramon Moner; 1333-1338: Marc Lloreta; 1333-1341: Joan

Guerau; 1333–1357: Jaume Solà, Francesc Morató; 1334: Jaume Falcó, Bernat Palol (Pallola?); 1334–1335: Bartomeu Florit, Ramon Figuera; 1334–1336: Francesc Rafart; 1334–1339: Francesc Rosell; 1334–1341: Pere Rabadà; **1335**: Pere Florit; 1336: Francesc Andreu, Guerau Cardona, Pere Comella, Guillem Ogern?, Guillem Ramad[er]a, Jaume Rosell; 1336–1337: Francesc d'Arenys, Maties Pons; 1336–1342: Francesc d'Hostòles; 1336–1343: Galcerán Tomàs; 1336–1345: Jaume de Vilatenim; 1336–1374: Joan Carmenço; 1336–1375: Guillem de Campllong; 1336–1382: Pere de Sicília; 1337: Guillem de Clapers, Mateu Coll, Bartomeu Pardo, Berenguer Segura; 1337–1338: Bernat Andreu, Jaume Morell, Guillem Vilar; 1337–1372: Francesc Gener; 1337–1374: Francesc Ros; 1338: Joan Bartolí, Pere de Bell-lloc, Francesc Berga, Pere de Buigues, Mateu Gormar, Guillem Mercader, Pere Perpinyà, Guillem de Pi, Berenguer Raffeques?; 1338–1339: Bernat d'Araveig; 1338–1341: Jaume Tint[or]er; 1338–1343: Bernat de Cases; 1338–1344: Francesc Ventalló; 1338–1355: Guillem Teixidor; 1338–1359: Llorens Moner; 1338–1373: Nicolau Tanyà; 1339: Pere de Sa Carrera; 1339–1397: Nicolau Sa Costa; 1339–1345: Guillem Crespià; 1339–1351: Berenguer Serra; 1339–1391: Francesc Colteller; **1340**: Lluis Llombart; 1340: Jaume Sa Farrera; 1340–1343: Joan Llombart; 1340–1344: Uguet Felip; 1340–1370: Pere de Pont; 1341: Benet, Guillem Curçavell?, Francesc Fares, Guillem Jover; 1341: Pere Roqueta, Francesc Turell; 1341–1342: Joan Bernat; 1342: Berenguer Borrell, Francesc de Roca; 1343: Bernat Mestre, Berenguer Moragues, Berenguer Roig, Bernat Soler, Domènec dez Soler, Bernat Vilardemí; 1343–1348: Bernat de Piles; 1343–1350: Berenguer Rovira; 1343–1385: Jaume de Mora; 1344: Guillem Bagés, Joan Giralt, Jaume Jordà, Francesc Martí, Pere Mora, Bartomeu Quirze, Pere de Valmanya; 1344–1347: Arnau Preixana; 1344–1352: Guillem Llobet; 1344–1374: Arnau Renart; 1344–1375: Guillem Jordà; **1345**: Guillem de Bas, Castelló de Font, Guillem Ivern, Jaume Julià, Arnau Lledó, Bernat Sa Horta, Francesc Segura, Ramon Vidal; 1345–1346: Bartomeu Babau, Francesc Taulers; 1345–1350: Ramon de Torrents; 1345–1361: Francesc Torrents; 1346: Bonanat Feliu, Esteve de Limoges, Gombau Perués, Ramon Serena; 1346–1347: Romeu Mar, Guillem de Soler; 1347: Bernat Castell; 1347: Pere d'Esparreguera, Arnau d'Espasens, Berenguer Surribes, Jaume Vicens, Bernat Vilanova; 1347–1348: Ramon Banc, Berenguer de Vilamarics; 1347–1376: Francesc Burriana; 1347–1386: Bernat Bru; 1348: Francesc de Muntanyana, Arnau de Piles

HUESCA (founded in the 1220s or early 1230s)
1232–1278: Il.luminat; 1236–1278: William (or Peter) of the See; 1273: Gil; 1279: Martín de Rosal; 1283–1308: Rodrigo de Gúdar; 1297–1316: Romeu de Bosom; 1299–1344: Ramón de Huesca; 1302: Bernardo de Ahones; 1305–1320: Martín de Alcolea; 1305–1337: Nicolás de la Naya; 1320: Bartolomeo de Alcalá; 1325–1329: Martín Romeo; 1328: Sancho de Marra; 1329–1346: Sancho López de Ayerbe; 1334–1337: Pedro de Huesca

JACA (founded before 1246)
1260–1316: Domingo de Jaca; 1302–1321: Ramon de Borau; 1305: Lamberto

CHRONOLOGY OF CONVENT RESIDENTS 377

LERIDA (founded ca. 1227)
Date unknown: Lluis d'Escala; 1234-1237: Jaume Arnau; 1234-1238†/1239†: Arnau; 1236: Guillem de Cervera; 1246-1276: Miguel de Tudela; 1247: Pere Tarragona; 1254-1255: Bernat de Bach; 1257: Segrià; 1270-1316: Pere Esteve; 1283-1286: Joan de Barriac; 1291-1305: Miquel Jordà; 1293-1307: Pere d' Esplugues; 1294: Guerau Botet; 1301-1333: Guillem Treballós; 1304-1317: Guillem Castelló; 1305-1353: Jaume Ferrer; 1307-1318: Bernat de Déu; 1307-1343: Domènec Martí; 1308-1315: Pere de Puig; 1312-1315: Simó de Puigcerdà; 1314-1336: Bernat Pintor; 1316: Bernat de Pim; 1316-1338: Bernat Esteve; 1318-1335: Antoni Andreu; 1320: Bernat de Rocanova: 1321-1337: Guillem Jornet; 1328-1349: Ramon de Bas; 1330-1334: Joan Maler; 1333: Jaume Altés; 1339-1391: Francesc Colteller

MAJORCA (founded ca. 1229)
1232: Simeó; 1234-1237: Jaume Arnau; 1234-1238†/1239†: Arnau; 1244: Albert de Milans; 1281: Ramon Tortosa, Pere de Vilagrassa; 1281-1292: Berenguer de Lledó; 1281-1327: Pere de Quadres; 1282: Guillem Bonet; 1282-1316: Arnau Oliba; 1286: Joan Bautista; 1286-1295: Berenguer Grau; 1292: Pere de Llívia; 1298-1316†: Pere Guerau (Third Order); **1300**-1310: Francesc de Vilagrassa; 1302-1325: A[rnau] d'Armenter; 1306: Jaume; 1306-1329: Pere Arnau; 1307-1348: Pons Carles; 1308: Pressivald Claver; 1311-1348: Pere Muntaner; 1317: Pere Cima; 1317-1322: Bernat Fuster; 1319: Antoni de Mora; 1322: Ferrer Reial; **1325**: Jaume Teuler, Guillem Caporer, Pere Massot, Pere Ses Oliveres; 1325-1330: Bernat Bort; 1325-1347: Jaume de Lacera; 1326: Pere Calahug; 1326-1327: Domènec Salvela; 1326-1338: Francesc Clarà; 1327: Antoni Camps, Pere Forner; 1329: Francesc Campanyó, Nicolau Estany, Joan Marçal; 1329-1345: Bernat Sans; **1330**: Joan Sa Granada; 1330-1339: Guillem Soberats; 1330-1342: Francesc Miquel; 1331-1338: Bertran Salmó; 1332-1348: Francesc Durant; 1333-1335: Salvador de Terrades; 1334-1338: Guillem Vidal; 1334-1346: Pere Seioll; 1336-1375: Guillem de Campllong; 1337: Antoni Cabot, Bernat Llorens, Guillem Massanet, Miquel de Sentís, Ramon de Terrassa, Miquel Torner, Jaume Trobat; 1338: Roderic Bergundia, Bonanat Roger; 1339: Pere Berrales, Bernat d'Olorda, Bernat de Salús, Pere Xiró; **1340**: Antoni Cabissó, Pere de Camps, Pere Cabiol; 1340-1344: Uguet Felip; 1343: Jaume Laberes; 1345: Guillem, Berenguer Martorell; 1345-1393: Bartomeu Sant Martí; 1346: Antoni Capó, Jaume Capó, Gabriel Ortolà, Felip? Pere; 1346-1365: Pere Domènec; 1346-1366: Jordi Amat; 1347-1386: Bernat Bru; 1348: Joan Palol (Pallola?); 1348-1382: Pere Marc

MANRESA (no convent, but there was a hospice there in the 1290s)

MINORCA (Ciutadella; founded 1287)
1273-1295: Berenguer Garí; 1273-1324: Guillem de Lles; 1304: Bernat de Garrigella, Obert Masmolí, Francesc de Pujada, Guillem de Torre; 1325-1347: Francesc Esteve

MIRAMAR, Majorca (founded 1276)
1291–1292: Bernat Folc

MOLINA (founded 1286?)
1293: Pedro de Chilliella, Domingo López, Nicolás de Morella (Moriella)

MONTBLANC (founded in the 1230s)
1305–1316: Guerau de Valls; 1305–1322: Guillem de Valls; 1320: Andreu de Guàrdia; 1330–1343: Jaume Ros

MONTPELLIER (founded ca. 1220)
1233: Dominique; 1282: Esteve Dardas, Pa[rdo] Tornat (Trobat?); 1282–1294: Arnau de Rocafull (at Lunel); 1294: Eustace (at Lunel), Guillem

MONZÓN (founded before 1261)
1232–1278: Il.luminat; 1236–1278: William (or Peter) of the See; 1269: Guillem de Fraumir; 1272: Miguel de Conchel, Pere de Copons; 1275–1295: Francisco; 1305–1322: Guillem de Valls; 1313: Andreu de Copons, Martín Dendestre; 1347: Ade de Tenat

MORELLA (founded between 1232 and 1249)
1271: [–] Amargós; 1272: Antonio Bonarres

MURVIEDRO (modern Sagunto; founded ca. 1248)
1302–1306: Domènec Fontana; 1304–1306: Fernando de la Reina

PAMPLONA (founded before 1245)
1246–1276: Miguel de Tudela; 1345: Pedro Paternué

PEDRALBES, Barcelona (no convent but there was a hospice there from 1327)

PERPIGNAN (founded ca. 1220)
Date unknown: Pere de Font de Llop; 1265–1338: Guillem Ferrer; 1292–1295: Ramon; 1295: Guillem Ferranco, Pere Malol; 1301–1327: Jeroni de Catalunya; 1314–1315: Ramon de Bignera; 1319: Francesc Raynaud; 1320–1337: Bernat Simó; 1320–1348: Pere Seguí; 1321: Berenguer Talló; 1323: Bernat Nau; 1330–1348: Bernat Geli; 1332–1348: Francesc Durant; 1337: Francesc Bosc, Joan Dinet, Francesc Guinya; 1342–1348: Berenguer Juli; 1348: Pere Masseguer, Ramon Nau, Arnau Rostan, Francesc Terreni; 1348–1382: Pere Marc

PUIGCERDÀ (founded 1320)
The friars listed with dates prior to the foundation spent their first years in the Order in other convents and their names appear there too.
1295–1337: Pere de Palau; 1299–1344: Ramón de Huesca; **1301**–1337: Ramon Puig; 1304–1329: Guillem de Sant Feliu; 1305–1338: Guillem Catelli; 1310–

1354: Bernat Puig; 1312-1315: Simó de Puigcerdà; 1314-1347: Tomàs Pere; 1315-1348: Bernat Espanyoll; 1315-1362: Pere Llaguna; 1319-1320: Ramon Talló; **1320**: Pere Feliu, Joan Plomer, Bernat Vicens; 1320-1321: Mateu Llinyà; 1320-1329: Ramon de Sant Feliu; 1320-1346: Bernat Colomer; 1321: Bernat Arcegell; 1321-1323: Ramon Llunada; 1323-1329: Joan Escatar; 1324: Arnau Colomer, Pere Gelera; **1330**: Bernat Galredoner, Joan de Vilallobent, Ramon; 1330-1338: Francesc Guillem; 1330-1348: Bernat Geli; 1331-1338: Arnau Duran; 1332: Arnau Pedrissa; 1333: Berenguer Tolrà; 1335: Ramon Ger; 1335-1341: Guillem Canals; 1335-1348: Pere Tasquer; 1336: Joan Engomader?; 1336-1339: Ramon Boixador; 1336-1341: Jaume Duran; 1336-1343: Cerdà d'Urús; 1336-1347: Pere Batlle; 1336-1348: Pere Santesteva; 1336-1351: Ramon Colomer; 1338: Pere d'Arcís, Bernat Baster, Bernat Borrell, Pere Canals, Pere Capdevila, Cerdà de Casca, Bernat Cerdà, Pere Cerdà, Francesc Fabra, Pere Ger, Pere Lora, Ramon Neva, Ramon Quer; 1338-1341: Guillem Juli; 1338-1346: Bernat Colom; 1338-1347: Pere Gomar; 1338-1348: Pere de Conomines; 1338-1351: Jaume Capdevila; 1339: Guillem Borrell, Jaume Roquer; 1339-1348: Guillem Tasquer; 1339-1362: Bernat Calva, Ramon Domenge; **1340**: Bernat Canals, Arnau Ramon; 1341: Francesc Baner, Guillem Bo, Pere Domenge, Guillem Orla, Arnau Pere, Cerdà de Viure; 1341-1342: Joan Bar; 1341-1348: Jaume Fabra, Ramon Santesteva; 1341-1353: Jaume Domenge; 1342: Ramon Ansurrà, Pere Colomer, Jaume Escariu, Esteve Fabra, Bernat Juli, Ramon Mora; 1342-1343: Pere Redon; 1342-1348: Berenguer Juli, Joan dez Trenils; 1343: Francesc Boera; 1344: Ramon Avezurrán?; 1346: Francesc Arguelaguers, Guillem Corell, Ramon Pagès, Guillem de Sarrià; 1346-1347: Ramon Malanyea (Manlleu?), Joan dez Torrents; 1347: Pere Colom, Guillem Guitard, Jaume Pintor; 1347-1348: Pons de Capbreu, 1347-1355: Guillem Torner; 1348: Guillem Bar, Jaume Bosc, Bernat Bruguera, Jaume de Conomines, Francesc Isogol

SARAGOSSA (founded in the 1220s)
1220: Nicolás Orbita, Bernat Vidal; 1220-1231†: Félix; 1234-1238†/1239†: Arnau; 1277: Miquel de Montagut; 1280-1316: Pascasi de Vall-llebrera; 1281-1316: Bernat Gil; 1283: Guillem de Roig; 1283-1313: Guillem de la Cort; 1285-1308: Rodrigo de Gúdar; 1286-1316†: Romeo Ortiz; 1288: Ramon de Gudal; 1299-1344: Ramón de Huesca; 1305-1311: Domingo de Lares; 1306-1312: Domingo de Ros; 1311-1368: Joan d'Aragó; 1320: Miguel Borau; 1320-1334: Guillem de Rubió; 1320-1336: Juan de Ximénez; 1321: Juan de Ejea; 1322-1330: García de Ayusa; 1325: Enégo Oblit; 1328-1332: Aparicio Serra; 1329-1346: Sancho López de Ayerbe; 1330: Miguel de Almenara; 1330-1345: Pardo Serra; 1348-1350: Martín Sancho de Antillón

SARIÑENA (founded 1282)
1285: Pascasi Vall-lloreta; 1320-1337: Nicolás de la Naya

SASSARI, Sardinia (founded ca. 1326)
Date unknown: Antoni de Sassari; 1316-1347: Arnau de Canelles

TARAZONA (probably founded in the 1220s)
1297-1305: Bertran Ahones; 1314-1320: García de Biesa; 1315-1326: Arnulf; 1320: Juan de Bonell; 1325-1329: Martín Romeo; 1337-1338: Pere de Maler; 1338: Eximeno de Maler

TARRAGONA (founded ca. 1227)
1246-1276: Miguel de Tudela; 1248-1267: Bernat Ferrer; 1249-1276: Ramon de Castelló; 1254-1255: Guillem d'Ager; 1302-1319: Guillem Sa Roca; 1306: Pere de Segarra; 1306-1332: Bernat Perpinyà; 1330: Guillem Alegre; 1337-1339: Francesc; 1340: Francesc Llena

TÀRREGA (founded 1318)
1316-1321: Pere de Cervera; 1321-1327: Pere Ses Gunyoles; 1342: Ramon Gornall

TERUEL (founded ca. 1225)
1220-1231: Bernat; 1281-1296: Marc Pérez; 1284: Bartomeu Manta; 1286-1316†: Romeo Ortiz; 1307-1335: García Martínez; 1317: Martín Catani; 1324: Guillem de Marimón; 1325: Garino Valentín; 1325-1329: Joan de Montfort; 1326-1339: Pedro Nicolás; 1330: Rodrigo Navarret; 1346: Eximeno de Sayas

TORTOSA (founded in the 1230s)
1248-1267: Bernat Ferrer; 1276: Andreu de Pamplona, Palazino de Baón, Berenguer de Guàrdia, Berenguer de Valls, Balaguer de Zabadía; 1276-1299: Guerau de Puigalt; 1302-1306: Domènec de Fontana; 1315: Balaguer Guasch, Martí Llomber; 1315-1326: Arnulf; 1318-1329: Pere de Cab[an]elles; 1322-1383: Guillem Guardiola; 1330-1333: Bernat de Vilagrassa; 1343-1385: Jaume de Mora

TUNIS (founded in the 1230s)
1249-1276: Ramon de Castelló; 1260-1280: Bernat Ferrer; 1303-1317: Guillem Guitard; 1306-1328: Joan de Roure; 1310: Arnau de Vilanova; 1314: Francesc Comte; 1317: Berenguer de Ca[s]tella, Miguel de Ca[s]tella, Jaume; 1317-1345: Romeu de Falques; 1337: Pere Comte

VALENCIA (founded ca. 1230)
Date unknown: Ferrer Terrassa; 1220-1231: Bernat; 1254: Ramón Cortell; 1262-1296: [-] Gómez; 1268: Sauner; 1277: Miquel de Montagut; 1278-1288: Martín de Vilella; 1280-1316: Pascasi de Vall-llebrera; 1282-1294: Arnau de Rocafull; 1283: Pere de Tous; 1286-1292: Romeo de Teruel; 1289: [Bernat?] Simó; 1290: Pere de Belchite; 1292-1326?: Fernando García; 1293-1310: Albert; 1296: Gil de Malvenda; 1297-1316: Romeu de Bosom; 1304-1306: Fernando de la Reina; 1306-1347: Sancho de Navarra; 1307-1343: Domènec Martí; 1310-1334: Andreu Albalat; 1313-1329: Bernat Constans; 1313-1326: Ramon de Mieres; 1315-1348: Bernat Espanyoll; 1318: Sancho de Castellany, Ramon de Rei; 1321-1337: Guillem Jornet; 1326-1334: Gil Alvárez; 1326-

1337: Berenguer d'Ivorra; 1329†: Ramon de Font; 1329-1333: Jaume de Montfort; 1329-1345: Gil de Medina; 1335: Guillem d'Agramunt, Francesc Miró; 1336-1374: Joan Carmenço; 1343: Francesc Calvo, Jaume Just; 1344-1374: Arnau Renart; 1347-1386: Bernat Bru

VIC (founded 1225)
Date unknown: Nicolau de Porra; 1232: Segimon des Lledó; 1247: [-] Olivera; 1257: Guillem de Montseny; 1260: Pere de Noguer; 1262-1284: Guillem de Blanes; 1263-1288: Arnau de Forn; 1263-1265†: Pere Vidal; 1265-1338: Guillem Ferrer; 1268-1280: Guerau Miró; 1271-1273: Guillem de Montmajor; 1273-1295: Berenguer Garí; 1273-1324: Guillem de Lles; 1275: Arnau de Fontanelles; **1280**: Pere de Fluvià, Berenguer de Vilagranada; 1280-1302: Berenguer de Sa Nespleda; 1281-1292: Berenguer de Lledó; 1281-1327: Pere de Quadres; 1285-1291: Bernat Draper; 1287: Guillem Folc; 1288: Bernat Riera; 1288-1308: Ramon de Sotsroca; **1290**-1302: Pere Mir; 1291-1306: Guerau d'Osor; 1292-1298: Ramon de Morera; 1293: Bernat Dubà, Berenguer Mercadal; 1293-1309: Pons Rossinyol; 1293-1324: Pere de Forn; 1299: Bernat Mora (?); 1299-1344: Ramón de Huesca; **1300**-1307: Tomàs de Caldes; 1301-1337: Ramon Puig; 1303: Francesc d'Arena; 1303-1317: Guillem Guitard; 1305-1316: Bernat de Vilajoan; 1306-1332: Bernat Perpinyà; 1307-1314: Guillem de Sa Carrera; 1307-1316: Ramon de Costa; 1308: Berenguer d'Osor; 1314-1347: Tomàs Pere; 1315: Bernat de Vilar; 1316-1364: Guillem Sala; 1317: Guillem Ses Pujol; 1318: Bernat Colteller, Guillem Espanyol; **1320**: Guillem Batlle; 1322: Pere de Terrassa; 1322-1326: Arnau Oller, Pere de Terrer; 1324-1333: Pere de Terradelles; 1324-1357: Pere Fuixà; 1333: Bernat Comas, Berenguer Roca, Bernat de Vilafant; 1333-1356: Francesc Rovira; 1335-1351: Francesc Batlle; 1337: Ramon Olomar, Berenguer de Puignibi; **1342**-1381: Antoni de Vilanova; 1343-1348: Bernat de Piles; 1344: Arnau Serra; 1344-1348: Pere Oriol; 1344-1375: Guillem Jordà; 1345: Bernat Rosell, Arnau de Soler, Bernat Vilaplana; 1345-1348: Guillem Pascasi; 1346: Domènec de Mastoro; 1347: Pere de Gualba; 1348: Gilabert, Pere Marquet, Pere Rabó, Gilabert Roura, Bartomeu Terrer

VILA IGLESIAS, Sardinia (founded ca. 1326)
1316-1325: Andreu d'Aguilar; 1321-1327: Pere Ses Gunyoles

VILAFRANCA DEL PENEDÈS (founded before 1230)
Date unknown: Ferrer Sala; 1262-1322: Ferrer d'Alemany; 1281-1327: Pere de Quadres; 1298-1314: Bernat Fuster (Third Order); 1298-1316†: Pere Guerau (Third Order); 1300-1336: Pons Carbonell; 1304-1329: Guillem de Sant Feliu;1308: Bartomeu; 1314: Ramon Alemany; 1314-1347: Tomàs Pere; 1317-1345: Romeu de Falques; 1320-1334: Guillem de Rubió; 1333: Borraç Baró; 1333-1356: Francesc Rovira; 1335: Pere Mercer; 1335-1368: Bernat Pellicer; 1344-1375: Ramon Moliner; 1345: Antoni Burdils, Guillem Crebayno, Jaume Julià, Pere de Marimón, Ramon Ricart

VILLEFRANCHE DE CONFLENT (probably founded before 1276; many of the early Puigcerdà friars lived in this convent until their house was founded in 1320)

XÀTIVA (founded 1248)
1264–1284: [Pere?] Marc; 1281–1316: Bernat Gil; 1283: Pere Roc (Sa Roca?) 1290: Pere de Belchite, Enric; 1291–1305: Miquel Jordà; 1292–1326?: Fernando García; 1306–1347: Sancho de Navarra; 1307: Simó Bertran; 1326: Benvingut de Granollers

Appendix 5

Alphabetical List of Friars

Abat, Berenguer d' (1307)
Abat, Jaume d' (1307)
Abeyà, Berenguer (1307)
Abeyà, Ferrer d' (1325-1335)
Abeyà, Miquel (1315)
Ade, Bernat (1305-1306)
Ager, Guillem d' (1254-1255)
Agramunt, Guillem d' (1335)
Aguda, Berenguer d' (1307)
Aguilar, Andreu d' (1316-1325)
Aguilar, Berenguer (1300-1307)
Agut, Nicolau (1342-1345)
Ahones, Bernardo de (1302)
Ahones, Bertran (1297-1305)
Aimeric (1246-1247)
Aimeric (1312-1315)
Albalat, Andreu (1310-1334)
Alberic (1290-1309)
Alberot (Alberic?) (1310)
Albert (1293-1310)
Alcalá, Bartolomeo de (1320)
Alcalá, Guillermo de (1300)
Alcolea, Martín de (1305-1320)
Alegre, Guillem (1330)
Alegre, Pere (1301-1306)
Alemany, Bernat d' (1307-1311)
Alemany, Ferrer d' (1262-1322)
Alemany, Ramon (1314)
Alfam[er]a, Bernat d' (1324)
Almenara, Miguel de (1330)
Alós, Arnau d' (1324)
Aloysius (1294)
Alp, Bernat d' (1295)
Alp, Joan d' (1296-1307)
Altés, Jaume (1333)
Alvarez, Gil (1326-1334)
Amalui, Jaume (1284)

Amargós, [-] (1271)
Amat, Jaume (1317)
Amat, Jordi (1346-1366)
Amorós, Berenguer d' (1340-1347)
Andreu, Antoni (1318-1335)
Andreu, Bernat (1337-1338)
Andreu, Francesc (1336)
Ansurrà, Ramon (1342)
Antillón, Martín Sancho de
  (1348-1350)
Antoni, Llorens d' (1324)
Aperrer?, Ramon (1286)
Aragó, Ferran d' (1348-1356)
Aragó, Joan d' (1311-1368)
Aranyó, Guillem (1310)
Araveig, Bernat d' (1338-1339)
Arbitre, Bernat (1288)
Arcegell, Bernat (1321)
Arcís, Pere d' (1338)
Arec, Martí (1301)
Arena, Francesc d' (1303)
Arenós, Domènec (1348)
Arenys, Francesc d' (1336-1337)
Arenys, Pere d' (1302)
Arguelaguers, Francesc (1346)
Argilés, Berenguer (1329-1334)
Armenter, A[rnau] d' (1302-1325)
Arnau (1234-1238†/1239†)
Arnau, Guillem (1285)
Arnau, Jaume (1234-1237)
Arnau, Pere (1306-1329)
Arnulf (1315-1326)
Artamara, Pere d' (1325)
Artasona, Pere d' (1339)
Artau, Pere (1329)
Atarravia, Pere d' (1317-1324)
Augre, Pere (1301)

Avezurrán?, Ramon (1344)
Ayusa, García de (1322–1330)
Babau, Bartomeu (1345–1346)
Bach, Bernat de (1254–1255)
Bagés, Guillem (1344)
Ballester, G[uillem] (1326)
Banc, Guillem (1297–1303)
Banc, Ramon (1347–1348)
Bancal, Ramon (1326–1327)
Baner, Francesc (1341)
Bano (Bancal?), Ramon (1326)
Baón, Palazino de (1276)
Bar, Guillem (1348)
Bar, Joan (1341–1342)
Barberà, Guillem de (1278)
Bardina, Guillem (1325)
Baró, Borraç (1333)
Barriac, Joan de (1283–1286)
Bartolí, Joan (1338)
Bartomeu (1308)
Bas, Guillem de (1345)
Bas, Ramon de (1328–1349)
Basella, Berenguer (1331–1332)
Bassols, Joan (date unknown)
Baster, Bernat (1338)
Batlle, Andreu (1326)
Batlle, Arnau (1349–1360)
Batlle, Francesc (1335–1351)
Batlle, Guillem (1320)
Batlle, Pere (1336–1347)
Bautista, Joan (1286)
Belchite, Pere de (1290)
Bell-lloc, Pere de (1338)
Bellfort, Pere de (1280–1298)
Benet (1341)
Berga, Francesc (1338)
Bergundia, Roderic (1338)
Bernat (1220–1231)
Bernat, Joan (1341–1342)
Berrales, Pere (1339)
Bertís, Ferran (1322)
Bertran, Simó (1307)
Besalú, Pere (1317–1324)
Bianya, Bernat de (1285–1288)
Biesa, García de (1314–1320)

Bignera, Ramon de (1314–1315)
Blanes, Guillem de (1262–1284)
Bo, Guillem (1341)
Boada, Pere (1270)
Boera, Francesc (1343)
Bogar, Guillem (1324)
Boià, Jaume (1302)
Boixador, Ramon (1336–1339)
Bolla, Ferrer (1325)
Bonarres, Antonio (1272)
Bonastre, Arnau (1278–1325)
Bonastre, Guerau (1300–1307)
Bonastre, Guillem de (1307)
Bondemà, Castelló de (1303)
Bonell, Juan de (1320)
Bonet, Guillem (1282)
Bonet, Nicolau (1343)
Bonhom (Bononia?), Jaume de (1319–1325)
Borau, Miguel (1320)
Borau, Ramon de (1302–1321)
Borrell, Berenguer (1342)
Borrell, Bernat (1338)
Borrell, Guillem (1339)
Bort, Bernat (1325–1330)
Bosc, Bartomeu de (1300–1307)
Bosc, Francesc (1337)
Bosc, Jaume (1348)
Bosom, Bartomeu (1278)
Bosom, Jaume de (1302–1324)
Bosom, Nicolau (1307)
Bosom, Romeu de (1297–1316)
Botet, Guerau (1294)
Botinyà, Castelló (1314–1330)
Briva, Guillem (1246)
Bru, Bernat (1347–1386)
Bruguera, Bernat (1348)
Bruno (1286)
Bruny, Francesc (1290?)
Brusca?, Pons (1325–1334)
Bueno, Beneyto (1317–1319)
Buigues, Pere de (1338)
Bullada, Simó de (1324)
Burdils, Antoni (1345)
Burdils, Bernat (1307)

ALPHABETICAL LIST OF FRIARS

Burdils, Pere de (1324)
Burgué, Pere (1321-1336)
Burgués, D[-] (1323)
Burriana, Francesc (1347-1376)
Busquet, Guillem (1324)
Cabà, Francesc(1330-1336)
Cab[an]elles,Pere de (1318-1329)
Cabiol, Pere (1340)
Cabissó, Antoni (1340)
Cabot, Antoni (1337)
Calahug, Pere (1326)
Calatayud, Simón de (1304)
Calatayud, Juan de (1300)
Caldes, Tomàs de (1300-1307)
Calva, Bernat (1339-1362)
Calvet, Guillem (1326)
Calvo, Francesc (1343)
Campanyó, Francesc (1329)
Campllong, Guillem de
 (1336-1375)
Camps, Antoni (1327)
Camps, Pere de (1340)
Canals, Bernat (1340)
Canals, Guillem (1335-1341)
Canals, Guillem de (1296)
Canals, Pere (1338)
Canavells, Guillem (1297-1317)
Canelles, Arnau de (1316-1347)
Capbreu, Pons de (1347-1348)
Capdevila, Jaume (1338-1351)
Capdevila, Pere (1338)
Capó, Antoni (1346)
Capó, Jaume (1346)
Caporer, Guillem (1325)
Caral, Berenguer de (1307)
Carbonell, Francesc (1326)
Carbonell, Pere (1307-1321)
Carbonell, Pons (1300-1336)
Carcassó, Bernat (1311)
Cardona, Berenguer de (1302)
Cardona, Bernat (1302)
Cardona, Francesc de (1310)
Cardona, Guerau (1336)
Carles, Pons (1307-1348)
Carmenço, Joan (1336-1374)

Carrall, Berenguer de (1307)
Casca, Cerdà de (1338)
Casells, Bernat (1326)
Cases, Arnau de (1326)
Cases, Bartomeu (1302)
Cases, Bernat de (1302-1308)
Cases, Bernat de (1338-1343)
Castell, Bernat (1347)
Ca[s]tella, Berenguer de (1317)
Castella, Juan de (1307)
Castella, Mateo de (1307)
Ca[s]tella, Miguel de (1317)
Castella, Pedro de (1332)
Castellany, Sancho de (1318)
Castelló, Guillem (1304-1317)
Castelló, Joan de (1302-1336)
Castelló, Ramon de (1249-1276)
Castllà, Arnau de (1307-1344)
Català, [-] (1248?)
Català, Francesc (1292†/1306†)
Catalunya, Jeroni de (1301-1327)
Catani, Martín (1317)
Catelli, Guillem (1305-1338)
Cendròs, Guillem (1335-1342)
Cerdà, Berenguer (1318-1331)
Cerdà, Bernat (1338)
Cerdà, Pere (1338)
Cervera, Guillem de (1236)
Cervera, Pere de (1316-1321)
Cetina, Fernando de (1275-1277)
Chilliella, Pedro de (1293)
Cida?, Miguel de la (1316)
Cima, Pere (1317)
[Ciscar], Ramon de (1339)
Ciurana, Joan de (1280-1316)
Clapers, Guillem de (1337)
Clarà, Francesc (1326-1338)
Clarà, Guillem (1300-1307)
Claver, Pressivald (1308)
Closa, Firm[íc] (1329)
Coll, Mateu (1337)
Colom, Bernat (1338-1346)
Colom, Pere (1347)
Colomer, Arnau (1324)
Colomer, Bernat (1320-1346)

Colomer, Pere (1342)
Colomer, Ramon (1336–1351)
Colteller, Bernat (1318)
Colteller, Francesc (1339–1391)
Comabella, Pere (1334)
Comas, Bernat (1333)
Comella, Pere (1336)
Company, Bernat (1307)
Comte, Francesc (1314)
Comte, Pere (1337)
Conchel, Miguel de (1272)
Conomines, Jaume de (1348)
Conomines, Pere de (1338–1348)
Constans, Bernat (1313–1329)
Copons, Andreu de (1313)
Copons, Pere de (1272)
Cordelles, Berenguer (1347)
Corell, Guillem (1346)
Cornudella, Pere de (1300–1307)
Cort, Guillem de la (1283–1313)
Cortell, Ramon (1254)
Coscollola, Eximeno (1340)
Costa, Ramon de (1307–1316)
Crebayno, Guillem (1345)
Crespià, Guillem (1339–1345)
Cros, Pons de (1286)
Cruilles, Ferrer de (1267)
Cuiga, Guillem de (1300)
Curçavell?, Guillem (1341)
Dalmau, P[ere] (1326)
Dardas, Esteve (1282)
David, Ramon (1326)
Demestre, Pere (1307)
Dendestre, Martín (1313)
Desideri (1246–1276)
Desquo?, Pere (1345–1346)
Déu, Bernat de (1307–1318)
Déu, Ramon de (1333–1334)
Dinet, Joan (1337)
Domènec, Pere (1346–1365)
Domenge, Jaume (1341–1353)
Domenge, Pere (1341)
Domenge, Ramon (1339–1362)
Dominique (1233)
Draper, Bernat (1285–1291)

Dubà, Bernat (1293)
Duran, Arnau (1331–1338)
Duran, Jaume (1336–1341)
Durant, Francesc (1332–1348)
Ebrí? (1308)
Eimeric (1314–1315)
Ejea, Juan de (1321)
Ejea, Martín de (1294)
Ejea, Nicolás de (1302)
Emberart, Pere (1287)
Engomader?, Joan (1336)
Enric (1290)
Escala, Lluis d' (date unknown)
Escariu, Jaume (1342)
Escarrer: see Esquerrer
Escatar, Guillem (1240)
Escatar, Joan (1323–1329)
Espais, Guillem d' (1322)
Espanyol, Guillem (1318)
Espanyoll, Bernat (1315–1348)
Esparreguera, Pere d' (1347)
Espasens, Arnau d' (1347)
Esplugues, Arnau d' (1292–1317)
Esplugues, Pere d' (1293–1307)
Esquerrer (Escarrer), Pere (1290)
Estagell, Arnau d' (1342)
Estalella, Simó d' (1333)
Estany, Nicolau (1329)
Estany, Ramon d' (1317–1336)
Esteve (1237)
Esteve, Bernat (1316–1338)
Esteve, Francesc (1325–1347)
Esteve, Pere (1270–1316)
Eustace (1294)
Fabra, Berenguer (1303)
Fabra, Esteve (1342)
Fabra, Francesc (1338)
Fabra, Jaume (1341–1348)
Falcó, Jaume (1334)
Falcó, Pere (1281)
Falgar, Guillem de (date unknown)
Falques, Romeu de (1317–1345)
Fares, Francesc (1341)
Felip, Uguet (1340–1344)
Feliu, Bernat (1336)

Feliu, Bonanat (1346)
Feliu, Pere (1320)
Félix (1220–1231†)
Fernando, Martín (1297†)
Ferranco, Guillem (1295)
Ferrer, Berenguer (1324–1326)
Ferrer, Bernat (1248–1267)
Ferrer, Bernat (1260–1280)
Ferrer, Bernat (1327–1335)
Ferrer, Guillem (1265–1338)
Ferrer, Jaume (1305–1353)
Ferrer, Pere (1311–1345)
Ferrer, Ramon (1307)
Ferrer, Simó (1303)
Figuera, Ramon (1334–1335)
Figuerola?, Juan de (1337)
Fiveller, Berenguer (1300–1309)
Florit, Bartomeu (1334–1335)
Florit, Pere (1335)
Fluvià, Pere de (1280)
Folc, Bernat (1291–1292)
Folc, Guillem (1287)
Folcrà, Berenguer (1307–1328)
Font, Castelló de (1345)
Font, Ramon de (1329†)
Font de Llop, Pere de (date unknown)
Fontana, Domènec de (1302–1306)
Fontanelles, Arnau de (1275)
Forn, Arnau de (1263–1288)
Forn, Jaume de (1295–1296)
Forn, Pere de (1293–1324)
Forner, Pere (1327)
Fort, Berenguer de (1300–1307)
Francesc (1324)
Francesc (1337–1339)
Francisco (1275–1295)
Fraumir, Guillem de (1269)
Frimago? (1286)
Fuixà, Joan de (1327)
Fuixà, Mateu de (1307)
Fuixà, Pere (1324–1357)
Fuixà, Romeu de (1300–1307)
Fustenyà, Berenguer de (1339)
Fuster, Bartomeu (1328)
Fuster, Bernat (1317–1322)
Fuster, Bernat (Third Order) (1298–1314)
Fuster, Guillem (1348)
Galcerán, Bernat (1302)
Galcerán, Tomàs (1336–1343)
Galícia, Juan de (1307)
Gallego, Vicente (1292)
Galredoner, Bernat (1330)
García, Fernando (1292–1326?)
Gargeto, Juan de (1316)
Garí, Berenguer (1273–1295)
Garisa, García (1327)
Garrigella, Bernat de (1304)
Gavarra, Guillem (1339)
Gelera, Pere (1324)
Geli, Bernat (1330–1348)
Gener, Ferrer (1331)
Gener, Francesc (1337–1372)
Gener (Janua), Pere de (1261–1293)
Gener (Janua), Rafael (1302)
Genoa, Angelo de (1322)
Ger, Pere (1338)
Ger, Ramon (1335)
Geraldo (1321–1322)
Gil (1273)
Gil, Bernat (1281–1316)
Gilabert (1348)
Gilabert, Guillem (1307–1327)
Giméno (1336). *See also* Hospital, Giméno de
Giniac, Ramon de (1309–1310)
Giralt, Joan (1344)
Godencs, Marc (1298–1307)
Gomar, Pere (1295)
Gomar, Pere (1338–1347)
Gómez, [–] (1262–1296)
Gonter, Alfredo (1322–1325)
Gonter, Bernat (1301–1313)
Gormar, Mateu (1338)
Gornall, Ramon (1342)
Gosalt, Francesc (1332–1335)
Granell, Ramon (1348)
Granollers, Benvingut de (1326)

Grau, Berenguer (1286–1295)
Gravera, Guillem de (1324)
Gualba, Bernat de (1262)
Gualba, Pere de (1347)
Guàrdia, Andreu de (1320)
Guàrdia, Berenguer de (1276)
Guàrdia, Ramon de (1296)
Guardiola, Guillem (1322–1383)
Guasch, Balaguer (1315)
Gudal, Ramon de (1288)
Gúdar, Rodrigo de (1283–1308)
Guerau (1236)
Guerau, Joan (1333–1341)
Guerau, Pere (Third Order)
  (1298–1316†)
Guillem (1294)
Guillem (1345)
Guillem, Francesc (1330–1338)
Guinya, Francesc (1337)
Guitard, Guillem (1303–1317)
Guitard, Guillem (1347)
Guzmán, Juan Pedro (1318)
[H]ispano (1302)
Hospital, Giméno de (1325)
Hostòles, Francesc d' (1336–1342)
Huesca, Pedro de (1334–1337)
Huesca, Ramón de (1299–1344)
Il.luminat (1232–1278)
Isern, Pere (1326–1339)
Isogol, Francesc (1348)
Ivern, Guillem (1345)
Ivern, Pere (1307)
Ivorra, Berenguer d' (1326–1337)
Ixar, Jaume d' (1330)
Jaca, Domingo de (1260–1316)
Jaume (1306)
Jaume (1317)
Jaume (1348)
Jerusalén, Antoni de (1346)
Joan (1313)
Jofre, Pere (1300–1309)
Jordà, Guillem (1344–1375)
Jordà, Jaume (1344)
Jordà, Joan (1325)
Jordà, Miquel (1291–1305)

Jornet, Guillem (1321–1337)
Jover, Guillem (1341)
Juli, Bernat (1342)
Juli, Berenguer (1342–1348)
Juli, Guillem (1338–1341)
Julià, Jaume (1345)
Junyer, Pere (1317–1331)
Just, Jaume (1343)
Laberes, Jaume (1343)
Lacera, Jaume de (1325–1347)
Lamberto (1305)
Lares, Domingo de (1305–1311)
Lavinyac, Pere (1331)
Lillet, Jaume de (1332)
Limoges, Esteve de (1346)
Llac, Martí de (1317)
Llàcer, Bernat de (1321)
Lladó, Francesc (1304)
Llaguna, Pere (1315–1362)
Llaurador, Francesc (1330–1336)
Lledó, Arnau (1345)
Lledó, Berenguer de (1281–1292)
Lledó, Segimon des (1232)
Llena, Francesc (1340)
Llenguida, Marc (1333)
Lleonart (1296)
Llers, Jaume (1324)
Lles, Guillem de (1273–1324)
Llinyà, Mateu (1320–1321)
Llívia, Pere de (1292)
Llobet, Ferrer (1329–1344)
Llobet, Guillem (1344–1352)
Llombart, Joan (1340–1343)
Llombart, Lluis (1340)
Llomber, Martí (1315)
Llop, Pere (1307)
Llorens, Bernat (1337)
Lloreta, Marc (1333–1338)
Lluçà, Joan de (1306–1307)
Lluch, Esteve (1333)
Llunada, Ramon (1321–1323)
Lope, Jaume (1336)
López, Domingo (1293)
López de Ayerbe, Sancho
  (1329–1346)

Lora, Pere (1338)
Major, Jaume (1347)
Malanyea (Manlleu?), Ramon (1346–1347)
Maler, Eximeno de (1338)
Maler, Joan (1330–1334)
Maler, Pere de (1337–1338)
Malol, Pere (1295)
Malvenda, Gil de (1296)
Mansolí, Dalmau (1300–1340)
Mansueto (1330–1332)
Manta, Bartomeu (1284)
Manuel (1286)
Mar, Romeu (1346–1347)
Marbres, Joan (1329)
Marc, [Pere?] (1264–1284)
Marc, Pere (1348–1382)
Marcador, Barceló (1334)
Marçal, Joan (1329)
Màrgens, Francesc (1345)
Marginet, Pere (date unknown)
Marimón, Guillem de (1324)
Marimón, Pere de (1345)
Marquet, Pere (1348)
Marra, Sancho de (1328)
Marsili, Pere (1310)
Martí, Domènec (1307–1343)
Martí, Francesc (1344)
Martí, Jaume (1302)
Martí, Pere (1329–1334)
Martín, Alfonso (1236)
Martínez, García (1307–1335)
Martorell, Berenguer (1345)
Mas, Berenguer de (1336)
Maserac, Guillem de (1307)
Masmolí, Obert (1304)
Massanet, Guillem (1337)
Masseguer, Pere (1348)
Massó, Guerau (1295)
Massot, Pere (1325)
Mastoro, Domènec de (1346)
Matamala, Pere de (1336)
Mateu, Pere (1324)
Meder, Pere (1333)
Media, Simó de (1318)

Medina, Gil de (1329–1345)
Mellot, Francesc (1334)
Menor, Guillem (1324)
Menorca, Ferrer de (1345)
Mercadal, Berenguer (1293)
Mercader, Guillem (1338)
Merced, Domingo (1296)
Mercer, Pere (1335)
Merlet, Guillem (1330†)
Messeguer, Ombert (1339–1343)
Mestre, Bernat (1343)
Mieres, Domènec (1307)
Mieres, Ramon de (1313–1326)
Milans, Albert de (1244)
Miquel, Francesc (1330–1342)
Miquel, Guillem (1333)
Mir, Joan Pere (1292)
Mir, Pere (1290–1302)
Miralles, Pons (1348)
Miravet, Sancho de (1296–1337)
Miró, Francesc (1335)
Miró, Guerau (1268–1280)
Moler, Jaume (1325–1342)
Molina, Joan de (1317)
Molina, Pascual de (1333)
Moliner, Ramon (1344–1375)
Moner, Llorens (1338–1359)
Moner, Ramon (1333–1336)
Montagut, Miquel de (1277)
Montfalcó, Arnau de (1340)
Montfort, Jaume de (1329–1333)
Montfort, Joan de (1325–1329)
Montlleó, Joan de (1324–1325)
Montmajor, Guillem de (1271–1273)
Mon[t]reclús, Ramon (1326)
Montsec, Jaume de (1330–1336)
Montsec, Simó de (1297–1309)
Montseny, Guillem de (1257)
Mora, Antoni de (1319)
Mora, Bernat (1299)
Mora, Jaume de (1343–1385)
Mora, Pere (1344)
Mora, Ramon (1342)
Moragues, Berenguer (1343)

Morató, Francesc (1333-1357)
Moré, Andreu (1307)
Morell, Guillem (1325)
Morell, Jaume (1337-1338)
Morell, Miquel (1327)
Morella (Moriella), Nicolás de (1293)
Morera, Ramon de (1292-1298)
Morés, Joan de (1290)
Muñoz, Pedro (1312)
Muntaner, Pere (1311-1348)
Muntanyana, Francesc de (1348)
Mura, Joan de (1330)
Museros, Guillem de (1307)
Nadal, Jaume (1299-1333)
Nàpols, Jaume de (1323)
Narlot, Guillem de (1320)
Nau, Bernat (1323)
Nau, Ramon (1348)
Navarret, Rodrigo (1330)
Navarra, Gil de (1323-1336)
Navarra, Pere de (1304)
Navarra, Sancho de (1306-1347)
Naya, Nicolás de la (1320-1337)
Neco, Juan (1333)
Negre, Pere (1296-1299)
Negrell, Jaume (1325)
Neva, Ramon (1338)
Nicolás, Pedro (1326-1339)
Noguer, Pere de (1260)
Notó, Prisc de (1332)
Nuca, Sancho de la (1337)
Oblit, Enégo (1325)
Ogern?, Guillem (1336)
Oliba, Arnau (1282-1316)
Oliba, Jaume (1311)
Oliba, Pere (1309)
Olít, Martín de (1333)
Oliver, Bernat (1277)
Oliver, Guillem (1324-1344)
Oliver, Pere d' (1324-1325)
Olivera, [-] (1247)
Oller, Arnau (1322-1326)
Ollers, Guillem (1307)
Olloghet?, Pere (1307)

Olm, Bernat d' (1286)
Olomar, Guillem (1348)
Olomar, Ramon (1337)
Olorda, Bernat d' (1339)
Onís?, Ramon (1330)
Orbita, Nicolás (1220)
Oriol, Pere (1344-1348)
Orla, Guillem (1341)
Ort, Arnau d' (1324)
Ortiz, Martín (1317)
Ortiz, Romeo (1286-1316†)
Ortolà, Gabriel (1346)
Orts, Andreu d' (1307)
Orvay, Martín (1246)
Osor, Berenguer d' (1308)
Osor, Guerau d' (1291-1306)
Otger, Gil R[amon] (1302)
Ozari?, Berenguer (1279)
Pagès, Ramon (1346)
Palau, Jaume de (1303)
Palau, Pere de (1295-1337)
Palmerola, Berenguer de (1279-1289)
Palol (Pallola?), Bernat (1334)
Palol (Pallola?), Joan (1348)
Pamplona, Andreu de (1276)
Paquet (1326)
Paradís, Guillem (1302)
Pardo, Bartomeu (1337)
Pascasi, Guillem (1345-1348)
Pasqual, Pere (1321†)
Paternué, Pedro (1345)
Pau, Pons de (1307)
Pedret, Joan de (1300)
Pedrissa, Arnau (1332)
Peiró, Joan (1324-1325)
Pellicer, Bernat (1335-1368)
Peravalls? (1302)
Pere, Arnau (1341)
Pere, Felip? (1346)
Pere, Guerau: *see* Guerau, Pere
Pere, Ramon (1301-1303)
Pere, Tomàs (1314-1347)
Peregrí, Bartomeu (1303)
Peregrí, Bernat (1282-1300)

Perellada, Arnau de (1307)
Pérez, Juan (1344)
Pérez, Marc (1281–1296)
Perpinyà, Bernat (1306–1332)
Perpinyà, Pere (1338)
Perués, Gombau (1346)
Perugia, Alexandre de (1324)
Perugia, Bonadono de (1324)
Perugia, Pelegrí de (1307)
Pi, Guillem de (1338)
Picalquers, Ramon de (1289)
Piles, Arnau de (1348)
Piles, Bernat de (1343–1348)
Pim, Bernat de (1316)
Pinta, Gil (1304)
Pintor, Bernat (1313–1314†)
Pintor, Bernat (1314–1336)
Pintor, Jaume (1347)
Pintor, Mateu (1334–1336)
Plomer, Joan (1320)
Pocoví?, Ramon (1305)
Polinyà, Jaume (1280)
Pomar, Guillem (1326)
Pons, Maties (1336–1337)
Pont, Pere de (1340–1370)
Porra, Nicolau de (date unknown)
Porta, Guillem (1348)
Porta, Pere de (1276)
Porta, Rafael de (1302)
Portell, Pere de (1328)
Portugal, Martim de (1307)
Prat, Guerau de (1297–1329)
Prat, Guillem de (1326)
Prat, Pere de (1307)
Preixana, Arnau (1344–1347)
Preixana, Ferrer de (1307)
Preixana, Francesc de (1300–1307)
Prim, Joan (1300)
Proeta, Pere (1317)
Provençal, Firm[íc] (1329)
Puig, Bernat (1310–1354)
Puig, Guillem de (1307–1339)
Puig, Nicolau de (1333)
Puig, Pere de (1308–1315)
Puig, Pere de (1346–1382)

Puig, Ramon (1301–1337)
Puigalt, Bernat: *see* Puigalt,
    Guerau de
Puigalt, Guerau de (1276–1299)
Puigcerdà, Simó de (1312–1315)
Puigfort, Pere de (1288)
Puignibi, Berenguer de (1337)
Pujada, Francesc de (1304)
Pujol, Guillem de (1259)
Quadres, Pere de (1281–1327)
Quer, Ramon (1338)
Queralt, Berenguer (1331–1343)
Queralt, Galter (Galcerán) (1302)
Quintana, Bernat (1326)
Quintana, Pere (1329)
Quirze, Bartomeu (1344)
Rabadà, Pere (1334–1341)
Rabó, Pere (1348)
Rafart, Francesc (1334–1336)
Rafart, Guillem (1344–1375)
Rafart, Guerau (1340)
Raffeques?, Berenguer (1338)
Ramad[er]a, Guillem (1336)
Ramon (1292–1295)
Ramon (1330)
Ramon, Arnau (1340)
Ramon, Guillem (1305)
Ramón, Pedro (1334)
Raolf, Joan (1284)
Raynaud, Francesc (1319)
Reate, Pere de (1330–1342)
Redon, Pere (1342–1343)
Rei, Ramon de (1318)
Reial, Ferrer (1322)
Reina, Fernando de la (1304–1306)
Renart, Arnau (1344–1374)
Requesens, Bernat (1332)
Revell, Guillem (1348)
Rexach, Guillem Pere de
    (1339–1378)
Ricart, Ramon (1345)
Riera, Arnau de (1300–1309)
Riera, Bernat (1288)
Riquer, Joan (1322–1332)
Riucoll, Bernat de (1322)

Riuprimer, Jaume de (1273–1281)
Roc (Sa Roca?), Pere (1283)
Roca, Berenguer (1333)
Roca, Francesc de (1342)
Roca, Guillem de (1301–1302)
Roca, Guillem de (1319–1339)
Roca, Pere: see Sa Roca, Pere de
Roca, Ramon de (1301)
Rocafull, Arnau de (1282–1294)
Rocanova, Bernat de (1320)
Roger, Bonanat (1338)
Roig, Berenguer (1343)
Roig, Guillem de (1283)
Roirós, Jaume (1313)
Romaní, Berenguer de (1295)
Romaní, Pere de (1277)
Romeo, Martín (1325–1329)
Roquer, Jaume (1339)
Roqueta, Pere (1341)
Ros, Domingo de (1306–1312)
Ros, Francesc (1337–1374)
Ros, Guillem (1307)
Ros, Jaume (1330–1343)
Ros, Llorens (1311–1312)
Rosal, Martín de (1279)
Rosell, Bernat (1345)
Rosell, Francesc (1334–1339)
Rosell, Jaume (1336)
Rossinyol, Pons (1293–1309)
Rostey, Pere de (1324)
Rostan, Arnau (1348)
Roura, Gilabert (1348)
Roure, Joan de (1306–1328)
Roure, Salvador de (1300–1307)
Rovira, Arnau de (1271)
Rovira, Bartomeu (1326)
Rovira, Berenguer (1343–1350)
Rovira, Francesc (1333–1356)
Rovira, Jaume de (1284)
Rubera, G[uillem] de (1324)
Rubió, Bernat de (1302)
Rubió, Guillem de (1320–1334)
Sa Costa, Nicolau (1339–1397)
Sa Capella, Pere (1326–1333)

Sa Carrera, Guillem de (1307–1314)
Sa Carrera, Pere de (1339)
Sa Farrera, Jaume (1340)
Sa Granada, Joan (1330)
Sa Horta, Bernat (1345)
Sa Mas, Bertran (1328)
Sa Nespleda, Berenguer de (1280–1302)
Sa Roca, Guillem (1302–1319)
Sa Roca, Pere de (1302–1350)
Sabé, Pere de (1307)
Sabenyà, Pere de (1300–1307)
Sala, Ferrer (date unknown)
Sala, Guillem (1316–1364)
Salas, Jaume de (1334)
Salines, García (1341)
Salmó, Bertran (1331–1338)
Salús, Bernat de (1339)
Salvela, Domènec (1326–1327)
Samaní, Pedro (1330)
Samara, Martín de (1320–1321)
San Tiberi, Serafí (1238)
Sans, Bernat (1329–1345)
Sans, Domènec (1330)
Sant Domí, Arnau (1348)
Sant Feliu, Guillem de (1304–1329)
Sant Feliu, Ramon de (1320–1329)
Sant-Hipòlit, Pere Guerau de (1317)
Sant Jordi, Pons de (1307)
Sant Martí, Bartomeu (1345–1393)
Sant Miquel, Ferrer de (1284)
Santa Eugènia, Pere de (1307)
Santa Maria, Bartomeu (1331)
Santesteva, Pere (1336–1348)
Santesteva, Ramon (1341–1348)
Saquer, Francesc (1326)
Sarrià, Bernat de (1311)
Sarrià, Guillem de (1346)
Sarrià, Marc de (1301)
Sars, Gil de (1301–1302)
Sassari, Antoni de (date unknown)

Sauner (1268)
Savinyac, Pere de (1329–1331)
Savolla, Jaume (1330)
Sayas, Guillermo (1326–1327)
Sayas, Jaime de (1334)
Sayas, Eximeno de (1346)
See, William (or Peter) of the (1236–1278)
Segarra, Francesc (1326–1328)
Segarra, Guillem (1336–1340)
Segarra, Pere de (1306)
Segrià (1257)
Seguí, Pere (1320–1348)
Segur, Jaume (1317)
Segura, Berenguer (1337)
Segura, Francesc (1345)
Seioll, Pere (1334–1346)
Senechs, Bernat (1307)
Senechs, Ferrer (1326–1345)
Sentís, Miquel de (1337)
Serena, Ramon (1346)
Serra, Aparicio (1328–1332)
Serra, Arnau (1344)
Serra, Berenguer (1339–1351)
Serra, Ferrer (1273)
Serra, Pardo (1330–1345)
Ses Gunyoles, Pere (1321–1327)
Ses Oliveres, Pere (1325)
Ses Pujol, Guillem (1317)
Sevilla, Juan de (1324)
Sicart, Ramon (1345)
Sicília, Pere de (1336–1382)
Sifré, Joan (1311)
Simeó (1232)
Simó (1289)
Simó, [Bernat?] (1289)
Simó, Bernat (1320–1337)
Sinibald (1278)
Soberats, Guillem (1330–1339)
Sobrí, Bartomeu (1284)
Solà, Francesc (1326–1328)
Solà, Jaume (1333–1357)
Soler, Arnau de (1345)

Soler, Bernat (1343)
Soler, Domènec dez (1343)
Soler, Guillem de (1346–1347)
Sotsroca, Ramon de (1288–1308)
Surribes, Berenguer (1347)
Talló, Berenguer (1321)
Talló, Ramon (1319–1320)
Tanyà, Nicolau (1338–1373)
Tarragona, Pere (1247)
Tarravia, Pere de (1320)
Tasquer, Guillem (1339–1348)
Tasquer, Pere (1335–1348)
Taulers, Francesc (1345–1346)
Tauste, Pons (1297)
Taxonera, Sancho de (1301–1302)
Teixidor, Guillem (1338–1355)
Teixidor, R[amon] (1327)
Tenat, Ade de (1347)
Térmens, Pere (1348)
Terra Llaurador, Angel de (1324)
Terradelles, Pere de (1324–1333)
Terrades, Salvador de (1333–1335)
Terrassa, Bernat de (1284)
Terrassa, Ferrer (date unknown)
Terrassa, Francesc (1326–1328)
Terrassa, Pere de (1322)
Terrassa, Ramon de (1337)
Terreni, Francesc (1348)
Terrer, Bartomeu (1348)
Terrer, Pere de (1322–1326)
Terrer (Terreni), Jaume de (1303–1306)
Terrós, Bernat (1303)
Teruel, Romeo de (1286–1292)
Teuler, Jaume (1325)
Tint[or]er, Jaume (1338–1341)
Tolrà, Berenguer (1333)
Tomàs, Galcerán (1336–1343)
Tomàs, Pere: *see* Pere, Tomàs
Tomàs, [Pere?] (1280–1297)
Torelló, Guillem (1306)
Tornat (Trobat?), Pa[rdo] (1282)
Tornavell, Pere de (1307)
Torner, Guillem (1347–1355)

Torner, Miquel (1337)
Torralta, Gonzalo (1346)
Torre, Guillem de (1304)
Torrents, Bernat (1300–1308?)
Torrents, Francesc (1345–1361)
Torrents, Joan dez (1346–1347)
Torrents, Pere de (1299–1307)
Torrents, Ramon de (1345–1350)
Tortosa, Ramon (1281)
Tous, Pere de (1283)
Trassera, Bernat (1333)
Treballós, Guillem (1301–1333)
Trenils, Joan dez (1342–1348)
Trilla, Jaume de (1324)
Trobat, Jaume (1337). *See also* Tornat, Pa[rdo]
Tudela, Gonzalo de (1299)
Tudela, Miguel de (1246–1276)
Turell, Francesc (1341)
Ullà, Bernat d' (1291–1318)
Ullà, Pons (1287–1307)
Urús, Cerdà d' (1336–1343)
Valentín, Garino (1325)
Vall-llebrera, Pascasi de (1280–1316)
Vall-lloreta, Pascasi (1285)
Valls, Berenguer de (1276)
Valls, Guerau de (1305–1316)
Valls, Guillem de (1305–1322)
Valmanya, Pere de (1344)
Valseca, Guillem de (1338–1339)
Velasco (1275)
Venècia, Jaume de (1301–1302)
Ventalló, Francesc (1338–1344)
Vernet, Jaume de (1302–1324)
Vicens, (Bernat?) (1289)
Vicens, Bernat (1320)
Vicens, Jaume (1347)

Vidal, Bernat (1220)
Vidal, Guillem (1334–1338)
Vidal, Pere (1263–1265†)
Vidal, Ramon (1345)
Vigana, Eneco Martín (1316)
Vigué, Pere (date unknown)
Viladolç, Marc de (1347)
Vilaert, Bernat de (1291)
Vilafant, Bernat de (1333)
Vilagranada, Berenguer de (1280)
Vilagrassa, Bernat de (1330–1333)
Vilagrassa, Francesc de (1300–1310)
Vilagrassa, Pere de (1281)
Vilajoan, Bernat de (1305–1316)
Vilallobent, Joan de (1330)
Vilamajor, Guillem (1298)
Vilamarics, Berenguer de (1347–1348)
Vilanova, Antoni de (1342–1381)
Vilanova, Arnau de (1309)
Vilanova, Bernat de (1307–1315)
Vilanova, Bernat (1347)
Vilanova, Pere de (1295–1302)
Vilaplana, Bernat (1345)
Vilar, Bernat de (1315)
Vilar, Guillem (1337–1338)
Vilardemí, Bernat (1343)
Vilatenim, Arnau de (1295–1331)
Vilatenim, Jaume de (1336–1345)
Vilatenim, Pere de (1305)
Vilella, Martín de (1278–1288)
Viure, Cerdà de (1341)
Vivià? (1246)
Ximénez, Juan de (1320–1336)
Xiró, Pere (1339)
Zabadía, Balaguer de (1276)
Zamora, Alfonso de (1316)

Appendix 6

Chronological List of Friars

1220: Nicolás Orbita
    Bernat Vidal
1220–1231: Bernat
1220–1231†: Félix
1232: Segimon des Lledó
    Simeó
1232–1278: Il.luminat
1233: Dominique
1234–1237: Jaume Arnau
1234–1238†/1239†: Arnau
1236: Guerau
    Guillem de Cervera
    Alfonso Martín
1236–1278: William (or Peter) of
    the See
1237: Esteve
1238: Serafí San Tiberi
1240: Guillem Escatar
1244: Albert de Milans
1246: Guillem Briva
    Martín Orvay
    Vivià?
1246–1247: Aimeric
1246–1276: Desideri
    Miguel de Tudela
1247: [–] Olivera
    Pere Tarragona
1248?: [–] Català
1248–1267: Bernat Ferrer
1249–1276: Ramon de Castelló
1254: Ramon Cortell
1254–1255: Guillem d'Ager
    Bernat de Bach
1257: Guillem de Montseny
    Segrià
1259: Guillem de Pujol
1260: Pere de Noguer

1260–1280: Bernat Ferrer
1260–1316: Domingo de Jaca
1261–1293: Pere de Gener (Janua)
1262: Bernat de Gualba
1262–1284: Guillem de Blanes
1262–1296: [–] Gómez
1262–1322: Ferrer d'Alemany
1263–1265†: Pere Vidal
1263–1288: Arnau de Forn
1264–1284: [Pere?] Marc
1265–1338: Guillem Ferrer
1267: Ferrer de Cruilles
1268: Sauner
1268–1280: Guerau Miró
1269: Guillem de Fraumir
1270: Pere Boada
1270–1316: Pere Esteve
1271: [–] Amargós
    Arnau de Rovira
1271–1273: Guillem de Montmajor
1272: Antonio Bonarres
    Miguel de Conchel
    Pere de Copons
1273: Gil
    Ferrer Serra
1273–1281: Jaume de Riuprimer
1273–1295: Berenguer Garí
1273–1324: Guillem de Lles
1275: Arnau de Fontanelles
    Velasco
1275–1277: Fernando de Cetina
1275–1295: Francisco
1276: Palazino de Baón
    Berenguer de Guàrdia
    Andreu de Pamplona
    Pere de Porta
    Pere de Romaní

1276: Berenguer de Valls
Balaguer de Zabadía
1276–1299: Guerau de Puigalt
1277: Miquel de Montagut
Bernat Oliver
1278: Guillem de Barberà
Bartomeu Bosom
Sinibald
1278–1288: Martín de Vilella
1278–1325: Arnau Bonastre
1279: Berenguer Ozari?
Martín de Rosal
1279–1289: Berenguer de
Palmerola
1280: Pere de Fluvià
Jaume Polinyà
Berenguer de Vilagranada
1280–1297: [Pere?] Tomàs
1280–1298: Pere de Bellfort
1280–1302: Berenguer de Sa
Nespleda
1280–1316: Joan de Ciurana
Pascasi de Vall-llebrera
1281: Pere Falcó
Ramon Tortosa
Pere de Vilagrassa
1281–1292: Berenguer de Lledó
1281–1296: Marc Pérez
1281–1316: Bernat Gil
1281–1327: Pere de Quadres
1282: Guillem Bonet
Esteve Dardas
Pa[rdo] Tornat (Trobat?)
1282–1294: Arnau de Rocafull
1282–1300: Bernat Peregrí
1282–1316: Arnau Oliba
1283: Pere Roc (Sa Roca?)
Guillem de Roig
Pere de Tous
1283–1286: Joan de Barriac
1283–1308: Rodrigo de Gúdar
1283–1313: Guillem de la Cort
1284: Jaume Amalui
Bartomeu Manta
Joan Raolf
Jaume de Rovira

1284: Ferrer de Sant Miquel
Bartomeu Sobrí
Bernat de Terrassa
1285: Guillem Arnau
Pascasi Vall-lloreta
1285–1288: Bernat de Bianya
1285–1291: Bernat Draper
1286: Ramon Aperrer?
Joan Bautista
Bruno
Pons de Cros
Frimago?
Manuel
Bernat d'Olm
1286–1292: Romeo de Teruel
1286–1295: Berenguer Grau
1286–1316†: Romeo Ortiz
1287: Guillem Folc
1287–1307: Pons Ullà
1288: Bernat Arbitre
Ramon de Gudal
Pere de Puigfort
Bernat Riera
1288–1308: Ramon de Sotsroca
1289: Ramon de Picalquers
Simó
[Bernat?] Simó
[Bernat?] Vicens
1290: Pere de Belchite
Enric
Pere Esquerrer (Escarrer)
Joan de Morés
1290?: Francesc Bruny
1290–1302: Pere Mir
1290–1309: Alberic
1291: Bernat de Vilaert
1291–1292: Bernat Folc
1291–1305: Miquel Jordà
1291–1306: Guerau d'Osor
1291–1318: Bernat d'Ullà
1292: Vicente Gallego
Pere de Llívia
Joan Pere Mir
1292†: Francesc Català (or 1306†)
1292–1295: Ramon
1292–1298: Ramon de Morera

1292–1317: Arnau d'Esplugues
1292–1326?: Fernando García
1293: Pedro de Chilliella
  Bernat Dubà
  Domingo López
  Berenguer Mercadal
  Nicolás de Morella (Moriella)
1293–1307: Pere d'Esplugues
1293–1309: Pons Rossinyol
1293–1310: Albert
1293–1324: Pere de Forn
1294: Aloysius
  Guerau Botet
  Martín de Ejea
  Eustace
  Guillem
1295: Bernat d'Alp
  Guillem Ferranco
  Pere Gomar
  Pere Malol
  Guerau Massó
  Berenguer de Romaní
1295–1296: Jaume de Forn
1295–1302: Pere de Vilanova
1295–1331: Arnau de Vilatenim
1295–1337: Pere de Palau
1296: Guillem de Canals
  Ramon de Guàrdia
  Lleonart
  Gil de Malvenda
  Domingo Merced
1296–1299: Pere Negre
1296–1307: Joan d'Alp
1296–1337: Sancho de Miravet
1297: Martín Fernando†
  Pons Tauste
1297–1303: Guillem Banc
1297–1305: Bertran Ahones
1297–1309: Simó de Montsec
1297–1316: Romeu de Bosom
1297–1317: Guillem Canavells
1297–1329: Guerau de Prat
1298: Guillem Vilamajor
1298–1307: Marc Godencs
1298–1314: Bernat Fuster (Third Order)
1298–1316†: Pere Guerau (Third Order)
1299: Bernat Mora
  Gonzalo de Tudela
1299–1307: Pere de Torrents
1299–1333: Jaume Nadal
1299–1344: Ramón de Huesca
1300: Guillermo de Alcalá
  Juan de Calatayud
  Guillem de Cuiga
  Joan de Pedret
  Joan Prim
1300–1307: Berenguer Aguilar
  Guerau Bonastre
  Bartomeu de Bosc
  Tomàs de Caldes
  Guillem Clarà
  Pere de Cornudella
  Berenguer de Fort
  Romeu de Fuixà
  Francesc de Preixana
  Salvador de Roure
  Pere de Sabenyà
1300–1308?: Bernat Torrents
1300–1309: Berenguer Fiveller
  Pere Jofre
  Arnau de Riera
1300–1310: Francesc de Vilagrassa
1300–1336: Pons Carbonell
1300–1340: Dalmau Mansolí
1301: Martí Arec
  Pere Augre
  Ramon de Roca
  Marc de Sarrià
1301–1302: Guillem de Roca
  Gil de Sars
  Sancho de Taxonera
  Jaume de Venècia
1301–1303: Ramon Pere
1301–1306: Pere Alegre
1301–1313: Bernat Gonter
1301–1327: Jeroni de Catalunya
1301–1333: Guillem Treballós
1301–1337: Ramon Puig
1302: Peravalls?
  Bernardo de Ahones

1302: Pere d'Arenys
    Jaume Boià
    Berenguer de Cardona
    Bernat Cardona
    Bartomeu Cases
    Nicolás de Ejea
    Bernat Galcerán
    Rafael Gener (Janua)
    [H]ispano
    Jaume Martí
    Gil R[amon] Otger
    Guillem Paradís
    Rafael de Porta
    Galter (Galcerán) Queralt
    Bernat de Rubió
1302–1306: Domènec de Fontana
1302–1308: Bernat de Cases
1302–1319: Guillem Sa Roca
1302–1321: Ramon de Borau
1302–1324: Jaume de Bosom
    Jaume de Vernet
1302–1325: A[rnau] d'Armenter
1302–1336: Joan de Castelló
1302–1350: Pere de Sa Roca
1303: Francesc d'Arena
    Castelló de Bondemà
    Berenguer Fabra
    Simó Ferrer
    Jaume de Palau
    Bartomeu Peregrí
    Bernat Terrós
1303–1306: Jaume Terrer (Terreni)
1303–1317: Guillem Guitard
1304: Simón de Calatayud
    Bernat de Garrigella
    Francesc Lladó
    Obert Masmolí
    Pere de Navarra
    Gil Pinta
    Francesc de Pujada
    Guillem de Torre
1304–1306: Fernando de la Reina
1304–1317: Guillem Castelló
1304–1329: Guillem de Sant Feliu
1305: Lamberto
    Ramon Pocoví?

1305: Guillem Ramon
    Pere de Vilatenim
1305–1306: Bernat Ade
1305–1311: Domingo de Lares
1305–1316: Guerau de Valls
    Bernat de Vilajoan
1305–1320: Martín de Alcolea
1305–1322: Guillem de Valls
1305–1338: Guillem Catelli
1305–1353: Jaume Ferrer
1306: Jaume
    Pere de Segarra
    Guillem Torelló
1306†: Francesc Català (or 1292†)
1306–1307: Joan de Lluçà
1306–1312: Domingo de Ros
1306–1328: Joan de Roure
1306–1329: Pere Arnau
1306–1332: Bernat Perpinyà
1306–1347: Sancho de Navarra
1307: Berenguer d'Abat
    Jaume d'Abat
    Berenguer Abeyà
    Berenguer d'Aguda
    Simó Bertran
    Guillem de Bonastre
    Nicolau Bosom
    Bernat Burdils
    Berenguer de Carrall
    Juan de Castella
    Mateo de Castella
    Bernat Company
    Pere Demestre
    Ramon Ferrer
    Mateu de Fuixà
    Juan de Galícia
    Pere Ivern
    Pere Llop
    Guillem de Maserac
    Domènec Mieres
    Andreu Moré
    Guillem de Museros
    Guillem Ollers
    Pere Olloghet?
    Andreu d'Orts
    Pons de Pau

CHRONOLOGICAL LIST OF FRIARS

1307: Arnau de Perellada
    Pelegrí de Perugia
    Martim de Portugal
    Pere de Prat
    Ferrer de Preixana
    Guillem Ros
    Pere de Sabé
    Pons de Sant Jordi
    Pere de Santa Eugènia
    Bernat Senechs
    Pere de Tornavell
1307-1311: Bernat d'Alemany
1307-1314: Guillem de Sa Carrera
1307-1315: Bernat de Vilanova
1307-1316: Ramon de Costa
1307-1318: Bernat de Déu
1307-1321: Pere Carbonell
1307-1327: Guillem Gilabert
1307-1328: Berenguer Folcrà
1307-1335: García Martínez
1307-1339: Guillem de Puig
1307-1343: Domènec Martí
1307-1344: Arnau de Castllà
1307-1348: Pons Carles
1308: Bartomeu
    Ebrí?
    Pressivald Claver
    Berenguer d'Osor
1308-1315: Pere de Puig
1309: Pere Oliba
    Arnau de Vilanova
1309-1310: Ramon de Giniac
1310: Alberot (Alberic?)
    Guillem Aranyó
    Francesc de Cardona
    Pere Marsili
1310-1334: Andreu Albalat
1310-1354: Bernat Puig
1311: Bernat Carcassó
    Jaume Oliba
    Bernat de Sarrià
    Joan Sifré
1311-1312: Llorens Ros
1311-1345: Pere Ferrer
1311-1348: Pere Muntaner
1311-1368: Joan d'Aragó

1312: Pedro Muñoz
1312-1315: Simó de Puigcerdà
1313: Andreu de Copons
    Martín Dendestre
    Joan
    Jaume Roirós
1313-1314†: Bernat Pintor
1313-1326: Ramon de Mieres
1313-1329: Bernat Constans
1314: Ramon Alemany
    Francesc Comte
1314-1315: Ramon de Bignera
    Eimeric
1314-1317: Aimeric
1314-1320: García de Biesa
1314-1328: Joan de Roure
1314-1330: Castelló Botinyà
1314-1336: Bernat Pintor
1314-1347: Tomàs Pere
1315: Miquel Abeyà
    Balaguer Guasch
    Martí Llomber
    Bernat de Vilar
1315-1326: Arnulf
1315-1348: Bernat Espanyoll
1315-1362: Pere Llaguna
1316: Miguel de la Cida?
    Juan de Gargeto
    Bernat de Pim
    Eneco Martín Vigana
    Alfonso de Zamora
1316-1321: Pere de Cervera
1316-1325: Andreu d'Aguilar
1316-1338: Bernat Esteve
1316-1347: Arnau de Canelles
1316-1364: Guillem Sala
1317: Jaume Amat
    Berenguer de Ca[s]tella
    Miguel de Ca[s]tella
    Martín Catani
    Pere Cima
    Jaume
    Martí de Llac
    Joan de Molina
    Martín Ortiz
    Pere Proeta

1317: Pere Guerau de Sant-Hipòlit
    Jaume Segur
    Guillem Ses Pujol
1317–1319: Beneyto Bueno
1317–1322: Bernat Fuster
1317–1324: Pere d'Atarravia
    Pere Besalú
1317–1331: Pere Junyer
1317–1336: Ramon d'Estany
1317–1345: Romeu de Falques
1318: Sancho de Castellany
    Bernat Colteller
    Guillem Espanyol
    Juan Pedro Guzmán
    Simó de Media
    Ramon de Rei
1318–1329: Pere de Cab[an]elles
1318–1331: Berenguer Cerdà
1318–1335: Antoni Andreu
1319: Antoni de Mora
    Francesc Raynaud
1319–1320: Ramon Talló
1319–1325: Jaume de Bonhom
    (Bononia?)
1319–1339: Guillem de Roca
1320: Bartolomeo de Alcalá
    Guillem Batlle
    Juan de Bonell
    Miguel Borau
    Pere Feliu
    Andreu de Guàrdia
    Guillem de Narlot
    Joan Plomer
    Bernat de Rocanova
    Pere de Tarravia
    Bernat Vicens
1320–1321: Mateu Llinyà
    Martín de Samara
1320–1329: Ramon de Sant Feliu
1320–1334: Guillem de Rubió
1320–1336: Juan de Ximénez
1320–1337: Nicolás de la Naya
    Bernat Simó
1320–1346: Bernat Colomer
1320–1348: Pere Seguí

1321: Bernat Arcegell
    Juan de Ejea
    Bernat de Llàcer
    Pere Pasqual†
    Berenguer Talló
1321–1322: Geraldo
1321–1323: Ramon Llunada
1321–1327: Pere Ses Gunyoles
1321–1336: Pere Burgué
1321–1337: Guillem Jornet
1322: Ferran Bertís
    Guillem d'Espais
    Angelo de Genoa
    Ferrer Reial
    Bernat de Riucoll
    Pere de Terrassa
1322–1325: Alfredo Gonter
1322–1326: Arnau Oller
    Pere de Terrer
1322–1330: García de Ayusa
1322–1332: Joan Riquer
1322–1383: Guillem Guardiola
1323: D[–] Burgués
    Jaume de Nàpols
    Bernat Nau
1323–1329: Joan Escatar
1323–1336: Gil de Navarra
1324: Bernat d'Alfam[er]a
    Arnau d'Alós
    Llorens d'Antoni
    Guillem Bogar
    Simó de Bullada
    Pere de Burdils
    Guillem Busquet
    Arnau Colomer
    Francesc
    Pere Gelera
    Guillem de Gravera
    Jaume Llers
    Guillem de Marimón
    Pere Mateu
    Guillem Menor
    Arnau d'Ort
    Alexandre de Perugia
    Bonadono de Perugia

1324: Pere de Rostey
    G[uillem] de Rubera
    Juan de Sevilla
    Angel de Terra Llaurador
    Jaume de Trilla
1324-1325: Joan de Montlleó
    Pere d'Oliver
    Joan Peiró
1324-1326: Berenguer Ferrer
1324-1333: Pere de Terradelles
1324-1344: Guillem Oliver
1324-1357: Pere Fuixà
1325: Pere d'Artamara
    Guillem Bardina
    Ferrer Bolla
    Guillem Caporer
    Giméno de Hospital
    Joan Jordà
    Pere Massot
    Guillem Morell
    Jaume Negrell
    Enégo Oblit
    Pere Ses Oliveres
    Jaume Teuler
    Garino Valentín
1325-1329: Joan de Montfort
    Martín Romeo
1325-1330: Bernat Bort
1325-1334: Pons Brusca?
1325-1335: Ferrer d'Abeyà
1325-1342: Jaume Moler
1325-1347: Francesc Esteve
    Jaume de Lacera
1326: Ramon Bano (Bancal?)
    G[uillem] Ballester
    Andreu Batlle
    Pere Calahug
    Guillem Calvet
    Francesc Carbonell
    Bernat Casells
    Arnau de Cases
    P[ere] Dalmau
    Ramon David
    Benvingut de Granollers
    Ramon Mon[t]reclús

1326: Paquet
    Guillem Pomar
    Guillem de Prat
    Bernat Quintana
    Bartomeu Rovira
    Francesc Saquer
1326-1327: Ramon Bancal
    Domènec Salvela
    Guillermo Sayas
1326-1328: Francesc Segarra
1326-1328: Francesc Solà
    Francesc Terrassa
1326-1333: Pere Sa Capella
1326-1334: Gil Alvarez
1326-1337: Berenguer d'Ivorra
1326-1338: Francesc Clarà
1326-1339: Pere Isern
    Pedro Nicolás
1326-1345: Ferrer Senechs
1327: Antoni Camps
    Pere Forner
    Joan de Fuixà
    García Garisa
    Miquel Morell
    R[amon] Teixidor
1327-1335: Bernat Ferrer
1328: Bartomeu Fuster
    Sancho de Marra
    Pere de Portell
    Bertran Sa Mas
1328-1332: Aparicio Serra
1328-1349: Ramon de Bas
1329: Pere Artau
    Francesc Campanyó
    Firm[íc] Closa
    Nicolau Estany
    Ramon de Font†
    Joan Marbres
    Joan Marçal
    Firm[íc] Provençal
    Pere Quintana
1329-1331: Pere de Savinyac
1329-1333: Jaume de Montfort
1329-1334: Berenguer Argilés
    Pere Martí

1329–1344: Ferrer Llobet
1329–1345: Gil de Medina
 Bernat Sans
1329–1346: Sancho López de
 Ayerbe
1330: Guillem Alegre
 Miguel de Almenara
 Bernat Galredoner
 Jaume d'Ixar
 Guillem Merlet†
 Joan de Mura
 Ramon Onís?
 Rodrigo Navarret
 Ramon
 Joan Sa Granada
 Pedro Samaní
 Domènec Sans
 Jaume Savolla
 Joan de Vilallobent
1330–1332: Mansueto
1330–1333: Bernat de Villagrassa
1330–1334: Joan Maler
1330–1336: Francesc Cabà
 Francesc Llaurador
 Jaume de Montsec
1330–1338: Francesc Guillem
1330–1339: Guillem Soberats
1330–1342: Francesc Miquel
 Pere de Reate
1330–1343: Jaume Ros
1330–1345: Pardo Serra
1330–1348: Bernat Geli
1331: Ferrer Gener
 Pere Lavinyac
 Bartomeu Santa Maria
1331–1332: Berenguer Basella
1331–1338: Arnau Duran
 Bertran Salmó
1331–1343: Berenguer Queralt
1332: Pedro de Castella
 Jaume de Lillet
 Prisc de Notó
 Arnau Pedrissa
 Bernat Requesens
1332–1335: Francesc Gosalt
1332–1348: Francesc Durant

1333: Jaume Altés
 Borraç Baró
 Bernat Comas
 Simó d'Estalella
 Marc Llenguida
 Esteve Lluch
 Pere Meder
 Guillem Miquel
 Pascual de Molina
 Juan Neco
 Martín de Olít
 Nicolau de Puig
 Berenguer Roca
 Berenguer Tolrà
 Bernat Trassera
 Bernat de Vilafant
1333–1334: Ramon de Déu
1333–1335: Salvador de Terrades
1333–1336: Ramon Moner
1333–1338: Marc Lloreta
1333–1341: Joan Guerau
1333–1356: Francesc Rovira
1333–1357: Francesc Morató
 Jaume Solà
1334: Pere Comabella
 Jaume Falcó
 Barceló Marcador
 Francesc Mellot
 Bernat Palol (Pallola?)
 Pedro Ramón
 Jaume de Salas
 Jaime de Sayas
1334–1335: Ramon Figuera
 Bartomeu Florit
1334–1336: Mateu Pintor
 Francesc Rafart
1334–1337: Pedro de Huesca
1334–1338: Guillem Vidal
1334–1339: Francesc Rosell
1334–1341: Pere Rabadà
1334–1346: Pere Seioll
1335: Guillem d'Agramunt
 Pere Florit
 Ramon Ger
 Pere Mercer
 Francesc Miró

1335-1341: Guillem Canals
1335-1342: Guillem Cendròs
1335-1348: Pere Tasquer
1335-1351: Francesc Batlle
1335-1368: Bernat Pellicer
1336: Francesc Andreu
    Guerau Cardona
    Pere Comella
    Joan Engomader?
    Bernat Feliu
    Giméno
    Jaume Lope
    Berenguer de Mas
    Pere de Matamala
    Guillem Ogern?
    Guillem Ramad[er]a
    Jaume Rosell
1336-1337: Francesc d'Arenys
    Maties Pons
1336-1339: Ramon Boixador
1336-1340: Guillem Segarra
1336-1341: Jaume Duran
1336-1342: Francesc d'Hostòles
1336-1343: Tomàs Galcerán
    Galcerán Tomàs
    Cerdà d'Urús
1336-1345: Jaume de Vilatenim
1336-1347: Pere Batlle
1336-1348: Pere Santesteva
1336-1351: Ramon Colomer
1336-1374: Joan Carmenço
1336-1375: Guillem de Campllong
1336-1382: Pere de Sicília
1337: Francesc Bosc
    Antoni Cabot
    Guillem de Clapers
    Mateu Coll
    Pere Comte
    Joan Dinet
    Juan de Figuerola?
    Francesc Guinya
    Bernat Llorens
    Guillem Massanet
    Sancho de la Nuca
    Ramon Olomar
    Bartomeu Pardo

1337: Berenguer de Puignibi
    Berenguer Segura
    Miquel de Sentís
    Ramon de Terrassa
    Miquel Torner
    Jaume Trobat
1337-1338: Bernat Andreu
    Pere de Maler
    Jaume Morell
    Guillem Vilar
1337-1339: Francesc
1337-1372: Francesc Gener
1337-1374: Francesc Ros
1338: Pere d'Arcís
    Joan Bartolí
    Bernat Baster
    Pere de Bell-lloc
    Francesc Berga
    Roderic Bergundia
    Bernat Borrell
    Pere de Buigues
    Pere Canals
    Pere Capdevila
    Cerdà de Casca
    Bernat Cerdà
    Pere Cerdà
    Francesc Fabra
    Pere Ger
    Mateu Gormar
    Pere Lora
    Eximeno de Maler
    Guillem Mercader
    Ramon Neva
    Pere Perpinyà
    Guillem de Pi
    Ramon Quer
    Berenguer Raffeques?
    Bonanat Roger
1338-1339: Bernat d'Araveig
    Guillem de Valseca
1338-1341: Guillem Juli
    Jaume Tint[or]er
1338-1343: Bernat de Cases
1338-1344: Francesc Ventalló
1338-1346: Bernat Colom
1338-1347: Pere Gomar

1338–1348: Pere de Conomines
1338–1351: Jaume Capdevila
1338–1355: Guillem Teixidor
1338–1359: Llorens Moner
1338–1373: Nicolau Tanyà
1339: Pere d'Artasona
    Pere Berrales
    Guillem Borrell
    Ramon de [Ciscar]
    Berenguer de Fustenyà
    Guillem Gavarra
    Bernat d'Olorda
    Jaume Roquer
    Pere de Sa Carrera
    Bernat de Salús
    Pere Xiró
1339–1343: Ombert Messeguer
1339–1345: Guillem Crespià
1339–1348: Guillem Tasquer
1339–1351: Berenguer Serra
1339–1362: Bernat Calva
    Ramon Domenge
1339–1378: Guillem Pere de Rexach
1339–1391: Francesc Colteller
1339–1397: Nicolau Sa Costa
1340: Pere Cabiol
    Antoni Cabissó
    Pere de Camps
    Bernat Canals
    Eximeno Coscollola
    Francesc Llena
    Lluis Llombart
    Arnau de Montfalcó
    Guerau Rafart
    Arnau Ramon
    Jaume Sa Farrera
1340–1343: Joan Llombart
1340–1344: Uguet Felip
1340–1347: Berenguer d'Amorós
1340–1370: Pere de Pont
1341: Francesc Baner
    Benet
    Guillem Bo
    Guillem Curçavell?
    Pere Domenge

1341: Francesc Fares
    Guillem Jover
    Guillem Orla
    Arnau Pere
    Pere Roqueta
    García Salines
    Francesc Turell
    Cerdà de Viure
1341–1342: Joan Bar
    Joan Bernat
1341–1348: Jaume Fabra
    Ramon Santesteva
1341–1353: Jaume Domenge
1342: Ramon Ansurrà
    Berenguer Borrell
    Pere Colomer
    Jaume Escariu
    Arnau d'Estagell
    Esteve Fabra
    Ramon Gornall
    Bernat Juli
    Ramon Mora
    Francesc de Roca
1342–1343: Pere Redon
1342–1345: Nicolau Agut
1342–1348: Berenguer Juli
    Joan dez Trenils
1342–1381: Antoni de Vilanova
1343: Francesc Boera
    Nicolau Bonet
    Francesc Calvo
    Jaume Just
    Jaume Laberes
    Bernat Mestre
    Berenguer Moragues
    Berenguer Roig
    Bernat Soler
    Domènec dez Soler
    Bernat Vilardemí
1343–1348: Bernat de Piles
1343–1350: Berenguer Rovira
1343–1385: Jaume de Mora
1344: Ramon Avezurrán?
    Guillem Bagés
    Joan Giralt
    Jaume Jordà

1344: Francesc Martí
   Pere Mora
   Juan Pérez
   Bartomeu Quirze
   Arnau Serra
   Pere de Valmanya
1344–1347: Arnau Preixana
1344–1348: Pere Oriol
1344–1352: Guillem Llobet
1344–1374: Arnau Renart
1344–1375: Guillem Jordà
   Ramon Moliner
   Guillem Rafart
1345: Guillem de Bas
   Antoni Burdils
   Guillem Crebayno
   Castelló de Font
   Guillem
   Guillem Ivern
   Jaume Julià
   Arnau Lledó
   Francesc Màrgens
   Pere de Marimón
   Berenguer Martorell
   Ferrer de Menorca
   Pedro Paternué
   Ramon Ricart
   Bernat Rosell
   Bernat Sa Horta
   Francesc Segura
   Ramon Sicart
   Arnau de Soler
   Ramon Vidal
   Bernat Vilaplana
1345–1346: Bartomeu Babau
   Pere Desquo?
   Francesc Taulers
1345–1348: Guillem Pascasi
1345–1350: Ramon de Torrents
1345–1361: Francesc Torrents
1345–1393: Bartomeu Sant Martí
1346: Francesc Arguelaguers
   Antoni Capó
   Jaume Capó
   Guillem Corell
   Bonanat Feliu

1346: Antoni de Jerusalén
   Esteve de Limoges
   Domènec de Mastoro
   Gabriel Ortolà
   Ramon Pagès
   Felip? Pere
   Gombau Perués
   Guillem de Sarrià
   Eximeno de Sayas
   Ramon Serena
   Gonzalo Torralta
1346–1347: Ramon Malanyea
   (Manlleu?)
   Romeu Mar
   Guillem de Soler
   Joan dez Torrents
1346–1365: Pere Domènec
1346–1366: Jordi Amat
1346–1382: Pere de Puig
1347: Bernat Castell
   Pere Colom
   Berenguer Cordelles
   Pere d'Esparreguera
   Arnau d'Espasens
   Pere de Gualba
   Guillem Guitard
   Jaume Major
   Jaume Pintor
   Berenguer Surribes
   Ade de Tenat
   Jaume Vicens
   Marc de Viladolç
   Bernat Vilanova
1347–1348: Ramon Banc
   Pons de Capbreu
   Berenguer de Vilamarics
1347–1355: Guillem Torner
1347–1376: Francesc Burriana
1347–1386: Bernat Bru
1348: Domènec Arenós
   Guillem Bar
   Jaume Bosc
   Bernat Bruguera
   Jaume de Conomines
   Guillem Fuster
   Gilabert

1348: Ramon Granell
    Francesc Isogol
    Jaume
    Pere Marquet
    Pere Masseguer
    Pons Miralles
    Francesc de Muntanyana
    Ramon Nau
    Guillem Olomar
    Joan Palol (Pallola?)
    Arnau de Piles
    Guillem Porta
    Pere Rabó
    Guillem Revell
    Arnau Rostan
    Gilabert Roura
    Arnau Sant Domí
    Pere Térmens
    Francesc Terreni
    Bartomeu Terrer

1348–1350: Martín Sancho de Antillón
1348–1356: Ferran d'Aragó
1348–1382: Pere Marc
1349–1360: Arnau Batlle

Dates unknown
No dates for the following friars' names were found in the extant documents
    Joan Bassols
    Lluis d'Escala
    Guillem de Falgar
    Pere de Font de Llop
    Pere Marginet
    Nicolau de Porra
    Ferrer Sala
    Antoni de Sassari
    Ferrer Terrassa
    Pere Vigué

PART THREE

Glossary, Archival Sources, Bibliography and Index

ON THE PREVIOUS PAGE
The law code of Aragon:
the title page from the *Summa de todos los fueros* (Saragossa, 1589)

An eighteenth-century map of Barcelona showing a Franciscan house near the waterfront

Glossary

This glossary is not a comprehensive list of terms used. It contains only those words that occur frequently in the text and a few other terms, which although explained there, are nevertheless unusual or especially significant.

batlle	bailiff or mayor (judicial/municipal officer)
cana, canes	measurement equivalent to 1.555 mm.
carrer major	principal street
censal	a bond with annual interest on property
Consell	council, often municipal
conventet	small convent
corts	royal parliament
curia	court or gathering for royal, municipal and ecclesiastical affairs
custodi, custos	custodian: officer in charge of group of convents
diner	*denarius* (monetary unit); of differing value, but usually there were 8 or 12 diners to the sou
elemosinarius	almoner
emphiteosis	emphyteusis: a long-term rental agreement in return for a small annual payment
estudio general	*studium generale*: Franciscan house of study
fueros (*furs*)	local laws
guardian	superior of Franciscan house
jurados (*jurats*)	rulers/councillors
lector	reader or lecturer on theology in a Franciscan house
mà major	upper classes
maravedis	monetary unit: Castilian term for *morabatins* (see below)
masia	country house
mazmutina, mazmutines	(Arabic *maṣmūdī*) a gold coin of Arabic origin
menoretes	Poor Clares
merino	royal judicial representative
mestre racional	Keeper of the Royal Purse
morabatin, morabatins	a gold coin similar in value to the diner (see above)
òbol	small monetary unit
paers	councillors (province of Lerida)
procurator	a person appointed to handle financial affairs

reial, ral	(Castilian *real*) a Valencian monetary unit
salmedina	magistrate
sesmerino	(alternatively *sesmero*) local magistrate in Aragon
superjuntario	regional judge in Aragon
vila	small town
violarium	annual payment to ecclesiastics

Archival Sources

In the course of my research on the Franciscans in the Crown of Aragon I tried to visit all the archives in Spain and southern France that might possibly contain relevant materials. I was not successful in obtaining access to every archive listed below, nor was I always able to consult all the holdings in the archives to which I did gain admittance. The following list includes brief descriptions of materials consulted, and explanations regarding collections not seen. I examined all available documents dating from the beginning of the thirteenth century to the time of the Black Death (1348), and in some cases (specified below) extended my search as far as 1430. Useful records were also obtained from local libraries, especially in Calatayud, Saragossa, Tarazona and Teruel, where most of the medieval records pertinent to this study are no longer extant.

BARCELONA

ARXIU CAPITULAR DE LA CATEDRAL (AC)

All holdings up to 1430 were examined. The most relevant documents are in the collections *Pia Almoina, Obra de la catedral, Sagristía* and *Caritat o mensa capitular*. These include *llibres notarials,* the notarial records of Bernat Vilarrúbia (1295-1348), Jordi Vilarrúbia (1332-1346), Guillem Borrell (1316-1337) and Pere Borrell (1334-1348); *pergamins,* miscellaneous wills or testaments and other parchments; *llibres d'Obra,* miscellaneous books and papers concerned with the fabric of the cathedral; and the *Administració de la caritat* for the year 1351. These records provided much material relating to the lives of individual Franciscans.

ARCHIVO DE LA CORONA DE ARAGÓN (ACA)

Cancillería real

The most relevant collections are the *Registros de la Cancillería* (RC), registers of the royal chancellery; and the *Cartas reales,* loose sheets from the chancellery registers (frequently undated, and stored in *cajas,* boxes). The documents consulted cover the period of the reigns of James I to Peter III from 1213 to 1350: *registros* 9-34, 38-658, 858-886, 979, 1052-1062, 1113-1130, 1295-1312, 1406-1412, 1492 and 1524; and *cartas* from *cajas* 1-165 (reigns of James I, Peter II, Alfonso II and James II), 1-27 (reign of Alfonso III), and 1-37 (reign of Peter III).

Ordenes religiosas y militares (ORM)
The most relevant collections consulted in this section of the archives are: the *carpeta Franciscans*, a set of about sixty parchments (*pergamins*) of the fourteenth century, comprising records of the Franciscans; *Gran Priorato de Cataluña*, miscellaneous parchments from the records of the Hospitallers (Knights of the Hospital of Saint John of Jerusalem); and *Monacales de Hacienda*, archival records (manuscripts) from the houses of the Dominicans, Mercedarians and other religious orders.

Real Patrimonio (RP)
Registers from the series *Maestro racional* for the years 1293–1350, and from the *Tesorería real de Aragón* for the years 1297–1350.

ARXIU DEL MONESTIR DE PEDRALBES (AMP)
Parchments, dating from the foundation of the monastery in 1327, on the history of the convent of Saint Clare at Pedralbes (Barcelona); also included is the convent chronology, *Chronologia de la regla de Santa Clara*, compiled in 1798.

ARXIU DELS CAPUTXINS
The notes of P. Martí de Barcelona, contained in several files; and Franciscan periodicals, especially *Estudis franciscans/Estudios franciscanos* (*EF*).

ARXIU DELS PROTOCOLS
Protocols (notarial records) from 1297 to 1400.

ARXIU DE SANT JUST
Parchments concerned with the Eiximenis and Malla families; and the register of deaths for the parish in the fourteenth century.

ARXIU DE SANT PERE DE LES PUELLES
All parchments and records for the period up to 1400. As this is a Benedictine house, the principal material relevant to this study deals with legacies to the mendicant orders.

ARXIU DIOCESÀ (AD)
The collections *Col.lacions* and *Registra beneficiorum, communium, dotaliarum, gratiarum* and *ordinatorum*. These comprise various materials relating to the diocese, including documents pertaining to disputes with the mendicant orders and the Third Order of Saint Francis (especially in Vilafranca), and ordinations of the Barcelona Franciscans.

ARXIU HISTÒRIC DE LA CIUTAT
The collections *Consell de Cent, Lletres closes* and *Llibres del Consell;* and miscellaneous parchments up to 1400, comprising material relating mostly to the latter half of the fourteenth century, useful here for comparative purposes only.

ARXIU HISTÒRIC DELS FRANCISCANS DE CATALUNYA (AHFC)
Extant parchments for the houses of Berga and Gerona; the *Repertori de actes del convent de Girona,* an inventory of Gerona parchments compiled in the eighteenth century; and collections of Franciscan periodicals and secondary sources. Invaluable for the collection of Gerona parchments and for the secondary materials on the Franciscans in Aragon and beyond.

CERVERA
ARXIU HISTÒRIC COMARCAL
Fons general: Convents (franciscanos), a collection of documents concerned with the Franciscan house; *llibres de Clavaría; llibres del Consell;* miscellaneous registers relating to the functioning of municipal affairs up to 1400; and notarial records of Jaume Ferrer, Pere Dan, Ramon Rama and others, for the same period.

GERONA (GIRONA)
ARXIU DE LA CATEDRAL
Llibre verd, a cartulary of material concerning the cathedral; and parchments up to 1400 (unclassified at the time of my visit, but now arranged according to geographical location).

ARXIU DIOCESÀ (AD)
The collections *Registra litterarum, Libri notularum, Pergamins de la Mitra* (recently reorganized) and *Ordres sagrades,* comprising episcopal letters, diocesan notarial records and ordination registers, mostly for the latter half of the fourteenth century but some for the 1330s.

ARXIU HISTÒRIC (AH)
Pergamins from the Hospital de Girona; and protocols (notarial records) for Gerona (G), Castelló d'Empúries (C) and Perelada (P), as follows: Gerona (from 1300 to 1400): Guillem Banyils, Jaume Compte, Arnau Delmás, Arnau Despoll, Guillem Desqués, Pere Massanet, Ramon Serra, Francesc Simón, Jaume Transfort, Ramon Viader and many others; Castelló (1279-

1328): Bernat Fontcuberta, Bernat Junquera, Pere Perrini and Pere Serra; Perelada (from 1280): Jaume Barraca.

ARXIU HISTÒRIC MUNICIPAL (AHM)
Collections mainly concerned with the affairs of the city: *Correspondència* of the *jurats; Cartes reials; Acords;* and *Pergamins,* unclassified parchments, together with other records of municipal affairs up to 1400.

HUESCA
ARCHIVO DE LA CATEDRAL
Access to the collections was not granted, but rapid consultation of the catalogue on site suggested that there was no relevant material.

ARCHIVO DIOCESANO
I was able to consult this archive's set of photocopies of the parchments belonging to the convent of Saint Clare, access to which was not granted.

ARCHIVO HISTÓRICO MUNICIPAL (AHM)
Privilegios reales for the thirteenth and fourteenth centuries; and *Documentos eclesiásticos* for the thirteenth to seventeenth centuries.

ARCHIVO HISTÓRICO PROVINCIAL
Protocols for the towns of Barbastro, Huesca and Jaca for the years 1365–1418.

JACA
ARCHIVO DE LA CATEDRAL
Access not granted; the archive was closed for reorganization.

ARCHIVO DIOCESANO
A perusal of the complete catalogue found no relevant holdings.

ARCHIVO HISTÓRICO MUNICIPAL
As the archive was in the process of reorganization at the time of my visit, I was able to consult only a catalogue of extant parchments.

LERIDA (LLEIDA)
ARXIU CAPITULAR DE LA CATEDRAL
Access to the archive is limited, and most of the parchments for the period of my study are uncatalogued and unavailable for examination.

ARXIU HISTÒRIC MUNICIPAL (AHM)
Privilegis, statuts e ordinacions de la ciutat de Lleida 1299–1413, a cartulary of documents relative to the city of Lerida.

MADRID
ARCHIVO DE LA ACADEMIA DE HISTORIA
Records of royal wills.

ARCHIVO HISTÓRICO NACIONAL (AHN)
Parchments (*pergamins*) of the section *Clero (regular y secular)* for Dominicans, Franciscans and other religious orders; and papal bulls to 1400.

MANRESA
ARXIU HISTÒRIC MUNICIPAL
Protocols dating from the late thirteenth century up to 1330; and the *Manualia consilii* (*manuals del Consell*) for the years 1322–1352.

MARSEILLE
ARCHIVES DÉPARTEMENTALES DE BOUCHES-DU-RHÔNE
Miscellaneous parchments and secondary material covering the period up to 1400, very little of it pertinent to this study.

MONTPELLIER
ARCHIVES DÉPARTEMENTALES DE L'HÉRAULT
Material (mostly parchments) relating to religious orders; and secondary material concerned with the Montpellier district in the late thirteenth and early fourteenth centuries.

ARCHIVES DE LA VILLE DE MONTPELLIER
Parchments relating to the privileges of the city, taken from the *Inventaires et documents;* and *cartulaires* up to 1400.

MONTSERRAT
ARXIU DE L'ABADIA DE MONTSERRAT
Unclassified parchments for La Cerdanya; together with relevant secondary material.

MORELLA
ARXIU HISTÒRIC ECLESIÀSTIC DE L'ARXIPRESTAL BASÍLICA DE SANTA MARIA LA MAJOR
Being reorganized at my visit; parchments were not available for study.

ARXIU DEL NOTARIAT
This private collection is mainly about Valencian notaries; none of the manuals for the period include anything significant for the Morella house.

NARBONNE
ARCHIVES MUNICIPALES
Inventaries, cartularies and parchments up to 1400.

PALMA DE MALLORCA
ARXIU CAPITULAR DE LA CATEDRAL (AC)
Cartularies of documents concerning the cathedral, gathered in volumes known as *Llibre de la cadena, Llibre groc, Llibre vermell* and *Llibre verd;* protocols from 1314 to 1400; and *Documents eclesiàstics i judicials* covering the years 1232–1400.

ARXIU HISTÒRIC DEL REGNE DE MALLORCA (AHRM)
In the section *Governació: Lletres reials* and *Lletres comunes*, royal registers of letters. In the section *Reial Patrimoni: Dades*, the amounts paid out by the royal house to religious orders and others; *Llibres dels comptes*, accounts; and registers from the *Escribanía de cartes reials* (ECR). In the section *Notaris:* protocols for the first decades of the fourteenth century. Miscellaneous parchments and numerous secondary sources on Majorca for the period up to 1400 were also consulted.

BIBLIOTECA MARCH
The *Documenta maioricarum* assembled by Joaquim Maria Bover.

PERPIGNAN
ARCHIVES DE LA BIBLIOTHÈQUE MUNICIPALE
Nineteenth-century secondary sources, mainly concerned with the bishopric of Elne and mostly relating to the latter half of the fourteenth century.

ARCHIVES DÉPARTEMENTALES DES PYRÉNÉES-ORIENTALES
Protocols and parchments from *série B* (religious orders).

PUIGCERDÀ
ARXIU HISTÒRIC COMARCAL (AHC)
Protocols: *Libri firmitatis, testamentorum, extraneorum* etc. from notaries such as Ramon de Coguls, Arnald Embertad and Bernat Manresa, from the late thirteenth century to 1370 (a full list of these notaries and their records has been published: see Bosom i Isern in the Bibliography); miscellaneous other records, including privileges of the city, accounts of the *clavari* (city treasurer) and notations from the *veguer* (judicial officer) on jurisdictional proceedings; and secondary material relating to the area.

REUS
ARXIU HISTÒRIC COMARCAL
Protocols and other documents for the period up to 1400, useful only for legacies to the Franciscans in Montblanc and Tarragona.

SARAGOSSA (ZARAGOZA)
ARCHIVO CAPITULAR DE LA SEO (AC)
The *Cartulario menor,* documents of the cathedral in the thirteenth century.

ARCHIVO HISTÓRICO DE PROTOCOLOS
Notarial records for the fourteenth century (only two extant for the period under review).

ARCHIVO HISTÓRICO MUNICIPAL
Parchments relating to the history of the city up to 1400; and secondary material specific to Saragossa. Very little of relevance to this study.

SEU D'URGELL, LA
ARXIU CAPITULAR DE LA SEU
The section *Cartularis àntics;* parchments and manuals of wills relating to the religious orders. The Franciscans had no house in La Seu d'Urgell; the archive only contains indirect references to the Lerida Franciscan house.

SEVILLE (SEVILLA)
ARCHIVO DEL DUQUE DE MEDINACELI (ADM)
Records for the county of Ampurias, or Empúries (stored in bundles, *legajos*), up to 1400. Very few have direct relevance for this study.

TARAZONA
ARCHIVO CAPITULAR DE TARAZONA
A fire in the late 1300s destroyed most of the archival material of the period. I found nothing relevant to this study.

TARRAGONA
ARXIU CAPITULAR DE LA CATEDRAL
The cartulary of Archbishop Benet of Rocabertí (most of this has been published in *Franciscalia:* see the Bibliography); and notarial records for the first half of the fourteenth century.

ARXIU HISTÒRIC
Notarial records for the late fourteenth century.

TÀRREGA
ARXIU HISTÒRIC MUNICIPAL (AHM)
Llibres del Consell; and parchments relating to the functioning of municipal affairs up to 1400.

TERUEL
ARCHIVO CAPITULAR DE LA CATEDRAL
Parchments of wills.

ARCHIVO HISTÓRICO MUNICIPAL
Cartularies and other records up to 1400. These were mostly not relevant to this study.

ARCHIVO HISTÓRICO PROVINCIAL
Parchments up to 1400 (in the process of reorganization at the time of my visit).

TORTOSA
ARCHIVO DE LA CATEDRAL (AC)
Cartularies for the thirteenth and fourteenth centuries; miscellaneous parchments for the fourteenth century; *Registra litterarum* for the reign of James I; and *Común de cabildo* no. 53, an undated collection of documents referring to the cathedral chapter.

ARXIU HISTÒRIC MUNICIPAL
Wills, *Provisions municipals* and *Diversorum,* all fourteenth-century.

VALENCIA
ARCHIVO CAPITULAR DE LA CATEDRAL (AC)
Parchments containing wills; and notarial records.

ARCHIVO DEL REAL COLEGIO-SEMINARIO DE CORPUS CHRISTI (PATRIARCA)
Notarial records for the latter part of the fourteenth century.

ARCHIVO DEL REINO DE VALENCIA
Protocols, wills and receipts up to 1400; and secondary material concerning Valencia.

ARCHIVO HISTORICO DE LOS FRANCISCANOS
Notes of the late Fr. Andrés Ivars, who was working on the history of the Franciscans in the Crown of Aragon and, like Fr. Marti of Barcelona, was assasinated at the beginning of the Spanish Civil War. Although his notes are not directly relevant to the period before 1348, interested readers may wish to consult Benjamin Agulló Pascual, "Fray Andrés Ivars Cardona, OFM (1885-1936)," *AIA* 49 (1989), 51-77. The archive also contains secondary material relating to Teruel and Valencia.

ARCHIVO HISTÓRICO MUNICIPAL (AHM)
Manuals del Consell from 1306 to 1350; and *Lletres missives,* letters from the municipality of Valencia to a variety of recipients, from 1378 to 1422.

VALLDOREIX
ARXIU GAVÍN
A vast photographic archive of Catalan religious buildings assembled and directed by Josep Maria Gavín and located near Barcelona. It is published in part in his *Inventari d'eglésies* (25 volumes to date; Barcelona: Artestudi Edicions; Kapel S.A.; Arxiu Gavín; Editorial Pòrtic S.A., 1977-).

VALLS
ARXIU HISTÒRIC COMARCAL
Protocols and other documents relating to the area. As there was no Franciscan house in Valls, the records are mainly of interest for references to Tarragona and Montblanc.

VIC
ARXIU ECLESIÀSTIC (AE)

The name of the archive is an all-embracing term used to denote the archives housed in the bishop's palace in Vic; these include the Arxiu capitular (AC) and the Arxiu de la Curia Fumada (ACF), the archives of most relevance to this study. The material consulted includes manuals of wills or testaments (T) from the late thirteenth century to 1400; notarial records (N) for the same period; parchments from the capitular collection; the *veguería,* jurisdictional records; hospital records; and a number of unique secondary sources.

Bibliography of Printed Sources

Aguillo López de Turiso, Jerónimo. *La provincia seráfica de Cataluña.* Barcelona: La Hormiga de Oro, 1902.

Agulló Pascual, Benjamin. "Iglesia de San Francisco de Teruel." In *Celebración del 750 aniversario del martirio de los santos fray Juan de Perusa y fray Pedro de Saxoferrato, copatronos de Teruel, Valencia-Teruel, 1228-1978,* pp. 43-96. Proceedings of a conference held in Teruel Cathedral, 1978. Valencia: privately printed, 1979.

———. "Los restos del rey moro Zeit Abu Ceid, en el monasterio de la Puridad de Valencia." In *Crónica de la XI asamblea de cronistas oficiales del Reino de Valencia 1976,* pp. 1-6. Valencia: n.p., 1978.

Alexander IV. *La documentación pontificia de Alejandro IV (1254-1261).* Ed. Ildefonso Rodríguez de Lama. Monumenta Hispaniae Vaticana, sección registros 5. Rome: Instituto español de história eclesiástica, 1976.

Alfonso X, el Sabio. *Las siete partidas del rey don Alfonso el Sabio.* 3 vols. Madrid: Lope de Vega, 1972.

Alomar Esteve, Gabriel. *Cátaros y occitanos en el Reino de Mallorca.* Colección Eura 2. Palma de Mallorca: Luis Ripoll, 1978.

Amberes, Fregando de. "La orden tercera de San Francisco de Asís: Su difusión e influencia política en el siglo XIII." *EF* 29 (1923), 42-53.

Amorós Payá, León. "Anfredo Gontero, OFM, discípulo de Escoto y lector en el estudio general de Barcelona." *Revista española de teología* 1 (1941), 545-572.

———. *Los inventarios del antiguo archivo del convento de San Francisco de Teruel.* Teruel: Instituto de estudios turolenses, 1960.

Analecta Franciscana 3 (1897): *Chronica XXIV generalium ordinis Minorum cum pluribus appendicibus, inter quas excellit hucusque ineditus Liber de laudibus S. Francisci Fr. Bernardi a Bessa.* Covers the period from 1209-1374.

Andrés Antón, María Pilar. *El monasterio de la puridad: Primera fundación de Clarisas en Valencia y su reino, siglos XIII-XV.* Valencia: Monasterio de la puridad de Valencia, 1991.

Arnaldus de Villanova. See Vilanova, Arnau de.

Arribas Palau, Antonio. *La conquista de Cerdeña por Jaime II de Aragón.* Barcelona: Instituto español de estudios mediterráneos, 1952.

Batlle i Gallart, Carme, and Montserrat Casas i Nadal. "La caritat privada i les institucions benèfiques de Barcelona (segle XIII)." In *La pobreza y la asistencia a los pobres en la Cataluña medieval,* ed. Manuel Riu, 1: 117-190. Anuario de estudios medievales, anejo 9, 11. 2 vols. Barcelona: CSIC, 1980-1982.

Barcelona, Antoni Maria de. "La regla del terç orde franciscà." *EF* 27 (1921), 246-261.

Barcelona, Martí de. *La cultura catalana durant el regnat de Jaume II.* Ed. Valentí Serra. Sarrià (Barcelona): Provincias capuchinas iberoamericanas, 1991. Also published in three parts in *Estudios franciscanos* 91 (1990), 213-295; 92 (1991), 127-245; and 92 (1991), 383-492. A work that won a prize from the Institut d'estudis catalans in 1936, but was not published at that time due to the outbreak of war.

Bayerri y Bertomeu, Enrique. *Història de Tortosa y su comarca.* 8 vols. Tortosa: Algueró y Baiges, 1933-1959.

Benedict XI. *Le Registre de Benoit XI: Recueil des bulles de ce pape.* Ed. Ch. Grandjean. Paris: Albert Fontemoing, 1905.

Bevan, Bernard. *History of Spanish Architecture.* New York: Charles Scribner's Sons; London: B.T. Batsford, 1939.

Bisson, Thomas N. *The Medieval Crown of Aragon: A Short History.* Oxford: Clarendon Press, 1986.

—. "Prelude to Power: Kingship and Constitution in the Realms of Aragon, 1175-1250." In *The Worlds of Alfonso the Learned and James the Conqueror,* pp. 23-40.

Blanch, Josep. *Arxiepiscopologi de la santa església metropolitana i primada de Tarragona.* 2 vols. Tarragona: Diputació provincial de Tarragona, 1985.

Boades, Bernat. *Libre de Feyts d'armes de Catalunya.* Ed. Enric Bagué. Els nostres clàssics, Col.lecció A, 29, 45, 52, 60, 61. 5 vols. Barcelona: Barcino, 1930-1948.

Bofarull y Sans, Francisco de A. de. "Jaime I y los judíos." In *Congrés d'història de la Corona d'Aragó dedicat al rey en Jaume I y a la seva època,* 2: 819-943. Proceedings of the first conference, held in June 1908. 2 vols. Barcelona: F. Altés, 1909-1913.

Boniface VIII. *Les Registres de Boniface VIII: Recueil des bulles de ce pape.* Ed. Georges Digard, Maurice Faucon, Antoine Thomas, and Robert Fawtier. 4 vols. Paris: Ernest Thorin, 1884-1885 (vols. 1-3); E. de Boccard, 1939 (vol. 4).

Bono, José. *História del derecho notarial español.* 2 vols. Madrid: Junta de decanos de los colegios notariales de España, 1979-1982.

Bosom i Isern, Sebastià. *Homes i oficis de Puigcerdà al segle XIV (un document inèdit de 1345).* Puigcerdà: Institut d'estudis ceretans, 1982.

Bosom i Isern, Sebastià, and Salvador Galcerán i Vigué. *Catáleg de protocols de Puigcerdà.* Barcelona: Fundació Noguera, 1983.

Boswell, John. *Christianity, Social Tolerance and Homosexuality.* Chicago: University of Chicago Press, 1980.

Brooke, Rosalind B. *The Coming of the Friars.* London: George Allen and Unwin; New York: Barnes and Noble, 1975.

Bullarium Franciscanum Romanorum pontificum. Ed. J.H. Sbaralea (G.G. Sbaraglia) and D.A. Rossi de Pisauro. 7 vols. 1759-1904. Repr. Santa Maria degli Angeli: Edizioni Porziuncola, 1983- .

Bullarium pontificium quod exstat in archivo sacri conventus S. Francisci Assisiensis (nunc apud bibliothecam Assisii). Ed. Laetus Alessandri-Franciscus Pennacchi. Quaracchi: College of St. Bonaventure, 1920.

Bullough, Vern L. "Prostitution in the Later Middle Ages." In *Sexual Practices and the Medieval Church,* pp. 176-186. Ed. Vern L. Bullough and James Brundage. Buffalo: Prometheus Books, 1982.

Burns, Robert I. "Castle of Intellect, Castle of Force: The Worlds of Alfonso the Learned and James the Conqueror." In *The Worlds of Alfonso the Learned and James the Conqueror,* pp. 3-22.

——. "Príncipe almohade y converso mudejar: Nueva documentación." *Sharq al-Andalus: Estudios árabes* 4 (1987), 109-122.

——. *El Reino de Valencia en el siglo XIII (iglesia y sociedad).* 2 vols. Valencia: Del Cenia al Segura, 1982.

——. *Society and Documentation in Crusader Valencia.* Princeton: Princeton University Press, 1985.

Cabanes Pecourt, María Desamparados, and Ramon Ferrer Navarro, eds. *Libre del Repartiment del Regne de Valencia.* Facsimile ed., in progress. Textos medievales 66- . 3 vols. to date. Saragossa: Anubar, 1979- .

Campillo, Toribio del. *Documentos históricos de Daroca y su comunidad.* Saragossa: Imprenta del Hospicio provincial, sección histórico-doctrinal, 1915.

Castro, Américo. *The Spaniards: An Introduction to Their History.* Trans. Willard F. King and Selma Margaretten. Berkeley, Los Angeles and London: University of California Press, 1971.

Chabás y Lloréns, Roque. "Çeid Abu Çeid." *El archivo* (Denia and Valencia) 4 (1890), 215-221; 5 (1891), 143-166, 283-304, 362-376.

Chazan, Robert. *Daggers of Faith: Thirteenth-Century Christian Missionizing and Jewish Response.* Berkeley: University of California Press, 1989.

Clay, Rotha Mary. *The Mediaeval Hospitals of England.* London: Frank Cass, 1966.

Cohen, Jeremy. *The Friars and the Jews: The Evolution of Medieval Anti-Judaism.* Ithaca and London: Cornell University Press, 1982.

Coll, Jaime. *Crónica de la província franciscana de Cataluña: Parte primera.* 1738. Facsimile ed. with intro. and indices by José Martí Mayor. Crónicas franciscanas de España 21. Madrid: Cisneros, 1981.

Comes, Bernardo. *Libro vero è original.* 2 vols. Barcelona, n.p., 1725. Original of vol. 1 burnt during Tragic Week of 1909, but a copy was published in *Revista de la Asociación artístico-arqueológica barcelonesa* (Barcelona, 1900). Copy of vol. 1 and original of vol. 2 are both now in the Arxiu provincial dels Franciscans de Catalunya, Barcelona.

Corral Lafuente, José Luis. *La comunidad de aldeas de Daroca en los siglos XIII y XIV: Orígenes y proceso de consolidación.* Saragossa: Institución "Fernando el católico" (CSIC), 1987.

Coulton, G.G. *From St. Francis to Dante: Translations from the Chronicle of the Franciscan Salimbene (1221-1288).* 1906. 2nd ed., rev. and enl. London: Nutt, 1907. Paperback ed. Philadelphia: University of Pennsylvania Press, 1972.

——. *Two Saints: St. Bernard and St. Francis.* Cambridge: Cambridge University Press, 1932; repr. Folcroft, Pa.: Folcroft Library Editions, 1974.

Courtenay, William J. *Schools and Scholars in Fourteenth-Century England.* Princeton: Princeton University Press, 1987.

Cuadrado Sánchez, Marta. "Arquitectura franciscana en España (siglos XIII y XIV)." *AIA* 51 (1991), 15-70, 479-552.

Daniel, E. Randolph. *The Franciscan Concept of Mission in the High Middle Ages.* Lexington: University Press of Kentucky, 1975.

Davis, Charles T. "Le Pape Jean XXII et les spirituels: Ubertin de Casale." In *Franciscains d'Oc: Les Spirituels ca. 1280-1324,* pp. 263-283. Cahiers de Fanjeaux 10. Toulouse: Edouard Privat, 1975.

Delcor, Maties. "Le Diétari de Puigcerdà: Texte et notes, deuxième partie." *Etudes Roussillonnaises: Revue d'histoire et d'archéologie méditerranéennes* (Perpignan) 4 (1954-1955), 135-150.

Dufourcq, Ch.-E., and J. Gautier Dalché. *História ecónomica y social de la España cristiana en la edad media.* Barcelona: El Albir, 1983.

Durieux, F.-R. "Approches de l'histoire franciscaine du Languedoc au XIIIe siècle." In *Les Mendiants en pays d'Oc au XIIIe siècle,* pp. 79-100. Cahiers de Fanjeaux 8. Toulouse: Edouard Privat, 1973.

Durliat, M. *L'Art dans le royaume de Majorque.* Toulouse: Edouard Privat, 1962.

Duvernoy, Jean. "Le Catharisme en Languedoc au début du XIVe siècle." In *Effacement du Catharisme? (XIIIe-XIVe s.),* pp. 27-56. Cahiers de Fanjeaux 20. Toulouse: Edouard Privat, 1985.

———. *Le Registre d'Inquisition de Jacques Fournier, évêque de Pamiers (1318-1325).* 3 vols. Toulouse: Edouard Privat, 1965.

Eiximenis, Francesc. *Contes i faules.* Ed. Marçal Olivar. Els nostres clàssics 6. Barcelona: Barcino, 1925.

———. *Lo Crestià (selecció).* Ed. Albert Hauf. Les millors obres de la literatura catalana 98. Barcelona: Edicions 62, 1983.

———. *Dotzè llibre del Crestià: Segona part.* Ed. Curt Wittlin, Arseni Pacheco, Jill Webster et al. 2 vols. Girona: Col.legi universitari de Girona, Diputació de Girona, 1986-1987.

———. *Regiment de la cosa pública.* Ed. Daniel de Molins de Rei. Els nostres clàssics 13. Barcelona: Barcino, 1927.

España sagrada: Teatro geográfico-histórico de la iglesia de España. Comp. Enrique Florez et al. 1747-1879. 3rd ed. 56 vols. Madrid: José Rodriguez, 1879-1957.

Eubel, Conradus. *Hierarchia Catholica medii aevi.* 1898-1910. Vol. 1, *Series ab anno 1198 usque ad annum 1431 perducta.* 2nd ed. Regensberg: Monasterii sumptibus et typis librariae Regensbergianae, 1913.

———. *Provinciale ordinis Fratrum Minorum.* Quaracchi: Collegium S. Bonaventurae, 1892.

Finke, Heinrich, ed. *Acta Aragonensia: Quellen zur deutschen, italienischen, französischen, spanischen, zur Kirchen- und Kulturgeschicte aus der diplomatischen Korrespondenz Jayme II. (1291-1327).* 3 vols. Berlin and Leipzig: Dr. Walther Rothschild, 1908-1922.

Fleming, John V. *An Introduction to the Franciscan Literature of the Middle Ages.* Chicago: Franciscan Herald Press, 1977.

Frago Gracia, Juan A. *Toponimia del campo de Borja: Estudio lexicológico.* Saragossa: Institución "Fernando el católico" (CSIC), 1980.

Franciscalia, en la convergència centenària del trànsit del "Poverello." Barcelona: Editorial Franciscana, 1928.

Freed, John B. *The Friars and German Society in the Thirteenth Century.* Cambridge, Mass.: Mediaeval Academy of America, 1977.

Galcerán Vigué, Salvador. *Dietari de la fidelíssima vila de Puigcerdà: Transcripció literal del text i comentari original.* Barcelona: Fundació Salvador Vives Casajuana, 1977.

Gams, Pius Bonifacius. *Series episcoporum ecclesiae Catholicae.* 1873. 2nd unaltered ed. 3 vols. Leipzig: Karl W. Hiersemann, 1931.

García i Sanz, Arcadi, and Maria-Teresa Ferrer i Mallol. *Assegurances i canvis marítims medievals a Barcelona.* 2 vols. Barcelona: Institut d'estudis catalans, 1983.

Garcías Palou, Sebastián. *El Miramar de Ramon Llull.* Palma de Mallorca: Diputacion provincial de Baleares, Instituto de estudios baleáricos, CSIC, 1977.

Geremek, Bronisław. *The Margins of Society in Late Medieval Paris.* Trans. Jean Birrell from the French ed. of 1976. Cambridge: Cambridge University Press; Paris: Editions de la Maison des sciences de l'homme, 1987.

Giné i Torres, Anna M. "El convent de Sant Francesc de Barcelona: Reconstrucció hipotètica." *Acta historica et archaeologica medievalia* 9 (1988), 221-243.

Giordani, Bonaventura. "Statuta consortii B. Mariae Virginis et S. Francisci Parmae saec. XIV." *AFH* 16 (1923), 356-368.

Goffen, Rona. *Spirituality in Conflict: Saint Francis and Giotto's Bardi Chapel.* University Park, PA and London: Pennsylvania State University Press, 1988.

Golubovich, Hieronymus. "Series provinciarum ordinis Fratrum Minorum, saec. XIII et XIV." *AFH* 1 (1908), 1-22.

Gonzaga, Francisco. *De origine seraphicae religionis.* 1587. 2nd ed. Venice, 1603.

González i Betlinski, Margarida, and Anna Rubió i Rodón. "La regla de l'orde de Santa Clara de 1263: Un cas concret de la seva aplicació, el monestir de Pedralbes de Barcelona." *Acta historica et archaeologica mediaevalia* 3 (1982), 9-46.

Gual Camarena, Miguel. *Vocabulario del comercio medieval.* Barcelona: El Albir, 1976.

Gudiol, Josep, and Santiago Alcolea i Blanch. *Pintura gótica catalana.* Barcelona: Polígrafa, 1986.

Hillgarth, J.N. "The Problem of a Catalan Mediterranean Empire, 1229-1327." *English Historical Review* Supplement 8. London: Longman, 1975.

——. *The Spanish Kingdoms: 1250-1516.* 2 vols. Oxford: Clarendon Press, 1976.

Hinnebusch, William A. *The History of the Dominican Order.* 2 vols. Staten Island, NY: St. Paul Publications, Alba House, 1965.

Honorius III. *Regesta Honorii papae III.* Ed. Petrus Pressutti. 2 vols. Rome: Typographia Vaticana, 1888-1895.

Hurtebise, Eduardo González. *Libros de tesorería de la casa real de Aragón.* Vol. 1, *Reinado de Jaime II.* Barcelona: Luis Benaiges, 1911.

Innocent IV. *La documentación pontificia de Inocencio IV (1243-1254).* Ed. Augusto Quintana Prieto. Monumenta Hispaniae Vaticana, sección registros 7. 2 vols. Rome: Instituto español de historia eclesiástica, 1987.

Ivars, Andrés. "Sepulcro de Alfonso IV de Aragón en la iglesia de los frailes menores de Lérida." *AIA* 30 (1928), 107-113.

James I (Jaume I of Catalonia, Jaime I of Aragon). *Documentos de Jaime I de Aragon.* Vol. 2, *1237-1250.* Ed. Ambrosio Huici Miranda and María Desamparados Cabanes Pecourt. Textos medievales 50. Valencia: Anubar, 1976.

Jantzen, Hans. *High Gothic.* London: Constable, 1962.

Junyent, Eduard. *La ciutat de Vic i la seva història.* Documents de cultura 13. 1976. 2nd ed. Barcelona: Curial, 1980.

Knowles, David. *The Religious Orders in England.* 3 vols. Cambridge: Cambridge University Press, 1948-1959, repr. 1979.

Lavedan, Pierre. *L'Architecture gothique religieuse en Catalogne, Valence et Baléares*. Paris: Henri Laurens, 1935.

Ledesma Rubió, María Luisa, and María Isabel Falcón Pérez. *Zaragoza en la baja edad media*. Saragossa: Librería General, 1977.

Linehan, Peter. *The Spanish Church and the Papacy in the Thirteenth Century*. Cambridge: Cambridge University Press, 1971.

Little, Andrew G. *The Grey Friars in Oxford*. Oxford: Clarendon Press, 1892.

Lladonosa Pujol, José. *Lérida medieval*. 2 vols. Lerida: Dilagro, 1974–1975.

Llobregat, Enric A., and J.F. Yvars. *Història de l'art al país valencià*. 2 vols. Valencia: Eliseu Climent, 1986–1988.

Llompart, Gabriel. *La pintura medieval mallorquina*. Colección Eura 1. 4 vols. Palma de Mallorca: Luis Ripoll, 1977–1980.

López, Atanasio. *La província de España de los frailes menores*. Santiago: El Eco Franciscano, 1915.

López de Meneses, Amada. "Documentos acerca de la peste negra en los dominios de la Corona de Aragón." *Estudios de edad media de la Corona de Aragón* 6 (1956), 291–447.

Manuel, Juan. *Libro de los estados*. Ed. R.B. Tate and I.R. Macpherson. Oxford: Clarendon Press, 1974.

Marquès i Casanovas, Jaume. *Girona vella*. Gerona: Ajuntament de Girona, 1979.

Martínez Ferrando, J. Ernest. *Jaime II de Aragón: Su vida familiar*. 2 vols. Barcelona: CSIC, 1948.

—. *Jaume II o el Seny Català, Alfons el Benigne*. 1961. 2nd ed. Barcelona: Aedos, 1963.

—. *La tràgica història dels reis de Mallorca*. 1960. 2nd ed. Barcelona: Aedos, 1979.

Masià i de Ros, Angel. *Jaume II: Aragó, Granada i Marroc*. Barcelona: CSIC, 1989.

Mestres y Brea, Francisco de Asis. *Galería seráfica, o sea Vida del gran padre y patriarca, San Francisco de Asís*. 2 vols. in 1. Barcelona: José Ribet, 1857.

Miravall, Ramon. *Necròpolis, sepultures i inhumacions a Tortosa*. Tortosa: Dertosa, 1986.

Miret i Sans, Joaquím. *Itinerari de Jaume I, "el Conqueridor."* Barcelona: Institut d'estudis catalans, 1918.

Molar, Nolasc del. "Una traducció antiga del *Lignum vitae* de Sant Bonaventura." *EF* 79 (1978), 63–81.

Moll, Francesc de B. *Els llinatges catalans*. Els treballs i els dies 23. 1959. 2nd augm. ed. Palma de Mallorca: Moll, 1982.

Mollat, Michel. *The Poor in the Middle Ages: An Essay in Social History.* Trans. Arthur Goldhammer from French ed. of 1978. New Haven: Yale University Press, 1986.

Montoliu, Manuel de. *Les grans personalitats de la literatura catalana.* Vol. 4, *Eiximenis, Turmeda i l'inici de l'humanisme a Catalunya: Bernat Metge.* Barcelona: Alpha, 1959.

Moorman, John R.H. *A History of the Franciscan Order from its Origins to the Year 1517.* Oxford: Clarendon Press, 1968; repr. Chicago: Chicago University Press, 1988.

—. *Medieval Franciscan Houses.* St. Bonaventure, NY: Franciscan Institute, St. Bonaventure University, 1983.

Mora, Pau, and Lorenzo Andrinal. *Diplomatari del monestir de Santa Maria de la Real de Mallorca.* Tarragona: Abadia de Poblet, 1982.

Moreu-Rey, Enric. *Els nostres noms de lloc.* Els treballs i els dies 22. Palma de Mallorca: Moll, 1982.

—. *Renoms, motius, malnoms i noms de casa.* Barcelona: Millà, 1981.

Mundy, John H. *Europe in the High Middle Ages 1150–1309.* London: Longman, 1973.

Muntaner, Ramon. *Crónica.* Ed. Enric Bagué. Col.lecció popular Barcino 19, 141–148. 9 vols. (2nd ed. of vol. 1). Barcelona: Barcino, 1927–1952.

Mutgé Vives, Josefa. *La ciudad de Barcelona durante el reinado de Alfonso el benigno (1327-1336).* Anuario de estudios medievales, anejo 17. Madrid and Barcelona: CSIC, 1987.

Nicholas III. *Les Registres de Nicolas III (1277-1280): Recueil des bulles de ce pape.* Ed. Jules Gay and Suzanne Vitte. 5 fascs. in 1 vol. Paris: Albert Fontemoing, 1898–1904 (fascs. 1–3); E. de Boccard, 1932–1938 (fascs. 4–5).

Nicholas IV. *Les Registres de Nicolas IV: Recueil des bulles de ce pape.* Ed. Ernest Langlois. 2 vols. Paris: Ernest Thorin, 1886–1891.

Oliveros de Castro, María Teresa. *História de Monzón*. Saragossa: Institución "Fernando el católico" (CSIC), 1964.

Ollich i Castanyer, Immaculada. "Aplicació sistemàtica d'ordinadors a la documentació medieval de la plana de Vic." Doctoral dissertation, University of Barcelona, 1981.

Ollich i Castanyer, Immaculada. "Les entitats eclesiàstiques d'Ausona al segle XIII a través de les donacions testamentàries." Treball realitzat mitjançant la beca "Mossén Gudiol" per a estudis històrics, concedida pel Patronat d'estudis Ausonencs, Vic, Curs. 1974-1975.

Omaechevarría, Ignacio. "La 'Regla' y las reglas de la orden de Santa Clara." *Collectanea Franciscana* 46 (1976), 93-119.

Panofsky, Erwin. *Gothic Architecture and Scholasticism*. Latrobe, PA: Archabbey Press, 1951. Paperback ed. New York: Meridian Books, 1957.

Parsons, John Carmi. *The Court and Household of Eleanor of Castile in 1290*. Studies and Texts 37. Toronto: Pontifical Institute of Mediaeval Studies, 1977.

Perarnau, Josep. *L'"Alia informatio beguinorum" d'Arnau de Vilanova*. Barcelona: Facultat de teología de Barcelona, secció de Sant Pacià, 1978.

—. "Una altra carta de Guiu Terrena sobre el procés inquisitorial contra el franciscà fra Bernat Fuster." *EF* 82 (1981), 383-392.

—. "*Beatus Franciscus per Gerundam transiens*: Tradició del pas de Sant Francesc d'Assis per Girona." *EF* 85 (1984), 237-240.

—. "Noves dades sobre béguins de Girona." *AIEG* 25 (1979-1980), 237-246; 26 (1981), 383-392.

Pérez Martínez, Lorenzo. "Corpus documental Balear (V): Reinado de Jaime I." *Fontes rerum Balearium* (Palma de Mallorca) 3 (1979-1980), 1-48.

Peter III (Pere III of Catalonia, Pedro IV of Aragon). *Chronique catalane de Pierre IV d'Aragon, III de Catalogne, dit le Cérémonieux ou del Punyalet*. Ed. Amédée Pagès. Bibliothèque méridionale, 2nd ser. 31. Toulouse: Edouard Privat; Paris: Henri Didier, 1941.

—. *Crònica general de Pere III el Ceremoniós, dita comunament Crónica de Sant Joan de la Penya*. Ed. Amadeu-J. Soberanas Lleó. Barcelona: Alpha, 1961.

Peter III (Pere III of Catalonia, Pedro IV of Aragon). *Pere III of Catalonia (Pedro IV of Aragon): Chronicle.* Trans. Mary Hillgarth and J.N. Hillgarth. Mediaeval Sources in Translation 23-24. 2 vols. Toronto: Pontifical Institute of Mediaeval Studies, 1980.

Pinaga, Epifanio de. "Testamento de la infanta doña Blanca de Molina, fundadora del convento de San Francisco de Molina de Aragón, año 1293." *AIA* 27 (1927), 394-400.

Pla Cargol, Joaquín. *Gerona histórica.* 1940. 2nd ed. Gerona and Madrid: Dalmáu Carles, Pla, 1945.

Pladevall, Antoni, and F. Català Roca. *Els monestirs catalans.* 1968. 4th ed. Barcelona: Destino, 1978.

Pons, Antoni. *Historia de Mallorca.* Vol. 6, *História del Reino de Mallorca.* Palma de Mallorca: Gráficas Miramar, 1970.

Portet, Renada-Laura. *A la recerca d'una memòria: Els noms de llocs del Rosselló (Microtoponímia).* Premi Vila de Perpinyà, 1981. Perpignan: Publicacions del CDACC, 1981.

Pou y Martí, José María. *Visionarios, béguinos y fraticelos catalanes (siglos XIII-XV).* 1930. Rev. ed. with new bio-bibliography by J. Martí Mayor and introductory study by J.M. Arcelus Ulibarrena. Madrid: Colegio "Cardenal Cisneros," 1991.

Powers, James F. *A Society Organized for War: The Iberian Municipal Militias in the Central Middle Ages, 1000-1284.* Berkeley: University of California Press, 1988.

Puig y Puig, Sebastián. *Episcopologio de la sede Barcinonense.* Barcelona: Biblioteca Balmes, 1929.

Les quatre grans cròniques. Ed. Ferran Soldevila. Biblioteca perenne 26. 1971. 2nd ed. Barcelona: Selecta, 1983.

Reeves, Marjorie. *The Influence of Prophecy in the Later Middle Ages: A Study in Joachimism.* Oxford: Clarendon Press, 1969.

Riquer, Martín de. *História de la literatura catalana: Part antiga.* 3 vols. Barcelona: Ariel, 1964.

Romero, Jordi. "Sant Francesc d'Assis i la tradició de que va posar a Can Codina de Sant Joan Despí." *La font del be* (Sant Joan Despí) 57 (juliol-desembre 1984), 19-21.

Rubí, Basili de. "La escuela franciscana de Barcelona y su intervención en los decretos inmaculistas (siglos XIII-XIV)." *EF* 57 (1956), 363-406.

Rubió i Lluch, Antoni, ed. *Documents per l'història de la cultura catalana mig. eval.* 2 vols. Barcelona: Institut d'estudis catalans, 1908-1921.

Rubió Vela, Agustín. *Pobreza, enfermedad y asistencia hospitalaria en la Valencia del siglo XIV.* Valencia: Institución Alfonso el magnánimo, Diputación provincial de València, 1984.

Rubió Vela, Agustín, and Mateu Rodrigo Lizondo. "Els béguins de València en el segle XIV: La seva casa, hospital i els seus llibres." In *Estudis en memoria del professor Manuel Sanchís Guarner: Estudis de llengua i literatura catalanes.* 2 vols. Valencia: Universitat de València, 1984.

Ruiz, Juan (Arcipreste de Hita). *Libro de buen amor.* Ed. G.B. Gybbon-Monypenny. Clásicos Castalia 161. Madrid: Editorial Castalia, 1988.

Russell, Jeffrey B., ed. *Religious Dissent in the Middle Ages.* New York: John Wiley and Sons, 1971.

St. Francis of Assisi, Writings and Early Biographies: English Omnibus of the Sources for the Life of St. Francis. Ed. Marion A. Habig. London: SPCK, 1972; Chicago: Franciscan Herald Press, 1973.

Salavert y Roca, Vicente. *Cerdeña y la expansión mediterránea de la Corona de Aragón 1297-1314.* 2 vols. Madrid: CSIC, Escuela de estudios medievales, 1956.

Saldes, Ambròs de. "Documentació franciscana (1267-1285)." *EF* 45 (1933), 130-149.

——. "Documentació franciscana (1282-1285)." *EF* 42 (1930), 86-96, 97-107.

——. "Documents inèdits per a la història de l'antiga província franciscana d'Aragó (segles XIII-XIV)." *EF* 46 (1934), 98-107.

——. "Franciscanismo: Documentos franciscanos." *EF* 17 (1916), 64-74.

——. "La orden franciscana en el antiguo Reino de Aragón: Colección diplomática." *REF* 1 (1907), 90-92, 219-222, 279-282, 354-358, 414-417, 478-482, 537-540, 608-612, 753-757.

Salimbene da Parma. *The Chronicle of Salimbene de Adam.* Trans. Joseph L. Baird, Giuseppe Baglivi and John Robert Kane. Binghampton, New York: Center for Medieval and Early Renaissance Studies, University Center at Binghamton, 1986.

Salrach, Josep M., and Eulàlia Duran. *Història dels paisos catalans dels orígens a 1714.* 2 vols. Barcelona: Edhasa, 1982.

Sanahuja, Pedro. *História de la seráfica provincia de Cataluña.* Barcelona: Editorial Seráfica, 1959.

Sanahuja, Pedro. "El monestir de framenors de Berga." *EF* 43 (1931), 354–406.

———. "El monestir de framenors de Cervera." *EF* 45 (1933), 47–97.

———. "El monestir dels Framenors observants de Lleida." *Analecta sacra Tarraconensia* 11 (1934), 179–195.

Sangorrín y Diest-Garcés, Dámaso. *El libro de la cadena del concejo de Jaca*. Saragossa: F. Martínez, 1920.

Sant Francesc d'Assís, "el Pobrissó" (1181[2]-1226): El seu pas per Catalunya. Les nostres devocions 18. Reus: Torrell de Reus, 1968. Pamphlet, paginated 481–507.

Santi, Francesco. *Arnau de Vilanova: L'obra espiritual*. Història i societat 5. Valencia: Diputació provincial de València, 1987.

Sanz Artibucilla, José Maria. *El convento e iglesia de San Francisco en Tarazona y el santisimo Cristo de la V.O.T.* Tarazona: L. Martínez-Moreno, 1924.

———. *História de la fidelisima y vencedora ciudad de Tarazona*. 2 vols. Madrid: E. Maestre, 1929–1930.

Sarret i Pons, Lluis. *Privilegis de Tàrrega*. 1930. Facsimile ed. by Ignasi de L. Camps i Sarró. Tàrrega: A.G. Camps, 1982.

Scott, Martin. *Medieval Europe*. London: Longmans, 1964.

Segarra i Malla, Josep Maria. *Història de Tàrrega amb els seus costums i tradicions, I (segles XI–XVI)*. Tàrrega: Museu comarcal, 1984.

Sesma Muñoz, J. Angel, and Angeles Líbano Zumalacárregui. *Léxico del comercio medieval en Aragón (siglo XV)*. Saragossa: Institución "Fernando el católico" (CSIC), 1982.

Sobrequés, Santiago. "La época del patriciado urbano." In *História de España y América social y económica*. Vol. 2, *Baja edad media*, ed. J. Vicens Vives, pp. 7–406. 2nd ed. Barcelona: Vicens-Vives, 1971.

Soldevila, Ferran. *Pere el Gran*. 2 vols. in 4. Barcelona: Institut d'estudis catalans, 1950–1952.

Southern, R.W. *Robert Grosseteste: The Growth of an English Mind in Medieval Europe*. Oxford: Clarendon Press, 1986.

Sticca, Sandro. *The "Planctus Mariae" in the Dramatic Tradition of the Middle Ages*. Trans. Joseph R. Berrigan. Athens, GA and London: University of Georgia Press, 1988.

Teixidor, P. *Antigüedades de Valencia*. 2 vols. Valencia: P. Aguilar, 1895.

Thomas of Celano. "The First Life of St. Francis." Trans. with intro. and notes by Placid Hermann in *St. Francis of Assisi: Omnibus of Sources*, pp. 225-355.

Trens, Manuel. *Ferrer Bassa i les pintures de Pedralbes.* Institut d'estudis catalans: Memòries de la secció històrico-arqueològica 6. Barcelona: Institut d'estudis catalans, 1936.

Turull i Rubinat, Max. *El règim municipal de Paeria, Cervera, 1331-1333: Dinàmica social i política.* Lerida: Virgili & Pagès, S.A., 1986.

Ubieto, Agustín. *Toponimia aragonesa medieval.* Valencia: Anubar, 1972.

Ubieto Arteta, Antonio. *Ciclos económicos en la edad media española.* Valencia: Anubar, 1969.

Vila, Pau. *Selecció d'escrits de geografia.* Vol. 2, *Aspectes geogràfics de Catalunya.* Biblioteca de cultura catalana 32. Barcelona: Curial, 1978.

Vilanova, Arnau de. *Aphorismi de gradibus.* Ed. Michael R. McVaugh. Vol. 2 of *Arnaldi de Villanova opera medica omnia,* ed. L. Garcia-Ballester, J.A. Paniagua, and M.R. McVaugh. Granada and Barcelona: Seminarium historiae medicae Granatensis, 1975.

———. "Raonament d'Avinyó." In *Obres catalanes.* Vol. 1, *Escrits religiosos,* ed. Miquel Batllori, pp. 167-221. Els nostres clàssics, Col.lecció A 53-54. Barcelona: Barcino, 1947.

Villapadierna, Isidoro de. "La tercera orden franciscana de España en el siglo XV." In *Il movimento francescano della penitenza nella società medioevale,* ed. Mariano d'Alatri, pp. 125-144. Atti del 3º convegno di studi francescani, Padova, 25-26-27 settembre 1979. Rome: Istituto storico dei Cappuccini, 1980.

Vincke, Johannes, ed. *Documenta selecta.* Barcelona: Biblioteca Balmes, 1936.

Wadding, Lucas, comp. *Annales Minorum.* 1625-1654. 3rd ed. 28 vols. Quaracchi: Collegium S. Bonaventurae, 1931-1947.

Waley, Daniel. *Later Medieval Europe from Saint Louis to Luther.* 1964. 2nd ed. London and New York: Longman, 1985.

Webster, Jill R. "Els anys formatius dels franciscans i carmelites a Montpeller i Perpinyà." In *Montpellier, la Couronne d'Aragon et les pays de langue d'Oc (1204-1349): Actes du XII Congrès d'histoire de la Couronne d'Aragon, Montpellier, 26-29 septembre 1985,* pp. 241-253. Mémoires de la Société archéologique de Montpellier 15. Montpellier: Société archéologique, 1987.

Webster, Jill R. "L'art gòtic i els framenors segons alguns documents de Barcelona i de Vic." *Ausa* (Vic) 12 (1987), 203-208.

———. "Col.lecció de documents del convent de Sant Francesc de Girona (1224-1399)." *AIEG* 28-30 (1985-1989), 28: 157-189, 29: 27-86, 30: 141-226.

———. "La contribución de los registros del patrimonio real a la história de los frailes menores durante la primera mitad del siglo XIV." *AIA,* in press.

———. "El convent de Santa Clara, Puigcerdà: Algunes consideracions preliminars." *Ceretania: Quaderns d'estudis cerdans* (Puigcerdà and Bourg-Madame) 1 (1991), 107-116.

———. "El desconocido convento de Puigcerdà." *AIA* 49 (1989), 167-194.

———. "Documents relacionats amb els convents de Sant Francesc, Santa Clara i Santa Maria del Carme de Vic a l'edat mitjana." *Studium Vicensia* (Vic), in press.

———. "Dos siglos de Franciscanismo en Cataluña: El convento de San Francisco de Barcelona durante los siglos XIII y XIV." *AIA* 41 (1981), 223-255.

———."The Early Catalan Mendicants in Sardinia." *Biblioteca francescana sarda* (Oristano, Sardinia) 2 (1988), 5-16.

———. "Eiximenis and the Society of His Day." M.A. dissertation, University of Nottingham, 1964.

———. *Excerpts from the Works of Francesc Examenis.* Folklore Seminar Papers 3. St. Andrews: University of St. Andrews, [1982].

———. "Una familia de mercaderes: Los Examenis." *AIA* 47 (1987), 63-78.

———. "Els framenors de Manresa." *Miscel.lània d'estudis bagencs* (Manresa) 5 (1987), 127-137.

———. "Els orígens socials dels franciscans." In *Actes del segon col.loqui d'estudis catalans a Nord-Amèrica, Yale, 1979,* ed. Manuel Duran, Albert Porqueras-Mayo, and Josep Roca-Pons, pp. 415-424. Montserrat: Abadia de Montserrat, 1982.

———. *Per Déu o per diners.* Valencia: Generalitat, forthcoming. A transcription of the arbitration judgment in the conflict between the mendicant friars and the dioces of Valencia, with a brief study.

———. "Política reial i suport ciutadà per a les cases religioses del Regne de Mallorca." In *XIII Congrés d'història de la Corona d'Aragó (Palma de*

Mallorca, 27 setembre-1 octubre 1987): *Comunicacions 1*, pp. 263-270. Palma de Mallorca: Institut d'estudis baleàrics, 1989.

Webster, Jill R. "La reina doña Constanza y los hospitales de Barcelona y Valencia." *AIA* 51 (1991), 375-390.

——. "Tradiciones y datos medievales para la história franciscana." *AIA* 44 (1984), 199-210.

——. "Unlocking Lost Archives: Medieval Catalan Franciscan Communities." *Catholic Historical Review* 66 (1980), 537-550.

The Worlds of Alfonso the Learned and James the Conqueror: Intellect and Force in the Middle Ages. Ed. Robert I. Burns. Princeton: Princeton University Press, 1985.

Zurita, Gerónimo. *Anales de la Corona de Aragón, Libro II [1137-1228].* Ed. Antonio Ubieto Arteta, Maria Desamparados Pérez Soler, and Laureano Ballesteros Ballesteros. Valencia: Anubar, 1967.

JOURNALS CONSULTED

Acta historica et archaeologica mediaevalia, Departament d'història medieval, Universitat de Barcelona, 1980- .

Acta mediaevalia, Universitat de Barcelona, 1987- .

Analecta sacra Tarraconensia, Barcelona, 1958- .

Annals de l'Institut d'estudis gironins (AIEG), Gerona, 1958- .

Archivo ibero-americano (AIA), Madrid, 1914- .

Archivum Franciscanum historicum (AFH), Rome, 1931- .

Butlletí de la Reial acadèmia catalana de belles arts de Sant Jordi, Barcelona, vol. 1, 1986.

Estudis franciscans (EF) 1923-1936; or *Estudios franciscanos (EF)* 1916-1922, 1948- .

Franciscalia, 1928.

Franciscan Studies, 1914-1963.

Ilerda, Lerida, 1943- .

Revista catalana de teología, Barcelona, 1976- .

Revista de estudios franciscanos (REF), 1907.

Textos catalans antics, Barcelona, vols. 1-6, 1982-1987.

Index

Abad, Guerau de 98
abbesses: *see* Poor Clares: election of abbesses of
Abinaffia, Aaron 89
Aboabdille Abnazach 37, 128
Abu Zayd, Sayyid 22, 34n72, 122; friar descendants of 34–35, 58–59, 60, 122
Aciba, Ramon de 44n116
Ager, viscount of (count of Urgell) 276
Agnes (sister of Saint Clare) 221
Agnès, Sr. (proposed abbess of Xàtiva) 208, 239
Agnès, Sr. (sister of Fr. Pere Guerau) 225, 226n14
Aguilar, Fr. Galcerán d' (apostate) 217
Agut, Berenguer d' 37, 41
Ahones, Bertran 280
Ahones de San Vicente, Pedro 280
Aimeric, Fr. 153
Alagón, Artaldo de 210
Alagón, Blasco de 34
Alamanda (widow of Pere Metge) 113–114
Alazaicis (wife of Arnau Fabri) 172n70
Albercha, Pere 30
Alberic, Fr. 184n26
Albert, Fr. 188n38, 264
Albigensian Crusade 21, 190. See *also* heresy
Alcira: friars in 71
Alegre, Fr. Pere 286
Alemany, Ochoa 123, 124n50
Alexander IV, pope 230n29
Alexander, Fr. (provincial minister) 50

Alfons, Fr. Felip 253
Alfonso II, king of Aragon 92–93, 210
Alfonso III, king of Aragon 93, 94n61, 217; and resettlement of Sardinia 69; and support for friars 83–92 passim
Alfonso X, king of Castile: legal code of (*Siete partidas*) 5, 91, 136nn95–96, 170n62, 173n78, 185
Algeciras 190
Almatà (Almazán, site of Franciscan convent of Balaguer) 47–48
Almazán, Clarissan convent of 231. *See also* Almatà
Almenara, Fr. Miguel de 263n5
Alou, Pere d' 44n116
Aloysius, Fr. (of Sicily) 264
Amat, Pere 193n45
Amorós, Fr. Berenguer d' 97
Ampurias, counts of 48n132
Anagni, Treaty of 167
Andrés, Guillermo 188
Anglesola, Aldiarts d' (Cistercian, abbess of Valldaura) 44
Anjou, Charles of, king of Sicily 166
Añone, Domingo de 277
Antillón, Sancho de 138
Antillón, Sr. Sibil.la de 238
Antony, Saint 261, 285, 286, 287
Aparicio, Fr.: *see* Serra, Fr. Aparicio
Aperrer?, Ramon, and son Fr. Ramon 267
apostasy among friars 170–173, 179–181, 184, 217–218, 294
apostates, position of regarding wills 91

Aragó, Fr. Joan d' (bishop of Cagliari) 176–177; his father Joan d'Aragó 177
Aragó, Joan d' (archbishop of Tarragona, patriarch of Alexandria) 214–215
Aragón, Fr. Juan de 177n5
Aragon, James of (cardinal bishop of Valencia) 161
Arnau (archdeacon of the Ampurdán) 52
Arnau (bishop of Valencia) 123
Arnau, Fr. 117, 128
Arnau, Fr. Pere (Spiritual) 172, 216
Arnau, Master 52, 56, 57, 59, 63, 64
Arnold (cardinal protector) 234
Arnulf, Fr. 188–189
Artamara, Fr. Pere d' 168, 172
Artasona, Fr. Pere d' 208
Assisi 271n29. *See also* chapters of Friars Minor: in Assisi
Atarravia, Fr. Pere d' 33
Athenulf, Raymond (Raimondo) 248
Augustinians 15n5, 121, 141, 152, 190, 237, 295, 296
Ayusa, Blasco de 275

Bach, Fr. Bernat de 154
Bagès: *see* Manresa
Balaguer, Clarissan convent of 48, 229
Balaguer, Franciscan convent of (Almatà) 44, 47–48
Balearic Islands 39, 74. *See also* Majorca; Minorca; Ibiza
Bancal, Fr. Ramon 233
Banyeres, Pons de 40
Barbastro, citizens of: relations with friars 280, 283–284
Barbastro, Franciscan convent of 49, 61, 136n95, 187n35, 198n63, 283–284; bequests to 52, 62–63, 280; foundation of 62–63
Barberà, Fr. Guillem de (Dominican) 62

Barberà, Fr. Miquel de (Dominican) 62
Barcelona 107–112, 143–144; hospital of 94–95, 210; relations between Christians and non-Christians in 103n2, 131, 132–134; visit of Saint Francis to 19, 21, 23, 25
Barcelona, Clarissan convent of (Sant Antoni) 205, 223, 224–225, 231, 261. *See also* Pedralbes
Barcelona, Franciscan convent of 107–112, 198nn63–64, 217–218, 293; art and architecture of 272–273, 280, 283; association of, with Clarissan convents 69, 70, 234–235; bequests to 25–26, 109–112, 232, 295; burial of royalty in 93, 144, 159, 209, 213, 217; as centre of study 263–264, 266; foundation of 23, 25–26; relations of, with clergy and ecclesiastical authorities 158–161, 211, 215n146; relations of, with Jews 49, 132, 133–134, 136n95; relations of, with local population 143–144
Barriac, Joan de 97n65
Barriac, Ramon de 26–27, 116, 117
Bas, Fr. Ramon de 185n30, 187n35, 238
Bassa, Arnau 240, 283
Bassa, Ferrer 240, 283, 285
Basseda de la Llaguna, Francesc 139n104. *See also* Llaguna family
Bassols, Joan 266
Bastida, Arnau 184n26
Bavaria, Lewis of, emperor 167, 173, 243, 244
Beatriz, Sr. 207, 239–240
Bede, Fr. William: *see* See, Fr. Peter (or William) of the
béghards: *see* béguin(e)s
béguin(e)s 35n77, 41, 244, 247–253, 257, 258, 291. *See also* Spirituals
Bellfort, Fr. Pere de 40

Bell-lloc, Pere de 98, 99
Bell-tall, Bernat de 124
Belló, Pere 118
Benedict XI, pope 159
Benedict XII, pope 215
Benedict XIII, pope 188, 266
Benedict, Saint, rule of: and Franciscan apostates 173
Benedictines 172, 223
bequests: *see under individual convents*
Berenguera (wife of Cerdany Unnes) 231n36
Berenguera (wife of Joan Gili) 250n100
Berenguera (wife of Martí Ferran) 129
Berga: *see* Pere (of Berga)
Berga, Franciscan convent of 43–47, 49; bequest to friar in 44; grant to 46
Bernard (bishop of Oporto) 81
Bernat (bishop of Elne) 31
Bernat, Fr. (royal chaplain) 286
Biel, Fr. Martín Pedro de (apostate) 171n65
Black Death, the 101, 131, 152, 289, 296, 297–298
Blanca, princess (daughter of Alfonso III) 236n48, 237, 238
Blanca, queen of Aragon: *see* Naples, Blanca of
Blanes, Fr. Guillem de 178n11, 282
Blegua de Campdalchu, García Pedro de 98
Boadella (Valencia) 36
Bomilla, Sr. Margarita de 233n42
Bonafonat: *see* Vall-llebrera family
Bonaventure, Saint 83, 223, 265, 270, 287, 288
Boniface VIII, pope 158–159, 167, 173, 204, 242; bull of 234
Boniles, Ferrer de 179n11
Bonvila, Sr. Margarida de 233n42

books: friars as copiers of 267, 268, 286; importance of, to friars 178, 268. *See also* education of friars
Borberali, Domingo: *see* Spinelli, Domingo
Borja, Franciscan convent of 61, 64, 118, 136n95, 199; bequests and grants to 65, 277; foundation of 65
Borrassà, Lluis 285–286
Borrell, Bartomeu 194n46
Bou, Ramon 25n37
Boules 179n11
Boyl, Ramon de 184n26
Bruni, Navarra (mother of Fr. Pons Bruni) 249n94
Bruny, Fr. Francesc 213n131
bulls, papal: *Ad conditorem canonum* 243; *Ad fructus uberes* 151–152; *Clara ordinis vestri* 53; *Cum inter nonnullos* 243; *Etsi animarum* 151; *Gloriosam ecclesiam* 243; *Inter cunctas* 159, 159n28, 161; *Ordinem vestrum* 150; *Quo elongati* 150; *Quorumdam exigit* 243; *Super cathedram* 158, 159, 161, 162; *Super omnia* 243; *Supra montem* 246, 257
Burgos, Saint Francis in 19
Burguet, Fr. Arnau 253
burial of laity (royal and civil): as cause of conflict among friars and secular clergy 156–159; in Franciscan cemeteries 91, 92–94, 158; in mendicant habit 93n55, 93n58, 232; as source of revenue for friars and secular clergy 91, 138n103

Cagliari, Franciscan convent of 68–69, 72
Cahors, Constitutions of 84
Calatayud, Clarissan convent of 223, 231
Calatayud, Franciscan convent of 39, 49, 118, 136n95, 171, 184,

198n63; bequests, concessions to 52, 56, 86n29; foundation of 55–57
Calatrava, Order of 203
Calou, Jaume de 210
Caltabellota, Treaty of 167
Calvet, Ramon 144–146
Cambridge: centre of Franciscan study at 84, 263
Camdeuna, Pere de 142–143
Campdalchu, García Pedro de Blegua de 98
Campllong, Fr. Guillem de 201
Can Codina 24
Canelles, Fr. Arnau de 91, 94n61, 216–218
Canet: *see* Puig, Fr. Bernat de
canonical quarter 156–159
Cantaventayuelo, Juan Guillermo de 278
Capdevila, Jaume 228
Capuchins 65, 244, 289
Carbonell, Fr. Pons 82, 211, 212–216, 266
care of the sick: *see* work of friars: care of the sick and lepers
Carmelites 87n32, 104, 152, 169, 215n146, 249n94, 296; establishment of houses of 15n5, 70, 112, 121, 225, 237; and Franciscans 16, 30, 141, 295
Casale, Ubertino de 242
Castellbisbal, Fr. Berenguer de (Dominican, bishop of Gerona) 118
Castellbó, lord of (count of Foix) 132
Castellet, Sr. Clara de 233n42
Castellet family: Bernat 128; Saurina (wife of Bernat) 128; Sibil.la (daughter of Bernat, wife of García Examenis) 110, 128
Castelló, Fr. Ramon de 114
Castelló d'Empúries 113, 114, 253n110
Castelló d'Empúries, Clarissan convent of 226, 273
Castelló d'Empúries, Franciscan convent of 39, 136n95, 273; bequests to 48–49, 128, 267; foundation of 49
Castellón del camp de Burriana (hospice?), Franciscans in 71
Castile, Eleanor of, queen of England: gifts to friars 87, 89
Castllà, Fr. Arnau de 145, 185, 212
Català, Arnau (or Ramon Guillem) 247
"catalanesc" poetry of Jofre de Foixà 52, 272
Catharism 16, 133. *See also* heresy
Cato of Theodosius 268
Cauders, Pere, and wife Jacma 185n29
Caynt, Simó 279n59
Celano, Thomas of 19
Celestine V, pope 167
Centelles, Fr. Pere de (Dominican, bishop of Barcelona) 155n19
Centelles family: Gilabert (grandson of Bernat) 47; Bernat 47, 48
Cerda, Alfonso de la 204
Cerdà, Guillem (husband of Matea) 138n103
Cervera, Fr. Guillem de 117
Cervera, Fr. Pere de 54
Cervera, Clarissan convent of 226–227
Cervera, Franciscan convent of 44, 49, 136n95, 187n35, 281; bequest to 29; foundation of 26, 29; grant of leprosarium to 186; papal indulgence granted for donations to 261
Cescala, Pere 238
Cesena, Fr. Michael de 172–173, 216, 218, 243
Cestanyol: and Clarissan convent of Vic 229
Ceuta, martyrs of 41
chapter: confraternity, in Huesca 255–256; Dominican, in Oxford 87

chapters of Friars Minor 84, 86, 90, 140, 189, 196, 242, 243; in Assisi (Porziuncola) 22, 38, 189, 205, 210, 218; in Barcelona 26; in Calatayud 86; in Lerida 206; in Monzón 52, 53; in Naples 205; in Puigcerdà (Clarissan) 228; in Saragossa 33, 121; in Tàrrega 278-279; meetings, list of general and provincial 360-362
Charles II, king of Naples 167, 273
Charles of Anjou: *see* Anjou, Charles of
Chaucer: *Friar's Tale* 182
Chiarenti Company: *see* Pistoia
Chilliella, Fr. Pedro de 58
Cistercians 50; nuns 44, 45
Ciutadella, Pedro de 274
Ciutadella, Clarissan convent of 230
Ciutadella, Franciscan convent of 39; foundation of and grant of land to 40
Clare, Saint 221-222; order established by: *see* Poor Clares
Clareno, Angelo of 242
Clarí, Berenguer 45
Clarissans: *see* Poor Clares
Clement IV, pope 159n28
Clement V, pope 161
Clement VI, pope 84, 240, 242
clergy, secular: *see* conflicts of friars: with secular clergy
Cobis, Bernat de 42
Coch, Agnès 228
Codina family 24
cofradía: see confraternity
Colomer, Fr. Arnau 138n103
Colomer family 196n54
Comes, Francesc 286
concessions: *see under individual convents; see also* royal support for friars
conflicts of friars 45, 54, 75, 118; with hired workers 283-284, 285; with local population 75, 80-81, 141-147; with lay heirs over bequests 110, 139-141; with secular clergy and church authorities 27, 59-60, 63, 64, 75, 76, 79, 80, 101, 149-152, 154-165, 211, 291-292
confraternities 54, 112, 254-259, 288; relationship of, to Third Order 246-247, 254, 293
Conques de Tremp, Clarissan house of 229
Conrad (son of Frederick of Habsburg) 166; his illegitimate son Manfred 166
Consell de Cent 108-109
Constance, queen of Aragon: *see* Hohenstaufen, Constance of
Consuetudines ilerdenses 116
conventet: see hospices
convents: burial of laity in 91-94 passim, 158; endowment of churches and chapels in 94, 111, 286, 287; establishment of 21-72; lay residents in 193-194; secular use of 52, 74n3, 119, 198, 199n65, 202, 278, 294; support for building and maintenance of 169, 261, 274-280, 282-283. *See also* convents, Clarissan; convents, Franciscan
convents, Clarissan: *see under* Almazán; Balaguer; Barcelona; Calatayud; Castelló d'Empúries; Cervera; Ciutadella; Conques de Tremp; Gerona; Huesca; Lerida; Majorca; Manresa; Messina; Montblanc; Morella; Murviedro; Pamplona; Pedralbes; Perpignan; Puigcerdà; Saragossa; Tarazona; Tarragona; Tàrrega; Teruel; Tortosa; Valencia; Vic; Vilafranca; Xàtiva
convents, Franciscan: *see under* Balaguer; Barbastro; Barcelona; Berga; Borja; Cagliari; Calata-

yud; Castelló d'Empúries; Castellón del camp de Burriana (a hospice?); Cervera; Ciutadella; Daroca; Ejea de los Caballeros; Estella; Gerona; Huesca; Inca; Jaca; Lerida; Majorca; Molina; Montblanc; Montpellier; Monzón; Morella; Murcia; Murviedro; Oleron; Pamplona; Perpignan; Puigcerdà; Saragossa; Sariñena; Sassari; Tarazona; Tarragona; Tàrrega; Teruel; Tortosa; Tudela; Tunis; Valencia; Vic; Vila Iglesias; Vilafranca del Penedès; Villefranche de Conflent; Xàtiva
Conventual Franciscans 192, 244, 288, 289, 291
Copons, Fr. Andreu de 184n27
Corsica 167
Cortell, Fr. Ramon 124
Cortona, Fr. Elias de 38
Coscollola, Fr. Eximeno de 280
Crestià: see Eiximenis, Francesc
Crònica de Pere III 97
crown aims and policies: association of friars with 68–69, 72, 73–74, 78, 104, 121, 165–168, 170, 189–190. *See also* work of friars: in service of crown
crown support of friars: *see* royal support for friars
Cruilles family: Ferrer, and wife Dolça 177; Fr. Ferrer (son of Ferrer) 177, 178
custodians of Friars Minor: function of 190; list of names of 355
custodies, Franciscan: Barcelona 39–43, 159–160; Lerida 43–47; Narbonne 65–68, 107; Navarre 33, 39, 74; Saragossa 33, 39, 61, 204, 267; Serrania 39, 55; Valencia 39, 55–61, 279

Da Fiore, Joachim 66, 241, 251, 266, 288, 290. *See* Joachimism
Daniel, Fr. and Saint 41

Daroca, Franciscan convent of 39, 49, 55, 118, 119n37, 136n95, 276, 277–278, 287; alms, bequests, concessions to 52, 86n29, 276; foundation of 57
Delfrau, Pere 54
Dendestre, Fr. Martín 184n27
Denis (Dinis), king of Portugal 82
Desideri, Fr. 152–153
Deslledó: *see* Lledó
Dezcastlar, Arnau: *see* Castllà, Fr. Arnau de
Digne, Hugh of: *Expositio regulae* 242
Dinis: *see* Denis
Domingo, Fr.: *see* Jaca, Fr. Domingo de
Dominic, Saint 15n5, 261, 295
Dominican nuns (at Valencia) 236n50
Dominicans 92, 127, 197n60, 211, 215; in Barcelona 45, 264, 295; as beneficiaries or executors of wills 32n62, 45, 78, 79, 92, 128, 295; in Berga 45; development and influence of 3, 15n5, 17, 62, 130, 155, 294–296; in Gerona 112; in Lerida 96; in Manresa 70, 71, 295; privileges and concessions to 85, 87, 169; in Puigcerdà 115, 172n70, 295; relations of, with Jews 49, 131, 132, 133; relations of, with secular clergy 149, 157; in Saragossa 119, 295; similarity to Franciscans of, in aims and practices 16, 73, 76, 93, 141, 150, 190, 258n124, 264; in Tarragona 215; in Tortosa 50; in Tunis 43; in Valencia 121, 264, 295. *See also individual Dominicans:* Castellbisbal, Fr. Berenguer de; Ferrer, Fr. Vicent; Martí, Fr. Ramon; Penyafort, Fr. Ramon de; Puig, Fr. Bernat de
Dublet, Fr. Ramon (apostate) 171n65
Duzenem, Jucef (of Pedral) 277

education of friars 83–85, 179, 180, 262–267. *See also* books
Eiximenis, Fr. Francesc 31, 34, 99, 129, 260, 272; relatives of: *see* Examenis; and studium in Valencia 96, 99, 125, 264. Writings of: *Contes i faules* 270n26; *Libre del Crestià* 23, 166, 197; *Regiment de la cosa pública* 186
Ejea, Fr. Juan de 267
Ejea, Fr. Martín de 204–205
Ejea de los Caballeros, Franciscan convent of 49, 61, 118, 136n95, 198n63, 204; bequests to 52, 64; foundation of 64
Eleanor, queen of England: *see* Castile, Eleanor of
Eli(c)senda, queen of Aragon (2nd wife of James II) 218, 224, 232
Elne, see of: Franciscans in 31
Emberart, Fr. Pere 44
Empúries, count of: *see* Hug (Huguet), Pons
endowments: *see* bequests, gifts, grants *under individual convents*
Entenza, Saurina de 239
Ermengol, Fr. (apostate) 171n65
Ermengol, Martí 114
Ermesenda (sister of Bernat de Palau) 25n37, 109
Escarrer: *see* Esquerrer
Escodo, *masia* of 44
Espanyoll family 196n54
Esplugues, Fr. Pere d' 96, 213n133
Esquerrer, Fr. Bernat (apostate) 171n65, 172
Esquerrer (Escarrer), Fr. Pere 213n131
Estella, Franciscan convent of 107
Esteve, Bernat 114
Esteve, Fr. 132
Esteve, Fr. Francesc 139n104
Esteve, Fr. Pere 132n85, 209
Eulàlia, Saint 23
Examenis, Francesc: *see* Eiximenis
Examenis family 126–127, 137; Francesc (son of Jaspert) 160n30, 198n64, 293; Francesc (son of Francesc) 160n30; García (husband of Sibil.la de Castellet) 128; Jaspert (Gisbert) 178n11, 198n64, 212; Pere 126
executors of wills or estates, friars as 45, 91, 128, 201; Franciscan 34, 83, 138, 139n104, 186n30, 205, 207, 209, 210

Fabri, Arnau (husband of Alazaicis) 172n70
Fernando, Fr. Martín 184
Ferran, Martí (husband of Berenguera) 129
Ferrer, Fr. (bishop of Barcelona) 208
Ferrer, Fr. (bishop of Neopatria) 214
Ferrer, Fr. (bishop of Valencia) 122
Ferrer, Fr. Bernat 50
Ferrer, Fr. Pere 216n148
Ferrer, Fr. Vicent (Dominican) 161, 264
Finesterra, Sr. Constanza 233n42
Fivaller: *see* Fiveller
Fiveller, Fr. Berenguer 190n42
Fiveller, Sr. Constanza 233n42
Fiveller, Sr. Serena 233n42
Flequer, Fr. Guillem 249n94
Foix, count of (lord of Castellbó) 132
Foix, Pere 111
Foixà, Fr. Jofre de (apostate, later Benedictine) 52, 173, 181, 272, 275
Folcrà, Fr. Berenguer 206
Foligno, Angela of 242, 265
Fonollars, Bernat de 211
Fontana, Fr. Domènec de 210
foros: see fueros
Four, Fr. Vidal de 210
Franca (widow of Andreu de Vall-llebrera) 138

Francis, Saint 14-15, 18-19, 169, 190, 196; and Saint Clare 221-222; missionary journey of, to Spain 19-21, 22, 42, 169; legends surrounding travel of and foundation of convents by 19, 23-33 passim, 40-41; popular appeal of 16, 272, 287-288, 295; as subject for artists 261, 285-286

Franciscans: contribution of, to learning and literature 262, 265-266, 288 (*see also* education of friars); control of, by crown 99-100, 201 (*see also* crown aims and policies); convent life of 193-199; and divergence from ideals of Saint Francis 72, 75, 101, 140-141, 176, 179, 181, 242, 290-291; foundation and organization of 18-20, 176, 181, 190-202, 246; function of socius among 183, 194; and heresy: *see* heresy; impact of, on development of art, architecture and culture 261, 268-274, 280-282, 285-287, 288; and Inquisition: *see* Inquisition; lay brothers among 169, 194, 280, 293; officers of: *see* custodians, guardians, lectors, procurators, provincial ministers; popularity and influence of 287-288, 290, 294; preaching ability of: *see* preaching of friars: power of; priests among 169; problems of: *see* conflicts of friars; provisions of rule of 141, 180, 260, 290, 292; social and family backgrounds of 109, 148, 194, 261; societal attitudes of 147, 186-188, 294; support for (material and moral): *see* merchant/papal/royal support for friars; and Third Order 246-247, 249, 258n124; work of: *see* work of friars. *For a complete list of convents see* convents, Franciscan. *See also* custodies, Franciscan; provinces, Franciscan

Fraticelli 4, 241. *See also* Spirituals; Third Order of Saint Francis

Frederick (infant brother of Peter III) 93

Frederick II (of Habsburg), king of Sicily 43, 166-167, 204, 215, 245n78

Friars Minor, Order of: *see* Franciscans

Friars of the Sack 31, 66, 115, 151, 248

Friars Preacher, Order of: *see* Dominicans

Fuentes, Domingo de 187n35

fueros of Aragon 119, 247, 277

Fuster family 97, 181, 250-252; Bernat 250; Fr. Bernat (tertiary, brother of Guerau) 97, 250, 251; Fr. Bernat (son of Fr. Bernat) 181-182, 251; Guerau 97

Galindi, Fr. Jaume (apostate) 171n65
Gambe, Juan Pedro de 277
Garcès, Juan (apostate) 179-180
García, Fr. Fernando 188n38, 189n40
Gardiola, Bernat (husband of Guilleuma) 93n58
Garsias (canon of Huesca cathedral) 163
Gener, Fr. Francesc 185
Gener, Sr. Clara de 205
Geoffroi, Raymond 242
Gerard, Fr. (minister general) 185n30, 207, 217, 239-240
Gerona 24, 98, 106, 112-115, 132, 144-146, 253
Gerona, Clarissan convent of 226, 227, 232
Gerona, Franciscan convent of 106, 109, 127, 198n63, 201, 202n72; art and architecture of 281; bequests and concessions to 28, 85n29, 178; foundation of 26,

27–29; grants of land to 112–115; and hospice in Manresa 71; and preaching to Jews 49, 136n95; and problems with local population 90, 144–146
Gil, Fr. 21–22
Gili, Joan (husband of Berenguera) 250n100
Giotto 271n29
Godofred, Fr. 124
Gómez, Fr. 34, 122
Gondissalvo, Fr. 161, 188n38
Gonter, Fr. Alfredo 263nn8–9; *Quaestio de paupertate Christi* 266
Gonter, Master Bernardo 286–287
Gornall, Fr. Ramon 197n57
Gosalt, Fr. Francesc 292
Granada 19; wars in 170, 189n40
Granollers, Fr. Benvingut de 279
grants: *see under individual convents*
Gregory IX, pope 132, 150; bulls of 224, 225
Gregory X, pope 151
Gregory XI, pope 214
Gregory, Saint: *Letters* 267
Gros, Bernat 113–114
Grosseteste, Robert 84
Gualba, Pons de (bishop of Barcelona) 159, 160, 161
Guàrdia, Fr. Berenguer de 156
guardians of Friars Minor: functions and powers of 42, 124, 134, 190–191, 196, 198, 234, 278, 294; involvement of, in confraternities 246n81, 255; involvement of, in execution of wills 34, 45, 92, 95, 122, 139n104, 194n46; list of names of 356–358; qualities desired in 201–202
Gudal, Assalia de 128
Guerau, Fr. (of Lerida) 118
Guerau family 24, 98, 99, 114–115, 137; Fr. Joan (son of Jofre) 24, 99, 171; Fr. Pere (tertiary) 225–226, 250–251; Jofre (son of Pere) 24, 98, 99; Pere 98, 99, 114; Sr. Agnès (sister of Fr. Pere) 225, 226n14
guilds: *see* confraternities
Guillem (of Sant Boi) 24
Guillem, Arnau 195. *See also* Morlans
Guilleuma (daughter of Guillem Porquet) 117
Guilleuma (widow of Bernat Gardiola) 93n58
Guilleuma (wife of Guillem Hug) 128
Gunter: *see* Gonter

heresy 16, 21, 75, 133, 141, 166, 190, 296; friars and tertiaries condemned for 172, 211, 216, 251, 253; royal policy against 132, 133, 136; and Spirituals 66, 172, 242–243, 249, 252. *See also* Inquisition
heretical groups: Albigensians 21, 75, 190; Cathars 16, 133; Humiliati 16; Joachimists 242, 244; Waldensians 16, 75, 190
Hohenstaufen, Constance of, queen of Aragon (wife of Peter II) 93, 209, 293; legacy of 94–96, 157–158, 210, 213, 232
homosexuality 146–147. *See also* prostitution
Honorius III, pope 169
hospices (*conventets*) 48, 69–71, 202, 224; of Balaguer 229; of Manresa 223; of Pedralbes (Barcelona) 234–235; of Puigcerdà 68
Hospital, Joan de l', and Ermesenda 29
Hospital de la Reina (Valencia) 95–96
Hospitallers 45, 54, 238
hospitals: run by Franciscans 94–96, 109, 186; run by tertiaries 253.

See also work of friars: care of the sick and lepers
Huesca, Fr. Pedro de 85, 207–208, 239
Huesca, Fr. Ramón [de Ola] de 98, 275. *See also* Ola family
Huesca 162–165
Huesca, Clarissan convent of 231, 238n57
Huesca, Franciscan convent of 49, 64, 89n39, 118, 136n95, 198n63, 207; bequests and concessions to 52, 62, 88; foundation of 61–62
Hug, Guillem (husband of Guilleuma) 128
Hug (Huguet), Pons, count of Empúries 48, 49
Humiliati 16. *See also* heresy
Hungary, Violant of, queen of Aragon (wife of James I) 62, 120–121

Ibiza 39, 40
Il.luminat, Fr. 35, 36, 52, 62, 117
Inca, Franciscan convent of 40
indulgences 59, 63, 170, 261
Innocent III, pope 73, 77, 141, 150, 169
Innocent IV, pope 133, 150, 151, 153, 166, 224–225, 261; bulls of 63, 170
Inquisition 16, 134, 135, 172n70; friars and tertiaries accused under 35n77, 100n77, 207, 249, 251; friars as inquisitors 132, 168, 253, 266; friars as witnesses 249n94. *See also* heresy
Isabel, Saint, queen of Portugal 82, 176, 203n77
Isidore, Saint: *Sentences* 267
Ivorra, Fr. Berenguer d' 239, 279

Jaca, Fr. Domingo de 82, 120, 203–204, 209, 264, 281
Jaca 62, 204
Jaca, Franciscan convent of 49, 61, 118; concessions to 63; foundation of 63–64; papal indulgence granted for donations to 63
Jacopone da Todi: *see* Todi, Jacopone da
James (Jaume) I, king of Aragon 17, 73, 77, 91–92, 103, 104, 107–108, 126, 152–153; *Chronicle* 74; friars as part of policies of 35, 73–74, 77–78, 297; and reconquest and Christianization of Moorish territories 17–18, 74, 121, 133, 272; and support of friars 36, 73–92 passim, 96, 126
James (Jaume) II, king of Aragon 166–167, 170, 189–190, 204, 251n103, 252, 266; support of friars 53–54, 55, 82–92 passim, 98
James (Jaume) III, king of Majorca 236
Jaume, Fr. (béguin at Castelló) 250n100
Jaume, Joan 283
Jerome, Saint 197n61
Jerusalem 77
Jews 49, 57–58, 72, 103, 130–137 passim, 152, 298. *See also* Tarasco, Guillem de; Roda, Mahil de
Joachimism 242, 244, 245, 291. *See also* Da Fiore, Joachim; heresy
Joan, Fr. Francesc (tertiary) 253
Jofre, Fr. Pere 190n42
John (cardinal deacon of Saint Nicholas, protector of Order of Saint Clare) 233–234
John XXII, pope 53, 165, 172–173, 207, 216, 232, 234, 249, 257
Jonques, Sr. Saurina de 233n42
Juan, Fr.: *see* Parente, Fr. John
Jungría, Nicolás de 124
Junqueres, Sr. Sauria de 233n42

La Zaidia, Cistercian abbey of 83
"Ladies of Penitence" 248. *See also* béguin(e)s
Ladrón, Doña Toda 36

Languedoc 21, 133
Laurador, Fr. Pere (apostate) 171n65
Lavinyac, Fr. Pere de 217n150
lectors of Friars Minor: list of names of 358-359; office and function of 134, 194n46, 262, 263; privileges of 264
legacies: *see* bequests, gifts, grants *under individual convents*
Leonor, queen of Sicily 84
lepers: *see* work of friars: care of the sick and lepers
Lerida 115-117; *Consuetudines ilerdenses* 116; *Llibre vert* 115
Lerida, Clarissan convent of 223, 225
Lerida, Franciscan convent of 44, 49, 93, 96, 97n65, 106, 116-118, 136n95, 206, 216n148; bequests to 27, 52, 117-118; foundation of 26-27, 28, 29, 78; studium generale founded in 262
Les, Pedro de 62
Lewis of Bavaria: *see* Bavaria, Lewis of
Libro de buen amor: see Ruiz, Juan
Libro de los estados: see Manuel, Juan
Lille, Alain de 265, 267
Lillet, Ferrer de 279
Llaguna family 138, 139, 196n54; Berenguer 139n104; Berenguera 67; Guillem, and wife Ermesenda 138n103; Matea 138n103; Pere, and wife Guilleuma 138n103; Fr. Pere 67, 138. *See also* Basseda de la Llaguna, Francesc
Llambilles: *see* Morell, Ferrer
Llaurador, Berenguer 187n35
Lledó, Fr. Berenguer de 142
Lledó, Fr. Segimon des 283
Llibre del consolat del mar 107-108
Llivià, Bernat de 98
Llor, Simó de 203
Lloriz, García 278

Llotger, Fr. Joan (Dominican) 216
Llull, Ramon 37, 43, 125, 128, 135, 137, 184, 205, 266; *Ars consilii* 137n97, 206
Llull, Ramon (father of writer?) 128
Lluvià, Fr. Ramon de (apostate) 171n65
Lombard, Peter: *Sentences* 262, 267
Lope (butcher in Murviedro) 61
López, Fr. Domingo 58
López de Ayerbe, Fr. Sancho 83, 100, 183, 184n26, 207-209, 275-276, 281
Loria, Ruggiero di 166
Louis IX, king of France (Saint) 256
Louis, Saint, of Toulouse 213, 256, 272-273; as subject for artists and craftsmen 90, 261, 285, 287
Lulla, Sr. Dolça 233n42
Lulla, Sr. Maria 233n42
Lusignan, Marie of, queen of Aragon (3rd wife of James II) 111, 153n13, 188, 189n39
Luxembourg, Henry of, emperor 167
Lyons, Council of 15n5, 124, 151, 241-242

Majorca 67, 68, 107, 125-130, 140; béguin(e)s in 35n77, 248, 253; reconquest of 17, 36, 79, 116, 209
Majorca, Clarissan convent of 230, 232n39, 286
Majorca, Franciscan convent of 35n77, 38, 39, 87, 125-130, 178n11, 198n63, 216, 273-274, 282, 286; bequests, concessions and grants to 37, 74, 79, 125, 128, 129, 140, 253n111; foundation of 36-37. *See also* Miramar, missionary college of
Malayn, Beatrix de 45
Malla 179n11
Manethedei (Florentine merchant) 228
Manresa 24, 288

Manresa, Clarissan convent of 70, 71, 223, 224, 229, 295
Mansolí, Fr. Dalmau 190n42, 211
Mansolí, Sr. Alamanda de 233n42
Manuel, Juan 185, 189, 247; *Libro de los estados* 214
Marc, Pere 215n145
Margarida (slave) 193n45
Margarida (wife of Guillem of Sant Boi) 24
Maria (wife of Macià Portaioyes) 36
Maria, princess (daughter of Alfonso III) 236n48, 237, 238
Maria (Marie), queen of Aragon: *see* Lusignan, Marie of
Martí, Fr. Ramon (Dominican) 132, 245
Martí, Pere 158
Martin IV, pope 151
Martín, Fr. Pedro (apostate) 171n65, 171n67
Martínez, Ferrant 135n93
Martorell, Pedro de 275
Mas, Berenguer de 70
Mas-Lino, Sr. Alamanda 233n42
Mataplana, Hug de (bishop-elect of Saragossa) 81
Matea (wife of Guillem Cerdà) 138n103
Mayoles, Felip, and wife Berenguera 27
menoretes: see Poor Clares
Mercader, Fr. Gil 171
mercantile class: its importance to mendicant cause 67, 105–106, 147–148. *See also* merchant support for friars
Mercedarians 50, 112. *See also* Rafart (stonemason)
merchant support for friars 68, 108–130 passim, 261. *See also* bequests, concessions, grants *under individual convents; see also* mercantile class
Messina, Clarissan convent of 158, 231

Metge, Bernat 114
Metge, Pere (husband of Alamanda) 113
Mieres, Fr. Ramon de 131
milennium 241, 243
Minorca 39, 40
Minorca, convents of: *see* Ciutadella
Miramar, missionary college of 37, 125, 126, 137
missionary work of Franciscans: *see* work of friars: missionary
Mohamet (slave) 193n45
Mohammed III, ruler of Granada 189, 206
Molina, Doña Blanca de 57–58
Molina, Franciscan convent of 39, 296; foundation of and bequests to 57–58
Molins, Sr. Constanza de 233n42
Moltó, Guillem 51
Monrodó, Guillem 266
Montblanc, Clarissan convent of 225
Montblanc, Franciscan convent of 40, 44, 49, 87n32, 136n95, 279; alms and concessions to 199n65, 273; foundation of 41
Montfort, Simon de 73
Montpellier 66, 73, 242n70, 262, 264
Montpellier, Franciscan convent of 107
Montros, Joan de 278, 279n59
Montserrat, Benedictine monastery of 172
Monzón, Franciscan convent of 44, 49, 136n95, 199; bequest to 52; foundation of 51–53
Moors 122, 123, 189–190, 197, 236, 277; conversion of, as missionary aim of church and crown 77–78, 133, 135, 136–137, 152
Mora, Fr. Bernat 178n11
Morell, Ferrer (tertiary, of Llambilles) 253
Morella (Moriella), Fr. Nicolás de 58

Morella 51, 274
Morella, Clarissan convent of 231
Morella, Franciscan convent of 44, 53, 58, 198n63, 282; foundation of 50–51; gift, grant to 188, 274
Morera, Fr. Francesc de (apostate) 171n65
Moriella: *see* Morella
Morlans, Arnau Guillem de 123
Mornach, Andreu 228
Mornach, Bernat de 68
Morocco 19, 41, 42
Moros, Bartolomea de 123
Muñoz, Sancho 184n27
Mur, Ramón de 187n35
Murcia 17, 74, 116, 126
Murcia, Franciscan convent of: concession to 86n29
Murovalle, Fr. John of 210
Murviedro (modern Sagunto), Clarissan convent of 230
Murviedro (modern Sagunto), Franciscan convent of 55; foundation and bequest to 61
Muslims: *see* Moors

Nagera, Sr. Sancia 233n42
Naples, Blanca of, queen of Aragon (1st wife of James II) 225
Naples 205
Navarra, Fr. Gil de 84
Nédélec, Fr. Hervé (Dominican) 162
Negro, Juan 283–284
Nicholas IV, pope 170n62
novices: age requirement of 170, 195, 242

Observants 129, 192, 244, 288, 291; convents of 48, 277n54
Ockham, William of 263, 265
Ola family: Juan 98; Pedro Ximéno 98. *See also* Huesca, Fr. Ramón de
Oleron, Franciscan convent of: concessions to 86n29, 89

Oliba, Bernat 211
Oliba, Fr. Arnau 92, 100n77, 186n30, 203, 209–212, 213, 215n146, 216
Oliba, Fr. Pere 190n42
Olivi, Peter John 66, 241, 242, 243, 244–245, 266, 290
Oltzinelles, Bernat de 184n26
Olzet: *see* Saus
On[ten]iente, Fr. (apostate) 171n65, 171n67
Onyar (river): and convent of Gerona 29, 145, 146
ordenanzas (of Saragossa) 120
orders: *see* Augustinians; Benedictines; Calatrava, Order of; Capuchins; Carmelites; Conventual Franciscans; Dominicans; Franciscans; Friars of the Sack; Hospitallers; Mercedarians; Observant Franciscans; Poor Clares; Third Order of Saint Francis; Trinitarians
Oriol, Pere 266
Orsini, John Gaetano 223
Orta, Artau d' 275
Ortiz, Fr. Romeo 83, 120, 137n97, 184n27, 204–207, 209–210, 212, 238n57, 263n6, 267, 281, 286
Ortiz, Lope 206
Ortiz family (of Setia) 206
Otger, Pons 159
Otina, Felip de 143–144, 145n113
Ovid: works of, possessed by friars 262n4, 268
Oxford 87; centre of Franciscan study at 84, 263, 265

Palau, Bernat de (brother of Ermesenda) 25n37, 109
Palazini, Guillermo 275
Pallarés, Ferrer, and wife Berenguera 117
Pallars, count of 250
Pallars, Fr. Roger de 84

Palma de Mallorca: *see* Majorca
Palmerola, Fr. Berenguer de 81–82
Palou, Berenguer 155n19
Pamiers: heresy in 249n94
Pamplona, Clarissan convent of (Santa Engracia) 223
Pamplona, Franciscan convent of 107; bequest to 52
Papa Luna: *see* Benedict XIII, pope (Pedro de Luna)
papal support for friars 63, 66, 149, 150–152, 158–159, 168–174, 261. *See also* work of friars: in service of papacy
Pardo, Fr.: *see* Serra, Fr. Pardo
Parente, Fr. John 22, 26, 31, 32, 35n77, 38, 114, 121
Paris: university of 162; and Franciscan studies 84, 85, 263, 265, 266
Parma: religious consortium in 255
Pedral: *see* Duzenem, Jucef
Pedralbes, Clarissan convent of 69, 202, 224, 232–235
Pedralbes: Franciscan hospice near 69, 70, 202, 224
Pedregal, Cistercian monastery of 54
Pedro, Fr.: *see* Huesca, Fr. Pedro de
Peirón, Guillermo Pedro d'En 284
Peirón, Tolomeo d'En 280
Penitents of Jesus Christ, Order of: *see* Friars of the Sack
Penyafort, Fr. Ramon de (Dominican) 43, 62, 132
Pere (of Berga) 44
Pere, Fr. (socius of Fr. Francesc Gener) 185n29
Pere, Fr. Guerau: *see* Guerau, Fr. Pere
Pere, the Infant 176; *Relevations* 245
Pere family: *see* Guerau family
Peregrí, Fr. Bernat (bishop of Barcelona) 159, 160n30, 211
Perelada 268, 295
Pérez, Fernando 34, 122
Pérez, Fr. Marc 58–59

Pérez, Pedro 124
Peris, Simó 282
Perpignan, Clarissan convent of 67, 231
Perpignan, Franciscan convent of 26, 65, 107, 185n29, 295; foundation of and bequests to 30–31
Perugia, Fr. John of 33, 58
Peter (bishop of Barcelona) 212, 224–225
Peter (Pedro) I, king of Castile 231n35
Peter (Pere) I, king of Aragon 21
Peter (Pere) II, king of Aragon 62, 83, 119n39, 166, 205
Peter (Pere) III, king of Aragon 46, 94, 100, 199n66, 208, 231n34, 231n35; and conquest of Majorca 4, 67, 209; *Crónica* 97
Peter, Fr.: *see* See, Fr. Peter (or William) of the
Pex, Audalle 197n62
Philip III, king of France 166
Pim, Fr. Bernat de 216n148
Pistoia: Chiarenti Company of 204
plague: *see* Black Death
Poblet 24, 94; Cistercian monastery of 24, 54
Polinyà, Bernat de 26
Pons, Fr. Antoni de (apostate) 171n65
Pons, Fr. Rodrigo (Order of Calatrava) 203
Pont, Fr. Pere de 185
Poor Clares 69, 93, 71, 158, 220–240, 245, 246; duties of Franciscans towards 202, 222–224, 234–235, 238; election of abbesses of 207–208, 229, 239–240, 292; rule of 221–223, 233. *For a complete list of convents see* convents, Clarissan
Porquet, Guillem (father of Guilleuma) 117
Portaioyes, Macià (husband of Maria) 36

Portella, Ismael de 44
Porziuncola: *see* chapters of Friars Minor: in Assisi
Posanes, Fernando 187n35
Pouilly, Fr. John of (Dominican) 162
Pozo, Andrés de 184n27
Prades: legend of Saint Francis in 24
Prat, Fr. Jordi (bishop of Belgrade) 193n45
preaching of friars: power of 49, 76, 131, 270n26
procurators of Friars Minor: enfranchisement of 47, 51, 70, 97, 181, 246; list of names of 362-364; and membership in Third Order 182, 241, 252; office and function of 90, 96-97, 150, 240, 292-293
prostitution 80, 147, 186, 187, 294. *See also* homosexuality
provinces, Franciscan: Aragon 38, 39; Castile 38; Provence 67, 185n29, 210; Santiago 38; Spain 38
provincial ministers of Friars Minor: initial appointment of 31-32, 77; list of names of 355; office and function of 22, 180, 190, 222, 232
Pugio fidei 132
Puig, Fr. Bernat de (Dominican) 100n77
Puig, Fr. Bernat de (of Canet) 268
Puig, Ramon de, and wife Ramona 50
Puig family 196n54
Puig de Reig 229
Puigalt, Fr. Bernat de 178n11
Puigalt, Fr. Guerau de 178n11
Puigcercós, Fr. Bernat de (Dominican) 216
Puigcerdà, Fr. Simó de 137n97, 205-206
Puigcerdà 115, 127, 172n70, 202, 296; béguin(e)s in 248; convents of Dominicans and Friars of the Sack in 115; Dominicans and Franciscans in 295
Puigcerdà, Clarissan convent of 202, 227-228, 231
Puigcerdà, Franciscan convent of 65, 66, 107, 115, 130, 172n70, 191, 196n54, 202, 274; bequests to 67, 68, 138n103, 139n104; foundation of 67-68, 115
Pujol, Berenguer de 145n114

Quadres, Fr. Pere de 40
Quaestio de paupertate Christi: see Gonter
Quintaval, Fr. Bernard of 20, 21, 22, 33

Rabassà, Guillem 237
Rafart (stonemason) 283
Ramon, Bernat (of Tamarit) 96, 97
Raymond IV, count of Toulouse 21
Razazol, Martín Alfonso de 65
reconquest: *see* James (Jaume) I, king of Aragon
Repartiment 35, 36, 126, 128
Rena (Vic), Bernat de 211
Renovart, Fr. Pere (apostate) 171n65
Reus: legend of Saint Francis in 24
Revelations: see Pere, the Infant
Rial Aboabdille Abnazach 37, 128
Ribas, Pons de 42n110
Ripoll, Benedictine monastery of 172
Riusec, Jaume de (father and son) 267
Robert, Fr. Jaume (apostate) 171n65
Robert, king of Naples 215
Robert, king of Sicily 82
Roca: *see* Sa Roca
Roca, Fr. Pere de (Dominican) 70
Rocabertí, Benet de 155
Rocafort, Umbert de, and wife Sibil.la 110
Rocafull, Guillem de 71
Roda, Mahil de 275
Romaní, Fr. Pere de 48

Roquetaillade, Jean de 245n79, 288
Rossell, Fr. Nicolau 211
Roure, Fr. Joan de 145, 159
royal support for friars 73–92 passim, 100–102, 130, 149, 199. *See also* bequests, concessions, grants *under individual convents; see also* safe-conducts; work of friars: in service of crown
Rubí, Berenguer de 143
Rubió, Fr. Guillem de 217n150, 266
Ruiz, Juan: *Libro de buen amor* 182
Ruzafa 35, 36, 52, 123

Sa Costa, Francesc 253n111
Sa Guàrdia, Fr. Nicolau 185n29
Sa Portella, Sr. Francesca 233n42
Sa Roca, Fr. Guillem 216n148
Sa Sala, Clara 229
Sabater, Bernat 111
Sack Friars: *see* Friars of the Sack
safe-conducts 62, 79, 84, 165, 200, 203n77, 252
Sagunto: *see* Murviedro
Saint Cyriacus in Thermis 185n30
Saint Damian, church of 221
Saint Damian, "Poor Ladies" of 221. *See also* Poor Clares
Saint John of Jerusalem, Order of: *see* Hospitallers
Saint Nicholas, chapel and hospital of (Barcelona) 23, 25–26
Sala, Ferrer de 70
Salimbene de Adam (da Parma) 183; *Chronicle* 194–195, 197
Sánchez, Pedro 52
Sancho, king of Majorca 127, 130
Sanguinyols, Sr. Romeva de 233n42
Sant Boi 24, 250
Sant Celoni: legend of Saint Francis in 24
Sant Cugat, Benedictine monastery of 54, 158
Sant Feliu, collegiate church of (Gerona) 178

Sant Feliu de Guixols, Benedictine monastery of (Gerona) 173, 178
Sant Joan Despí: legend of Saint Francis in 24
Sant Just, church of (Barcelona) 273
Sant Miquel de Cruilles, chapel of (Gerona) 178
Sant Pere de Galligans, church of (Gerona) 178
Santa Cecilia de Fígols, parish of (Berga) 44
Santa Clara la vella: and Clarissan convent of Vic 229
Santa Elisabet: *see* Saragossa, Clarissan convent of
Santa Engracia: *see* Pamplona, Clarissan convent of
Santa Eugènia, Pere de 47
Santa Pau, Pons de 236n50
Santes Creus: legend of Saint Francis in 24; Cistercian monastery of 53, 54, 40, 93
Santiago de Compostela 20, 21, 22
Sanz, Don Domingo 32n62
Sanz, Fr. Martín (apostate) 171n65
Saracens: *see* Moors
Saragossa 119–120; confraternity in 254–257
Saragossa, Clarissan convent of (Santa Elisabet) 207, 223, 230, 236n50, 238
Saragossa, Franciscan convent of 33, 87, 93, 107, 119, 120–121, 187n35, 188, 191, 197, 198n63, 207; bequests and concessions to 52, 85n29, 86n29, 88, 208, 275, 295; foundation of 24, 31–32, 57; and preaching to Jews 49, 136n95
Saragossa, Franciscan province of 276
Sardinia 68–69, 88, 99, 167, 292; concessions to Franciscans in 85n29
Sariñena, Franciscan convent of 61, 64–65
Sarrià, Bernat de 97, 204

Sassari, Franciscan convent of 69, 72
Sassoferrato, Fr. Peter of 26, 33, 58
Saurina (wife of Bernat de Castellet) 128
Saus (Olzet), Sr. Sobirana de (abbess of Pedralbes) 233
Scotus, Duns 262n4, 263, 265, 266
Second Order: *see* Poor Clares
See, Fr. Peter (or William) of the 35, 52, 62, 81, 117
Seguera, Sr. Constanza 233n42
Sentfores: and Clarissan convent of Vic 229
Serra, Fr. Aparicio 162–165, 208
Serra, Fr. Pardo 162–163, 208
Sesa, castle of 163, 164
Setia: *see* Ortiz family
Sibil.la, Sr. (daughter of Sibil.la de Castellet and Umbert de Rocafort) 110
Sibil.la, Sr. (nun in Pedralbes) 233n42
Sicily, kingdom of 166–167, 205
Siete partidas: see Alfonso X, king of Castile
slaves and servants, Moorish: employed in convents 236
Soler, Pons de (husband of Ramona Torpina) 123
Soquet, Ramon 97n65
Soriana, Sr. 247
Spinelli (Borberali), Domingo 283–284
Spirituals 72, 129, 165–166, 186n30, 205, 216, 218, 220, 252, 263; and Jews 131; in Provence 210; in Sicily 215; in Vilafranca 250; and Third Order 241–243, 253. *See also* béguin(e)s
studium generale 262, 267; in Barcelona 266–267, 268; in Cambridge 84; in Lerida 262; in Paris 84, 85; in Valencia 96, 266–267. *See also* education of friars

Tamarit 188. *See also* Ramon, Bernat
Tamarit, Pedro de 50
Tarasco, Guillem de (of Vilacubells) 268
Tarazona 32, 56
Tarazona, Clarissan convent of 223, 231
Tarazona, Franciscan convent of 32, 49, 61, 118; foundation of 33
Tarragona, Fr. Pere de 154
Tarragona 24, 41, 78, 211; and actions towards Jews 130–131, 133; archbishops of 42, 83, 133, 155, 160, 209, 215; Constitutions of 161, 215n146
Tarragona, Clarissan convent of 225, 226
Tarragona, Franciscan convent of 40, 44, 49; bequest and grant to 42, 279; foundation of 41–42
Tàrrega 55, 257; Privileges of 54
Tàrrega, Clarissan convent of 202, 227
Tàrrega, Franciscan convent of 44, 187n35, 201–202, 267, 278–279; alms to 200n67; foundation of 53–55, 106, 115, 202; grant of leprosarium to 54, 186
Tauste, Gil Pérez de 263n5
Teresa Gil de Vidaure: *see* Vidaure, Teresa Gil de
Terreni, Fr. Guy (Carmelite) 251
tertiaries: *see* Third Order
Teruel, Bertrán de 124
Teruel, Clarissan convent of 231
Teruel, Franciscan convent of 39, 55, 59–60, 156–157; art and architecture of church of 59, 90, 280–281, 285; bequests and concessions to 52, 89; foundation of 58; and preaching to Jews 49, 136n95
Teruel, martyrs of 34, 58

Third Order of Saint Francis 97, 181–182, 241–253, 254, 291, 293; rule of 246, 256, 257–258
Todi, Jacopone da: poems 265
Toledo, Franciscan convent of (San Juan de los Reyes) 214
Tolosa, Hug de 117
Tomàs, Bernat 268
Torpina, Ramona (wife of Pons de Soler) 123
Torre, Berenguer de 158
Torrents, Fr. Pere de 263n6
Tortosa 50
Tortosa, Clarissan convent of 226, 239
Tortosa, Franciscan convent of 44, 156–157, 198n63, 278; alms and bequests to 50, 199n65; foundation of 49–50
Treballós, Fr. Guillem (apostate) 171n65
Trinitarians 50
Tudela, Fr. Miguel de 154, 166
Tudela, Franciscan convent of 107, 154; bequest to 52
Tunis: Franciscan convent of 39, 42–43, 205; missionaries in 38, 43, 137
Turmeda, Fr. Anselm (convert to Islam) 43

Ugolino, cardinal 221–222
union, Aragonese 97, 204n82
universities: see Cambridge; Oxford; Paris
Unnes, Cerdany (husband of Berenguera) 231n36
Urban IV, pope 223
Urban V, pope 170n62, 195, 242
Urgell, count of (viscount of Ager) 276
usury 134, 135

Valencia 121–125, 161, 165; hospitals of béguin(e)s in 247, 248, 253; Franciscans martyred in 22, 121–122; Hospital de la Reina in 94–96; reconquest of 4, 79, 81, 230
Valencia, Clarissan convent of 34, 230, 236, 238–239
Valencia, Franciscan convent of 87, 123, 124, 125, 187n35, 191, 285; bequests to 36, 53, 78, 124, 295; foundation of 35–36; grants and concessions to 52, 79, 85n29, 123; and preaching to Jews 49, 136n95; studium in 96, 125, 262, 264, 266
Valdes: see Waldo, Peter
Valldaura, Cistercian monastery of 44, 46
Vall-llebrera family: Andreu 138; Bonafonat 138; Franca (wife of Andreu) 138; Fr. Pascasi 138
Valls, Bertran de 208
Valls, Fr. Berenguer de 156
Vallsanta, Cistercian monastery of 54
Varra, Garcias Fernando de 60
Venrell, Bernat 144–146
Verdaguer, Guillem de 282
Vic (Rena), Bernat de 211
Vic, Guillem de, and wife Berenguera 143
Vic 24, 27, 295
Vic, Clarissan convent of 229, 285–286, 292, 295
Vic, Franciscan convent of 39, 49, 142, 274, 282–283; bequests to 78, 140, 156, 178n11; foundation of 26, 27, 28; and hospice in Manresa 70, 71
Vicens, Fr. (apostate) 171n65
Vidal family: Berenguer 178n11; Fr. Pere 178n11, 179n11
Vidaure, Teresa Gil de (clandestine wife of James I of Aragon) 83
Vienne, Council of 161, 162, 205
Vigne, Pier delle 258n124
Vila Iglesias, Franciscan convent of 69, 72
Vilacubells: see Tarasco, Guillem de

Vilafranca del Penedès 41, 211, 248, 250
Vilafranca del Penedès, Clarissan convent of 225-226
Vilafranca del Penedès, Franciscan convent of 39, 49, 187n35, 281, 285, 286; foundation of 40-41
Vilagrassa, Fr. Francesc 159, 160
Vilanova, Arnau de 241, 244-245, 249, 251-252, 264, 266; works condemned as heretical 216
Vilanova, Fr. Arnau de 245n77
Vilanova, Fr. Bernat de 215
Vilar, Bernat de 123
Vilardell, Sr. Constanza de 233n42
Vilaric, Arnau de 49
Villefranche de Conflent, Franciscan convent of 65, 66-67, 107, 115
Violant, queen of Aragon: *see* Hungary, Violant of
Violant de Vilaragut, queen of Majorca (wife of James III) 236

Waldensians 16, 18, 75, 190. *See also* heresy
Waldo (Valdes), Peter 15
Wales, John of 262n4
William (of the See), Fr.: *see* See, Fr. Peter (or William) of the
witnesses, friars as: to legal documents 126, 201, 208; to wills 48, 58, 117, 178, 210
work of friars: care of the sick and lepers 54, 55, 109, 147, 186 (*see also* hospitals); missionary 34, 38, 42-43, 78, 126, 130-137, 189; pastoral 142-146, 155, 200; as physicians 188-189; as scribes 267, 268, 286; secular 105, 191-192, 200-201 (*see also* executors of wills or estates; witnesses, friars as); in service of crown 62, 81-83, 105, 165, 174, 192-193, 294, 267-268, 286; in service of papacy 62, 152-154

Xàtiva, Clarissan convent of 207-208, 230, 237, 238-240
Xàtiva, Franciscan convent of 49, 55, 136n95, 171, 279, 282; concessions to 60, 85n29; foundation of and bequests to 60-61, 123
Ximéno de Ayerbe, Sancho 163, 164
Ximéno de Ola, Pedro: *see* Ola family

Zaidia: *see* La Zaidia
zelanti 242. *See also* Spirituals

1 Morella, cloister and well

2 Morella, cloister

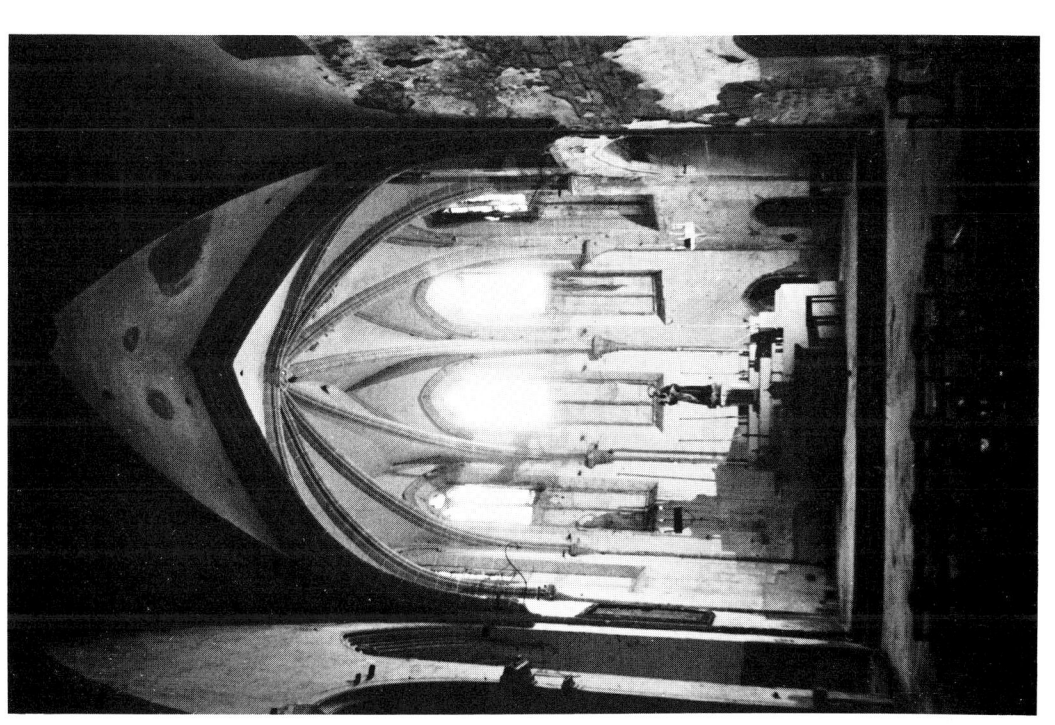

4 Cervera, interior of the Church of Sant Antoni de Padua

3 Cervera, part of the nave of the Church of Sant Antoni de Padua

5 Cervera, cloister of the Church of Sant Antoni de Padua

6 Cervera, well and cloister of the Church of Sant Antoni de Padua

7 Vilafranca, cloister of the Church of Sant Francesc

8 Miramar, Majorca

9 Tortosa, the Church of Sant Francesc

10 Santa Clara, Tortosa

11 Montblanc, apse of the Church of Sant Francesc

12 Montblanc, entrance of the Church of Sant Francesc

13 Castelló d'Empúries, wall of the Convent of Sant Francesc

14 Castelló d'Empúries, part of the Convent of Sant Francesc